the TOOLS & TECHNIQUES of

RISK MANAGEMENT & INSURANCE

STEPHAN R. LEIMBERG
DONALD J. RIGGIN
ALBERT J. HOWARD
JAMES W. KALLMAN
DONALD L. SCHMIDT

The
NATIONAL
UNDERWRITER
Company
PROFESSIONAL PUBLISHING GROUP

P.O. Box 14367 • Cincinnati, Ohio 45250-0367
1-800-543-0874 • www.nationalunderwriter.com

ISBN 0-87218-701-2

Library of Congress Control Number: 2002115351

THE NATIONAL UNDERWRITER COMPANY

Copyright © 2002
The National Underwriter Company
P.O. Box 14367
Cincinnati, Ohio 45250-0367

Printed in the United States of America

DEDICATION

Albert J. Howard

To my wife Christine, my brother William, and all of our many children.

James W. Kallman

To students of risk management with the hope that they will make our future safer and more profitable.

Stephan R. Leimberg

To Jo-Ann, my first mate and the love of my life!

Donald L. Schmidt

To all students, educators, and business professionals hoping you will realize that risk management is much more than simply financing risk.

ABOUT THE AUTHORS

Stephan R. Leimberg, J.D., Lead Editor

Stephan R. Leimberg is CEO of LISI, an email commentary and tax law news service; CEO of Leimberg and LeClair, Inc., an estate and financial planning software company; and president of Leimberg Associates, Inc., a publishing and software company in Bryn Mawr, Pennsylvania. He is a lecturer-in-law in the Masters of Taxation Program of Villanova University School of Law, holds a B.A. from Temple University, and a J.D. from Temple University School of Law.

Leimberg is the author of numerous books on estate, financial, and employee benefit and retirement planning and a nationally known speaker. He is the creator of the *Tools and Techniques* series, which includes *The Tools and Techniques of Estate Planning, The Tools and Techniques of Financial Planning, The Tools and Techniques of Employee Benefit and Retirement Planning, The Tools and Techniques of Life Insurance Planning, The Tools and Techniques of Charitable Planning,* and *The Tools and Techniques of Risk Management and Insurance.* Leimberg is co-author of *Tax Planning with Life Insurance* with attorney Howard Zaritsky, *The New Book of Trusts - Post '97 Tax Law* with attorneys Charles K. Plotnick and Daniel Evans, and *How to Settle an Estate* with Charles K. Plotnick.

Leimberg is co-creator of many software packages for the financial services professional including *NumberCruncher* (estate and financial planning), *Business QuickView* (business valuation, projection, and analysis), *IRS Factors Calculator* (actuarial computations), and *Financial Analyzer II.* His most recent software packages are *Estate Planning Quickview* (estate planning flow charts), *Gifts That Give, Gifts That Give Back, Long-term Care,* and *Toward a Zero Estate Tax* (PowerPoint Client Seminars).

A nationally known speaker and writer, Leimberg was awarded the Excellence in Writing Award of the American Bar Association's Probate and Property Section. He has been honored as Estate Planner of the Year by the Montgomery County Estate Planning Council and as Distinguished Estate Planner by the Philadelphia Estate Planning Council. He is also a recipient of the President's Cup of the Philadelphia Life Underwriters, a two time Boris Todorovitch Lecturer, and the First Ben Feldman Lecturer.

Leimberg was named 1998 Edward N. Polisher Lecturer of the Dickinson School of Law.

Donald J. Riggin, CPCU, ARM

Donald J. Riggin is a risk management and insurance consultant with Schiff, Kreidler-Shell, Inc. (SKS) in Cincinnati, Ohio. He created, edits, and writes *Financing Risk & Reinsurance (FRR),* a monthly journal devoted to enterprise risk management, insurance-linked securitization, and the convergence of the insurance and capital markets published by International Risk Management Institute, Inc. (IRMI).

Riggin was also principal author and editor of IRMI's *Risk Financing,* a two-volume reference service. Riggin's consulting practice includes the analysis, formation, and operation of alternative risk financing structures, including captives. He frequently writes on risk financing issues for various insurance and risk management publications and speaks at a variety of industry functions, including the annual RIMS conference.

Albert J. Howard, CPCU

Albert J. Howard currently teaches classes in insurance planning, retirement, and employee benefits planning through the CyberCampus at Golden Gate University. These courses are for students preparing for the Certified Financial Planner (CFP) examination and for candidates for the master's degree in financial planning.

Prior to 2000, Howard was president of Howard Risk Management, Inc. He spent more than twenty years as vice president of risk management and insurance for First Interstate Bancorp, a multistate bank holding company. His responsibilities included service as president of First Interstate's captive insurance company, Western Bonding and Casualty Company, and president of First Interstate Life Insurance Company. In addition, he headed the actuarial team leading to the formation of Bankers Insurance Company Ltd., a banking-industry-owned captive insurance company.

Howard owned an independent life and property/casualty brokerage firm and was licensed to transact life and disability insurance. He also served as an underwriter for the Commercial Union and the Fire Association of Philadelphia Groups.

Howard's education includes a bachelor's degree from San Francisco State University and a masters of science – finance from California State University. He is a lifetime member of the Business Honor Society and a recipient of the *Wall Street Journal* Award for Academic Excellence.

James W. Kallman, Ph.D., ARM

James W. Kallman holds a doctoral degree in risk management and insurance from the University of Wisconsin, a masters of science degree in business from the University of Wisconsin, and a bachelor of science degree in finance from the University of Minnesota. In addition, he has earned the Associate in Risk Management (ARM) designation.

Kallman is a full-time professor at St. John's University, the School of Risk Management (formerly The College of Insurance). He principally teaches graduate and undergraduate classes in corporate risk management, risk control, financial management, and risk management and insurance. He also teaches property and liability insurance, life and health insurance, financial management of insurers, financial risk management, the psychology of risk, and global risk management.

Prior to teaching, Kallman was an insurance agency owner, bringing more than twelve years of business experience to his academic research and teaching. He has served as the coordinator of graduate studies, graduate student advisor, and the school's liaison for RIMS national and New York chapter activities. Kallman also teaches professional education courses in financial management, risk management, risk control, and risk financing. His seminars are presented internationally to organizations including Marsh, Aon, RIMS, GNP – Mexico, A.M. Best, General-Cologne Reinsurance, the Insurance Education Institution, the International School of Management – Paris, and the U.S. Department of Commerce. His global presentations have been in Bermuda, Canada, China, Mexico, Puerto Rico, and Paris.

His work has earned several academic honors including two Spencer Educational Foundation Grants, the State Farm Companies Foundation Doctoral Dissertation Award in Insurance, and a pilot project research grant from the Center to Protect Workers' Rights, the research arm of the Building & Construction Trades Department, AFL-CIO, as well as several teaching awards, including ARIA's Lester B. Strickler innovation in instruction award.

Donald L. Schmidt, ARM

Donald L. Schmidt is senior vice president, managing consultant, and national practice leader for emergency response planning within the Risk Consulting Practice of Marsh in Boston, Massachusetts. He provides management consulting services in the areas of risk assessment and business impact analysis, mitigation, and emergency management.

Schmidt is the co-author of *Business at Risk: How to Assess, Mitigate, and Respond to Terrorist Threats* published by The National Underwriter Company. He also is the author of *Emergency Response Planning: A Management Guide* published by Marsh in 1994 and in part by *Facility Manager* magazine. He has been interviewed for and quoted in many periodicals and broadcast media including *NFPA Journal, The National Underwriter, Stores Magazine, Retail Challenge, Global Risk,* New England Cable News, and WBIX radio. He is a frequent lecturer on the subject of emergency management and has spoken to groups including the American Society of Safety Engineers, American Society for Industrial Security, National Retail Federation, Ford Motor Company, and a conference sponsored by FEMA's Project Impact.

Schmidt's twenty-four plus year career has included positions within the HPR insurance industry, heavy manufacturing, and a federal fire prevention agency as well as a being fire fighter with two fire departments. He graduated Summa Cum Laude from the University of Maryland with a bachelor of science degree in Urban Studies - Fire Science. Schmidt is a member of the Society of Fire Protection Engineers, National Fire Protection Association, and is a Professional Member of the American Society of Safety Engineers. He serves as a principal member on two National Fire Protection Association technical committees including *Disaster/Emergency Management and Business Continuity Programs* (NFPA 1600) and *Pre-Incident Planning* (NFPA 1620).

PREFACE TO THE FIRST EDITION

The subject matters! Without insurance and the other tools and techniques explained in this book, life as we know it, both business and personal, would not be possible. Skyscrapers would not be built and airlines would not fly. Our commercial institutions could not function and our economy would have no stability—were it not for the various assurances and methods used to eliminate, reduce, or shift the risk taken by investors. Managing risk through insurance and the many other methods described in this book is an exciting, challenging, and rapidly evolving field of growing importance to the success—and in many cases the survival—of enterprise in our highly complex economy.

Above all, the single most important goal of this resource is to help you learn how to help others in the risk management problem-solving process. Your greatest challenge will often be to communicate effectively with others—particularly with and to management at its highest levels—the urgency and significance of seeing and solving risk management problems. To accomplish that objective, you must first be able to identify and quantify a multiplicity of risks and then bring to bear the various tools and techniques that will eliminate, reduce, or shift the potential loss that risk represents.

For many readers, this book will be the first venture to the land of people, property, perils, and hazards. Venturing into this brave new world will be vigorously challenging.

It is a foreign land where the language is alien and guides who speak the native tongue and who can translate it clearly are invaluable. Fortunately, our authors: Don Riggin, Al Howard, James Kallman, and Don Schmidt; The National Underwriter Company's *FC&S Bulletins* staff: Karen Combs, Bruce Hillman, Mike McCracken, Susan Massmann, Diane Richardson, and David Thamann; and technical editor, Diana Reitz—your guides—possess a wealth of practical as well as academic experience, are blessed with the ability to take complex information and make it understandable, and have been generous in their sharing. Take a moment to look at their bios and you'll begin to appreciate the knowledge and wisdom they have to impart.

We have designed this text to provide students and practitioners with concise, accurate, and objective sources of information and commentary—packaged in a way that significantly reduces the time it takes to learn, research, or review complicated and broad-based risk management concepts. Although there are many scholarly texts on risk management covering one or more segments of the subject, there was no single professional level resource that incorporated all the aspects of the process and was designed as a practical guide for a student, novice practitioner, or long-term professional who needed to quickly grasp or revisit or train others in the uses and pros and cons of the various tools and techniques and understand which (or which combination) would meet the targeted objectives.

We were fortunate that so many risk management and insurance professionals were willing to share their knowledge with us. They are listed in the Acknowledgments. It is important to note that a number of property and casualty insurance companies, as well as companies that provide services to the industry, allowed us to reprint samples of their insurance coverage forms and documents. Our use of this material is for illustrative purposes and is not intended to endorse one company or service provider over another.

This is the first edition of *The Tools and Techniques of Risk Management & Insurance*. But it is the sixth in a series including *Tools and Techniques of Estate Planning, Tools and Techniques of Financial Planning, Tools and Techniques of Employee Benefit and Retirement Planning, The Tools and Techniques of Life Insurance Planning,* and *Tools and Techniques of Charitable Planning*. They all have one thing in common: they are all specifically designed to promote education for performance.

As with the other books in this series, the information is discussed in an easy-to-use format that is aimed at answering the professional's major questions:

WHAT IS IT? provides a brief description of the technique or tool.

STEPS TO IMPLEMENT outlines the order in which information is used and decisions made.

BUSINESS USES outlines some of the major reasons why a particular tool is needed.

ADVANTAGES and DISADVANTAGES illustrate the pros and cons of a particular tool or technique.

DESIGN FEATURES summarize the characteristic features of the tool and the options that are available.

WHERE CAN I FIND OUT MORE ABOUT IT? provides a list of references for further study and information.

QUESTIONS AND ANSWERS discusses some specific problems and their solutions and may offer auxiliary material that is not covered in depth in the text.

GLOSSARY provides the key terms and their definitions for each chapter. Glossaries are attached to individual chapters because some terms may have a special significance in terms of the material discussed in the chapter.

APPENDICES are attached to several chapters instead of being consolidated at the end of the book. This was done in an effort to facilitate use of the material.

Where appropriate, some chapters deviate from this format in order to provide the best approach to understanding the material.

A first edition is always just that—a work-in-progress. So please, share your comments, suggestions, and constructive criticism. Let us know what we can add to the second edition that will make this an even more useful educational, learning, reference, and training tool.

Stephan R. Leimberg

ACKNOWLEDGMENTS

A resource of this dimension isn't possible without the assistance and cooperation of many people and companies. There are hundreds of charts, forms, checklists, and specimen documents that are available to our readers because of their courtesy. The editors and authors would like to express particular appreciation to the following:

ACORD (Rick Gilman, Vice President, Communications, and Michael Mahle, Media Relations Specialist), for access to and permission to reprint samples of ACORD standardized forms.

Several representatives from Aon Corporation for general advice and assistance.

Chubb & Son and The Chubb Group of Insurance Companies (Mark L. Schussel, AVP and Public Relations Manager; Alan Driscoll, Senior Vice President, Risk Management Worldwide; Maureen Waterbury, CCI Marketing/Communications; Ned Mann, Media Relations, Chubb Specialty Insurance; and Holly Giordano) for access to and permission to use worldwide coverage forms.

Several representatives from Marsh, Inc., for general advice and assistance.

National Conference of Insurance Guaranty Funds (NCIGF) (Kevin D. Harris, Vice President, Secretary & General Counsel; and Barbara F. Cox, Counsel and Assistant Secretary) for permission to reprint NCIGF data sheets.

National Union Fire Insurance Company of Pittsburgh, Pa, A Member Company of American International Group, Inc. (AIG)(Martin J. Sullivan, Co-chief Operating Officer, and Albania Lara, Marketing Coordinator) for access to and permission to use D&O coverage forms.

Robert Glicksteen, Senior Vice President and CFO, Becher + Carlson Companies, who offered ideas to illustrate computer modeling, and Aaron Newhoff, FCAS, Vice President and Chief Actuary, Becher + Carlson Companies, who provided technical advice and a fine piece of writing.

Jack J. Hampton, Executive Director of the Risk and Insurance Management Society (RIMS), Inc., for assistance in locating potential authors.

James R. Jones, CPCU, AIC, ARM, AIS, Director of the Katie School of Insurance and Financial Services, Illinois State University, for reviewing selected chapters.

James Kuhl of Kemper Insurance companies for information on bonding.

John R. Phelps, a corporate risk manager, who provided information and insight into some of the information contained in this book.

Dr. Deborah J. Pretty of Oxford Metrica for permission to use research material on brand value.

Kevin Quinley, CPCU, ARM, AIC, AIM, ARe, Senior VP, Risk Services, Medmarc Insurance Co., for reviewing selected chapters.

A.M. Best Co., Inc., for permission to use rating definitions and assistance in reviewing them.

Fitch Ratings, for permission to use rating definitions and assistance in reviewing them.

Moody's Investors Service, for permission to use rating definitions and assistance in reviewing them.

Standard & Poor's, for permission to use rating definitions and assistance in reviewing them.

Weiss Research, for permission to use rating definitions and assistance in reviewing them.

A very special acknowledgment to Diana B. Reitz CPCU, AAI, editor of the *RF&S Bulletins* and associate editor with the Risk and Insurance Markets (RIM) Division of the National Underwriter Company, without whom this book would not be what it is. Serving as technical editor as well as well as an author, her expertise in property and casualty insurance and risk management is illustrated throughout the text. Diana was instrumental and essential in every major—and minor—— phase of this publication. Her creativity, persistence, and meticulous care are evident in every paragraph.

Thanks to Bruce Hillman, J.D., editorial director of the National Underwriter Company's RIM division; David D. Thamann, J.D., CPCU, ARM, managing editor of the National Underwriter Company's *FC&S* *(Fire, Casualty, & Surety) Bulletins;* Diane W. Richardson, CPCU, associate editor of the *FC&S;* and Mike K. McCracken, CPCU, ASLI, associate editor of the *FC&S,* for the contributions to and unfailing support for this project. A special thanks goes to Susan Massmann, RIM staff writer, who diligently read every word written and contributed hours of research to the project.

CONTENTS

Techniques of Risk Management & Insurance

Tools of Risk Management & Insurance

Chapter Glossaries

Chapter Appendices

Chapter 1

INTRODUCTION TO TRADITIONAL RISK MANAGEMENT

UNDERSTANDING THE NATURE OF RISK

The notion that *risk* is something that can be managed and controlled is a relatively new idea. While organizations face a multitude of complex risks, historically only *event* risk was deemed worthy of attention. Event risk is also known as insurable risk. Traditionally, insurers literally defined risk based on its insurability; if it can be insured, it's either a "good" risk or a "bad" risk. If it cannot be insured, it's a business risk, and thus considered just another cost of doing business.

Insurable risk is also known as fortuitous risk. Fortuitous risk connotes solely the risk of loss; it does not contemplate the notion that (conceptually) risk cuts both ways. For example, an investment in stocks represents both the risk of loss and the risk of gain, also known as speculative risk. While we generally do not associate the term risk with the possibility of a favorable outcome, that definition is just as valid as the fortuitous risk definition because each outcome represents deviation from the norm.

Regardless of the type, risk is just another way of defining *volatility*. The words risk and volatility are essentially synonymous. The absence of risk denotes *certainty*, and certainty denotes a lack of volatility. Volatility is expressed as deviation from the expected. For example, if losses are forecast to be x, the volatility associated with the loss forecast can be expressed as x-1, x+1, x-2, x+2, and so on. We use the term risk to define the degree of volatility as well as recognize the fact that volatility exists. Consider event risk in this context. If first-dollar (no significant deductible) insurance is used to transfer a particular event risk— for example, the risk of fire destroying a building— the volatility associated with the peril of fire has been removed. Assuming the insurance coverage and limits are appropriate, the insured has incurred a cost (the premium) for reducing the financial consequence of the risk of fire to effectively zero.

Next, consider the volatility associated with the risk that the building could burn to the ground in the absence of insurance. Of course, the volatility of the event does not change regardless of who ends up paying for the loss, but, in this case, it's the building owner who must understand the volatility and manage it.

Historically, insurance has been the only viable alternative for managing fortuitous risk. The primary goal of the insurance mechanism is to restore the insured to its preloss condition. However, since insurance can be a costly method of managing volatility, other, potentially more effective techniques, have emerged over the years. The remainder of this chapter will discuss risk management as it applies to fortuitous risk. Other chapters in this book will address more advanced risk management concepts that consider all aspects of risk.

A BRIEF HISTORY OF RISK MANAGEMENT

Risk management has been recognized as a viable technique for mitigating the effects of fortuitous loss to corporations and public entities since the early 1960s. Prior to that time, risk was not considered to be worthy of *management* per se; it was generally handled by the purchase of insurance, with insurance companies providing not only risk transfer capacity but also loss control engineering services. Large deductibles and active self-insurance programs were relatively rare. The employee responsible for buying the insurance also had another primary function, for example, the treasurer, chief financial officer, safety manager or, in some cases, corporate counsel.

In the 1960s and 1970s reliance on insurance companies as sole providers of risk services began to wane. Visionary academicians such as Robert Hedges and George Head developed new ways of managing the myriad of risks faced by corporations and public entities. It was recognized that while insurance was an effective means of moving fortuitous risk off the balance sheet, there was no systematic approach to evaluating risk. The centerpiece of this research became known as the *Risk Management Process*.

THE RISK MANAGEMENT PROCESS

A process, regardless of the subject matter, connotes a series of sequential activities leading to a stated result given a predetermined goal. In the conventional sense, risk management's results can be expressed in terms of the loss that did not occur, or, more accurately, the catastrophic loss that did not have a catastrophic impact on the organization. Managing risk does *not* mean that every conceivable loss has been analyzed and factored out; to the contrary, risk management is primarily focused on the firm's ability to recognize and correct faulty and potentially dangerous operations, trends, and policies that could lead to a catastrophic loss.

Risk management is, by definition, a *preloss exercise* that reflects an organization's *postloss goals,* which are discussed in a subsequent chapter. The risk management process does not occur in a vacuum; the degree to which risk is mitigated must be defined by the goals of the organization. For example, firm A may be comfortable with a minimum of risk management controls. Its post-catastrophic loss goal may be simply to remain in business, without regard for how many customers or employees it may lose as a consequence, as long as it is not forced into bankruptcy. Alternatively, firm B's risk management goal may be diametrically opposite, that is, to retain every customer, lay off no employees, and conduct business as usual. Clearly, firm B will incur considerably greater preloss risk management costs than will firm A. Yet to firm B, the costs can be justified given its postloss goals.

STEPS IN THE PROCESS

The conventional risk management process is comprised of *five* distinct steps or activities.

- Step 1. *Identify* actual and potential risks facing the organization.

- Step 2. *Quantify and analyze* actual and potential risks relative to their impact on the organization.

- Step 3. *Evaluate* potential treatment options, including specific risk control measures and risk financing techniques.

- Step 4. *Implement* selected treatment options.

- Step 5. *Monitor* the effectiveness of the chosen treatment options and *make adjustments* as necessary.

This chapter provides an overview of each step. Detailed discussions appear later in the book.

Risk Identification

That which cannot be identified cannot be managed. Risk identification is the critical first step in determining exactly what constitutes a risk commensurate with the postloss goals of the organization. In general, a firm's risks emanate from two major sources: assets and operations. These categories roughly define what are known as *first-party* risks and *third-party* risks. The expression *first party* connotes risks associated with owned assets, while the term *third party* indicates liability arising from operations.

Risks that must be financed or transferred (insured) in accordance with state law are generally considered *baseline risks* and should be the first to be identified. These include injury to employees (workers compensation) and statutory requirements to fund the legal liability for or derived from operating motor vehicles (third-party risks). Additional third-party risks include liability arising from operations, products, contractual obligations, and/or ownership of real property. As a general rule of thumb, third-party risks represent the greatest threat of financial loss to any organization. Automobile ownership represents both first- and third-party risks. Damage to the vehicle constitutes a first-party risk, while property damage or injury to persons (other than the driver) caused by operating the vehicle are third-party risks.

Quantitative Analysis

Risk quantification is accomplished through a variety of tools and methods. But, at its core, risk quantification means predicting the maximum and expected financial loss associated with each identified risk. For example, if fire destroys a building with a replacement cost of $1 million, its *maximum* potential loss can be set at $1 million. However, the building's fire-resistive construction, for example, might suggest that the *expected* potential loss should be no more than $500,000.

While physical assets allow relatively easy risk quantification, risks such as public liability (third-party risk) and worker safety (third-party risk) are considerably more difficult to quantify. When measuring third-party risks, organizations often ask two questions: One, "How much potential loss can we withstand as a result of this exposure?", and two, "How much potential loss can we withstand and *still remain financially viable*?" The answers to these questions will be dramatically different. Yet they help to form the parameters of the risk management process.

Evaluating Risk Treatment Options (Financing & Control)

Having identified and quantified a variety of loss exposures deemed important enough to warrant action, the risk manager must identify the options available to treat the exposures. Treating identified loss exposures is accomplished through two means: risk financing and risk control.

Financing

The spectrum of risk financing options is extremely broad. However, each financing technique falls into one of two major categories: *on-balance sheet* and *off-balance sheet*.

Risks that remain on-balance sheet are known as retained risks. Those considered off-balance sheet have been transferred to an unrelated third-party, usually for financial consideration. Examples of on-balance sheet risks include insurance policy deductibles and self-insured loss exposures. Off-balance sheet transactions include insurance policies and contractual transfers of risk, among others.

The concept of *self-insured* differs significantly from that of *uninsured*. Self-insurance connotes managing the loss exposure, such as establishing a fund from which to pay losses; this is also known as *active loss retention*. *Uninsured* simply means that nothing has been done to recognize the exposure from a financial standpoint. The term *passive retention* is also used in this context. The primary example of off-balance sheet financing is insurance. Chapters 7 and 8 cover conventional and alternative risk financing techniques in detail.

Control

Controlling risk means controlling the volatility inherent in organizational life. For example, a metal stamping machine represents a risk to its owners and operators. A stamping machine without the proper guarding equipment increases the potential for operator injury (increases volatility). Installing proper machine guards lowers the probability that the operator will become injured. Notice that the *risk* itself (owning and operating a metal stamping machine) is not controlled; the likelihood that the risk will result in a loss *is* controlled (its volatility).

Transferring risks off-balance sheet does not constitute adequate risk control. This is because the transfer is not free. If the volatility of the transferred risk is not controlled, future transfer and/or financing costs will increase, along with the possibility that affordable (and available) financing and transfer options may become nonexistent. Using the stamping machine example, workers operating the machine may be insured through a workers compensation insurance policy (off-balance sheet). But, if the volatility associated with the machine is not controlled and workers are repeatedly injured while using the machine, the workers compensation premiums will increase proportionately.

Risk control is the *most important* risk management activity. Without effective risk control, financing and transfer techniques become virtually meaningless or prohibitively expensive.

Risk control is comprised of two main activities— *risk prevention* and *risk reduction*. Risk prevention is only feasible if the person, thing, service, product, or operation capable of causing a loss is effectively removed or neutralized. In the above example, the metal stamping machine cannot be discarded. So prevention is not a reasonable risk control option. Risk reduction is most often associated with the notion of risk control. The metal stamping machine's risks cannot be eradicated. But with a few precautions—such as machine guarding and operator training—the risk of operator injury can be reduced.

Risk Administration— Monitoring and Adjusting

The final step in the risk management process is program oversight. Nothing remains static, especially the risks encountered by successful organizations. They must be monitored and adjusted continuously.

Continuous monitoring requires a structured approach that includes regular program reviews performed in conjunction with a reliable information database and (ideally) an automated risk management information system (RMIS). This step also should include planning for future contingencies such as market changes.

IMPORTANCE OF RISK MANAGEMENT TO THE ORGANIZATION

Risk management is an integral part of a successful organization's overall management strategy. In order to survive (and thrive) in today's competitive economic environment, simply transferring every known risk via insurance is *not* a viable option. Risk management has proven that the excessive use of insurance can be an extremely expensive and inefficient use of capital. Since capital is the lifeblood of any organization, it must be managed effectively. Risk management's most fundamental contribution has been to provide senior management with an array of techniques designed to manage risk, and, by doing so, manage *capital* as well. While insurance plays a critical part, it is by no means the lone or lead actor. In fact, in the most sophisticated risk management programs, insurance plays a relatively minor role.

Large and complex organizations usually employ risk managers. The primary duty of a risk manager is to design and execute a management regimen in accordance with the preloss and postloss goals of the organization and the process summarized in this chapter. Since risk management is a reflection of an organization's culture, it must be considered in every important decision. The risk manager must have complete and unconditional support from senior management. Because risk permeates every facet of the organization, only senior management has the authority to enforce the requirements set forth in a comprehensive risk management program.

Virtually every successful organization is driven by sales, regardless of their product. Manufacturers sell tangible goods, banks sell financial services, universities sell education, and hospitals sell health care. Organizations that are successful over time understand the need to incorporate risk management into these sales cultures.

Keep in Mind

Risk management provides the framework that balances the need for sales with an understanding of the risks that could jeopardize the organization's continued growth and existence.

A risk management program can be costly to develop and implement. Senior management will lend its support only if the benefits are perceived to outweigh the costs. The costs associated with risk management must be considered *investments*, because in most cases the benefits are only realized after an extended period of time. It is true that the initial costs may appear excessive given the minimal (if any) short-term return on investment. Senior management therefore must be willing to focus on long-term results.

It is extremely difficult to measure tangible benefits against a nonevent (i.e., the catastrophic loss did *not* occur due to our highly effective risk management program). Yet this is the challenge facing all risk managers. Ultimately, the metrics that senior management uses to gauge success—for example, earnings growth and return on invested capital—must also serve as the yardsticks used to measure the effectiveness of risk management.

THE RISK MANAGEMENT POLICY STATEMENT

No risk management effort can succeed unless its goals and objectives are clearly defined and communicated continuously and completely throughout the organization. This is commonly accomplished through the use of a formal risk management policy statement.

The policy statement is similar to a mission statement in that it reflects the organization's stated values relative to risk. It recognizes and gives importance to addressing the major risks facing the organization, and it outlines the breadth and scope of the mitigation efforts. Policy statements differ as to content depending on the organization's goals and risk appetite, as well as it primary constituents, such as customers, employees, suppliers, and shareholders. For example, banks and insurance companies generally wish to be perceived as cautious and conservative institutions, whereas a fast growing software firm may want to portray itself as a leading-edge risk taker.

Accordingly, the bank or insurance company's risk management policy statements rely heavily on financial protection and redundant security measures, each designed to reassure their constituents that they have recognized and taken steps to prevent loss events that could diminish brand quality or compromise the organization in any way. The software company's risk management policy statements may stress similar sentiments, albeit in the context of a high risk / high reward economic environment.

TRADITIONAL RISK MANAGEMENT VERSUS ENTERPRISE RISK MANAGEMENT

In this chapter we have broadly defined risk management in its traditional and historical context—that is, relative to specific events, either first-party (loss or damage to owned assets) or third-party (loss or damage to third parties and/or their property for which the organization is held liable). Traditional risk management has historically been closely related to the insurance industry. The risk manager position evolved from the insurance buyer since insurance was such an important component of risk management. However, organizational life is not static, and neither is the risk management function.

Large, complex organizations employ *two* separate and distinct forms of risk management—event (insurance) risk management as discussed thus far, and financial risk management. Financial risk management, as the name implies, is designed to protect the financial assets of an organization from risks that the insurance industry cannot assume. These risks include interest rate movements, commodity price fluctuations, credit risk, and foreign currency exchange (FX) risk. The processes used to manage these risks are similar to those discussed in this book, but the risk management techniques employ financial hedges created in the capital markets. Some of these hedging techniques also are used to address traditional event risk. This process is known as *securitization,* which is discussed in detail in Chapter 24. Conversely, the insurance industry is beginning to create insurance-based products that replicate the effects of a financial hedge for certain noncore financial risks. This is known as *insuratization.* These phenomena have become jointly known as *convergence*—the convergence of the insurance and capital markets.

The evolving convergence movement has spawned a new generation of risk management that attempts to combine event and financial risk into an entirely new discipline—Enterprise Risk Management (ERM). In addition to event and financial risk, ERM addresses so-called *business risk.* Business risk includes that which cannot easily be quantified, financed, or transferred. Examples include operational risks and strategic risks. Chapter 2 discusses ERM and its implications for the future of event risk management.

The following chart provides examples of the various risks within each major category.

Event Risk	Financial Risk	Operational Risk	Strategic Risk
Destruction of Owned Property (First-party Risk)	Market Risk	Hiring Practices	Mergers & Acquisitions
Theft of Owned Property (First-party Risk)	Foreign Exchange	Quality Control	New/Discontinued Products and Services
Worker Injury (Third-party Risk)	Credit	Regulatory Compliance	Reorganizations
Damage to the Property of Others (Third-party Risk)	Interest Rates	Customer Service	Joint Ventures
Injury to Others (Third-party Risk)	Commodity Prices	Brand & Reputational Risk	

Chapter 1

GLOSSARY

Baseline risk. Event risks that must be financed or insured in accordance with state law, often without regard to fault.

Business risk. Risks that are associated with the cost of doing business, which usually are not insurable.

Enterprise Risk Management. A management process that identifies, defines, quantifies, compares, prioritizes, and treats all of the material risks facing an organization, whether or not it is insurable.

Event risk. The risk of loss without possibility of gain; risks that traditionally have been insurable.

Financial risk management. A management process designed to protect an organization's financial assets from risks the insurance industry cannot assume.

First-party risk. Event risks associated with potential damage to owned assets; the risk that owned property or goods will be damaged by a fortuitous event.

Fortuitous risk. The risk of loss; risks that traditionally have been insurable.

Insuratization Insurance-based products that replicate the effects of a financial hedge for specific financial risks.

Off-balance sheet risk Risks that an organization transfers to others through vehicles such as insurance policies or contracts.

On-balance sheet risks. Risks that an organization chooses to finance itself, such as insurance policy deductibles and self-insured loss exposures.

Risk Management. A preloss exercise that reflects an organization's postloss goals; a process to recognize and manage faulty and potentially dangerous operations, trends, and policies that could lead to loss and to minimize losses that do occur.

Risk management policy statement. A statement that reflects an organization's stated values relative to risk.

Risk quantification. Predicting the maximum and expected financial loss associated with identified risks.

Securitization. The use of financial hedges created in the capital markets to address traditional event risk.

Self-insured. A conscious decision by an organization to manage a loss exposure and to retain its financial consequences; active loss retention.

Speculative risk. The risk of either loss or gain, such as the risks that are associated with investing in the stock market.

Third-party risk. Event risks associated with potential injury or damage to third parties or their property.

Uninsured. Failing to recognize a loss exposure and doing nothing to finance its consequences; passive loss retention.

Volatility. A deviation from the expected.

Chapter 2

ENTERPRISE RISK MANAGEMENT

WHAT IS IT?

Enterprise risk management (ERM) is a framework for identifying, defining, quantifying (individually and together), comparing, prioritizing, and treating all of the material risks facing an organization (whether insurable or not).

Enterprise risk management (ERM) is a relatively new risk management model that purportedly manages all material risks facing an organization, regardless of their origin or impact. As of this writing, the need for and utility of ERM is the focus of intense debate within the risk management community, the ultimate outcome of which will literally define the risk management discipline and the role of the risk manager for many years to come.

The debate is being argued from two points of view. Those advocating ERM maintain that, while it is not a panacea for all risks, it does represent a quantum leap in risk management thinking. Advocates also believe that conventional risk managers may be an endangered species. Risk managers who have (or can acquire) the skills required to execute a successful ERM program will flourish within the organization, while those who do not have such skills will either lose their jobs or find themselves demoted to insurance buyers. Those opposed to, or skeptical of, ERM claim that its purported benefits are overstated and its implementation can be extremely expensive and time consuming.

ERM was first developed for use in the financial services industry to coordinate the considerable financial and operational risks associated with banking, investment banking, and investment houses' underwriting and selling of securities. The concept has recently been expanded to accommodate virtually any large and complex organization. Enterprise risk management has been in use for many years in some European countries, the United Kingdom, Australia, and New Zealand. These countries have enacted specific corporate governance legislation that mandates a standardized enterprise-wide approach to risk management. The Australians and New Zealanders created the first national risk management standard in 1995 (ANZ Standard 4360:1995, 1999, and 2000). The Canadians followed in 1997 (CSA-Q850-97) with their version, and the British have published BS 6079-3:2000. No such standard exists in the United States.

ERM disregards the firewall dividing risks considered insurable and those considered uninsurable *business risks*. The fundamental basis of the insurance transaction is *fortuitous risk*, the risk of only loss. *Speculative risk*, which implies the possibility of gain as well as loss, is the basis for all risks faced by organizations except that which is transferable through insurance or other means. Proportionally, a firm's speculative risk far exceeds the value of its insurable risk. Yet until recently there has been little recognition of this reality.

PURPOSE OF ERM

Enterprise Risk Management describes a universal *approach* to risk management, not a specific product or service. It involves a wide range of tools and methodologies designed to facilitate an understanding of the relationship between an organization's risk profile and its impact on earnings and shareholder value.

Enterprise Risk Management	
Pros	Cons
Quantum leap in way to think about risks	Benefits are overstated
Adds importance to risk management efforts	Time-consuming and costly
Looks at entire risk spectrum	Chief Risk Officer is a redundant position

ERM has two primary objectives:

1. The reduction of earnings volatility

2. The maintenance and growth of shareholder value

Volatility

Risk is nothing more than variation from expected outcomes. If all possible outcomes are known in advance, no risk exists and there is no volatility. Theoretically, a guaranteed cost, no-deductible insurance policy effectively eliminates volatility (for the perils covered under the policy) and thus converts unknown risk factors (losses) into a known (and acceptable) outcome (the premium). Insurance is only effective for a small subset of an organization's risk profile, which is why risk management exists as a professional discipline. Enterprise Risk Management (ERM) is the newest expression of risk management that attempts to refine a concept that began in the mid-1990s. ERM has become the accepted term of art for a concept known variously as "integrated" risk management and "holistic" risk management.

An organization's earnings are subject to a wide variety of influencing factors. These include the variability of market share, economic downturns, and the organization's ability to anticipate and understand risk and its potential effects. It is almost impossible to expect consistent and predictable earnings growth in an environment of unchecked volatility. Unlike conventional risk management, ERM focuses on identifying the sources of volatility that can have a direct impact on earnings.

Shareholder Value

Today, consistent growth in shareholder value is *the* most important goal of senior management. Enterprise risk management's ultimate objective is to protect shareholder value from as many sources of potential loss as possible. In this context, shareholder value is equivalent to an organization's stock price (for publicly traded firms).

As Figure 2.1 illustrates, the single largest cause of shareholder value loss is not meeting analysts' earnings expectations. For example, if Multinational Cor-

Figure 2.1

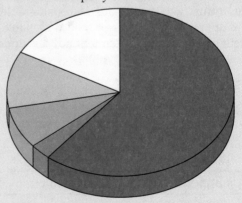

Risk Management Can Enhance Shareholder Value

➤ Over the past 5 years, 10% of the Fortune 1000 watched shareholder value erode 25% (or more) in one month's time, resulting in depressed stock prices

➤ Over two-thirds of these risks could have been mitigated

➤ Major stock drops usually occur in months when quarterly earnings are announced

➤ Closely-held companies face identical problems even though their earnings reductions are not translated as stock price reductions

What Causes Stock Prices to Plummet?

☛ Earnings Shortfall Announcement 61%
☛ Unknown 3%
☛ Discovery of Accounting Irregularities 8%
☛ External Market Forces 11%
☛ Other Company Announcements 17%

poration, Inc., is expected to earn $.50 per share in a given quarter, but it actually earns $.40 per share, investors may sell the stock and drive down the price, thus reducing shareholder value for the remaining stockholders. Proponents of enterprise risk management claim that the majority of earnings shortfalls can be traced back to risks that could have been prevented (or managed) had an ERM program been in place.

RISK CLASSIFICATIONS IN ERM

While there is no firm consensus among risk professionals as to the various categories of risk, for the purposes of this discussion we focus on the following four main categories:

- Hazard/Event

- Financial

- Strategic

- Operational

Additionally, risks derive from two primary sources:

- External

External risks are those that are imposed upon the organization from outside sources.

- Internal

Internal risks are inherent in the organization's business and are more predictable and controllable than externally driven risks.

Event/Hazard Risks

That which can be managed by the conventional risk management process discussed in Chapter 1 is the typical definition of event risk, which is also known as hazard risk. Event risk can generally be insured against, transferred contractually to another party, or in some cases, avoided altogether. Internally driven examples include damage to owned property and liability to third parties arising from operations. An example of an external event risk is the statutory requirement to insure against worker injury (workers compensation).

Financial Risks

Financial risks include both the risk of pure loss *and* the risk of inadequate gain, the latter being an example of *speculative* risk. Financial risks emanate from financial transactions. Every financial transaction is designed to either create value for the organization (make money) or hedge against the loss of value. For example, banks' earnings are heavily dependent on interest rates, either as a result of direct investments in the money markets or indirectly through the rates they charge on loans. Interest rate fluctuation is a typical externally driven financial risk. Cash managers are concerned with maintaining a minimum level of interest income on invested cash reserves. Money market funds usually provide floating interest rates. In times of falling interest rates, cash managers seek to protect their investments using interest rate swaps designed to replace their floating rate with a fixed rate. Another example of financial risk is credit. Every organization is exposed to credit risk, whether from account receivables, performance contracts, or loans. For example, a real estate owner is exposed to credit risk each time he leases a building if the lessee cannot pay the rent.

All significant financial risk is externally derived.

Strategic Risks

Every organization faces significant strategic risks. Strategic risk can be defined as the risks associated with the execution of a business plan, that is, the major decisions made by senior management that ultimately lead to success or failure. Examples include decisions involving mergers and acquisitions, new product lines, and joint ventures. Strategic risks are generally internally driven.

Operational Risk

Just as every organization must manage strategic risk, it must also manage *operational* risk. Operational risk derives from an organization's people and operations, not including that which can be defined as event risk and thus insured or transferred. Examples of operational risk include clearance/settlement systems (found in banks), quality control, hiring practices, customer interface, and work rules. Each of these activities contains risks that cannot be easily identified or quantified, yet can have a wide-ranging and devastating impact on an organization. The most celebrated examples of operational risk involve the various rogue traders that

Figure 2.2

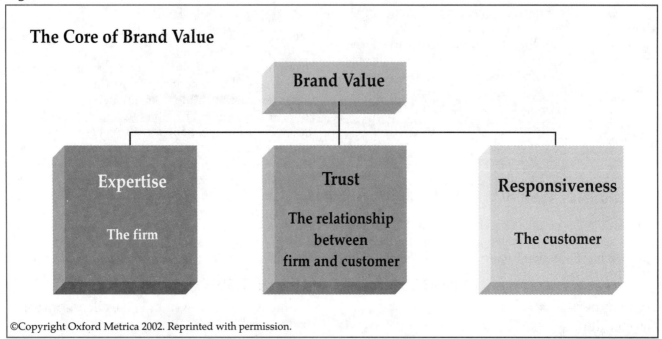

The Core of Brand Value

Brand Value

Expertise

The firm

Trust

The relationship between firm and customer

Responsiveness

The customer

violated their banks' trading parameters and subsequently caused billions of dollars of losses since the mid-1990s. Another example of operational risk is the apparent quality control problems that led to Firestone/Bridgestone's recent alleged tire failures.

Figure 2.3

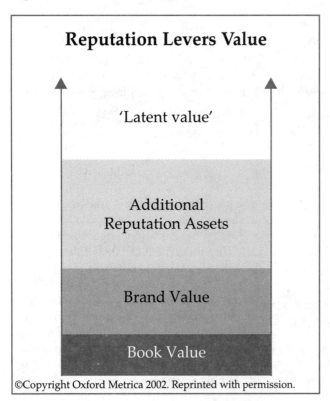

Reputation Levers Value

'Latent value'

Additional Reputation Assets

Brand Value

Book Value

Another aspect of operational risk is *reputational risk.* Reputational risk, also known as brand risk, involves the loss of market share and reputational value due to the management (or mismanagement) of a crisis. In 2002, Rory F. Knight and Deborah J. Pretty of Oxford Metrica, a risk management advisor based in Oxford, England, published an exhaustive study of twenty-five well-known companies that were involved in various reputational crises, including Johnson & Johnson's Tylenol poisoning crisis and the more current travails of Bridgestone/Firestone's alleged tire failures. The study tracks each company's management of its particular crisis and calculates the reputational risk impact on each firm.

Figure 2.2 illustrates how these researchers define the core of brand value, which is comprised of expertise, trust, and responsiveness. Figure 2.3 shows how the value of a company increases as brand value and other reputational assets are added. Loss of reputation can have a dramatic impact on a company's total value.

OVERLAY OF RISKS

Figure 2.4 illustrates the overlay and interaction of the four categories of enterprise risk.

CONCEPTS IN ERM

The Theory of Enterprise Risk Management is comprised of three main concepts:

Figure 2.4

Enterprise Risk Management

External Risks

New Markets   Political & Social
Competition   Capital Availability
Economic Trends   Legal & Regulatory
Technology   Stakeholders

Event & Operational Risks

Customer Retention   Quality Control

Financial Risks

Brand Erosion   Credit   Taxation   Product Pricing

Strategic Risks

Service Failure   Counter-party   Pension Funding   Illegal Acts

Market Share

Human Resources   Derivatives   Mergers/Acquisitions   Investment Management   Health & Safety

Contract Commitment   Manpower Planning   Logistics

Liquidity   Interest Rates

Customer Satisfaction   Market Planning   Environ-mental

Joint Ventures

Information Security   Portfolio Concentration (Lack of Covariance)   FX

Third-Party Liability   Property Damage Business Interruption

- Risk Interdependency

- Correlation/Noncorrelation

- Modern Portfolio Theory

Risk Interdependency

Risk is traditionally quantified as separate and distinct profiles; it is ultimately managed as such. For example, the risk of loss from an event (fire) and the risks associated with a reduction in the company's stock price are usually quantified and managed as separate and unrelated risks, that is, within their own treatment silos. Enterprise Risk Management explores the potential interdependencies and noninterdependencies among an organization's risks. In the above example, it may be discovered that a devastating fire at a key manufacturing plant would have a material downward impact on the firm's stock price. Given this knowledge, there is much that can be done to protect against both scenarios.

Another type of risk interdependency is known as the inflation effect. In this context, the term inflation refers to the magnified effects of two or more unrelated risks causing individual and collective damage to the organization. For example, assume that a company with a traditional risk management program experiences the following losses within the same quarter:

- A tornado destroys a major product manufacturing location.

- The Federal Reserve Board (Fed) raises short-term interest rates.

- The FBI discovers product tampering affecting the firm's most profitable product.

Individually, there is a risk management response to each of these events. The tornado damage may be insured in excess of a sizeable deductible or self-insured retention. The interest rate risk (a financial risk) may be hedged by an interest rate derivative. The firm also might carry a limited form of product recall insurance. While the large property insurance deductible, the imperfect interest rate hedge, and the deductible or self-insured retention in the product recall insurance policy may represent anticipated expenses that the organization is prepared to bear, the *combined effect* of the three losses could produce a wholly unanticipated result. For example, the tornado would shut down production for an indeterminate period of time. Assuming adequate property and business interruption insurance were in effect, the loss of physical assets and the subsequent loss of income would be manageable. However, since the tornado destroyed production equipment, the firm's ability to borrow short-term money may be compromised, albeit temporarily, because the firm's creditworthiness may be diminished. In this case, the derivative used to hedge the Fed's interest rate rise would prove thoroughly inadequate. Finally, the product recall insurance may be rendered invalid because the tornado destroyed not only the production equipment in question but also crucial data required by the products recall insurer, such as batch run data. Without the ability to retrieve the information necessary to isolate the defective batch, not only would recovery costs increase significantly; the firm's reputation also may be severely damaged.

Each risk management response would have been appropriate *but for* the fact that all three losses occurred in the same quarter. If these three risks were managed within an enterprise risk management program, it is possible that their potentially catastrophic combination would be recognized and managed.

Correlation and Noncorrelation

Correlation and noncorrelation are extremely important concepts in enterprise risk management. Similar to the risks inherent in any financial investment, all of the risks facing an organization either correlate with one another to some degree or do not correlate at all. Correlation is defined as the degree to which two or more investments, or in this context, risks, respond similarly to identical stimulus. In the investment example, stocks traded as part of the Dow Jones Industrial Averages (the Dow) index will respond similarly to the same risk factors. This is true because as the Dow rises and falls so would each of these stocks. They are considered highly correlated relative to market risk. Conversely, little correlation exists between an investment-grade municipal bond and a risky Internet stock traded over-the-counter (OTC), because each responds to a different set of risk factors. The concept of correlation had not traditionally been applied to the risks of an entire organization until it appeared in the ERM context.

In regard to the correlation of risks, many might say that there is no correlation between the risk of an earthquake and the risk of worker injuries, but that there is a high correlation between worker injuries and customer injuries in retail stores. However, the risk of an earthquake and worker injuries may be highly correlated if the earthquake occurs on a Tuesday at 2 p.m. in downtown Los Angeles.

Risk managers have discovered that correlation can have a significant impact on an organization's ability to retain risk. For example, unlike the three risk scenarios used to describe risk interdependency, other risks can have the opposite effect—they can be managed so that they check (i.e., counterbalance) one another's volatility—a process known as *internal hedging*. The overarching term used to express these phenomena is *Portfolio Theory*.

Portfolio Theory

A portfolio is an aggregation of either tangibles or intangibles designed to create a whole or a result greater than the sum of its parts. The best example is an investment portfolio wherein the desired result (financial gain) can only be reasonably expected within a balanced portfolio of investments. In this context, the term *balanced* (aka diversified) means that the portfolio will perform within expected ranges, that is, enough noncorrelation exists between and among the various investments that the variability of outcomes is reduced to an acceptable level. Losses in one type of investment will be balanced by increases in other types of investments.

In the context of enterprise risk management, portfolio theory suggests that risks heretofore insured or managed in a silo, that is, separately, could be more effectively managed as part of a portfolio of noncorrelated risks. Figure 2.5 illustrates the concept of risk silos. While the risks are not perfectly noncorrelated, that is, one loss may include both general liability *and* errors and omissions, they are separate and distinct enough to be considered noncorrelated.

WHY USE ERM IN LIEU OF CONVENTIONAL RISK MANAGEMENT?

Global business is now more focused on maintaining shareholder value than at any other time in history. As technologies are developed that make communication and access to information easier than ever before, shareholders are becoming acutely aware of the impact of management decisions on the value of their holdings. One of the areas affected by this is risk management. Enterprise risk management, according to its proponents, represents the natural and necessary evolution of traditional insurance-based risk management, because it concerns itself with and affects all facets of the organization.

Only within the last several years has the risk management function been viewed as having an impact on

Figure 2.5

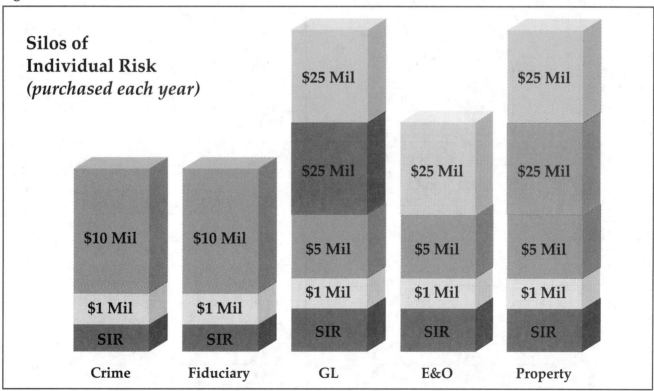

shareholder value, aside from the dreaded "uninsured loss," such as flood damage in the absence of flood insurance. The ability to establish an undeniable and tangible link between improved shareholder value and the implementation of an ERM program is technically possible. Yet because ERM must be customized to meet the needs of diverse organizations, its success can only be measured one organization at a time.

The central message of enterprise risk management is this—risks managed *separately* are not the same as when managed together. The nature of risks' impact on the organization changes when two or more disparate risks are managed from the same perspective. The notion that "risk is risk" regardless of its origins leads to the conclusion that an enterprise approach to risk can be effective in realizing the desired results:

- An increase in cost predictability

- A decrease in risk-based expenses

- Realignment of insurance plans with a multirisk, integrated program to eliminate multiple placements

- Improvement in financial security as a result of partnering with fewer insurers

- A comprehensive understanding of all risks that permits limited corporate resources to be allocated for optimal outcomes

- The creation of a detailed awareness of risk scenarios and their potential impacts

- A reduction in cash flow and earnings volatility

- Improved stock performance (for publicly traded companies) and reduced capital costs

- The building of stockholder and stakeholder confidence that risks are understood and managed

Figure 2.6

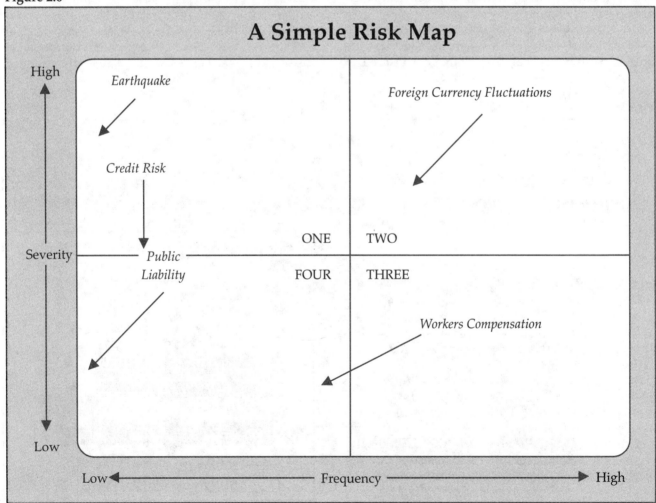

A Simple Risk Map

Enterprise risk management is not unlike conventional risk management relative to the process discussed in Chapter 1. The major differences lie in the types of risks subject to the process, the treatment options and methodology, and the degree to which the organization supports the risk management effort.

RISK ASSESSMENT AND ANALYSIS

Risk Mapping

Risk mapping is a graphical analytical tool that allows all material risks of an organization to be identified, understood, and prioritized. It is an efficient way to assess elements in all quadrants of the organization: hazard, financial, strategic, and operational areas. Risk maps may be simple or complex. Regardless of their complexity, the results can be a powerful representation of a firm's vulnerability to unforeseen loss exposures. Risk maps are one of the most effective means available to convey important risk information to senior management. Risk maps are also useful for the following:

- Making certain risk control decisions

- Determining risk financing decisions

- Modeling the effects of potential exposure scenarios that might develop in the future (risk inflation)

- Tracking risk reduction results

- Monitoring changes in exposures over time

A simple risk map consists of a graph divided into four (4) quadrants, each reflecting a different blending of frequency and severity characteristics for each risk.

In Figure 2.6 the arrows represent the desired movement of the risk exposures—from right to left. Frequency on the map refers to how often a loss occurs over a period of time. Severity measures the impact of the loss. Risks that can be placed in quadrant four tend toward low frequency and low severity. Each quadrant relates to costs—the further up and to the right, the more costly the risk. Ideally, organizations take precautions to avoid or transfer the effects of risks that represent extreme frequency

and severity. Risks that inhabit quadrant one can be extremely dangerous. Low frequency means that actuarial predictability is extremely low or nonexistent, yet the severity of potential losses is high.

FINANCIAL SOLUTIONS IN AN ERM ENVIRONMENT

Integrated Risk (IR) insurance structures make up the general category of platforms used in an ERM environment. Two types of IR structures are

- Cross-Class Multiyear Insurance

- Dual Trigger Programs

Integrated Risk Insurance Structures

Many of the concepts central to ERM are based on integrated risk platforms. While ERM is a newly evolving conceptual alternative to traditional risk management, *Integrated Risk* (IR) is the term that describes the underlying programmatic details. Integrated Risk is a risk financing/transferring *technique*. By integrating certain risks into a single risk management framework, many of the goals of ERM can be realized. An *integrated structure* is one in which noncorrelated risks (usually event and financial) are managed *together* to create a portfolio. This can result in less combined volatility and more predictable outcomes.

Figure 2.7

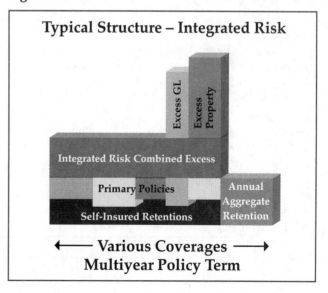

Typical Structure – Integrated Risk

Excess GL
Excess Property
Integrated Risk Combined Excess
Primary Policies
Annual Aggregate Retention
Self-Insured Retentions

◄── **Various Coverages** ──►
Multiyear Policy Term

Figure 2.7 illustrates a typical integrated risk approach that could be used to address catastrophic exposures. In this example, five separate risks are integrated into one risk financing/transfer program. Each risk is subject to a *self-insured retention (SIR).* Directly above the SIR, individual risk transfer limits in the form of primary insurance policies apply. For example, auto, general liability, crime, property, and professional liability exposures could be insured through these primary insurance policies. The integrated risk layer attaches above the individual risk transfer limits. This would be in the form of a combined excess insurance policy that would respond when the underlying self-insured retention or any primary insurance policy coverage is exhausted. Figure 2.7 shows that additional insurance limits are placed above the integrated layer for general liability and property exposures. Note that the program's policy period is comprised of multiple years. This is a necessary feature of all integrated risk structures as a multiyear policy term allows for better loss predictability than does the traditional one-year horizon. The program also aggregates the self-insured retentions on an annual basis.

Impact of Financial Accounting Standard 133 on IR

Financial Accounting Standard 133 (FAS 133) is a relatively new directive developed by the Financial Accounting Standards Board that instructs corporations on the correct accounting for the value of derivative contracts. This discussion will not purport to cover FAS 133 in great detail. It is included here only by way of introduction and to provide a framework for the understanding of how financial risk is traditionally managed and its applicability to integrated risk programs. FAS 133 became effective on June 15, 2000. Its primary impact is on how corporations account for their financial risk management activities, that is, their use of financial derivatives as hedges against certain types of financial loss.

A *derivative* is a type of investment that derives its market value from another asset. For example, credit derivatives are commonly used to hedge against credit risk—the risk of incurring an excess amount of bad debt. When derivative investments are used for risk management purposes, the use of *hedge accounting* is essential. Hedge accounting simply means that a derivative's gains or losses are reflected in the same period as the income effects of the underlying hedged item.

Hedge accounting is necessary to properly match the timing of the income recognition between the derivative and its underlying asset. If these become mismatched, income distortions can result in greater earnings volatility. For example, assume ABC Corporation earned $100,000 on sales of widgets in Japan. Because the currency exchange rate is always in flux, the value of the Japanese sales could have been lower based on the dollar's value as compared to the yen's. To protect against currency exchange rate devaluation, ABC purchased a foreign exchange (FX) derivative contract. The derivative was designed to pay if the dollar/yen exchange rate fell below a predetermined point, known as the "strike price". If the FX is a qualified hedge (and the strike price is met), proceeds from the derivative will have effectively hedged the loss resulting from the currency devaluation, resulting in $100,000 of earnings. On the other hand, if the FX contract is not deemed to be a qualified hedge, it must be reflected on the books at its current market value. Doing so in the accounting period when the $100,000 earnings is recognized will not cause a problem; however, if the option period of the FX derivative extends beyond the initial accounting period, the derivative's value (either positive or negative) will be reflected in a period (or periods) that do not include the earnings being hedged. This can cause earnings distortions and introduce unwarranted volatility.

FAS 133 states that all derivatives of a certain type must be recognized on the balance sheet, that is, "marked to market" in order to determine its *effectiveness.* Marking-to-market involves valuing derivatives and their underlying positions in order to determine how to account for gains and losses. The portion of the hedge that *effectively* offsets the change in value of the underlying item is accounted for in "other comprehensive income" in the statement of shareholder's equity. The ineffective part of the hedge, that is, the part that is superfluous to the risk management objective, is reflected in earnings, and is not shown as a separate item.

Since a truly integrated risk program includes one or more financial risks, it is conceivable that the value represented by pre-FAS 133 hedge accounting may be available again through an insurance mechanism. This has been the primary motivation for the development of integrated risk structures. The only hard and fast rule is this: **the event risk and the financial risk must not be bifurcatible.** Put another way, it cannot be possible to separate the financial risk insurance component without the entire program collapsing. If bifurcation is possible, under FAS 133 the financial risk component will be deemed to be an *embedded derivative*, and thus subject to its rules.

For example, assume an integrated risk insurance program is designed to cover workers compensation and the movement of certain interest rates. The policy might state that, in the event that a key short-term interest rate rises above a predetermined level (the trigger or strike price), the policy would respond. If the policy simply paid the difference between the strike price and a predetermined upper limit interest rate (the strike price being the interest rate level above which the company would begin to lose money), that would be an example of a derivative embedded in an insurance contract. If the policy's response was *not* a direct payoff but was in the form of a lower deductible on the company's workers compensation insurance—that scenario would theoretically satisfy the nonbifurcatible requirement since both components—workers compensation AND interest rate risk—must exist in order for the contract to be valid.

Assume ABC Corporation insures its workers compensation subject to a $2 million annual aggregate self-insured retention. Once aggregate losses exceed this amount, the insurer provides coverage for all claims from dollar one. Also assume that the policy contains an endorsement that automatically reduces the $2 million aggregate retention in direct proportion to a documented reduction in investment income that is earned through several money market funds, in the event that interest rates fall below a predetermined level. So, if investment income falls by $300,000 during the policy term, the workers compensation aggregate retention becomes $1,700,000. This concept is not flawless and is largely untested; however, it represents an innovative use of insurance.

The Theoretical Benefits of Integrated Risk Structures

Integrated risk structures can provide tangible benefits to an organization. However, the concept is relatively new, and there have been few successful examples. Insurance market conditions also have an impact on the viability of integrated risk programs. When insurance rates are rising, insurers are less willing to exhibit the creativity necessary to structure an IR program, concentrating instead on their core products and services. The theoretical benefits of IR are as follows.

- The portfolio approach reduces the variation of potential outcomes (volatility), which allows for a reduction of the risk transfer costs as compared to a conventional program.

- The use of fewer insurers eliminates multiple placements and reduces the credit risk associated with dealing with a multitude of insurers.

- There are reduced administrative costs because the number of policies and insurers being used is reduced.

- The use of fewer insurers reduces or eliminates potential claims disputes among insurers.

- There is customized and improved protection for balance sheet risk (FAS 133).

- Overall risk management is more efficient.

Perceived Disadvantages of Integrated Risk Structures

Integrated risk represents a significant change in the way risk is financed and transferred. Regardless of its potential merits, those who it affects rarely, if ever, universally embrace change. The following are some often heard objections to integrated risk:

- There is a lack of integrated risk management expertise and experience.

- Multiline insurers and reinsurers may not support integrated risk, especially in a hard market environment.

- Corporate treasury personnel are unable and/ or unwilling to relinquish control over financial risk management issues.

- There often is entrenched organizational resistance to anything new and otherwise untested elsewhere—a "wait and see" attitude

Types of Integrated Risk Structures

Multiline–Multiyear Insurance

A multiline-multiyear (MLMY) insurance arrangement, sometimes known as a *cross-class* program, can provide some of the benefits of an integrated risk structure without the financial risk component. MLMY programs combine primary and excess insurance limits and retentions for hazard risks and utilize a multiyear policy term. The value can be twofold:

- Potentially lower overall premiums may result because of economies of scale, that is, the use of a single insurer.

- Expected losses may be better predicted (over the multiyear policy term) than that which would have been available using only a standard one-year term.

Figure 2.8

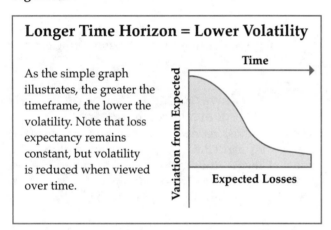

Figure 2.8 illustrates the effect of time on volatility.

Multiple Trigger Programs

A multiple trigger insurance policy is a form of integrated risk structure that covers two or more loss events that occur as a consequence of each other. For example, in a *dual trigger* program, the first trigger might be a property loss, and the second might be a drop in the company's stock price as a result of the property loss. When both occur, the policy responds.

Multiple trigger programs are usually designed to respond to the financial consequences (as well as the physical loss) of an insured loss event. These policies are not standardized, nor are they readily available from the major multiline insurers. They are customized financial arrangements usually structured by specialty insurers located in Bermuda and London.

Figure 2.9

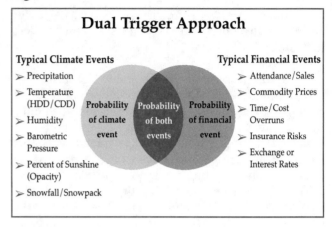

Figure 2.9 illustrates a dual trigger structure that incorporates the risks associated with weather and climate and various types of financial, event, and operational risks. The overlap of the two circles illustrates the probability of how often the policy will respond. For example, if the organization is an amusement park, the risk of rain is a factor in projecting sales based on attendance. Each risk can be measured independently, that is, the probability of it raining within a predetermined timeframe and the probability of attaining the projected sales and attendance targets can be identified.

The dual trigger policy is based on the *combined probability* of the occurrence of precipitation *and* meeting the sales and attendance targets.

THE CHIEF RISK OFFICER

The advent of the Chief Risk Officer (CRO) is a direct result of the enterprise risk management movement. Due to the centralized and highly focused nature of ERM, proponents are advocating the establishment of a new executive level corporate position—the Chief Risk Officer. Financial institutions, such as banks, originally adopted the CRO concept. Long before ERM became popular, many large banks understood the benefits of an enterprise-wide approach to managing risk, especially operational risk. The CRO is slowly beginning to gain currency among a cross section of global corporations.

The Goal of the CRO

In concert with enterprise risk management's goal of maximizing shareholder value and earnings, the CRO's mission is to protect and enhance shareholder value as efficiently and effectively as possible. To accomplish this goal, the Chief Risk Officer must embody the following characteristics and skills:

- The ability to provide overall leadership in the prosecution of the company's ERM program

- Excellent communication and persuasion skills

- The ability to generate organizational buy-in

- Proven ability to effectively manage people and tasks

- The ability to see the big picture

- An understanding of insurance risk analysis and the available treatment options

- Highly developed financial and analytical skills

- The ability to synthesize the efforts of the various staff members responsible for component parts of the ERM program and to effectively communicate results in appropriate financial language

Who Reports to the Chief Risk Officer?

Only a small number of people within most large corporations have risk management as their primary job function. Many others, however, are secondarily responsible for specific types of risk management. For example, the management information systems manager (MIS) not only is responsible for maintaining an efficient and properly functioning computer system. She must also take precautions (or make sure precautions exist) against hackers (computer vandals and saboteurs) both outside and inside the organization and be responsible for the net results of system malfunctions, among other things.

The CRO is responsible for both the traditional risk management activities, such as purchasing the proper insurance and executing the necessary financial derivatives trades, as well as the nontraditional risk management activities, such as the MIS manager's efforts to safeguard the company's computer system. This is most easily done when managers of the functions within the CRO's responsibility spectrum report to the CRO.

Figure 2.10

Figure 2.10 illustrates a possible organizational structure.

Benefits and Advantages

- The CEO is able to make decisions based on the best information available, confident that the CRO is constantly monitoring the company's entire risk profile.

- There is thorough and cost effective treatment of all risks facing the organization, with direct access to senior management.

- The goals that are consistent with ERM—reduction in earnings volatility and higher stock price multiples—are the CRO's highest priority.

Drawbacks and Disadvantages

The following disadvantages of the CRO concept seem to have a common theme—lack of confidence in the concept and its execution. The corporate culture objection stems from a skeptical viewpoint, which may be the most intractable obstacle to overcome. The fact is that some companies will 1) never recognize the value of the CRO position (although it may be good for the organization), and 2) will never be able to remake their organizational structure to accommodate a CRO, even if they recognize its value. Disadvantages include

- Lack of organizational buy-in

- Possibility of concentrating important corporate responsibilities in one potentially unqualified individual

- An absence of management controls

- Disruption of established relationships between former corporate risk decision-makers and service providers

- Unconvincing execution

- Inability to change the corporate culture

THE FUTURE OF THE CRO

There is growing evidence that, in the wake of the collapse of energy trader Enron, and the WorldCom accounting fraud, the role of the *audit committee* will be expanded to include enterprise risk management responsibilities. As of this writing, the Institute of Internal Auditors is preparing a position paper that includes specific corporate governance recommendations relative to the management of financial, operational, and strategic risks. If the audit committee assumes such oversight, the role of the traditional risk manager as well as the CRO will undergo significant changes.

Chapter 2

GLOSSARY

Bifurcation. Separating one component of an integrated program from another, such as separating the financial risk component from the event risk component in an integrated risk program.

Business risks. Risks that are encountered as a part of doing business, which are thought to be largely uninsurable.

Chief Risk Officer (CRO). An executive level corporate position whose mission is to manage material risks to protect and enhance shareholder value.

Correlation. When two or more investments or risks respond similarly to the same stimulus.

Derivative. A type of investment that derives its market value from another asset.

Enterprise risk management (ERM). A framework for identifying, defining, quantifying, comparing, prioritizing, and treating all of the material risks facing an organization (whether insurable or not).

Event or hazard risk. The risk of loss without possibility of gain; risks that traditionally have been insurable.

Financial risks. Risks that include the chance of loss and inadequate gain, which emanate usually from financial transactions.

Frequency. How often a loss occurs over a period of time.

Hedge accounting. The system of reflecting a derivative's gains or losses in the same period as the income effects of the underlying hedged item.

Holistic risk management. An early term coined to describe the enterprise risk management concept.

Inflation effect. The magnified effects of two or more unrelated risks causing individual and collective damage to an organization.

Integrated risk. A risk financing/transferring technique that integrates noncorrelated risks into one management structure.

Integrated risk management. An early term coined to describe the enterprise risk management concept.

Internal hedging. A process to manage risks so that they balance one another.

Multiline-Multiyear (MLMY) arrangement. A program that combines primary and excess insurance limits and retentions for hazard risks into a multiyear policy term.

Multiple trigger program. An insurance policy that covers two or more loss events that occur as a consequence of each other.

Noncorrelation. When two or more investments or risks do not respond similarly to the same stimulus.

Organizational buy-in. The process of getting various sectors of an organization to agree on (to buy into) the value of an initiative.

Operational risk. Risks that arise from an organization's people and operations other than event or hazard risk.

Portfolio. The aggregation of tangibles or intangibles that is designed to create a whole greater than the sum of its parts.

Portfolio theory. A term used to describe the fact that correlation can significantly impact an organization's ability to retain risk and that certain risk scenarios can be used to counterbalance the volatility of such correlated risks.

Reputational risk. The risk of losing market share and good reputation because of the management of a crisis; also called brand risk.

Risk mapping. A graphical analytical tool that allows an organization's material risks to be identified, understood, and prioritized.

Self-insured retention (SIR). That portion of pure risk an insured undertakes to handle on its own. A deductible is a form of self-insured retention.

Severity. The relative impact of a loss.

Silos. Segregation of responsibilities within an organization, which leads to little cross-department cooperation.

Strategic risk. Risks associated with the execution of a business plan.

Chapter 3

RISK ASSESSMENT: IDENTIFICATION

─── ■ ───

WHAT IS IT?

The expression *risk assessment* connotes two separate and distinct activities:

1. Risk identification, and

2. Risk quantification.

A company's ability to accurately identify and quantify its risk is directly related to the quality of its management controls, the effectiveness of its business plan, and the culture that drives its management philosophy. History is replete with spectacular examples of seemingly invincible companies that, through arrogance, negligence, or design, were brought down by a lack of effective management controls, a cavalier attitude towards risk, or a combination thereof. Fortunately, corporations are beginning to understand the value of high-quality risk assessment, as well as the skills necessary to do the job.

The Enterprise Risk Management discussion in Chapter 2 focused on assessing risk from a global perspective, using tools such as the *risk map* to help identify hidden loss exposures and the impact of two or more unrelated risks occurring within the same time period. In Chapter 3 we discuss a broad range of techniques risk managers use to recognize risk's financial impact on the company. As we discussed in Chapter 1, all loss exposures are derived from one of two major sources:

1. Owned and Nonowned Assets

2. Third-Party Liability

Of course, it can be argued that third-party liability risk actually describes the potential loss of an owned asset—money. But our purpose here is to review not only that which can be lost or damaged, but also the sources from which potential losses emanate.

STEP ONE: CATEGORIZING OWNED AND NONOWNED ASSETS

Owned and nonowned assets can be categorized into four separate and distinct groups:

1. physical assets,

2. financial assets,

3. intellectual capital (people), and

4. intangible assets.

Each of these assets can be susceptible to *direct loss* caused by a variety of perils, including fire, theft, and natural occurrences such as windstorm, flood, or earthquake. *Indirect loss,* which may be referred to as consequential loss because it arises as a consequence of a direct loss, is the loss of earnings and the need for additional expenditures following a direct loss.

Physical Assets

A company's physical assets are comprised of its real and personal property. These include buildings, furniture and fixtures, electronic equipment, décor, inventory, raw materials, work-in-process, and the systems that support the operations. These systems include all manufacturing equipment and heating, venting, and air conditioning (HVAC) systems. Physical assets also include nonowned assets such as property of employees (tools, etc.); rented property; property considered to be in the company's care, custody, or control; and any property in which a bailment has been created. (A bailment exists when one party is legally responsible for the property of others. For example, a dry cleaner is responsible for the safekeeping of its customers clothing.)

Financial Assets

Financial assets are comprised of all financial records and legally negotiable instruments (e.g., cash, stock certificates, bonds, notes, money orders, and checks), wherever they exist (in transit, in the bank, etc.). The accounts receivables document is one of the company's most important financial records, since it represents the company's cash flows. Accounts receivables are often leveraged against short-term borrowing, allowing a company to maximize the value of its capital. Although it could be argued that accounts receivables belongs in the physical assets category, we list them here because the financial impact of irreplaceable lost or damaged accounts receivables far exceeds the physical value of the records themselves.

While financial records such as the balance sheet and annual report are important, they are not considered financial assets per se, because they have no inherent intrinsic value.

Intellectual Capital

Most companies consider their employees to be their most important asset. However, some employees are more critical than others relative to the firm's survival and growth. These people include the senior management team, legal and financial experts, and those with specialized technical expertise and knowledge such as key engineers, programmers, and designers. However, in the wake of the tragic loss of life that occurred during the terrorist attack on the World Trade Center in New York City on September 11, 2001, the impact associated with the massive loss of human capital from a single event must also be considered when evaluating loss potential.

Intangible Assets

The most obvious and well understood intangible asset is goodwill. Goodwill can be converted into a dollar amount when a company is sold or merged with another. Goodwill is tantamount to reputation. When a firm's reputation is damaged, goodwill evaporates and the company is in danger of losing—or even going out of—business. (The former accounting firm, Arthur Andersen, is a case study example.) Other intangible assets include relationships with vendors and suppliers.

Nonowned intangible assets are comprised of the public infrastructure necessary to conduct business, for example, water, electricity, and communication lines.

STEP TWO: IDENTIFYING THIRD–PARTY LIABILITY

The second major source of loss exposures is third-party (public) liability. There are five major categories of public liability loss exposures:

1. Premises Liability
2. Liability for Operations (off premises)
3. Products Liability
4. Professional Liability
5. Liability for Employees

Premises Liability

Premises liability arises from the ownership or rental of real property and involves injury or damage that arises from a condition of those premises. The law recognizes three separate circumstances that connote varying degrees of responsibility: In order of responsibility and therefore degree of liability, they are:

1. Invitees
2. Licensees
3. Trespassers

The highest degree of care is owed to *invitees.* Invitees are people who, as the name implies, are invited onto the premises for a particular purpose other than within the context of a commercial contract. A repairperson invited to fix a faulty computer is considered an invitee. (This is covered in the next category, liability for operations.)

The term *licensee* describes those who have implicit permission to enter a company's premises. Door-to-door salespeople and delivery people fall into this category. They are not specifically invited, but neither are they unexpected. Liability to licensees is not as clearly defined as it is for invitees. However, unless extenuating circumstances prevail, licensees must be afforded a high degree of care.

Finally, *trespassers* are those who are implicitly and/or explicitly prohibited from entering the premises. For example, the existence of a locked fence may represent an *implicit* prohibition, whereas a fence and a sign warning against unlawful entry may represent an *explicit* prohibition. Trespassers are generally afforded the lowest standard of care. However, case law is full of examples in which even trespassers were awarded significant damages as a result of injuries sustained while trespassing onto the premises of others.

Liability for Operations

Companies are liable for injury to persons and damage to nonowned property resulting from their off-premises operations. Examples include building trades contractors working at a nonowned job site and repairpersons working at a customer's location.

Products Liability

Any company that manufactures and/or distributes a tangible product for sale to the general public or other businesses is liable for the potential injury to third parties and damage to nonowned property. It is important to understand the precise nature of the liability assumed. Many products are inherently dangerous if used improperly or for a purpose for which they were not designed. Examples include lawn mowers, power tools, and chemicals. However, even in court cases in which serious injury occurred as a result of improper use, judges and juries overwhelmingly have found in favor of the plaintiff (the injured party), citing missing or inadequate warning labels or insufficient operating instructions. Products liability does **not** extend to efficacy or warranty issues. If the product does not perform as advertised, liability cannot be assessed against the manufacturer or distributor—assuming the product did not cause physical injury or damage to property. While not exactly a separate category of liability, product efficacy and warranty loss exposures exist and may be transferred using specialized insurance products.

Professional Liability

The third-party liability described thus far is that which would be represented by what the law calls a *reasonable person*. For example, firm A sells cardboard boxes to firm B. Neither party is held to be superior to the other relative to the sales contract; each is assumed to be a reasonable person under the law. However, depending on the organization's business or purpose, legal liability can extend beyond that of a reasonable person to that of a *professional*. A professional is held to a higher standard of care than is a reasonable person, due to the fact that the relationship that exists between a professional and the general public is not deemed to be equal.

For example, a physician has specialized knowledge and skills that require a higher standard of care relative to the liability to which she is exposed each time she treats a patient. While this risk is similar to general or public liability, it must be specifically identified so that appropriate treatment options can be employed.

Liability for Employees

Employees occupy a special place relative to third-party liability issues. For some types of injury claims, they may be considered third parties. However, for the vast majority of work-related injuries, employees are covered by workers compensation. Every state in the United States—except Texas—requires employers to compensate injured workers, either by purchasing workers compensation insurance or through a formal self-insurance program. See Chapter 18, Workers Compensation, for additional information on this subject.

STEP THREE: CHOOSING THE RESOURCES

Except for insurers, reinsurers, and financial services firms, commercial enterprises are generally not in the business of taking risk. While risk is an inescapable part of business life, it is often regarded as just another expense item, similar to payroll and overhead. Management realizes that it must assume a certain amount of risk in order to run a successful business, but its threshold for most types of risk is fairly low. In order to determine the optimal risk threshold, loss exposures must be identified.

Risk managers have access to an effective array of information resources with which to identify loss exposures. They include the following:

- Surveys and Questionnaires

- Financial Documents

- Sales and Other Contracts

- Risk Management Committees

- Flow Charts

- Company Documents

- Physical Inspections

Surveys and Questionnaires

Large, diverse companies are generally managed on a decentralized basis. While senior management is preoccupied with overall strategic issues, line and staff managers actually run the business on a daily basis. Surveys and questionnaires can provide effective vehicles for identifying loss exposures because the questions can be tailored to conform to the recipients' responsibilities, whether they're staff functions (human resources, legal), or line functions (subsidiary presidents, production managers).

Surveys are used in two ways:

- to collect and document specific line-of-insurance underwriting information, and

- to collect and document insurance and risk management practices and procedures.

Line-of-insurance questionnaires contain straightforward questions relative to the exposures associated with a particular line of insurance. For example, a workers compensation survey will include questions pertaining to number of employees, job classifications, geographic location, and work hazards and safeguards. For property insurance purposes, questionnaires should include COPE (construction, occupancy, protection, and exposures) data.

The second type of questionnaire, that which deals with insurance and risk management practices and procedures, can be of greater value to risk managers than line-of-insurance surveys. This questionnaire covers a wide spectrum of risk management responsibilities and can be designed as a basic checklist of important issues and considerations. Figure 3.1 is an example of a typical insurance and risk management practices and procedures questionnaire.

Financial Documents

A company's financial records contain a wealth of information that is useful to the risk manager. Publicly held companies are required by the Security and Exchange Commission (SEC) to publish quarterly 10Q financial reports and annual 10K reports. Financial reports for publicly traded companies may be found at the SEC Web site, http://www.sec.gov/.

Whether the company is public or private, its financial statements reveal the amount of capital allocated to managing risk, the book value of company assets, how much reserve cash is available to cover self-insured (or uninsured) losses, and the company's debt load as it may affect its ability to collateralize self-insured loss exposures. Other sources of financial information include Dun & Bradstreet reports and a variety of online sources, including *Yahoo Finance* (http://finance.yahoo.com/?) and *Bloomberg,* (http://www.bloomberg.com/).

Sales and Other Contracts

The majority of contracts contain provisions for the shifting of liability. Since contracting parties are rarely, if ever, considered equal parties relative to one another, the party holding the upper hand in the contract is usually able to successfully transfer certain risks to the weaker party. Sales contracts and lease agreements can include contractual liability transfers and hold-harmless language that expose the company to potential risk. (In a *hold harmless agreement,* one party agrees to assume another party's responsibility for damages or injuries that occur due to the two parties' relationships.) Many contracts also require one party to name the other as an additional insured on its general liability insurance policy. This gives the additional insured entity certain rights to coverage under the insurance policy.

Risk Management Committees

Risk management committees are comprised of key members of each corporate staff department, plus a representative(s) from operations—for example, manufacturing. Staff departments can include finance, legal, and human resources. The committee is usually led by the risk manager and convenes at least once per quarter. Committee members are responsible for communicating specific risk-related information to the risk manager.

Flow Charts

A flow chart can be an effective tool in identifying potential exposures to loss that may exist between corporate functions such as manufacturing and sales, as well as between the company and its suppliers, vendors and other service providers. Flow charts graphically depict *communication* and *expectations.* Figures 3.2 and 3.3 depict the two types of flow charts: external and internal. In the example in Figure 3.2, the external flow chart tracks the movement of goods from materials suppliers to subcontractors and, finally, to wholesalers.

Figure 3.1

Insurance & Risk Management

Policies and Procedures

Document Management

Describe the company's document retention and retrieval system:

Insurance Policies	_____ years	
Premium Audits	_____ years	Retrieval System(s):
Certificates of Insurance	_____ years	Compact Disk_____
Lease Agreements	_____ years	Microfiche_____
Construction Contracts	_____ years	Paper Files_____
Other Contracts	_____ years	

Describe the company's system for accessing and maintaining currently valued loss information.

Is there a suspense system in place to assure timely renewals? [ ] Yes [ ] No

Is there a system to monitor & analyze Certificates of Insurance? [ ] Yes [ ] No

Management of Claims and Losses

Is the following claims training provided to employees and managers?

The importance of reporting occurrences [ ] Yes [ ] No

How to report a loss occurrence/accident [ ] Yes [ ] No

What to do with suit papers [ ] Yes [ ] No

How to handle inquiries by the press after a disaster/occurrence [ ] Yes [ ] No

Are regular case reserve meetings held with claims adjusters? [ ] Yes [ ] No If yes, frequency of meetings?
_____

Are open or closed claims audits performed? [ ] Yes [ ] No If yes, frequency?_____

By whom? _____

Are any claims self-administered? [ ] Yes [ ] No If yes, describe the program _____

_____

_____

Figure 3.1 (Cont'd)

Responsibilities of the Risk Manager

To whom does the risk manager report and why? _____
_____

Does the risk/insurance manager periodically visit the company's locations/subsidiaries? [ ] Yes [ ] No If yes, frequency of visits _____

Risk Manager's Responsibilities (check all that apply)

[ ]   Agent/Broker Selection

[ ]   Insurance Company Selection

[ ]   Property Value Establishment

[ ]   Property and Liability Insurance Purchasing

[ ]   Presentations to Board of Directors

[ ]   Preparation of Corporate Insurance/Risk Management Manual

[ ]   Determine/Recommend Retention Levels

[ ]   Property Claims Management

[ ]   Liability Claims Management

[ ]   Workers Compensation Claims Management

[ ]   Safety/Loss Control

[ ]   Quality Assurance

How are subsidiaries' insurance and risk funding needs met? Separately or consolidated?

Describe the arrangements.

_____

_____

Are the following costs allocated to subsidiaries or profit centers:

Premiums?   [ ] Yes [ ] No

Deductibles?   [ ] Yes [ ] No

R.M. Department operating costs?   [ ] Yes [ ] No

Figure 3.1 (Cont'd)

Describe the procedure/system of allocation of premiums/deductibles:

_____

_____

_____

_____

Is the company's "Cost of Risk" calculated each year and compared to industry benchmarks?

[ ] Yes   [ ] No

Figure 3.1 (Cont'd)

Complete the following chart for each of the last five policy years.

Coverage	Limits of Liability	Insurer & Policy Dates	Policy Form Occurrence/ Claims-Made	Risk Financing Arrangements, i.e. guaranteed cost insurance, large deductible, captive, self-insurance
Workers Compensation				
General Liability				
Products Liability				
Automobile Physical Damage				
Automobile Liability				
Professional Liability				
Employment Practices Liability				
Directors & Officers Liability				
Property				
Environmental Impairment Liability				

Figure 3.1 (Cont'd)

Loss Control and Engineering

Does the company have a safety/loss control program?   [   ] Yes   [   ] No   Who is responsible?

_____

Are the loss control program (if any) benefits evident in the company's earnings?   [ ] Yes [ ] No

Is the program supported by senior management? [   ] Yes [   ] No

Is there a formal safety committee? [   ] Yes [   ] No

Are regularly scheduled safety meetings held? [ ] Yes [ ] No

How often? [   ] Daily [   ] Weekly [   ] Monthly

Are safety audits by outside/independent consultants ever conducted? [ ] Yes [ ] No

Comments on loss control activities

_____

_____

_____

_____

Do employees/managers receive any form of formal safety training? [   ] Yes   [   ] No

Are regularly scheduled safety inspections held?   [   ] Yes [   ] No

[   ] Weekly   [   ] Monthly   [   ] Quarterly   [   ] Annually

Does the company have a written contingency/disaster plan?

Details:

_____

_____

_____

_____

Transportation risks are the dominant loss exposures in Figure 3.2. However, the chart also suggests the existence of products and contractual liability issues. The internal flow chart (Figure 3.3) represents the flow of goods within the company. Critical junctures include the materials inspection and quality control stations. In addition, final assembly of leather shoes is dependent on the coordination of the leather uppers assembly station and the leather and rubber sole fabricating station. A mechanical malfunction or a workers compensation-related accident at either station would cause a production bottleneck and the consequent potential financial loss.

Company Documents

A company's internal documents reveal much about its exposures to loss. Public and employee liability losses can often be traced to a company's documents, such as its employee handbook, equipment operating manuals, and promotional literature. Historical loss records provide data that may be used to predict future claims. The company's business plan and the minutes of corporate board meetings may include information about the firm's long-term strategic planning. Product packaging and advertising are also important sources of potential liability as they may exaggerate the product's efficacy, which could lead to advertising liability claims.

Physical Inspections

Once all the company documents (including financial statements and contracts) have been reviewed, and after the flowcharts have been analyzed, it's time to physically inspect the company's operations and locations. Inspections can be useful for a variety of reasons.

First, they allow independent verification of published material. For example, a metal stamping machine-operating manual may prescribe the use of a specific safety precaution designed to guard against employee injury. Without an on-site inspection, the risk manager would not be able to verify that all stamping machine operators were actually employing the safety device. (For this type of inspection it is best to arrive unannounced.) Another example of data verification might concern the COPE data records.

The risk manager's files may indicate that a particular building's construction is *fire resistive* (built with materials that have been tested to withstand exposure to high temperatures for specified periods of time) with a sprinkler system, only to discover that it is actually *noncombustible* (built with materials that resist bursting into flame) and that the water pressure at the sprinkler system is inadequate. Physical inspections not only provide an opportunity to verify and update risk management files but also give the risk manager the opportunity to meet with the local managers and discuss specific loss trends or safety concerns and receive and encourage their "on-the-spot" feedback and suggestions. This helps assure their cooperation in risk management compliance and improvement.

ADVANTAGES

The assessment of risks across an organization can serve a number of purposes in addition to risk identification. It provides risk managers with information that might not otherwise be readily shared and which could lead to enhanced risk management programs. Service on risk management or audit committees also helps to integrate the risk management process into operations.

DISADVANTAGES

There may be problems in obtaining certain documents, especially if the organization is decentralized. And a great deal of time must be committed to obtaining and reviewing company documents and inspecting properties. It may be difficult to physically inspect all locations, but inspections should be scheduled on a rotating basis so that all are visited periodically.

WHERE CAN I FIND OUT MORE ABOUT IT?

Most brokers, independent agents, and risk management consultants can offer valuable insight into risk assessment processes. Additional information may be obtained from:

- *Risk Financing* (Reference Service). Dallas: International Risk Management Institute (IRMI).

- *Risk Funding & Self-Insurance Bulletins (RF&S)*. Cincinnati: The National Underwriter Company, http://www.nationalunderwriter.com/nucatalog/.

- Church, Frederic C. Jr. *Avoiding Surprises, Second Edition*. Boston: Standard Publishing Corp.

Figure 3.2

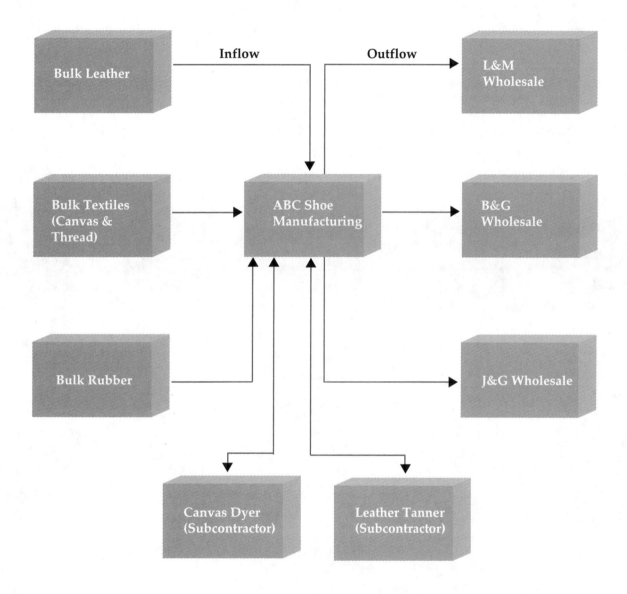

**External Flow Chart Example
ABC Shoe Manufacturing**

Each line represents a transportation exposure. The double arrow lines to and from ABC Shoe Manufacturing and the two subcontractors represent potential products liability exposures as well as contractual liability exposures.

Figure 3.3

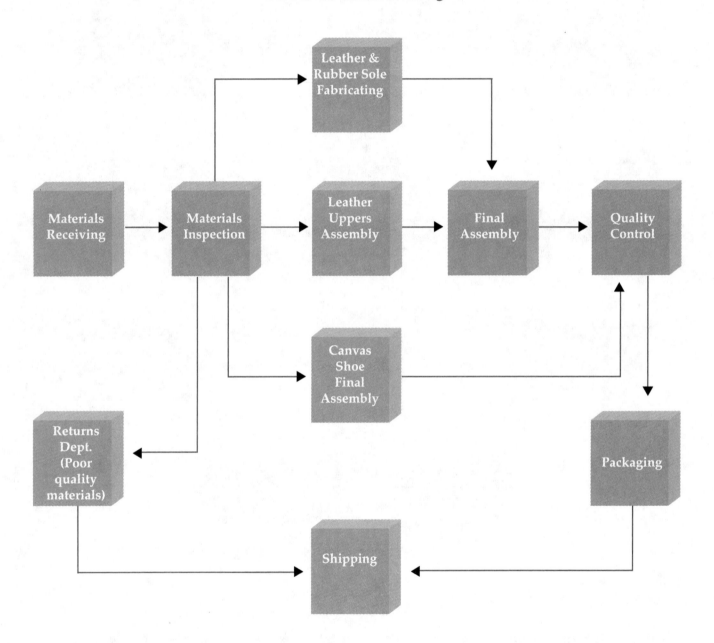

Internal Flow Chart Example
ABC Shoe Manufacturing

QUESTIONS AND ANSWERS

Question—How can risk managers determine which identification processes are best for their organizations?

Answer—There is no one *best* risk identification process. A number of company documents may first be reviewed to gain an overview of the organization's risk profile. That usually will uncover areas of prime importance, which then should be reviewed in more detail. A combination of processes is best, with physical inspections always recommended.

Question—Businesses are not static; they constantly change equipment, processes, and employees. As a result, their risks also are constantly evolving. Is there a way to build this into the risk identification process?

Answer—The best way to accomplish this is to institutionalize the risk identification process. For example, systems may be established so that the purchase of physical assets above a certain value are reported to the risk management department. Or a process may be established so that all proposed contracts are reviewed by the risk management department before they are executed. This is an excellent way to continuously identify new risks.

Participation in risk management or audit committees also offers the opportunity for ongoing monitoring of the risk profile.

GLOSSARY

Bailment. When one party is legally responsible for the property of others.

COPE. An acronym for the exposure categories that are associated with property. The acronym stands for Construction (what the property is constructed of), Occupancy (the type of business the property houses), Protection (the type of risk protection, such as alarms and sprinklers), and Exposures (the type of property that surrounds the building).

Direct loss. A loss that directly injures or damages a person or property. For example, a building fire is considered a direct property loss.

Employee liability. Liability that arises from an employer's responsibility for its employees.

Flow charts. Graphical depictions of the flow of goods and services throughout an organization (an internal flow chart) or from suppliers to subcontractors to wholesalers (an external flow chart).

Goodwill. An intangible asset that is equivalent in value to and results from a firm's reputation.

Indirect loss. The consequential losses that are associated with a direct loss, such as the loss of earnings that occurs when business is interrupted after a fire.

Intellectual capital. The value that people (employees) bring to an organization.

Legally negotiable instruments. Paper documents that represent financial value, such as cash, bonds, money orders, stock certificates, and checks.

Operations liability. Liability that arises from a business's operations that are conducted away from its premises.

Premises liability. Liability that arises from the ownership or rental of real property.

Products liability. Liability that arises from a tangible product that is sold to the general public or to other businesses.

Professional liability. Liability that arises from activities of a professional, whose activities are held to a higher standard of care than that of average individuals. Professionals usually have extensive education, are licensed, and perform services to others for a fee.

Risk assessment. A process through which a company's risks (exposures to loss) are identified and quantified.

Risk map. A tool to help identify loss exposures and the impact of two or more unrelated risks occurring within a certain time period. Risk maps are visual maps of a company's exposures and where they may overlap.

Risk quantification. A process to place a value on a business's risks; a system to evaluate the financial impact of a company's risks.

Chapter 4

RISK ASSESSMENT: QUANTIFICATION

As introduced in Chapter 3, the expression *risk assessment* connotes two separate and distinct activities:

1. Risk identification, and

2. Risk quantification.

Chapter 3 dealt with risk identification. This chapter deals with risk quantification.

WHAT IS IT?

Exposure quantification is an extremely inexact science. It relies on data that may or may not be complete and accurate. Unless the risk is transferred off-balance sheet in its entirety, such as by purchasing guaranteed cost, first-dollar insurance, quantifying its impact on the company is a function of probability and intuition. The better the input data, the better the result.

When we speak of exposure quantification, we are *not* implying that each identified loss exposure will be assigned a value. Exposure quantification is relative in that its value derives from the company's ability to absorb loss; if a risk is too expensive to absorb, it should be avoided or transferred, assuming the transfer costs are within reason.

At the bottom line, exposure quantification can be summed up in one sentence: *To determine the optimal amount of retained losses.* The notion of *optimal retained losses* assumes

1. insurance costs in excess of the retained loss level are optimized, and

2. retained losses are reasonably predictable.

If either one of these are not present, exposure quantification cannot be optimized. For example, when insurance premiums are extremely inexpensive, the company may not want to assume any risk at all, since, by doing so, they would expose themselves to potential loss greater than the premium expenditure. On the other hand, when insurance premiums are very expensive, it may not be reason-

able to purchase first-dollar insurance. The risk quantification process compares loss exposures relative to two criteria:

*   loss frequency versus loss severity, and

*   the cost of insurance.

STEP ONE: DETERMINING FREQUENCY VERSUS SEVERITY

The first point of analysis evaluates each loss exposure based on its potential dollar value of loss.

For example, earthquakes and hurricanes are considered to be catastrophic in nature and do not make good candidates for retained losses. If the company is prone to these types of losses, full retention is never advisable. Of course, if insurance is unavailable, the company has no choice. However, it should never intentionally assume a catastrophic risk. Conversely, in a large company, workers compensation losses are generally predictable and plentiful, a combination that suggests that a certain amount of loss retention may be more economical than purchasing first-dollar insurance.

Almost every loss exposure has the potential to produce catastrophic loss scenarios, including workers compensation. The idea is to strike a balance between affordable retained losses and affordable excess insurance. Figure 4.1 is a graph that shows the comparative relationships between frequent risks and severe risks. The smaller, more frequent risks should be retained, if only to avoid trading dollars with an insurance company. Medium-sized/medium-frequency losses should either be transferred or retained based on the cost of excess insurance, and large losses of any frequency should be transferred except for the most frequent, a percentage of which may be retained.

The Cost of Insurance

There is an old saying in risk management: "Don't risk a lot for a little." This idea can be applied when

Figure 4.1

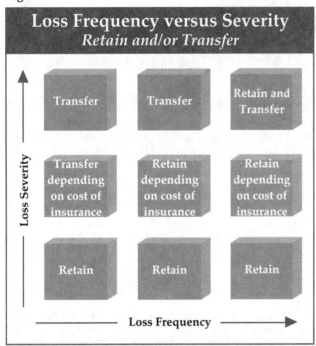

deciding how much risk to retain and how much insurance to purchase. Retained risk may be as simple as accepting a deductible, which requires that the insured business pays for the first level (deductible amount) of a claim, before the insurance company picks up the rest. Self-insurance is another example of a business retaining risk. In a perfect world, if the premium for insurance in excess of a $100,000 retention is $50,000, the premium for coverage in excess of $200,000 should be $25,000, and so on. Unfortunately, the relationship between retentions (or deductibles) and premiums does not proceed in a straight line. Insurance premiums are designed to pay for losses as well as to provide insurers a profit. Below a certain point, insurers cannot make any money due to the nonloss costs associated with the program (expenses). In the previous example, the incremental premium savings in excess of the $200,000 retention may only be 10 or 15 percent, making the premium for the $200,000 retention option somewhere between $42,500 and $45,000. Would it be prudent to risk $100,000 of loss for a mere $5,000 or $7,500 savings? Perhaps, but probably not. Unfortunately, exposure quantification is heavily dependent on the cost of insurance. But that fact does not mitigate the importance of accurately quantifying the retained risk.

STEP TWO: QUANTIFYING RETAINED RISK

Once it has been determined that a certain amount of risk must be retained, the question becomes "how

much?" There are several techniques used to arrive at this figure; however, they are extremely inexact and heavily dependent on the quality of the data used to support the conclusions. They include:

1. Loss Range Analysis
2. Loss Triangles
3. Projected Expected Losses

Loss Range Analysis

Loss range analysis places historical losses into defined ranges in order to determine the number of claims and the dollar value of those claims that fall under various thresholds. This analysis can be useful in determining the optimal value of retained versus transferred losses at a variety of potential retention levels, assuming the loss data can be considered credible. Figure 4.2 is an example of a simple loss stratification exercise. What can be gleaned from this example? Seventy-six percent of all losses did not exceed $100,000 per occurrence (all claims that arise from one accident or occurrence) for the five-year period. Of the remaining 26 percent (twelve claims), all but two did not exceed $250,000 per occurrence. The two losses that *did* exceed the $250,000 threshold did so by only $42,000. Without evaluating other factors, (for example, the company's financial ability to retain a given amount of loss), an argument for retaining loss under the $250,000 threshold in order to hold the excess risk transfer (insurance) costs to a bare minimum can be made based on the fact that only $42,000 of actual loss has breeched the $250,000 threshold in five years.

Figure 4.2

Simple Loss Range Example
Total Number of Claims: 50
Years: 1996-2001

Loss Ranger	Claims (cum)	% of Total	Claims (each)
$1,000 – $100,000	38	76	38
$100,001 – $150,000	42	84	4
$150,001 – $200,000	45	90	3
$200,001 – $250,000	48	96	3
Total within Ranges:			48
Claims in Excess of $250,000:			2
Ultimate projected Value:			1. $260,000
			2. $282,000

Loss Triangles

If we assume that our per occurrence retention will be $250,000 (based on the loss stratification exercise), we may then calculate loss development factors that assume that losses are limited to $250,000. The concept of *loss development* is relatively simple. A claim occurs in 2001. It is not immediately settled, but an estimated value is placed on it. As it matures, the claim value increases, or *develops*. By the time the claim is finally settled three years later, the claim value has increased from $100,000 to $145,000. The $145,000 is the *ultimate payout*. A loss triangle is a method for calculating loss development factors. Loss development factors are used to project historical loss data to estimate ultimate payout.

For example, an open workers compensation loss (one that has not been settled and closed) that occurred in 2001 will not be settled and closed until 2006. Its approximate ultimate value is a function of its *current value* times a loss development factor (LDF). The LDF is based on the development of similar workers compensation losses that settled and closed within the same period of time. Figure 4.3 is a loss triangle example. Calculating LDFs using one business's loss data is not considered to be a valid exercise unless the losses represent adequate actuarial credibility. *Actuarial credibility* refers to the ability of historical losses to predict future losses. If a company's own history of losses is not sufficient to calculate individual LDFs, then industry LDFs must be used in the expected loss projections.

Projected Expected Losses

The next step in quantifying exposures to loss is the calculation of expected losses. Using either individually calculated loss development factors, industry factors, or

Figure 4.3

A Loss Triangle Example					
Losses Valued at Each Annual Interval					
Losses Limited to $250,000					
		12 Months	24 Months	36 Months	48 Months	60 Months
1996	Losses	100,000	125,000	160,000	175,000	230,000
	Factor		1.25	1.28	1.10	1.31
1997	Losses	150,000	160,000	220,000	250,000	
	Factor		1.06	1.38	1.14	
1998	Losses	220,000	240,000	300,000		
	Factor		1.09	1.25		
1999	Losses	190,000	235,000			
	Factor		1.24			
2000	Losses	75,000				
	Factor					
Total Factors			4.64	3.91	2.24	1.31
Average of Factors			1.16	1.30	1.12	1.31

Loss Development Factors per Year:

2000:	2.21	(1.16 x 1.30 x 1.12 x 1.31)
1999:	1.91	(1.30 x 1.12 x 1.31)
1998:	1.47	(1.12 x 1.31)
1997:	1.31	(1.31)

a combination thereof, future losses can be predicted using historical loss data. Figure 4.4 illustrates a sample expected loss worksheet. The example in Figure 4.4 uses the loss development factors calculated in Figure 4.3 and the same incurred losses. It also assumes that incurred losses are limited to under $250,000.

STEP THREE: PROPERTY EXPOSURES

Maximum Probable Loss and Maximum Possible Loss

Loss range analysis, loss triangles, and projected expected losses pertain mainly to the casualty lines of insurance, for example, workers compensation, general liability, and automobile liability. The concepts of maximum probable and possible loss are related to first-party loss exposures, for example, real and personal property. The term *maximum probable loss* is used to define the maximum amount of loss that a structure will sustain given the facts of its COPE data. For example, a ten-story, sprinklered, fire-resistive office building located in any major metropolitan area may have a maximum probable loss of approximately three stories.

This means that, with respect to such a building, considering the construction, occupancy, and protection, the most that is likely to be lost in any single loss event, for example, fire, is three stories. The "E" part of COPE stands for *exposure*. Exposure in this case refers to

hazards that are close enough to the building to cause a potential loss. For example, if an office building were to be constructed within fifty feet of a fireworks factory, the office building's maximum probable loss would be far worse than three stories.

The expression *maximum possible loss* has assumed far greater importance since the terrorist attacks of September 11, 2001. As the term implies, maximum possible loss describes the absolute maximum amount of value considered to be at risk. In the above example, if the building's value was $10 million, the maximum *probable* loss might be pegged at $3 million. The building's maximum *possible* loss is $10 million. Prior to September 11, 2001, using maximum possible loss to describe the value-at-risk was rarely done. We have since learned that the total destruction of a building should not be considered such an extraordinary event. However, with the possible exception of super-tall skyscrapers such as the Sears Tower in Chicago, the maximum probable loss calculation using COPE data should suffice in determining real property loss probabilities.

STEP FOUR: CONSIDERING OTHER FACTORS

Impact of Actuarial Credibility on Insurance Pricing

While general insurance and risk management practitioners routinely use the models described in this chapter,

Figure 4.4

	A	B	C	D	E	F	G
Projected Expected Losses Worksheet							
Losses Valued 1/1/2001 and Limited to $250,000							
Policy Year	Incurred Losses	Trend Factor (Inflation)	Trended Incurred Losses (A x B)	Loss Development Factor	Trended and Developed Incurred Losses (C x D)	Payroll (00)	Loss Rate (E/F)
1996	230,000	1.15	264,500	1.00	264,500	1,000	2.65
1997	250,000	1.13	282,500	1.31	370,075	1,050	3.52
1998	300,000	1.10	330,000	1.47	485,100	1,150	4.22
1999	235,000	1.08	253,800	1.91	484,758	1,100	4.41
2000	75,000	1.00	75,000	2.21	165,750	1,200	1.38
				Weighted Average Loss Rate:			3.236
							x
				Projected 2002 Payroll:			1,250
				2002 Projected Losses:			404,500

they can be particularly effective when employed by an actuary. For example, an actuarial approach to the expected loss calculation includes *confidence levels*. That is, the expected loss result is displayed at a level of confidence based on the redundancy actuary's data inputs. For example, using standard industry loss development factors, an actuary's expected loss confidence level is about 50 percent. This means that the actuary is 50 percent confident that the loss figure will prove accurate. Market competition usually prohibits funding at confidence levels that exceed 50 or 55 percent, which is why most loss sensitive programs such as retrospectively rated plans have a built-in *swing*, also known as the *maximum premium*. Using such a swing means that, if losses exceed expected, the insurance company will not lose money.

The swing effectively makes up for the fact that the plan is funded at the 50 percent confidence level. Of course, if the plan were funded at, say, an 80 percent confidence level, the swing would not be necessary.

Cash Flow Analysis

Understanding the cash flows associated with any risk transfer/risk retention program is critical to the risk quantification process. Cash flow analysis is used to measure a plan's economic efficiency and represents the *true long-term value* of all risk transfer/risk retention programs. Once loss range analysis, loss triangles, and projected expected losses have been calculated and the optimal amount of risk retention has been determined, cash flow analysis measures the relative economic benefit of competing risk transfer/risk retention plans. These plans can be grouped into two main categories:

1. guaranteed cost insurance (pure risk transfer)

2. self-insurance combined with excess insurance

Guaranteed cost insurance cash flows are relatively easy to understand. The annual premium is paid either at the beginning of the policy year or periodically during the year. If the premium is paid at the beginning of the year, there is no cash flow benefit (outflow with no inflow). If the premium is paid monthly over the course of the year, the cash flow benefit can be calculated as the present value of the annual premium assuming twelve equal payments and the company's cost of capital, also known as the discount rate.

Self-insurance programs can differ dramatically in terms of the amount of cash flow they afford. For ex-

ample, an incurred loss retrospective plan (an insurance program in which the final premium is adjusted on an annual basis as claims develop) requires payment of the full annual premium during the twelve-month policy year. Adjustments to the premium based on incurred losses are made at twelve-month intervals beginning six months after the expiration of the policy period. If it takes sixty months to close out every claim, there will have been five annual adjustments (one per year for five years), during which premium is either returned to the insured or collected from the insured.

Because losses are green in the early years, premium is usually returned to the insured. As losses mature in the later years, the insurance company must collect additional premium. This back and forth cash flow can be properly evaluated *only* by discounting it back to today's cost. Conversely, a large deductible plan allows the insured to retain control of the loss funds until a loss must be paid. Because there is no give and take with the insurance company, large deductible cash flows tend to be better than those associated with incurred loss retrospective plans. However, the only way to know the precise cost savings is to compare the plans on a discounted (net present value) basis.

Benchmarking

Benchmarking is a comparison of one company's cost of risk, insurance premiums, or retention levels with others in the same or similar industries. So benchmarking is not a risk assessment method per se. A composite *cost of risk* benchmark, which would include the cost of any insurance purchased, as well as amounts the business pays for claims, may be calculated depending upon the industry and the amount of available data. Benchmarking is considered a valuable exercise because it is assumed that an entire industry's cost of risk data will reflect the norm or standard for that industry.

ADVANTAGES AND DISADVANTAGES

Impact of Risk on Financial Health

Risk's impact on a company's financial health cannot be overstated. While every other facet of the business may be expertly managed, strong product lines, robust market share, an inspired business plan, and happy, motivated employees will not make up for a lack of risk management strategy and foresight.

Risk is nothing more than uncertainty. In the long run, a business cannot function properly and meet its shareholders' expectations in the presence of unchecked uncertainty.

Conversely, too much risk aversion can have an equally detrimental effect on the financial health and profits of a company. For example, purchasing costly and excessive insurance limits squanders resources and erodes earnings. Routinely avoiding business opportunities because they may expose the company to an unaccustomed level of risk restricts profitability and growth and can force shareholders to sell their interests in favor of better-performing investments The best companies are those that are able to identify and measure risk, to find the optimal mixture of risk retention and risk transfer.

WHERE CAN I FIND OUT MORE ABOUT IT?

- *Risk Financing* (Reference Service). Dallas: International Risk Management Institute (IRMI).

- *Risk Funding & Self-Insurance Bulletins (RF&S)*. Cincinnati: The National Underwriter Company, http://www.nationalunderwriter.com/nucatalog/.

- Church, Frederic C. Jr. *Avoiding Surprises, Second Edition*. Boston: Standard Publishing Corp.

QUESTIONS AND ANSWERS

Question—A business has good historical data about the frequency and severity of claims. This company wants to use its own data to develop its own loss development factors, but the insurer they are dealing with is unwilling to permit it. Do most insurance companies permit companies to use their own losses to develop LDFs?

Answer—Many insurers prefer to use the loss development factors that they have developed, so this situation is not unusual. However, if an individual company's loss history is credible, and if the individual LDFs that are developed from it are lower than the insurer's, it is worth the time negotiating for their use in the business's risk financing program. A good deal of time and information may be required, however, before the insurer will agree to use the company's own data instead of industrywide information.

Question—Where can businesses obtain benchmarking information for their cost of risk?

Answer—A number of organizations may develop this type of measurement tool. For example, the Risk and Insurance Management Society (RIMS) annually publishes a benchmark survey, which is available for purchase at http://www.rims.org/Template.cfm?Section=OnlineStore. Industry trade associations also frequently gather and compile this information. In addition, some information may be available from insurers that write insurance for companies in various sectors.

Question—What are some of the methods that a business may use to select how much risk they should retain, either through deductibles and self-insured retentions or through other risk-sharing programs?

Answer—There are a number of methods that businesses often use to establish their loss retention levels. Some may use liquidity ratios, such as from 1 to 5 percent of current obligations; financial strength ratios, such as from .2 to 1 percent of total revenues; or performance ratios, such as from 2 to 3 percent of shareholder equity. While these may be of value, they should be considered in context with other measurements. For example, historical loss data may be used to project future loss frequency and severity. A simple example of this type of simulation is found in the illustration entitled *How Much Risk Should a Business Retain? A Simple Loss Simulation Example,* which is found in the chapter appendix.

In the practical world of insurance, businesses at times must defer to what is available in the marketplace. For example, one year a business may be able to buy insurance coverage at a reasonable price and retain only the first $10,000 of each property loss. However, in the following year, that business may be forced to accept a $100,000 property deductible because the insurance marketplace will not offer coverage with a lower deductible. Or coverage for specific types of catastrophic risks—such as earthquake or terrorism—may not even be available so the business is forced to retain all of those risks.

It is important that attention be paid to other risk management techniques—such as loss control and claims management—besides insurance as the best approach to minimizing the amount of risk that is retained.

Question—Is there a simple way to better understand the concept of how future loss severity and frequency can be projected?

Answer—Refer to Figure 4.5. After reviewing this exercise, distribute bags of jelly beans to students, and have them count the pieces and colors. Collect the information from each class member. Then follow the exercises in Figure 4.5 to show the range of colors (value of claims) and pieces of candy (number of claims) across the student population. That information then can be reviewed further and compiled to illustrate the range of claim costs that a business might incur in future years.

Figure 4.5

How Much Risk Should a Business Retain?
A Simple Loss Simulation Example[1]

When a company sets out to establish the optimum insurance program to cover its loss exposure for the coming year, one factor that must be given careful consideration is the retention of a certain portion of that loss exposure. Depending on risk transfer alternatives available to the company, some level of retention may be desirable or unavoidable. Market conditions may result in first-dollar guaranteed cost coverage being prohibitively expensive, or such coverage may simply not be offered at all.

Risk retention may be accomplished through a variety of mechanisms, the most common being the deductible and the self-insured retention (SIR). In most SIR programs, a company will pay the first portion of a claim itself and purchase insurance for claim amounts that exceed that point. For example, if a company maintains a $250,000 SIR and they experience a loss of $1 million, the company will pay $250,000 and insurance will cover the remaining $750,000. Any loss less than $250,000 will be paid entirely by the company. Certain situations may result in an SIR program being more advantageous than a deductible program, and state regulations may make one preferable. But, for purposes of this discussion, we will assume that they are identical.

Once a company has determined that an SIR is an option to explore, the key question that must be answered is "What amount of loss should I retain?" Again, it is possible that market conditions may have already provided the answer to this question, but in general a company will have some flexibility in making this decision.

There are many benchmarks upon which a company may base their retention decision. Ratios based on liquidity or financial strength can provide guidance. However, these ratios typically generate a wide range of outcomes and may be of limited value in making a final decision.

A very useful tool in the selection of appropriate retention levels is an analysis of historical loss data, including a loss simulation. By examining both the frequency (how many) and severity (how much) of a company's claim history, valuable insights may be gained regarding what to expect in the future. If a company's data is sufficiently credible (credibility is a statistical measure of the value of information, generally based on its volume and consistency) that data may be used to make actuarial predictions of future losses.

A loss simulation can provide a company with not only an idea of what total losses might be expected next year, but also losses at various retention levels. Just as important, simulation results identify the variability in possible outcomes. A simplified example will clarify the simulation process as well as the value of the results.

Suppose our loss experience in a given year is defined by a bag of jelly beans. Each jelly bean represents a loss, and the color of the jelly bean determines the size of that loss as defined:

Pink	=	$	500
Yellow	=	$	5,000
White	=	$	25,000
Red	=	$	100,000
Orange	=	$	400,000
Green	=	$ 1,000,000	
Misshapen	=	$10,000,000	(catastrophes)

Next year we will open a new bag, and what we find inside will determine our loss payments for the year. But we have to decide what amount of these losses to retain and what amount to insure before we peek into the bag. It is critical that we make the best prediction possible regarding the contents of that bag before deciding on our retention. We must also be prepared for the fact that what we actually find in the bag will not be exactly what we had predicted, thus we also need to explore the range of likely outcomes. A simulation can help.

Before we can begin the simulation process, we need some historical information on which to base our predictions. Let's assume that we've already looked in five bags of jellybeans (five historical years of data) and seen their contents:

	Bag 1	Bag 2	Bag 3	Bag 4	Bag 5
Pink	15	12	17	13	21
Yellow	9	11	9	10	6
White	3	7	10	7	14
Red	13	9	6	10	6
Orange	9	12	8	12	2
Green	11	6	7	7	6
Misshapen	0	0	0	0	1
Total	**60**	**57**	**57**	**59**	**56**

We see that the number and color of jellybeans varies from bag to bag. This results in a different total loss amount for each bag. For example, losses in Bag 1 would be as follows:

	Count	Loss Amount	Loss Amount
Pink	15	500	7,500
Yellow	9	5,000	45,000
White	3	25,000	75,000
Red	13	100,000	1,300,000
Orange	9	400,000	3,600,000
Green	11	1,000,000	11,000,000
Misshapen	0	10,000,000	0
Total	**60**		**16,027,500**

So we see that our losses based on Bag 1 were over $16 million. However, if we had retained only the first $100,000 of each loss, our losses would have been $3,427,500 (all claims less than $100,000 and $100,000 for each of the 33 claims $100,000 or larger). From looking at the contents of this one bag, we start to get an idea of what we might expect when we open up the "mystery bag" that represents next year's losses. But just looking at one bag is not sufficient, so let's look at all five of the open bags:

	Bag 1	Bag 2	Bag 3	Bag 4	Bag 5
Pink	7,500	6,000	8,500	6,500	10,500
Yellow	45,000	55,000	45,000	50,000	30,000
White	75,000	175,000	250,000	175,000	350,000
Red	1,300,000	900,000	600,000	1,000,000	600,000
Orange	3,600,000	4,800,000	3,200,000	4,800,000	800,000
Green	11,000,000	6,000,000	7,000,000	7,000,000	6,000,000
Misshapen	0	0	0	0	10,000,000
Total	**16,027,500**	**11,936,000**	**11,103,500**	**13,031,500**	**17,790,500**

Now we start to get some idea as to the variability of possible outcomes. Frequency was relatively consistent (each bag had from 56 to 60 beans) but total losses vary substantially (from just over $11 million to almost $18 million). Based on this information, we may reasonably guess that when we open our next bag of jellybeans, the contents will represent about $14 million in losses (the average of the five open bags). However, as the chart below shows, this does not tell the whole story:

Beware of Averages!

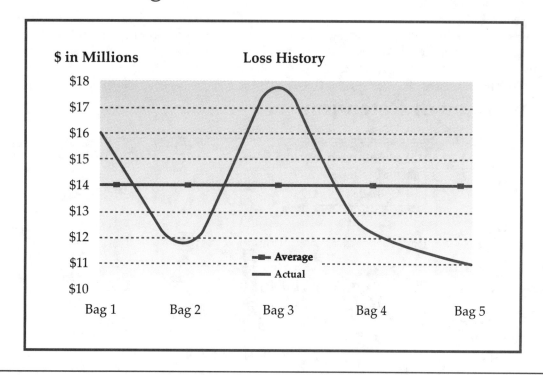

An actuary who told his risk manager to expect $14 million in losses in the coming year might have a lot of explaining to do when actual losses emerged at the $18 million level. And pointing out that "I clearly stated in the footnote to Exhibit XXXVII that actuarial estimates contain a substantial degree of variability and it is likely that actual results will differ from the projections contained here," will probably not give anyone a lot of comfort. It would be far preferable to give a reasonable quantification of that variability before important decisions were made. Loss simulation to the rescue!

Based on our analysis of the contents of the five open bags, we may select frequency and severity parameters upon which to base a computer simulation. We then simulate the opening of the new bag and reveal its contents. For example, the first time we run the model, we may find that our simulated bag contains 58 jellybeans representing $13.2 million of losses. To be certain we fairly represent the full range of possible outcomes, we will run our model 10,000 times (let's hear it for today's high speed computers). We then sort the results from low to high and determine the likelihood of losses at various levels. The likelihood of a given outcome is expressed in terms of percentiles. A sample of simulation outcomes and percentiles is shown below:

Order of Projections	Loss Amount	Percentile
1	$4,975,380	
2	$5,479,377	
100	$6,900,206	1st Percentile
5,000	$12,995,092	50th Percentile
9,900	$32,208,686	99th Percentile

The value at the 50th percentile (number 5,000 of the 10,000 total simulations) tells us that there is a 50 percent chance that next year's losses will exceed $12,995,092 and a 50 percent chance that losses will be less than this amount. Similarly, the value at the 99th percentile tells us that there is a 1 in 100 chance that losses next year will exceed $32.2 million.

This type of simulation can also generate results at various retention levels. Thus a risk manager will have the ability to review the likely range of outcomes for a variety of insurance options, and thus make an informed decision as to the most appropriate program. The chart below presents the results of our simulation at selected retention levels.

Comparison of Retention

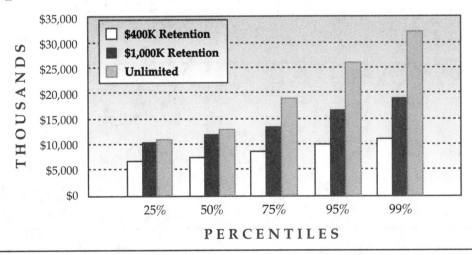

In this example we see that at the 50th percentile losses at the $1 million and unlimited retention levels look very similar. Thus a risk manager looking only at averages might conclude that coverage above the $1 million retention level is not very valuable. "Why should I pay $2 million for the coverage when it's only expected to save me a few hundred thousand in loss payments? I'll just retain the risk and the savings will go straight to our bottom line. I'll be a hero!" Ah, if only our would-be hero had the above chart to guide him. He would see that at the 75th percentile, his good intentions look more like a dangerous roll of the dice. Losses at the $1 million retention are about $14 million and unlimited losses are around $18 million. A $2 million payment for coverage in that layer would have been a bargain. If our hero had known that there was a 25 percent chance (chance of losses exceeding the 75th percentile) he would become the goat, would his decision have been the same? The additional variability resulting from higher retentions must not be overlooked.

Of course, real world application of this process is generally much more complicated than the example provided above. Parameters for frequency and severity distributions may be more difficult to divine than the contents of jelly bean bags. Also, risk managers often require analysis of several lines of business, with an examination of different retention levels for each line.

Computer simulations of loss experience cannot provide a definitive answer to those charged with choosing the optimum insurance program for their company. However, they can provide useful information to assist in making an informed decision.

END NOTES

1   The idea of using candy to illustrate a loss simulation came from a presentation made by Robert Glicksteen, senior vice president and chief financial officer, Becher + Carlson Companies, an insurance consultant and broker based in Woodland Hills, CA, http://www.maglobalservices.com/.

Chapter 4

GLOSSARY

Benchmarking. Comparing one operation or program against another in the same or a similar industry.

Cash flow analysis. A process to measure a plan's economic efficiency; the timing of cash outflows.

Claim frequency. The number of claims that occur within a given period of time.

Claim severity. The potential dollar value of a loss.

Confidence levels. The percentile level at which actuaries regard the loss information they develop to be accurate. For example, a confidence level of 50 percent means that the actuary believes that losses will be less than the projected amount half of the time and more than the projected amount the other half of the time. The actuary is 50 percent confident that the loss projection will prove to be accurate.

Loss development factors (LDFs). Factors that show the percentage increase in the value of claims over several 12-month periods of time.

Loss range analysis. Placing a company's historical losses into defined ranges to determine the number of claims and the dollar value of those claims that fall under various thresholds.

Loss triangles. A method for calculating loss development factors, which show the percentage by which claim values increase as they mature.

Maximum possible loss. The absolute maximum amount of value that is considered to be at risk in a property; often, this may be equated with the replacement cost of the structure.

Maximum probable loss. The maximum amount of loss that a structure probably will sustain in light of its construction, occupancy, protection system, and outside exposures.

OVERVIEW OF RISK TREATMENT ALTERNATIVES

WHAT IS IT?

The loss exposure treatment options available to risk managers are limited to four fundamental choices. You might remember these as ANRI:

- Avoidance
- Noninsurance Transfer (Contractual)
- Retention
- Insurance Transfer

Some texts also include loss prevention and loss reduction as alternative risk exposure treatments. As noted subsequently in this chapter, these also are key to managing loss exposures.

The order in which the options appear above is based on their relative costs. Avoidance costs nothing assuming the risk is avoided for sound economic reasons. Transferring risks by contract costs little or nothing, assuming the trade-offs (if any) make sense. Risks that cannot be avoided or transferred contractually must either be retained or transferred to an insurance company. For most losses, retention is the less expensive risk management technique.

Risk managers are faced with the challenge of choosing the best method for each loss exposure. However, the term *best* is highly subjective and is largely defined by the company's perspective on risk and its corporate culture. To some, *best* means the cheapest out-of-pocket cash outlay alternative. To others, a fully insured program that shifts essentially all or the bulk of the risk to another party is their definition of the best method. Others define *best* in terms of how much risk they can successfully retain. This discussion defines the four basic risk management methods in terms of their utility within a balanced risk management regimen.

Risk represents both uncertainty and opportunity. Uncertainty is an analogy for risk, because without uncertainty there would be no risk. Risk represents opportunity because without risk life would be boringly predictable—and no gain would be possible. The goal is to find an efficient middle ground using the four methods listed previously that is within keeping with the client's risk-taking propensity and comfort levels.

THE OPTIONS

Avoidance

While not all risks can or should be avoided, the concept of avoidance is a valid and useful risk management tool. Virtually every important business decision involves a calculated risk. If the potential benefits cannot be proven to exceed the risk, the endeavor should not be undertaken. For example, a company decides to study the feasibility of developing a new product line. Preliminary sales and cost projections indicate that the project should go forward, until the risk manager submits her evaluation. Unfortunately, the projected cost of products liability insurance, expected losses within deductibles and self-insured retentions, and the costs of defending self-insured products liability claims negate the projected earnings for each year in the study. The final—and appropriate decision (absent some extenuating circumstance or justification beyond the pure economics)—is to shelve the project and avoid the risk.

Avoidance as a risk management technique can be employed in many other business environments. The choice of purchasing an existing building, leasing one, or building a new one often rests on the scope of the risks associated with each choice. An existing building's systems may not be "up to code" or it may not have a sprinkler system, causing higher than normal fire rates. New construction might cost more in the beginning, but its insurance costs probably would be less over time. A cost/benefit analysis would dictate which risk to take and which to avoid.

Noninsurance Transfer

Risks can be transferred to other parties without employing an insurance transaction. This is commonly accomplished through contracts. Contractual risk transfer consists of an agreement between two parties in which one party assumes certain risks of the other.

Examples include *hold-harmless* and *indemnification agreements* and *additional insured provisions* in insurance policies. Hold-harmless and indemnification agreements both outline the circumstances in which one party will assume liability from another. Hold-harmless agreements effectively remove the nonliable party from the risk altogether, while indemnification agreements state that once the loss is adjudicated and paid by one party, the other will provide indemnification. Neither hold-harmless nor indemnification agreements are specifically tied to the availability of insurance proceeds. Additional insured status, however, is directly related to an insurance contract. Many contracts—for example, lease agreements—usually require one party to be named as an additional insured on the other's general liability insurance policy. (Lessors are usually required to add their landlords to their general liability policy as additional insureds.) There is a limit to the types of liability that can be transferred via contract. For example, tort liability cannot be transferred to another party.

Additional information on noninsurance (contractual) transfers is contained in Chapter 6.

Retention

For small, frequent, predictable losses, retention is far less expensive than insurance. For example, if a company has had $5,000 of workers compensation losses each year for the past ten years, that loss amount should probably be retained. Insurance premiums for small, frequent losses usually cost far more than retaining them because premiums not only must cover the losses. They must also pay for the associated expenses, such as for adjusting the losses, issuing the policy, and providing a profit for the insurer.

Loss retention can be accomplished through a wide variety of methodologies. The simplest method is the deductible. More exotic forms of self-insurance include captives, risk retention groups, and rent-a-captives, which are discussed in Chapter 8. For loss exposures that represent catastrophic potential—for example, flood and earthquake—retention is not a viable management technique. There is no universal rule of thumb regarding how much loss to retain; every company must find its own balance between risk retention and risk transfer.

Information on methods that may be used to select an appropriate risk retention amount is included in Chapter 4.

Insurance Transfer

Insurance is the final risk management technique. Risks that cannot be avoided, transferred via contract, or successfully retained should be transferred to an insurance company. Insurance should be considered one of four viable risk management techniques, but many companies focus on insurance as their primary means of managing risk. However, in a balanced risk management program, insurance should be used sparingly. In economic terms, insurance is an expensive product; only about 65 percent of every insurance dollar is used to pay losses. The remaining 35 percent pays for expenses, such as for underwriting, policy administration, taxes, loss control, auditing, claims handling, marketing, insurer profit, and sales commissions.

Given the fact that insurance is such an expensive way to manage risk, it should be used only if its value can be demonstrated. For example, the risk that a thirty-story, $100 million fire-resistive building will be destroyed by fire is minimal. Its PML (probable maximum loss) is approximately $3,000,000, roughly one story. The insurance premium to cover this building with a small ($1,000) deductible might be roughly $300,000 assuming a thirty-cent rate per 100 dollars of value. Given the extremely small chance of a total loss, there is no economic value in insuring the full $100 million. Instead, the building owner could assume the first $100,000 of each loss. This might reduce the fire rate to about fifteen cents, reducing the annual premium to $150,000. For every loss-free year, the building owner saves $150,000. Of course, he runs the risk of having to pay retained losses of up to $100,000 each, but, given the circumstances, it is a risk worth taking. The $150,000 premium has value because it provides protection against catastrophic loss at a reasonable premium.

DECREASING THE COST OF RISK

Loss Prevention and Reduction

Regardless of which alternative is chosen, businesses ultimately will decrease their cost of risk by preventing and reducing losses when possible. This is especially true when the business elects to retain all or some of its risks because there should be a direct impact on the amount of retained losses.

Efforts must be made to prevent retained losses and to reduce the impact of losses that cannot be prevented. Just because a company has decided that it can afford to retain a portion of its insurable loss does not mean that it should not look for ways to prevent those losses from occurring and to reduce the severity of those that do. On the contrary, the greater the retention, the more it makes sense—and dollars—for a company to maintain an active and on-going loss prevention program.

Similar to the balance that must be found between the four primary risk management techniques, a balance must also be found between the cost of retaining losses and the costs associated with preventing them and mitigating their impact. The costs of loss prevention and reduction efforts must be factored into the total costs associated with retaining any loss. As seen in Chapter 10, a cost-benefit analysis of possible prevention and reduction techniques often is valuable in deciding which loss control activities offer the greatest financial impact.

Fortunately, the benefits of sound loss prevention and reduction measures can extend far beyond the time periods in which their expenses are incurred. For ex-

ample, the installation of a sprinkler system in a one-story warehouse is a one-time expense that can be amortized over several years. The fire suppression benefits of the system, however, far exceed the amortization period of the initial expense.

Figure 5.1 is a simplified risk management decision flow chart.

ADVANTAGES AND DISADVANTAGES

Risk managers who have mastered the concepts of the four categories of risk treatment alternatives have a distinct advantage in being able to use them together to create a complete risk management program. Some businesses may be under the impression that, since buying insurance is the easiest of the alternatives, it is the best. However, when premiums increase—or if a claim is unexpectedly not covered because of a policy exclusion—they may not be prepared to absorb the additional costs. Considering all the alternatives and choosing the best for each risk situation creates a flexible program that can be more easily revised as business conditions change.

As with all risk management techniques, a great deal of time may be required to decide which alternative is best for various risk situations. In addition, risk managers who advocate *avoidance* too often may lose credibility in the organization. Their input may be solicited less frequently if they get a reputation for wanting to avoid risk too often. Avoidance should be chosen only when the potential benefit of the activity clearly is outweighed by the cost.

WHERE CAN I FIND OUT MORE ABOUT IT?

- The American Institute for Chartered Property Casualty Underwriters and the Insurance Institute of America offer a number of courses in the risk management field. Two of the primary designation programs are the Associate in Risk Management (ARM) and the Associate in Risk Management for Public Entities (ARM-P), http://www.aicpcu.org/programs/index.htm.

- *Contractual Risk Transfer*. Dallas: International Risk Management Institute, www.irmi.com.

- Malecki, Donald S., and Pete Ligeros and Jack P. Gibson. 2000. *The Additional Insured Book, 4th*

Figure 5.1

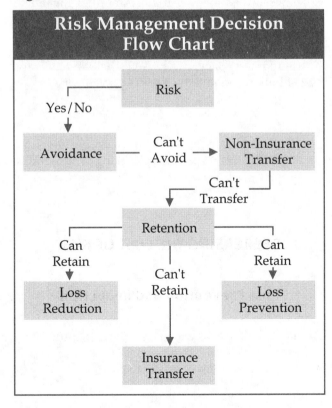

Edition. Dallas: International Risk Management Institute.

- *Practical Risk Management*. Irvine, CA: ARMTech, http://www.pracrisk.com/.

QUESTIONS AND ANSWERS

Question—What is the difference between noninsurance and insurance transfer? Don't both of them transfer risk from one party to another?

Answer—Both techniques do transfer risk from one party to another. However, noninsurance transfers are not tied to any insurance proceeds. For example, a building tenant (a restaurant) agrees in a lease to hold the building owner harmless and indemnify him for damages that restaurant customers may suffer if they fall in the parking lot of the restaurant, even though the building owner is responsible for maintaining the parking lot. This is a contractual transfer of risk. If the restaurant owner does not purchase general liability insurance to cover the assumption of liability, she will have to fund the exposure herself. Purchasing a general liability policy to cover the risk would be an insurance transfer.

Question—When should a business select *avoidance* as the appropriate risk management technique?

Answer—Avoidance should be chosen when the projected cost of the risks associated with the project outweighs its benefits. For example, a real estate developer is considering purchasing an office building, which it will remodel and lease. The price of the building is well within the range that the developer wants to pay, and its location is within a prime development area. However, during the review process, an environmental analysis is done, and it is discovered that the building is full of asbestos. The developer will have to remove all the asbestos during the remodeling phase at a cost of twice the asking price of the building. The developer would have to remove it even if it decided to demolish and rebuild the building at the prime site. This is a case in which the project probably should be avoided.

Question—An HVAC contractor agrees in a contract to hold the general contractor (GC) harmless, to indemnify the GC for damages that result from the HVAC company's work, and to add the GC as an additional insured on its commercial general liability policy. The HVAC company fails to initiate the additional insured status, and the GC is sued because of the HVAC contractor's work. Who will be responsible to handle the claim? Will the HVAC contractor's insurance policy defend this claim?

Answer—In this case, the HVAC contractor initiated a noninsurance transfer of risk through the hold harmless and indemnification clauses to which it agreed. These transfers are not dependent on insurance proceeds. As long as a court does not invalidate them, the HVAC contractor is responsible for the damages that the GC incurs. Since the GC was not added as an additional insured on the HVAC company's policy, the HVAC's liability coverage will not respond to the claim against the GC.

Chapter 5

GLOSSARY

Additional insured. One who qualifies as insured under the terms of a policy even though not the named insured. Additional insureds are given access to the benefits of the named insured's insurance coverage.

Avoidance. Deciding not to take on a risk exposure.

Contractual transfer. Another name for noninsurance transfer of risk. Transferring risk(s) from one party (a business) to another party (a business) that is not an insurance company. Examples of contractual transfer are hold-harmless and indemnification agreements.

Hold-harmless agreement. Contractual agreement in which one party removes the nonliable party from the risk altogether. One party assumes the risk of a second party.

Indemnification agreement. Contractual agreement in which one party agrees to reimburse another party for damages it incurs because of the actions of the first party. Insurance policies are forms of indemnification agreements. Indemnification means to "make whole."

Insurance transfer. Transferring risk(s) from one party (a business) to an insurance company.

Noninsurance transfer. Transferring risk(s) from one party (a business) to another party (a business) that is not an insurance company. Noninsurance transfer is achieved through contracts. (Also called contractual transfer.)

Retention. Affirmatively deciding to keep (retain) all or some portion of a risk. Examples of retention tools are deductibles, self-insured retentions (assuming a certain amount of each loss), self-insurance, and other risk-sharing techniques.

Chapter 6

Noninsurance Transfer of Risk

WHAT IS IT?

A noninsurance transfer of risk is a technique by which an entity transfers its exposures to loss to a party other than an insurance company. The party to whom the exposures are transferred (the transferee) can be any entity that the transferor believes is an adequate receptacle for the exposures. A company can transfer its loss exposures when it deems it to be an appropriate business decision based on the goals and the capabilities of the company. For example, if a company decides it cannot profitably transport its products to its customers, the company can contract with a trucking firm to handle the transportation. Or, if the company decides it does not want to continue manufacturing an article due to its past loss experiences, the company can contract with another firm to have the article manufactured elsewhere.

All businesses face the possibility of suffering some kinds of loss that could hurt profitability or even cause the entity to cease to exist. To protect against such a loss, a business can transfer the risk of that loss to another entity other than an insurance company. This can be done either before or after the loss actually occurs. This means, for example, that Company A can transfer its risk of loss to Company B so that A does not ever suffer the loss. This is an example of a *before-loss* transfer. Alternatively, A can transfer the cost of paying for the loss after the loss has occurred. This is an *after-loss* transfer.

BEFORE–LOSS TRANSFERS

Potential before-loss transfers of risk include various options, such as

- incorporation,

- leases,

- subcontracts,

- surety and performance bonds,

- waivers,

- maintenance agreements, and

- licensing.

Incorporation

When individuals incorporate, they create a legal entity and, to the extent possible, transfer their potential individual exposures to liabilities and responsibilities to that corporation.

For example, Jim and his friends decide to start a business. They form a corporation—Buddies, Inc.—in accordance with the laws of their state. Property is bought and business contracts are drawn up with Buddies, Inc., as the contracting party. If the company's main building burns down, Jim and his friends will not have individually incurred the property damage. The corporation will suffer the loss.

Also, if a customer is hurt while using a product made by Buddies, Inc., and sues for damages, the personal assets of Jim and his friends will not be at risk. The assets of Buddies, Inc., would be in jeopardy. In both instances, Jim and his friends have transferred the risk of loss from themselves as individuals to another legal entity—a corporation.

The same type of noninsurance transfer of risk is possible when forming a limited liability company (LLC), which is another type of business authorized by most states. The limited liability company is somewhat like a hybrid between a corporation and a partnership. The LLC is similar to a partnership in the way that income, deductions, and losses flow through to the members of the LLC, who are taxed individually. Under the normal corporate structure, tax is imposed at the corporate rather than the personal level. An LLC is similar to a corporation in that its assets are held in the company's name. Those assets, and not the individual members' personal assets, are at risk from, for example, a lawsuit filed by an aggrieved customer. Additional information on this type of noninsurance transfer is available in *The*

Tools & Techniques of Estate Planning, 12th Edition, www.nationalunderwriter.com.[1]

Leases

A lease is a contract by which one party grants to another party legal interest in—that is, the right to use or possess—some item. When this is done, a transfer of risk can occur. The following examples illustrate how a lease can be used to transfer risk.

Leases Involving Property

The Smith Company owns property that it wants to develop and use as the site of a manufacturing plant. Smith, as the owner of property, can be held liable for injuries occurring on that property simply because he is its owner. In addition, property ownership can add to Smith's financial liabilities through mortgage and tax assessments (the latter will even escalate once the property is developed). To transfer these owner responsibilities, Smith sells the land to the Jones Company and then leases it back. Smith has actual possession and use of the property, but that company has transferred its risk exposures as a land owner to Jones. Jones gets the lease payments and can deduct the depreciation of the property (if any) or the property taxes from his income tax payments, as well as the other benefits a landowner enjoys.

Of course, this transfer of risk can work both ways. Using the above example, if Smith owned the land and Jones wanted to build on it, Smith could lease the property to Jones. Jones could agree to assume all liabilities in accordance with the terms of the lease agreement. This still effects a transfer of risk through a lease.

Leased Workers

Another example of this process involves leased workers. A leased worker is loaned by one company to another. The intention is that the leased individual will work under the control of and at the direction of the latter company for some definite period of time. The main risk exposures in this situation involve injury to the leased worker (the workers compensation exposure) and the leased worker causing injury to an outside party, such as a customer (the third-party liability exposure).

Normally, when a company (the lessee) leases an employee from a labor leasing firm (the lessor), the lessee is responsible for the workers compensation exposure. However, to transfer this risk exposure, the lessee can negotiate a contract with the lessor in which the lessor retains the responsibility for workers compensation benefits. The lease agreement can contain such provisions, which would be recognized and accepted by legal authorities.

There also is the risk that the leased employee could injure someone while performing his duties for the lessee. As with workers compensation, the lessee—under the *respondeat superior maxim*—would usually be responsible for the actions of the employee. (Respondeat superior literally means: let the master answer.) For example, the employer is liable under certain circumstances for the acts of his employee if someone is injured as a result of those acts. But, as occurs with workers compensation in an employee-leasing situation, the lessee could transfer these liability exposures to the lessor.

The point is that, while liability for workers compensation and injury to outsiders can be transferred, the objective of the transfer may fail (for example, the lessor may go out of business or never buy proper or adequate insurance to finance the assumption of risk). In such cases, the lessee would be ultimately responsible for damages that arise from the risks. So, for a transfer of risk under a lease to attain its goal, the party seeking the transfer needs to make sure the agreement is contractually sound, strictly enforced, and adequately backed financially.

Subcontracts

A subcontract allows the parties to the agreement to share work, and, consequently, the risk exposures that accompany the work. Subcontracts are frequently used by general contractors to parcel out work on jobs that the general contractor has undertaken.

For example, Brown Builders, as the general contractor, has taken on the job of constructing a three-story office building. The construction job includes plumbing, electrical work, and bricklaying, none of which Brown is equipped to do. So Brown enters into subcontracts to have these specific parts of the overall job done by an individual plumber, electrician, and bricklayer. Brown has shared its overall responsibilities to complete the construction job on time and in a satisfactory manner with these subcontractors. Brown also needs to share the risk exposures, especially since he does not have the expertise needed to do competent plumbing, electrical, or bricklaying jobs.

The subcontract agreement that Brown negotiates and executes with the plumber, electrician, and bricklayer should contain clauses that transfer the risks involved in those particular parts of the construction job from Brown to the individual subcontractors. These include risks associated with workers compensation, liability towards the general public, and liability toward the owner of the construction project.

The subcontractors may have employees who are subject to the state workers compensation law. The subcontractor should be primarily responsible for providing workers compensation insurance. But this risk may ultimately be pushed onto Brown if the subcontractor fails to acquire the coverage. Since the responsibility for providing workers compensation benefits is statutorily required, it is a risk exposure that the general contractor does not wish to have transferred to him. The general contractor needs to require that the workers compensation exposure is retained by the subcontractor and make that requirement a part of the subcontract agreement.

As an example of the liability risks that involve the general public, a passerby may be injured or have his property damaged because of the work of the subcontractor. If that happens, the subcontractor should bear the responsibility. However, Brown would be held ultimately responsible should the subcontractor somehow default on this duty. Just like the workers compensation exposure, this is a risk that the general contractor does not want to be transferred to him.

Finally, there is the issue of liability to the owner of the building. The building has to be completed by a certain date, and the finished product has to be appropriate for its stated purpose. If the general contractor does not meet either of these objectives, penalties will be assessed. It may be difficult, if not impossible, for the general contractor to transfer the risk of these penalties to another party because he is a competent party to the main contractual agreement. However, the various subcontracts that Brown negotiates could contain clauses that transfer at least some of the exposure of not completing the job on time and in a quality fashion to the subcontractors who actually are doing the work—something like a share-the-risk-and-blame plan. Subcontracting is, after all, a share-the-work idea, so sharing the loss exposures is not completely out of line.

In addition to the liability risks that arise from the activities of subcontractors, Brown also has a risk exposure arising from his general supervision of the building project. The general contractor may not be able to transfer this risk entirely as a matter of law. This means that public policy, a law, or a government regulation might prevent the general contractor from transferring all his risk exposures. For example, strict liability, such as the liability that arises from a hazardous operation such as dynamite blasting, cannot be transferred as a matter of law. Despite this, the subcontract agreements should at least try to transfer all of Brown's risks.

The bottom line is that subcontracting should be used by a general contractor for two main purposes:

- to make sure the risk exposures of the subcontractors are not transferred to the general contractor; and

- to attempt to have the risk exposures that are inherent in the position of a general contractor transferred to the subcontractors.

Surety, Guaranty, and Performance Bonds

Another way to effect a noninsurance transfer of risk is to enter into surety and guaranty agreements or performance bonds. Through these efforts, one party can shift its liability to perform certain tasks to another party.

A surety is one who promises to pay money or to perform a task in the event that the principal fails to do his duty. For example, Smith contracts with Jones to build a dam. Jones is new to the business, so Smith wants some kind of a guaranty that the job will be performed in accordance with the terms of the contract. Jones has his brother—an experienced dam builder—act as a surety for the job, guaranteeing to Smith that the contract will be fulfilled should Jones falter along the way. Jones has transferred his potential liability exposure for not living up to the terms of the contract to his brother. In this example, Jones is the principal, the brother is the surety, and Smith is the obligee (the party to whom someone else is obligated under a contract).

A surety guarantees that a duty will be performed. However, there is a difference between a surety and a guarantor. According to *Black's Law Dictionary, 5ᵗʰ Edition*, a surety is usually bound with the principal by the same instrument, which is executed at the same time and for the same consideration. In other words, the agreement is a joint undertaking between the surety and the principal, with both joining in the same promise and both being primarily liable for a breach of duty. A guarantor, however, is in a separate undertaking in which the principal does not join. The guarantor enters into a contract separate from the principal and usually for separate consideration.

We can illustrate these relationships with the example of Smith, Jones, and Jones's brother.

- Under a surety agreement, Jones and his brother join in the same promise and are primarily liable to Smith.

- Under a guaranty, Jones's brother would make his own separate agreement with Smith and becomes secondarily liable. That is, his liability is contingent on the default of Jones and does not begin unless and until that occurs.

Both a surety agreement and a guaranty make Jones's brother answerable for Jones's lack of performance (risk has thus been transferred). But the approaches used by the two agreements to resolve the problem are a bit different.

Types of Contractor Bonds

In general there are four types of contractor bonds:

Bid bonds, which guarantee that, when the contract is awarded, the contractor will enter into the contract and provide the necessary performance and payment bonds.

Performance bonds, which guarantee that the work will be done according to contract specifications.

Maintenance bonds, which guarantee that faulty work or defective materials that are discovered within a certain period of time will be corrected and/or replaced.

Completion bonds, which guarantee the completion of a project.

A performance bond is basically a type of surety agreement in that it can be used to transfer risk by guaranteeing the fulfillment of contract obligations. The performance bond guarantees to the owner (or obligee) that work will be completed according to the contract

specifications. It protects against loss due to the inability or refusal of a contractor to perform his contract. A performance bond normally is required on public works projects, as well as for many private construction projects. Performance bonds also may be used to guarantee that a contract to provide services is properly fulfilled.

Major Difference Between Insurance and Surety Bonding

What is one of the most important differences between insurance and bonding? Insurance companies expect that they will have to pay claims that arise from the exposures they insure. Surety companies do not expect that they will have to pay claims. In writing a bond, they are attesting to the ability of a principal to complete a job as promised in the contract. Contractors must meet rigorous standards before being able to obtain performance bonds. And surety companies retain the right to recover any payments or work they do under the bond from the company that is bonded.

For example, ABC Contractors is hired to construct a building. After reviewing ABC's ability to complete the project, XYZ Surety Company provides a performance bond, which guarantees that the building will be built according to the specifications and contract. ABC unexpectedly experiences difficulty with its workforce and is not able to complete the job. XYZ Surety engages another contractor to complete the work and pays to have the job completed. XYZ then takes action against ABC Contractors to recover the money spent.

Waivers

A waiver is the intentional and voluntary relinquishment of a known legal right. For example, an individual may give up (waive) her right to sue an entity if the entity causes her harm. A waiver acts as a somewhat different transfer-of-risk mechanism because the person granting the waiver transfers a risk back to herself instead of transferring it to another party.

Waivers are often used to facilitate business deals. For example, the White Corporation may want Brown Construction to do some work. Or White may want Brown to manufacture or sell White's products. To facilitate such an arrangement, White Corporation may sign a waiver to the effect that, if the work is faulty or the product is not up to par, White will not sue Brown for possible damages. The risks that Brown could face if it fails to perform the job are not retained by that company because White chooses to waive the right to recover those losses.

A waiver is legally binding as long as the one granting the waiver does so on a voluntary basis. Even insurance contracts recognize the validity of waivers since the insurer demands that the insured do nothing after loss to impair subrogation rights. Subrogation is the assumption by one party of the legal rights of another to recover an amount paid as damages. For example, when an insurer pays damages to a claimant on behalf of the insured, the insurer is entitled to the insured's rights to seek reimbursement from some other party who was ultimately responsible for the claimant's injuries. As long as the waiver of subrogation is given prior to the loss, an insurer accepts the practice.

Maintenance Agreements

Maintenance agreements, or service contracts, are used to transfer the risk exposures surrounding maintenance services—usually from the owner of the item to the maintenance person or company.

An example of this is an elevator maintenance contract. Smith Realty owns a five-story office building that has two elevators. Naturally, the elevators need maintenance to insure they function properly. Smith Realty knows nothing about servicing elevators, so the company contracts with ACE Elevator Service to keep the elevators in working order. As part of the contract, ACE also agrees to accept responsibility for injuries or damages caused by the failure of the elevators to work properly. This is called a *hold harmless* agreement, which is discussed in the section on after-loss transfers.

Through this contract, Smith Realty has transferred its elevator maintenance exposures and responsibilities to ACE. The work of maintaining the elevators is no longer Smith's responsibility. And, any possible future lawsuits or claims based on the faulty working of the elevators is passed onto ACE.

Licensing

Licensing involves formally permitting an entity to engage in a specific activity that otherwise would not be permitted. A license agreement can be used to transfer such risk exposures as long as the parties to the agreement are aware of the transfer and accept it. Just as a governmental body can grant licenses for people or businesses to act, a business can also grant a license to another business. An example of a business-to-business license is a *franchise*.

Under a franchise, the owner of a registered trade name or process permits another party to use that trade name or process. As part of the franchise agreement, the owner of the process or name can require that the franchisee assume all the risks associated with the particular business activity. So, for example, if My Burgers, Inc., owns a trade name and has a special process of making hamburgers but does not want to invest the capital to open new restaurants itself and incur the additional risk exposures that are entailed with ownership, it can grant Mr. Worker a franchise. However, along with this franchise comes the contractual transfer of the risks from My Burgers, Inc., to Worker.

AFTER–LOSS TRANSFERS

A person or a business may try to transfer risk exposures so that the entity is protected from the exposures both before and after a loss. The before-loss transfers, as noted previously, attempt to keep the transferor from even suffering a loss. This is a sensible risk management tool. To complement this strategy and implement another safeguard, risk managers should also plan to transfer the costs of paying for losses that do occur.

Insurance is one way to address this after-loss scenario. Insurance as a risk-transfer technique is discussed in Chapter 7. Entities that choose not to use insurance to transfer risk may opt for a noninsurance after-loss transfer. This type of transfer of risk involves just about any contractual arrangement that an attorney can skillfully and legally craft. However, two of the most common transfers are

- hold-harmless agreements and
- loss sharing arrangements.

Hold–Harmless Agreements

A *hold-harmless agreement* is when one party agrees to assume another party's responsibility for damages or injuries that occur due to the two parties' relationships.

For example, Brown Construction may obtain an easement from White Corporation to use a parcel of White's land for Brown's business activities, White may insist that the easement contract contain a hold-harmless clause. Brown agrees. If a customer comes onto that easement and is injured, she will seek compensation from Brown (as the business owner) and from White (as the property owner). Since White has transferred its loss cost liabilities to Brown through the hold harmless agreement, Brown must pay for the loss without any involvement from White. And the payment by Brown encompasses defense costs from a lawsuit if it is filed, since the hold-harmless agreement contains wording to that effect.

The applicability of a hold-harmless agreement is limited only by the abilities of the attorney drawing up the agreement and by the laws of the jurisdiction that the agreement specifies. For example, the agreement between Brown and White may require that all questions and disputes over the agreement be settled in accordance with the laws of Delaware. This means, then, that any disputes over the meaning or scope of the hold-harmless agreement will be determined by applying Delaware law.

Furthermore, the subject matter of a hold-harmless agreement can deal with just about any legal transaction. For example, the elevator maintenance agreement discussed previously includes a hold-harmless provision. As long as the liability of one entity for a loss is transferred to and assumed by another, a hold-harmless agreement has been used to transfer risk for any losses that do arise from it.

Even though the sweep of hold-harmless agreements is a general one, one subject does need clarification. That is, just what is the extent of the transfer of risk? As an example, in the Brown and White hold-harmless agreement discussed previously, are the liabilities resulting from the sole fault of White included? Or do the covered liabilities have to be the result of the joint liability of Brown and White? Sole liability is simply when one party is totally responsible for causing injuries or damages, whereas joint liability is when more than one person is responsible for causing injuries or damages.

The agreement could proceed in one of the following paths.

Referencing the Brown-White agreement discussed previously, the hold-harmless agreement could be limited by rejecting any transfer of risk arising solely from White's activities. For example, White enters the easement and leaves an obstacle in the pathway by accident. A customer trips over the obstacle and is injured. The injury was the sole fault of White, so that company should pay for the injury.

As a corollary, the agreement could limit itself to cover White's liability only on a vicarious basis. *Vicarious liability* arises when one person or entity is responsible for the actions of another person or entity. White's liability solely as the property owner, when it is not directly responsible in any way for the injury, is an example of vicarious liability. The hold harmless agreement would hold White harmless for claims arising from such indirect (vicarious) liability.

The hold-harmless agreement could apportion the responsibilities of the exposures. Brown could agree to assume White's liability exposures but specify that the transfer of risk is only for instances when there is joint fault, that is, when an injury occurs due to the fault of both Brown and White. For example, White accidentally leaves an obstacle in the pathway. Brown notices but ignores it, believing that no one will trip over it. Someone does trip, and both Brown and White are held responsible. The hold-harmless agreement in this instance would have Brown assuming the entire loss cost.

Or, the agreement could dictate that all of White's risk exposures involving the easement are transferred to Brown. This would apply with respect to the premises and operations in their entirety so that, even if White were the sole cause of the injury, those liabilities would still be transferred to Brown. While this type of hold harmless agreement would certainly benefit White, there is a question of whether a court would approve such a complete transfer of liability since the law does not readily accept a party who is responsible for injuring another abandoning his duty to the injured person. A court could throw out such an agreement, depending on several factors. These factors include the comparative negotiating power between Brown and White (the David v. Goliath syndrome), the protection afforded to an innocent member of the public (does Brown have the financial wherewithal to compensate an injured party), and how state law views such agreements, that is, whether the agreements are against public policy or in actual violation of state law.

A similar type of agreement that may be contained in a contract is an *indemnification agreement*. Under a hold-harmless agreement, one party agrees to assume another party's responsibility for damages or injuries that occur due to the two parties' relationships. An indemnification agreement provides for the reimbursement by one party to the other for the financial consequences of the other's act or liability. Liability is not assumed as it is in a hold harmless agreement. Only the duty to pay for damages arising from this liability is assumed. Insurance policies are indemnity agreements because, after damage occurs, the insurer pays the damages for the insured.

Loss Sharing Arrangements

This type of after-loss transfer of risk is actually most appropriate for associations or entities that have a common interest. For example, a condominium association or an association of dry cleaners is able to share losses among the members of the association. The risks are spread among all owners instead of one condominium unit owner or one Mom and Pop dry cleaner bearing all of them.

The arrangement could be set up the way a risk retention group (RRG) is, except that the insurance aspect of the RRG is left out of the mix. Indeed, the concept here is quite similar to insurance: share the losses so that one member of the association is not overwhelmed by his one loss. This type of arrangement has to be worked out in advance of losses occurring and has to be contractually sound. But, if all the members of the association have a common interest and all voluntarily contribute to the transfer of risk arrangement, it should function properly.

As noted previously, a single condominium unit owner or one small dry cleaning store cannot as easily transfer its risk exposures as can a large association. But an individual entity could still try to transfer some or all of its after-loss costs through contractual arrangements with other individual entities. For example, the small dry cleaning store sends out expensive silk dresses to another dry cleaning store that is better equipped to clean them. To transfer its exposure for a dress being damaged, the small dry cleaning store contracts with the other store so that damages will be paid by the other store, which actually cleans the dresses. As long as the transfer of risk is contractually fair and sound, even small businesses can arrange to share after-loss costs.

STEPS TO IMPLEMENT

The steps that any parties take to transfer risks can be generalized. Risk managers (or the persons charged with making such business decisions) must look at all the possible loss exposures facing the entity and decide which to keep and which to transfer. This decision is based on costs, legal issues, company objectives, and other factors.

Once the decision has been made as to which risk exposures to transfer, the entity needs to decide whether it would be better if that transfer were through insurance or a noninsurance transaction. If the noninsurance transfer is chosen, the question is whether a before-loss or after-loss technique is the better choice. Of course, this need not be an either/or choice. Both before-loss and after-loss techniques can be used if they help to achieve the goals of the entity.

Then it simply becomes a matter of implementing the choices as efficiently and as cost effectively as possible. Since the noninsurance transfer of risk will require contracts, attorneys familiar with contract law and state regulations should review the transactions, or, better yet, draw up the contracts.

After the transfers have been implemented, the entity, through its risk manager or other designated individual, needs to monitor the results. If the results are satisfactory, fine; if not, look for another way to correct the problem.

These steps are general in nature. But individual entities have specific problems, issues, goals, and risk exposures that should be applied to and considered in the decision-making process. One size does not necessarily fit all when it comes to risk-transfer transactions.

ADVANTAGES AND DISADVANTAGES

There are no big secrets here. The advantages and disadvantages of a noninsurance transfer of risk have to be reviewed by a risk manager based on the particular goals of the company. But, there are some general guidelines that an entity can follow.

Advantages

One obvious advantage is the transfer of risk itself. If a company doesn't have to worry about and plan for a certain type of loss, the time and money that would otherwise be spent on a response can be spent on other activities that are designed to aid the profitability, continuing operations, and survival of the company. And, should a loss occur, if the transfer has been made, company resources won't be spent paying for it.

Another advantage is that, if a risk exposure is transferred, the company need not purchase insurance for that risk. Some exposures are so subject to frequent or severe losses that trying to provide insurance for those exposures would either be a futile exercise or would cost a huge amount in premium dollars. Transferring the risk of those frequent or severe exposures would enable the company to have the money to buy insurance for its less frequent and less severe exposures at a premium that is acceptable.

One more advantage is that after the risk is transferred and a loss occurs, the bad news and potential economic debt need not be put on a balance sheet. This could affect a company's ability to obtain loans at a good rate from financial institutions. The quality of planning that went into transferring the risk might also impress the lending institutions.

Disadvantages

A disadvantage is the time and effort needed to identify the risk that should be transferred. After this, time and effort and even some money have to be spent implementing the transfer.

Another disadvantage is that, by transferring the exposure, the company is giving up control over how it is handled and over the process of paying for a loss arising from it. This may not be a problem but, if the exposure is managed negligently or irresponsibly by the transferee and an injured person complains, a court may order all the responsibility back onto the transferor. And, what if the transferee goes into bankruptcy? A competent attorney for an injured plaintiff will not hesitate to revise a complaint to include the transferor of a risk exposure if there is no available party available to pay for the loss. The transferee has to be a reliable and capable choice or the transferor will pay and the decision to transfer risk will turn out to be a bad one.

Another disadvantage arises not so much from the actual transfer of risk, but from the process itself. If the process is not legal or not contractually sound, the transfer could be voided. The transferor could get into a dispute with both the legal system and the transferee and end up paying for a loss or, at the very least, having the responsibility for the exposures returned.

The bottom line is that there are advantages and disadvantages to any business decision to transfer a risk exposure. These could be long-term or short-term, serious or mild. But they should always be identified before the transfer occurs.

TIME AND CASH COMMITMENT

The time and cash required to accomplish these transfers vary from company to company, depending on the individual company's own management and economic situation. However, if the transfer is to be legal, competent, and as advantageous as possible, a firm commitment of time and cash is necessary. And, this commitment should come from every level of management.

WHERE CAN I FIND OUT MORE ABOUT IT?

- Annual ACE/SCLA Conference, produced by *Claims Magazine*, the National Underwriter Company, and the Society of Claim Law Associates. This annual claims conference offers an educational forum for claims adjusters and managers as well as a hall of exhibitors that spotlights vendors that provide service in the area of claims management. Contact at www.ace-scla.com

- Associate in Risk Management (ARM) courses offered by the Insurance Institute of America. Contact at www.aicpcu.org

- Brooks, Harry F., and Donald S. Malecki. 1989. *Insuring the Lease Exposure*. Cincinnati: National Underwriter Company.

- Leimberg, Stephan R., et al. 2001. *The Tools & Techniques of Estate Planning, 12th Edition*. Cincinnati: National Underwriter Company.

- Risk and Insurance Management Society (RIMS) annual conference. Contact at www.rims.org

- The National Underwriter Company, the leading voice in the risk management field, offering various publications on risk and insurance management issues. Contact the company at www.nuco.com/nucatalog.

Attorneys familiar with contract law and brokers can act as valuable resources for a noninsurance transfer of risk. Contact local bar associations and agents and brokers associations.

QUESTIONS AND ANSWERS

Question—When it comes to paying for injury or damage to a claimant, why is incorporation better for an entity than forming a partnership?

Answer—Incorporation allows only the assets of the corporation to be subject to the payment of damages, whereas a partnership subjects the personal assets of the individual partners to the damage claim.

Question—If a company needs an experienced worker to help with a certain project and decides to lease that worker, what is an important item for the company risk manager to remember?

Answer—A company leasing a worker from a labor leasing firm is considered the lessee. The lessee is responsible for the workers compensation benefits to the leased worker unless the leasing contract calls for the leasing firm to keep the responsibility. Also, even though the leased employee is not a regular employee, the lessee can be held responsible for the actions of that leased worker if he injures someone while doing work for the lessee.

Question—What are some ways in which a general contractor can be held responsible for the acts of a subcontractor?

Answer— If the subcontractor defaults on his duties, such as by not providing workers compensation coverage, the duty would fall upon the general contractor as a matter of law. Also, the general contractor can be held responsible due to his position as the general supervisor of the total work project.

Question—The company risk manager is not sure whether to request a surety agreement or a guaranty to cover the risk exposure of a new project. What information about the two agreements can help him decide?

Answer— A surety agreement and a guaranty both obligate someone to perform a duty in the event that another (the principal) fails to perform. The differ-

ence is that a surety agreement is a joint undertaking of both the principal and the surety; that is, both are bound by the same agreement and both are primarily liable for a breach of duty. A guaranty is a separate undertaking, a separate contract in which the principal has no part. Under a guaranty, the principal and the guarantor are bound by separate and distinct contracts with the guarantor only secondarily liable. This liability is contingent on the default of the principal.

Question—What instruments guarantee the fulfillment of contract obligations?

Answer—In general, there are four types of contractor bonds:

Bid bonds—guarantee that, when the contract is awarded, the contractor will enter into the contract and provide the necessary performance and payment bonds.

Performance bonds—guarantee that the work will be done according to contract specifications.

Maintenance bonds—guarantee that faulty work or defective material discovered within a certain time period will be corrected and/or replaced.

Completion bonds—guarantee the completion of a project.

Question—What is the difference between a waiver and a hold-harmless agreement?

Answer—A waiver is the intentional and voluntary relinquishment of a known legal right, as for example, an individual giving up her right to sue someone who causes her harm. A hold-harmless agreement is an agreement between two entities to the effect that one agrees to hold the other without responsibility for damages or injuries that occur due to the activities of the two entities. A hold-harmless agreement usually involves damages or injuries that occur to an outside third party, while a waiver usually involves damages or injuries just between the entities agreeing to the waiver.

Question—What is the difference between sole liability and vicarious liability?

Answer—Sole liability is when one entity is totally and primarily legally responsible for the injuries and damages done to another because of that entity's acts or omissions. Vicarious liability is indirect legal responsibility wherein one entity can be held liable for the injuries and damages done to another, but only because of the specific relationship between that entity and another who actually does the damage; for example, an employer being held responsible for the acts of his employee.

SAMPLE NONINSURANCE TRANSFER CLAUSES

Contractual transfers, such as hold-harmless and indemnity agreements, attempt to shift liability to others. Typical examples are found on tickets for parking lots, amusement parks, or sports arenas, as well as in property and equipment leases and injury waivers. Each will usually contain a statement that the owner is not responsible for any losses to the visitor or lessee or to their property.

The wording of these agreements differs according to purpose. The risk manager may not be an attorney and may not be qualified to give legal advice.

Figure 6.1 includes sample wording for several types of hold-harmless and indemnity agreements. Wording for specific situations should be carefully worked out between risk managers and legal counsel.

Figure 6.1

Facility Usage

ABC Companies, its heirs, and assigns, voluntarily agree to release, waive, discharge, hold harmless, defend and indemnify XYZ Company, its owners, agents, officers, and employees from any and all claims, actions, or losses for bodily injury, property damage, wrongful death, loss of services, or otherwise that may arise out of the use of _____equipment and facilities. ABC Companies releases, discharges, and waives any claims or actions that may arise in the present or future for the negligent acts or other conduct by the owners, agents, officers, and employees of XYZ Company.

* * * *

Garage Waiver

Owner and company agree. All claimed damage or loss must be reported and itemized by customer to attendant in writing before car is taken from park, after loss occurs and if not so made is waived. Company has option to make repairs at its own expense of any claimed damage within 48 hours after filing a claim. In all court actions burden of proof to establish claim remains with customer. Court actions by customer for any claims must be filed within 90 days from date of parking, in court of jurisdiction where claimed loss occurs. Company not responsible for damage by fire, or defective brakes, or parts, or for articles left in car unless separately checked with attendant, charge being $.25 per article. Total liability of company limited to $250 for all damage or loss to customer. Company not responsible for loss of use. Company not responsible for cars after closing time. Customer must set emergency brake before leaving car. This is the entire contract and no employee can modify it. It is not assignable. Customer waives all laws in conflict with the foregoing.

When you park car in unoccupied stall, you agree that it is at your sole risk, that you will lock same, and that possession and control of your car are yours.

* * * *

Property Rental

Lessee shall indemnify and agree to indemnify and save lessor, its successors, and assigns, harmless from any and all liability, damages, or loss, including reasonable legal fees, arising out of the ownership, selection, possession, leasing, renting, operation, control, use, condition (including but not limited to latent or other defects whether or not discoverable by the lessee), maintenance, delivery, and return of the equipment or in the event that the lessee shall be in default hereunder arising out of the condition of any item of equipment sold or disposed of after use by the lessee.

* * * *

Employee Use of Fitness Room

In condition of _____
Company's sponsorship of certain nonemployment-related recreational activities, including the company health and fitness center, I,

_____(an employee) of _____Company agree for myself and my successors, assigns, heirs, executors, and administrators to indemnify and hold harmless _____Company, its subsidiaries, divisions, affiliates, and their respective directors, officers, employees, agents from and against any and all claims, actions, causes of action, damages, suits, liabilities, and demands whatsoever in the event of any injury, loss, or damage I may sustain while participating in any company-sponsored sports or recreational activity, including the health and fitness center.

I understand the nature and purpose of the health and fitness center and am aware that any strenuous physical activity involves certain risks. It is my responsibility to consult with my doctor before beginning a physical exercise program. I am a voluntary participant in _____Company's health and fitness center and hereby assume the risk of any and all accidents or injuries of any kind that may be sustained by me by reason of or in connection with my participation in activities at the health and fitness center. I agree for myself and my successors, assigns, heirs, executors, and administrators to hereby release, discharge, and absolve _____Company, its subsidiaries, divisions, affiliates, and their respective directors, officers, employees, and agents from and against any and all claims, actions, causes of action, damages, suits, liabilities, and demands whatsoever in the event of any injury, loss, or damage I may sustain while participating in activities at the health and fitness center.

END NOTES

[1]   Leimberg, Stephan R., et al. 2001. _The Tools & Techniques of Estate Planning, 12th Edition._ Cincinnati: National Underwriter Company.

Chapter 6

GLOSSARY

Bid bond. Surety bonds that guarantee that, when a contract is awarded, the contractor will enter into it and provide the necessary performance and payment bonds.

Completion bond. A surety bond that guarantees the completion of a project.

Franchise. A business-to-business license, in which a license to conduct a certain activity or process is granted by one business to another business.

Hold-harmless agreement. An agreement in which one party agrees to assume another party's responsibility for damages or injuries that occur because of the two parties' relationships.

Incorporation. The creation of a legal entity that, to the extent possible, transfer potential individual exposures to liabilities and responsibilities to the corporation.

Indemnification agreement. An agreement in which one party agrees to reimburse another party for damages or injuries that occur as a result of the two parties' relationship.

Lease. A contract in which one party grants to another legal interest in some item.

Maintenance bond. A surety bond that guarantees that faulty work or defective materials that are discovered within the bond period will be corrected or replaced.

Performance bond. A surety bond that guarantees that work will be done according to contract specifications, at the price listed and in the time frame provided in the contract.

Risk retention group (RRG). A group of similar entities that is formed to share risk and the financial consequences of those risks.

Service contract. Similar to a maintenance agreement, this type of agreement transfers the risk exposures that surround maintenance services to a service person or company.

Subcontract. A contract that provides for parties to share the work that is covered by the contract.

Vicarious liability. The liability that arises when one party is responsible for the actions of another party, such as the liability that a general contractor might have for the actions of subcontractors.

Waiver. The intentional and voluntary relinquishing of a known legal right.

Chapter 7

INSURANCE AS A RISK TRANSFER MECHANISM

WHAT IS IT?

Insurance is a risk transfer device. It operates in much the same manner as other risk transfer devices, such as lease or hold harmless agreements. By contract, one party agrees to be responsible for another party's acts or to indemnify another party for the financial consequences of a loss.

Through the purchase of insurance, the financial consequences of a loss are transferred to another party, the insurer. The insurer may be an insurance company, a risk retention group, or another type of alternative risk mechanism.

A risk manager may see insurance as a means of budgeting a relatively small, known amount up-front (the premium) in place of funding a much greater amount at the time of a large—and possibly catastrophic—unknown future event (a possible loss).

The classic textbook definition of insurance says that it is "a device for reducing risk by combining a sufficient number of exposure units to make their individual losses collectively predictable. The predictable loss is then shared proportionately by all units in the combination."[1] In other words, the losses of the few are shared among the premiums of the many.

The need for a large number of similar exposure units is called the *law of large numbers*. Insurers must be certain that they have enough similar exposure units insured so that they can accurately predict their losses. The law of large numbers is based on the regularity of events. Mehr and Cammack say that the law may be stated as follows:

The greater the number of exposures, the more nearly will the actual results obtained approach the probable result expected with an infinite number of exposures. Thus, if a coin is flipped a sufficiently large number of times, the results of the trials will approach half heads and half tails—the theoretical probability if the coin is flipped an infinite number of times.[2]

An insurer collects premiums from the many, pools those premiums, and out of that pool pays its insureds' losses and company expenses. Anything left is profit to be reinvested or distributed to shareholders.

Historical Perspective

Insurance may have started as early as 4000 BC in the rice paddies of China. There, grain merchants divided their cargo among several boats in order to minimize the economic impact of any one boat sinking. However, most historians place the beginning of insurance as the 17th century in London, with the founding of Lloyd's of London.

STEPS TO IMPLEMENT

The first part of developing an insurance program is to determine what exposures (risks of loss) face a business or organization. Businesses will own their own property; have liabilities arising out of custody of property belonging to others; have liability exposures to others arising from premises, operations, and products; and encounter a host of other situations in which loss might cause the business to suffer financially.

Therefore, risk managers should first explore what their company's exposures to loss are. As noted in Chapter 3, there are various methods that may be used to identify and assess exposures. They include surveys and questionnaires, financial statements, risk management committees, risk management audits, inspections, risk mapping, flow charts, and computer modeling. Many good loss surveys are published and referenced in the section of this chapter entitled **Where Can I Find Out More About It?**

In this chapter it is that *exposure to loss* (specifically bodily injury and property damage) that is used to define the word *risk*. However, the word risk is also used by insurance professionals to include any of the following:

- The property insured.

- The person insured.

- The perils being insured against.

- Any hazards that may increase the chance of loss from a peril.

STEP ONE: BEGINNING THE PROCESS

Ideally, a risk exposure survey will show most of a company's potential loss exposures. A risk manager should then solicit proposals for insurance coverage. In some cases, corporations interview and solicit insurance proposals from various *intermediaries*. An intermediary is an individual or company that is licensed to sell insurance, such as an independent agent, a retail broker, or a surplus lines agent. Another name for intermediary is *producer* or *broker*. The risk manager should then select the producer she feels would deliver the best insurance coverage, providing that producer with a *broker-of-record* letter. The broker-of-record letter appoints that producer as the corporation's representative to all insurance carriers, and it permits the producer to approach the market for insurance coverage and pricing options on behalf of the client. (See Step Two for more about the process of selecting an intermediary.)

Broker-of-record Letters

A business may issue a broker-of-record letter either during the proposal process or midterm, during an actual policy period. A midterm broker-of-record letter transfers the company's business from one intermediary to another while insurance is in place. A broker-of-record letter that is issued during the proposal process usually is effective for the purpose of obtaining insurance quotations, placing the insurance, and then managing the coverage throughout the policy term.

Insurance companies vary in the way they treat such letters. The contract between the intermediary and the insurance company outlines the procedure that must be followed. Most contracts provide a waiting period of five or ten days during which the incumbent broker may attempt to obtain a rescinding broker-of-record letter from the insured. Unless the waiting period is waived by the incumbent producer, the account is not transferred until the waiting period elapses.

Midterm Broker-of-record Letters

Not all insurance companies permit business to be transferred midterm. Those that do often require that the policy(ies) involved be canceled and rewritten for the new broker of record, who must submit a new application to the carrier. This is an effort to keep possible errors and omissions from transferring from the incumbent broker to the new one. In addition, the policy(ies) may be transferred from one underwriter to another at the insurance company or even from one underwriting branch to another when a broker-of-record letter is presented. The new underwriter usually requires a new application and supporting underwriting information in order to complete the underwriting file. He also may underwrite the account differently from the original underwriter.

In addition, the agency contract often specifies that, if the coverage is not canceled and rewritten, the annual commission stays with the prior agent. Also discussed in the contract between the insurance company and the agent or broker are issues about who is responsible to collect any additional premiums due on endorsements or audits of the policy and which broker receives—or must refund—commission on those transactions. The agency contract also specifies which broker or agent is charged with losses on the account. It also is important to remember that the broker or agent that accepts the broker-of-record letter must represent the carrier that writes the policy(ies) in order to present a valid letter.

Broker-of-record Letters for Marketing Purposes

In other cases, a risk manager may select two or three producers she feels would meet the service needs of her corporation. These producers then are assigned insurance companies that they will approach to insure the business. They are given broker-of-record letters to use in dealing with those particular insurance companies. This process often is referred to as *going to market with an account* or *marketing an account*.

Each producer approaches the insurance carriers it is assigned to negotiate the best insurance coverage and pricing options it can negotiate. The producers then present their proposals to the corporate risk manager, who chooses one. That producer then is appointed the corporation's broker-of-record for all policies and insurance companies and is directed to place the insurance coverages.

The following is a sample broker-of-record letter.

SAMPLE BROKER-OF-RECORD LETTER

Important: The letter should be on the client's (insured business's) stationery.

(Insured's Name)
(Insured's Address)

(Date)

(Insurer Name)
(Street Address)
(City, State, Zip)

Dear (Underwriter Name—if known):

RE: (Client Name)
     (Policy Type, Policy Number, Policy Term)
     (Policy Type, Policy Number, Policy Term)
     (Policy Type, Policy Number, Policy Term)

Please be advised that, effective (date), we have appointed (Broker or Agency Name, Address) as our exclusive agent and broker for the above noted insurance policies (and bonds). You are authorized to provide representatives of (Broker or Agency Name) with any information they request regarding our insurance contracts, schedules, loss data, rating worksheets, and other miscellaneous items.

The (Broker or Agency Name) is not responsible, however, for any errors or omissions that may have occurred in insuring the account prior to the effective date of this broker-of-record assignment. This letter supersedes any previously issued broker-of-record letters.

Sincerely,

(Authorized Representative, Named Insured)

Risk Management Tip

In general, insurance companies provide only one quotation for each piece of business that is submitted to them. Quotations for insurance coverage and premium are provided to the broker or agent that reaches the insurance company first.

Take, for example, the situation of ABC Restaurants, which wants to market its insurance program. If ABC's risk manager tells three different brokers to solicit insurance proposals, and all three approach Ajax Insurance Company, the broker that submits the first complete coverage application to Ajax will receive that company's quotation. In order to avoid a stampede to the insurance marketplace, risk managers often assign specific insurance companies to specific brokers or agents through broker-of-record letters that are tailored to individual insurance companies. In this way, only one broker will approach each possible insurance company.

STEP TWO: CHOOSING AN INTERMEDIARY

Proposals may be solicited from several different types of insurance intermediaries. Since individuals that sell insurance must be licensed in the state in which the prospective insured is located, the intermediary must be licensed in that state. In most states, all these intermediaries are now referred to and licensed as *producers*. However, there are different types of producers, including

- independent agents,
- exclusive agents,
- employee agents,
- direct-writing agents,
- brokers, and
- surplus lines brokers.

The risk manager should consider the advantages and disadvantages of working with each type of intermediary.

Independent Agents

A producer who is an *independent agent* is an independent businessperson who represents the insurer. In fact, he may be the agent of several insurers. The independent agent is appointed by the insurer to represent it in a given state (although an insurance agent may hold licenses to transact insurance business in multiple states). Independent agents are said to *own the expirations* of the policies they write. When the policy expires, an independent agent may offer the renewal to any insurance company he represents. And, he has the right to sell those policy rights to anyone else. If either the insurance company or the independent agent for any reason terminates the agency agreement, the customers remain with the agent. He may then place them with any other company he represents.

It is important to remember that it is the insurer that creates the agency relationship through the contract with the independent agent. The independent agent's first duty and loyalty must be to the insurer that appointed him. The agency contract spells out the agent's rights and responsibilities. One of an agent's important rights is the right to bind the insurer to an insured. Once the agent tells a customer that a risk is covered, the risk is covered. Among the agent's responsibilities are loyalty to the principal, truthfulness in dealings with the insurer, and accurate accounting of any funds that belong to the insurer.

The advantage of working with an independent agent is that with the availability of several markets, the agent should be able to find a good match for the customer—both in terms of coverage and price. Examples of insurers who market their products through independent agents are the Cincinnati Insurance Companies, Travelers Property Casualty, and The Hartford.

Independent agents usually are compensated with commission that insurance companies pay.

Exclusive Agents

The exclusive agent is also an independent businessperson. However, exclusive agents represent only one insurance company. Unlike the independent agent, the exclusive agent may or may not own policy expirations, depending on the company. Either party may terminate the arrangement at any time. State Farm Insurance® is an example of an insurer that markets its products through exclusive agents.

Exclusive agents usually are compensated with commission that their company pays.

Employee Agents

Employee agents are licensed as insurance agents (producers) but are employees of the insurer. They do not own their expirations and are usually employed at will by the insurer. The Allstate Corporation and Liberty Mutual insurance are examples of insurers that market their products through employee agents.

Employee agents usually are compensated through a salary paid by the company for which they work.

Direct-writing Agents

A direct-writing agent is an employee agent, but only does business over the telephone or Internet. Insurers that use direct-writing agents often are referred to as *direct writers*. GEICO is an example of a direct writer. Direct writers usually are compensated with salary.

Brokers

A broker is considered an agent of the insured. In general, there is no agency contract between the insurer and the broker. There may or may not be a formal service agreement between the broker and the insured business. The broker has permission to place coverage with certain insurers. It is important to note that a broker, typically, does not have binding authority. When a customer goes to a broker, the broker will try to place the customer with one of the companies with whom he has a relationship. However, the broker usually may not bind coverage for that customer without the express permission of the insurer.

In many cases, a business that uses a broker for insurance and risk management services will issue a broker-of-record letter to that broker to establish the relationship. In others, a service agreement or contract may be executed. In recent years, many brokers have refrained from making commission on the insurance they write for larger businesses. In lieu of commission, they negotiate a service fee with the insured businesses they represent. This agreement outlines the level of service the broker has agreed to provide and the fee amount the business will pay for that service.

The reasoning behind this is that a fee arrangement is thought to prevent brokers from placing business with insurers from whom they get the most commission, as well as encouraging them to seek noninsurance solutions to risk management problems. Some risk managers believe that a fee keeps brokers independent from specific insurance companies.

In larger commercial settings, brokers have the advantage of finding the best match for the applicant, without being tied to any company or system. Brokers may be compensated by insurance policy commissions or by fees paid by the businesses they represent.

Surplus Lines Brokers

A surplus lines broker is a specialized insurance producer. A surplus lines broker has relationships with *nonadmitted insurers*, which are described more completely in Chapter 15, Insurance Companies. Nonadmitted insurers are not subject to rate and form regulation by the various states. An insured cannot approach a surplus lines broker directly. Rather, a licensed intermediary must approach the surplus lines broker.

Premiums paid to a surplus lines company are not protected by state guaranty funds. So, if a surplus lines insurer becomes insolvent and not able to pay claims, the insured has no way of recovering premium that it

may have paid. The insured also may have to assume responsibility for outstanding claims.

The advantage of working with a surplus lines broker is that these companies can quickly adapt their forms and underwriting to accommodate a risk. As mentioned, they do not need regulatory approval. The biggest disadvantage is that the insured's premium is not protected by the state's guaranty fund, so claims may not be paid in the event that the nonadmitted company becomes insolvent. Any business considering surplus lines coverage should thoroughly investigate the company's financial rating.

Surplus lines brokers usually are compensated with insurance company commission.

STEP THREE: BINDERS OF INSURANCE

If several intermediaries are marketing the coverage, their proposals should be reviewed for both breadth and cost. After they are received, the risk manager should interview those that appear to offer the best option. It is here that the risk manager can ask questions about levels of service, coverage, exclusions, rate credits, and premium levels. In addition to discussing the insurance coverage that is being offered, it is important for the insured and the intermediary to discuss areas such as the insurer's financial rating and its service reputation.

After selecting an intermediary's proposal, the customer should receive binders of insurance that reference the insurance coverage that is in place. The binders take the place of the insurance policies until they are issued.

The binders will contain information similar to the declarations page of a policy:

1. Name and address of the insured, insurer, and intermediary.
2. Forms that apply.
3. Effective and expiration dates.
4. Binder premium.
5. The exposures covered, such as general liability, auto liability, and property.
6. Limits of insurance that have been bound.

Figure 7.1

ACORD™ INSURANCE BINDER		DATE	

THIS BINDER IS A TEMPORARY INSURANCE CONTRACT, SUBJECT TO THE CONDITIONS SHOWN ON THE REVERSE SIDE OF THIS FORM.

PRODUCER	PHONE (A/C, No, Ext):	COMPANY	BINDER #
	FAX (A/C, No):		

	EFFECTIVE			EXPIRATION	
	DATE	TIME		DATE	TIME
			AM		12:01 AM
			PM		NOON

CODE:	SUB CODE:	THIS BINDER IS ISSUED TO EXTEND COVERAGE IN THE ABOVE NAMED COMPANY PER EXPIRING POLICY #:

AGENCY CUSTOMER ID:	DESCRIPTION OF OPERATIONS/VEHICLES/PROPERTY (Including Location)
INSURED	

COVERAGES LIMITS

TYPE OF INSURANCE	COVERAGE/FORMS	DEDUCTIBLE	COINS %	AMOUNT
PROPERTY CAUSES OF LOSS ☐ BASIC ☐ BROAD ☐ SPEC				
GENERAL LIABILITY ☐ COMMERCIAL GENERAL LIABILITY ☐ CLAIMS MADE ☐ OCCUR		EACH OCCURRENCE		$
		DAMAGE TO RENTED PREMISES		$
		MED EXP (Any one person)		$
		PERSONAL & ADV INJURY		$
		GENERAL AGGREGATE		$
	RETRO DATE FOR CLAIMS MADE:	PRODUCTS - COMP/OP AGG		$
AUTOMOBILE LIABILITY ☐ ANY AUTO		COMBINED SINGLE LIMIT		$
☐ ALL OWNED AUTOS		BODILY INJURY (Per person)		$
☐ SCHEDULED AUTOS		BODILY INJURY (Per accident)		$
☐ HIRED AUTOS		PROPERTY DAMAGE		$
☐ NON-OWNED AUTOS		MEDICAL PAYMENTS		$
		PERSONAL INJURY PROT		$
		UNINSURED MOTORIST		$
				$
AUTO PHYSICAL DAMAGE DEDUCTIBLE	☐ ALL VEHICLES ☐ SCHEDULED VEHICLES	ACTUAL CASH VALUE		
☐ COLLISION:		STATED AMOUNT		$
☐ OTHER THAN COL:		OTHER		
GARAGE LIABILITY ☐ ANY AUTO		AUTO ONLY - EA ACCIDENT		$
		OTHER THAN AUTO ONLY:		
		EACH ACCIDENT		$
		AGGREGATE		$
EXCESS LIABILITY ☐ UMBRELLA FORM		EACH OCCURRENCE		$
		AGGREGATE		$
☐ OTHER THAN UMBRELLA FORM	RETRO DATE FOR CLAIMS MADE:	SELF-INSURED RETENTION		$
WORKERiS COMPENSATION AND EMPLOYERiS LIABILITY		WC STATUTORY LIMITS		
		E.L. EACH ACCIDENT		$
		E.L. DISEASE - EA EMPLOYEE		$
		E.L. DISEASE - POLICY LIMIT		$
SPECIAL CONDITIONS/ OTHER COVERAGES		FEES		$
		TAXES		$
		ESTIMATED TOTAL PREMIUM		$

NAME & ADDRESS

	☐ MORTGAGEE ☐ ADDITIONAL INSURED
	☐ LOSS PAYEE
	LOAN #
	AUTHORIZED REPRESENTATIVE

ACORD 75 (2001/01)   NOTE: IMPORTANT STATE INFORMATION ON REVERSE SIDE   © ACORD CORPORATION 1993

Figure 7.1 (cont'd)

CONDITIONS

This Company binds the kind(s) of insurance stipulated on the reverse side. The Insurance is subject to the terms, conditions and limitations of the policy(ies) in current use by the Company.

This binder may be cancelled by the Insured by surrender of this binder or by written notice to the Company stating when cancellation will be effective. This binder may be cancelled by the Company by notice to the Insured in accordance with the policy conditions. This binder is cancelled when replaced by a policy. If this binder is not replaced by a policy, the Company is entitled to charge a premium for the binder according to the Rules and Rates in use by the Company.

Applicable in California

When this form is used to provide insurance in the amount of one million dollars ($1,000,000) or more, the title of the form is changed from "Insurance Binder" to "Cover Note".

Applicable in Delaware

The mortgagee or Obligee of any mortgage or other instrument given for the purpose of creating a lien on real property shall accept as evidence of insurance a written binder issued by an authorized insurer or its agent if the binder includes or is accompanied by: the name and address of the borrower; the name and address of the lender as loss payee; a description of the insured real property; a provision that the binder may not be canceled within the term of the binder unless the lender and the insured borrower receive written notice of the cancellation at least ten (10) days prior to the cancellation; except in the case of a renewal of a policy subsequent to the closing of the loan, a paid receipt of the full amount of the applicable premium, and the amount of insurance coverage.

Chapter 21 Title 25 Paragraph 2119

Applicable in Florida

Except for Auto Insurance coverage, no notice of cancellation or nonrenewal of a binder is required unless the duration of the binder exceeds 60 days. For auto insurance, the insurer must give 5 days prior notice, unless the binder is replaced by a policy or another binder in the same company.

Applicable in Nevada

Any person who refuses to accept a binder which provides coverage of less than $1,000,000.00 when proof is required: (A) Shall be fined not more than $500.00, and (B) is liable to the party presenting the binder as proof of insurance for actual damages sustained therefrom.

ACORD 75 (2001/01)

Each of these sections is shown in Figure 7.1, a sample Binder of Insurance form, developed and distributed by ACORD (Association for Cooperative Operations Research and Development). In order for coverage to apply, the appropriate box on the form must be checked and, where applicable, a limit of insurance entered. As noted under the Conditions section of page 2 of the binder, the insurance indicated on the binder is "subject to the terms, conditions and limitations of the policy(ies) in current use by the Company." If special coverage forms or wording applies, it must be indicated on the binder. Copies of all binders are sent by the intermediary to both the insured business and the insurance companies they reference.

Typically binders are issued for a period of thirty days. If the customer has not received the policy within that thirty-day period, a new binder should be issued. Many claims have been adjusted and settled based on the information that is contained in the binder. So it is important that they accurately represent the coverage and are renewed if they expire.

STEP FOUR: RECEIVING AND REVIEWING POLICIES

Receiving the Policies

The insurance policy is a contract that spells out the terms and conditions of coverage. Any discrepancies between the proposal, binder, and insurance policy will be controlled by the insurance policy. Therefore, it must meet expectations. Any questions or discrepancies should be referred to the intermediary as soon as possible, before problems develop. The intermediary should act as an advocate for the insured in resolving any discrepancies. As noted in Chapter 15, Insurance Companies, the financial rating of insurance companies selected is very important. Financial ratings gauge the financial strength of an insurance company and provide one means of determining whether the chosen insurer will be able to pay claims. Other items that are discussed in Chapter 15 include the insurance company's claims-handling and risk management philosophies and ability to provide adequate services.

Contract of Adhesion

Insurance differs from other contracts in that it is typically not negotiated. Most insureds, other than very large businesses, have little, if any, say in the content or language of the policy. Most insurance contracts are written by the insurance company, filed for approval in the states in which the policies are being used, and then offered to potential customers on a take-it-or-leave-it basis. Large businesses may negotiate for specific coverage wording, or they may seek out a nonadmitted insurance company that may be able to offer customized coverage language. Policy wording that has been negotiated between an insurance company and an insured is called *manuscript wording*. Besides the difficulty that is encountered in getting an underwriter to agree to change the language on a form, problems may arise with regulators that are charged with approving policy language. Therefore, manuscript wording usually is confined to policies for very large businesses in situations that do not involve regulators. In addition, manuscript wording has not been tested in the courts as has standardized wording. A court may not interpret manuscript policy language in the way in which an insured business expected.

General Rule

The insurance departments in most states do review policy language and approve or disapprove wording. But most insureds have little or no input into the policy language.

Thus, an insurance policy is a *contract of adhesion* — the insurer has drafted the contract and the insured must adhere to it. Although this may not seem advantageous to the insured, it is important to remember that, because of this, courts typically interpret insurance policies in the light most favorable to the insured. If the insurer was not clear about the intent, the benefit of the doubt must be given to the insured. Coverage grants will be interpreted broadly and exclusions narrowly. Also, any undefined words will be given their ordinary meaning.

It is also a generally true statement that the states have established minimum coverage requirements that insurance policies must meet. Most of these statutes are based on the coverage that was statutorily mandated in the 1943 New York Standard Fire Policy. States have adjusted their requirements in the intervening years but still set minimum requirements. These requirements involve such items as minimum notices of cancellation and nonrenewal, allowable exclusions, and policy terms.

States set minimum standards because of the so-called public policy aspect of the insurance transaction. The importance of the insurance contract to the general welfare of the public-at-large requires that insurance transactions meet a high standard of review. In addition to the adhesion contract aspects of the insurance policy, there are also other differences between the insurance policy and other contracts. One of the most important differences is that breach of a contract in a usual business situation does not allow the breached party to recover punitive damages awards. However, the issue of bad faith in insurance transactions has developed at law such that insureds who can prove breach of an insurance contract by an insurer can, in some circumstances, sue for and recover punitive damages or bad faith dealing awards.

Reviewing the Insurance Policy

Risk managers should review insurance policies as soon as they receive them. It is incumbent upon the insured to make sure that the policy as delivered by the insurer matches the proposal sent to the underwriter for coverage. Are all of the requested coverages in place? For all the right property? For all appropriate perils?

Declarations Page

The first section of the policy is the *declarations page*. This section of the policy contains much important information—it is a guide to the rest of the policy. Figure 7.2 shows a common policy declarations page for a property policy. This declarations page was filed with state regulators by the *Insurance Services Office (ISO)*. ISO is an organization that provides statistical information, actuarial analyses, policy language, and related services for the insurance industry. The common declarations page indicates which coverage forms and endorsements are included in the policy.

Figure 7.3 is a sample declarations page for the commercial property coverage part of a standard ISO form. This page lists specific information about what properties are covered, to what extent they are covered, and which forms and endorsements apply to the property coverage.

The following items are included on either the common policy declarations or the declarations page of a specific coverage part. They include:

1. **Named Insured**. In most insurance policies the named insured has special rights and responsibilities above and beyond those of an *insured*. One responsibility is the payment of the premium. One right is the right to be notified of policy cancellation. Some policies automatically confer insured status on all family members or all subsidiaries of a company. However, the best advice is, of course, to read the policy.

   If the named insured is a partnership, joint venture, or limited liability company, coverage under the policy for partners and members of the joint venture or limited liability company is addressed here.

2. **Address.** This is the mailing address to which premium notices, policy changes, and cancellation notices should be sent.

3. **Address of Insured Location**. Coverage—especially property insurance—may apply to only certain locations or properties of the insured. Those locations are listed here.

4. **Forms and Endorsements that Apply**. This section lists the coverage forms and endorsements that apply. For example, the property coverage part, auto part, or liability part form numbers would be listed. In general, the coverage *form* provides the basic insuring language. *Endorsements* modify the contract by broadening or limiting coverage and must be read in context with the coverage part. For example, one endorsement may exclude coverage for certain activities or locations of an insured. Another type of endorsement may add coverage for an additional insured, loss payee, or mortgage company that has a financial interest in the insured business or property.

5. **Policy Period**. This states when coverage begins and when it ends. Most policies begin at 12:01 a.m. on the inception date of the policy and end at 12:01 a.m. on the expiration date. The exact time is important when determining which insurance policy applies to claims that may happen near the expiration date of a policy.

6. **Agent's Name and Address.** This is the information on the intermediary used to secure coverage. This is where the insured should turn with any questions.

Figure 7.2

POLICY NUMBER:

IL DS 00 07 02

COMMON POLICY DECLARATIONS

COMPANY NAME AREA	PRODUCER NAME AREA

NAMED INSURED: _____

MAILING ADDRESS: _____

_____

POLICY PERIOD: FROM _____ TO _____ AT 12:01 A.M. STANDARD
TIME AT YOUR MAILING ADDRESS SHOWN ABOVE.

BUSINESS DESCRIPTION	

IN RETURN FOR THE PAYMENT OF THE PREMIUM, AND SUBJECT TO ALL THE TERMS OF THIS POLICY, WE AGREE WITH YOU TO PROVIDE THE INSURANCE AS STATED IN THIS POLICY.

THIS POLICY CONSISTS OF THE FOLLOWING COVERAGE PARTS FOR WHICH A PREMIUM IS INDICATED. THIS PREMIUM MAY BE SUBJECT TO ADJUSTMENT.

	PREMIUM
BOILER AND MACHINERY COVERAGE PART	$ _____
CAPITAL ASSETS PROGRAM (OUTPUT POLICY) COVERAGE PART	$ _____
COMMERCIAL AUTOMOBILE COVERAGE PART	$ _____
COMMERCIAL GENERAL LIABILITY COVERAGE PART	$ _____
COMMERCIAL INLAND MARINE COVERAGE PART	$ _____
COMMERCIAL PROPERTY COVERAGE PART	$ _____
CRIME AND FIDELITY COVERAGE PART	$ _____
EMPLOYMENT-RELATED PRACTICES LIABILITY COVERAGE PART	$ _____
FARM COVERAGE PART	$ _____
LIQUOR LIABILITY COVERAGE PART	$ _____
POLLUTION LIABILITY COVERAGE PART	$ _____
PROFESSIONAL LIABILITY COVERAGE PART	$ _____
	$ _____
_____	$ _____
TOTAL:	$ _____

Premium shown is payable: $_____ at inception. $ _____

IL DS 00 07 02

Page 1 of 2

FORMS APPLICABLE TO ALL COVERAGE PARTS (SHOW NUMBERS):

_____
_____
_____
_____
_____
_____
_____
_____

Countersigned:	By:
(Date)	(Authorized Representative)

NOTE

OFFICERS' FACSIMILE SIGNATURES MAY BE INSERTED HERE, ON THE POLICY COVER OR ELSEWHERE AT THE COMPANY'S OPTION.

Figure 7.3

COMMERCIAL PROPERTY
CP DS 00 10 00

COMMERCIAL PROPERTY COVERAGE PART DECLARATIONS PAGE

POLICY NO.   EFFECTIVE DATE   ___ / ___ / ___   "X" If Supplemental
                                                                      Declarations Is Attached

NAMED INSURED _____

DESCRIPTION OF PREMISES _____

Prem. No.	Bldg. No.	Location, Construction And Occupancy

COVERAGES PROVIDED   Insurance At The Described Premises Applies Only For Coverages For Which A Limit Of Insurance Is Shown

Prem. No.	Bldg. No.	Coverage	Limit Of Insurance	Covered Causes Of Loss	Coinsurance*	Rates

*If Extra Expense Coverage, Limits On Loss Payment

OPTIONAL COVERAGES   Applicable Only When Entries Are Made In The Schedule Below

Prem. No.	Bldg. No.	Agreed Value			Replacement Cost (X)		
		Expiration Date	Cov.	Amount	Building	Pers. Prop.	Including "Stock"

Inflation Guard (%) Bldg.	Pers. Prop.	*Monthly Limit Of Indemnity (Fraction)	Maximum Period Of Indemnity (X)	*Extended Period Of Indemnity (Days)

*Applies to Business Income Only

MORTGAGEHOLDERS _____

Prem. No.	Bldg. No.	Mortgageholder Name And Mailing Address

DEDUCTIBLE _____

$500. Exceptions:

FORMS APPLICABLE _____

To All Coverages:
To Specific Premises/Coverages:

Prem. No.	Bldg. No.	Coverages	Form Number

7. **Name of Insurance Company.** This denotes the insurer. The insured needs to verify that it is the same as on any binder or the same name discussed with the intermediary. The financial rating should be checked again, as well.

8. **Premium.** This is the amount the customer pays for coverage. If it differs from what was agreed upon, clarification should be obtained. The premium section may also show a breakdown into a payment plan.

The insured may be presented with either a monoline or package policy. A *monoline policy* covers only one line of insurance, such as a property policy covering building and contents. A *package policy*, on the other hand, covers more than one line. Quite often package policies combine property, general liability, auto, and excess liability coverage forms.

Package Policy Example

One example of a package policy is the businessowners package policy (BOP). It covers the building(s), other structures, and personal property of the insured. The liability section covers damages the insured may have to pay because of its liability to someone else for bodily injury or property damage. Auto and business income coverage can also be provided through the package concept.

Coverage Parts

If all of these items on the declarations page are correct, then move to the policy itself. This is a comprehensive review of the coverage parts of the policy. Does the policy presented to the insured match the binder and insurance specifications?

In general, an insurance policy is made up of an insuring agreement that describes the property or liability risk covered, a definitions section, exclusions, and policy conditions. Any applicable endorsements are also attached to the policy. Each section should be reviewed with the agent or broker delivering the policy to see that it matches the specifications. The insured should become familiar with the policy exclusions, particularly as it is this section of the form that is frequently misunderstood and troublesome.

Use of Deductibles

One way to keep the premium down is through the use of higher *deductibles*. A deductible is the amount for which the insured is responsible on any property loss before the insurance pays. If the property deductible is $1,000 and the loss is $10,000, the insured would pay $1,000 and the insurer, $9,000.

A *self-insured retention* functions in a similar way. The specific wording of deductible and self-insured retention language should be reviewed to determine exactly how they would work.

A higher deductible shows the insurer that the insured is willing to share in a greater portion of any loss, and the insurer rewards this willingness with a reduced rate. However, the insured must be certain that in case of a loss, it can quickly and easily come up with the amount of the deductible. The important thing is how much premium is being saved for choosing the higher deductible. With a $10,000 deductible, risk managers need to see how much credit they are getting for taking on the exposure to that extra $9,000. In some cases, insurers may insist that an insured assume a higher deductible or it will decline to write the business.

The typical deductible is a *flat deductible* or *straight dollar deductible*, which means that a dollar amount applies to any loss. Flat deductibles usually apply on a per claim basis, which means that the deductible is subtracted from each claim, even when more than one claim arises from one accident or occurrence. However, some flat deductibles apply on a per occurrence basis, which means that only one deductible applies to all claims that arise from the same accident or occurrence. The distinction is very important!

Per Claim Versus Per Occurrence Deductibles

For example, ABC Restaurants selects a $10,000 per claim deductible for its general liability program. Unfortunately, one of its restaurants offers a Mother's Day buffet that includes salmonella-tainted tuna salad. On Mother's Day, 291 people are victims of food poisoning. Since the restaurant has a per claim deductible, the restaurant must pay the first $10,000 of each of the 291 individual claimant's negligence claim.

Conversely, ABC selects a $10,000 per occurrence deductible. If the same situation occurred, the restaurant probably would have to pay only one $10,000 deductible.

Another type of deductible is a *percentage deductible,* which is represented as a percentage of the limit of liability for covered property. Some policies combine flat and percentage deductibles. For instance, a policy may be written with a $1,000 deductible, but that does not apply to loss from earthquake. In that case, the deductible for earthquake can range from 2 percent of the limit to 25 percent of the limit.

Another thing to look for is whether or not the form being used is a *bureau* (e.g., ISO) or an independently filed form. A bureau is another name for an organization that regulates and publishes insurance-related documents and rates. ISO is the largest rating bureau. A rating bureau collects premium and loss statistics from its members. From this information, it calculates rates to be charged in the various lines of insurance, by its members. Some insurers who are ISO members use the rates as developed by ISO, while others may apply surcharges or credits to those rates, as their individual situations dictate.

ISO also writes policy language. Since ISO language is so widely used, it is accepted as the industry standard. Again, some ISO member companies may use the ISO policy without modification. Others may change it to meet their own needs, while others may write their own policy language entirely.

If a company charges its own rates or uses its own forms, the rates and forms are referred to as being *independently filed.* That means the company has filed (or submitted) the rates and forms to the various state insurance departments separately from a bureau.

For an insured looking for a specific type of coverage or credit, an independently filed form may be the answer. If the situation is unique, it may not be addressed in a bureau form. An agent should have knowledge of which independently filed forms may offer a coverage or rate advantage.

When purchasing insurance, the buyer must be aware of any coverage overlaps or coverage gaps. The best way to do this is with a survey.

After analyzing the coverage needs, deciding on an agent or broker, and choosing the policy, what happens if the companies used by that agent or broker won't accept the submission? If all of the avenues through the agent or broker have been exhausted, the options for the insured become rather limited.

One place to look is the *surplus lines market* (also called the *nonadmitted market*). Surplus lines companies often write business that standard (or admitted) companies cannot or will not write. However, this may often be at a considerably higher premium and with limited perils.

An insurer is referred to as *admitted* if it applies for admission to do business in a state. In order to be admitted, an insurer must meet certain financial standards. If a state does admit an insurer, then that insurer must also participate in the state's guaranty fund. All admitted insurers pay into a guaranty fund. Then, if one of those admitted insurers becomes insolvent, the guaranty fund is available to refund any part of a premium that has not yet been used up on a policy. The availability and protection of the guaranty fund protection is obviously a big advantage of doing business with an admitted insurer. Usually admitted companies must submit their rates and forms to a state for its approval.

A *surplus lines company* is not admitted to a state. It does not have to meet those same financial standards and it does not have to get its rates and forms approved. However, the premiums paid to a surplus lines company are not protected by most states' guaranty funds. Thus, if a surplus lines company becomes insolvent, then the insured is without protection.

As mentioned previously, the surplus lines market may be thought of as the *market of last resort.* If an intermediary cannot find coverage for a risk among admitted companies, she may then take that risk to the surplus lines market. Typically, a market for most risks can be found.

As also mentioned, the premiums paid to a surplus lines company are not protected by a guaranty fund. In addition, the state regulator has not reviewed the insurer's forms or rates. But this is part of the price to be paid in order to find insurance for some risks.

Another outlet for property insurance is a state's FAIR (Fair Access to Insurance Requirements) plans. FAIR plans were born out of the urban riots of the 1960s and 70s. After those riots, insurers stopped writing property insurance in areas that had experienced a riot. A FAIR plan is a state-sponsored insurer that provides basic property insurance to insureds who cannot find it elsewhere. Like the surplus lines market, FAIR plan coverage may be expensive and limited in scope.

ADVANTAGES

There are a number of advantages to using insurance as a risk transfer mechanism. They include:

- Insurance presents the risk manager with the opportunity to incur a known, up-front cost (the premium) in exchange for the insurer's taking on the large, possibly catastrophic unknown (the potential for a large loss).

- Securing an insurance policy may satisfy a contractual requirement. If a retail customer leases a building, the lease will probably require that he carry insurance that will cover any damage done to the building. The vast majority of all types of contracts include insurance requirements.

- Banks and other financial institutions usually require that insurance be purchased to protect their interest in the buildings on which they hold mortgages. Loans on other types of property, such as cars, furnishings, and equipment, often are conditional on evidence that insurance on the items is in place.

- Most insurance policies provide that the insurance company adjust and pay claims on behalf of the insured business. This takes a burden off company managers, who probably are not experts in claim-management procedures.

- Insurance may be used to satisfy certain statutory or regulatory requirements. For example, state laws in all but Texas require that insurance be purchased to cover workers compensation exposures, unless the business is a qualified workers compensation self-insurer.

DISADVANTAGES

The following are some of the disadvantages to using insurance as a risk transfer mechanism:

- Spending money for insurance means that the insured has that much less to invest elsewhere—whether in new plant and equipment, new personnel, new training methods, or the acquisition of other businesses. If the risk manager can measure that loss, perhaps a trade-off can be made between less insurance and an aggressive investment policy.

- Unfortunately, even the broadest of insurance policies may not cover every loss. Some business owners and executives may be under the false impression that all claims will be covered by their insurance policies, but that is not possible. As noted previously, the selection of a good intermediary will help ease this situation.

- The way in which most intermediaries are compensated—through commission on the insurance they sell—has given rise to concern among some risk managers. An alternative is to compensate the intermediary on a fee basis.

- Despite the advent of simplified insurance policies, with language that is designed to be more easily understood, insurance policies are difficult to read and understand. It is easy to assume coverage is broader and more complete than it actually is.

WHERE CAN I FIND OUT MORE ABOUT IT?

- Many insurers that specialize in particular industries or groups may have developed checklists. Another source are coverage applications, which ask many of the questions that are necessary to determine what exposures need to be addressed.

- Risk and Insurance Management Society (RIMS), www.rims.org.

- Council of Insurance Agents and Brokers (CIAB), http://www.ciab.com/index.jsp.

- Independent Insurance Agents and Brokers of America (IIABA), www.iiaa.org.

- Professional Insurance Agents association, http://www.piaonline.org/.

- *The FC&S Bulletins* Cincinnati: The National Underwriter Company. www.nationalunderwriter.com.

QUESTIONS AND ANSWERS

Question—What if a business's exposures are unique and very hazardous?

Answer—In this case, the surplus lines market may be the only place to find coverage. The surplus lines company that does insure this business will not have the advantage of a large number of exposure units upon which to base its premium because it writes fewer accounts than the mainstream insurance companies. Therefore, the premium may be higher, and coverage may be restricted.

Risk managers who find themselves in this position also may need to consider assuming a higher retention or looking for alternative risk transfer mechanisms, which are discussed in Chapter 8.

Question—What is the meaning of the word *risk*?

Answer—While the word *risk* has several meanings and uses in the insurance world, its meaning for purposes of this chapter is "exposure to damages that arises from property damage or bodily injury."

Question—How important is a binder of insurance? Is it a legal document?

Answer—A binder of insurance is a legal document that stands in place of an insurance policy or policies until issued. When claims occur before the actual policies are issued, the coverage noted on the binder will be used when adjusting the claim. Therefore, it is critical that the binder accurately reflects the insurance coverage that has been purchased.

An example of the importance of insurance binders is the property claim filed after the destruction of the World Trade Center on September 11, 2001. The property insurance policies had not been issued when the structures were destroyed, so the binder of insurance became critical in the litigation process.

Refer to Figure 7.1, a sample ACORD binder of insurance. Review each box on the document to determine the type of information included on the binder. List the types of insurance that may be represented on the binder. Note that the exact minute that coverage is to begin is listed in the top right of the form.

END NOTES

1   Principles of Insurance; by Robert I. Mehr and Emerson Cammack; Richard D. Irwin, Inc.; 1980.

2   Ibid.

Chapter 7

GLOSSARY

Admitted market. An insurance company that is licensed to do business (write insurance) in a state.

Binder of insurance. A legal document that stands in place of the insurance policy(ies) until issued.

Broker: An insurance intermediary who is the agent of the insured and not the agent of an insurance company.

Broker-of-record letter. A document that is used to appoint an insurance intermediary to represent the insured to insurance companies.

Contract of adhesion. A contract that is offered as is and not subject to negotiation. Insurance policies are considered to be contracts of adhesion.

Declarations page. Usually the first page of an insurance policy. Lists information such as the insurance company, effective period of coverage, forms and endorsements, named insured, and limits of coverage.

Deductible: A deductible is the amount for which the insured is responsible on any loss.

Direct-writing agent (direct writer). An employee insurance agent who does business only over the telephone or Internet.

Employee agent. An insurance intermediary who is employed by a specific insurance company.

Exclusive agent. An independent insurance agent who represents only one insurer.

Flat deductible. A deductible that is a specific dollar amount and is applied to each claim.

Going to market. The process of soliciting insurance coverage proposals from the insurance companies that will write a particular type of risk.

Independent insurance agent. An insurance intermediary that represents a number of insurance companies.

Independently filed forms and rates. Insurance forms and rates that are filed by specific insurance companies, independently from bureau filings.

Insurance: A device for reducing risk by combining a large number of similar exposure units. This combination makes individual loss exposure collectively more predictable.

Insurance Services Office (ISO). An organization that provides statistical information, actuarial analyses, policy wording, and related services to the insurance industry.

Manuscript wording. Wording on an insurance policy that has been negotiated between an insured and insurance company.

Nonadmitted insurers. Insurance companies that are not licensed in a particular state or territory. Specific provisions of state or territorial law control placements, and nonadmitted insurers are not covered by state guaranty funds.

Percentage deductible. A deductible that is represented as a percentage of the limit of coverage, which often is used with catastrophic property insurance, such as earthquake coverage.

Producer. An insurance intermediary, especially a broker or agent, who is licensed to sell insurance.

Self-insured retention. The amount of risk that an insured elects to retain (finance).

Surplus lines broker: A surplus lines broker is a specialized insurance producer that represents nonadmitted insurance companies.

Surplus lines company. Also known as a nonadmitted market or nonadmitted company, this is an insurance company that is not licensed to write business in a state.

OVERVIEW OF ALTERNATIVE RISK TRANSFER TECHNIQUES

WHAT IS ALTERNATIVE RISK TRANSFER (ART)?

Alternative risk transfer is the term-of-art used to describe a collection of property and casualty risk financing techniques. In insurance industry vernacular, ART is often referred to as a *market*, as in the expression *alternative risk transfer market*. However, there is no market, per se, where one can find alternative risk transfer products and services. The spectrum of ART products and services is diverse, but there is one common thread that connects each and every ART technique: *significant risk retention*. ART is simply a fancy expression for various forms of self-insurance. Risk retention is at the heart of every ART program.

In this chapter, we discuss the subject in the following chronology:

- ART Options
- Funding Loss Retentions
- Understanding Types of Captives
- Direct versus Fronted Captives
- Choosing a Captive Domicile
- Advantages and Disadvantages of Group Captives
- The Captive Feasibility Study
- Understanding Captive Tax Issues
- Other Alternative Risk Financing Techniques

STEP ONE: THE OPTIONS

Risk Retention: Self–insurance versus Noninsurance

There are only two basic options for managing risk—transfer it to another party, such as an insurance company, or retain it. Another name for risk retention is *self-insurance*. While this expression may sound like a mis-

nomer, it is actually an effective means of describing everything involved in risk retention. Insurance is another term for risk transfer. When risk is transferred to another party, that party also assumes responsibility for managing that risk. Risk management techniques such as loss control, claims management, and the placement of reinsurance become the transferee's (insurer's) responsibilities. Self-insurance, therefore, connotes the retention of risk *and* the responsibilities for managing it. Comprehensive self-insurance programs include loss control and claims management, as well as a reinsurance component. Reinsurance (insurance that pays in excess of the self-insurance) is the critical factor in all self-insurance schemes.

> Self-insurance connotes the retention of risk *and* the responsibilities for managing it.

Companies cannot and should not retain every dollar of risk. Retained losses must exhibit three distinct characteristics:

1. They must be reasonably predictable in amount and frequency.

2. They must not represent catastrophic loss potential.

3. Their market insurance premiums must not represent significant value based on the limits purchased. Self-insurers should live by the adage, "Don't risk a lot for a little."

Small, frequent, predictable losses should not be insured (transferred). Doing so adds unnecessary costs and requires human resources that could be better applied elsewhere in the company. Insuring such small, predictable losses is known as "trading dollars" with an insurance company, except that, for every dollar spent for premiums, only about 65 cents comes back as claims payments.

Conversely, large and infrequent losses should never be retained. The premiums spent to insure against earthquake, for example, represent an exceptionally good value whether or not a catastrophic earthquake occurs. Retaining losses with catastrophic potential might save a few premium dollars, but the risk to the company is usually considered unacceptable. Finally, risks for which significant insurance capacity (limits) are available for a reasonable premium should generally not be retained. For example, the insurance markets usually offer employment practices liability insurance (EPLI) limits at a reasonable cost. While it is possible to self-insure against the risks arising from employment practices, it makes little sense to knowingly expose the balance sheet to such a risk.

Noninsurance—otherwise known as being *uninsured*—is far different from self-insurance. Self-insurance is a conscious and deliberate act—the risks and benefits are known prior to the initiation of the program. No insurance, on the other hand, connotes a lack of planning and analysis. For example, due to either ignorance or neglect, many companies do not insure against employment practices liability (EPL). Unless a company actively decides to retain the risk, that is, establishes a fund dedicated solely to paying EPL claims or identifies a percentage of retained earnings earmarked to pay for these claims, that company is uninsured for EPL. The consequences of being uninsured for certain risks can be devastating.

Using the EPL example, the company would be forced to pay an unanticipated and potentially enormous claims settlement (plus legal costs). Worse yet, its reputation in the marketplace would suffer and its stock price (for a public company) may plummet.

Deductibles and Self-insured Retentions

The most common form of risk retention is the deductible. There are several types of deductibles:

- Per-loss Deductibles
- Annual Aggregate Deductibles
- Percentage Deductibles
- Franchise Deductibles
- Waiting Period Deductibles
- Self-insured Retentions

Per-loss Deductible

This deductible is expressed as a dollar amount of loss. It is also known as a *straight-dollar* deductible. For example, a $10,000 property loss is subject to a $1,000 deductible. The insured pays $1,000 while the insurer pays the remaining $9,000. This type of deductible is applied to each and every loss.

Annual Aggregate Deductible

While per-loss deductibles apply to each and every loss, an annual aggregate deductible is often used as a way to limit the amount of total loss the insured must retain in any one policy year. In the above example, the per-loss deductible could be limited by an annual aggregate of $5,000. This means that, once this threshold is breached, either by five $1,000 losses or any combination of deductible losses totaling $5,000, the insurer would cover every subsequent claim from the first dollar of loss.

Percentage Deductible

Percentage deductibles are per-loss deductibles expressed as a percentage. The percentage may be of each loss, or in the case of property, a percentage of the values at risk. Flood and earthquake coverages often have percentage deductibles.

Franchise Deductible

A franchise deductible is a per-loss deductible that disappears once the amount of the loss exceeds the deductible amount. For example, once a loss exceeds a $5,000 per-loss deductible, the policy reverts to first dollar coverage and the deductible disappears.

Waiting Period Deductible

This type of deductible is expressed as a period of time rather than a specific dollar amount or percentage of loss or value. Business interruption losses are often subject to waiting period deductibles in order to eliminate small, often questionable, claims.

Self-insured Retentions

Another common form of risk retention is known as a self-insured retention (SIR). An SIR differs from a deductible relative to the responsibilities of the insured and the insurer. Legally, a deductible is not considered self-insurance because the insurer must pay every claim from dollar-one. Once the claim is paid, the insured must then reimburse the insurer the amount of the deductible.

An SIR is bona fide self-insurance in that the insurer is not responsible for any loss that falls within the SIR limit. For example, a company has a general liability SIR of $10,000 and $10 million of insurance limits in excess of the SIR. Losses valued $10,000 and under are the sole responsibility of the insured; the insurer is under no obligation to participate in the loss until its value breeches the SIR limit. Of course, regardless of the technicalities, both deductibles and SIRs represent retained risk that must be managed and financed.

Because deductibles and self-insured retentions usually pertain to a specific line of insurance coverage, it is important to understand the potential for *deductible stacking*. Stacking occurs when one loss triggers several different coverages. For example, a fire could cause damage to real property, personal property, fine arts, and business earnings. If each of these coverages were subject to its own deductible or SIR, the accumulated retention could result in a wholly unanticipated expense.

Qualified Self-insurance

Some types of liability are subject to state financial responsibility laws. These include workers compensation and automobile liability. While each state's laws are slightly different, each of these laws requires employers and operators of motor vehicles to demonstrate their ability to pay for a loss. In most cases this is accomplished through insurance. However, many businesses choose to become *qualified self-insurers*. The term *qualified self-insurance* connotes compliance with a state's financial responsibility regulations. Each state that permits businesses to self-insure their workers compensation and automobile liability has a set of qualifying rules. These rules include minimum number of employees, the amount of security provided to the state (self-insurer's bond), and the amount of liability that may be self-insured (insurers provide excess insurance over qualified self-insured retentions.)

STEP TWO: FUNDING LOSS RETENTIONS

There are a variety of ways to fund retained losses. These methods fall into two main categories:

1. Informal
2. Formal

Informal Loss Funding Techniques

Informal loss funding is not tantamount to noninsurance as discussed previously. The term *informal* means that there is no specific financing technique devoted to the self-insured loss exposures. Losses may be expensed as they are paid from cash flow (accounting rules do not allow the expensing of self-insured losses as they occur), assuming the company can afford to do so. Companies may also establish an unfunded reserve on the balance sheet. This creates financial recognition of the liability without actually creating a funding vehicle.

Formal Loss Funding Techniques

Formal loss funding techniques may be divided into two categories:

1. Postloss
2. Preloss

Postloss Funding Techniques

Postloss funding means that the company has either made a formal arrangement with another party to fund the loss without actually transferring it, or it has made specific internal arrangements that do not entail establishing a loss fund. Examples of the former include bank lines of credit and debt financing (borrowing). Issuing equity to raise funds after a loss is another postloss funding technique.

Preloss Funding Techniques

A preloss funding technique is a formalized program designed to accumulate funds for the purpose of financing retained losses. Reserve funds and trusts are examples of preloss funding techniques, however, the most popular and arguably the most effective preloss funding technique is the captive insurance company.

STEP THREE: UNDERSTANDING TYPES OF CAPTIVES

Captives and Risk Retention Groups

According to the risk consulting firm Tillinghast-Towers Perrin (http://www.tillinghast.com/tillinghast/), a captive is a "closely held insurance company whose insurance business is primarily supplied by and controlled by its owners, and in which the original insureds are the principal beneficiaries. Furthermore, a captive's insureds have direct involvement and influence over the company's major operations, including underwriting, claims management policy, and investments."

A captive's principal goals are to reduce and/or stabilize costs, provide and arrange specific risk management services, and take advantage of certain tax opportunities. Risk retention groups are similar to captives except for the types of risks they are permitted to insure and where they may be domiciled. These are discussed later in this chapter.

Classifications and Types of Captives

There are two major classifications of captives:

1. Owned
2. Rented (rent-a-captive)

Within these classifications there are two main types of captives:

1. Pure (single-parent)
2. Group (multiple parents)

Owned versus Rented

An owned captive, as the name implies, is owned by its policyholder(s). This arrangement follows the basic definition of a captive (described previously). The policyholder(s) own the capital, and thus form the board of directors as well as the various operating committees. Conversely, rent-a-captives are licensed offshore insurers owned by an outside organization. The term *offshore* refers to the fact that the company is domiciled outside the United States of America.

Types of Owned Captives

Pure Captives

Pure captives, also known as single parent captives, are closely held insurance companies primarily insuring the risks of their owner, typically one large firm.

Group Captives

Group captives are owned by multiple, nonrelated organizations. Group captive members are both shareholders *and* policyholders. Any group of companies can form a group captive, assuming they meet the minimum qualifications. They may be either homogeneous, in which members are in the same business, or heterogeneous, in which members are in different businesses.

Subsets of group captives include:

Association Captives

Association captives are similar in purpose and structure to group captives. They are formed to insure the risks of companies involved in the same or similar industries. The captive is either sponsored by or owned by a trade association.

Agency Captives

Agency captives are owned by insurance agencies formed to insure the risks of the agency's clients. The agency does not take the place of the insurer; it shares low level premiums and losses with the insurer.

Risk Retention Groups (RRG)

Risk retention groups are a special kind of group captive formed under the Risk Retention Act of 1986. While there is almost no limit as to what a captive may insure, RRGs are limited to providing liability coverages for its owners/insureds. Risk retention groups are exempt from state insurance regulatory requirements.

Types of Rented Captives

Rent-a-captives and Protected Cell Companies (PCC)

While no precise reports are available, it is estimated that annual premiums for rent-a-captives are close to $1 billion. Unlike owned captives, rent-a-captives and protected cell companies (PCCs) rent their capital to other organizations for a fee. Investors (brokers, reinsurers, insurance companies, banks, or other business enterprises) own the capital and the company's license. The owner maintains a minimum amount of *core capital*, and the renters must capitalize their own risk. Neither rent-a-captives nor PCCs take any risk. Risk is segregated by policyholder in order to avoid risk sharing.

The way that risk is segregated by policyholder defines the difference between a rent-a-captive and a PCC. In a rent-a-captive, the accounts of the various members are segregated by contract, that is, the agreement between each member (renter) and the rent-a-captive states that the rent-a-captive will not use the assets of one member to subsidize the losses of another member.

PCCs do not rely on private contracts to maintain asset separation. They rely on special enabling legislation enacted in the captive's domicile that provides a statutory firewall between cell assets. Members usually receive one preferred (nonvoting) share of stock, which entitles them to dividends. The rent-a-captive owner determines the amount of investment income and underwriting profit (excess premium) returned to the member (dividends), as well as the timing of such payments. Each rent-a-captive and PCC has its own minimum premium; however, $1 million is considered realistic.

Brief History of Captives

The captive insurance company concept is not new and has been used in many different forms. For instance, during the late 1800s, a group of New England textile manufacturers formed a captive in response to the high fire insurance rates of the period. The company ultimately evolved into what is known as the Factory Mutual System and now the FM Global Insurance Company.

Other notable captive insurers formed in the first half of the twentieth century included the Church Insurance Company (formed by the Episcopal Church in 1929) and Mahoning Insurance Company (established by Youngstown Sheet & Tube Company in 1935). Ocean marine insurers in the form of various clubs have used the captive concept. Protection and indemnity (P&I) clubs such as the Steamship Mutual have been in existence in one form or another for centuries.

In spite of these early entries, captive insurers did not become prevalent until the 1950s. At the end of that decade, it is estimated that there were close to 100 in operation. A more recent example of a captive evolving into a global multiline insurer is ACE. ACE was started in 1985 by several visionary investors responding to the lack of available insurer capacity in directors and officers and high excess liability coverage limits.

The next thirty-five years witnessed explosive growth, and, by 2001, about 4,500 captives had been established. Annual written premiums are presently in the neighborhood of $25 billion, while capital and surplus are estimated at $45 billion.

Characteristics of Captive Ownership

- Control over claims and reserving practices
- Control over investments made by the captive
- Recapture of investment income and underwriting profit
- Potential tax advantages

STEP FOUR: CHOOSING A CAPTIVE DOMICILE

Captive insurers are subject to the laws and regulations of their domiciles and cannot be formed in jurisdictions that do not have specific captive-enabling legislation. There are many captive domiciles around the world, and (as of this writing) twenty-two U.S. states have enacted captive legislation. Every state has minimum capital and surplus requirements for insurance companies domiciled in that state. These requirements are extremely difficult to attain. For example, the state of California requires insurers to have at least $85 million in share capital, and $15 million working capital. These requirements exist to protect the consumer. While captives are also insurance companies, they sell no insurance to the general public—only to their shareholders. Because of this, they are required to have far less capital than are normal insurers.

Captives that are domiciled in the United States of America are called *onshore captives*. Captives that are formed in other countries—such as Bermuda or the Cayman Islands—are called *offshore captives*.

Domicile Selection Criteria

Regulatory Environment

All captive domiciles are considered *regulation friendly* towards captives. This means that there is a minimum of reporting requirements, and the application process is a standardized, streamlined affair. Some domiciles have established various classes defined by captive type, and the majority of domiciles have investment regulations.

Required Capitalization

Capitalization requirements do not differ very much from domicile to domicile. Bermuda, for example, requires a minimum of $120,000 in share capital for pure (single-parent) captives, while Vermont's minimum requirement is $250,000.

Few, if any, captives qualify to remain at the minimum capitalization level, since their capital must conform to solvency rules (rules that govern the amount of premium that may be written per each dollar of capital and surplus). For example, the majority of captives require minimum solvency of 5:1, premium to capital and surplus. This means that for every dollar of premium, the captive must also have twenty cents of capital.

Local Service Infrastructure

The older, established domiciles such as Bermuda and Vermont have highly qualified service providers. These include attorneys, auditors, actuaries, brokers and captive managers. Newer domiciles (of which there are many) may not have the same quality of infrastructure.

Taxes and Fees

No captive domicile except Luxembourg levies an income tax on earnings. They do, however, charge various government fee and duties. These fees are usually based on the size of the captive's premium writings and are charged annually.

Permitted Business

Offshore domiciles have few restrictions relative to the type of business that may be written by the captive. In Bermuda, for example, if the business plan makes good sense and the opening capital is adequate, the captive is usually approved. Offshore domiciles also allow captives to write third-party

business. Third-party business is business that is *not related* to the captive's owners. For example, a large general contractor may provide insurance for its best subcontractors through its Cayman-based captive. Onshore domiciles, however, do not generally permit such third-party business.

Investment Regulations

Each domicile has its own set of rules concerning the investment of captive assets. Bermuda, for example, requires that at least 75 percent of assets be considered *relevant assets*. Relevant assets are highly liquid, since the captive must have enough liquidity to pay claims as they come due.

Geographic Convenience

Companies that are located in California usually do not form captives in Vermont; they go to Hawaii. And U.S. companies generally do not use European domiciles such as Guernsey or Dublin.

Offshore versus Onshore

Aside from the issue of permitted business as discussed above, there are other important things to consider when evaluating onshore and offshore domiciles. First, companies that are sensitive to customer or shareholder perceptions often choose to remain onshore. While there is nothing wrong with offshore domiciles, some companies choose to avoid the perception that they are doing business in some offshore "haven." Second, there are certain tax ramifications of doing business offshore that cannot be duplicated in an onshore domicile. Tax issues are discussed later in this chapter.

Political Climate

No company wants to do business in a country (offshore) that is not politically stable. Fortunately, the established offshore domiciles such as Bermuda, Cayman Islands, and the British Virgin Islands recognize the value of American investment. Although their political climates may fluctuate from left to right and back over the years, their business environments are not materially affected.

Figure 8.1

Domicile Comparison – Four Popular Domiciles		
Domicile	**Bermuda**	**Cayman**
Minimum Capitalization	Class I: $120,000 Class II: $250,000 Class III: $1 million	Unrestricted Class B: $120,000 General Business $240,000 Long-term Business $360,000 Both Restricted Class B: No Minimum (Single Parent)
Registration & Incorporation Expenses	Registration: $4,000 - $9,000 (based on amount of capital)	Annual license and government fees CI $5,000 (US$6,098) Cost of incorporating ranges from US $15,000 to US$20,000 depending on the complexities of its structure
Investment Restrictions	General business - 75% of general insurance liabilities must be in relevant assets None for long-term (life, disability) business	None for restricted Class B companies but other investments may be restricted
Taxes & Fees	Income tax exemption until 2016; Annual fees range from $800 to $15,000	None
Applicable Act	Insurance Act - 1978 (effective 1/1/80) and related regulations; Companies Act 1981; 1995 amendments	The Insurance Law (#24) of 1979 (1995 revision) Companies Law, 1969 The Insurance (forms) Regulations (1980) Monetary Authority Law 1996
Tax Treaties	Yes, but no U.S. FET exemption	No
Supervisory Jurisdiction	Registrar of Companies Inspector of Companies Government Administrative Building 30 Parliament Street Hamilton, HM 12, Bermuda	Superintendent of Financial Institutions Acting Head of Insurance Supervision Monetary Authority, Elizabethan Square P.O. Box 10052, George Town, Grand Cayman, Cayman Islands BWI
Reserve & Underwriting Requirements	Solvency must equal a minimum of 5:1 premium to capital & surplus up to $6 million in premium; above $6 million solvency ratio may rise to 10:1	No underwriting requirements; shareholders' equity at least greater than amount prescribed or amount superintendent considers necessary to maintain solvency. Minimum $100,000 in reserves required after initial registration
Reporting Requirements	Annual audited financial statements filed annually; annual actuarial certification	Application for registration; audited financial statements to be filed annually; annual actuarial certification: two-year projection (including premium revenue) and audited financial statements of the parent corporation
Local Office Requirements	Registered office required	Registered office required
Estimated Number of Captives	Approximately 1500 (includes all classes)	Approximately 550

Figure 8.1 (cont'd)

Domicile Comparison – Four Popular Domiciles		
Domicile	Hawaii	Vermont
Capitalization	Class 1, Reinsurance Only: $100,000 Class 2, Pure: $250,000 Class 3, Group: $500,000 Class 4, Leased Capital Facility: $1,000,000 Class 5, Reinsurance Facility $50,000,000	Statutory minimum: Pure: $250,000 Association: $750,000 Industrial insurers and RRGs: $500,000 Sponsored: $1,000,000
Registration & Incorporation Expenses	$1,000 application fee $300 registration fee Outside application review fee: approximately $3,500 (pure) to $7,500 (assn. and RRGs)	$200 application fee $300 license fee $3,200 actuarial review Incorporation fees vary
Investment Restrictions	Must follow same investment restrictions as regular insurance companies in the state. May request exemption from the commissioner	None for pure and industrial insured; same as for other admitted insurers for association captives and RRGs
Tax Issues	Premium tax 0.25% for pure and 1% on association and RRGs premiums for all Hawaii-located risks and on premiums not otherwise taxed	Direct Reinsurance $1-$20M 0.40% 0.225% $20M-$40M 0.30% 0.15% $40M-$60M 0.20% 0.05% over $60M 0.075% 0.025% (on gross premiums written)
Applicable Act	Captive Insurance Law 431, Article 19 (eff. July 1, 1987; major amendments eff. July 1, 1998)	Public Act 28, Title 8, Vermont Statutes, Chapter 141, 1981 Amendment S-105, 1988 Amendment H.422, 1989 Amendment S.163 and H.164, 1991
Supervisory Jurisdiction	Commissioner of Insurance, Dept. of Commerce and Consumer Affairs 250 South King Street P.O. Box 3614 Honolulu, HI 96811-3614	Department of Banking, Insurance, Securities & Health Care Administration Vermont Department of Captive Insurance 89 Main Street, Drawer 20 Montpelier, VT 05620-3101
Reserve & Underwriting Requirements	Vary; conservatively set for each company, 3:1 minimum premium to capital is goal	Actuarial opinion on reserves required annually; discounting sometimes allowed
Reporting Requirements	Annual GAAP financial statements; statutory convention statement for association captives and RRGs $315 renewal fee	Annual GAAP financial statement; NAIC convention statement for RRGs and association captives only; $300 annual fee
Local Office Requirements	Annual board of directors meeting in Hawaii; principle office in Hawaii; use of local management company and lawyer advised; books and records must be kept in Hawaii	Office in Vermont; one directors meeting in Vermont annually; use of resident agent required; financial records must be kept in Vermont
Estimated # of Captives	Approximately 80	Approximately 470

STEP FIVE: REVIEWING THE DIFFERENCES

Fronted versus Direct Captives

For workers compensation and automobile liability, states require that insurers be licensed and admitted to do business there. Further, several types of businesses (e.g., contractors) are regularly required to provide evidence of insurance purchased from admitted insurers that hold acceptable claims-paying ratings from the A.M. Best Co., and captives usually do not qualify for such financial rating. Since captives and other forms of alternative risk funding structures cannot satisfy state capital and surplus requirements, they are not licensed and admitted. Therefore, a licensed, admitted *fronting company* must be utilized.

When a fronting company is employed, the insured (captive owner) pays premium to the fronting company. Next, the fronting company *cedes* (transfers) the portion of the premium designated to pay losses (predetermined based upon share of risk) to the captive so that the captive is functioning as a *reinsurer* for the fronting insurer. (Sometimes, the fronting company retains a minimal share of the risk and premium; 10 percent is most common.) The fronting company issues a policy to the insured (captive owner) and pays insured losses to claimants. These claims payments are then recovered from the captive. The fronting company provides services and use of its license. In return for these services, the insurer receives a fronting fee.

Figure 8.2

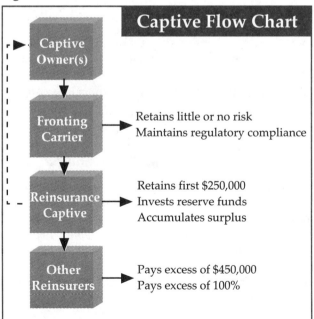

Direct-writing captives do not utilize a fronting insurer. Coverages such as general liability and products liability do not require a fronting insurer. However, if the captive owner must provide certificates of insurance, a direct-writing captive may not be feasible, although direct-writing captives can be less expensive than fronted captives as there is no fronting fee.

Figure 8.2 illustrates how a fronting company interacts with the captive insurance company, outside reinsurers, and the captive owners.

Figure 8.3 outlines the steps that are necessary to the process of establishing a group-owned captive insurance company.

Figure 8.3

Steps Towards Implementing a Group-Owned Captive

1. Completion of feasibility study, business plan, financial projections, and limits structure.
2. Selection of fronting insurer and reinsurer(s).
3. Group acceptance of business plan—program structure, effective dates, board and committee decisions, etc.
4. Escrow bank account opened in name of captive, and collection of good faith deposits from each participant.
5. Creation and delivery of Private Placement Memorandum—shareholders agreement, stock structure, etc.
6. Selection of service providers, such as captive manager, auditor, actuary, lawyers, and third party administrator.
7. Formal application to domicile via law firm.
8. Preparation of company by-laws, and obtaining license and charter.
9. Paid-in capital remitted by participating group members.
10. Initial board meeting—vote in by-laws, resident (domicile) board members, etc.
11. Commence writing business.

ADVANTAGES OF A GROUP CAPTIVE

Reduced Operating Costs

Captives can potentially reduce the cost of normal overhead items. Normal insurer overhead generally includes agent's commissions, insurer services (e.g., underwriting, claims, loss control), general overhead (e.g., rent), insurer profit, and stockholder dividends. These items typically constitute 30 to 40 percent of a traditional insurance premium. Offsetting some of these cost reductions are the costs of forming and operating a captive. Nevertheless, a captive can be expected to generate expense savings of between 10 and 25 percent off conventional insurance expenses.

Pricing

Insurance pricing is influenced by two factors:

1. the underwriting quality of the risk, and

2. the state of the insurance market.

In a perfect world only the underwriting would matter; however, insurance market pricing is cyclical. In a hard (expensive) market, many companies increase premiums simply because the market permits them to do so, regardless of the underwriting quality of the risk. In addition, premiums can fluctuate drastically on a year-to-year basis, making the planning and budgeting processes difficult. A captive's pricing is based primarily on the loss experience of its owner(s). While some premium uncertainty cannot be avoided—for example, fluctuation in reinsurance costs—captives can offer a stable pricing environment for many companies.

Investment Income and Underwriting Profit

Captives provide the opportunity for their owners to earn investment income on loss reserves (the amount of money allocated to future claim payments). In conventional insurance plans, the insurance company establishes loss reserves and is the primary beneficiary of investment earnings on them. Traditional loss-sensitive programs, such as incurred loss retrospectively rated programs (the final premium is adjusted to reflect claim values), provide potential return premiums, but the formula does *not* include a provision for investment income. Underwriting profit is generated when the reserves set aside to pay for losses exceed the ultimate value of the losses at the end of the payout period. Conventional programs can return varying amounts of underwriting profit to insureds, depending upon the type of plan, but captives can provide their owners with the opportunity to keep all of the underwriting profit.

Broader Coverage

Unlike their commercial counterparts, most captive insurers (especially those domiciled offshore) are generally subject to fewer limitations in coverage format. This may not always be true, however, given the terms of some fronting arrangements.

Equitable Premium Rating

Rating equity in a captive insurance company manifests itself in two forms. In the long term, traditional insurance arrangements require insureds with good loss records to subsidize those with poor ones. Under the captive concept, the organization can develop rates that accurately reflect its own expected loss levels. Traditional insurance arrangements often do not provide adequate credit when an organization assumes a high level of potential loss. Insurance companies are oriented to providing coverage for low-level losses—even for large organizations that have the financial strength to absorb substantial claims. Captives can use rating structures that provide more realistic premium credits for the levels of loss their owners are willing to assume. (Note that the advantages of expanded policy scope and rate flexibility more often apply to direct-writing captives than to captives using a fronting arrangement. This is because a fronting company can only issue a policy form that has been filed with insurance regulators with all of the standard restrictions, and the fronting company often controls rating.)

Coverage Availability/Stability

A captive mitigates the extent to which the underwriting cycle can cause radical short-term swings in premium levels and coverage breadth. Captives increase the probability that both the availability of coverage as well as the price stability of that coverage will track more closely with the risks inherent in its own exposures, rather than those built into the marketplace over which the organization has no control.

Direct Reinsurer Access

Reinsurers' customers are primary insurance companies. Insureds can usually approach the reinsurance markets only if they own an insurance company. (This is slowly changing.) The ability to deal directly with reinsurers allows captives to:

1. eliminate or reduce the cost of commissions paid to reinsurance intermediaries,

2. obtain pricing that is driven by the captive's own exposures and loss record (rather than those of the marketplace), and

3. access reinsurance pools that have been established by captive owners.

Improved Service

Underwriting, loss control, and claims adjusting services are oriented to the captive owner's special needs—rather than in the manner offered by an insurance company. More specifically, this could entail greater accuracy in rating (underwriting), better safety engineering (loss control), and more input into and control over sensitive loss settlements (claims adjustment).

Reduction in the Long–Term Cost of Risk

A reduction in the long-term cost of risk is the most important result of successful captive ownership. Captives provide a financial focus for the identification and management of risk. The *cost of risk* involves far more than insurance premiums and uninsured loss costs. A captive provides a vehicle to accurately measure corporate risk and, over time, recognize tangible financial benefits.

Enhanced Risk Management Perspective

A number of intangible but meaningful benefits accrue from establishing a captive insurer. These benefits include:

1. Increased visibility and enhanced appreciation of the risk management function within the organization.

2. The ability of the firm to select an *optimal retention level* (rather than one imposed on an insured by an insurer).

3. Facilitation of more equitable cost allocation between divisions of a company, and creation of a potential profit center.

4. The investment income generated by a captive should be attributed to the risk management department, rather than being absorbed in the general funds of the owner. Therefore, the investment income accrues to the risk management effort.

Fewer Regulatory Restrictions

A number of states do not permit or place onerous restrictions on the self-insurance of workers compensation and automobile liability exposures. Additionally, for certain lines of coverage, some states have restrictions in the areas of policy forms, rates, and evidence of financial security. The use of a captive insurer assists an organization to overcome many such constraints.

POTENTIAL DISADVANTAGES OF A CAPTIVE

Internal Administrative Costs

Participation in a captive requires more time of administrative/risk management personnel and senior management than does an insured program. This perceived negative feature may be more than offset by the benefits of captive ownership. Nonetheless, the additional personnel time—and the costs associated with this time—must be factored into the overall analysis to determine whether or not the captive can be justified.

Capitalization and Commitment

Establishing a captive generally requires a substantial initial outlay of capital. Depending on the specifics of the company, this could range from one-third to one-half of the insured's annual premium for the line of coverage the captive insures. The organization must commit these funds for at least three to five years. However, the capital contribution is not an expense, rather, it is an investment. As an investment, its value must be measured against any opportunity cost incurred by the company as a result of committing the funds to the captive.

Dependent upon Service Providers

The captive's owners must ultimately control and approve the recommendations, actions, and decisions of adjusters, attorneys, safety and loss control personnel, reinsurers, actuaries, accountants, and regulatory authorities, among others.

Inadequate Loss Reserves and Potential Losses

Unlike a traditional insurance arrangement, captive owners must be prepared for the fact that the captive may suffer losses greater than originally expected. This situation could trigger the need for an additional infusion of capital and/or a sharply increased renewal premium rate. Similarly, owners should be prepared for the possibility of having to increase inadequate loss reserves. This increases the importance of timely actuarial reviews. Most captive domiciles require annual loss reserve certification by a Fellow of the Casualty Actuarial Society (FCAS).

Increased Cost and Reduced Availability of Other Insurance

Use of a captive insurer for a certain line of coverage may cause the premium for other lines that remain commercially insured to increase in price. This is known as *account pricing* (offering discounts on rates when more than one type of insurance is purchased from an insurer). By removing one or more lines, an insurer may increase the price of the remaining lines or in some cases refuse to offer a renewal.

STEP SIX: THE CAPTIVE FEASIBILITY STUDY

The next step in the development of a captive insurance program is the feasibility study. A feasibility study is an analysis of the facts and circumstances surrounding a potential captive candidate. The value of a feasibility study is directly related to the following factors:

Unbiased Perspective

Captive feasibility studies should (ideally) be written by an independent consultant with no stake in the outcome of the study. Many insurance agents and brokers are capable of performing feasibility studies. But if the same agent or broker also sells the company insurance, a conflict of interest could taint the utility of the effort.

Cost

Quality captive feasibility work is expensive. Free captive feasibility work is usually worth the price.

Qualified Professional

The decision to create a captive is a potentially expensive mistake. Only experienced and objective professionals should be relied on to sort out all of the complex details and provide a truthful, unbiased assessment. Figure 8.4 outlines the basic elements that should be included in any captive feasibility study.

In some cases a feasibility study is not required because the decision to form a captive has already been made. In these situations, however, the chosen domicile may still require that a feasibility study be included in the application documents.

STEP SEVEN: UNDERSTANDING CAPTIVE TAX ISSUES

While insurance premiums are generally considered deductible from a company's federal income taxes, premiums paid to a captive are subject to a complex set of rules promulgated by Congress in the Internal Revenue Code and by the Treasury and Internal Revenue Service (IRS) in Regulations and Rulings. Since captives are bona fide subsidiaries of their corporate owners, their earnings are similarly subject to U.S. federal taxation. This discussion provides an overview of the basic tax issues faced by captives. There are two major questions relative to captive taxation:

1. Is the premium paid to the captive deductible from the shareholders' U.S. federal income tax?

2. When must the captive (or its shareholders) pay U.S. federal income tax on captive earnings? *(Timing of income tax payments).*

Tax Deductibility

Premiums paid to a group captive by multiple nonrelated owners may qualify for a tax deduction. The precise number of members required to attain tax deductibility is highly subjective since the IRS has not prescribed a minimum.

Likewise, captives with a percentage of nonrelated business, that is, business not related to the shareholders, can also qualify for a tax deduction, however, there is no stated percentage.

Tax Timing

The question relative to the timing of U.S. federal income taxes pertains solely to offshore captives. Onshore captives must pay U.S. federal income tax on earnings annually. It is important to note that the captive pays the taxes, and not the shareholders or parent company(s).

OTHER ALTERNATIVE RISK FINANCING TECHNIQUES

Finite Risk Reinsurance

Finite risk reinsurance is another type of alternative risk transfer technique. Traditional insurers and reinsurers must write a diversified book of business to spread the risk among many insureds. Conversely, finite risk reinsurance is not dependent upon spread of risk.

Figure 8.4

Captive Feasibility Study Basic Elements

Introduction
1. Goals and objectives of the feasibility analysis
2. Sources of information—currently valued, highly detailed losses
3. Executive summary of results

Candidate Overview
1. Current insurance, risk-financing arrangements, premiums
2. Loss history
3. Summary of actuarial report (if any)

Captive Basics
1. Risk/reward discussion (potential benefits)
2. Minimums: solvency, capital requirements, premiums
3. Structure: fronting, reinsurance, retentions
4. Rented versus owned; domicile overview

Financial Analysis
1. Expected loss calculation (if no actuarial study) at various retention options
2. Discounted, after-tax cost comparison of captive to existing risk financing program
3. Captive pro forma financial statements

Tax Issues
1. Premium deductibility
2. Captive taxation

Legal Issues
1. SEC requirements
2. Domicile requirements

Incorporation
1. Start-up and ongoing expenses (sources and probable amounts)
2. Business plan and incorporation procedures
3. Service providers (on and offshore)

Timeline for completion

Finite risk reinsurance can be used for almost any loss exposure; however, certain exposures are better suited to the finite risk approach. These include the following:

1. product-recall exposures
2. warranty programs
3. environmental impairment liability
4. commodity price fluctuations
5. credit risk

Typically, a prototype finite risk prospect is a firm with a high severity, low frequency exposure for which adequate coverage is either unavailable or prohibitively priced.

Each finite risk contract is designed to be as *fully funded* as possible. This means that, instead of spreading the risk over a large number of exposure units, finite risk uses *time* to create the loss funding necessary to pay for losses. Finite risk programs have multiyear policy terms, usually at least three years and often as many as ten years. Multiyear policy terms permit the accumulation of investment income over time. Another reason finite risk reinsurance is designed as a multiyear approach concerns expected losses. Because finite risk reinsurance is used to provide funding for nontraditional risks, loss expectations cannot be restricted to a single policy year, as in conventional insurance. Instead, finite risk reinsurance recognizes an event horizon of up to ten years. It is far easier to predict that a given loss scenario will occur within a span of five years, for example, than within a one-year policy term. In finite risk plans, aggregate limits apply over the entire policy term, not one year at a time.

How a Finite Risk Program Works

Once the risk is identified, a reinsurer establishes the premium (covered later in this chapter). The majority of the premium is known as an *experience account*. This account is held by the reinsurer and invested on behalf of the insured. The reinsurer guarantees a rate of interest on the experience account that accrues to the insured. This rate is called a *preset interest rate* and often corresponds to a *risk-free* rate such as LIBOR (London Interbank Offered Rate).

The reinsurer keeps all interest earned in excess of the preset rate. The reinsurer pays losses from the experience account during the policy period, and whatever is left at the end is commuted back to the insured, includ-

ing the interest earned at the preset rate. In addition to interest earned in excess of the preset rate, the reinsurer also charges a fee that can range from 5 to 25 percent.

Risk Transfer in Finite Risk Contracts

Pure finite risk contracts contain no actual risk transfer. Blended programs, however, contain a layer of risk transfer over the finite risk experience account. This approach is used in order to justify taking a tax deduction on the entire transaction.

Types of Finite Risk Contracts

There are three main types of finite risk contracts:

1. Loss Portfolio Transfers (LPT)
2. Prospective Aggregate Contracts
3. Retrospective Aggregate Contracts

Loss portfolio transfers are designed to transfer known, incurred self-insured losses off the balance sheet. A self-insurer or a captive can use an LPT to convert unknown liabilities, that is, the ultimate cost of self-insured losses, to a known quantity, a finite risk contract premium. Figure 8.5 illustrates a sample LPT transaction.

Prospective aggregate contracts are similar to conventional insurance as they are designed to fund unknown prospective losses. Companies that cannot obtain conventional insurance often use these contracts. Figure 8.6 illustrates a prospective aggregate contract.

Retrospective aggregate contracts are similar to loss portfolio transfers but with one important difference: instead of transferring a portfolio of known losses, retrospective aggregate contracts fill in uninsured gaps in prior insurance policy periods.

Calculating a Finite Risk Reinsurance Premium

Finite risk contracts rely on the accumulation of investment income. As such, the initial premium in any finite risk contract is the present value of the loss fund (experience account). For example, if the experience account is $1 million, and it is paid in over a five-year policy period, the annual payments would equal the net present value of $1 million paid over five years. Once this figure has been calculated, other charges may be added, such as a charge for premature payout, credit risk, or interest rate risk. Reinsurers assume one or all of these risks depending on how the program is structured. Finally, an expense provision is added. The reinsurer charges for program administration and policy issuance.

The Potential Accounting Effects of Finite Risk Reinsurance

Finite risk reinsurance is best suited to exposures that are known to occur, are infrequent, and tend to be large and expensive. For these reasons and others, multiyear policy periods are utilized. Companies know that the loss will probably occur, but they cannot predict *when* it

Figure 8.5

Loss Portfolio Transfer
Blended Finite Risk Reinsurance Example

G&J Manufacturing is a bottler located in ten states. Over the past twenty years it has accumulated a portfolio of self-insured workers compensation losses. An actuary has determined that reserves on outstanding losses equal $8 million and IBNR (incurred but not reported) reserves are $2 million, for a total of $10 million. It will be ten years before all known and unknown losses from the twenty-year period will be closed. The company wants to rid itself of all of its outstanding workers compensation liabilities as it prepares to be sold to a nationwide bottler.

Finite Contract Details

- Contract limit of liability: $12 million
- Preset policy interest rate: 7%
- Payout (policy) period: 10 years
- Premium payment: Annual Installments
- Discount Rate for NPV: 7%

Premium Calculation

- Net present value (NPV) of expected losses
  (expected losses = $10 million): $4,970,000
- Premium for premature loss payout: $ 300,000
- Premium for interest rate risk
  (the reinsurer's exposure for losses between
  the contract's $10 million limit and the
  NPV of $4,970,000): $100,000
- Premium for $2 million coverage in
  excess of expected losses: $25,000
- Reinsurer's fee (10 percent): $574,000

Total premium: **$5,969,500**

Commutation Provision

The reinsurer establishes an experience account from which losses are paid. The insured will share in any profits under the contract in excess of the reinsurer's 10% fee, either at the end of the policy period or upon cancellation of the policy. If the insured cancels the policy midterm, the insured will receive 90% of the fund balance.

will occur. So, a finite risk contract has the potential to smooth earnings by converting a large loss that will occur sometime over a five-year timeframe, to predictable annual premiums. To do this, a company must account for the finite risk contract as if it were a standard insurance contract; that is, the premiums must be deducted from U.S. federal income taxes and earnings will not be affected by claims activity. This tactic has proven to be an extremely aggressive tax/accounting position and should only be undertaken at the advice of competent tax counsel.

WHERE CAN I FIND OUT MORE ABOUT IT?

- Bawcutt, P.A. 1997. *Captive Insurance Companies: Establishment, Operation and Management,* Fourth Edition. London: Witherby Publishers of UK.

- *Financing Risk & Reinsurance.* Dallas: International Risk Management Institute (IRMI).

- *Risk Financing* (Reference Service). Dallas: International Risk Management Institute (IRMI).

- *Risk Funding & Self-Insurance Bulletins (RF&S).* Cincinnati: The National Underwriter Company,

http://www.nationalunderwriter.com/nucatalog/.

QUESTIONS AND ANSWERS

Question—What is the primary criterion for determining whether captive insurance premiums qualify for tax deductibility?

Answer—The primary criterion for determining whether premiums qualify for tax deductibility is whether or not the captive is defined as an insurer by the IRS. This determination is made on a case-by-case basis because the IRS has never provided a *bright line* definition of what constitutes an insurer. The IRS relies on the *economic family theory* as described in IRS Revenue Ruling 77-316 as the basis upon which a captive may or may not be deemed an insurer. Revenue Ruling 77-316 established two major tests for insurance company status:

1. Risk Shifting

2. Risk Distribution (Risk Sharing)

Under Revenue Ruling 77-316, premiums paid to a wholly owned captive are deemed not to be a tax-

Figure 8.6

Prospective Aggregate Contract Example

Toxic Services, Inc. is a large asbestos removal contractor. Although it employs highly trained and experienced people, it cannot obtain environmental impairment liability (EIL) insurance coverage in either the standard or specialty markets due to poor loss experience. In order to attract business, the company must show evidence of insurance to prospective general contractors. Toxic desires a policy with a $3 million limit.

Contract Details and Premium Computation

The contract will extend for three years and will offer a $3 million aggregate limit of liability coverage per year. The first year premium is $2 million with $1.5 million due in years two and three. The experience account loss fund will accumulate and all funds not used to pay claims (less the reinsurer's 10 percent fee) will be returned to the insured at the termination of the policy.

Benefit to Insured

The contractor will obtain the needed $3 million annual aggregate limit of liability despite the unavailability of coverage elsewhere and will be able to provide evidence of insurance.

Benefit to Reinsurer

Unless interest rates plummet or the sky falls, the reinsurer will be able to lock in an almost risk-free profit on the transaction.

deductible expense because there was no *risk distribution*—the premiums were merely transferred from one member of the same economic family to another.

In the case of *Humana, Inc. v. Commissioner*, 881 F.2d 247 (6th Cir. 1989) the brother-sister doctrine was created. The brother-sister doctrine states that, if a company has a number of subsidiaries that each pay insurance premiums directly to the captive and there is no financial relationship between the captive and the subsidiaries, a brother-sister relationship exists between the subsidiaries and the captive. Therefore, the premiums paid by the subsidiaries are considered tax deductible. In 2001, the IRS issued Revenue Ruling 01-31. This ruling is a follow-up to Revenue Ruling 77-316, in that it retains the economic family argument. But it formally recognizes the brother-sister relationship established by the *Humana* case.

Currently, the IRS *insurance company test criteria* includes the following:

1. Brother-sister subsidiary relationship (pure captives)

2. Multiple nonrelated shareholders (group captive)

3. Significant percentage of nonrelated business (any captive)

4. Proper and adequate capitalization (all captives)

5. Legitimate business purpose (all captives)

Question—What is the IRS stance in regard to the timing of offshore captive insurance company tax payments?

Answer—The timing of offshore captive tax payments is complex. Offshore captives can be classified as one of the following:

1. Controlled Foreign Corporation (CFC) (for insurance companies)

2. Related Person Insurance Income (RPII) CFC

3. Noncontrolled Foreign Corporation (NCFC)

4. CFC that has elected to pay U.S. federal income tax as if it were located in the United States

IRS Rules and Controlled Foreign Corporation (CFC)

The following is a discussion of the Internal Revenue Service's rules and regulations relative to the taxation of offshore captives. All offshore captive income falls under IRC Subpart F. Subpart F imposes tax on income of a foreign corporation that qualifies as a Controlled Foreign Corporation (CFC). Any foreign subsidiary of a U.S. company is a CFC unless it makes specific provisions otherwise. (CFCs of noninsurance companies are subject to different rules than are CFCs of insurance companies. They are not covered in this discussion.)

Insurance Controlled Foreign Corporation (CFC) Status

A *qualified U.S. shareholder* owns 10 percent or more of the total combined voting power of all classes of stock that is entitled to vote. More than 25 percent of voting power or stock is owned by or attributed to a U.S. person (corporation, partnership, trust, individual, or estate). The captive must generate income from insurance or reinsurance contracts, and the captive's gross amount of premiums from risks arising outside the company's country of incorporation (the domicile) must exceed 75 percent of all gross premiums. The captive has not elected to be taxed as a U.S. entity {IRC 953(d)}.

Each U.S. shareholder must pay U.S. federal income taxes on annual earnings based on ownership percentage and individual federal tax rate. This presents a timing problem—cash distributions from the captive cannot easily be coordinated with required tax payments. The insurance CFC insures *only* unrelated business—it earns no related person insurance income (RPII).

RPII (Related Person Insurance Income) Controlled Foreign Corporation (CFC) Status

RPII is defined as insurance income that is attributable to insuring or reinsuring U.S. shareholders of a foreign corporation. The definition of qualified U.S. shareholder (see previous discussion) does not apply to RPII CFCs. In this type of captive, all U.S. persons owning stock in the captive are considered U.S. shareholders (without the 10 percent threshold). More than 25 percent of voting power or stock must be owned by or attributed to a U.S. person (corporation, partnership, trust, individual, or estate). The captive must generate income from the sale of insurance or reinsurance, and its gross amount of premiums from risks arising outside the foreign company's country of incorporation (the domicile) must exceed 75 percent of all gross premiums.

Identical to the Insurance CFC above, the captive has not elected to be taxed as a U.S. entity {IRC 953(d)}. Each

U.S. shareholder must pay U.S. federal income taxes on annual earnings based on ownership percentage and individual federal tax rate. Again, there is a timing problem—cash distributions from the captive cannot easily be coordinated with tax payments.

Non-Controlled Foreign Corporation (NCFC)

Less than 25 percent of voting power or stock is owned by or attributed to a U.S. person (corporation, partnership, trust, individual, or estate, and no RPII is permitted—this type of captive insures only unrelated business). No individual U.S. shareholder can own more than 9.9 percent of the voting stock, which means the captive must have at least eleven shareholders. Earnings avoid U.S. federal taxation until they are repatriated into the U.S. This can represent a significant (legal) tax arbitrage opportunity.

Logistical Restrictions Associated with CFC and NCFC Status

Captive business cannot be conducted in the U.S. under CFC and NCFC status. This is known as the prohibition against ETB (engaging in trade or business). It prohibits local offices, U.S. business meetings, and discussion of business between U.S. correspondents over the telephone or fax or through email. Potential IRS penalties include a 30 percent withholding tax on certain income received by foreign companies.

Making the "Domestic Election" to Be Taxed as a U.S. Entity {IRC section 953 (d)}

Insurance and RPII Controlled Foreign Corporations (CFC) may elect to be taxed as though they were physically domiciled in the U.S. A captive may be qualified to make the domestic election if it is deemed to be an insurance company for U.S. tax purposes. The election is irrevocable. Most captives make this election because it alleviates the timing problem associated with the above captive types—the captive pays the taxes, not the individual shareholders, so there is no need to coordinate dividend payments to shareholders and tax payments to the IRS. Also, there are no ETB (engaged in trade or business) issues or problems because the captive is deemed to be a U.S. company.

Chapter 8

GLOSSARY

Account pricing. A process in which insurance companies offer premium discounts to businesses that place more than one type of insurance coverage with them.

Alternative risk transfer (ART). A term used to describe a collection of property and casualty risk-financing techniques; various types of risk-financing programs that include significant elements of risk retention.

Agency captive. A captive insuer that is formed to insure the risks of an agency's clients and which usually is sponsored and owned by the agency.

Association captive. A captive insurer that is formed to insure the risks of companies involved in the same or similar industries and which often is owned by members of a trade association.

Captive. A closely-held insurance company that mainly insures the risk of its owners.

Captive domicile. The jurisdiction (country) in which a captive is organized.

Captive feasibility study. An analysis by a professional, independent consultant to determine whether insuring risk through a captive is financially and managerially feasible.

Deductible. One type of risk retention.

Finite risk reinsurance. An ART technique in which time is used to create the funding necessary to pay losses.

Fronting company. A licensed insurance company that issues an insurance policy that is reinsured by a captive.

Group captive. Captive insurance companies that are owned by a group of nonrelated companies or organization.

Hard market. An insurance marketplace that is categorized by high premiums and restricted availability of coverage.

Loss-sensitive insurance program. A traditional type of insurance program in which the insured business shares the financial impact of losses with an insurance company. An example is a retrospectively rated insurance plan.

Loss trigger. An event that causes an insurance policy to pay.

Minimum capitalization level. The minimum amount of capital (financial assets) that is needed to establish a captive insurance company.

Noninsurance. Being uninsured; operating a business without planning how its risks will be managed.

Offshore captive. A captive insurance company that is organized in a country outside the United States of America.

Onshore captive. A captive insurance company that is organized in one of the states of the U.S.

Protected cell company (PCC). A captive that rents its capital to other organizations for a fee. Assets of members who participate in this type of captive insurance are separated from one another by special legislation enacted in the jurisdiction in which the PCC is domiciled.

Pure or single-parent captive. Closely-held insurance companies that primarily insure the exposures of their owners.

Qualified self-insurer. A business that complies with a state's financial responsibility regulations and has been authorized to self-insure exposures that fall under those regulations, such as the workers compensation exposure.

Reinsurance. In terms of ART programs, insurance coverage that is purchased to back-up a self-insured program or to pay in excess of the self-insured limits.

Rent-a-captive. Captive insurers that rent their capital to other organizations for a fee. Instead of setting up their own captive insurer, a business may rent the capital of a rent-a-captive and participate in that fashion. The accounts of the various members are separated according to contractual terms so one member does not subsidize the losses of another.

Risk retention group (RRG). A type of group captive that is formed under the federal Risk Retention Act of 1986.

Self-insurance. Retaining risk and the responsibilities for managing that risk.

Self-insured retention (SIR). That portion of pure risk an insured business decides to retain and manage itself. A deductible is a form of self-insured retention.

GLOBAL RISK MANAGEMENT

WHAT IS IT?

In general, there are three types of foreign exposures that a U.S.-domiciled company may encounter:

- Temporary exposures,

- Export exposures, and

- Permanent multinational exposures.

You may want to remember these with the acronym TEP.

The process of identifying foreign risks, implementing steps to reduce such risks, and deciding whether to retain or transfer them is similar to the process for domestic exposures. It often is difficult, however, to manage global exposures both because they are physically distanced from corporate headquarters and because managers may not be aware of how foreign risks differ from domestic ones.

Other difficulties may be encountered because of

- limitations in standard domestic insurance policies for foreign exposures,

- local insurance requirements in foreign jurisdictions,

- requirements for local admitted insurance coverage,

- the possibility of political unrest in specific foreign countries,

- differences in healthcare standards,

- claims-management challenges, and

- currency conversion.

Each of these is introduced in this discussion, with information provided on additional resources that may be of importance.

CATEGORIES WITHIN TEP

The categories of temporary exposures, export exposures, and permanent multinational exposures may be further divided into these risk areas:

- Property risks,

- Premises and operations risks,

- Products risks,

- Auto risks,

- Employee risks, and

- Political Risks.

A simple matrix may be established to visualize potential foreign exposures. FIgure 9.1 is a starting point; as information is gathered, the risk areas will be expanded.

The location of foreign exposures has a direct impact on the degree of risk. For example, the risk of political unrest and terrorism is much greater in some countries than in others. Risk managers should become familiar with vendors that provide information on the political climate in various countries. Some vendors are listed at the end of this chapter.

STEPS TO IMPLEMENT

The five steps to implement a global risk management process are essentially the same as the general domestic risk management process:

1. Identify risks

2. Quantify and analyze risks

3. Evaluate treatment options

4. Implement selected options

5. Monitor and adjust

Figure 9.1

Categories	Temporary Exposures	Export Exposures	Permanent Multinational Exposures
Property			
Owned or leased premises			X
Personal property			X
Cargo		X	X
Contingent exposures	X	X	X
Political unrest	X	X	X
Premises/Operations			
Foreign sales offices		X	X
Foreign production facilities			X
Employee travel	X	X	X
Owned or leased premises		X	X
Political unrest	X	X	X
Employee injury to others	X		X
Credit risk	X	X	X
Products			
US goods distributed in foreign country		X	X
Goods manufactured & distributed in foreign country		X	X
Cargo		X	X
Political unrest		X	X
Credit risk		X	X
Auto			
Rented autos	X	X	X
Owned/leased autos			X
Employees			
Workers compensation	X	X	X
General healthcare standards	X	X	X
Endemic disease	X	X	X
Repatriation	X	X	X
Political risk	X	X	X
Kidnap/ransom	X	X	X
Accidents	X	X	X

This process is explained in Chapter 1. We continue that discussion into the global arena in this chapter.

Step One: Identifying Risks

Identifying foreign risks may be the most difficult step in the process because of the distances involved and sometimes dramatic variations in legal climate between domestic and foreign locations. Ideally the risk manager will meet periodically with senior executives and key managers to discuss new corporate initiatives and to explain the entity's risk management program. Such meetings should stress the need for providing the risk management department with advanced notice of any changes in the entity's operations. At a minimum the meetings should include managers from finance, audit, production, marketing, product research and development, and mergers and acquisitions. If a formal meeting cannot be arranged it is important for the risk manager to network with such individuals. The topic of global exposures should be included in these meetings.

In addition, risk managers should include questions about foreign initiatives (such as export programs, employee travel, or marketing initiatives) when gathering information for the renewal of insurance policies. For example, in a holding company environment, subsidiaries should verify the list of their own subsidiaries and divisions to reveal changes in the structure that have not yet reached the parent company's risk management department. Another source of information is the minutes of key committees. Foreign risks also may be identified through communication with the corporate travel agency and through the annual updating of the schedule of properties or the company's annual financial statement. Extensive information on assessing risks in general is contained in the first five chapters of this book.

Step Two: Quantifying and Analyzing Risks

The matrix shown in Figure 9.1 may be used as a starting point to analyze the types of risks that may be involved. Once it is determined whether the exposures are temporary, export-oriented, or permanent multinational, risk managers can proceed to determine their extent.

For example, temporary exposures often take the form of employees traveling outside the United States territory on sales or development trips. The corporation's exposure with these trips involves injury to the employees themselves (workers compensation-related) as well as injury the employees may cause third parties (premises/operations liability-related). Export exposures involve not only employee risks but also products risks. Permanent multinational exposures encompass all the same risks as a domestic operation. Added to each of these are the risks of political unrest, currency exchange, and foreign laws that may dictate how insurance should be arranged. Cultural differences also must be considered.

Step Three: Evaluating Treatment Options

The actual risk to foreign operations varies with such factors as the likelihood of political unrest and the quality of a country's healthcare standards. Risk managers with extensive foreign exposures must obtain real-time information about the countries involved.

For example, less developed countries may not have readily available health clinics or hospitals that are able to treat traveling employees or expatriates. Political upheaval may place both employees and properties in grave danger. Such conditions will affect whether insurance will be the main treatment option or whether additional risk management programs dedicated to the foreign exposures are needed.

One way to learn about and handle these exposures—especially for corporations that insure their domestic risks—is to take advantage of services offered by the corporations' insurance companies.

Several insurers have teamed up with foreign brokers, healthcare facilities, security firms, and medical-assistance companies to help corporations handle such foreign exposures. Vendors may offer services independently of or in tandem with insurers. Either way, they offer analyses of the potential for political unrest, and corporations should consider subscribing to one of them if they have employees traveling overseas or at permanent foreign installations. The Central Intelligence Agency Web site also offers information about prospective political unrest. Information on some of these services is contained in the section of this chapter entitled **Where Can I Find Out More About This Topic?**

An option that may provide both loss control and financial protection is to have the entity's insurance program automatically include new foreign exposures with premiums to be adjusted on audit. This makes the difficult task of identifying foreign risks somewhat less burdensome. When risks are identified, the insurer can be approached for assistance with loss control. However, to begin this process, insurers will require basic information about foreign initiatives. The selection of insurers and the degree to which the insurance program has to be amended will depend upon the basic types of foreign risks involved.

Step Four: Implementing Selected Options

Among the treatment options are

1. avoidance or prevention (such as refraining from doing business in countries with high political risks or countries that are prone to economic turmoil),

2. retention (such as establishing a guideline of accepting a limited amount of uninsured credit risk from customers in certain countries or deciding to self-insure a portion of property exposures in foreign countries),

3. noninsurance transfer avoidance or prevention (such as modifying foreign sales contracts to require payment in U.S. dollars in an effort to avoid the risk of a drop in the value of a foreign currency), and

4. insurance transfer (such as purchasing property and liability insurance on foreign exposures and goods in transit or, when appropriate, purchasing political risk and credit insurance).

Step Five: Monitor and Adjust

Monitoring the global risk management program and amending it as necessary is the fifth step in implementing the program.

These five techniques are discussed extensively in the first five chapter of this book. A corporation may employ many of these alternatives, especially retention and contractual transfers, to handle foreign exposures. If those options are selected, it is important to keep in mind that legal considerations undoubtedly will be different from those encountered with domestic exposures.

Risk Management Tip

When a corporation decides to handle certain foreign exposures through contractual transfers, legal counsel that specializes in international matters should be consulted.

The rest of this chapter outlines the issues that should be considered when transferring foreign risks to an insurance company.

THE INSURANCE OPTION

Admitted versus Nonadmitted Coverage

It is extremely important to recognize and remember that, in most cases, policies purchased to cover an entity's domestic operations will not automatically provide coverage when the firm initiates operations overseas.

One solution is for the entity to attempt to replicate its domestic insurance program by purchasing policies in each of the foreign countries in which the entity operates. One of the basic issues when considering this is that of *admitted* versus *nonadmitted* coverage. Admitted insurers are authorized by a given country to transact insurance business within its borders. Nonadmitted insurers are not authorized to do so.

Some countries may permit certain classes of insurance on a nonadmitted basis while requiring that other classes of insurance be written only on an admitted basis. The types of insurance that are classified as admitted or nonadmitted vary from country to country, and some jurisdictions may even require that policies be purchased from state-owned insurers.

Advantages of Admitted Insurers

The advantages to using admitted insurers are:

1. The premiums may be tax deductible, whereas nonadmitted insurance premiums may not be tax deductible.

2. The handling of claims and recoveries from third parties that may have caused or contributed to the loss may be easier.

3. Fines and penalties for failing to conform to local insurance requirements may be reduced or eliminated.

4. There may be intangible benefits to patronizing a local insurer or broker such as favorable local connections

Disadvantages of Admitted Insurers

Admitted coverage may be required, but there are disadvantages to purchasing individual admitted policies in each country where there is an exposure:

1. Policies purchased in a foreign country may be written in a foreign language and based upon that jurisdiction's legal system.

2. The coverage may be denominated in a foreign currency of varying value.

3. The financial strength and claims-paying record of the local or admitted insurer may be difficult to evaluate

4. Communicating the entity's insurance needs to local agents in each country can be difficult and require constant monitoring.

5. The local coverage may be more expensive than coverage purchased domestically as part of a worldwide program.

6. Risk managers may have a difficult time managing a program consisting of many individual policies with provisions that may vary widely, and loss control and claims management programs may be inconsistent.

Advantages of Nonadmitted Insurers

The advantages of using nonadmitted insurers are, quite naturally, opposite to the disadvantages of using admitted insurers. They include:

1. Policies will be written in English and based on the U.S. court system.

2. The coverage limits will be valued in U.S. dollars.

3. The financial strength of the insurer can be determined.

4. A relationship with a U.S.-based underwriter and broker can be established.

5. There are fewer contact individuals so the program may be more easily monitored.

Disadvantages of Nonadmitted Insurers

When nonadmitted coverage is permitted, the issue of taxes should be considered. Tax counsel should be asked to respond to at least the following questions:

1. Will the premiums for nonadmitted insurance be deductible?

2. Will claim payments from a nonadmitted insurer to a foreign subsidiary be treated as in-

come or as the transfer of capital? If so, are they subject to any recapitalization taxes?

3. If a U.S.-domiciled parent company has the right to receive payment for losses occurring at or from a foreign subsidiary, will the proceeds be taxed as income to the parent? Does the situation change if the proceeds are paid directly to the subsidiary or transferred from the parent to the subsidiary?

The process of obtaining coverage for an overseas exposure begins with determining the local insurance requirements of each country in which it operates, identifying the territorial limitations in each of its domestic insurance policies and whether these policies meet local insurance requirements, and then deciding whether the domestic program should be amended or additional insurance purchased. In this chapter the term *domestic insurance* means the policies covering the entity's U.S. operations. The term *local insurance* refers to the insurance covering the entity's operations in a particular foreign country.

DETERMINING LOCAL INSURANCE REQUIREMENTS

Some insurers specializing in worldwide coverage provide country-by-country summaries of local insurance requirements and regulations and the approved use of nonadmitted insurance. These carriers will often make the information on local insurance requirements available to agents and brokers using their facilities. Some U.S. brokers with offices throughout the world may gather this information on their own.

It is important to remember that some countries may require certain types of coverage that is not normally a part of a domestic insurance program. For example, state-sponsored health insurance may be required for all individuals working in the country. Some municipalities may require that historic buildings be replaced exactly as they stand, thus requiring special coverage.

For more information on this topic, a sample of information sources is contained at the end of this chapter.

Risk Management Tip

Gathering information about insurance requirements in foreign countries may be difficult. A number of resources—including worldwide insurance companies, service vendors, and insurance brokers—are available to help in this process. Risk managers need to select vendors who can provide more than simple summaries of a particular country's insurance requirements.

IDENTIFYING TERRITORIAL LIMITS

Identifying the territorial limits of the entity's domestic insurance program involves more than just reading policies. Understanding the impact of such limitations requires that risk managers clearly understand the entity's operations. Following the order of Figure 9.1, we discuss how foreign operations may differ from domestic operations and how the wording on various insurance policies impacts the global risk management program.

Property

The Insurance Services Office (ISO) commercial property policy coverage territory is the United States of America (including its territories and possessions); Puerto Rico; and Canada. Therefore, any property that is located outside this territory, including personal property temporarily outside it, would not qualify for coverage. As a result, specifically designed property coverage may be needed.

To address these needs, a risk manager may need to obtain separate admitted policies where required and then structure a comprehensive program to coordinate the entity's worldwide insurance program. This process is described later in this chapter, under the heading **Structuring a Worldwide Insurance Program.**

The Impact of Political Risks on Property

An additional threat to foreign-located property is that of political risk, which is not a common risk to domestic properties. Political risk is a broad category of loss potential, in which a local foreign government or force causes an insured to lose or vacate its property. Many activities may fall within the broad category of political risk, but the following set of definitions provides an overview of them. The appendix to this chapter also includes a copy of a sample Political Risk Insurance application, and an insurance policy that will respond to various political risks to permanent overseas invest-

ments. These illustrate the type of information that must be gathered to underwrite the risk, as well as one method of insurance treatment.

Types of Political Risks:

Confiscation—an act of the government of a host country to take without permission the corporation's property and deprive the enterprise of the benefits of the property.

Currency inconvertibility—an inability to convert currency of the host country into currency of the insured's country through normal currency exchange channels and transfer it out of the host country.

Expropriation—the action of a host country in taking or modifying the property rights of an individual or corporation in the exercise of its sovereignty.

Forced abandonment—the abandonment of a foreign enterprise for more than a brief period as the result of a directive of the host country to leave the foreign country.

Nationalization—when the government of a host country takes over the corporation's business and property and makes it a national operation of the host country.

Political violence—violence that results from political upheaval, including, but not necessarily limited to, civil war, riot, revolution, strikes, coups, sabotage, terrorism, civil commotion, and insurrection.

Since September 11, 2001, American citizens have become much more aware of the dangers of political risks. Although no country is immune from it, the degree of political risk varies from country to country and period to period. Therefore, risk managers should consult specialists that track the likelihood of political unrest. An application form and sample policy for Political Risk Insurance is reprinted at the end of this chapter. Careful study of both illustrates the types of exposures that may be subject to political risk, as well as one method of insuring the risk. A review of these documents will assist risk managers in learning more about this topic.

Transportation of Property

Import or export goods—as well as products, equipment, and other property destined for permanent for-

110

Tools & Techniques of Risk Management & Insurance

eign installations—are usually shipped by air or ocean liners. Cargo losses often are exacerbated because of the lost freight charges and the delivery delay that a loss may cause. Even when the shipper is responsible for the goods during transit, risk managers may choose to purchase insurance in order to speed financial recovery. In such cases, the cargo owner should notify the carrier responsible for the lost or damaged goods and then file a claim against its ocean cargo insurer. The insurer will take action to adjust the claim and then take action to effect recoveries from any third parties that may have been responsible for or contributed to the loss.

Cargo coverage may be purchased on individual shipments or on an open cargo form. An open cargo policy provides coverage for shipments that meet certain conditions—such as value, type of property, type of packing, and destinations—on an ongoing basis. The insured then reports shipments as they occur. Corporations that import or export goods on a regular basis usually purchase open cargo policies because of the ease of use.

Who Owns the Goods?

The terms of sale dictate when ownership of goods being shipped passes from seller to buyer. They indicate which party has an insurable interest in the property at different periods from manufacturing to delivery. They also indicate which party—seller, buyer, or shipper—is responsible for the property (and who bears risk of loss) while it is being transported.

Some terms of sale include:

Ex point of origin—the buyer takes delivery of the property at a specified place and within a specified period of time. The buyer is responsible and should consider insuring the property while it is being shipped.

Free on board (FOB)—the seller is responsible until the property is on board a specific carrier at a specific place. The seller should consider insuring the goods from the point of origin until they are loaded, and the buyer, from loading until final delivery.

Free along side (FAS)—the seller is responsible for the property until it is on a specified dock or alongside a carrier. The buyer should consider insuring the goods from arrival at this specified location until final delivery; the seller may want to insure them from the point of origin to the dock.

Cost and freight (C&F), named point of destination—the selling price includes freight costs for the entire trip, but the buyer is responsible for the insurance during transit. The seller is responsible for the goods before they reach the carrier.

Cost, insurance, and freight (CIF), named point of destination—similar to C&F, but the selling price includes cost of the goods, insurance, and freight to the named point of destination. The seller is responsible for the goods—and insurance on them—until they reach the named point of destination.

General Liability

As with domestic operations, liabilities arising from operations overseas may be formidable. The corporation may face exposures created by its premises and operations, such as from employee actions or ongoing operations. Products liability may arise from import-export operations as well as permanent multinational facilities, which may involve manufacturing products for either U.S. or foreign consumption. The ISO commercial general liability form provides coverage for injury or damage arising from both premises/operations and products liability. The policy states that:

This insurance applies to "bodily injury" and "property damage" only if:

(1) The "bodily injury" or "property damage" is caused by an "occurrence" that takes place in the "coverage territory";

(2) The "bodily injury" or "property damage" occurs during the policy period. . .

"Coverage territory" later is defined as:

a. The United States of America (including its territories and possessions), Puerto Rico and Canada;

b. International waters or airspace, but only if the injury or damage occurs in the course of travel or transportation between any places included in a. above; or

c. All other parts of the world if the injury or damage arises out of:

(1) Goods or products made or sold by you in the territory described in a. above; or

(2) The activities of a person whose home is in the territory described in a. above, but is away for a short time on your business; or

(3) "Personal and advertising injury" offenses that take place through the Internet or similar electronic means of communication

provided that the insured's responsibility to pay damages is determined in a "suit" on the merits, in the territory described in a. above or in a settlement we agree to.

The last phrase in this section specifies that lawsuits must be brought in the territory cited in order for coverage to apply. Thus, lawsuits that are filed in a foreign country would not trigger the policy.

Risk Management Tip

Certain countries that are hostile to the United States are often excluded from coverage in worldwide insurance policies. Risk managers should take time to review coverage for such exclusions and take adequate risk management steps if exposures in those countries exist.

At a minimum the test for the worldwide insurance program includes three prongs:

1. Will it cover losses, accidents, or injuries occurring anywhere in world?

2. Will it respond to claims, suits, or settlements made anywhere in world?

3. Will it afford coverage regardless of where the products are made?

In regard to products liability, these limitations mean that the global insurance program should be tailored to respond to claims, suits, or settlements anywhere in the world arising from injuries sustained anywhere in the world and caused by products made:

1. Within the United States for sale outside the United States

2. Outside the United States for sale outside the United States

3. In one foreign country for sale in a another country

4. Using parts produced in the United States or foreign countries and sold overseas

Using a Separate Policy

A separate international liability policy may fill this gap. An example of an international coverage territory clause, which is used in the Chubb Group International Commercial General Liability Insurance form, reads:

International General Liability Coverage Territory means anywhere, provided that the insured's responsibility to pay damages to which this insurance applies is determined in a claim, suit, or settlement outside the United States and Canada.

Carriers may exclude coverage in certain countries, however, so it is important to review the territory and territory exclusionary endorsements that are included in the policy.

Amending Coverage Territory

Another approach to the issue of coverage territory may be for an insurer to amend the domestic general liability policy to read simply "anywhere in the world." Although this may appear to be a simple and quick solution, the problem is that this type of amendment to the domestic CGL policy may be difficult to obtain, depending upon the extent and location of the foreign exposures.

In most cases using a separate policy or amending the coverage territory without coordinating them with the requirements for local insurance is not recommended There are cases in which a claim or suit may be filed in a foreign jurisdiction that requires admitted coverage. In such jurisdictions, risk managers may need to investigate their own claims, handle the defense of lawsuits, and pay settlements if an admitted carrier does not write their coverage. Their nonadmitted international insurer would then reimburse them for claims expenses that fall within the coverage grant. Such a possibility increases the importance of having a network of international claims and legal experts available for assistance. Many of the prominent international insurers, as well as risk management consultants and brokers, may provide access to such networks.

The section entitled **Structuring a Worldwide Insurance Program** will outline the techniques for coordinating insurance purchased domestically and locally.

Automobiles

Employees traveling overseas, even on a temporary basis, often rent cars. Operations with permanent foreign installations also face potential liabilities from their use of autos, and foreign jurisdictions may specifically regulate the type of financial responsibility that must be available to pay for these liabilities. Insurance is one method to comply with these regulations, but standard domestic business auto policies only apply in the following coverage territory:

> The coverage territory is:
>
> a. The United States of America;
>
> b. The territories and possessions of the United States of America;
>
> c. Puerto Rico: and
>
> d. Canada.

We also cover "loss" to, or "accidents" involving, a covered "auto" while being transported between any of these places.

This wording makes it clear that the policy would not extend to autos in foreign countries. Many jurisdictions may require compulsory admitted insurance on autos licensed there, and risk managers should check the specific regulations in the jurisdictions where they own vehicles.

An international auto liability policy may be used to insure the liabilities that may arise from hired autos, such as short-term rentals or cars hired with drivers.

Even when the local jurisdictions do not require admitted automobile liability coverage, risk managers may place minimum coverage of, for example, $100,000 U.S. with a local admitted insurer in order to facilitate local claims handling.

Employees

Another situation involves problems associated with employee exposures. An employee who is hired in the United States and working there usually is subject to the workers compensation law of the state of hire. If this employee is temporarily assigned to work overseas, the domestic workers compensation policy may provide coverage for the temporary foreign employment.

There is no defined coverage territory in part one (workers compensation section) of the standard National Council of Compensation Insurance workers compensation policy. However, part two (employers liability) states that employers liability insurance does not cover "bodily injury occurring outside the U.S., its territories or possessions, and Canada." There is an exception, however, in that this exclusion "does not apply to bodily injury to a citizen or resident of the United States of America or Canada *who is temporarily outside those countries . . .*" (emphasis added).

"Temporary" is not defined on the policy. So risk managers should check with the workers compensation carrier to determine whether coverage applies in a particular situation. It also would be wise to notify the carrier in advance of temporary foreign assignments. In addition, there may be other issues that arise because of temporary foreign travel. For example, endemic diseases that occur overseas may not fall within the coverage grant of a state workers compensation law. There also may be additional costs to return an injured or ill employee to the United States, which would not automatically be covered by the workers compensation policy. This additional cost is called *repatriation expense*. From a risk management standpoint, healthcare facilities in foreign countries may not meet U.S. standards. So it is important to know where the closest quality healthcare facility can be found and what types of transportation facilities are available.

Coverage for endemic diseases and repatriation expenses may be available from the workers compensation carrier, but it is not automatic.

Risk Management Tip

If employees are traveling overseas, consider purchasing additional coverage for endemic disease and repatriation expenses.

If foreign nationals are being hired or U.S. citizens are being assigned permanently (or for longer than a *temporary* period) outside the territory, other arrangements should be made. The foreign country may provide or require some type of coverage that must be obtained there. Or an accident and health policy might be chosen.

Some carriers also offer coverage that is in addition to benefits provided by required insurance. Such policies should be individually reviewed to determine how they would apply to the situation.

Risk Management Exercise

A sample International Voluntary Workers Compensation policy is reprinted at the end of this chapter. Study the definitions and coverage grant, and compare it with the standard NCCI workers compensation policy that is reprinted after Chapter 18. How do the definitions differ? How does the coverage differ? Are there differences in how employers liability coverage is provided?

Risk managers who use a domestic policy for protection should be aware that the employers liability section only provides coverage for suits that are brought within the domestic coverage territory. In addition, state workers compensation funds may not include any temporary foreign coverage, making a voluntary foreign compensation policy necessary. Risk managers should check with the insurance carrier or state fund that provides the domestic workers compensation coverage to be sure that the international policy dovetails properly with it.

A foreign compensation policy, or equivalent coverage, also is necessary if the entity assigns individuals hired in the United States to work permanently overseas or hires third-country or foreign nationals. (See the sample policy at the end of this chapter on wording for coverage of various types of international employees.) For the purposes of this chapter, the term *local hires* is used to mean employees hired in a particular country to work in that country. The term *third-country national* is used to mean employees hired in one foreign country to work in a different foreign country.

Besides checking the corporate insurance portfolio for coverage, risk managers should be aware that various countries might have their own methods to deal with injuries to workers. For example, a country may include worker benefits in its national health or welfare programs with coverage being paid for through employer payroll or other taxes. Even when worker injuries are covered through a national social insurance program, employee suits may not be included under that coverage. As a result, separate employers liability coverage may be needed.

STRUCTURING A WORLDWIDE INSURANCE PROGRAM

Most U.S. based risk managers would like to develop a worldwide program with a few policies written in English. But that is not always possible.

A Basic Problem

One of the major problems that a risk manager may face when using admitted policies is the potential language barrier. It is difficult to interpret insurance coverage when it is written in French, Spanish, or Portuguese and you don't speak that language. This is another argument to support the use of a worldwide insurance program that fills potential gaps in the admitted program.

The worldwide program will usually result in a combination of admitted and nonadmitted policies with the admitted policies forming the base of the program. One method of structuring a worldwide program is to use a *difference-in-conditions* (DIC) policy to wrap around individual admitted policies. Another is to use a *controlled master program* to control the implementation of the local coverage.

Using a DIC Approach

A difference-in-conditions policy can be used to bring locally purchased admitted policies up to the level of coverage set for the domestic insurance program. A DIC policy provides coverage for the difference in the amount and type of coverage carried locally and the amount and type provided in the domestic program. For example, an admitted policy in a foreign country may provide a $100,000 limit of general liability coverage, and the domestic policy may provide a $1,000,000 limit. The DIC policy would make up the difference ($900,000) in limits between the $100,000 foreign policy and the $1,000,000 domestic policy.

In addition, the difference-in-conditions policy will provide uniform insurance terms and conditions in areas such as covered causes of loss (perils). For example, the broadest available foreign country's locally admitted policy might offer only specified causes of loss for property coverage. The domestic program may provide special perils coverage. The DIC policy would provide coverage for causes of loss that are included in the domestic program but not included in the locally admitted foreign policy.

Advantages and Disadvantages of a DIC Policy

The main advantages of a DIC policy are that it fills in coverage and limit gaps, and provides uniform coverage. It brings consistency to the international risk management program.

The disadvantages of using a difference-in-conditions policy include the fact that local admitted policies must be individually policed, and, if a loss exceeds the limits of the local coverage, the claim settlement likely will involve more than one insurance company.

Using a Controlled Master Program

An insurer that has extensive international insurance operations can issue a controlled master program of insurance to cover the insured's international exposures. A uniform set of terms, conditions, amounts of insurance, and pricing are negotiated for the entire program. Policies in jurisdictions that require admitted coverage might be issued in any of three ways:

1. If the insurer is admitted to do business in the jurisdiction, it will issue the appropriate local policies.

2. If the insurer is not admitted, it may direct one of its admitted subsidiaries or an admitted carrier in which it has a controlling interest to issue the coverage.

3. If the insurer is not admitted and does not have an admitted subsidiary, it will work with an insurer with which it has a close working relationship to issue the policy.

The use of a nonaffiliated admitted insurer might involve reinsurance to the underwriter for the controlled master program. It should be noted that some countries restrict or prohibit the use of reinsurance from nonadmitted carriers.

Advantages of a Controlled Master Program

The advantages of a controlled master program include:

1. It gives the entity uniform coverage for its international operations and improves claims management. In the event of a loss, a single insurer

handles the claim on behalf of both the local admitted and the nonadmitted policies.

2. One insurer handles arrangements for placing coverage in admitted jurisdictions.

3. The number of parties involved in implementing the entity's international coverage is reduced, which simplifies the conveying of insurance requirements and improves the monitoring of the international insurance program.

4. One insurer handles documents such as certificates of insurance.

Some factors that should be considered when measuring an international insurer's ability to handle claims in foreign jurisdictions are shown in Figure 9.2.

Risk Management Tip

A company with large-scale overseas operations may find some underwriters reluctant to offer a controlled master program. An insurer's appetite for underwriting a controlled master program will vary with market conditions. In addition, a company that gives local control to foreign subsidiaries may feel it is best to buy as much coverage as it can locally in order to solve problems of cost allocation. This also may protect the worldwide operation's loss experience with its domestic underwriters.

OTHER EXPOSURES

Kidnap and Ransom (K&R)

Extortion threats against persons and property occur in all parts of the world, including the United States of America. However, the threat is more prevalent in some parts of the world. Kidnap and ransom coverage for such extortion demands and expenses is available from a number of insurers.

The major categories of exposure are:

1. Ransom demands that arise from the actual or threatened kidnapping of an insured person;

2. Extortion demands that arise from threats to do bodily injury to or abduct an insured person;

Figure 9.2

Evaluation Checklist for Choosing a Worldwide Insurer	
Category	Evaluation (Excellent, Good, Average, Fair, Poor, Not Acceptable)
Financial strength	
Ability to provide information on local insurance requirements and regulations.	
Knowledge of foreign laws.	
Countries in which it has a local presence. How well does it match the jurisdictions in which the corporation is operating?	
Ability to provide loss prevention and safety programs in foreign jurisdictions.	
Worldwide claims-management ability.	
Ability to integrate foreign losses into online risk management information system.	
What type of communication systems is in place to facilitate communication with insurance representatives (claims adjusters, safety engineers, etc.) located in foreign jurisdictions?	
If a broker is used, will it assist with foreign claims management?	
If a broker is used, will it help to place admitted coverage if a DIC program is used?	
Can the insurer provide a complete list of local policy conditions that differ from the DIC or controlled master policy?	

3. Extortion demands that arise from threats to damage the insured's property; and

4. Extortion demands that arise from threats to contaminate the insured's property.

Insured persons are outlined on the policy but usually include corporate executives, employees, relatives and guests of designated insureds, and customers of the named insured.

Most K&R policies include access to a security service, such as The Ackerman Group or Corporate Risk Services, which would provide recovery assistance in the event of an incident. Of course, risk managers also

could subscribe to such services directly, without purchasing K&R insurance.

Exchange–rate Risk (Exporters)

Exporters may arrange to sell goods under a contract that stipulates payment in a foreign currency. When the sale is completed at a future date, the foreign currency may be of lesser value. This means that the exporter will not be able to exchange the foreign currency for as many U.S. dollars as he could have on the date of the export contract.

There are a number of ways to handle exchange-rate risk.

Checklist for Offshore Claims Handling and Management	
Category	Evaluation (Excellent, Good, Average, Fair, Poor, Not Acceptable)
Are there provisions to assist with language barriers?	
Will the carrier accept notice of loss via email or fax?	
Is an online claims-notification system available?	
Does the list of the insurer's local claims offices dovetail with the insured's foreign locations? List should include main contact's name, address, phone and fax numbers, and email address.	
Does sending notice of loss to the admitted carrier constitute notice of loss under the controlled master program?	
Does sending notice of loss to the controlled master program carrier constitute notice of loss to the admitted carrier?	
Does the insurer provide access to a worldwide medical assistance agency, which can provide emergency medical evacuation services?	
When a broker is used, what assistance will it give in foreign claims management?	
When a broker is used, does notice to the broker constitute notice to the carrier?	
Does the broker offer access to worldwide correspondent brokers that can provide assistance?	

One is to enter into a *forward contract* with a bank. The essence of such a contract is that the bank and the exporter agree that, on the payment date of the exporter's receivable, the bank and the exporter will exchange the foreign currency for dollars at a specified rate.

For example, an exporter ships goods to Japan and is to be paid in one month with 12,000,000 Yen. At the time the deal is struck, the exporter could exchange the Yen for $100,000 at an exchange rate of 120 Yen to the dollar. Since the payment is not due for a month, there is a risk to the exporter that the value of the Yen may drop and the 12,000,000 Yen worth fewer dollars. The forward contract allows the shipper to set the exchange rate at 120 Yen to the dollar one month from the export date, less a fee for the forward contract. The fee for the forward contract will vary with market conditions. The fee increases if the length of

time between export date and conversion date is lengthened.

In addition, if the foreign currency has increased in value, the exporter will lose the opportunity to profit from it.

Export Credit Risk

An exporter must deal with the creditworthiness of its overseas buyers. Two commonly accepted methods of addressing this risk are:

- Letters of credit and/or
- Credit insurance.

Letters of credit often are used as security for credit offered to a foreign purchaser. Under this arrangement, the exporter and importer come to an agreement on the terms of the sale. The importer then has its bank issue an irrevocable letter of credit subject to the exact terms of the agreement. Once the exporter has documented that he has shipped the goods and met the terms of the letter of credit, the exporter can take that document to the foreign bank's U.S. correspondent bank and draw down the funds in payment for them.

Letters of credit remain the principal method of guaranteeing the credit extended by the exporter. Disadvantages of this method to the importer are that the letter of credit reduces borrowing capacity, and there is a charge for the letter of credit. In the case of the exporter shipping property valued at 12,000,000 Yen, the buyer's bank would be guaranteeing the payment with the letter of credit. In making this guarantee, the buyer's bank would either require that the customer set aside funds to back the letter of credit or reduce the amount of its unused line of credit. The fee for such a transaction depends upon the overall relationship between the bank and its customer, as well as credit market conditions.

When an exporter is trying to enter a market in which the importers have been used to dealing on an open credit account basis, the request for a letter of credit may hinder the exporter's sales efforts. Another disadvantage to the exporter is that if the exact terms of the letter of credit are not met, even due to circumstances outside the exporter's control, the issuing bank may refuse to honor the letter of credit and not make payment.

Such disadvantages have led to increases in the use of *export credit insurance* as an alternative. In some cases export credit insurance supplements letters of credit.

The Export-Import Bank of the United States was created to promote the export of United States goods. As part of its activities, it helps businesses and financial institutions satisfy their need for foreign credit insurance in connection with export activities. Subject to its underwriting guidelines, the Export-Import Bank can arrange for insurance against commercial and political risks or for political risks alone. The coverage may be issued for 90 percent or more of the principal and interest receivable. The commercial risk may also be subject to a deductible.

The deductible and lack of 100 percent coverage for commercial risk is one disadvantage for the exporter. Another disadvantage is that the exporter

pays the cost of the insurance. However, if the exporter is able to adjust pricing to include some or all of the costs of insurance, this disadvantage may be lessened. In addition, the existence of credit insurance may help the exporter obtain financing for his export operations.

Export–Import Terms

The Export-Import Bank offers insurance for two types of risk, which the bank defines as:

Political risks—foreign government's inability to convert local currency into U.S. dollars (transfer risk); specified changes in import or export regulations that occur after shipment; and war, civil strife, revolution, or expropriation by a government authority. Additional information on political risks is included in the section of this book entitled **Identifying the Territorial Limits of the Domestic Insurance Program**.

Commercial credit risks—nonpayment for reasons other than political risk, including default, insolvency, and bankruptcy but excluding product disputes between the exporter and buyer.

The *Overseas Private Investment Corporation*, (OPIC) was created to assist and encourage international investment by the U.S. private sector. Its activities include the financing of businesses overseas, loans and loan guarantees, and the providing of insurance against losses arising out of overseas operations. OPIC's obligations are backed by the full faith and credit of the United States of America.

Subject to its underwriting guidelines and actual policy terms, the OPIC describes the types of coverage that it can arrange as currency inconvertibility, expropriation, and political violence.

Several commercial insurers also offer significant amounts of coverage for both credit and political risks.

GLOBAL ASPECTS OF THE INTERNET

The Internet also presents a type of global risk. It permits corporations to do business around the world. That seeming advantage, however, opens them to potential liabilities that may differ from those commonly found in the United States. Some of the prominent risk areas that *wired* companies face are:

- Difference in legal structures among the various jurisdictions;

- Differences in privacy requirements between the United States and other parts of the world, primarily the European Union; and

- The need to institutionalize information security systems.

The Internet presents exposures that are unique in the areas of intangibility and speed, which are coupled with its lack of jurisdictional boundaries. Additional information on Internet risks and treatments is contained in the book, *e-Risk: Liabilities in a Wired World* (The National Underwriter Co. 2000).

WHERE CAN I FIND OUT MORE ABOUT IT?

The Ackerman Group

http://www.ackermangroup.com/

This company provides analysis of risks in eighty-seven countries through a subscription service as well as kidnap/ransom recovery and negotiating services.

American International Group, Inc.

http://home.aigonline.com/country_view/0,4605,1350,00.html

This site includes country risk summaries and information on country insurance practices.

From this site the reader can branch to the **American International Underwriters** site at

http://home.aigonline.com/AIGOnline/region_view/0,2043,650,00.html

For information on its political risk products within a country.

http://home.aigonline.com/aig_product_listing/body_international/0,2246,,00.html

For information on international products and services

Central Intelligence Agency

http://www.cia.gov/cia/publications/factbook/index.html

This site contains political and economic information on foreign countries.

Chubb Group of Insurance Companies

http://www.chubb.com/businesses/mrg/

This site includes information on political risks insurance and trade credit insurance. It also includes information on property, casualty, and employee-related coverages normally required by an entity with multinational operations.

http://www.chubb.com/businesses/export/exporters.pdf

Chubb group's Exporter Package Portfolio

Corporate Risk International

http://www.corprisk.com/

This company offers security services and kidnap/ransom recovery and negotiating services. This Web site links to the Worldwide Advisory Intelligence Service, which provides threat assessments for various countries through a subscription service.

http://www.corprisk.com/wais/index.asp

Export-Import Bank

http://www.exim.gov/

This is the site of the bank's home page. The reader can branch from this site to get more information on its operations. Its insurance operations are summarized at:

http://www.exim.gov/minsprog.html

Headquarters toll free number: 800-565-EXIM

International SOS

http://www.internationalsos.com/

This company provides global emergency assistance, medical, healthcare management, and security services to subscribers.

Medex Assistance

http://www.medexassist.com/index.html

This company offers travel insurance and medical assistance to foreign travelers and expatriates.

Overseas Private Investment Corporation

http://www.opic.gov/Insurance/

Sovereign Risk Insurance Ltd.

http://www.sovereignbermuda.com/

This site includes information on long term political risk insurance.

U.S. Department of State

http://www.state.gov/

This site provides links to travel warnings and assistance and emergencies abroad.

Zurich North America

http://www.zurichna.com/

This site includes information on its political risk insurance and multinational property and casualty coverages.

QUESTIONS AND ANSWERS

Question—A company has multinational operations. Parts from its plant in Germany are required for the completion of its product in the United States of America. Will a standard Commercial General Liability policy provide sufficient coverage for the products liability exposure?

Answer—The coverage territory on a standard CGL policy encompasses all parts of the world if the bodily injury or property damage arises out of products made or sold in the United States of America, Canada, or Puerto Rico. In addition, lawsuits must be adjudicated within that same territory.

Therefore, the products liability exposure of this multinational company is not properly addressed by a standard CGL policy.

Question—Consider the case of a company that has its major operations in the United States but maintains offshore sales and service offices. What are some of the ways that such a company could structure its worldwide insurance program?

Answer—

- Its property insurance policy might be written on a global basis to cover both U.S. and foreign exposures.

- General and automobile liability insurance policies in the amount of $1,000,000 might be written to cover U.S. operations, with companion policies written on an international basis covering the off-shore operations in the amount of $1,000,000.

- A Foreign Voluntary Compensation policy could be written with a $1,000,000 limit on employers liability coverage.

- The entity's excess liability program should be structured to attach in excess of both the primary domestic and foreign general and automobile liability policies, as well as both domestic and foreign employers liability insurance.

- Specific admitted country policies would be used to

  a. meet the requirements for compulsory coverage,

  b. meet requirements forbidding nonadmitted insurance, and

  c. comply with any special insurance practices of a particular country.

- In addition in those countries where foreign general liability and auto liability insurance coverage is not compulsory, local coverage in a minimal amount may be purchased to provide for the rapid handling of claims.

- When required, local workers compensation coverage (or its equivalent) should be placed with the appropriate governmental schemes or purchased from a local insurer.

- If employers liability insurance is not included in the local workers compensation coverage, a local employers liability policy should be purchased.

GLOSSARY

Admitted insurance. Policies that are issued by a state fund or an insurer licensed or legally permitted to do business in the jurisdiction in which an exposure is located.

Admitted insurer. An insurance company that is authorized by a particular country to transact insurance business within its borders.

Cause of loss. The underlying source or cause of damage, such as fire, windstorm, or hail.

Causes of loss basic form. A property coverage form that provides coverage for specified causes of loss plus vandalism, sprinkler leakage, sinkhole collapse, and volcanic action. The form lists these covered causes of loss (perils).

Causes of loss broad form. A property coverage form that provides coverage for the basic causes of loss plus falling objects; weight of snow, ice, or sleet; and certain types of water damage.

Causes of loss special form. A property coverage form that provides coverage for risks of physical loss except those specifically excluded in the form. Previously known as all-risk coverage.

Compulsory insurance. Coverage that is required to be in-force by a given jurisdiction, such as a particular country.

Compulsory admitted insurance. Admitted insurance that is required to satisfy a particular jurisdiction's legal requirements; synonymous with compulsory insurance for purposes of this chapter.

Controlled master program. A system of policies that are controlled through one insurer. The insurer issues policies where it is admitted to do so and arranges for admitted subsidiaries or correspondent admitted carriers to issue policies in jurisdictions where it is not permitted.

Difference-in-conditions (DIC) policy. A policy that brings a locally admitted foreign policy up to the coverage standards set in the domestic insurance program.

Domestic insurance. Policies that cover a corporation's operations and properties within the United States of America, its territories and possessions; Puerto Rico; and Canada, and, for some policies, international waters or airspace.

Employers liability. The liability of an employer for injury to workers, or consequential injury to the family members, that is job-related but not encompassed by a state workers compensation or similar employee disability law.

Endemic disease. Infectious diseases that are peculiar or restricted to certain regions or countries and are not usually covered by state workers compensation laws.

Expatriate. A U.S. citizen who is assigned to work in a foreign country for an extended period of time.

Foreign nationals. Citizens hired in a foreign country to work in that foreign country.

Forward contract. A contract in which a bank and an exporter agree that, on the payment date of the exporter's receivable, the bank and the exporter will exchange the foreign currency in which payment is made for dollars at a specified rate.

Insurance Services Office (ISO). An organization providing statistical information, actuarial analyses, policy language, and related services for the insurance industry.

Letter of credit. An arrangement in which an importer's bank issues an irrevocable letter of credit subject to the exact payment terms of the import agreement. Once the exporter has documented that he has shipped the goods and met the terms of the letter of credit, the exporter can take the document to a U.S. correspondent bank and draw down the funds in payment for the goods.

Local insurance. Policies that cover an entity's operations in a specific foreign (non-U.S.) country or that are issued by insurers domiciled in the country or operated by the country.

Local national employees. Foreign citizens hired to work outside the U.S. or Canada to which the corporation does not voluntarily offer to provide statutory workers compensation benefits of a state within the United States of America.

Nonadmitted insurer. An insurance company that is not authorized by a specific country to transact insurance within its borders.

Nonadmitted jurisdiction. Jurisdictions in which an insurance company is not licensed or permitted by law to issue insurance policies or to handle claims.

Peril. A potential cause of loss, such as fire, windstorm, or hail.

Repatriation expenses. The additional cost to return an ill or injured U.S. employee to the United States from the foreign country above the cost to return to the United States if the employee were not injured or ill.

Specified causes of loss. The most basic group of causes of loss to property. Individual policies list the specified causes of loss that they cover, but typically they are fire, lightning, windstorm, civil commotion, smoke, hail, aircraft, vehicles, explosion, and riot.

Subrogation. The right of the party that has paid for a loss of a second party to recover those costs from the third party that is responsible.

Third-country nationals. Individuals hired in one foreign country to work in another foreign country.

Workers Compensation Part One. The coverage part of a workers compensation policy that provides medical and wage loss benefits for workers injured on the job in compliance with the state workers compensation statute. Also known as workers compensation coverage.

Workers Compensation Part Two. The coverage part of a workers compensation policy that provides coverage for the liability of employers for injury to workers that is not encompassed in the state workers compensation or similar disability law. Also known as employers liability coverage.

Appendix

The Chubb Group of Insurance Companies provided the application and coverage forms contained in the Appendix to Chapter 9.

©Copyright Chubb Group of Insurance Companies. Reprinted with permission.

Confiscation, Expropriation, Nationalization (CEN)
Insurance Policy
Permanent Investment

Contract

Words and phrases that appear in **bold** print have special meanings and are defined in the definition section of this contract.

Throughout this contract the words "you" and "your" refer to the Named Insured shown in the Declarations of this policy. The words "we", "us" and "our" refer to the company providing this insurance.

Insuring Agreement

In consideration of payment of premium, and in reliance upon statements made to the **company** by the **insured** and subject to the Conditions, Warranties, Exclusions and other terms of this policy, the **company** agrees as follows:

To indemnify the **insured** for the **covered percentage** of **loss** suffered by the **insured** caused solely and directly by a Covered Cause of Loss (as described below) occurring during the **policy period**.

Covered Causes Of Loss

1. EXPROPRIATORY CONDUCT

    Expropriatory conduct means confiscation, expropriation, nationalization, requisition, sequestration or **willful destruction** by law, order or administrative action of the **government of the host country** which:

    a. expressly and permanently deprives the **insured** of all or part of its shareholding in the **foreign enterprise**; or

    b. expressly and permanently deprives the **foreign enterprise** of all or part of its fixed or current assets;

    c. expressly and selectively prevents or restricts the operation of the **foreign enterprise** so as to cause **permanent cessation**; or

    d. expressly and permanently deprives the **insured** of inventory and equipment, used by the insured in connection with the **foreign enterprise,** carried on the **insured's** financial records and located in the **host country**,

    unless such conduct is formally represented by the **government of the host country** as temporary.

2. CURRENCY INCONVERTIBILITY

    Currency inconvertibility means the inability of the foreign enterprise or the **insured**, after all reasonable efforts to convert and transfer outside the host country available funds through normal currency exchange channels in order to remit in **policy currency** a distribution of earnings from the **insured** investment.

3. DEPRIVATION

    Deprivation means the **insured** being deprived of the use or possession of the whole or part of its inventory or equipment outside the **host country** or its territorial waters by reason of the **insured** and/or its agents being prevented from exporting its inventory or equipment from the **host country** or its territorial waters because the **insured** is unable to obtain an export license from the **government of the host country.**

    The **insured** shall be deemed to have been prevented from exporting its inventory or equipment after six months pass from the date the **insured** advised the **company** that it could not export the inventory or equipment from the **host country** or its territorial waters.

Covered Causes Of Loss (Continued)

4. SELECTIVE DISCRIMINATION

Selective Discrimination means the imposition of any law, order, decree, regulation or import/export restriction, selectively and discriminately, against the **foreign enterprise** by the **government of the host country** which, in circumstances beyond the control of the **insured**, expressly and selectively prevents or restricts the operation of the **foreign enterprise** so as to cause **permanent cessation**.

5. THIRD PARTY BLOCKADE OR QUARANTINE

Third Party Blockade or Quarantine means the use of military force or the direct threat thereof, by one or more third party sovereign nations preventing the **insured** from removing **mobile assets** from the **host country**. The **insured** will have been deemed to have been prevented from removing **mobile assets** after six months pass from the date the **insured** advised the **company** that it could not remove the **mobile assets**.

6. FORCED ABANDONMENT

Forced Abandonment means the **insured's** abandonment of the **foreign enterprise** for a period of more than six months from the date the **insured** advised the **company** of such abandonment, due to:

a. circumstances beyond the **insured's** control; and

b. solely and directly in consequence of the **insured** being required or advised by the government of the **insured's** country or official representative(s) thereof to leave the **host country** if such requirement or advice was generally applicable to all nationals of the **insured's** country, in the **host country**.

For the purpose of this policy, an advisory against travel by a governmental authority alone shall not constitute the above referenced requirement or advisement.

7. FORCED DIVESTITURE

Forced Divestiture means the imposition of any law, order, decree, regulation or restriction, by the government of the **insured's** country that requires the **insured** to permanently divest itself of all or part of its shareholding in the **foreign enterprise** so as to cause **permanent cessation**.

8. FORCED PROJECT RELOCATION

Forced Project Relocation means efforts undertaken by the **insured** to re-establish the **foreign enterprise** in a location outside the **host country** as a result of a **loss** amounting to at least fifty percent of the applicable **limit of liability**.

9. POLITICAL VIOLENCE

Political Violence means **civil war** and **insurrection**, revolution, **rebellion, coup d'Etat, strikes, riots, civil commotion, sabotage or terrorism**.

General Terms And Conditions

NOTICES

Unless otherwise indicated, in writing, by the parties, notices of loss, policy change requests or any other communications provided for in this policy shall be in writing and mailed to the **insured** at its principal address shown in the Declarations and to the **company** at 15 Mountain View Road, Warren, New Jersey 07059.

General Terms And Conditions (Continued)

INSPECTION AND AUDIT

Upon reasonable notice to the **insured**, the **company** shall have the right at all times to inspect, copy and examine the books and records of the **foreign enterprise** and the **insured** and gain access to relevant documentation of third parties.

EXCHANGE RATE

Local currency shall be determined by using the average exchange rate over the fifteen days prior to the **date of loss** as quoted by Chase Manhattan Bank in New York, New York.

OTHER INSURANCE

This insurance is excess over the applicable limit of any other valid bond, insurance or other indemnity available to the **insured**.

SUBROGATION

In the event of **loss** under this policy, the **company** shall be subrogated to all rights of recovery, which the **insured** may have. After **loss**, the **insured** shall assign and transfer to the **company** or its designee any such rights of recovery.

DEDUCTIBLE

The **company's** obligation to pay for **loss** shall apply in excess of the deductible amount, if any, shown in item 5. of the Declarations.

WARRANTY AGREEMENTS

The **insured** warrants and agrees that it has no knowledge at the inception of the **policy period** of any circumstance which could give rise to a **loss** hereunder and that all information provided to the **company** by the **insured** is true and correct and that no material information has been withheld.

In addition, the **insured** expressly warrants to the **company** that:

1. all arrangements, agreements, licenses, permits and understandings applicable to the **foreign enterprise** have been duly and validly authorized and executed, are and will be available for inspection by the **company**, and are or will be in full force and effect as soon as possible;

2. the **insured** has complied and will use its best efforts to continue to comply in all respects with all contracts and laws of which the **insured** should have reasonably been aware which relate to the **foreign enterprise** or to the **insured** (unless prohibited from such compliance by a law, order, regulation or decree in force in the **insured's** country);

3. the **insured** will attempt, as required by law, to extend, renew, or modify licenses and will comply with any non-arbitrary and reasonable licensing requirements relating to the **foreign enterprise**;

4. the **insured**: (a) has no knowledge or information of any matter, fact, or circumstance which may reasonably give rise to a **loss**; (b) will give written notice to the **company** within fifteen days after receiving such notification or knowledge at its corporate headquarters; (c) will diligently monitor and oversee the **foreign enterprise**, and (d) will not incur further expenses or costs associated with operation of the **foreign enterprise** after receiving such notification or knowledge, unless first receiving the prior written consent of the **company**;

5 the **insured** will not disclose the existence of this policy to any third party; and

General Terms And Conditions (Continued)

6.   the **insured**, at its own expense, will: (a) take all reasonable and ordinary measures to avoid, prevent or minimize **loss**; (b) pursue and preserve for the **company** all administrative or judicial remedies which may be available to contest the **loss**; (c) cooperate in full with the **company** in attempting to negotiate a settlement with the **government of the host country**; (d) take no action without the prior consent of the **company** (whether before or after the payment of any claim) which might adversely affect the **company's** actual or potential subrogation rights; (e) take all action as may reasonably be required (following the payment of any claim) to effect recoveries and assist in preserving and prosecuting any claims transferred to the **company**, including permitting the **company**, at the **company's** expense, to bring actions in the name of the **insured**; and (f) in all instances, exercise due diligence in meeting all warranties, terms and conditions of this policy.

ACCOUNTING PRINCIPLES

All financial statements and accounts, as well as the calculation of any **loss**, shall be in accordance with the principles of accounting generally accepted in the **insured's country**, and used by the **insured** in its certified financial statements.

ARBITRATION

Should any dispute arise between the **insured** and the **company** under this policy, the matter in dispute shall, if agreed by the **insured** and the **company**, be referred for arbitration to a three-person panel. Each party to the arbitration shall appoint one arbitrator experienced in political risk or the property and casualty insurance industry who shall, in turn, select a third arbitrator to act as umpire. The arbitration shall be conducted pursuant to the rules of the American Arbitration Association and judgment upon the award rendered may be entered in any court having jurisdiction thereof. The arbitration shall be held in Warren, New Jersey. No award may exceed the applicable **limits of liability**.

ASSIGNMENT

This policy is assignable only with the prior written consent of the **company**. No assignment by the **insured** of any right, title or interest to any amount payable under this policy shall be valid and binding upon the **company** unless the **insured** notifies the **company** thereof and the **company** endorses the policy in the manner provided for in the changes condition which follow.

CANCELLATION

1.   No cancellation of this policy is permitted by the **insured** except in the event of termination of the **foreign enterprise**.

2.   No cancellation of this policy is permitted by the **company** except in the event of non-payment of premium.

3.   In the event of cancellation as per paragraph (2) above, the policy may be canceled by the **company** in the manner provided by mailing written notice stating when, not less than ten (10) days thereafter, the cancellation shall be effective. The mailing of such notice shall be sufficient proof of notice and the effective date and hour of cancellation stated in the notice shall become the end of the **policy period**. If the **company** cancels in accordance with this paragraph, earned premium shall be computed pro rata.

4   In the event of cancellation in accordance with paragraph 1. above, the **company** shall refund the unearned premium as computed at customary short rates.

General Terms And Conditions (Continued)

CHOICE OF LAW

The construction, validity and performance of this policy shall be governed by the laws of the United States of America and the State of New York.

FALSE OR FRAUDULENT STATEMENT, REPORTS OR CLAIMS, CONCEALMENT

If the **insured** makes any statement, report or claim, knowing it to be false or fraudulent, or if the **insured** knowingly conceals any material fact, this policy shall become void and all rights under this policy shall be forfeited.

LOANS NOT DENOMINATED IN POLICY CURRENCY

If the **insured** makes loans to the **foreign enterprise**, or **guarantees** loans made to the **foreign enterprise**, and these loans provide for repayment in a currency other than the **policy currency**, for the purpose of calculating the amount of **policy currency** payable, the rate of exchange which shall be used shall be that offered on the **date of loss** by the **company's commercial** bank. If, however, the **insured** makes payment under the **guarantee** in **policy currency**, the **company** will also pay in **policy currency**.

PAYMENT OF PREMIUM

The Premium set forth in Item 6. of the Declarations shall be payable to the **company**.

When premium is payable in installments (or otherwise not in full at inception), the full Premium shall be fully due and payable immediately in the event a claim for **loss** is submitted.

RECOVERIES

After payment of any **loss**, any sums which are recovered from any source shall be immediately paid to the **company** and shared between the **company** and the **insured** as follows:

1. The **company** shall receive the **covered percentage** of all sums recovered, including the **company's** cost of recovery, until the amount of the payment of a **loss** has been fully reimbursed;

2. All further sums recovered shall inure to the benefit of the **insured**.

PROOF AND PAYMENT OF LOSS

Payment for **loss** shall be made promptly on the condition that:

1. a written proof of loss, acceptable to the **company** has been submitted; and

2. the **insured** has submitted such written proof of loss within (i) twelve months after the **date of loss** or (ii) in the event of a demand by the **company** for submission of such proof of loss, the **insured** shall file such proof of loss with the **company** within thirty days thereafter; and

3. the **loss** was caused solely and directly by a Covered Cause of Loss.

The responsibility for proving a **loss** under this policy shall at all times rest with the **insured**.

LOSS REDUCTION - DISPUTES

The **insured** will use its best efforts to reduce the **loss**. The **company** will pay, subject to the applicable **limit of liability**, for extraordinary expenses, which are necessarily incurred in reducing such **loss**. In no event shall the aggregate of such expenses exceed the amount by which the **loss** is reduced.

Policy Exclusions

The **company** shall not be liable for **loss** caused by, contributed to by, or resulting from:

1   **war** (whether before or after the outbreak of hostilities) between any of the following five countries. The People's Republic of China, France, the United Kingdom, the Russian Federation and the United States of America;

2.   destruction or **physical property damage** caused by **war** or any event except **willful destruction** by the **government of the host country** or **civil war** and **insurrection**, subject always to Exclusion 1. above;

3.   a.   ionizing radiation from or contamination by radioactivity from any nuclear fuel or from any nuclear waste or from the combustion of nuclear fuel;

    b.   the radioactive, toxic, explosive or other hazardous or contaminating properties of any nuclear installation, reactor or other nuclear assembly or nuclear component thereof;

    c.   any weapon employing atomic or nuclear fission and/or fusion or other like reaction or radioactive force or matter;

    d.   nuclear reaction, nuclear radiation or radioactive contamination however caused.

4.   wrongful or dishonest acts or omissions of the **insured**, or to the extent within the **insured's** control, the **foreign enterprise**;

5.   insolvency, bankruptcy or financial default of any party or person whatsoever; except the official exchange control authority of the host country; or currency fluctuation or devaluation;

6.   any contract in which the **insured** or the **foreign enterprise** may be a party; or the repossession of property by any titleholder;

7.   business interruption, delay, deterioration, loss of market or profits, or other consequential loss;

8.   the actual, alleged, or threatened discharge, dispersal, seepage, migration, release, or the actual escape of **pollutants** at any time.;

9.   goods in transit in respect of political violence;

10.   any:

    a.   request, demand or order that any **insured** or others test for, monitor, clean up, remove, contain, treat, detoxify or neutralize, or in any way respond to, or assess the effects of **pollutants**; or

    b.   claim or suit by or on behalf of a governmental authority for damages because of testing for, monitoring, cleaning up, removing, containing, treating, detoxifying, or neutralizing or in any way responding to, or assessing the effects of **pollutants**.

Definitions

Book Value means historical cost less accumulated depreciation, as reflected in the **insured's** most recent financial records prior to the **date of loss.**

Civil Commotion means a substantial disturbance of the public peace by three (3) or more persons assembled together and acting with common interest.

Civil War means a hostile contention by means of armed forces carried on between opposing citizens or subjects of the **host country**.

Coup d'Etat means the overthrow of an existing government by a group of its citizens or subjects.

Definitions (continued)	**Company** means the stock insurance company shown in the Declarations.

Covered Percentage means the applicable percentage shown in Item 5. of the Declarations.

Date of Loss means the date on which the Covered Cause of Loss first occurred.

Extraordinary Costs means those reasonable, unavoidable, necessary, and extraordinary non-mitigatable costs, penalties, and expenses, net of tax benefit (if any), which are incurred by the **insured**, with prior consultation with the **company**, as a result of Forced Relocation provided that in no event shall there be included as **extraordinary costs** any earned or anticipated revenues or profits.

Foreign Enterprise means the entity shown in Item 2. of the Declarations.

Government of the Host Country means the present or any succeeding governing authority, (without regard to the method of its succession) or any of its authorized agents, in effective control of all or part of the **host country** or of any political or any of its territorial subdivisions.

Guarantee means a written unconditional guarantee by the **insured** to pay a debt of the **foreign enterprise**, which is due, and payable, if the **foreign enterprise** has not paid according to the terms of the underlying obligation.

Host Country means the country shown in Item 1. of the Declarations.

Insurrection means a violent rising of citizens or subjects in resistance to the **government of the host country.**

Insured means the entity shown in the Declarations or anyone authorized to act on behalf of such entity.

Insured Assets means tangible assets, used by the **insured** in connection with the **foreign enterprise**, which are located in the **host country**

Investment means the **insured's** financial interest in the **foreign enterprise**, as well as any equipment or inventory owned directly by the **insured**, which is located in the **host country**.

Local currency means the currency of the **host country**.

Loss means the lesser of:

1   the applicable **limit of liability** for each Covered Cause of Loss shown in Declarations subject always to **maximum policy limit of liability**; or

2   the amount of loss as calculated using the method described below applicable to each Covered Cause of Loss, less any salvage, funds or other compensation recovered from the **government of the host country** or from any other source prior to any loss payment.

    a   Expropriatory Conduct: The **book value** of the portion of the **net investment** in the **host country** which has been subject to Expropriatory Conduct or the lesser of replacement, **book value** or repair cost of any **physical property damage** caused by **willful destruction**.

    b   Deprivation: The lesser of replacement cost or **book value** of the **insured's** inventory or equipment of which the **insured** is deprived.

    c.   Selective Discrimination: The **book value** of the portion of the **net investment** in the **host country**, which has been subject to Selective Discrimination.

Definitions (continued)

d. Third Party Blockade or Quarantine: The **book value** of **mobile assets**, which have been subject to the Third Party Blockade or Quarantine.

e. Forced Abandonment: The **book value** of the **net investment** in the **host country**, which has been subject to Forced Abandonment.

f. Forced Divestiture: The difference between the **book value** of the **net investment**, which has been divested, and any sums received by the **insured** from the sale of such divested shares. The **insured** hereby agrees to consult with the **company** prior to agreeing to sell the divested shares.

g   Forced Relocation Coverage: The value of all **extraordinary costs** incurred by the **insured** in relocating (but not in operating) the **foreign enterprise** outside the **host country** in a country with the same physical characteristics as the **host country**; plus, all **extraordinary costs** actually incurred in the performance of non-cancelable third party obligations which pertain to the **foreign enterprise**, that existed at the **date of loss**. Costs of rebuilding or replacement leasing are hereby included in the loss payment, but such rebuilding or replacement leasing costs will reduce the applicable **limit of liability** for political violence or expropriatory conduct.

h   Currency Inconvertibility: The lesser of the **policy currency** equivalent of the currency of the **host country** sought to be transferred as of the end of the **waiting period** less the **insured percentage** of the amount of any other compensation or monetary benefit realized by the **insured** by the reason of the **loss**. The equivalent value shall be determined by applying the net exchange rate prevailing at the end of the **waiting period** in the normal exchange market or channel through which **policy currency** is generally available for the type of transaction involved. Any **loss** shall be computed and paid in **policy currency**.

i. Political Violence: The lesser of replacement, **book value** or repair costs to **insured assets**.

Limit of Liability means, subject to the **maximum policy limit of liability**, the **limits of liability** shown in Item 5. of the Declarations for each Covered Cause of Loss, which is the most we will indemnify the **insured** for loss caused solely and directly be such Covered Cause of Loss. Each payment for **loss** made by the **company** shall reduce the applicable **limit of liability** by the same amount.

Maximum Policy Limit of Liability means the **maximum policy limit of liability**, shown in Item 5. of the Declarations, which is the most we will indemnify the **insured** for all **losses** during the **policy period**. Each payment made by the **company** shall reduce the **maximum policy limit of liability** by the same amount. The **maximum policy limit of liability** applies separately to each **policy period** and is non-cumulative with prior or subsequent **policy periods**.

Mobile Assets means those assets scheduled in the Application which are owned or legally held by the **insured**, used by the **insured** in connection with the **foreign enterprise,** are not on the books of the **foreign enterprise**, and are physically present in the **host country**.

Net Investment means the sum of:

1   the **insured's** original equity contribution to the **foreign enterprise** plus the **insured's** share of retained earnings adjusted by the **insured's** ratable share of profits and losses of the **foreign enterprise** from the date of investment; and

2   principal and interest (accruing up to the **date of loss**) on loans made to the **foreign enterprise** by the **insured**; and

Definitions (continued)

3   principal and interest (accruing up to the **date of loss**) on debts of the **foreign enterprise** which are **guaranteed** by the **insured**; and

4   the amount of the **foreign enterprise's** accounts payable to the **insured** less the amount of the **foreign enterprise's** accounts receivable for the **insured**; and

5   the lesser of the costs to repair or replace, or **book value**, on the day immediately prior to the **date of loss**, for any equipment or inventory:

        a.   located outside of the **insured's** country with proper documentation; and

        b.   carried on the **insured's** financial records,

as of the **date of loss**, less the value of any goodwill, operating rights, franchise agreements, trademarks, capitalized expenses, research and development and other intangible assets.

Permanent Cessation means the complete cessation of the operations of the **foreign enterprise**, under the control of the **insured**, with the understanding that such operations will never resume under such control.

Physical Property Damage means destruction, impairment, or damage to **insured assets** (excluding cash, jewelry, other valuables, marketable securities, or other financial instruments).

Policy Currency means the currency shown in the Declarations and shall be the currency in which:

1.   the premium is payable;

2.   any **loss** is payable; and

3.   all **limits of liability** and deductibles are stated.

For the purpose of calculating the amount in 2. above, for **loss** denominated in currency other than **policy currency**, the rate of exchange to the **policy currency** shall be that rate offered on the date of loss payment by the **company's** commercial bank.

Policy Period means that period of time shown in the Declarations.

Pollutants means any solid, liquid, gaseous or thermal irritant or contaminant, including smoke, vapor, soot, fumes, acids, alkalis, chemicals or waste. Waste includes materials to be disposed of, recycled, or reclaimed.

Rebellion means a deliberate, organized and open resistance by force and arms to the laws or operations of the **government of the host country** committed by its citizens or subjects.

Riot means a violent disturbance by three (3) or more workers to enforce demands made on an employer or to protest against an act or condition.

Sabotage or Terrorism means politically motivated destruction of or damage to **insured assets** (1) as a result of state-sponsored and government-directed terrorism, or (2) by an organized political group which advocates the overthrow of the established political authorities in the **host country**.

Strike means a work stoppage by three (3) or more workers to enforce demands made on an employer or to protest against an act or condition.

Sublimit of Liability means, subject to the **limit of liability** for Expropriatory Conduct, the sublimits of liability shown in Item 5. of the Declarations for each Covered Cause of Loss, which is the most we will pay for **loss** caused solely and directly by such Covered Cause of Loss.

Definitions (continued)

War means hostile or warlike action, including action in hindering, combating, or defending and actual, impending, or expected act by (1) any government or sovereign power or any authority maintaining or using military, naval, or air forces; (2) any military, naval, or air forces; or (3) any agent of any such government, power, authority, or forces.

Willful destruction means **physical property damage** to the **foreign enterprise** caused solely and directly by, or under the order of, the **government of the host country**.

Tools & Techniques of Risk Management & Insurance   135

International Voluntary Workers' Compensation

Contract

Table Of Contents

COMPENSATION WORKERS'

CONTRACT

INTERNATIONAL VOLUNTARY WORKERS' COMPENSATION

International Workers' Compensation Insurance

Form 11–02–0603(Rev. 2–99)   Contract

International Voluntary Workers' Compensation

Contract

Words and phrases that appear in **bold** print have special meanings and are defined in the definitions section of this contract.

Throughout this contract the words "you" and "your" refer to the Named Insured shown in the Declarations of this policy. The words "we", "us" and "our" refer to the company providing this insurance.

Coverages

International Voluntary Workers' Compensation

We agree, at your option and on your behalf, to pay voluntarily to your **International Executive Employees** the compensation, medical and other benefits specified in the **Workers' Compensation Law** of the State(s) designated in the Declarations, in the same manner as if such **International Executive Employees** were covered under the provisions of said Law or Laws; we also agree, at your option and on your behalf, to pay voluntarily to your **Other International Employees** the compensation, medical and other benefits specified in the respective **Workers' Compensation Law–Country of Origin**.

We further agree, at your option and on your behalf, to pay to your **International Executive Employees** and **Other International Employees** the compensation, medical and other benefits, in lieu of voluntary payments, for which you become liable under the provisions of a **Workers' Compensation Law** or **Workers' Compensation Law–Country of Origin** of jurisdictions other than those you have chosen as Voluntary Statutory jurisdictions in the Declarations.

We will cover **endemic disease** as if it were occupational in nature and as if it were included in the provisions of the respective **Workers' Compensation Law** or **Workers' Compensation Law–Country of Origin**.

We will pay on your behalf, up to the corresponding Limits of Insurance for Repatriation Expense, for such additional expenses as may be reasonably incurred, over and above **normal transportation costs**, for the repatriation or relocation of injured or sick **International Executive Employees**, **Other International Employees** or **Local National Employees**, including repatriation expenses associated with accompanying spouse and children during temporary business travel provided that:

1. the relocation or repatriation is from the country of injury or disease to a destination in any country other than the country of injury or disease, including the **United States** or Canada and

2. the relocation or repatriation is necessary, in the opinion of competent medical authorities.

We will also pay, up to the corresponding Limits of Insurance stated in the Declarations, certain expenses related to the death of your covered employees:

1. the cost of embalmment to meet U.S./Canadian or other National health standards;

2. all reasonable expenses of transportation to return the remains of the deceased to the country of burial or funeral.

Coverages
(continued)

Employer's Liability

We agree to pay, up to the corresponding Limits of Insurance stated in the Declarations, all sums you legally must pay as damages because of bodily injury to your **International Executive Employees**, **Other International Employees** and **Local National Employees**, provided that the bodily injury arises out of **endemic disease** or arises out of and in the course of the injured employee's employment by you and provided that the bodily injury is covered by this Employer's Liability insurance.

The damages we will pay, where recovery is permitted by law, include damages:

1. for which you are liable to a third party by reason of a claim or suit against you by that third party to recover the damages claimed against such third party as a result of injury to your employee;

2. for care and loss of services;

3. for consequential bodily injury to a spouse, parent, child, brother or sister of your injured employee;

    provided that these damages are the direct consequence of bodily injury that arises out of and in the course of the injured employee's employment by you; and

4. because of bodily injury to your employee that arises out of and in the course of employment, claimed against you in a capacity other than as employer.

In some countries, this insurance will serve as primary Employer's Liability insurance because you are not required to purchase **admitted** Employer's Liability insurance and you do not elect to do so.

In other countries, this insurance will serve as excess insurance over **admitted** Employer's Liability insurance which you are required to purchase or you elect to purchase.

Who Is Insured

You are insured if you are an employer named in the Declarations. You are also insured if that employer is a partnership and you are one of its partners.

Limits Of Insurance

WHAT WE WILL PAY

Workers' Compensation

1. We will pay promptly when due the benefits of the applicable **Workers' Compensation Law** or **Workers' Compensation Law–Country of Origin**.

2. Repatriation Expense–Each Employee

    The limit shown in the Declarations is the most we will pay for all repatriation expenses covered by this insurance and arising out of bodily injury by accident or bodily injury by disease, including **endemic disease**.

3. Repatriation Expense–Policy Limit

    The limit shown in the Declarations is the most we will pay for all repatriation expense covered by this insurance and arising out of bodily injury by accident or bodily injury by disease, including **endemic disease**, regardless of the number of employees who sustain bodily injury by accident or bodily injury by disease or bodily injury by **endemic disease**.

International Voluntary Workers' Compensation

Limits Of Insurance

Workers'Compensation (continued)

4. We will not pay any claims for repatriation expense after we have paid the applicable limit of our liability under this coverage.

Employer'sLiability

Our liability to pay for damages is limited to the Limits of Insurance stated in the Declarations. They apply as explained below:

1. Bodily Injury by Accident. The limit shown in the Declarations for "bodily injury by accident–each accident" is the most we will pay for all damages covered by this insurance because of bodily injury to one or more employees in any one accident.

   A disease, including an **endemic disease**, is not bodily injury by accident unless it results directly from bodily injury by accident.

2. Bodily Injury by Disease. The limit shown for "bodily injury by disease–policy limit" is the most we will pay for all damages covered by this insurance and arising out of bodily injury by disease, including **endemic disease**, regardless of the number of employees who sustain bodily injury by disease. The limit shown for "bodily injury by disease–each employee" is the most we will pay for all damages because of bodily injury by disease, including **endemic disease**, to any one employee

3. Bodily injury by disease, including **endemic disease**, does not include disease that results directly from a bodily injury by accident.

4. We will not pay any claims for damages after we have paid the applicable limit of our liability under this insurance.

Additional Coverages

Workers'Compensation– Defense

We have the right and the duty to defend at our expense any claim, proceeding or suit against you for benefits payable by this insurance. We have the right to investigate and settle this claim, proceeding or suit.

We have no duty to defend a claim, proceeding or suit that is not covered by this insurance.

Employer'sLiability – Defense Or Indemnification

We have the right and duty to defend, at our expense, any claim, proceeding or suit against you for damages payable by this insurance, except in a **non–admittedjurisdiction**. We have the right to investigate and settle these claims, proceedings and suits.

We have no duty to defend a claim, proceeding or suit that is not covered by this insurance. We have no duty to defend or continue defending after we have paid our applicable Limit of Insurance as stated in the Declarations.

Miscellaneous Coverages

Workers'Compensation/ Employer'sLiability

We will also pay these costs, in addition to other amounts payable under these insurances, as part of any claim, proceeding or suit we defend, or you defend after consultation with us:

International Workers' Compensation Insurance

Form 11–02–0603(Rev. 2–99)   Contract   *Page 5 of 7*

Miscellaneous Coverages

Workers'Compensation/ Employer'sLiability (continued)

1. Reasonable Expenses incurred at our request, but not loss of earnings;

2. Premiums for bonds to release attachments and for appeal bonds in bond amounts up to the amount payable under Workers' Compensation coverage or the Limit of Insurance stated in the Declarations for Employer's Liability coverage;

3. Litigation costs taxed against you;

4. Interest on a judgment as required by law until we offer the amount due under this insurance; and

5. Expenses we incur.

Exclusions

Workers'Compensation

This insurance does not apply to any payments for which you are responsible in excess of the benefits regularly provided by the applicable **Workers' Compensation Law** or **Workers' Compensation Law–Countryof Origin**, including those required because:

1. of your serious and willful misconduct;

2. you knowingly employ an employee in violation of law;

3. you fail to comply with a health or safety law or regulation; or

4. you discharge, coerce or otherwise discriminate against any employee in violation of the applicable **Workers' Compensation Law** or **Workers' Compensation Law–Countryof Origin**.

If we make any payments in excess of the benefits regularly provided by the **Workers' Compensation Law** or **Workers' Compensation Law–Countryof Origin** on your behalf, you will reimburse us promptly.

In addition, this insurance does not apply:

5. to **Local National Employees**

BUT

this exclusion does not apply to repatriation expense for **Local National Employees**.

Employer'sLiability

Under Employer's Liability coverage, we will not cover:

1. Liability assumed under a contract. The exclusion does not apply to a warranty that your work will be done in a workmanlike manner;

2. Punitive or exemplary damages because of bodily injury to an employee employed in violation of law;

3. Bodily injury to an employee employed in violation of law with your actual knowledge or the actual knowledge of any of your executive officers;

4. Any obligation imposed by a workers' compensation, occupational disease, unemployment compensation or disability benefits law or any similar law;

5. Bodily injury intentionally caused or aggravated by you;

International Voluntary Workers' Compensation

Exclusions

Employer's Liability
(continued)

6. Damages arising out of the discharge of, coercion of, or discrimination against any employee in violation of law;

7. bodily injury sustained by any:

   a. master or crew member of any vessel;

   b. employee in the course of any employment subject to the Longshore and Harbor Workers' Compensation Act (33 USCA Sections 901–950); the Defense Base Act (42 USCA Sections 1651–1654); or the War Hazards Compensation Act (42 USCA Sections 1701–1706; Sections 1711–1717);

   c. member of the flying crew of any aircraft.

International Workers' Compensation Insurance

Form 11–02–0603(Rev. 2–99)   Contract

Workers' Compensation Conditions

Contract

Table Of Contents

SPECIMEN

WORKERS' COMPENSATION

CONTRACT

WORKERS' COMPENSATION CONDITONS

International Workers' Compensation Insurance

Form 11–02–0604(Ed. 2–87)   Contract

Page 1 of 8

Workers' Compensation Conditions

Contract

Words and phrases that appear in **bold** print have special meanings and are defined in the definitions section of this contract.

Throughout this contract the words "you" and "your" refer to the Named Insured shown in the Declarations of this policy. The words "we", "us" and "our" refer to the company providing this insurance.

Conditions	**HOW THIS INSURANCE APPLIES**
Workers' Compensation	This Workers' Compensation insurance applies to bodily injury by accident or bodily injury by disease, including **endemic disease**. Bodily injury includes resulting death.

1. Bodily injury by accident must occur during the policy period.

2. Bodily injury by disease must be caused by or aggravated by the conditions of your employment. Bodily injury by **endemic disease**, however, must be caused or aggravated by environmental conditions. The employee's last day of last exposure to the conditions causing or aggravating such bodily injury by disease or bodily injury by **endemic disease** must occur during the policy period.

Employer's Liability

This Employer's Liability insurance applies to bodily injury by accident or bodily injury by disease, including **endemic disease**. Bodily injury includes resulting death.

1. The bodily injury must arise out of and in the course of the injured employee's employment by you or arise out of **endemic disease**.

2. The employment must be necessary or incidental to your work in the policy territory.

3. Bodily injury by accident must occur during the policy period.

4. Bodily injury by disease must be caused or aggravated by the conditions of your employment. Bodily injury by **endemic disease**, however, must be caused or aggravated by environmental conditions. The employee's last day of last exposure to the conditions causing or aggravating bodily injury by disease, or bodily injury by **endemic disease**, must occur during the policy period.

Premium Calculations And Audit

The premium for the operations covered by this insurance is stated in the Premium Statement.

If the premium for this coverage is based upon the number of trips made outside the **United States** and Canada, then you will give us an estimate of the number of trips and, at our option, the length of trips for the upcoming year.

If the premium for this coverage is based on payroll, the entire gross remuneration estimated to be earned by all covered employees shall be disclosed to us. This remuneration includes Cost of Living, Housing Allotments and other such cash benefits as form part of the Overseas Compensation Package of your employees.

You may elect which employees (including partners, if any) of your company fall within the coverage categories of this insurance by allocating the appropriate payroll amounts for premium purposes.

International Workers' Compensation Insurance

Form 11–02–0604(Ed. 2–87)	Contract	*Page 3 of 8*

Conditions

Premium Calculations And Audit
(continued)

The premium shown on this statement is a deposit premium only. You shall maintain records of the information necessary for premium computation and shall send copies to us at such times during or after the policy period as we may direct.

You will let us examine and audit all your records that relate to this insurance. These records include ledgers, journals, registers, vouchers, contracts, tax reports, payroll and disbursement records and programs for storing and disbursing data. We may conduct the audits during regular business hours during the policy period and within three years after the policy period ends. Information developed by audit will be used to develop the final premium.

Loss Provisions

Your Duties If Injury Occurs

Tell us at once if injury occurs that may be covered by this policy. Your duties are listed here:

1. Provide for immediate medical and other services required by the applicable Workers' Compensation Law.

2. Give us or our Agent the names and addresses of the injured persons and of witnesses, and other information we may need.

3. Promptly give us all notices, demands and legal papers related to the injury, claim, proceeding or suit.

4. Cooperate with us and assist us, as we may request, in the investigation, settlement or defense of any claim, proceeding or suit.

5. Do nothing after an injury that would interfere with our right of recovery from others.

6. Do not voluntarily make payments, assume obligations or incur expenses, except at your own cost.

Our Options

1. We can request you, on our behalf, to make payment directly to any person entitled thereto. Upon receipt of proof of payment, we will reimburse you for any such payments.

2. In a **non-admitted jurisdiction** we can ask you to investigate, defend and settle claims, proceedings and suits involving your employees. We will reimburse you for the reasonable cost of such investigation, defense and settlement.

Arbitration

We are entitled to exercise your rights in the choice of arbitrators and the conduct of any arbitration proceeding.

Our Rights To Recover From Others

Under Workers' Compensation coverage, we have your rights and the rights of persons entitled to the benefits of this insurance to recover our payments from anyone liable for the injury.

Under Employer's Liability coverage, we have your rights to recover our payment from anyone liable for an injury covered by this insurance.

In all cases, you will do everything necessary to protect those rights for us and to help us enforce them.

International Workers' Compensation Insurance

Form 11-02-0604(Ed. 2-87)   Contract

Workers' Compensation Insurance

Loss Provisions
(continued)

Actions Against Us

For Employer's Liability coverage, there will be no right of action against us unless:

1. You have complied with all terms and conditions of this policy.

2. The amount you owe has been determined with our consent or by actual trial and final judgment.

This insurance does not give anyone the right to add us as a defendant in an action against you to determine your liability.

Other Insurance

WORKERS' COMPENSATION

This insurance is intended to be primary insurance for your covered employees whose bodily injuries arise out of and in the course of employment by you outside the **United States** and Canada or who contract **endemic disease** while in your employ outside the **United States** and Canada.

If an injured **International Executive Employee** or **Other International Employee** is eligible for Workers' Compensation benefits under the laws of countries other than the **United States** or other than the **Country of Origin** to which the employee would be eligible under this insurance, we will not require that said employee or his dependents file claim under that foreign program as a pre-condition to filing claim under this policy.

If an injured employee or his dependents, as described above, actually file claim and receive benefits under such other Workers' Compensation or Social Security plan, whether private or State-sponsored, then we will not pay more than the difference, if any, between the benefits received or payable under that foreign plan and the benefits payable under the applicable Workers' Compensation Laws of:

1. the **United States**;

2. the **Country of Origin**; or

3. any other country for which you become liable.

We will only pay such difference when the amount of benefit under the foreign plan has been determined and we have satisfactory evidence of such determination.

EMPLOYER'S LIABILITY

If your **admitted** Employer's Liability insurance responds to a claim, proceeding or suit, we will provide excess insurance. If your **admitted** Employer's Liability insurance does not respond to a claim, proceeding or suit for which this insurance grants coverage, we will provide primary insurance.

If you do not have in-force **admitted** Employer's Liability insurance, we will provide primary insurance for a claim, proceeding or suit for which this policy grants coverage.

Loss Provisions

Other Insurance
(continued)

We will not pay more than our share of damages and costs covered by this insurance and other insurance or self–insurance, including self–insurance which results from your failure to comply with **compulsory admitted** Employer's Liability insurance requirements, if any. Subject to any Limits of Insurance that apply, all shares will be equal until the loss is paid. If any insurance or self–insurance is exhausted, the shares of all remaining insurance and self–insurance will be equal until the loss is paid.

Special Loss Provisions

Workers' Compensation

We may request you to pay benefits directly to injured employees or their dependents. We will reimburse you for payments you make on our behalf, and with our approval.

In most cases, we will make payments directly, at your option and on your behalf. We will make voluntary payments only on condition that the employee or dependents receiving such payments execute a full release of all claims against you on account of such injuries or disease as may be required by us and, in addition, execute an assignment to us of any right of action which they may have against any person, firm, corporation or estate, other than you, who is or may be liable for such injury. If we collect by virtue of such assignment an amount in excess of the voluntary payments made or agreed to be made, we will be entitled to, and shall retain from the amount recovered, our expenses incident to such recovery and the amount of payments made or agreed to be made. We will pay any remaining balance of the amount recovered to the person or persons executing such assignments. We will have full power and discretion to proceed against the party at fault or settle with such party upon such terms as may seem desirable to us, either without litigation or during pendency thereof.

Amended Currency Provision–Workers' Compensation

We will pay Workers' Compensation losses to your **Other International Employees** in the same currency in which you pay the premium of this insurance, which means that we will generally pay our losses in the currency of the **United States**.

We will convert the foreign currency benefit level of the applicable **Workers' Compensation Law–Country of Origin** to U.S. dollars at the free rate of exchange published by Citibank, N.A. as of the date of loss, or, for ongoing disability or medical payments as of the date of the respective payment.

We may also pay losses, at our option and upon request of the injured employee or his dependents, in the currency of the **Country of Origin**.

Workers' Compensation Insurance

Definitions

Country Of Origin

means any country (except the **United States**) of which your **Other International Employee** is a citizen.

Endemic Disease

means an infectious disease, including diseases which are borne by air, arthropods (i.e., arachnids, crustaceans, insects), blood, food or water, provided that the disease: 1) is indigenous to a particular region outside the **United States** and Canada; or 2) occurs in epidemic proportion outside the **United States** and Canada.

International Executive Employee

means any partner assigned by you, or employee hired or assigned by you, to work outside the **United States** and Canada, provided that you choose, under this insurance, to offer voluntarily to said partner or employee the Statutory Workers' Compensation benefits of the **Workers' Compensation Law** of any jurisdiction of the **United States**, except those Workers' Compensation benefits governed by Federal Statutes.

Local National Employee

means any partner assigned by you, or employee hired or assigned by you, to work outside the **United States** and Canada, provided that you do not choose, under this insurance, to offer voluntarily to said partner or employee any Workers' Compensation benefits (except repatriation expense). **Local National Employees** are, however, included in your Employer's Liability coverage.

Normal Transportation Costs

means the cost of transporting an employee in good health, and in conformance with your business travel policy, from the country of injury or sickness to a given country of relocation or repatriation.

Other International Employee

means any partner assigned by you, or employee hired or assigned by you, to work outside the **United States** and Canada, provided that you choose, under this insurance, to offer voluntarily to said partner or employee the Statutory Workers' Compensation benefits of the **Workers' Compensation Law–Country of Origin** of the respective partner or employee.

Workers' Compensation Law

means the Workers' Compensation Law and any Occupational Disease Law of any jurisdiction of the **United States** which you voluntarily designate in the Declarations, or those of any jurisdiction of the **United States** for which you become liable.

Workers' Compensation Law does not mean:

1. Federal Workers' Compensation Statutes, the inclusion of which may be arranged by amendment to this insurance;

2. provisions for non–occupational disability benefits;

3. **compulsory admitted** Workers' Compensation insurance.

International Workers' Compensation Insurance

Form 11–02–0604(Ed. 2–87)   Contract   Page 7 of 8

Definitions

Workers'Compensation Law (continued)

Workers' Compensation Law is extended to include 24–hour coverage for: 1) **International Executive Employees** employed by you in the **United States**, while traveling outside the **United States** and Canada; 2) **International Executive Employees** employed by you in a country other than the **United States** and Canada, while traveling outside the country to which they are assigned.

Workers'Compensation Law ˘ Country Of Origin

means the Workers' Compensation Law, Social Security Law and any Occupational Disease Law of any sovereign state other than the **United States**, from which your employee or partner is voluntarily offered, under this insurance, Workers' Compensation benefits based on citizenship.

Workers' Compensation Law–Countryof Origin also means the Workers' Compensation Law and related Laws, as described above, of any sovereign state (except the **United States**) for which you become liable to pay Workers' Compensation benefits on a basis other than the citizenship of your covered employees or partners.

Workers' Compensation Law–Countryof Origin does not mean:

1. provisions for non–occupational disability benefits;

2. **compulsory admitted** Workers' Compensation insurance.

Workers' Compensation Law–Countryof Origin is extended to include 24–hour coverage for: 1) **Other International Employees** employed by you in the **United States**, while traveling outside the **United States** and Canada; 2) **Other International Employees** employed by you, in a country other than the **United States** and Canada, while traveling outside the country to which they are assigned.

CHUBB

International Workers' Compensation Insurance

Declarations

Chubb Group of Insurance Companies
15 Mountain View Road
Warren, NJ 07059

Named Insured and Mailing Address

EXPORT PKG INC.

15 CHUBB WAY
WARREN, NJ
07059

Policy Number   2288-04-64

Effective Date   APRIL 01, 1999

Issued by the stock insurance company
indicated below, herein called the company.

GREAT NORTHERN INSURANCE COMPANY

Producer No.   0051252

Producer   MCSWEENEY & RICCI INSURANCE AGENCY, INC.
               420 WASHINGTON STREET
               BRAINTREE, MA 02184-0000

Incorporated under the laws of
MINNESOTA

SPECIMEN

Policy Period

From: APRIL 1, 1999   To: APRIL 1, 2000
12:01 A.M. standard time at the Named Insured's mailing address shown above.

Insurance applies only to those coverages and employee categories for which a Limit of Insurance/Benefits Limit is shown.

Coverage	Covered Employees		Benefits Applicable
International Voluntary Workers' Compensation	**International Executive Employees**	[X]	STATUTORY, according to the Laws of the State(s) as declared STATE OF HIRE
	Other International Employees	[ ]	STATUTORY - according to the Laws of the COUNTRY OF ORIGIN

International Executive Employees and **Other International Employees** employed by you in the **United States** are covered on a 24-hour basis, while traveling outside the **United States** and Canada. **International Executive Employees** and **Other International Employees** employed by you in a country other than the **United States** and Canada are covered on an employment-only basis, while working in the country to which they are assigned, but on a 24-hour basis while traveling outside the country to which they are assigned.

Repatriation Expense coverage applies to **International Executive Employees**, **Other International Employees**, and **Local National Employees**, subject to a Limit of Insurance of $250,000   each employee and $500,000   policy limit.

International Workers' Compensation Insurance   *continued*

Form 11-02-0988 (Ed. 4-99)   Declarations   Page 1

Coverage	Covered Employees	Limits Of Insurance
Employer's Liability	**International Executive Employees**, **Other International Employees**, and **Local National Employees**	Bodily Injury by Accident each accident. $1,000,000
		Bodily Injury by Disease policy limit. $1,000,000
		Bodily Injury by Disease each employee. $1,000,000

Where This Insurance Applies

This insurance applies to bodily injury by accident or bodily injury by disease arising out of and in the course of employment outside the **United States** and Canada and to bodily injury by accident or bodily injury by disease arising out of and in the course of temporary employment in the **United States** and Canada.

Employers Liability does not apply in the UK or Ireland. This exclusion does not apply to employees while traveling to the UK or Ireland on a temporary basis.

Forms Applicable:

AS PER SCHEDULE OF FORMS ATTACHED

Authorized Representative _Robert Hamburger_

CHUBB

Application   **Political Risk Insurance**

Expropriation - Permanent Investments

Should answers to any of the following questions require more space than provided, attachments providing particulars are welcome, especially in the case where more than one host country is involved.

Insured Information:

Name: _____

Mailing Address: _____

_____

Nationality: _____

Date and place applicant established: _____

Business of applicant: _____

_____

Person Chubb should contact for information concerning this application:

Name: _____   Telephone: _____

Title: _____   Fax: _____

Authorized Representative (e.g. broker):

Name: _____

Company: _____   Address: _____

Telephone: _____   Fax: _____

Foreign Enterprise:

Name: _____

Mailing address: _____
_____

General location and physical address of foreign enterprise: _____
_____

Describe the business of the foreign enterprise: _____
_____
_____

Is this a new or existing enterprise: _____

Year of start-up: _____

Year in which investor became involved in enterprise: _____

Ownership of Foreign Enterprise:

Describe ownership of foreign enterprise and note any equity participation controlled by governments or their agencies:

Equity	Participant	Nationality	Participation %

If enterprise is a joint venture, has the partner ever had a political risk loss? _____
_____

If yes, please explain: _____
_____

What is the expertise that the local partner brings to the table? _____
_____
_____

Describe any existing provisions or plans to divest ownership in foreign enterprise: _____
_____
_____

List all foreign or multilateral institutional lenders to the foreign enterprise:

Lender	Nationality	Type of Loan	Amount

Investment to be Insured:

Exposed investment:

Investor's equity contribution to foreign enterprise   _____

Investor's share of retained earnings   _____

Investor's loans to foreign enterprise
(including accrued but unpaid interest)   _____

Investor's guarantees of obligations
to the foreign enterprise   _____

Payables due investor (average)   _____

Receivables due from investor (average)   _____

Total exposed investment   _____

Desired limit of liability   _____

       (Note: _____ The limit requested in any policy year can be less than but not greater than the exposed limit)

Nature of investment:

Form of investor's equity contribution (cash, equipment, technology, other): _____

_____

Form and terms of investor's debt contribution (notes, letters of credit, maturities, etc.): _____

_____

Names of guaranteed third parties: _____

_____

Has the investor pledged shares in the Foreign Enterprise to a third party? If yes, please explain: ___

_____

_____

Operations of Foreign Enterprise in Host Country

Please answer the following questions concerning the foreign enterprise in the host country. If this is a new enterprise, estimates should be made as to the level of operations after a reasonable start-up period:

Breakdown of foreign enterprise's assets: (This information is used for underwriting purposes and not for determining limits of liability).

Cash/Securities _____

Accounts Receivables _____

Inventories _____

Mobile Equipment and plant _____

Fixed Plant and machinery _____

Buildings _____

Land _____

Other Assets _____

Total Assets _____

What accounting basis is used in determining value of assets: (e.g. book, replacement, or repair): _____

Basis of depreciation of assets: _____

Foreign exchange impact of foreign enterprise: _____

If this is a new enterprise, estimates should be made as to the initial level of operations after start-up.

Total exports as a percentage of annual revenues _____ %

Exports to investor as a percentage of annual revenues _____ %

Total imports as a percentage of annual revenues _____ %

Imports from investor as a percentage annual revenues _____ %

What countries does foreign enterprise export to?: _____

_____

How dependent is foreign enterprise on technology inputs from investor?: _____

_____

Labor and management of foreign enterprise:

Does the investor control the management of the foreign enterprise? _____

Number of local nationals in managerial positions? _____

Number of local national employees? _____

Number of foreign employees and nationality? _____

Is work force unionized? _____

Foreign Enterprise/Host Government Agreements:

Have all documents necessary for legal operation in host country been obtained and are they currently valid? _____

Have any special agreements been negotiated between the investor and the host country beyond those normally afforded foreign investors under the investment code of the host country (e.g. tax holidays, monopoly agreements, subsidies, special tariff or quota concessions, etc.)? Please explain. _____
_____
_____
_____

Describe any effects on the host country by the foreign enterprise that you consider noteworthy (e.g. impact on local suppliers, local employment, creation of downstream economic activity, training programs, development of social services, etc.). _____
_____
_____
_____

Does investor have operations in the host country other than the subject of this application? Please describe. _____
_____
_____
_____

Does the Investor have any knowledge of any facts which might give rise to a claim under the policy? It is agreed that if such knowledge or information exists, any claim arising therefrom is excluded from the policy. _____
_____
_____
_____

Has the Applicant, its partner, joint venture, affiliates or subsidiaries ever suffered a loss as a result of acts of a foreign government? Please explain. _____
_____
_____
_____

Has the applicant ever carried expropriation insurance? If yes, please provide details below: _____
_____
_____
_____

Has any carrier declined or canceled similar coverage? If yes, please provide details below: _____
_____
_____
_____

Is the applicant aware of any legislation, pending legislation, discussions, disputes, negotiations or litigations with the host government regarding pollution or other environmental impact relations to the foreign enterprise? _____

_____

_____

_____

Physical Property Damage: Please indicate the type of construction, any unusual exposures, and fire protection features of all buildings or properties to be insured._____

_____

_____

_____

Does the project have an independent power source? _____

_____

Is the property insurance for the foreign enterprise is written by Chubb, and if not, does the property insurance include coverage for strikes, riots, civil commotion, malicious mischief, sabotage, and terrorism and is it written on an 'all risk' or named-peril basis? _____

_____

_____

Describe security at foreign enterprise:

     Is there a guard force? _____ How many?_____
     Is the security force paramilitary or private? _____
     Are there intrusion detection and CCTV systems? _____
     Is there a perimeter fence? _____ Is it lighted? _____
     Is there an access control system (i.e., card access, sign-in, etc.)?_____

     Other   _____

            _____

Are there any strategic, political, economic or military installations, locations, or operations near the foreign enterprise? _____

_____

Have there been any prior threats, by any party whatsoever, against the foreign enterprise or its employees? _____

_____

Please provide a short description of the physical characteristics of the foreign enterprise and the surrounding areas. _____

_____

_____

_____

Please attach the applicant's most recent Annual Report and that of the foreign enterprise. Other material relating to the application or foreign enterprise you may wish to provide is welcome. The undersigned authorized officer of the applicant declares that to the best of his/her knowledge the statements set forth in this application are true and no material information has been withheld. The undersigned agrees that the existence of any policy that may be issued will not be disclosed to the host government. All information in this application will be treated confidentially by the company. Signing of this application does not bind the undersigned to complete the insurance, but it is agreed that this application shall be the basis of insurance should a policy be issued and will be attached to form a part of the policy.

Signed: _____

Title: _____

Corporation: _____

Date: _____

LOSS CONTROL TECHNIQUES

THE IMPORTANCE OF LOSS CONTROL

The future of a new business owner ruined. Two loved dogs dead. An untold loss of property. All could have been prevented with the application of loss control. Sure, there was insurance to pay off the creditors but does risk financing ever truly indemnify the owners? Losses like this one are not a risk that business owners intend to take when they open their doors.

WHAT IS IT?

Loss control is an intentional act aimed at decreasing the probability of losses, the severity of losses, or both. Entrepreneurs engage in ventures in order to capitalize on speculative risks; they are not rewarded for failing to manage pure risks. Thus it is essential for risk managers to be aware of and use loss control techniques to help their firms achieve the intended goals. These loss control techniques contribute to the firm's value by decreasing the likelihood of losing money, by protecting physical and intangible assets, and by protecting the people who have a stake in the firm's success.

Large organizations may incorporate loss control staff members within the risk management department. Others may outsource loss control responsibilities to an independent contractor or avail themselves of loss control services from their insurance company. Regardless of who staffs the loss control function, the organization must ultimately decide whether to implement recommended projects or not. Often it is the business decision of whether or not to implement a recommended loss control project that poses the greatest friction between risk management personnel and the rest of the organization.

In order to better understand how loss control can enhance company value, the sage risk manager will learn from the experiences of other risk managers. The history of formal loss control is rather brief. It wasn't until the industrial revolution, and the accompanying concentration of human and physical assets, that managers were made aware of the need for loss control. An appalling increase in the rate of worker injuries and deaths made it clear that some accident prevention and mitigation control was needed. During the last half of the nineteenth century, employer liabilities and a gradual shifting of the legal responsibility for selling products and using the environment further accentuated the need for loss control.

OVERVIEW

As the demand for loss control increased, risk managers examined several loss control theories to help them understand how to efficiently manage their risks. Using the latest theory, the authors suggest a loss control program for contemporary risk managers. Next we discuss the advantages and disadvantages of a loss control program, loss control regulation, and where to start to search for more loss control information. We conclude by answering some typical loss control questions.

As stated by a Philadelphia law firm on its Web site,

Ford Motor Company no longer produces a car that explodes and bursts into a ball of flames when struck from behind. Work places have fewer guard-less punch presses and other machines capable of maiming and disfiguring. Life-threatening birth control and other medical devices have been removed from the market and the industry exercises more caution before introducing new devices. Asbestos is no longer used as an insulator, infants' toys are safer and, in general, manufacturers are simply producing safer products. What has motivated manufacturers? Perhaps the greatest incentive has been products liability lawsuits (Monheit, Silverman, & Fodera, Attorneys at Law, 2002).

Risk managers protect their firms with product liability insurance. But the educated risk manager also uses loss control to decrease the likelihood and severity of losses.

LOSS CONTROL THEORIES

Why should you examine some of the more popular loss control theories? By understanding the theories, you will be more efficient in implementing your loss control program. Unless you have unlimited time and money to experiment with your own loss control models, studying these models may lead to valuable insight into helping others in your firm be safer and more productive, and, ultimately, to the creation of more value.

The Domino Theory

One of the earliest theories advanced to explain industrial losses occurred during the industrial revolution. In the mid-1920s H. W. Heinrich proposed the *domino theory* of accident causation. An industrial engineer with the Travelers Insurance Company, Heinrich suggested that a sequence of five events (or conditions) results in injuries. The first domino is a fault in society, culture, or the environment. This fault causes the domino to topple over onto the second domino, a fault in the individual. This fault topples the third domino, an unsafe act of the person (or an exposure to an unsafe condition). This unsafe action topples the fourth domino, an accident. The accident causes the fifth domino to fall—which represents the injury (Heinrich, Petersen, & Roos, 1980). Heinrich further suggested the most efficient loss control activities should be focused on the third domino—the unsafe act or mechanical condition. While this early theory is not universally accepted, it still appeals to common sense and has proven to be quite robust in application. Unfortunately, the global economic conditions of the 1930s shifted management's attention away from safety and necessarily toward production.

General Methods of Control

The military response to losses during the 1940s was a structured loss control program. The focus of this theory is to modify the unsafe physical environment and establish a disciplined method for performing hazardous tasks. It was felt that a carefully controlled process would be a significant contribution to loss control. Procedures were carefully reviewed and documented; formal plans were written for every process—from cleaning rifles to assembling airplanes. Following the war, a surge in consumer demand once again shifted management's focus from safety to production.

Engineering Approach

The huge demand for goods following World War II caused industrialists to produce goods in record quantities. The rush for production, combined with the accelerating discoveries in science and technology, also caused a dramatic increase in the size of factories and machinery, and the consumption of energy. The accompanying damage from the increased output resulted in a large increase in industrial accidents. In the 1960s industrial engineers proposed that a major cause of accidents was the uncontrolled release of energy. An example of the engineering approach was proposed by Dr. William Haddon Jr., an expert in highway safety and public health. Haddon's Release of Energy theory presents ten steps for preventing or reducing the harm caused by the uncontrolled release of energy. The engineering approach to loss control emphasizes creating safe working environments. For example, tools, machinery, and processes are engineered to be safe. The engineering movement culminated in the early 1970s with the creation of the Occupational Safety and Health Administration (OSHA).

Technique of Operations Review

First proposed by D.A. Weaver and enhanced and promoted by Dan Petersen in the 1980s, the technique of operations review theory suggests that management is the key to safety. Because management controls the work environment and labor activities, the theory proposes that management must be held responsible for workplace safety. By shifting the emphasis to management responsibility, the true cost of safety is also shifted from labor to management. With this theory safety became a management priority.

System Safety Approach

During the 1990s the four previous theories—the Domino Theory, the General Methods of Control, the Engineering Approach, and the Technique of Operations Review—were combined into one model—the *system safety approach*. This theory suggests that all four previous theories contain valid points. It combines the Domino theory's concept of controlling the unsafe acts of workers, the General Methods of Control theory's concept of creating a safe operating method, and the ideas of the Engineering Approach in creating safe workplaces, machinery, and equipment with the Technique of Operations Review's theory of management responsibility. Thus, the system safety approach incorporates all these loss control program components.

Behavior Modification

By the end of the century, the labor force was shrinking and consumers began demanding quality goods. The demographics of the country once again shifted management's attention to safety and quality control. A loss control theory that is currently popular is that safety and quality control can be achieved through behavior modification. Applying psychology to labor and management is key to achieving the desired loss control goals. The Behavior Modification Theory suggests that providing management and labor with incentives will motivate them to perform at the intended levels of efficiency.

This latest loss control theory is wonderfully similar to Heinrich's original theory. It also brings to mind the words of philosopher George Santayana, "Those who do not remember the past are condemned to repeat it." Hopefully risk managers will learn from their predecessors.

DEVELOPING A CONTEMPORARY LOSS CONTROL SYSTEM

A Management Approach

The modern risk manager is a business manager. She is aware of, and able to implement, the latest management approach to loss control. Like the system safety approach, the contemporary management approach is a systems approach. Its five-step process, outlined below, focuses on achieving the organization's goals. In addition, it promotes the coordination of activities among all the organization's departments. With all team players working together, the organization avoids the *silo effect* and the *agency problem*.

The silo effect is where risk managers focus only on one particular problem area to the exclusion of all else. In other words, they don't see the forest for the trees. The agency problem is the economic concept in which the risk manager's goals may not be in harmony with the owner's goals. The manager is the agent, but the manager is not acting in the best interests of the owner, who is the principal.

When the risk manager creates a loss control system that is integrated with the entity's other departments, loss control is promoted throughout the entire organization.

THE FIVE-STEP PROCESS

The five steps to developing a contemporary loss control system are part of the larger risk management process:

- program development,

- risk analysis,

- loss control solution analysis,

- loss control decision process, and

- system administration.

Within this process the loss control manager contributes in many ways.

Step One: Program Development

The first step in developing the loss control management system is to create a holistic risk management program. Planning and creating goals, organizing the risk management department, and writing a risk management business plan achieves this.

1. **Planning loss control activities.** The first part of step one is to establish the loss control goals. These goals include setting both preloss and postloss goals. For a retail grocer, an example of a preloss goal might be to decrease the number of customer falls in the produce aisle from two a month to zero. It is important that managers focus on goal-setting at this juncture so they understand why they are in the job.

   The grocer will also set postloss goals at this time. In the event a customer does fall, the store may have an economic goal to decrease the amount of money for each claim. For example, a postloss goal for this merchant might be to decrease the average cost of claims for customer falls from $2,500 per occurrence to $250 per occurrence.

   In setting these goals and the activities to reach them, the risk manager must understand what level of probability and severity of losses are acceptable to the owners and relevant stakeholders. In addition, the risk manager must integrate the loss control goals with all other organizational goals. The most effective way to achieve these two activities is to consult and continually interact with other managers. Direct and constant communication with others creates loss control goals that are compatible with the objectives of all affected stakeholders.

2. **Organizing loss control activities.** Next, the risk manager must create an organizational structure to facilitate achieving the organization's risk goals. First, lines of authority and responsibility must be defined. Empowering labor and management with loss control authority and responsibility reflects the wisdom of the System Safety Approach and Technique of Operations Review loss control theories. For certain organizations, the risk manager may outsource some or all loss control activities. The decision to outsource will depend upon the availability of internal resources to implement the activities and the comparative cost of the use of internal versus external re-

sources. Many competent loss control consulting firms are available to assist the risk manager.

3. **Writing a loss control plan.** Standard Operating Procedure (SOP) manuals have long been a part of effective management. Risk managers should include loss control activities in the SOP manual. This written reference contributes to the stability and consistent application of accepted loss control techniques. As suggested in the General Methods of Control theory, safety is optimized if management and workers understand the procedures to follow in performing their duties. Once the loss control SOP is written it must be shared with the relevant stakeholders, who might include middle management and employees. People who are affected by loss control procedures need to be aware of the methods to prevent and mitigate losses and should be encouraged to provide suggestions as to how. Share the information by providing copies to workers, holding brief meetings, and posting notices in appropriate locations.

Step Two: Risk Analysis

A risk manager has scarce resources of people, money, and time. Therefore, it is important to understand which loss control techniques are appropriate for particular risks. To efficiently allocate these scarce resources the risk manager must have performed a complete analysis of the organization's risks, which is discussed in Chapters 3 and 4. This analysis includes the identification, measurement, and evaluation of the risks. Given this foundation, the risk manager is prepared to move on to analyzing the set of loss control solutions.

Step Three: Loss Control Solution Analysis

The myriad of common loss control solutions is described in the Chapter 25, Loss Control Tools. These solutions represent some, but not all, of the opportunities available to the risk manager to control losses. The risk manager should be aware that new loss control techniques are being developed simultaneously with advances in technology.

1. **Identify Loss Control solutions.** Risk managers must make themselves aware of the many loss control tools at their disposal. Some of the

common tools are described in Chapter 25. The common methods for identifying these tools include:

a. Checklists—lists of common solutions available to risk managers,

b. References and texts—discuss many different loss control solutions,

c. Flow charts—such as the risk management solution tree,

d. Asking inside experts—such as managers and workers, and

e. Asking outside experts—such as loss control engineers, risk management consultants, suppliers, trade associations, competition, and coopetition.

2. **Measuring Loss Control Solutions—Quantitative Analysis.** Once the risk manager has identified potential loss control solutions the next procedure is to measure the costs and benefits of each proposed solution. The solution's impact on the organization is measured both quantitatively and qualitatively. In this section, we consider the quantitative impacts.

a. *Effects on loss frequency.* The first measure to consider is the impact of the loss control solution on the loss event's likelihood of occurring—sometimes referred to as the probability of a loss occurring. We use the symbol 'p(L)' (read: 'probability of loss') to designate this measure. The risk manager may be able to obtain data on the probability of certain losses occurring from a loss control service provider or from an insurer. Otherwise, the risk manager must either accumulate his own data or use professional judgment to estimate the new probabilities. Loss control projects that decrease the probability of loss are regarded as prevention projects.

b. *Effects on the value of loss.* This second measure is referred to as the loss severity, and is denoted by '$(L)' (read: 'severity of loss'). The risk manager forecasts the loss control project's impact on the value of

each possible solution. Loss control projects that decrease the severity of loss are regarded as reduction projects.

c. *Effects on expected value of loss – 'E(L)'.* A key result of implementing a loss control solution is the change in the average value of loss. The risk manager will often adopt loss control projects that decrease the mean loss value. The expected value is the sum of the product of each probability of loss and severity of loss. This measure of central tendency provides the risk manager one factor to consider in the decision process.

$$E(L) = \sum p(L_i) \times \$(L_i) \qquad \text{Eqn. LC-1}$$

d. *Effects on risk.* Another critical measure for the risk manager is the measure of dispersion about the mean loss value. An effective loss control project should also decrease the variability of the possible outcomes about the mean value. Typical measures of dispersion are the range and the standard deviation (we use the symbol 'S_L').

$$S_L = \{\sum [E(L)-\$(L_i)]^2 \times p(L_i)\}^{\frac{1}{2}} \quad \text{Eqn. LC-2}$$

The smaller the average difference from the new mean loss value, the more predictable is the loss. Better information helps the risk manager make better decisions.

e. *Relative effects of risk.* In order to compare one loss control project to another, or to itself over a time period, or to projects with different probability distributions, the risk manager needs a comparative quantitative measurement. The most common ratio used is the coefficient of variation (CV). The CV is the ratio of the dispersion to the mean. The risk manager may adopt a loss control projects that decrease the relative risk of a project.

$$CV = S_L \div E(L) \qquad \text{Eqn. LC-3}$$

f. *Financial analysis.* A final quantitative analysis performed by risk managers is to evaluate the Net Present Value (NPV) of a proposed loss control project. This common financial tool assumes the future cash flows and discount rates are reasonably well known so we can predict an expected NPV. This is a serious problem for loss control projects. As research has demonstrated, the consequential losses are often not well defined for loss control projects. As Frank Bird emphasized in his *Iceberg* theory, underestimating the consequential losses can have catastrophic financial results on the firm. Modern variants of this model employ computer simulation analysis to present outcome probability distributions and incorporate the risky future cash flows.

$$NPV = E\, PVCF_t \qquad\qquad \text{Eqn. LC-4}$$

3. **Measuring Loss Control Solutions—Qualitative Analysis.**

    a. *Strategic fit.* The quantitative analysis of a loss control project provides the risk manager with necessary but not sufficient information to make a decision. For example, loss control projects that have small positive NPVs may require a transgression of a strategic goal. This means that some loss control projects may violate some of the goals set at the beginning of the year. For example, a loss control safety project may decrease production to a level where the firm cannot grow at its planned rate. In such cases the loss

Figure 10.1

The following very simple data is provided to show how a risk manager might measure the effects of a loss control project. ABC Corporation's risk manager adopted a loss control project that was a risk prevention and reduction solution (both the probabilities and severities are expected to decrease.) The project was an employee training program to teach employees how to decrease the chance that they would get seriously injured. The program also trained them how to respond if one of their coworkers were injured in order to decrease the severity of the injury.

Data prior to loss control project initiated:

Probabilities of employee injury		Severity (Value) of employee injury	
P(Severe injury)	= .001	$ 100,000	
P(Moderate injury)	= .003	$ 20,000	
P(minor injury)	= .01	$ 5,000	
P(no injury)	= .986	$ 0	
Sum of probabilities	= 1.000		

Data after loss control project initiated:

Probabilities of employee injury		Severity (Value) of employee injury	
P(Severe injury)	= .0008	$ 80,000	
P(Moderate injury)	= .002	$ 15,000	
P(minor injury)	= .02	$ 4,000	
P(no injury)	= .9772	$ 0	
Sum of probabilities	= 1.0000		

Using loss control equation 1 (Eqn. LC-1), we calculate the expected value of loss before and after the adoption of the loss control project.

Expected loss prior to loss control project:

$$
\begin{aligned}
E(L) \; &= \sum p(L_i) \times \$(L_i) \\
&= (.001 \times \$100{,}000) + (.003 \times \$20{,}000) + (.01 \times \$5{,}000) + (.986 \times \$0) \\
&= \$100 \qquad\qquad + \$60 \qquad\qquad + \$50 \qquad\qquad + \$0 \\
&= \$210
\end{aligned}
$$

The risk manager expects a loss of $210 each year because of this operation.

Expected loss after adopting the loss control project:

$$E(L) = \sum p(L_i)\_\$(L_i)$$

$$= (.0008 - \$80,000) + (.0020 - \$15,000) + (.02 - \$4,000 + (.9772 - \$0)$$

$$= \$64 \qquad\qquad + \$30 \qquad\qquad + \$80 \qquad\qquad + \$0$$

$$= \$174$$

The risk manager expects a loss of only $174 each year after the loss control project is adopted. Now the risk manager uses loss control equation LC-2 to determine the standard deviation (S_L) from the expected outcomes.

Standard deviation before the loss control project:

$$S_L = \{\sum [E(L)-\$(L_i)]^2 \times p(L_i)\}^{\frac{1}{2}}$$

$$= \{([210-100,000]^2 \times.001) +([210-20,000]^2 \times.003) +([210-5,000]^2 \times.01) +([210-0]^2 \times.986)\}^{\frac{1}{2}}$$

$$= \{([-99,790]^2\_.001) +([-19,790]^2 \times.003) + ([-4,790]^2 \times.01) + ([210]^2 \times.986)\}^{\frac{1}{2}}$$

$$= \{(9,958,044,100 \times.001) + (391,644,100 \times.003) + (22,944,100 \times.01) + (44,100 \times.986)\}^{\frac{1}{2}}$$

$$= \{9,958,044 + 1,174,932 + 229,441 + 43,483\}^{\frac{1}{2}}$$

$$= \{11,405,900\}^{\frac{1}{2}}$$

$$= 3,377$$

This means the risk manager expects a loss of $210, and the usual difference from this loss amount is $3,377. Of course the smallest loss is never less than $0, so the usual range of losses is from $0 to $3,587 (3,377+210).

Standard deviation after the loss control project:

$$S_L = \{\sum [E(L)-\$(L_i)]^2 \times p(L_i)\}^{\frac{1}{2}}$$

$$= \{([174-80,000]^2 \times.0008) +([174-15,000]^2 \times.002) +([174-4,000]^2 \times.02) +([174-0]^2 \times.9772)\}^{\frac{1}{2}}$$

$$= \{([-79,826]^2 \times.0008) +([-14,826]^2 \times.002) + ([-3,826]^2 \times.02) + ([174]^2 \times.9772)\}^{\frac{1}{2}}$$

$$= \{(6,372,190,276 \times.0008) + (219,810,276 \times.002) + (14,638,276 \times.02) + (30,276 \times.9772)\}^{\frac{1}{2}}$$

$$= \{5,097,752 + 439,621 + 292,766 + 29,586\}^{\frac{1}{2}}$$

$$= \{5,859,724\}^{\frac{1}{2}}$$

$$= 2,421$$

This means the risk manager now expects a loss of only $174, and the usual difference from this loss amount is decreased to $2,421. The new usual range is from $0 to $2,595 (2,421+174).

Next, the risk manager uses equation LC-3 to determine the coefficient of variation (CV).

Coefficient of Variation before the loss control project:

$$CV = S_L \div E(L)$$

$$= \$3,377 \div \$210$$

$$= 16.08$$

This large number (16.08) means the usual difference, relative to the expected amount, is quite large; the conditions are very risky.

Coefficient of Variation before the loss control project:

$$CV = S_L \div E(L)$$

$$= \$2,421 \div \$174$$

$$= 13.91$$

The smaller result (13.91) means the loss control project has made the situation less risky! Relative to the new expected loss amount (174), there is proportionally less difference in outcomes. Of course the absolute differences are significantly less, so this may be a good loss control project.

Next, the risk manager performs a financial net present value (NPV) analysis of the proposed loss control project. Let's assume the following additional information. The training program will cost $800 today. The benefits of the loss control project will last two years. The firm purchases insurance to pay for employee injuries, and the insurer charges a premium equal to the expected value of loss plus one standard deviation. Before the loss control project the insurance premium was $ 3,587 ($210 + 3,377); after the loss control project the premium is $2,595 ($174+2,421). All cash flows occur at the end of the year. The firm pays 34 percent taxes. The cost of capital for equally risky projects is 6 percent. Now we complete a change in cash flow (DCF) table for each year.

Change in Cash Flow, at time 0
Cost of the project = $800

Change in Cash Flow, at end of each period
Δ Revenues	$ 0
Δ Expenses	
Δ Cost of Goods Sold	$ 0
Δ Selling & Admin.	$ 0
Δ Overhead	
Δ Insurance	-$ 992 (3,587-2,595)
Δ EBIT	$ 992
Δ Taxes	337
Δ Net Income	$ 655
Δ Cash flow for each period:	$ 655

Present Value of $655 from period one = $618 (655 ÷ 1.06)
Present Value of $655 from period two = $583 (655 ÷ [1.06]^2)

Net present Value of loss control project = $ 401 (-800 + 618 + 583)

This means the loss control project adds value to the firm when measured in today's dollars. Next the risk manager must perform a qualitative analysis of the proposed loss control project.

control project should be rejected. In other cases, a loss control project may have a small negative NPV but reinforce the organization's long-term strategy. In both situations the risk manager should ask if the loss control project fits with other goals, strategies, and objectives. If the new project does not violate any of the existing organizational goals, it is a good contender for adoption.

b. *Cultural fit.* Equally important for the risk manager is to consider how employees will respond to proposed loss control projects. Some financially favorable projects may have devastating effects on employee morale. The employees may reject the project entirely. For example, if management pressures workers for increased production then workers may reject safety equipment that impedes their work speed.

c. *Fit with other relevant stakeholders.* The risk manager should also consider how a loss control project will affect other stakeholders. For example, suppliers of capital may look favorably on loss control projects that protect assets financed by that capital. Government regulators may go easier on firms that have a history of adopting loss control projects that go beyond the minimum legal requirement. Finally, customers may prefer to buy from firms that have reacted positively to previous liability problems.

Step Four: Loss Control Decision Process

Once the risk manager has thoroughly analyzed the set of potential loss control projects, the next step is to choose among and implement them. Like any other risk management process, deciding among projects and allocating the firm's scarce resources is challenging. And loss control project decision-making holds some special challenges.

1. **Decision models.** Corporate risk managers have several models to use in making decisions, but perhaps the most common is a financial model. Typically the risk manager works closely with the financial manager to determine the impact of any risk management project on the firm's value. Each project can be evaluated using the Net Present Value (NPV) model. Equation 4 shows that the financial value added to the firm is the sum of the present value of future differential cash flows. The challenge for risk managers is to determine the appropriate cash flows and the appropriate discount rate. Estimating the decrease in future losses is highly subjective and the values are impossible to prove. Moreover, the time horizon of loss control projects is rather indeterminable. Finally, the proper discount rate for financial analysis is usually equal to projects with similar risk[1]. But determining the riskiness of a loss control project is equally as subjective. As a result, the financial analysis model, while necessary, should be used with discretion.

   Other decision models are also credible for evaluating loss control projects. Many risk managers rely upon their professional judgment to guide them. Others also use benchmarking to compare their organization to what others are doing. Benchmarks may be available from industry associations, insurers, or by observing the competition. An often-recommended model for loss control decisions is an ethical model. Some organizations adopt loss control projects because "it's the right thing to do." Most risk managers are careful to comply with legally mandated loss control projects (e.g., complying with OSHA), but it is difficult to decide how much further to go to do the right thing. It is likely that loss control projects, like other financial investments, may exhibit decreasing or negative marginal returns. That is why the decision of where to stop investing in safety must be made using a combination of financial, ethical, benchmarking, and professional judgment models.

2. **Support.** Once the risk manager decides to implement a loss control project, the next challenge is to garner support from relevant stakeholders. Of particular importance is buy-in from senior management. Without their support the project stands little chance of success. The risk manager next solicits support from middle managers and then from laborers. This top-down approach is suggested for firms that have abundant sources of labor. Another technique is the bottom-up approach. Here, the manager obtains the support from the rank-and-file before moving up the organizational ladder. This technique is suggested for firms with highly skilled laborers or in situations where the labor market is very tight.

   How does a risk manager gain support? First, the financial analysis must be done. The NPV usually should be positive. Moreover, the project should coincide with the firm's ethical guidelines. If the project is very compelling the risk manager is ready to present the proposal to various stakeholders. Start by asking for advice. For example, say, "Here's a project that looks pretty good to me. Will you look it over and tell me what you think?" Unless there are compelling reasons to reject the project, the stakeholders will probably recommend it. At this point, they have bought into the idea, adopted it as their own, and become a champion for the project. An old adage is to "get it in writing." This is valid advice for the risk manager who may have to revisit the project at some future date. This written evidence is proof that the project was synchronized with the organization's goals. Often it is sufficient to get stakeholders to simply initial the proposal so others can see whose idea it is.

3. **Implementation.** Given adequate support, the risk manager is ready to allocate the firm's scarce resources of people, money, and time. Allocating risk management budgets is always a challenge and loss control budgets are no exception. The risk manager may have to resell the project to affected stakeholders if inadequate support was generated.

Step Five: Loss Control System Administration

A loss control project requires the same administration as other risk management projects.

1. **Monitor.** First the risk manager must make provisions in the risk management information sys-

tem (RMIS) for loss control data. The initial loss data should be saved so a comparison can be made to post-project data. Proving the value of a loss control project is difficult without this reference point. For example, in the case of customer injuries in a retail grocer's produce section, historical information should be compiled for the number and value of the losses for the previous several years. After a nonskid floor is installed, customer fall injuries again are tracked. Changes in the frequency and/or severity of customer injuries are used to gauge the impact of the loss control initiative of installing nonskid flooring.

2. **Judgment.** When is a loss control program a success? The absence of losses suggests the risk manager has done a good job. Such a *results-based measure* is not always possible, however. Sometimes events beyond the risk manager's control (such as hurricanes or terrorism) may render the loss control project ineffective or overpower its benefits. In these cases the judgment of the risk manager's success should be an *activity-based measure*. That is, the risk manager should also be evaluated on the activities initiated, not just the results

3. **Communicate.** Finally, the risk manager must share the loss control project's success with relevant stakeholders. If the project is truly successful, then the organization may have no losses and people may wonder why the organization needs a risk manager in such a hazardless environment. One method of sharing the loss control activity is to distribute interim loss control reports. Timely reminders about the benefits of loss control projects reinforce understanding. Another method to communicate is to create reward systems, which reward employees for a reduction in employee injuries. These include awards programs, premiums, and compensation schemes. Some argue that these controversial programs improve safety; others suggest they only mask or cover up losses because employees will not jeopardize an award by reporting a legitimate loss. But they definitely communicate the risk manager's intent to control losses.

A final method to communicate the success of the loss control program is to include a section in the Risk Management Annual Statement to Senior Management. This document should highlight both the benefits and the costs of the loss control program.

Advantages

Why should an organization develop a loss control program? As outlined in the beginning of this chapter, loss control is an intentional act aimed at decreasing the probability of losses, the severity of losses, or both. The primary reason to implement a loss control program is to assist the organization in achieving some or all of the following goals:

1. **Decrease worry.** One key reason for loss control is to decrease the worry that results from operating under hazardous conditions. Worrying consumes valuable time and attention that could be better used in achieving the organization's goals. If workers are not occupied with worry, then they can focus on their jobs and productivity.

2. **Improved efficiency.** A related benefit of loss control programs is a more efficient allocation of the firm's scarce resources. If there are fewer and less severe losses, then fewer people and less time are needed to complete tasks.

3. **Decreased loss costs.** Another benefit of loss control programs is a reduction in the total cost of risk. Although the program requires a capital investment, the decrease in loss costs is usually greater than the cost. Given an appropriate time horizon, the NPV of loss control projects is frequently positive. A successful loss control program will decrease both the variance and the expected value of losses.

4. **Improved planning.** Loss control programs facilitate better goal setting and planning because they produce better information. Specifically, many loss control projects decrease the standard deviation from the expected value of losses. Thus the confidence intervals are tighter and the firm will be better able to set realistic goals.

5. **Improve likeliness of achieving goals.** Given the above advantages, the organization is more likely to achieve its intended results.

   a. **Corporate returns.** A common goal of for-profit corporations is to create the desired level of risk at the desired time to achieve a desired return. Risk managers who create an effective loss control program facilitate achieving this goal by creating the desired level of risk by controlling the probability and/or severity.

b. **Earnings stability**. Mature corporations' stockholders often seek a stable flow of dividends. Risk managers help to stabilize this cash flow by using loss control projects to reduce outflow of cash to finance unwanted risk.

c. **Market share**. Loss control programs are closely related to quality control programs. These improve customer satisfaction and brand loyalty. The risk manager assists in achieving the goal of market share by improving product quality and service.

d. **Service efficiency**. The risk manager also promotes service by creating a safe work environment that is conducive to efficient operations.

e. **Dividend growth**. Investors in small cap stocks expect dividends to grow by a factor commensurate with the risk of the stock. By decreasing the firm's losses the risk manager assures that capital is used for speculative growth projects.

f. **Social responsibility**. All firms set goals that include some level of ethical duty. Many loss control programs are designed to protect the worker or the environment. Thus the organization's social responsibility is enhanced through this subset of risk management. Preventing a loss of life is almost always superior to making provisions to fund a loss.

Disadvantages

1. **Competing for scarce resources.** All organizations have scarce resources of people, money, and time. Allocating these resources is a primary managerial function. The risk manager faces these same budgetary constraints in developing and implementing a loss control program. First, the risk manager must compete for the organization's people. To sell a loss control project the risk manager must get management and labor to participate in the program's creation and implementation. However, these same people are busy (and often rushed) to complete their immediate tasks. Second, loss control projects require money. All other departments are competing for the same assets. Finally, every worker has only so much time to achieve her production requirements. As loss control programs do not directly produce goods or services, managers will sometimes give priority to other speculative programs.

2. **The *invisible improvement* problem.** The effects of loss control projects are similar to those achieved by fine portrait photographer retouchers. If the artist does a really good job of retouching the wrinkles and blemishes, then the viewer will never see the brush strokes or artwork. They may not appreciate the hard work that went into improving the quality of the work. The risk manager faces the same dilemma. If losses are prevented or their severity reduced, then management may wonder why a loss control program is needed. They may not appreciate the hard work required to achieve such success.

3. **The *profit center* problem.** Sometimes departments are evaluated based on their contribution to the firm's profits. Because risk managers primarily focus on pure risk management, then the optimum outcome is zero losses but never a profit. Another related argument suggests that investors purchase stock because of the organization's risk-return characteristics. If a risk manager decreases the firm's risk, then the firm's returns are concurrently diminished.

4. **The *geek* problem.** Financial speculation is perceived as a sexy and exciting career. In contrast, loss control engineers are perceived as wearing pocket protectors, carrying slide rules, and having white tape on the bridges of their glasses. Senior managers may hesitate to reward geeks even if they complete a stellar performance in saving lives and protecting assets.

5. **Creating new risks.** Every loss control project adopted may decrease certain risks but simultaneously create new risks. For example, when developing safe machine operating procedures the risk manager may create a new hazard of misusing the equipment. If an OSHA inspector is invited to examine facilities, the examination may uncover new potential liabilities.

6. **Public relations issues.** Finally, adopting loss control projects may send signals to society that the firm seeks only a certain level of social responsibility. Regulators may become more aware of the operation and pay closer attention to the firm's activities. Consumers may consider the loss control program inadequate or misguided. Investors may think the company is too conservative and might not provide the desired level of risk and return.

Loss Control Regulation

Loss control and safety are highly regulated functions. It is beyond the scope of this chapter to list all possible laws and rules. For example, the Occupational Safety & Health Administration was created in 1971 under the federal Occupational Safety and Health Act. OSHA guidelines alone take up volumes. In addition, Section 18 of the OSH Act encourages individual states to develop and operate their own safety and health programs. Other federal, state, and local agencies are charged with enforcing laws and regulations dealing with building safety, environmental protection, transportation, and other organizational risks.

A brief listing of federal, state, and international organizations is provided at the end of this chapter. Some major regulatory bodies and brief descriptions of their responsibilities are provided as an introduction to this complex subject. An appendix lists some of the other regulatory bodies of interest to risk managers.

WHERE CAN I FOUND OUT MORE ABOUT IT?

There is a plethora of materials available in the growing field of loss control. Some of the most common references are provided in this chapter's references and source citations. The interested researcher can quickly find a rich body of information by checking the citations and reference lists in each source. The sources include publications, Web sites, government agencies, academic sources, consultants, and trade associations.

QUESTIONS AND ANSWERS

Question—How do I convince the CEO that our firm should spend our resources on loss control?

Answer—CEOs focus on the big picture; they are trying to achieve a desired risk profile for the firm. The risk

manager helps the CEO sculpt the desired risk by decreasing the adverse risks. Thus the risk manager allows the firm to concentrate its resources on speculative opportunities. Investing in people and spending money and time on loss control helps the CEO achieve the intended return to shareholders. Use of one of the quantitative analysis tools discussed previously, along with a qualitative analysis of proposed projects, may go a long way in convincing the CEO of their importance to the organization's value.

Question—I'm afraid that if I let an inspector in he'll discover more than we're prepared to handle. What should we tell the inspector?

Answer—Inspectors are trying to help the firm create a safer work environment and protect the firm's human resources. Many organizations claim their people are their greatest assets. Allowing inspectors in helps the firm protect its people and prevents even costlier losses and litigation.

In addition, your company may be eligible to participate in OSHA's free consultation service, which is designed to help employers uncover potential employee safety and health hazards and improve their occupational safety and health management systems without risk of being cited or penalized by OSHA. Smaller businesses may request this free consultation service, which seeks to identify and correct potential workplace hazards. OSHA also offers other programs that encourage voluntary safety improvement instead of forced, penalty-driven improvement.

Question—If I don't have to exceed regulations (such as OSHA), then why should I?

Answer—Regulations are dynamic; they have a way of changing—usually becoming more and more protective. By exceeding existing regulations the risk manager is taking a proactive stance on loss control. This sends a signal to regulators, inspectors, employees, and consumers that the firm is serious about safety. The results of a proactive position include fewer and less severe lawsuits, fewer workers compensation claims, and fewer or less severe property losses.

In addition, the total costs of claims are never fully recovered, even when an organization is able to recover from an insurance policy. The only way to truly remain whole is to prevent claims from happening. Decreasing the probability of a claim to a desired level is a realistic goal.

Figure 10.2

Standard Operating Procedures
ABC Corporation
(Excerpts Relating to Loss Control)

Purpose: This Loss Control SOP manual provides direction for risk managers to efficiently and effectively control losses at ABC Corporation. By consistently applying these procedures the risk manager is assured of efficiently using ABC's scarce resources. Moreover, experience verifies these procedures are the most effective method we know of to help ABC achieve its goals.

Loss Control Process: ABC applies the same five-step management process to all its activities, including loss control. These five steps are 1) creating a loss control program, 2) analyzing risks subject to losses, 3) analyzing solutions to these potential losses, 4) applying a logical decision processes, and 5) administrating the loss control system.

1. **Creating a loss control program.** ABC's board of directors, acting on instructions from our owners, has adopted the following loss control philosophies.

   a. *Preloss objectives*: ABC is a growing corporation. Its owners are willing to sacrifice small short-term losses to achieve long-term capital gains. Our loss prevention projects should focus on decreasing the probability of catastrophic events.

   b. *Postloss objectives*: To sustain the long-term growth objective ABC's owners are willing to bear up to a three month down-time period. This period may be required to rebuild our facilities after a major loss. However, we believe any period greater than three months will erode consumer confidence and will result in an unacceptable loss of market share. Therefore, we encourage developing loss control projects that get ABC back into production within three months.

   c. *Loss Control Organization*: Loss control activities are organized under the Risk Management department. The Chief Risk Officer is responsible for recruiting such personnel as are required to achieve the loss control objectives. The CRO reports directly to the CEO.

   d. *Risk Control Policy Statement*: A part of the risk management policy statement is ABC's loss control philosophy. This written document is approved by the board of directors and represents the owner's attitudes toward loss control.

2. **Analyzing risks subject to losses**: The SOP manual includes the usual risk management procedures for identifying, analyzing, and evaluating risks

3. **Analyzing solutions to these potential losses**: ABC Corporation adopts the common sense philosophy that "an ounce of prevention is worth a pound of cure." To engage this philosophy we authorize the risk manager and loss control team to use resources to decrease the probability and the severity of catastrophic events. Because ABC is located in an active earthquake area we encourage projects that mitigate the impact of earthquakes on long-term operations.

4. **Applying a logical decision process**

   a. *Decision Modeling*: ABC recognizes that many risk control projects require a long time to yield benefits. This is consistent with our strategy of achieving long-term growth for our owners. Therefore single period financial analyses must be tempered with long-term financial horizons and with qualitative variables. In addition, as an industry leader ABC does not rely on what our competition is doing to guide our management decisions. Moreover, we intend to be the industry leader when it comes to setting the standard in ethical behavior. Finally, we are endowed with a gifted and experienced management team. We encourage the risk manager to consult our experts regarding loss control projects.

---

b. *Support*: The board of directors and senior management are committed to employee safety, the preservation of our capital assets, and maintaining proactive community relations. We use multiple techniques to communicate our support with the goal of creating understanding by all our workers.

c. *Implementation:* To implement our loss control projects we are willing to commit our scarce resources of people, money, and time. Every other department will allocate a portion of their budgets to loss control so we can achieve our long term goals.

5. **Administrating the loss control system:**

a. The Risk Management Information System includes files for monitoring our loss control projects. These files are integrated with other risk management project files and system wide MIS data.

b. ABC's risk management projects are evaluated using a five-year, long-term horizon. They are regarded as successful if they help ABC achieve its strategies.

c. A part of the annual risk management statement includes a brief description of our loss control activities.

END NOTES

[1] standard deviation is a usual proxy for risk in financial analysis.

Chapter 10

GLOSSARY

Behavior Modification. A loss control theory that applies psychology to labor and management to achieve loss control goals.

Coopetition. The idea of a business cooperating with its competition.

Domino Theory. A loss control theory of accident causation that states that a sequence of five events or conditions result in injuries.

Energy-release Theory. A loss control theory that presents ten steps for preventing or reducing the harm caused by the uncontrolled release of energy.

General Methods of Control Theory. A loss control theory that aims to modify the unsafe physical environment and establish a disciplined method for performing hazardous tasks.

Loss control. An intentional act aimed at decreasing the probability of losses, the severity of losses, or both.

Net present value (NPV). A process to determine the net present value of an investment by discounting back the inflows over the life of the investment to determine whether they equal or exceed the required return.

Occupational Safety and Health Administration (OSHA). A federal agency created under the federal Occupational Safety and Health Act. Charged with occupational safety and health regulation.

Pure risk. The risk of loss; risks that traditionally have been insurable.

Silo effect. Segregation of responsibilities within an organization so there is little cross-department cooperation.

Speculative risk. The risk of either loss or gain, such as the risks that are associated with investing in the stock market.

System Safety Approach. A loss control theory that combines the domino, general methods of control, engineering, and technique of operations review theories of loss control.

Technique of Operations Review. A loss control theory that suggests that management controls safety.

Appendix

REFERENCES

Publications:

Dickson, G.C.A. 1995. *Corporate Risk Management.* London: Witherby & Co. Ltd.

Graves, Chris. 2002. Chris Graves is at cgraves@startribune.com .

Harrington, Scott E. and Gregory R. Niehaus. 1999. *Risk Management and Insurance.* Boston, MA: Irwin McGraw-Hill.

Head, George L., editor. 1995. *Essentials of Risk Control, Volumes I and II.* Malvern, PA: Insurance Institute of America.

Heinrich, H. W. 1931. *Industrial Accident Prevention, A Scientific Approach.* New York, NY: McGraw-Hill Book Company.

Heinrich, H.W., Dan Petersen, & Nestor Roos. 1980. *Industrial Accident Prevention, A Safety Management Approach.* Fifth edition. New York, NY: McGraw-Hill Book Company.

Krieger, Gary R. and John F. Montgomery, editors. 1997. *Accident Prevention Manual for Business and Industry, Administration & Programs,* 11th Edition. Itasca, IL: National Safety Council.

Monheit, Silverman & Fodera 2002. http://www.civilrights.com/prod.html. 215-561-2100; 1-800-220-LAW1. Eleven Penn Center, 1835 Market Street, Suite 1101, Philadelphia, PA 19103.

National Safety Council. 1997. *Accident Prevention Manual for Business and Industry: Administration & Programs,* 11th Edition. Itasca, IL: National Safety Council.

Vaughan, Emmett J. 1997. *Risk Management.* New York, NY: John Wiley & Sons, Inc.

Williams, C. Arthur Jr., Michael L. Smith, and Peter C. Young. 1995. *Risk Management and Insurance.* Eighth Edition. Boston, MA: Irwin/McGraw Hill.

Web sites

Type "loss control" into your search engine and you'll come up with many hits. Here are some to get you started:

http://www.hsbplc.com/. HSP Professional Loss Control Services. A commercial loss control service.

http://www.doa.state.wi.us/dsas/risk/slc.asp. State of Wisconsin Department of Administration. Contains many useful links.

http://www.iirsm.org/. The International Institute of Risk and Safety Management.

http://www.natlsco.com/property/liability/. NATLSCO Liability Consultants. A liability services program started in 1989 in response to growing concerns about product liability loss exposures.

Governmental Agencies

http://risk.das.state.or.us/index.htm. State of Oregon risk management site. Good references for other government links.

http://www.dehs.umn.edu/outsidelinks/ State of Minnesota Environmental and Health Safety site. Contains many good reference links.

http://www.osha.gov. Source of U.S. Department of Labor Occupational Safety & Health Administration resources.

Academic sources

http://www.dcp.ufl.edu/. University of Florida, College of Design, Construction, and Planning. A long history of excellence in loss control and safety.

http://www.uww.edu/muadmin.html University of Wisconsin-Whitewater. The Department of Occupational and Environmental Safety & Health (OES&H) in the UW-Whitewater College of Education prepares students for jobs that study employee behavior and the work environment to improve safety, health, and productivity.

http://www.aicpcu.org/ AICPCU/IIA Web site. The ARM and ARM-P designations greatly enhance your understanding of the risk management process, from analysis to implementation and monitoring. Both programs provide fundamental concepts. The information you learn is practical, and you will be able to apply it immediately to your daily risk management responsibilities.

http://www.stjohns.edu/ The School of Risk Management, St. John's University, 101 Murray Street, New York, NY 10007. Offers undergraduate courses in risk management & loss control.

Consultants

ABS Consulting, Inc. Government Institutes. 4 Research Place, Suite 200, Rockville MD 20850, Environmental, Safety, ISO 9000 & ISO 14001 consulting and information. An excellent source for Code of Federal Regulations (CFRs).

Many insurance companies and brokers have loss consulting services. For example:

http://www.nnng.com/entities/nnib/areas/irc/lc Near North Insurance Brokerage.

http://www.aontruckgroup.com/Products.htm Aon Transportation.

Trade associations

http://rims.org/ Risk & Insurance Management Society, Inc. A great start for your loss control research.

EMERGENCY RESPONSE PLANNING

WHAT IS IT?

Emergency response is the collective action taken at a site to stabilize an incident that has the potential to injure people, damage property, interrupt business operations, and contaminate the environment. Emergency response planning is the development and implementation of policies, procedures, and organized team(s) designed to prevent further damage by stabilizing the situation. Common examples include organizing and training individuals to administer first aid or CPR to injured employees; to use portable fire extinguishers on an incipient fire; and to evacuate building occupants that might be in danger.

The first and foremost goal of emergency response planning is to safeguard the health and safety of people, including members of the emergency response organization. Protection of property, business operations, and the environment are always secondary objectives. Prompt, effective response in the initial minutes often determines the ultimate impact of an emergency. CPR administered immediately after a heart attack has proven to save lives. On the other hand, waiting for paramedics to reach an upper floor of a high-rise building at rush hour could significantly delay treatment.

All facilities should have an emergency response plan. Small facilities with few occupants, limited hazards, and strong public emergency services require only a limited plan. However, larger facilities with many people at risk, vulnerability to many threats or perils, inadequate protection of hazards, and/or limited public emergency services require a strong capability and detailed plans. Successful stabilization of an emergency not only protects people, physical assets, business operations, and the environment—it also protects profits, market share, and the reputation of the firm, regardless of size.

STEPS TO IMPLEMENT

Development of an emergency response plan should follow a systematic process customized to the individual site and facility. Threats differ as well as the vulnerability and protection of people, buildings, equipment, and business operations. The availability and capabilities of public emergency services can vary widely requiring enhanced planning where local services could be delayed or may be inadequate.

Development and implementation of an emergency response plan involves the following nine steps:

1. Write a management policy statement

2. Organize a planning committee

3. Identify perils or threats; assess the vulnerability of people, property, business operations, and the environment; and quantify the potential severity

4. Assess the availability and capabilities of public emergency services, company personnel, and equipment resources

5. Decide the level of response capability based upon local needs and regulatory requirements

6. Organize the emergency response team(s) to take protective action

7. Write the plan

8. Train personnel

9. Exercise the plan

Step One: Management Policy

A policy statement signed by senior management is the foundation of an emergency response plan. The policy statement should define the scope and purpose of the plan; the basic roles and responsibilities of everyone; and the necessary support for the plan. Senior management must provide sustained commitment, direction, and support if planning efforts are to be successful over time. This includes financial support for training, equipment, and supplies. Managers should participate actively in the planning process, drills, and exercises; and they must hold personnel accountable for completing assigned tasks.

Step Two: Planning Committee

Organize an emergency planning committee to develop the plan. The committee can be very large for facilities with many departments, employees, operations, and hazards, or it can be very small. A small core group can actively develop the plan with ad hoc participation from departments or experts as needed.

Participation should include representatives from important departments including:

- executive management

- operations

- facilities or engineering

- environmental, health, & safety (EH&S)

- security

- risk management

- human resources

- finance

- public relations

- government or regulatory affairs

- legal

Assign members of the planning committee responsibility for completing the risk assessment, assessing available resources, determining the functions and organizing the emergency response team, and then developing and implementing plans.

Contact public emergency services including law enforcement, fire, emergency medical services, and environmental authorities to solicit their input and to review and or approve portions of the plan. For example, the public fire department should review evacuation plans; the types, locations, and use of any hazardous materials; and responses to fires. Firefighters must be aware of the number of people in a building, occupancy hazards, fire protection systems, and access points for their fire apparatus. If not, the strategy and tactics employed by firefighters could conflict with site plans or, at the very least, result in confusion and delayed or ineffective response. Figure 11.1 lists plan components and the public agencies that may have statutory responsibility to approve plans or who may provide input.

Step Three: Risk Assessment

Risk assessment is a process to identify and quantify the potential impact of threats, hazards, or perils that could injure people, damage property, interrupt business operations, or contaminate the environment. In most cases, the consequences will also be financial; however, there are many other possible consequences. A serious event can hurt an organization's reputation

Figure 11.1

Plan Components & Public Agency Review		
Agency		Plan Component to Be Reviewed
Fire Department	Local or county fire department	Evacuation, fire, hazardous materials spill or release, technical rescue, bomb threats and suspicious packages
Police or Law Enforcement	Local, county, and state police FBI	Bomb threats, suspicious packages, labor strife, civil disturbance, special events
Emergency Medical Services	Ambulance and/or paramedics; service may be provided by fire department, public or private service	Medical emergencies, hazardous materials spills or releases
Environmental Protection	Local Emergency Planning Committee (LEPC), State Emergency Response Commission (SERC), U. S. Coast Guard, U. S. Environmental Protection Agency	Hazardous materials spill or release, Risk Management Prevention Plan (RMPP), Spill Prevention Control and Countermeasures Plan (SPCC)
Emergency Management	Local or county emergency management agency	Hurricane, tornado, flood, earthquake, and other regional disasters

and incur the attention of regulators who can impose fines or penalties—if they can determine regulatory noncompliance.

Indirect costs are often hidden, but they can also be significant. Depending upon the type and magnitude of the incident, indirect costs may include lost productivity, costs to recruit and train replacement employees, insurance deductibles, third-party liability, and lost customers. Many small businesses that suffer major losses never recover.

There are many possible examples of threats, hazards, or perils such as:

- accidents involving employee or third party injury

- fire

- explosion

- hazardous materials spill or release

- natural hazards (flooding, hurricane/windstorm, earthquake, tornado, subsidence, landslide, and winter storms)

- utility outages (electricity, natural gas, steam, water, sewer, HVAC, LAN/WAN connectivity, and telecommunications, etc.)

- water leakage

- security incidents (workplace violence, strike, civil disorder, sabotage, and vandalism)

- terrorism (nuclear, chemical, or biological weapons)

The risk assessment should address both the relative probability (frequency) of an incident occurring as well as the potential consequences (severity) of the incident. Classify probability as low, medium, or high. The potential impact of each threat, hazard, or peril must be determined by systematically assessing the potential severity of each threat and the vulner-

Figure 11.2

Example Risk Assessment Matrix											
Threat, Hazard, or Peril / At Risk	Hurricane or Windstorm	Earthquake	Tornado	Flood	Fire	Explosion	Utility Outage	Machinery Breakdown	Hazardous Materials Spill or Release	Workplace Violence	Robbery	Terrorism
Probability (Annual Frequency)	M	L	None	M	L	L	M	M	M	L	L	L
People (on & off-site)	L	H		L	H	H	L	L	M	H	L	H
Buildings	H	H		L	H	H	L	L	L	L	L	M
Equipment	H	H		M	H	H	M	M	L	L	L	M
Raw materials/finished goods	H	H		M	H	H	L	L	L	L	H	M
Operations	H	H		M	H	H	M	M	L	L	L	M
Environment (air, water, land)	L	M		L	M	M	M	M	H	L	L	M
Market share	H	H		M	H	H	L	L	L	L	L	M
Reputation	L	L		L	L	L	L	L	H	M	L	L

ability of people, property, business operations, and the environment.

For many threats or perils, there are many possible scenarios. For example, small fires are common in some industrial plants and quickly extinguished by automatic suppression systems. Large fires are relatively infrequent but can occur if protection systems fail or are inadequately designed. Properties located along the Gulf of Mexico or Atlantic Coast are subject to hurricanes. Catastrophic, Category 5 storms only hit the United States mainland three times in the twentieth century; however, tropical storms and Category 1 hurricanes are relatively frequent. The risk assessment process must address probable and improbable scenarios. Assess the potential impact on people (employees, visitors, guests, and third parties such as people in the surrounding community), buildings, equipment, raw materials, finished goods, continuity of business operations, the environment (air, water and land), as well as market share and the reputation of the organization. Figure 11.2 is an example matrix that illustrates one company's evaluation of potential threats and their impact.

Address high frequency events, such as medical emergencies, in the emergency response plan. You can ignore low frequency/low severity incidents—unless regulatory requirements dictate otherwise. For instance, if a building is located along the Gulf of Mexico, then plans must address hurricane preparedness. Conversely, facilities located in the heartland of America can ignore hurricanes. Figure 11.3 summarizes both the frequency of possible threats as well as the severity. Address all threats located in the shaded areas in the plan.

Risk assessment also identifies opportunities for hazard mitigation. Mitigation of hazards to reduce the frequency of occurrences or the severity of consequences should be considered whenever cost-effective.

Example Risk Assessment Matrix

The frequency and severity of the scenarios depicted in Figure 11.3 can vary greatly from one site to another. In addition, for each peril the severity of consequences increases as the probability of occurrence decreases. Use the maximum foreseeable event (i.e., event with the greatest potential impact on people, property, business operations, and the environment) for planning purposes.

Figure 11.3

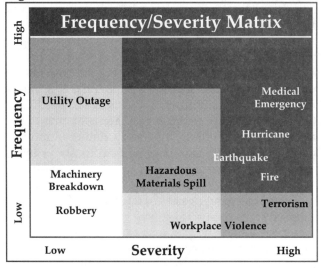

Step Four: Assess Available Resources

An emergency response plan requires trained personnel to utilize systems and equipment to stabilize an incident. Therefore, planning must identify available resources and assess their capabilities. Resources may include:

- public emergency services (e.g., fire, hazardous materials, police/law enforcement, and emergency medical services)

- other public agencies (e.g., public works)

- contractors and vendors

- in-house staff

- systems (e.g., fire detection, alarm, communication, and fire suppression systems; ventilation systems; emergency power supplies; and hazardous materials containment or pollution control systems)

- equipment and supplies (e.g., first aid equipment and hazardous materials clean-up supplies)

Examples of Primary and Secondary Responsibilities

Identify all resources that may be needed to respond to the types of threats identified in the risk assessment process. First, address those with primary responsibility for incident stabilization and those who play supporting roles. The public fire department may be called to suppress a fire, but corporate facilities and engineering staff typically supervise internal fire-protection systems under the direction of the fire department incident commander, and security would supervise evacuation. Conversely, police and fire authorities may play only a supporting role for a bomb threat lacking credible evidence (they would play a primary role if a suspect device is found, however). Identify contractors that provide or service critical machinery and equipment so they can be called upon quickly as well.

Some emergencies are handled in-house with only internal resources. A water leak may be controlled by facilities or engineering personnel and cleaned up by janitorial staff. However, many emergencies require a coordinated response involving both internal personnel as well as public emergency services. A major fire would require the response of the public fire department supported by any in-house emergency organization.

Many different resources may be utilized at an emergency. Personnel—both internal and external— are critical, but successful stabilization of an incident also requires systems and equipment. A leak of a hazardous chemical would require in-house staff to notify occupants in the affected area to evacuate, shut down process systems, and use ventilation systems to control the spread of hazardous vapors. A public hazardous materials response team or an outside contractor may be called—depending upon the size of the spill, hazards of the chemical involved, and threat to people and the environment. Personal protective equipment may be worn, and containment equipment such as absorbent and waste containers may be utilized by qualified personnel to clean up the spill.

Assess the availability of personnel, public agencies, or contractors that may be needed. This includes twenty-four hour, seven-day coverage for incidents that can occur at anytime (e.g., fire and hazardous materials spill or release) or coverage during operating hours only (e.g., medical emergencies). Assess response time because a service that is unavailable (or significantly delayed) when needed may be useless. How quickly would fire apparatus or an ambulance arrive on-site? Would the response time be slower during commuter rush hours, during a severe storm, or after a catastrophic regional disaster such as an earthquake, hurricane, flood, or major terrorist incident? Do they have enough equipment and personnel to meet peak demands?

Capability Assessment

The capability assessment addresses the ability of people, systems, and equipment to perform effectively during an emergency. The capability of people is a measure of their education and training and their ability to utilize systems and equipment to stabilize the situation. This applies to in-house personnel as well as the public emergency services or contractors that are called to assist. All responders must be familiar with buildings, occupants, systems, equipment, and the hazards of the situation that they may face. They must be able to assess the situation and determine the most effective strategy and tactics to stabilize the situation without jeopardizing anyone's safety. In-house personnel generally have the most in-depth knowledge of the facility, but often they are the least trained or the least experienced to handle emergencies. Conversely, public emergency services are well trained to respond to emergencies, but they may have limited or no knowledge of a building and its hazards. Are public emergency service agencies staffed with full-time, part-time, or volunteer personnel? Part-time or volunteer personnel may not be as well trained as full-time personnel, and they may not be immediately available.

Fire suppression systems such as sprinkler systems, if properly designed, installed, and maintained, can suppress or at least control most fires. Inadequately designed, installed, or maintained systems may fail to control a fire. If protection is inadequate and the potential consequences of an incident are significant, then enhanced planning may be warranted.

Assess other systems such as fire detection, alarm, notification, and communication systems; emergency power systems; and HVAC systems to determine how they detect a threat, could be used to warn building occupants, or stabilize an incident. For example, an HVAC system may be used to exhaust chemical fumes from a building and stabilize an incident. The adequacy of means of egress (e.g., number and arrangement of exits) also factors into the planning for different threats. If there is inadequate means of egress or the building is large or tall with many occupants, then evacuation could be very challenging. Plans must carefully address when to call for evacuation or sheltering in place, who will make the decision, and how to accomplish it.

Step Five: Determine the Level of Response

The level of response and the type of emergency organization depends upon multiple site-specific factors. The emergency planning committee must evaluate each factor when determining whether to organize a team to address identified threats or perils.

- **Frequency and severity of threats or hazards.** As outlined in the previous section, plan for threats or perils with moderate or higher frequency and those that occur relatively infrequently but have high potential severity. However, low frequency, moderate severity incidents should not be ignored completely.

- **Capabilities and response time of public emergency services.** A potentially limited or delayed response from public emergency services suggests the need for an enhanced on-site capability. "Limited" includes agencies that are unfamiliar with the nature of operations on-site, which could result in delayed or ineffective response. Facilities with hazardous materials and operations or facilities with many buildings and diverse operations present many challenges for unprepared responders.

- **Number and capabilities of employees who could serve on the emergency response team.** A small pool of personnel limits the functions of the emergency organization, especially when minimum staffing is dictated by regulatory requirements or national standards. Likewise, a full complement of responders may not be available to provide twenty-four hour coverage.

- **Senior management commitment and availability of resources to equip and train members of the emergency organization.** Training is one of the keys to an effective emergency organization. An emergency organization may include multiple teams, such as fire fighting, HAZMAT, and rescue teams. Management must provide time, money, and resources for personnel to be trained initially and periodically thereafter. Financial support to procure equipment and supplies must also be assured not only initially, but also for inspections, testing, or replacement over time.

- **Regulatory requirements.** There are many regulatory requirements that mandate emergency response planning. Other regulations or national standards address the scope of activities—if an organization chooses to engage in potentially hazardous emergency operations.

- **Insurance company recommendations.** Many property underwriters—particularly those that underwrite to highly protected risk (HPR) standards—require emergency planning as well.

Numerous OSHA standards require emergency planning. They include 1910.157, Portable Fire Extinguishers; 1910.119, Process Safety Management for Highly Hazardous Chemicals; 1910.120, Hazardous Waste Operations and Emergency Response; and others that address specific chemical hazards or high-hazard facilities. 29 CFR 1910.38, Employee Emergency Plans and Fire Prevention Plans, is the standard invoked by the three OSHA standards. It requires an employer to provide a means to notify occupants of an emergency, and it requires implementation of evacuation procedures and development of a fire prevention plan.

There are additional OSHA standards that apply to specific emergency procedures. Employers who choose to provide first aid or medical treatment for employees must comply with 1910.1030 (*Bloodborne Pathogens)*; those who engage in firefighting operations may have to comply with 1910.155, (*Fire Protection*), 1910.156 (*Fire Brigades*), and 1910.157-163 (*Fire Suppression Equipment*); those who engage in hazardous materials activities (as defined in the standard) must comply with 1910.120 (*Hazardous Waste Operations and Emergency Response*); and employees who engage in rescue of trapped occupants in confined spaces must comply with 1910.146 (*Confined Space Entry.*) Typically, OSHA standards dictate the selection and training for personnel; equipment requirements; and the scope of procedures, drills, or exercises.

Besides the OSHA standards that mandate emergency planning or specify requirements, there are dozens of standards and recommended practices[1] promulgated by the National Fire Protection Association (NFPA). OSHA and other regulatory agencies often adopt NFPA standards. Review them to determine minimum requirements prior to deciding whether to engage in firefighting, hazardous materials spill response, or technical rescue.

If regulatory requirements are met, management can then decide the functions and the level of response (e.g., no firefighting versus organized fire brigade) of the emergency organization.

Step Six: Organize the Emergency Response Team

The emergency response organization should include the minimum number of people necessary to carry out the minimum protective actions required by regulations. At the very least, the emergency organization should be capable of prompt evacuation of all buildings. Figure 11.4 identifies possible protective actions for many threats, hazards, or perils. Medical treatment for sick and injured people is not shown but should be addressed in the plan.

Since it may not be practical to train all members of the emergency organization for all types of incidents, organize individual teams for types of threats or specific functions. For example, organize a hazardous materials team with employees familiar with chemical hazards; organize security to handle site security, evacuation, strikes, civil disturbances, and workplace violence incidents. Assign a plant doctor and/or nurse to provide first aid. Facilities and engineering staff can address property conservation, using janitorial or housekeeping staff for non-hazardous cleanup. An effective incident

command system and command structure is essential to ensure proper coordination of all teams responding to a major incident.

Organize an emergency response team or teams with defined responsibilities and lines of authority. Accurate flow of information, clear communication of orders or instructions from leaders, and effective decision-making by a knowledgeable incident commander are critical. The leader of the emergency organization acts as the incident commander and must be known to all employees and responding public emergency services. Determine the leader's authority to take protective actions based upon the threat posed by the emergency—prior to an incident. Be sure to appoint incident commanders and team leaders to cover all operating shifts.

Executive management, facility management, and administrative functions such as finance, public affairs, and legal have important roles in support of the emergency plan. It is critical to provide them with periodic status reports, including a summary of action taken to stabilize an incident.

Figure 11.4

Protective Actions of the Emergency Organization

Threat, Hazard, or Peril	People (Employees, Visitors, Guests, Contractors)	Physical Assets (Buildings, Equipment, Stock)	Business Operations	Environment (Air, Water, Land)
Hurricane or Windstorm	Evacuation or Shelter-in-Place	Property Conservation Damage Assessment	Property Conservation Business Continuity	Containment & Clean Up (if necessary)
Earthquake	Evacuation First Aid			
Tornado	Shelter-in-Place First Aid			
Flood	Evacuation			
Fire	Evacuation First Aid	Firefighting		
Explosion				
Utility Outage	Evacuation or Shelter-in-Place	Property Conservation	Repair, Restoration and/ or Business Continuity	
Machinery Breakdown		Property Conservation		
Hazardous Materials Spill or Release	Evacuation (if Required) First Aid (if required)	Containment & Clean Up		
Workplace Violence		N/A		
Robbery				
Terrorism	Evacuation or Shelter-in-Place	Dependent upon the incident	Repair, Restoration and/ or Business Continuity	Containment & Clean Up (if necessary)

Write an organizational statement that defines the functions of the emergency organization and its command structure. For example, OSHA 1910.156, *Fire Brigades*, and NFPA 600, *Industrial Fire Brigades*, require a formal organizational statement, if a fire brigade is established. For each protective action or team, describe the required number of personnel, required equipment, minimum training, and the shifts when the organization will respond. Management should approve the organizational statement after ensuring it complies with the company's policy statement. This informs management of the support required for the team, and it outlines the boundaries for duties performed by members of the team.

The emergency organization depicted in Figure 11.5 is an integrated organization with multiple functions (e.g.,

evacuation, security, and firefighting) under the command of a single incident commander. Each of the eight functional areas could be expanded into dedicated teams (e.g., evacuation team or fire brigade as shown in Figure 11.5). In fact, many large industrial plants have industrial fire brigades, hazardous materials response teams, and technical rescue teams with full-time staff and equipment commensurate with public fire departments. Small businesses may develop a much simpler structure.

Incident Commander

The incident commander is the most critical member of the team and must be physically and mentally capable of handling the stress of an emergency operation.

Figure 11.5

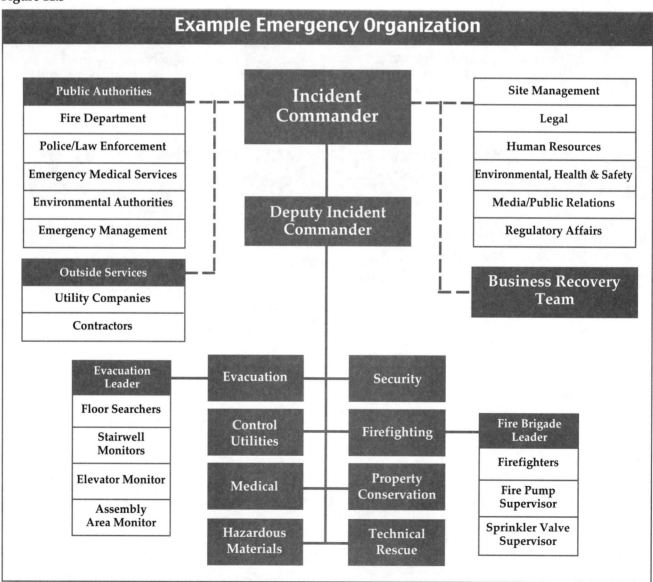

184

The commander must be very familiar with the facility's construction, occupancy hazards, fire suppression systems, and utility systems as well as the content of the emergency response plan and the personnel and agencies that will respond. Duties of the emergency coordinator include:

- developing emergency procedures in conjunction with the emergency planning committee,

- directing all emergency activities, including evacuation of personnel,

- coordinating pre-incident planning with outside agencies,

- ensuring that outside emergency services are called when necessary, and

- directing the shutdown of operations when necessary.

Emergency Response Team Members

All personnel assigned to fire brigades or hazardous materials response teams must be physically capable of performing their duties as required by OSHA standards; medical evaluations may be required. Train members who respond to medical emergencies in first aid, CPR, and universal precautions to prevent exposure to HIV, HBV, and other bloodborne pathogens. Electricians, plumbers, and other trades people from engineering, maintenance, or facilities departments can be assigned responsibility for operating mechanical and utility systems. Assign security to direct public emergency services and agencies to the scene of the emergency, prevent unauthorized access to the site, and evacuate building occupants. Janitorial staff is typically assigned to salvage and clean up operations.

Incident Command System

Coordination of internal resources and outside agencies during an emergency requires an incident management system. The Incident Command System (ICS) is the model tool for command, control, and coordination of individual groups or agencies as they work toward the common goal of stabilizing the incident. ICS identifies the persons in charge of each group or agency and responsible for each function.

ICS is very important at large facilities where it is necessary to coordinate the activities of multiple teams (e.g. fire, hazmat, and medical). Facilities with only a single team need only coordinate incident command with responding public agencies. The ICS should address:

- person in charge (organization, name, and title)

- chain of command

- advisory roles (technical recommendations) and veto powers, if any

- command post and emergency operations center activation and operation

- common terminology (organizational functions, resources and facilities)

- resource management

Step Seven: Write the Plan

The written plan is a compilation of all planning activities but must not become a document that is unusable or impossible to maintain. Keep in mind that the plan is a reference, and it must be easy to use. Today many plans are maintained electronically to enhance accessibility from multiple sites or from virtual command posts that exist on wide area networks. Electronic documentation also is easier to update. However, plan documentation must be available to everyone who will use the document during an emergency, and computer networks may be inaccessible or inoperable at that time. Therefore, maintain a hard copy of all documentation at the primary and secondary emergency operations centers.

Many companies create wallet cards or abbreviated versions of their emergency response plans for distribution to members of the emergency organization as well as to all employees. These documents provide basic information about emergency procedures, including evacuation, and the action each employee should take.

Write the emergency response plan as succinctly as possible, and clearly organize information for easy retrieval. Place supporting information in the appendix.

Figure 11.6 depicts the table of contents of an example plan.

Introduction

The introduction is a brief but important section of the document. It should include the policy and organizational statements that define the emergency organization and scope of emergency response. Define and provide examples of the types of incidents that warrant declaration of an emergency. In most cases, emergencies are very apparent, but some are not. An over-pressurized vessel can explode, releasing hazardous materials. Small chemical spills can spread toxic vapors or contaminate wastewater systems. Defining in advance what constitutes an emergency results in less confusion when an incident occurs.

Emergency Organization

Provide a detailed description of the emergency organization, including names, titles, command structure, and responsibilities. List the public agencies, contractors, and others that may respond to the facility, and define how activities will be coordinated.

The safety and health of all members of a company's emergency organization is a top objective. Prescribe the types, locations, and use of personal protective equipment (where required by specific procedures); procedures to account for all members; and other safety precautions. OSHA and NFPA standards specify requirements and provide other guidance.

Emergency Operations Center (EOC)

Establish primary and secondary emergency operations centers where leaders of the emergency organization and others can assemble to direct response operations. Two centers are needed in case one is uninhabitable due to the emergency. One can be located on-site. The second should be located far enough away to ensure it is not subject to the same incident—a location ten miles away or more may be appropriate if a regional disaster is possible.

The EOC should be located in a part of the building that is least vulnerable. Interior locations that are away from any windows and constructed with substantial walls are best. Size and equip the EOC to support extended operations lasting many days. Equip each EOC with communications equipment (telephones, fax, email, computer with Internet and network access, two-way radio, AM/FM radio, and television), supplies (paper, pens, pencils, flip charts,

markers, computer printer, and copier), and copies of the emergency response plan.

Communications

Effective communication is critical during emergencies. This includes notification to both public and in-house emergency services that an emergency exists; communication of emergency instructions to occupants of a building that may be endangered; communication among members of the emergency organization; and communication with responding public agencies, company management, employees, customers, and the news media.

First, define the preferred method for reporting fires and other emergencies (e.g., telephone call to an emergency number or manual fire alarm pull station). Then specify the means and methods to notify building occupants to take protective actions. Fire alarm systems, voice communication systems, and other means may be used depending upon the facility.

The communication needs of the emergency organization include twenty-four-hour means to notify members to respond as well as two-way communications during the emergency.

Compile a list of internal and external groups (e.g., management, employees, regulators, customers, suppliers, contractors, and the news media) and define when it is necessary to communicate with these groups. Write procedures or scripts for communicating with each group tailored to the nature of the emergency. Compile a list of telephone numbers for each group—both daytime/nonemergency as well as after-hours/emergency numbers. Include landline, cellular, and pager numbers and email addresses if available.

Emergency Procedures

Write detailed response procedures for each threat or type of emergency incident that is identified as credible during the risk assessment. This will probably include

- medical emergencies
- fire & explosion
- hazardous materials spill or release

- severe weather (winter storms, flooding)

- natural hazards (hurricanes, tornadoes, & earthquakes)

- bomb threats & suspicious packages

- terrorism (chemical, biological, & radiological scenarios)

- security threats (workplace violence, robbery, strike, civil disturbance, etc.)

- utility outages (water, gas, electricity, steam, heating, cooling, HVAC, telecommunications)

- mechanical breakdown (machinery & equipment, elevator, etc.)

- water leakage

- property conservation, including salvage

As a minimum, OSHA Standard 1910.38, *Emergency Action Plans*, requires:

- an evacuation policy and procedure;

- emergency escape procedures and route assignments, such as floor plans, workplace maps, and safe or refuge areas;

- names, titles, departments, and telephone numbers of individuals both within and outside the company to contact for additional information or explanation of duties and responsibilities under the emergency plan;

- procedures for employees who remain to perform or shut down critical plant operations, operate fire extinguishers, or perform other essential services that cannot be shut down for every emergency alarm before evacuating; and

- rescue and medical duties for any workers designated to perform them.

Each procedure should address protective actions, including evacuation or sheltering-in-place; notification procedures (building occupants, public emergency services, emergency organization, contractors, department managers); defensive actions to protect people, property, business operations, and the environment;

incident control or stabilization (e.g., firefighting, hazardous spill containment, and medical treatment); cleanup when safe to do so; and restoration of business operations.

Responses to fires, hazardous materials spills, terrorism, and natural hazards may require preparation of many tactical plans because there are many possible scenarios. For example, protective actions in preparation for the landfall of a tropical storm may be minimal; however, preparation for a major hurricane would be substantial. Terrorism can involve receipt of a suspicious package, dispersal of a chemical agent outside the building, or a catastrophic explosion. It is important to develop tactics for potential scenarios, and train the emergency organization to employ them.

Regulations dictate the complement of personnel as well as equipment and training for employees who are expected to respond to fires, hazardous materials spills or release, confined space rescue, and first aid. In addition, documentation must specify roles, lines of authority, and communication procedures; emergency medical and first aid treatment; site security and control; decontamination procedures; personal protective and emergency equipment; and evacuation routes and procedures. Additional required documentation may include procedures for reporting incidents to governmental regulators and coordination with the plans of local, state, and federal government agencies. All plans must be practiced regularly, reviewed periodically, and amended, as necessary, to keep them current with new or changing site conditions or information.

Step Eight: Train Personnel

An emergency response team is only as good as the capability of team members to evacuate occupants, control building systems, notify public agencies, or do any of the other tasks they may be called on to perform.

Outline training requirements in the plan. There are multiple tiers of training depending upon the role of the individual in the plan. Train all employees in the basic requirements of the Emergency Action Plan—initially when the plan is developed, whenever the employees' duties under the plan change, and whenever the plan is changed. In addition, inform all employees of the fire hazards of materials and processes to which they are exposed.

Figure 11.6

Example Emergency Response Plan

1. Policy & Organizational Statements

    1.1   Definitions of emergency situations

2. Emergency Organization

    2.1   Command System

    2.2   Responsibilities of Members

    2.3   Safety & Health Protection of Team Members

    2.4   Emergency Operations Center

    2.5   Coordination with Outside Authorities

3. Communications

    3.1   Emergency Alarm System

    3.2   Radio Communications

    3.3   Notification of Personnel On Site and Off Site

    3.4   Media Relations

4. Emergency Procedures

    4.1   Evacuation

    4.2   Medical Emergencies

    4.3   Fire & Explosion

    4.4   Hazardous Materials Spill or Release

    4.5   Severe Weather (Winter Storms, Flooding)

    4.6   Natural Hazards (Hurricanes, Tornadoes, & Earthquakes)

    4.7   Bomb Threats & Suspicious Packages

    4.8   Terrorism (Chemical, Biological, & Radiological scenarios)

    4.9   Security Threats (Workplace Violence, Robbery, Strike, Civil Disturbance, etc.)

    4.10   Utility Outages (Water, Gas, Electricity, Steam, Heating, Cooling, HVAC, Telecommunications)

    4.11   Mechanical Breakdown (Machinery & Equipment, Elevator, etc.)

    4.12   Water Leakage

    4.13   Property Conservation including Salvage

5. Training Requirements

6. Distribution of and Updating of the Plan

7. Recordkeeping Requirements

Train members of the emergency organization to fulfill their responsibilities as defined in the plan. Specialized training is required for members of the emergency response team in the following areas:

- Evacuation team members must memorize the location of primary and secondary exit routes, assembly points, and procedures to account for evacuees.

- Training for fire brigade members must be commensurate with the duties and functions that the members will perform. This may include use of portable fire extinguishers; hose streams; fire detection, alarm, and communication systems; and fire pumps, sprinkler systems, and water supplies. Where fire suppression systems have been provided, it is essential that fire brigade members understand how the systems operate; the locations and areas controlled by valves; and what to do if a system malfunctions.

- Train members of the emergency response team responsible for operating or shutting down building utility and process systems such as electrical distribution, emergency generators, HVAC systems, water, natural gas, steam, and mechanical or chemical process systems.

- The training required for hazardous materials teams varies according to the functions defined in the OSHA standard. The standard specifies the scope and number of hours of training as well as the demonstrated competency in the tasks specific to each assignment. Refresher training or verification of proficiency is required annually.

- Certify personnel who are expected to provide first aid and CPR. The American Red Cross schedules regular training and certification courses for employers. In addition, provide training on universal precautions to prevent exposure to bloodborne pathogens such as Hepatitis B or HIV.

- Train confined space entry rescuers as authorized entrants. They must have knowledge of the hazards in confined spaces; the use of personal protective equipment including respirators; and first aid and CPR. Practice exercises are required annually.

Instructors must be qualified to conduct the required training and must be able to demonstrate that they have a higher level of training than those they train. The frequency of training varies according to the duties of the emergency response team. Train the emergency organization at least annually, or as often as necessary to ensure proficiency. Review regulations periodically because many require more frequent training. Document all training in employee personnel files, and maintain a master training record for review by regulatory authorities and insurance representatives.

Step Nine: Exercise the Plan

The goal of the emergency response plan is to first protect the health and safety of people and then to protect property, business operations, and the environment. The first eight steps in the process outlined so far, if properly followed, will result in the compilation of a credible plan. However, no plan or organization is perfect, nor can a plan envision every threat or emergency.

Practice drills hone the skills of members of the team. For example, fire drills teach occupants to find their primary and secondary exit routes while the evacuation team can practice their tasks of notification, searching, and directing occupants to the proper evacuation route and assembly area. Other drills can provide practice in use of the fire alarm or public address systems, use of portable fire extinguishers, or supervision of critical protection systems.

Exercises will help determine whether parts of the plan are properly designed and participating team members can work well together. They afford an opportunity for members of the emergency organization to work together as a team, validate the logic or decisions that were made when the plan was developed, and identify weaknesses that can be addressed before a real event occurs. Exercises can involve the business continuity planning team as well as external public emergency services. Notification procedures can be tested, and the ability to communicate effectively can be practiced.

Four levels of exercises can be run depending on objectives, available time and resources, and effort. They include orientation, tabletop, functional, and full-scale exercises. Orientation exercises walk members of the team through established plans. Roles and responsibilities are reviewed as well as specific procedures. A tabletop exercise centers around a scripted event that provides the context for the exercise. Initially, members of the team evaluate the situation, determine what needs to be done, and then execute procedures in the plan. Once the team becomes comfortable with their roles and responsibilities and execution of scripted procedures, problems are posed to test the ability of the team to reevaluate a situation; identify possible implications; and determine how best to respond. Full-scale exercises involve many participants both within and outside the organization simulating an actual incident. A full-scale exercise simulating a chemical spill or release would require internal and public hazardous materials response teams to don personal protective equipment and work cooperatively to contain an actual (nonhazardous) spill.

Document the exercise and record gaps or inadequacies in plans, procedures, or execution. Utilize a checklist that identifies critical steps or activities. When concluded, participants should critique the exercise and compare results with the intended outcome. Identify improvements in plans and procedures, and focus on any problems or unresolved issues.

ADVANTAGES

Implementing an emergency response plan with an effective organization capable of protecting employees, physical assets, business operations, and the environment can result in faster response than public emergency services can provide. In many cases it can be more effective. There are many possible reasons:

- Public services must be notified to respond; then they must travel to the site. The interval of time between detection of an emergency to time of arrival of emergency apparatus can be considerable. Travel distance or traffic congestion can delay response; volunteers may have to respond to their station before responding to your site; or a regional disaster may overwhelm or overtax the capabilities of the public services.

- Public emergency services may have limited or no knowledge of the construction, occupancy hazards, and protection of private facilities. Limited knowledge is a handicap that could delay an incident commander's ability to develop strategy or tactics to stabilize an incident. Lack of knowledge of on-site hazards could also result in incorrect decisions and endanger personnel.

- Effective planning will also help ensure compliance with regulatory requirements including OSHA standards, fire codes, and possibly other laws, rules, or regulations.

Since there are varying degrees of response—use of portable fire extinguishers by a small group of employees or implementation of an industrial fire brigade commensurate with a public fire department—the advantages of enhanced planning can vary significantly.

The cost of preparedness increases with the scope of the organization and the plan. The advantage of minimal planning (i.e., to satisfy minimum regulatory requirements) is clearly financial.

DISADVANTAGES

The potential consequences for lack of preparedness can be significant. Delayed response to an incident allows conditions to worsen—a heart attack victim can die, an incipient fire can grow, or a chemical spill can contaminate a larger area.

Public emergency services focus their activities on protection of life and property. They typically do not respond to incidents that do not jeopardize life or property—a loss of power to an individual business, for example. Individual businesses have to fend for themselves.

Major regional disasters such as floods, hurricanes, and earthquakes have overwhelmed public emergency services or prevented them from reaching facilities in need. Lack of on-site preparedness can leave the facility with no organized means of response.

TIME AND CASH COMMITMENT

Time

Time is the biggest commitment for emergency planning. Senior management's time is limited to development of the policy statement, initial involvement in the planning committee, and then attendance at selected training sessions, drills and/or exercises. The planning committee can spend a few hours to many days assessing risk and writing a policy and procedures.

The leader of the emergency organization will probably have to commit the most time to recruiting members of the emergency organization; writing or revising policies and procedures; training members of the emergency organization; and coordinating planning with public emergency services and regulatory agencies. Considerable time is also required to develop site-specific drills and exercises.

Individual members will only have to attend scheduled training. All employees must be trained in the basic requirements of the Emergency Action Plan and the fire hazards of materials and processes to which they are exposed.

Cash Commitment

The cost to organize and train an emergency organization varies according to the scope of the organization and the functions it fulfills (e.g., first aid, firefighting, and hazardous materials response). An emergency organization that provides a high level of response—especially those covered by regulations—will require more funding for training and, in many cases, time away from work (overtime wages).

Equipment must be purchased for use by trained responders. As a minimum, procure first aid supplies and kits to prevent exposure to bloodborne pathogens. An incipient level fire brigade need only use portable fire extinguishers (all buildings should be equipped with them). An advanced interior or exterior fire brigade, however, would require personal protective equipment (helmet, eye and face protection, coat, pants and boots) that meets OSHA and other standards. Medical evaluations would also be required prior to appointment to a fire brigade and possibly annually thereafter. Likewise, members of a hazardous materials response team must be medically evaluated, equipped, and trained like members of a fire brigade.

Radios and communications equipment can be critical to the successful coordination of an incident response. The purchase of additional radios, chargers, and spare batteries may be warranted to meet the needs of the emergency organization.

IMPLEMENTING CHANGE WHEN NECESSARY

Emergency response plans are site-specific and hazard-specific. As physical conditions change, the emergency plan should be revised to reflect material changes. This includes changes in process hazards (e.g., changes in quantity or type of hazardous materials and changes in manufacturing processes that increase or decrease the relative hazard); an expansion of buildings or equip-

ment; provision of enhanced fire protection that may obviate the need for firefighting efforts; or other material changes that affect the hazard or protection level.

Changes in the availability or capability of public emergency services could warrant a change in preparedness levels. Addition of advanced life support, the opening of new fire station, or enhanced hazardous materials response capabilities may allow a reduction in the on-site functions of the emergency organization. Conversely, a reduction in the availability or capabilities of public services could justify enhanced preparedness.

The key to any emergency organization is the ability of its members. Members of the emergency organization who are unable to fulfill their role either because they have left the company, been reassigned to other duties, or are no longer medically fit to participate must be replaced.

Stay abreast of regulatory changes and technological advances and revise the plan accordingly.

Review the emergency organization and plan documentation at least annually, if there have been no changes in the prior year. Inspect, test, and maintain fire protection equipment weekly, monthly, or quarterly in accordance with applicable codes and standards. Inspect supplies and other equipment as often as needed to ensure it is available and in good condition. Confer with public emergency services at least annually to learn about changes in their capabilities and to ask them to visit the site to update their pre-incident plans.

Immediately after every emergency incident, critique the performance of the emergency organization and the effectiveness of the plan. The critique can identify deficiencies in the plan or the execution of the plan. Correct noted deficiencies or amend the plan as necessary.

WHERE CAN I FIND OUT MORE ABOUT IT?

Regulations

Occupational Safety and Health Standards (29 CFR 1910)

- Subpart E – Means of Egress

  - 1910.37 Means of egress

- 1910.38 Employee emergency plans and fire prevention plans

Appendix Means of egress

- Subpart H – Hazardous Materials

  ◦ 1910.119 Process safety management of highly hazardous chemicals

  ◦ 1910.120 Hazardous waste operations and emergency response

- Subpart I – Personal Protective Equipment

  ◦ 1910.133 Eye and face protection

  ◦ 1910.134 Respiratory protection

  ◦ 1910.135 Occupational head protection

  ◦ 1910.136 Occupational foot protection

  ◦ 1910.138 Hand protection

- Subpart J – General Environmental Controls

  ◦ 1910.146 Permit-required confined spaces

  ◦ 1910.147 Control of hazardous energy sources

- Subpart K – Medical and First Aid

  ◦ 1910.151 Medical services and first aid

- Subpart L – Fire Protection

  ◦ 1910.155-156 Fire protection and fire brigades

  ◦ 1910.157-163 Fire suppression equipment

  ◦ 1910.164 Fire detection systems

  ◦ 1910.165 Employee alarm systems

  ◦ Appendices A-E of Subpart L

- Subpart R – Special Industries, Electrical Power Generation, Transmission, and Distribution

- Subpart Z – Toxic and Hazardous Substances

  ◦ 1910.1030 Bloodborne pathogens

  ◦ 1910.1200 Hazard communication

Standards & Best Practices

- NFPA 1600, *Standard on Disaster/Emergency Management and Business Continuity Programs*, 2000 Edition. 2000. National Fire Protection Association, Quincy, MA.

- NFPA 1670, *Standard on Operations and Training for Technical Rescue Incidents*, 1999 Edition. 1999. National Fire Protection Association, Quincy, MA.

- NFPA 1620, *Recommended Practice for Pre-Incident Planning*, 1998 Edition. 1998. National Fire Protection Association, Quincy, MA.

- NFPA 471, *Recommended Practice for Responding to Hazardous Materials Incidents*, 2002 Edition. 2002. National Fire Protection Association, Quincy, MA.

- NFPA 600, *Standard on Industrial Fire Brigades*, 2000 Edition. 2000. National Fire Protection Association, Quincy, MA.

- NFPA 1, *Fire Prevention Code*, 2000 Edition. 2000. National Fire Protection Association, Quincy, MA.

- NFPA 101®, *Life Safety Code®*, 2000 Edition. 2000. National Fire Protection Association, Quincy, MA.

Organizations

- National Fire Protection Association, http://www.nfpa.org

- International Association of Emergency Managers, http://www.iaem.com/index.html

- American Red Cross, http://www.redcross.org

- Federal Emergency Management Agency, http://www.fema.gov

- U.S. Department of Labor, Occupational Safety and Health Administration, http://www.osha.gov

- U.S. Environmental Protection Agency, Chemical Emergency Preparedness and Prevention Office, http://www.epa.gov/ceppo/

Information Resources

- Quinley, Kevin M. and Donald L. Schmidt. 2002. *Business At Risk: How to Assess, Mitigate and Respond to Terrorist Threats.* Cincinnati: The National Underwriter Co.

- Jones, Radford W., Project Director. 2000. *Critical Incident Protocol — A Public and Private Partnership.* East Lansing: School of Criminal Justice, Michigan State University. http://www.securitymanagement.com/library/CIP0401.pdf

- *Emergency Management Guide For Business & Industry.* Federal Emergency Management Agency, http://www.fema.gov/library/bizindex.shtm

- *Hazardous Materials Response Handbook.* 2002. Quincy, MA: National Fire Protection Association.

- *How to Plan for Workplace Emergencies and Evacuations.* U.S. Department of Labor, Occupational Safety and Health Administration, OSHA 3088.

- Colonna, Guy R., editor. 2002. *Introduction to Employee Fire & Life Safety.* Quincy, MA: National Fire Protection Association.

- Alesch, Daniel J., James N. Holly, Elliott Mittler, and Robert Nagy. 2002. *Organizations at Risk: What Happens When Small Businesses and Not-for-Profits Encounter Natural Disasters.* Green Bay: Center for Organizational Studies, Univ. of Wisconsin. http://www.riskinstitute.orgptritem.asp?catid=1&itemid=1028

- *Permit-Required Confined Spaces.* U.S. Department of Labor, Occupational Safety and Health Administration, OSHA 3138.

QUESTIONS AND ANSWERS

Question — Do I have to prepare an emergency response plan?

Answer — Yes, all employers subject to OSHA standards must develop an Emergency Action Plan, which covers basic notification of emergencies and evacuation and related issues.

Question — How long does it take to prepare an emergency response plan?

Answer — The process can take a day or so for a small facility with few employees, or it could take many months for a large facility with complex hazards. Facilities that follow the nine steps in this textbook should expect to spend about three months developing and implementing the plan.

Question — Do I have to develop the plan on my own, or are there resources available to me?

Answer — The information resources listed in this textbook provide a wealth of information including examples that can be easily customized to address site-specific needs. You can also engage a consultant to help you develop your plan.

Question — What procedures should I focus on first?

Answer — Procedures required by OSHA standards are a good starting point. They include notification procedures and evacuation.

CASE STUDIES

Firefighting

There are multiple firefighting options, and each has personnel, training and equipment requirements. Options range from no firefighting to establishing an interior structural and advanced exterior fire brigade that is organized, trained, and equipped like a municipal fire department. For most facilities served by a public fire department, the best choice is to train designated employees to use portable fire extinguishers on incipient fires. In this case no medical evaluations are required, no protective clothing is permitted, and training and drills are only required annually. Large facilities with significant fire hazards that are remote from a strong public fire department can justify the cost and effort of organizing a fire brigade.

Hazardous Materials Spill or Release

Any facility with a significant quantity of highly hazardous chemicals should be prepared to handle spills or releases. Facilities mandated to comply with OSHA's *Hazardous Waste Operations and Emergency Response* standard *(HAZWOPER)* include government mandated cleanup sites; hazardous waste treatment, storage, and disposal facilities regulated pursuant to the

Resource Conservation and Recovery Act; and emergency response operations for releases of, or substantial threats of releases of, hazardous substances without regard to the location of the hazard.

Emergency response operation is defined by OSHA as "a response effort by employees from outside the immediate release area or by other designated responders (i.e., mutual aid groups or local fire departments) to an occurrence that results, or is likely to result, in an uncontrolled release of a hazardous substance. Responses to incidental releases of hazardous substances where the substance can be absorbed, neutralized, or otherwise controlled at the time of release by employees in the immediate release area, or by maintenance personnel are not considered to be emergency responses within the scope of the [OSHA HAZWOPER] standard. Responses to releases of hazardous substances where there is no potential safety or health hazard (i.e., fire, explosion, or chemical exposure) are not considered to be emergency responses.[2]

If a hazardous materials (hazmat) response team is provided, it must be organized, trained, and equipped in accordance with the OSHA standard.

Natural Hazards

Earthquakes, hurricanes, and flooding result in billions of dollars of losses annually. Public emergency services can do little to mitigate the effects of these events, so it is incumbent upon individual businesses to prepare. Each of these is a unique threat, although tropical storms and hurricanes can drop considerable rainfall causing significant flooding. Tropical Storm Allison dropped over thirty inches of rain in the Houston, Texas, area in 2001. Allison caused billions of dollars of damage in areas not thought subject to severe flooding.

Earthquakes occur without warning. So emergency preparedness efforts must take into account the varying amount of personnel available to respond to an event. This is especially important since off-duty personnel may not be able to travel to the site after a quake has occurred. In addition, those persons on-site at the time of the quake will be concerned about family members and may attempt to return home. Earthquakes and aftershocks may trigger secondary events such as fires, tsunamis, landslides, liquefaction, flooding and release or spread of hazardous materials.

Once the shaking abates, evacuate the building if there is significant structural damage or threat to occupants. Conduct a roll call of occupants to determine whether anyone is missing. Search for missing persons only if it is safe to do so. Shut off all building utilities including water, gas, and electricity if damaged.

Hurricanes can cause catastrophic damage. Inspect and repair as needed the exterior of buildings to ensure windows, doors, and roof coverings are in good condition. Protect vulnerable windows from flying debris by taping or covering with plywood. Update important records and move to a site out of the path of the storm. Anchor yard structures that can be moved by high winds. Move them inside, if possible. Assemble supplies for the emergency response team, including portable lights, lumber and nails, tape for windows, roofing paper, sandbags, tarpaulins, power and manual tools, chain saws, shovels, and axes. Fill emergency generator and fire-pump diesel engine driven fuel tanks. Clean out street catch basins and drains to prevent street flooding.

Terrorism

Terrorists can strike in many ways, and terrorism incidents can involve biological, chemical, or radiological hazards and explosive or incendiary devices. Cyberterrorists can also attack critical infrastructure. A good emergency response plan can be amended to address the threat of terrorism. Key components of the plan should include:

- threat or incident assessment

- notification of public emergency services

- alerting building occupants

- evacuation or sheltering of occupants

- supervision or control of building utility systems (HVAC, life safety, and fire protection)

- provision of first aid

- security of buildings and grounds

- rescue of trapped occupants

- firefighting (if trained)

- hazardous materials containment and cleanup (if trained and equipped)

Workplace Violence

Workplace violence is violence or the threat of violence against workers. It can occur at or outside the workplace and can range from threats and verbal abuse to physical assaults and homicide, one of the leading causes of job-related deaths.

In an effort to control workplace violence, employers should establish a workplace violence prevention program; train employees on what is acceptable behavior and what is not; ensure all employees know the policy; instruct employees what to do if they witness or are subjected to workplace violence; and investigate all incidents and claims of threats promptly and take action as the facts warrant.

Provide security commensurate with the vulnerability of both employees and property. Install video surveillance, extra lighting, and alarm systems and minimize access by outsiders through identification badges, electronic keys, and guards. Provide drop safes to limit the amount of cash on hand, and keep a minimal amount of cash in registers during evenings and late night hours.

Equip field staff with cellular phones and hand-held alarms or noise devices, and require them to prepare a daily work plan and keep a contact person informed of their location throughout the day. Instruct employees not to enter any location where they feel unsafe, and introduce a "buddy system," provide an escort service, or request police assistance in potentially dangerous situations or at night.

Following an incident of workplace violence, provide prompt medical evaluation and treatment. Promptly report all incidents to law enforcement authorities, and inform victims of their legal right to prosecute perpetrators. Discuss the circumstances of the incident with staff members, and encourage employees to share information about ways to avoid similar situations in the future. After serious incidents, offer stress debriefing sessions and posttraumatic counseling services to help workers recover.

END NOTES

1   NFPA 1, *Fire Prevention Code*; NFPA 600, *Industrial Fire Brigades*; NFPA 471, *Recommended Practice for Responding to Hazardous Materials Incidents*; and NFPA 1670, *Standard on Operations and Training for Technical Rescue Incidents*. NFPA 1600, *Standard on Disaster/Emergency Management and Business Continuity Programs*, provides criteria to "assess current programs or to develop, implement, and maintain a program to mitigate, prepare for, respond to, and recover from disasters and emergencies."

2   Ibid. Section (a) (3)

Chapter 11

GLOSSARY

Assembly points. The predetermined areas in which evacuees are to gather after evacuating a building. Primary and secondary assembly points should be designated in case one area is not safe.

Bloodborne pathogens. Pathogenic microorganisms that are present in human blood and can cause disease in humans. They include, but are not limited to, hepatitis B virus (HBV) and human immunodeficiency virus (HIV).

Bloodborne pathogens standard. A standard promulgated by the Occupational Safety and Health Administration (OSHA) on December 6, 1991, as the Occupational Exposure to Bloodborne Pathogens Standard. This standard is designed to protect workers in the healthcare and related occupations from the risk of exposure to bloodborne pathogens, such as the Human Immunodeficiency Virus (HIV) and the Hepatitis B Virus.

Category 1 hurricane. The intensity of tropical cyclones (hurricane in the Atlantic Basin) are measured by the Saffir Simpson Scale. A Category 1 storm has winds of 74 to 95 mph, and can generate a storm surge 4 to 5 ft above normal. A Category 1 hurricane poses no real damage to building structures, but unanchored mobile homes, shrubbery, trees and poorly constructed signs are vulnerable. Minor coastal road flooding and minor pier damage is also possible.

Category 5 hurricane. A category 5 hurricane produces sustained winds greater than 155 mph, and can produce storm surge greater than 18 ft above normal. Category 5 storms can cause complete roof failure on many residences and industrial buildings and extensive window and door damage. Many small utility buildings will be destroyed, blown over or away. The lower floors of all structures located less than 15 ft above sea level and within 500 yards of the shoreline will sustain major damage. All shrubs, trees, and signs will be blown down. Mobile homes will be destroyed.

Confined space entry. A term used by OSHA to describe employee entry/exit into work spaces that are so small or configured in such a way that their entry and exit, as well as activities within the confined spaces, are hindered. A confined space is large enough and so configured that an employee can bodily enter and perform assigned work; has limited or restricted means for entry or exit (for example, tanks, vessels, silos, storage bins, hoppers, vaults, and pits are spaces that may have limited means of entry.); and is not designed for continuous employee occupancy.

Emergency Operations Center (EOC). A fixed, designated area to be used in supporting and coordinating operations during emergencies.

Emergency response. Collective action taken at a site to stabilize an incident that has the potential to injure people, damage property, interrupt business operations or contaminate the environment.

Emergency response plan. A plan that documents the roles and responsibilities of people and organizations; equipment, systems and communications; and policies and procedures for responding to emergency incidents.

Emergency response planning. The development and implementation of policies, procedures, and organized team(s) designed to safeguard the health and safety of people, minimize property damage and business interruption, and prevent environmental contamination in an emergency.

Emergency organization (response team). An organization comprised of one or more teams each consisting of the minimum number of people necessary to carry out protective actions as specified in the emergency response plan.

Frequency. The relative probability that an incident will occur.

Incident Command System (ICS). (also known as "incident management system") The combination of facilities, equipment, personnel, procedures, and communications operating within a common organizational structure with responsibility for the management of assigned resources to effectively accomplish stated objectives pertaining to an incident.

Occupational Safety and Health Administration (OSHA). A federal agency created under the federal Occupational Safety and Health Act. Charged with occupational safety and health regulation.

Public emergency services. Public resources that are available to assist in emergency situations, such as public fire departments, hazardous materials cleanup teams, police and other law enforcement agencies, and emergency medical services organizations.

Risk assessment. A process to identify and quantify the potential impact of threats, hazards, or perils that could injure people, damage property, interrupt business operations, or contaminate the environment.

Severity. The potential relative consequences of an incident.

Shelter-in-place. To move personnel to safe locations within a building after an emergency incident has occurred. This is usually a temporary measure lasting no more than one to two hours.

Chapter 12

BUSINESS CONTINUITY PLANNING

WHAT IS IT?

A business continuity plan defines the processes and resources needed to sustain critical business functions (e.g., manufacturing, sales and marketing, order entry, inventory management, and invoicing) after a disruption. It requires identification of those business processes that are required to maintain an acceptable level of operations in the event of a disruption. Disruptions can result from a breakdown of critical systems or a natural or manmade hazard.

Disaster recovery planning is a component of the larger business continuity plan. It focuses on the restoration of information technology systems, applications, or the entire computer facility at an alternate site after an emergency. Emergency response planning, covered in Chapter 11, is the development and implementation of policies, procedures, and organized team(s) designed to stabilize the effects of an incident.

Business continuity planning is a multi-step process, not a one-time project or book that collects dust on a shelf. The business continuity process includes the following steps:

1. Project initiation and management support

2. Risk assessment

3. Business impact analysis

4. Recovery strategy selection

5. Recovery plan development

6. Implementation, testing, and maintenance

Once the plan has been developed and implemented, changing conditions, testing, and maintenance may require changes that require following and/or modifying steps two through six.

STEPS TO IMPLEMENT

Step One: Project Initiation and Management

Senior management commitment, direction, and support are critical to the successful development of a business continuity plan. Many aspects of the planning process require the input and/or participation of senior managers, so failure to gain their support will compromise the planning effort. The best way to gain management support is by effectively communicating the need for business continuity planning.

There are many reasons why business continuity planning is important.

- First and foremost is the potential survival of the business. A major loss affecting a critical facility or the disruption of an essential process could interrupt the ability to supply or service customers.

- Business continuity is part of corporate governance. Unprepared businesses can lose customers, profits, and market share and incur fines or penalties. Stock prices of companies can fall resulting in shareholder lawsuits against directors and officers. A study done at Templeton College, Oxford University found that of major public companies that suffered a catastrophic loss, well-prepared companies actually saw a modest boost (5 percent) in their market capitalization fifty days after the date of loss. Conversely, companies unprepared for a catastrophic loss saw a cumulative 15 percent drop in per-share value a year after the catastrophe.[1]

- Businesses in the financial services industry (banks, securities dealers, and investment managers) must comply with federal regulations[2], state regulations, and/or NASD regulations. As of 2003, The Health Insurance Portability and Accountability Act (HIPAA) requires hospitals, insurers, managed care providers, and employers to implement effective security and privacy policies and standards within their respective organizations.[3] Other standards have been promulgated that may be used as a standard or criteria in civil litigation to determine whether an organization exercised due diligence in their preparedness efforts. These include ISO 17799, *Information Technology Code of Practice for Information Security Management; NFPA 1600, Standard on Disaster/ Emergency Management and Business Continuity Programs* promulgated by the National Fire Protection

Association; and *Professional Practices for Business Continuity Planners* published by DRI International. Additional information on where to obtain these publications is included in the section of this chapter entitled **Where Can I Find Out More About It?**

• The reputation of the company is also potentially at stake. As noted in Chapter 2, loss of reputation following a major incident may seriously impact a company's value.

Begin the planning process by creating a mission statement or charter. Reference the reasons stated above that warrant business continuity planning, and define goals and objectives, the organization, and resources needed for the project.

Organize a steering committee comprised of senior managers representing information technology, operations, finance, and other functions as needed. The steering committee provides project oversight and should be authorized to make any decisions regarding declaration of an emergency and deployment of resources. Then appoint a business continuity planning leader to lead the development of the business continuity plan. The BCP leader then must recruit personnel from operating departments and define their roles and responsibilities.

Prepare a project plan that outlines the major activities and tasks and expected completion dates. Develop a preliminary budget for resources. Then package the project plan and present your findings to senior management to gain their approval.

Figure 12.1

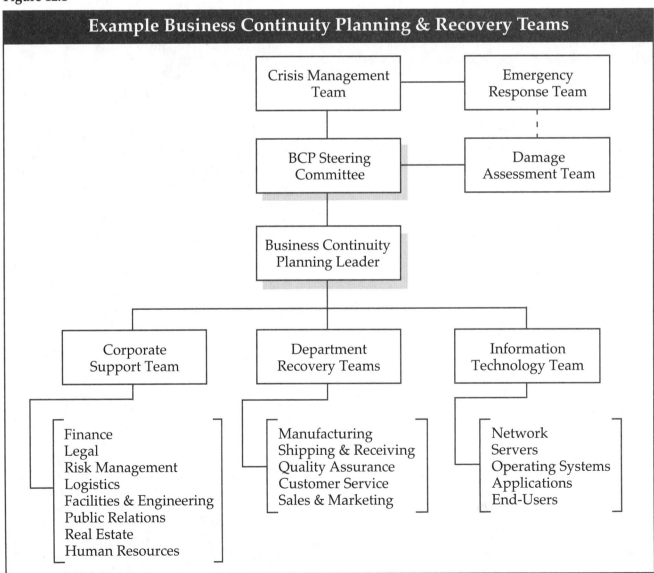

Example Business Continuity Planning & Recovery Teams

Crisis Management Team — Emergency Response Team

BCP Steering Committee — Damage Assessment Team

Business Continuity Planning Leader

Corporate Support Team

Department Recovery Teams

Information Technology Team

Finance
Legal
Risk Management
Logistics
Facilities & Engineering
Public Relations
Real Estate
Human Resources

Manufacturing
Shipping & Receiving
Quality Assurance
Customer Service
Sales & Marketing

Network
Servers
Operating Systems
Applications
End-Users

Step Two: Risk Assessment

Risk assessment is a process to identify potential threats and to assess the vulnerability of buildings, systems, equipment, inventory, and business operations to these threats. The goal of risk assessment is to identify the potential impact on business operations, which will be quantified in the next step.

There are many possible threats such as:

- Loss or disruption of supplier(s) or service provider(s) (e.g., single or sole sources suppliers, interdependencies with other company business units and functions, and foreign imports)

- Regulatory changes, controls, or enforcement action

- Political risk affecting the availability or cost of importing

- Damage or loss of information or communications equipment (servers, routers, voice-messaging systems, etc.)

- Damage or interruption of LAN/WAN connectivity and telecommunications links

- Loss or corruption of software applications, data, vital records, or information

- Loss or unavailability of key employees (e.g., employees unable to reach the workplace or strike)

- Fire and explosion

- Natural hazards (flooding, hurricane/windstorm, earthquake, tornado, subsidence, landslide, and winter storms)

- Utility outages (electricity, natural gas, steam, water, sewer, heating, ventilation or air conditioning, etc.)

- Water leakage (interior or exterior source)

- Terrorism (nuclear, chemical, or biological weapons)

Identify threats regardless of frequency of occurrence or potential severity. Develop scenarios based upon maximum severity and worst-case timing (e.g.,

end of month or quarter or holiday shopping season). Evaluate each threat to determine whether advance warning is possible to enable preparedness and mitigation efforts (e.g., hurricanes). Highlight threats that could reduce the availability of personnel (e.g., a regional disaster); interrupt critical infrastructure (e.g., telephone central office switching, other telecommunications links, electrical power, and natural gas); and disrupt transportation systems, preventing employees from reaching their assigned workplaces or recovery sites.

Evaluate each threat to determine the effects on buildings, systems, equipment, key personnel, information technology and data, intangible assets, business interruption, regulatory noncompliance, and the organization's reputation. Focus on the loss or disruption of information technology and its impact on end-users. Identify all end-users—whether within the company, customers who access technology directly, or business partners.

Security and protection of buildings and communication systems is critical. Evaluate the adequacy of physical and operational security controls for buildings, computer rooms, data storage areas, voice, and data communications, and networks (Internet, intranet, LAN, WAN, etc.). Assess the adequacy of protection against fire or other threats.

Information is at the heart of all businesses today, and many records—paper or electronic—are critical to ongoing operations. Identify vital records, and evaluate backup and restoration strategies to ensure availability after a major loss.

Investigate ways to mitigate the risk through enhanced protection; information, physical, or operational security; relocation away from the hazard; duplication or redundancy; data backup; segregation; or other means.

Step Three: Business Impact Analysis

The goal of the business impact analysis (BIA) is to identify business units, operations, and processes that are critical to the survival of the organization. The financial impact of loss or disruption of each critical function and the maximum downtime before irreparable harm is done to the organization will determine recovery priorities. This requires further analysis of the consequences resulting from damage to, disruption or loss of, physical assets, infrastructure, or suppliers.

Interview managers using a scripted questionnaire to conduct the business impact analysis. Questionnaires ensure consistent collection of information, and the interviews should follow the questionnaire. Ask the same questions of each manager and use consistent criteria for quantifying the impact of various loss scenarios. Conduct initial interviews with individual managers, and subsequently allow them to review the data collected.

The business impact analysis questionnaire and interviews should review each threat scenario and attempt to answer the following:

- What is the impact on sales, revenues, cash flow, and market share?

- How would it affect the ability to supply or service customers?

- How would it affect suppliers?

- How would the news media react, and would it affect the organization's reputation?

- Would there be any legal or regulatory implications? Major events often generate regulatory scrutiny, and investigations can identify noncompliance with regulations. Also, a major disruption to operations could affect the ability to satisfy regulatory requirements (e.g., loss of data or a computer system prevents on time payment of sales taxes).

- Would there be legal or contractual liability? Companies—especially those in the automotive industry—that supply *just-in-time* manufacturers can incur penalties if their failure to supply components on time shuts down a manufacturing line.

- What effect would the threat have on the environment, and would the environmental impact cause further consequences (e.g.., business interruption, cleanup, or regulatory scrutiny)?

Quantify the impact of each scenario in financial terms such as "revenue lost per hour of downtime." If loss or disruption does not have a direct financial impact, then evaluate whether there is any indirect impact such as liability, penalties, or increased administrative costs. Quantify the loss by estimating the value of each lost sale. If a store were closed for a day, the average sales volume for that store for a day would be the lost sales number (assuming no delayed sales were recovered in the following days.) Evaluate the impact of lost data that could result in lost sales or inability to invoice a customer. The downtime may extend back to the time of the last error-free data backup.

After completing initial interviews, schedule a workshop for managers to review the results of the interviews and obtain a broader perspective. Often the larger group can better assess the cumulative impact of a loss or disruption and can identify workarounds that would minimize the impact. Groups of senior managers can also better assess priorities. The BCP leader should facilitate the meeting and focus attention on the identification and validation of critical functions, necessary resources, and interdependencies.

Document the results of the workshop, assign responsibilities for action items, and follow-up to ensure resolution. Circulate the results of the workshop to participating managers and ask them to identify errors or omissions.

Critical Functions

Define the criteria for identifying a function as *critical* and review that criteria with senior management to ensure they approve. Next, identify the functional organization—what does each department do? Then determine who within the department has sufficient knowledge of its operations to determine critical functions. Most often the department manager will participate, but beware of false data since most department managers feel their department is critical. Critical functions can include both business operations (e.g., manufacturing, order entry, sales and marketing, and inventory management) and support functions (e.g., security, legal, and maintenance). Identify dependent operations both at intradepartmental and interdepartmental (e.g., technology applications and processes) levels.

Each critical function requires information and resources. Identify the facilities, systems, and equipment as well as vital records and information needed to support each critical business operation. Use the checklist depicted in Figure 12.2 to gather planning information, and then prioritize critical business functions.

Figure 12.2

Department Business Impact Analysis Checklist

Inputs from Other Departments

☐ Identify the inputs from other departments; record the department.

☐ Rate the criticality of each input.

☐ How often are they required? What is the minimum frequency or scheduled time?

☐ What is the form of the input? Can the input be provided in another format?

Outputs to Other Departments

☐ Identify the outputs from other departments; record the department.

☐ Rate the criticality of each output.

☐ How often are they required? What is the minimum frequency or scheduled time of delivery?

☐ What is the form of the output? Can the output be provided in another format?

Inputs & Outputs from Outside Contractors & Suppliers

☐ Identify the inputs and outputs from outside contractors and suppliers; record the name and telephone numbers of the outside contractors and vendors.

☐ Rate the criticality of each input and output.

☐ How often are they required? What is the minimum frequency or scheduled time of delivery?

☐ What is the form of the input or output? Can the input or output be provided in another format?

Alternative Contractors & Suppliers

☐ Identify alternative contractors and suppliers who could provide similar goods or services.

Computer Networks, Systems, Applications, & Data

☐ Identify the software applications (programs) and the business function that the application supports.

☐ Identify the maximum timeframe that the application can be down before irreparable harm is done.

☐ Where does the application reside (mainframe, LAN, WAN, individual PC, etc.)?

☐ What connectivity is required (e.g., Internet, LAN, WAN, business partners, etc.)

☐ How many PCs are required for end-users?

Telecommunications

☐ Identify telecommunications services and equipment (e.g., voice or fax).

☐ What is the minimum required number of incoming and outgoing lines?

Personnel Resources

☐ Identify the numbers of full-time and part-time personnel.

☐ Identify any key employees who have knowledge that is difficult to replace or irreplaceable.

Business Impact

☐ What is the worst possible time or date that a loss or disruption could occur (end of month, end of quarter, prior to season, etc.)?

☐ Describe the potential impact of a loss or disruption of operations within the department (e.g., revenue loss, impact on customers, contract performance, or regulatory implications).

Recovery Priorities

☐ Prioritize the importance of recovering the department's functions (1 = highest, 10 = lowest) and explain why.

Recovery Resources

☐ Identify vital records, data, or other information that is critical to restoring business functions.

Identify any other systems, equipment, and supplies needed to restore operations not listed elsewhere.

Recovery Objectives

Define recovery time objectives for each critical function beginning with the most critical function. *Recovery time objective* is the maximum allowable time that a critical function can be down before the organization suffers irreparable harm. The maximum allowable downtime is determined by careful examination of the business needs to satisfy valued customers; to meet contract deadlines or performance clauses before penalties are incurred; satisfy regulatory requirements; ensure cash flow management; etc.

Order the recovery time objectives with the shortest allowable downtime first. Next, determine the resources required to recover the critical function. Resources include people, desks, computers, technology platforms, applications, connectivity, telephones, fax machines, offices supplies, equipment, raw materials, etc.

Compile the results of the business impact analysis into a report and present the report to the BCP steering committee for validation and approval.

Step Four: Recovery Strategy Selection

Recovery strategies are the methods of restoring critical functions within the recovery time objectives. These strategies can include manual workarounds, reciprocal agreements (i.e., use someone else's system or equipment), relocate to an alternative site (owned or not owned), substitute an ingredient, source a raw material or subassembly from another supplier, outsource, arrange a consortium to service those with a common need, and mitigation. Effective threat mitigation means never having to deal with restoration (i.e., if you fix the problem before it becomes an emergency, then you do not have to deal with the emergency). Assess the risk of each proposed recovery strategy to identify dependability, practicality, cost, effort necessary to implement, and capacity.

Analyze each recovery strategy to determine whether it will meet business objectives and conform to any performance specifications or criteria. For example, outsourcing product manufacturing must meet rigid quality standards and customer requirements. A contract manufacturer must be able to meet those same standards of quality; otherwise, you fail to meet the expectations of your customer. Compare the cost of each recovery strategy with the benefit. Ultimately, senior management will have to validate the recovery strategy.

Recovery strategies involve procurement of supplies, equipment, buildings, communications, and many other assets and services. Procurement involves development of specifications; negotiation of pricing, terms, and conditions; and finalizing the agreement in a signed contract. Many vendors can help with recovery of critical functions, including building utilities, telephone services, and data communications.

Alternative operating strategies enable continuity of operations when there is a loss of functionality. One type is a manual workaround. For example, if an order entry computer system is unavailable, record orders on

paper and verbally communicate them to the intended recipient. After system restoration, all orders are input into the computer system. A substantial loss may require transfer of functions from one facility to a backup or redundant facility. Many large catalogue retailers, for example, have multiple call centers to receive and process customer orders. If one call center is lost, all calls are transferred to another call center. If critical data is backed up every sixty seconds or less, data cannot be lost by failure of computer hardware. For extreme events, many companies have established *hot sites* where they can relocate critical computer operations to a facility equipped to run their applications and data.

Step Five: Business Recovery Plan Development

The business recovery plan is the documentation of teams, procedures, and resources necessary to restore critical functions or utilize alternate strategies to replace critical functionality. Include the following in the plan:

- Define what constitutes a disaster and establish notification procedures to inform senior management.

- Organize business recovery team(s) for functions and departments.

- Organize a damage assessment team, and prepare procedures for preliminary and detailed assessments.

- Document agreed-upon recovery strategies and step-by-step procedures to implement them.

- Identify critical information, and implement secure back-up means to ensure availability of error-free data.

- Compile lists of, and specifications for, critical systems, equipment, and supplies as well as contacts and vendors who can provide or restore them.

- Establish primary and secondary emergency operations centers.

Define what constitutes a disaster or when interruption of critical functions becomes an emergency. Although loss of a major building is an obvious disaster, lesser events may not be recognized as such. Loss of network connectivity may not be an emergency—unless it affects critical functions such as order entry, inventory management, and product shipment. Establish criteria and reporting systems to inform high-level managers of situations that could constitute an emergency. Include escalation criteria so lower level managers know when to notify superiors. Escalation procedures should include after business hours notification to senior management.

A Contrast in Communications

On March 17, 2000, a fire occurred at a semiconductor plant in Albuquerque, New Mexico, operated by Royal Philips Electronics NV. Lightning caused the ten-minute fire in a clean room environment. It shut down manufacturing of cellular telephone handset components, and two major customers (Ericsson and Nokia) were affected. Nokia reported the loss to its management promptly, was able to arrange an alternate supplier of the critical component, and did not suffer a major impact. However, Ericsson's response to the loss was routine, and senior management was not notified for many hours. It was not able to

arrange an alternate supplier. Four months after the fire, Ericsson stunned analysts when they reported a $256 million pretax loss. It ultimately outsourced handset production to a competitor.

Organize a business recovery team and define the responsibilities of its members. The organization should include:

❑ business recovery team leader

❑ departmental teams

❑ corporate support team (provides administrative, financial, and other services required by individual recovery teams)

❑ information technology recovery teams (technical recovery of computer, voice, network, and application systems; verifying applications are functioning properly; and ensuring user connectivity)

❑ damage assessment team

Figure 12.3 further describes additional support teams.

Figure 12.3

Business Recovery Team Supporting Functions	
Department	**Support Function**
Finance	Funds recovery in accordance with rules of corporate governance; maintains records on funds disbursed; works with risk management on insurance claim
Risk Management	Notification of insurance companies or brokers, claim reporting and settlement
Legal	Prepares, reviews, negotiates, and/or approves contracts; supports any litigation
Information Technology	Supports business recovery operations by procuring and/or installing desktop/laptop equipment; ensures connectivity with servers, networks, and other IT resources
Logistics	Arranges transportation of equipment and personnel; procurement of housing accommodations and food service
Facilities & Engineering	Manages owned and leased facilities; primary contact for incidents involving buildings; installer of office equipment; responsible for other workspace requirements
Public Relations (or Crisis Management Team)	Communicates with external audiences including news media, shareholders, customers, and regulators
Real Estate	Procures new permanent or long-term office space, if warranted
Vital Records	Obtains vital records and arranges transportation to recovery site
Human Resources	Responsible for addressing employee issues, including notifications to employees, injuries to employees, and compensation of employees

Develop agreed-upon recovery strategies and document step-by-step procedures in a manner that will be easy to use and understand. Ensure that corporate governance policies for approving capital expenditures, leasing, and other appropriations are followed.

Prepare department plans that define operations necessary to support critical business functions. Identify information requirements, end-user computing requirements (e.g., personal computers, system and application software, telephones, facsimiles, and connectivity), furniture, equipment, and supplies needed for the necessary complement of staff. Document procedures for activation of the department plan as well as systematic procedures for restoration.

Prepare recovery plans for supporting functions (e.g., human resources, risk management, purchasing, transportation, legal, engineering, and security). Although not critical functions, each group plays an important role in support of the overall recovery process.

Identify the starting point for processing or handling of information. For example, if billing records are backed up every Monday, and records are lost on Wednesday, Monday would be the starting point for recovery of billing records. Procedures must document all tasks necessary to continue or restore critical functions of the organization and when. Define tasks; assign teams; identify resources; and compile the names and telephone numbers of key contacts, suppliers, and vendors required to assist in the completion of the task.

Information such as customer records, orders, shipments, invoices, accounts receivables, and accounts payable is critical to a business. Every organization also requires many reports. Loss of critical information could result in customer service problems, financial loss, and tax or regulatory penalties. Therefore, the information technology portion of the plan may be the most detailed.

It must address the equipment, systems, applications, and data needed to support many different functions, departments, and needs. Prioritize the critical technology functions, and address both the computer room needs as well as the end-user needs. Validate minimum requirements and timeframes so you can determine the most cost-effective means of recovery. Hot sites (preconfigured computer centers that allow quick installation of application software) offer quick recovery of computer functions—but at a high cost. Use of an alternate site within the same organization may not be suitable unless there is available space and the

resources necessary to support all required functions. Fast replacement of equipment and systems can work if recovery timeframe are longer; however, equipment vendors and contractors should verify the availability of equipment, which may vary over time. All options require use of backup data, so backup strategies and protection of vital records are critically important.

Identify vital records and data, how often data must be replicated or backed up, how records should be backed up; where data should be stored, how information should be transferred to the storage area, and how long the information should be kept. Ensure information storage is properly protected and secure. Information recovery requires compatible equipment and installation of operating systems and software in proper sequence. Prioritize

Example Business Recovery Plan

A. Introduction
  1. Policy Statement
  2. Assumptions
B. Business Recovery Organization
  1. Steering Committee
  2. Business Recovery Organization
  3. Emergency Response Team
  4. Crisis Management Team
C. Recovery Time Objectives
D. Recovery Strategies
  1. Communications
  2. Information Technology
  3. Call Center
  4. Manufacturing
  5. Distribution
E. Plan Activation
  1. Preliminary Evaluation
  2. Escalation
  3. Plan Activation
  4. Plan Deactivation
  5. Restoration
F. Recovery Plans
  1. Business Relocation
  2. Manual Workarounds
  3. Data Restoration
  4. Emergency Operations Center
G. Tests & Exercises
  1. Tests
  2. Exercises
  3. Schedules
H. Maintenance
  1. Plan Distribution
I. Appendix

system and application recovery based on criticality and required timeframe (e.g., order entry systems are a higher priority than human resource records).

Related to information technology is communications. Today, most businesses have extensive voice and data communications systems including wide area networks, local area networks, Internet connections, voice mail systems, electronic messages systems, and more. Customers expect their telephone calls, faxes, and email messages to be answered promptly; otherwise, they may direct their business to competitors. Address recovery strategies for communication systems in the plan. Arrange for alternate means of switching communications (e.g., to a backup call center) and provide temporary messaging facilities to communicate a short-term interruption of incoming communications.

Establish emergency operations centers on-site and off-site where members of the business recovery team can assemble. Ensure all business continuity documentation is available at all times for use at the on-site and off-site emergency operations centers and to members of the business recovery team wherever they will be deployed.

Document procedures for initial activation of the business continuity plan—who is authorized and when are they authorized to declare an emergency and mobilize necessary resources? Keep in mind that declaration of an emergency may result in substantial costs. Gain agreement on criteria and the escalating list of managers who must approve it. Include a twenty-four-hour notification procedure to contact all necessary members of the team.

Organize a damage assessment team to assess the scope of damage or interruption. Initially, assess the scope and estimate the expected duration of the interruption. Provide a preliminary situation report to the business recovery team, who can then decide whether to declare an emergency. Conduct a detailed assessment as soon as qualified personnel or outside contractors are available. The scope of damage will determine whether equipment must be replaced, cleaned, or otherwise restored.

Establish procedures for communication with news media, regulators, investors, important customers and suppliers as well as employees and unions. A corporate crisis management team may retain responsibility for all communications with the exception of site level communication with local media representatives.

Crisis Management

Many larger companies have corporate crisis management plans. A senior level crisis management team is organized to assess the situation; determine the potential impact on the corporation; and then determine how the corporation must respond. Corporate crisis management plans typically identify the internal and external stakeholders that must be addressed, as well as the authorized spokesperson and scripts.

Step Six. Plan Implementation, Maintenance, and Testing

Implementation

Distribute copies of the plan to those who have a need to know and the authority to review sensitive or confidential information contained in the plan. Provide copies for the primary and secondary emergency operations centers. Any electronic copies should be available on multiple servers, CD ROM, or other accessible electronic means. Implement procedures to restrict access to the plan to authorized users only and for the distribution of updates.

Procure redundant power suppliers or network connections, additional data storage or backup equipment, or contract with a hot site for emergency data processing—whatever management decides is necessary to reduce the probability of or to mitigate the consequences of an interruption.

Training

All members of the business continuity and individual department recovery teams must understand their roles and responsibilities as outlined in the plan. Therefore, education is important to build awareness of the plan and to ensure that, as business operations, facilities and equipment, or personnel change, the business continuity plan is reviewed and updated.

Formal training may be required for members of departments that will participate in the risk assessment, business impact, or recovery strategy development processes. The leader of the business continuity team should develop or facilitate training to ensure those who participate in the plan development process are able to correctly provide input or make decisions.

The leader and members of the business continuity team should receive additional training on the complex subject of business continuity and disaster recovery planning. Budget for professional conferences and seminars, membership in professional associations, and publications.

Tests and Exercises

Exercises describe activities to educate, train, and/or familiarize personnel with the plan. They provide opportunity for members of the business recovery team to work together, validate the logic or decisions that were made when the plan was developed, and identify weaknesses that can be addressed before a real event occurs. There are many means to exercise or test a plan to ensure all parts work together. Exercises can include simulations in which members of the business recovery team review the plan step by step, modular exercises that test a portion of the plan, functional exercises that test a specific function, or large-scale exercises that test much of the plan.

Conduct tests to develop confidence that the business continuity plan will work. Develop and document test procedures, schedules, and resource requirements. Create exercise scenarios based upon threats or perils identified in the risk assessment and business impact analysis, and inform participants of the scope, conduct, and expectations of the exercises. Stress to all participants that the goal is to enhance the plan rather than to assign blame. Exercise the fundamental procedures and responsibilities outlined in the recovery plan including notifications, reporting to the emergency operations center, and damage assessment. Appoint observers to evaluate the exercises and record questions, problems, or action items. The observers should utilize a checklist or evaluation guide with defined criteria to evaluate the exercise. Summarize the results of the tests noting action items, assignments, and completion dates. Distribute sections of the report to participants based upon their need to know.

Some plan components must be tested to ensure the processes, procedures, equipment, data, and other facets perform as required by plan objectives. A test may include restoration of data from backup tapes with zero errors. Schedule tests annually and whenever conditions change. It may not be practical to exercise the entire plan initially. Therefore, incremental exercises or tests that validate components of the plan may be done in succession until a full-scale exercise is conducted.

Design exercises to achieve specified objectives. For example, an exercise may test the recovery of a server that holds all customer information. Objectives may include recovery within eight hours with no database errors.

Identify editions of the plan with a revision number, and summarize changes to the plan with a revision history section. Ensure that all members of the business recovery team receive updates to their portions of the plan.

Management should verify that plans are updated and tested periodically. Persons charged with developing and maintaining the plans should be held accountable.

Audits

An independent audit of the business continuity plan can help identify shortcomings. Qualified personnel who are independent of the plan developers should complete the audit. The scope of the audit should encompass:

- review of the completeness of the risk assessment and any assumptions about probability

- business impact analysis

- identification of critical functions

- effectiveness of the recovery strategies to meet recovery time objectives and verification of resource requirements

- organization of the business recovery team(s)

- completeness and usability of the plan documentation

- awareness and training of management and members of the business continuity team

- identification, protection, and backup of vital records

- verification of contracts and confirmation of ability of suppliers and vendors to fulfill their defined role in the plan

- frequency, adequacy, and documentation of tests and exercises

- plan maintenance, updating, distribution, and accessibility during emergencies

- integration with emergency response and crisis management organizations and plans

ADVANTAGES AND DISADVANTAGES

There are multiple options for business continuity planning:

- do nothing

- develop plans to meet regulatory requirements

- develop, implement, and maintain business continuity plans in accordance with best practices

Most organizations are not required by regulation to develop business continuity plans. However, as pointed out in Step 1, there are many reasons to plan effectively, and there are many potential consequences if an unprepared organization suffers a serious loss or disruption.

The Bottom Line

Quite simply, the advantage of business continuity planning is the ability to restore critical functions before a loss or disruption causes irreparable harm to the organization.

The disadvantage is the time and cost to develop, implement, and maintain the plan as well as the costs to implement recovery strategies.

Many different recovery strategies can be employed to continue operations after a loss or during a disruption in a critical function. Since information technology is at the heart of many businesses, it is a good example to explore. There are many options for providing temporary functionality if computer processing is unavailable. These include:

- commercial recovery site—a hot site.

- mobile recovery center.

- cold and warm sites. (A cold site is a facility void of any resources or equipment except air-conditioning and electrical wiring; computer equipment must be installed before it is usable. A warm site is a facility partially equipped depending upon the location and contract.)

- displacement model (includes dedicated sites and displacement strategies).

- quick shipment of replacement equipment and use of vendor sites.

TIME AND CASH COMMITMENT

Development, implementation, and maintenance of a business continuity plan requires considerable time, but variable amounts of money. As the size of the businesses, number of departments, and functions grow, the greater the complexity of the planning effort. Businesses with little or no tolerance for downtime must have more robust plans and more extensive recovery strategies to continue operations. However, well-protected facilities less subject to physical damage or interruption of critical functions may require less planning. Regulatory requirements or mandates from customers that their suppliers must have plans could also increase the planning time and costs.

The total cost and the time commitments from senior managers, BCP leaders, and individual teams are hard to predict. Use of outside consultants or company-wide plans that share information and recovery strategies can reduce the time and cost expended by individual facilities.

Each business unit should budget sufficient time and money to address all steps in the development and implementation process. Inadequate project planning; failure to identify potential risks; or an incorrect business impact assessment analysis could result in poor decisions about the need or scope of recovery strategies. If recovery strategies are flawed, then the plan may not protect the business as intended. If training is inadequate, then employees don't know how to use the plan. Potential problems won't be identified if plans are not exercised and testing periodically.

IMPLEMENTING CHANGE WHEN NECESSARY

All plans must be updated over time to reflect changes in physical conditions, business operations, personnel, regulatory requirements, or deficiencies noted during exercises. Some portions of the plan require regular updating (e.g., membership rosters and vendor and

Figure 12.4

Advantages and Disadvantages of IT Recovery Strategies		
Recovery Strategy	Advantages	Disadvantages
Commercial "Hot Site"	• Near state-of-the-art, well-equipped facilities designed and equipped for companies to quickly restore information technology systems	• High costs just to maintain availability • High costs to declare an emergency and additional costs for duration of usage during an emergency • Contractual obligations • Regional emergency may result in significant demand by contracted users; first come, first served
Mobile Site	• Minimal personnel relocation requirements • Operational within one hour from delivery • Testing capability	• Availability—especially if demand following a regional disaster exceeds supply
Warm & Cold Sites	• Low fixed costs	• High recovery costs to procure equipment and configure environment • Extended recovery times • Limited or no testing capability
Displacement Model	• Expedited recovery capability • Scalable recovery capability • Cost control	• Impact to unaffected business areas • May require extensive resource commitments • May have limited testing capability
Quick Shipment of Replacement Equipment	• No costs	• Requires rebuilding or procurement of suitable room or facility • Delayed recovery until equipment arrives and is installed
Vendor Sites (e.g., application developers, overflow customer call center vendors, and other providers of partial recovery services)	• Low initial or fixed costs	• Impact to vendors • Limited testing capability • Limited or no control over recovery site

contractor contact lists). Other portions may be updated only as conditions change.

Changes in business operations require changes in the business continuity plan. Assess the risks and quantify the business impact of new business operations in the same manner as the original plan was developed. Validate changes to critical functions and review the recovery timeframes.

Review the protection and backup of vital records periodically to ensure that important information is backed up as frequently as necessary, properly pro-

tected against damage, and secure from theft or copying. Verify that electronic and paper records are available, properly cataloged, or otherwise usable.

Exercises and tests provide an excellent opportunity to identify necessary modifications to the plan.

Conduct a post-incident review after any loss or after the plan is utilized to respond to or recover from a disaster or interruption of normal functions. Critique the quality of the plan as well as the ability of members of the business recovery teams to follow the plan. Update the plan to correct any noted deficiencies.

WHERE CAN I FIND OUT MORE ABOUT IT?

Regulations and Standards

- BS ISO/IEC 17799:2000, Information Technology. *Code of Practice For Information Security Management*, British Standards.

- NFPA 1600, *Standard on Disaster/Emergency Management and Business Continuity Programs*, 2000 Edition. 2000. Quincy, MA: National Fire Protection Association.

Publications and Best Practices

- *Professional Practices for Business Continuity Planners*. 2002. Falls Church, VA: DRI International.

- *Contingency Planning Guide for Information Technology Systems*. 2001. National Institute of Standards and Technology, NIST Special Publication 800-34.

- *Risk Management Guide for Information Technology Systems, National Institute of Standards and Technology*, NIST Special Publication 800-30.

- Jones, Radford W., Project Director. 2000. *Critical Incident Protocol—A Public and Private Partnership*. East Lansing: School of Criminal Justice, Michigan State University. http://www.securitymanagement.com/library/CIP0401.pdf

- *Emergency Management Guide For Business & Industry*, Federal Emergency Management Agency, http://www.fema.gov/library/bizindex.shtm

- Alesch, Daniel J., James N. Holly, Elliott Mittler, and Robert Nagy. 2002. *Organizations at Risk: What Happens When Small Businesses and Not-for-Profits Encounter Natural Disasters*. Green Bay: Center for Organizational Studies, Univ. of Wisconsin. http://www.riskinstitute.org/ptr_item.asp?cat_id=1&item_id=1028

- *Establishing A Vital Records Program*. 2002. Association of Records Managers and Administrators, Inc., Draft Standard.

- *Threat and Risk Assessment Working Guide*. 1999. Government of Canada, Communications Security Establishment, P.O. Box 9703, Terminal, Ottawa, Ontario, Canada, K1G 3Z4.

- *Reputation & Value: The Case of Corporate Catastrophes*. 2001. Oxford Metrica, www.oxfordmetrica.com./executivesummary1.pdf

Regulatory and Professional Organizations

- U.S. Department of Health & Human Services, Office for Civil Rights, http://www.hhs.gov/ocr/

- DRI International, http://www.drii.org/

- Business Continuity Institute, http://www.thebci.org

- Federal Emergency Management Agency, http://www.fema.gov

- National Fire Protection Association, http://www.nfpa.org

QUESTIONS AND ANSWERS

Question—Does every organization have to develop a business continuity plan?

Answer—Legally, "No". However, businesses in the banking, securities, investment management, and those that must comply with the Health Insurance Portability and Accountability Act are required to develop business continuity plans. Many manufacturers with sole suppliers require their suppliers to have plans. Although there may be no legal or contractual duty to implement and maintain a business continuity plan, studies have shown that unprepared companies that have a loss suffer significant adverse consequences.

Question—What is the difference between emergency response, business continuity, business recovery, disaster recovery, and crisis management plans?

Answer—Many terms refer to preparedness, response, and recovery efforts. Emergency response typically deals with stabilization of an event or incident that occurs at an individual site. Firefighting is a good example. Business continuity is a planning process to maintain critical functions so an organization can satisfy its mission in the event of a loss or disruption.

Disaster recovery, in particular recovery of information technology, is the restoration of damaged buildings and/or equipment while continuity of operations are maintained using recovery strategies. Crisis management is the overarching senior level or corporate function intended to assess the impact of any incident or event on the organization as a whole. The crisis management team receives information from the site level emergency team, damage assessment team, and business recovery team. It has the ultimate authority to determine the overall response of the organization and to communicate with internal and external stakeholders. The crisis management team is solely responsible for protection of the company brand or image.

CASE STUDY

Planning for a manufacturing site is more challenging than planning for the recovery of a computer center because it is difficult to duplicate or quickly restore damaged buildings, manufacturing lines, and supporting infrastructure. In addition, the cycle for new products continues to decrease, with the shelf life less than twelve months for some products. Managers may question whether it is possible to address these challenging circumstances. However, manufacturing operations need to develop sound business continuity plans especially as companies focus on a select number of products with higher profit margin potential.

Recovery strategies for manufacturing operations may include multiple options:

- mitigation

- transfer of operations to other company-owned facilities

- outsourcing to competitor or third party manufacturer

- expediting reconstruction of damaged facilities

Ultimately, more than one of these options should be pursued, if possible. Mitigate hazards that threaten a facility where cost-effective and practical. The cost-benefit analysis to determine whether it is cost-effective to upgrade protection should include not only the potential saving from reduced insurance premiums (if any), but also the potential direct and indirect costs of a major loss (see Risk Assessment and Business Impact Analysis). Most protection improvements cannot be justified using return-on-investment financial models, since improved protection does not increase manufacturing output or enhance productivity.

Recovery strategies include transfer of operations to other company-owned facilities that manufacture the same or similar products. If other facilities have the space, excess manufacturing capacity, and equipment, they may be suitable recovery sites. Take into account the availability of employees and any excess capacity working twenty-four hours, seven days per week.

Commodity products—manufactured by many companies—present the opportunity to outsource production. Essentially, this involves paying a competitor or a third party to increase their production and place a different label on their product. The company that suffers the loss maintains responsibility for sales and marketing, distribution, and other functions.

The final strategy involves expediting reconstruction of the damaged facility. This requires maintenance of vital records such as the sources and design of manufacturing equipment, patterns, specifications, process flow diagrams, and other information needed to design the new facility and procure and install production equipment. Permitting processes may take considerable time depending upon the nature of the manufacturing operation and the political jurisdiction of the manufacturing site.

END NOTES

[1] *The Impact of Catastrophes on Shareholder Value*, Rory F. Knight and Deborah J. Pretty, Oxford Executive Research Briefings, Templeton College.

[2] Banks must comply with regulations of the Federal Financial Institutions Examination Council and state bank examiners. Broker dealers and investment managers must comply with Securities and Exchange Commission rules and/or NASD regulations.

[3] HIPAA specifies seven requirements for organizations that, in the normal course of business, come in contact with health information, whether oral or recorded, in any form or medium that is created or received by a healthcare provider, health plan, public health authority, employer, life insurer, school or university, or healthcare clearinghouse; and relates to the past, present, or future physical or mental health or condition of an individual; the provision of healthcare to an individual; or the past, present, or future payment for the provision of health care to an individual.

Chapter 12

GLOSSARY

Alternative operating strategies. Strategies that enable operations to continue when there is a loss of functionality. A manual workaround is an example of an alternative operating strategy.

Business continuity plan. The documentation of an ongoing process that identifies the impact of potential losses, maintains viable recovery strategies and recovery plans, and ensures continuity of services through personnel training, plan testing, and maintenance.

Business impact analysis (BIA). The process that identifies business units, operations, and processes that are critical to an organization's survival. The BIA is used to help determine business recovery strategies.

Business recovery plan. Documentation of the teams, processes, and resources needed to restore critical functions or utilize alternate strategies to replace critical functionality.

Corporate crisis management plan. A plan to assess a crisis situation, determine the potential impact on the corporation, and determine how the corporation must respond. The plan typically identifies the internal and external stakeholders that must be addressed at the time of a crisis, as well as how and by whom they should be addressed.

Disaster recovery planning. A part of the business continuity plan that focuses on restoring information technology systems, applications, or an alternative computer facility at an alternate site.

Exercises. Activities that are used to educate, train, or familiarize personnel with a business recovery plan and to identify any weaknesses in the business continuity plan or the execution of the plan.

Recovery strategies. The methods of restoring critical functions within the recovery time objectives.

Recovery time objectives. The maximum allowable time that a critical function can be down before an organization suffers irreparable harm.

Risk assessment. A process to identify potential threats and to assess the vulnerability of buildings, systems, equipment, inventory, and business operations to those threats.

Chapter 13

CLAIMS MANAGEMENT

WHAT IS IT?

Claims management is the technique used to decrease the financial impact of losses (claims) that occur. This contrasts with loss control, which attempts to stop or decrease the severity of losses before they happen. Claims management is a postloss activity, whereas loss control is a preloss activity.

This chapter discusses the important steps that risk managers (as well as the agents, brokers, and third-party administrators who work with them) should take to proactively manage the business's claims to reduce its financial impact.

Claims management is an important technique for corporations regardless of whether they use self-insurance, other types of risk-sharing mechanisms, or a traditional guaranteed cost program. Claims have both a direct financial impact (their actual dollar cost) and an indirect, or intangible, cost.

The direct financial impact is the amount of money spent to adjust and settle claims, such as investigation expenses and settlement amounts. Examples of the indirect cost of claims are the lost productivity that results from worker injuries, the loss-of-use of physical assets that are damaged, and the loss of time that must be redirected to resolve a claim. Since it is difficult to measure such intangibles, risk managers and claims adjusters tend to focus on managing the direct financial impact.

On the other side of the coin, insurance companies compile information on the dollar amount of claims an individual business sustains each year, as well as the expenses associated with those claims, to judge the underwriting profitability of the accounts it writes. Underwriting profitability is determined by weighing the cost to write the insurance policy and pay claims for an individual account against the premium received. The aggregate history of claims for an individual business over several years is referred to as its *losses, loss history,* or *loss experience.* Loss experience is critically important when a business negotiates pricing for a policy renewal or wants to

change insurance companies. Successful claims management activities lower the aggregate amount of claim payments in order to improve a business's loss experience. Loss experience—good or bad—can affect insurance premiums or even the insurability of the business.

Terminology Refresher

Under self-insurance, a business chooses to pay for its own claims and claim costs and may purchase insurance to protect against catastrophic losses above a specified level.

Risk-sharing mechanisms other than self-insurance include deductible and retrospectively-rated programs. Under these, a business pays a portion of its claims and claim costs along with a premium for insurance to pay for losses above a certain threshold.

In a fully-insured, guaranteed cost insurance program, a business purchases an insurance policy and the insurance company pays the cost of claims. A small deductible may apply to each claim under a guaranteed cost program.

Elements of Loss Experience

A business's loss experience may be separated into four categories:

- paid losses,

- reserves,

- incurred losses, and

- expenses.

Paid losses represent the amounts that insurance companies have paid on claims for a business. Paid losses often include both damage payments and expenses for adjusting and/or defending the claim.

Reserves represent the amount that is expected to be paid in the future on claims. Reserves are established by adjusters based on statistical information developed for various lines of insurance. Incurred losses represent the total of paid losses and reserves.

Expenses represent the money needed to adjust the claims, such as adjuster fees, data management expenses, and office expenses. There are two types of expenses: unallocated loss adjustment expenses and allocated loss adjustment expenses. Unallocated ex-

Figure 13.1

Loss History, ABC Restaurants, as of January 1, 2003

General Liability as of 1/1/03

Policy Term	# Closed Claims	# Open Claims	Paid Losses	Reserved Losses	Incurred Losses	ALAE	Premium
1/1/1997-98	85	0	$124,313	$0	$124,313	$4,298	$103,000
1/1/1998-99	62	0	$97,852	$0	$97,825	$3,100	$113,000
1/1/1999-00	72	1	$107,121	$27,899	$135,020	$3,842	$98,000
1/1/2000-01	63	3	$61,010	$43,212	$104,222	$2,301	$105,100
1/1/2001-02	76	17	$27,003	$65,729	$92,732	$1,621	$99,100
Total	358	21	$417,299	$136,840	$554,112	$15,162	$518,200

Auto Liability as of 1/1/03

Policy Term	# Closed Claims	# Open Claims	Paid Losses	Reserved Losses	Incurred Losses	ALAE	Premium
1/1/1997-98	1	0	$125,000	$0	$125,000	$0	$3,500
1/1/1998-99	0	0	$0	$0	$0	$0	$4,000
1/1/1999-00	2	0	$6,750	$0	$6,750	$0	$4,000
1/1/2000-01	0	0	$0	$0	$0	$0	$3,500
1/1/2001-02	0	2	$0	$12,000	$12,000	$0	$3,750
Total	3	2	$131,750	$12,000	$143,750	$0	$18,750

Property as of 1/1/03

Policy Term	# Closed Claims	# Open Claims	Paid Losses	Reserved Losses	Incurred Losses	ALAE	Premium
1/1/1997-98	12	0	$9,212	$0	$9,212	$0	$26,500
1/1/1998-99	12	0	$14,296	$0	$14,296	$0	$19,555
1/1/1999-00	19	0	$26,872	$0	$26,872	$0	$19,555
1/1/2000-01	13	0	$27,165	$0	$27,165	$0	$21,500
1/1/2001-02	8	2	$12,000	$9,800	$21,800	$0	$27,500
Total	64	2	$89,545	$9,800	$99,345	$0	$114,610

Workers Compensation as of 1/1/03

Policy Term	# Closed Claims	# Open Claims	Paid Losses	Reserved Losses	Incurred Losses	ALAE	Premium
1/1/1997-98	173	7	$152,398	$52,169	$204,567	$7,632	$375,000
1/1/1998-99	185	4	$183,111	$149,575	$332,686	$8,111	$382,000
1/1/1999-00	168	3	$116,321	$98,423	$214,744	$2,621	$376,000
1/1/2000-01	153	14	$89,325	$143,652	$232,977	$1,995	$392,000
1/1/2001-02	146	54	$69,253	$198,158	$267,411	$4,312	$405,000
Total	825	82	$610,408	$641,977	$1,252,385	$24,671	$1,930,000

Total paid	$1,249,002
Total reserves	$800,617
Total incurred	$2,049,592

penses reflect adjusting operations that cannot be segregated and assigned to an individual claim, such as adjuster salaries, office expenses, and staff attorney fees.

The second type of expense often shows up as a separate entry in a company's loss history. This is allocated loss adjustment expenses or ALAE. ALAE reflects adjusting expenses that can be specifically attached to an individual claim, such as special surveillance, expert witness fees, outside legal fees, and premiums on appeal bonds that can be assigned to a single claim.

The loss history for ABC Restaurants, a 25-location restaurant chain, may look something like Figure 13.1.

Substantial information may be obtained from the loss history.

Importance of Reserves

All four categories—paid losses, reserves, incurred losses, and expenses—are important in terms of claims management. However, once payments are made, there is little that can be done to recoup the payments, other than subrogation. *Subrogation* is the right of the party that has paid for a loss of a second party to recover those costs from the third party that is responsible. For example, an insurance company may pay a business for fire damage to its building so that it can be repaired and business resumed. However, assume the investigation determines that a vendor who was in the building negligently caused the fire. The property insurer then may subrogate against the vendor—or his general liability insurer—to try to recover the settlement.

Because subrogation is one of only a few possible payment recovery methods, risk managers typically concentrate on managing reserves. This is especially true when the business is sharing in the risk with the insurance company. Adjusters set reserves when claims are first investigated and then adjust the reserves as the claims age. For example, a worker may be burned while cooking French fries. His initial medical bills are more than $5,000, and it is expected that future medical bills will amount to more than $3,500. The adjuster may set a workers compensation medical reserve of $3,500. However, if an infection sets in, medical costs may escalate and the adjuster will increase the medical reserve to reflect the change in circumstances. Conversely, the employee may heal more quickly than anticipated and not need the entire $3,500. In that case, the adjuster will reduce the medical reserve.

In Figure 13.1, more than $800,000 remains reserved for the payment of claims that have not yet been settled. Successfully managing these claims until they are closed can mean the difference between a profitable and an unprofitable account. From their initial establishment, reserves should be as accurate as possible and reduced when positive steps are taken to decrease the ultimate cost of individual claims.

Figure 13.1 is a snapshot of ABC Restaurants' loss experience as of January 1, 2003. The paid and reserve amounts will change through the year. By January 1, 2004, there may have been significant changes as claims develop and are adjusted.

Chapter 14 focuses on monitoring loss reserves in detail.

WHY CLAIMS MANAGEMENT IS IMPORTANT

All claims need to be managed, regardless of what type of risk-financing program is involved. For example, a company may successfully manage a liability claim to avert a lawsuit. This immediately saves money. In the long term, that same company may protect its ability to negotiate lower future insurance premiums because claims are well-managed and under control. As mentioned previously, insurance company underwriters review a company's past history of claims when underwriting an insurance policy and establishing the premium. Certain lines of insurance—such as workers compensation—integrate the cost of claims into their experience rating systems.

When claims are submitted to insurance companies under guaranteed cost programs, their management falls primarily to insurance company adjusters. In risk-sharing programs, such as deductible or retrospectively-rated plans, the insured business has a larger stake in the outcome of claims and usually takes a larger role in managing them. Under a self-insured program, a business has the greatest vested interest in how claims are handled because their cost reverts back to the self-insured.

In general, once a claim is filed with an insurance company, that insurance company has the ultimate right to adjust the claim as it sees fit. However, courts have held that insurers hold the absolute right to settle claims only when it is solely their own money that is involved. Therefore, the insurer has some obligation to work with the insured business to manage claims when a risk-sharing plan—such as a retrospectively rated or large deductible program—is involved. This is because both the insurance company's and the business's money is at stake. An example is *Transport Indemnity Company v. Dahlen Transport, Inc.*, 161 N.W. 2d 546 (Minn. 1968), in which the Minnesota Supreme Court ruled that an insurer can be forced to produce evidence that settlements were made in good faith and not as a tool to avoid responsibility for making payments under excess insurance policies that it provided. A number of other cases also discuss such responsibilities in risk-sharing arrangements.

These cases illustrate why it is important for risk managers to become involved in claims management. It is simply a smart business practice through which a company may significantly decrease its cost of claims on both an immediate and long-term basis.

Society also has an interest in how well claims are managed. The loss of money and productivity that results from injury and property damage can never be fully regained, even when the claim is covered by insurance.

The immediate and long-term implications of claims are illustrated in Figure 13.2:

THE PARTIES IN A CLAIM

Several parties usually are involved in claims and their management. These parties include

- The injured party (called the claimant)

- An insured or self-insured business (the risk manager)

- An insurance company or other risk-sharing facility (represented by a claims adjuster)

- The vendor that manages the insured's risk program (the broker or agent)

Figure 13.2

Impact of Claims on Three Types of Risk-Financing Mechanisms		
Guaranteed Cost Program	**Risk-Sharing Program (large deductible or retrospectively rated)**	**Self-insured Program**
Claim payments may be reduced if losses are handled expediently	Claim payments may be reduced if losses are handled expediently	Claim payments may be reduced if losses are handled expediently
The business pays a premium to the insurance company, which then adjusts and pays claims	The business pays a premium to the insurance company but subsequently is billed for a portion of claim payments	The business sets up a fund to pay claims and purchases insurance only to protect against catastrophic events
The insurance company is given the authority to adjust and settle or defend claims	The insurance company has the final authority over how claims are adjusted, but the business has a financial interest in that process	The self-insured has authority to adjust and settle or defend claims, subject to possible overview by an insurance company providing catastrophic protection
The business's history of claim costs will affect the future cost of insurance	The business's history of claim costs will affect the future cost of insurance	The business's hisory of claim costs will affect the future cost of insurance
The business may have to pay a small deductible	The business will pay either a a large deductible amount ($100,000 or more) or most of the cost of the claim plus expenses	The business will pay the full amount of the claim plus expenses
Other than a possible deductible, the business is not assessed claim costs	The business is assessed a portion of or all claim costs after claims are settled	The business pays for claims as they are settled

For the purpose of this chapter, we will divide claims management into three segments:

First-party claims	Claims that arise from injury or damage to owned assets. Examples are a fire that burns down an owned building and physical damage to an owned or leased auto.
Third-party claims	Claims that arise from liabilities to others (third parties). Examples are negligent building maintenance that causes a customer to fall and be injured or an at-fault auto accident that injures occupants in another vehicle and demolishes that other vehicle.
Statutory responsibilities	Claims that arise from a state or federal law that require that a risk be insured or financed in another way (self-insured or bonded). The best example of this is employee claims for job-related injuries, which are regulated by state workers compensation laws. Although these are statutorily enacted, they also are considered third-party claims.

STEPS IN THE CLAIMS– MANAGEMENT PROCESS

Certain elements remain constant, regardless of whether first-party, third-party, or statutorily-regulated claims are involved. However, many first-party claims—especially those involving guaranteed cost insurance—are fairly straightforward and require less active management. Despite this, it is important to keep on top of even relatively simple first-party claims until they are settled so that potential issues with coverage or valuation are resolved before the insured and adjuster become polarized.

Since first-party losses involve fewer variables than third-party and statutorily-imposed responsibilities, this chapter will concentrate on the latter two types of claims. For illustration purposes we will assume that a traditional insurance company handles the risk-financing program being discussed.

Step One: Incident Occurs

All claims begin with an incident, which are also known as *accidents* or *occurrences*.

An individual slips in a department store. The brakes on a bicycle fail, and a child is injured. A worker is burned while deep-frying French fries.

Note than an incident does not necessarily result in a claim for damages. Many individuals fall but are not injured, do not request medical attention, and never file a claim against the store owner or operator. Thus, the incident may or may not lead to a claim. Note also that incidents that do not lead to claims still may be important in the claims-management process. This is because such incidents may point out areas of an operation that are not as safe as they should be.

Step Two: Claim Is Made

Claims usually are filed when an occurrence results in damage or injury. Some insurance policies define the terms *occurrence* or *claim*, but others do not.

For example, the commercial general liability (CGL) policy designed by the Insurance Services Office (ISO) states that it will pay damages that arise from bodily injury or property damage caused by an occurrence. The form defines the term occurrence on its most recent policy form as:

"Occurrence" means an accident, including continuous or repeated exposure to substantially the same general harmful conditions.

A directors and officers liability policy form may define "claim" to include written demands for civil damages, a civil proceeding that is commenced by a complaint, and a formal administrative or regulatory proceeding that is commenced by the filing of a notice of charges, formal investigative order, or similar type of legal document.

In general, a claim is made when a party seeks financial compensation for injury or damage. Therefore, a customer stopping to tell a store manager that she fell and got hurt, a parent calling a manufacturer to report the bicycle's brake failure and the child's injury, and the worker telling his manager about his burnt arm all constitute claims.

The business in turn notifies its insurance company of the claim.

Step Three: Claim Is Denied, Accepted, or Conditionally Investigated

The insurance company assigns an adjuster to the claim. After reviewing the details of the claim, the adjuster may

- deny the claim,

- accept the claim and begin the adjustment process, or

- conditionally investigate the claim.

Claim Is Denied

When denying a claim, the insurer states the reason(s) for denial. Common reasons are that the incident happened outside the policy term of coverage, an exclusion on the policy voids coverage for the damages, or the type of accident is not covered by the policy.

When a claim is denied, the risk manager may accept the denial or challenge it.

Claim Is Accepted

An adjuster is assigned to adjust the claim. At this stage it is critical that the risk manager supply any information the adjuster requests as quickly as possible. After the initial information is gathered, the adjuster will establish a *claim reserve*. The claim reserve is an estimate of what the claim will ultimately cost. Additional information on claim reserves is included in the section of this chapter entitled **Elements of Loss Experience** and in Chapter 14, Monitoring Loss Reserves.

Paid versus Reserve

First-party claim: Assume a fire damages a corporation's primary manufacturing plant. The adjuster estimates that the total cost of the loss will be $500,000. The risk manager requests an advance payment of $100,000, which will be used to clear debris and start repairs. The $100,000 represents a paid loss. The adjuster establishes a $400,000 reserve. As repairs are made, money is moved from the reserve amount to the paid column. The incurred loss for the fire is $500,000 plus expenses.

Third-party workers compensation claim: A worker is burned while cooking French fries. He needs immediate medical attention, will require plastic surgery on one arm, and is expected to be off work a total of six weeks. The initial medical bills, $5,342, are paid as they are received. The insurance company expects another $3,500 in medical bills for this type of injury so establishes a $3,500 medical reserve. In addition, the insurance company believes the employee will be off work for four weeks, which amounts to approximately $1,500 of wages. The initial paid amount on the claim is $5,342. The reserve amount is $3,500 for medical and $1,500 for work loss, or a total reserve of $5,000. The incurred value of this claim is $10,342.

Claim reserves and payments, as well as other activities taken to decrease the financial impact of claims, often are handled through *claim reviews*, which are outlined in Chapter 28.

Claim Conditionally Investigated

When an adjuster believes—but is not certain—that a claim is not covered by a particular policy, she may investigate the claim under a *reservation of rights*. A reservation of rights usually is invoked in writing with a *reservation of rights letter*. The reservation of rights letter is sent to the insured business and states that the insurance company will continue to investigate and/or defend the claim without admitting it is responsible for coverage and without waiving its right to later deny the claim.

Insurance companies use a reservation of rights letter for two main purposes:

- to keep the insured informed about the status of coverage for claim(s), and

- to avoid allegations that the insurance company misled the insured or acted in bad faith.

Bad faith allegations often are lodged against insurance companies if their actions lead the insured business to believe that coverage will be available for the claim and later deny it.

Risk managers should consider challenging the reservation of rights position taken by the insurer. They may appeal to their insurance broker or agent as the first step in disputing a reservation of rights notice. These vendors often can provide coverage information that is helpful. However, if unsuccessful in this attempt, the risk manager may consider hiring outside counsel to represent the company's interest in defending the claim.

Step Four: Claim Is Adjusted

Once it is established that the claim is covered by the insurance policy, the adjuster will collect additional information and work to either settle or defend the claim. Risk managers need to cooperate with the adjuster in this process by supplying requested information as quickly as possible. They also should maintain open lines of communication with the adjuster—regardless of the type of claim and whether an insurance company adjuster or in-house adjuster is involved. Communication and the free flow of information are paramount in this stage of the process because control of a claim easily can be either maintained or lost at this stage.

Clarifying Terms

The *tail* of a claim is a term used to describe the relative length of time that it takes to resolve various types of claims.

First-party property claims are said to have *short tails* because they typically are settled rather quickly once coverage is established. In addition, the value of damaged property is defined by the cost to replace or repair it. So there tends to be less volatility in setting the financial value of first-party property losses.

Third-party claims, including statutorily regulated responsibilities such as workers compensation exposures, are said to be *long-tail* exposures. This is because many variables can extend the life of third-party claims, such as legal maneuvering, volatility in the perceived value of a third party's damages, and factors that can intervene to increase their severity. For example, a worker who is injured on the job or a customer who is injured in a fall in a restaurant may not heal as quickly as anticipated. This increases the cost of medical treatment and other compensatory damages such as wage loss and pain and suffering.

First-Party Claims

Property policies specify that the insured provide a detailed inventory of damaged and undamaged property and a signed, sworn proof of loss. As stated in the standard commercial property policy written by the Insurance Services Office (ISO) under the section entitled Duties in the Event of Loss of Damage:

. . . (7) Send us a signed, sworn proof of loss containing the information we request to investigate the claim. You must do this within 60 days after our request. We will supply you with the necessary forms.

(8) Cooperate with us in the investigation or settlement of the claim.

Failure to abide by these conditions could result in the claim being turned down.

Business income and extra expense claims are filed after a direct loss to property. These request payment for the loss of net income and expenses that are incurred as a result of a direct property loss. They are among the most difficult of claims to manage because the coverage is based on the business's historical income figures. There may be substantial changes in the business's financial picture between the time the insurance is purchased and when the loss occurs.

Since they are so difficult to handle, risk managers often utilize the services of the business's chief financial officer, outside certified public accountant, or other accounting adviser to assist in preparing the proof of loss. As with all property claims, diligence in bringing the company back to normal operating levels also is paramount to successfully managing a business income loss.

Other difficult issues may arise in the adjusting of first-party property claims. At times, the risk manager may dispute the value that the adjuster assigns to the damaged property. When this happens, an appraisal may be requested. Other thorny issues may involve terms of the policy, such as coinsurance, the application of a deductible, or advance payments.

Despite the preceding caveats, most direct property claims are finite in nature. After all, a piece of property usually has a set value. Therefore, property claims usually are *short-tail* in nature, which means that they tend to be adjusted and settled more quickly than third-party claims.

Third-Party Claims

Auto

As noted in Chapter 1, auto claims may involve both first-party and third-party liabilities. Physical damage to a business's own vehicle is considered a first-party loss. It is similar to a direct property claim, mentioned earlier in this section, and usually involves prompt notice of loss, a damage appraisal, and settlement.

In contrast, third-party auto liability claims may present a different picture. Many liability claims are considered to be *long-tail* in nature because it often takes a substantial period of time—often seven years or more—between a liability claim being filed and subsequently settled.

Figure 13.1 shows an auto claim from 1997 that is now closed. This accident involved a restaurant manager, who was driving a company car, failed to heed a red light and hit another car in an intersection. Liability was fairly clear cut, and the insurance company and the injured third party negotiated the $125,000 settlement, which included medical bills for emergency room treatment, the cost of minor continuing medical treatment, the cost to replace the demolished car, and $50,000 settlement for the third party's pain and suffering. (Note that the cost to repair the restaurant car would be shown as a first-party auto claim. The restaurant manager's injuries would be included in the 1997-98 workers compensation loss experience in Figure 13.1.)

However, if the restaurant manager were not clearly responsible for the accident, negotiations may stall and the third party who was injured may sue the restaurant and the employee-driver. This not only increases the

costs but also delays settlement, stretching the case out for a much longer period of time. The extended length of time that often is required to settle liability claims makes them long-tail exposures.

General Liability

Most general liability claims involve either the business's *premises and operations* or its *products and completed operations*.

Premises and operations claims involve injury or damage that arises from a condition of the premises or work in which the business is engaging. For example, a customer slips inside one of the ABC Restaurants because water was spilled on the floor and not quickly mopped up. This claim involves negligence in maintaining the restaurant's premises.

Products liability claims involve allegations of property damage or bodily injury that result from a company's product or completed work. When the brakes fail on a bicycle and a child is injured, a products liability claim may be filed against the bike manufacturer.

Unlike a first-party property loss in which the damages usually are finite, the damages arising from liability claims usually are not limited. Theoretically they are as high as a jury wants them to be. These types of claims also involve third parties who may be unpredictable, a legal system that offers numerous potential sources of resolution, and potential disagreement over who is responsible for causing the accident. These variables extend the amount of time required to adjust and resolve many general liability claims, which leads to them being categorized as long-tail in nature.

Statutorily Imposed Responsibilities

Claims also arise from statutes that require businesses to be financially responsible for certain types of exposures. The most prominent and costly of these can be a business's responsibility for worker injuries and deaths.

Nearly every state requires that businesses with more than a set number of employees either

- purchase workers compensation insurance or

- become qualified self-insurers for the workers compensation exposure.

When a guaranteed cost workers compensation policy is purchased, the business pays a premium to an insurance company to provide coverage and adjust and pay claims. Aggressively managing workers compensation claims is important even when guaranteed cost insurance is purchased, however, because workers compensation is *experience rated*.

Experience rating compares a business's workers compensation losses with those of businesses engaged in similar types of work. If the business's loss experience is better than its peers, its workers compensation premium is discounted. If it is worse than its peers, the premium is increased.

Many workers compensation programs are not written on a guaranteed-cost basis. They may include financial arrangements—such as large deductibles or retrospective rating—that require the insured business to share in the cost of claims. These are called the workers compensation *financial plan* or *financial program*. Chapter 18 includes a discussion of workers compensation, various financial plans, and experience rating.

Both experience rating and the prospect of a financial plan that requires the business to share in losses makes claims management one of the most important aspects of any workers compensation program.

Businesses may be restricted in the steps they can take to manage claims because of state regulations. In most states, effective workers compensation claims management will include:

- Reviewing claim reserves frequently to be sure they are appropriate.

- Implementing cost management systems that are allowed by law, such as light-duty return-to-work positions for injured workers, conducting periodic review of claims with the adjuster, and holding managers responsible for maintaining a safe working environment.

- Adopting an approved panel of physicians to provide early medical treatment to injured workers as permitted by state law.

- Adhering to state-established timeframes for filing claim-related information and accepting or rejecting employee claims for workers compensation payments.

- Letting injured employees know that the business values their contribution, wants them to get well, and will make reasonable accommodations for their return to work.

Risk Management Tip

The longer that an injured employee remains off the job, the more expensive the claim will be. Therefore, employers should maintain contact with injured workers during their recuperation. They should try to get the employee back to work as quickly as possible—without risking further injury.

Step Five: Claim Is Settled or Closed

The final step is making the claim payment and closing the file. Before a file is closed, claimants usually are asked to sign a form accepting the resolution. Risk managers should follow up in two ways:

1. Be sure the loss history reflects that the claim has been closed and that the recorded payment amount is correct, and

2. Monitor reserve amounts to be sure they fall to zero after a claim has been closed.

Figure 13.3 shows the path of a typical claim through these five steps.

ADVANTAGES OF CLAIMS MANAGEMENT

Effectively managing claims can save a substantial amount of money both in the short- and long-term. In addition to such financial considerations, good claims management can

- mean the difference between a loyal customer and a lost customer,

- allow a business to resume operations as quickly as possible after its property is damaged,

- avert possible lawsuits,

- conserve property resources, and

- increase or maintain employee productivity.

Figure 13.3

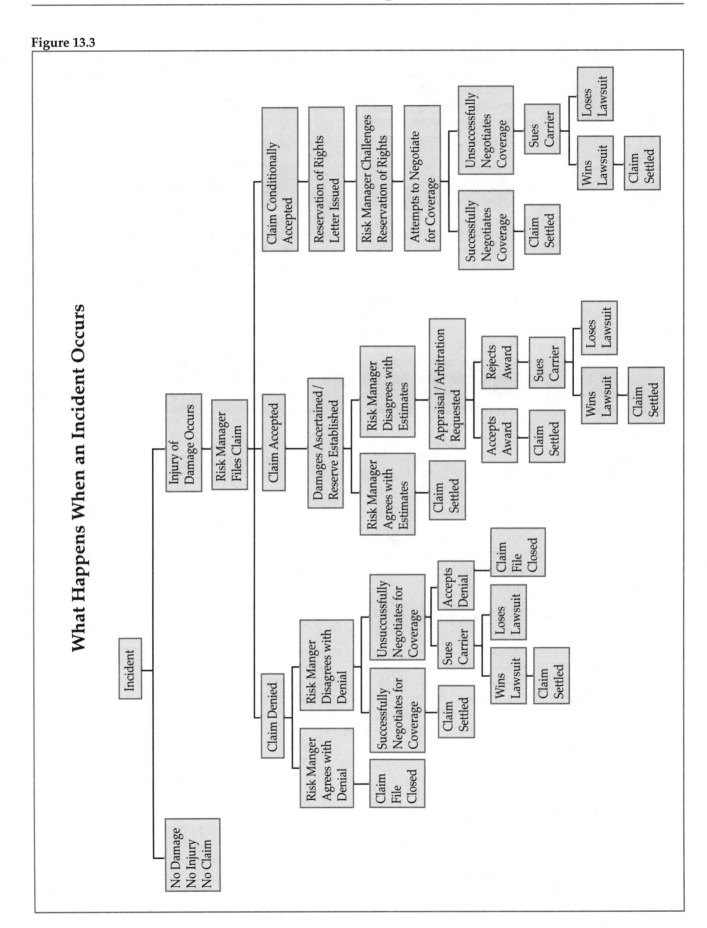

What Happens When an Incident Occurs

DISADVANTAGES OF CLAIMS MANAGEMENT

Claims should be managed. However, a substantial amount of time and internal resources are required to effectively manage the process.

TIME AND CASH COMMITMENT

Depending upon the volume of claims, the responsibility for claims management could reside with the risk manager. Larger companies may employ a full-time internal claims manager. In some companies, human resource departments manage workers compensation claims.

Cash will be needed to cover the salaries of employees who manage the claims process. Additional expenses may be incurred for a computer and software to record claim data, as well as the typical miscellaneous expenses to run an office.

WHERE CAN I FIND OUT MORE ABOUT IT?

- American Educational Institute (AEI), which offers claims law and coverage courses in Legal Principles, Liability, Automobile, Property, Workers Compensation, and Fraud. http://www.aeiclaimslaw.com/

- Annual ACE/SCLA Conference, produced by *Claims* magazine, The National Underwriter Company, and the Society of Claim Law Associates. This annual claims conference offers an educational forum for claims adjusters and managers as well as a hall of exhibitors that spotlights vendors that provide service in the area of claims management. http://www.ace-scla.com/

- Associate in Claims (AIC) designation program offered by American Institute for Chartered Property Casualty Underwriters and the Insurance Institute of America, a four-part program that covers the claims area. http://www.aicpcu.org/programs/index.htm

- Risk and Insurance Management Society, Inc. (RIMS) annual conference, held each spring. http://www.rims.org/

There are countless agents, brokers, third-party administrators, and claim-adjusting companies that can act as valuable resources in this area. Risk managers who are selecting insurance companies should pay particular attention to the claims-management philosophies of competing insurers.

QUESTIONS AND ANSWERS

Question—What if a customer says he was injured on a business's premises, but there's no evidence that he was injured there?

Answer—Situations such as this frequently happen and should not be ignored. The general liability insurance company should be notified of the claim so it can be investigated. Most insurance policies require that claims be reported as soon as practicable. Failure to do so—regardless of how the business views the merits of the claim—may invalidate potential coverage.

Question—What if a risk manager fails to notify his insurer of a claim and then a lawsuit is filed?

Answer—The lawsuit and other pertinent information about the claim should be forwarded immediately to the insurance company. If the carrier attempts to deny the claim because of late reporting, the business should take steps to defend the lawsuit itself. In the meantime, the risk manager should attempt to negotiate with the insurer for coverage.

Question—What if a carrier is paying claims that the risk manager believes should be fought?

Answer—The answer to this question differs depending upon the type of insurance policy involved:

Guaranteed Cost Policy

Under a guaranteed cost, fully-insured insurance policy, the insurer has the right to adjust claims as it feels is appropriate. The insured-business can tell the insurer that it feels the claim is not legitimate and should be defended, but the ultimate decision is up to the adjuster.

Risk—sharing Policy

Under policies in which the business shares the cost of claims with the insurance company, the insurance company retains the final right to adjust claims. However, several courts have ruled that a business may be entitled not to pay its share of claim(s) if it can prove that the insurance company acted unreasonably or negligently in paying claims.

A business that is contemplating purchasing risk-sharing policies should relay its philosophy of claims management and scrutinize the ability of the insurance company to meet its needs.

Self—insured Program

Businesses that self-insure their exposures pay their own claims. They therefore can establish guidelines on how claims are adjusted. However, they must operate within legal boundaries. In addition, choosing to fight legitimate claims may cause costs to escalate if they result in additional lawsuits.

Chapter 13

GLOSSARY

Accident. An unforeseen, unintended, and unexpected event, which occurs suddenly and at a definite place.

Aggregate loss history. The total amount of claims that an individual business has incurred over a specific number of years.

Allocated loss adjustment expenses (ALAE). Adjusting expenses that can be attached to specific, individual claims, such as special surveillance, expert witness fees, and outside legal fees.

Bad faith allegations. Allegations that may be filed against an insurance company, alleging that the company did not handle a claim situation according to the terms of the insurance contract.

Claim tail. A commonly used term to describe the relative length of time before various types of claims are fully adjusted and settled.

Claims management. A technique to manage losses so that their financial impact is decreased.

Financial plan or program. A term used to describe the risk-sharing programs that require a business to share in the cost of its claims as well as paying a premium for certain levels of insurance coverage.

First-party claims. Claims that arise from injury or damage to owned assets, such as a fire that damages an insured's office building.

Incurred losses. The value of claim payments plus reserves.

Loss control. A system of preloss activities that is geared to preventing (claims) losses from occurring.

Loss history. The total amount of claims that an individual business has incurred over a period of years.

Occurrence. An incident that triggers coverage under certain types of insurance policies.

Paid losses. The amounts that already have been paid on claims.

Premises and operations liability. Liability for injury or damage that arises from a condition of premises or ongoing work.

Products and completed operations liability. Liability for injury or damage that arises from a products or completed work.

Reservation of rights. An arrangement in which an insurer agrees to proceed with the defense of a case without commitment to provide coverage in the event that the facts disclosed during the investigation reveal that the occurrence is not covered.

Reserves. Loss or claim reserves represent the value of losses that have been estimated and set up for future payment.

Risk-sharing programs. Insurance programs in which a business pays a portion of its claims and claim costs in addition to a premium for insurance. Examples are programs that are retrospectively rated or include large deductibles.

Statutory-based claims. Claims that arise from a state or federal law that require that a risk be insured or officially financed in some fashion, such as statutory workers compensation requirements.

Subrogation. The right of a party that has paid for a loss that a second party has suffered to recover those costs from the third party that is responsible for the damage.

Third-party claims. Claims that arise from liabilities to others (third parties).

Unallocated loss adjustment expenses. Adjusting expenses that cannot be segregated and assigned to individual claims, such as adjuster salaries, office expenses, and staff attorney fees.

MONITORING CLAIMS FOR FINANCIAL ACCURACY

WHAT IS IT?

Managing loss reserves is the process of monitoring claims to be sure that the loss reserve amounts placed on them accurately reflect their ultimate financial value. Insurance companies, as well as self-insured programs, set up reserves in order to identify what portion of their assets will be required to pay claims in the future. In addition, regulatory statutes require that insurance companies maintain reserves as liability accounts in their financial statements. The same is true of self-insured programs.

Loss management is one of the most important financial missions for a risk manager because of the impact that a business's loss history has on the total cost of its risk management program. This process is important regardless of whether the business has a guaranteed cost insurance program, a risk-sharing program, or self-insured program. The accurate statement of all business liabilities—including loss reserves—is critical in the overall management of a business.

Individual claims have three financial elements:

1. Paid amounts

2. Reserve amounts

3. Expenses

Paid amounts or *paid losses* are what already has been paid on individual claims. Reserve amounts or *reserves* are what is expected to be paid out in the future. *Expenses* are what is being spent for administrative and adjusting activities.

Each of these three elements is shown on a business's *loss history*, which also may be referred to as *loss experience*. A loss history is an individual business's aggregate history of claims over several years. The term *aggregate* refers to the total financial value of all claims over past years. Risk managers need to understand their business's loss history in order to

- pinpoint areas where claims frequently occur,

- identify the types of claims that frequently occur,

- identify individual claims that have a high financial value,

- target areas of high claim frequency or severity for loss control and safety initiatives,

- identify problem areas for claims, and

- identify claims that need to be monitored closely.

Loss histories are not static. The financial value of claims changes frequently as new claims are filed and situations develop on existing claims to increase or decrease the ultimate claim payouts. A sample general liability loss history for ABC Restaurants is shown in Figure 14.1. The first set of figures shows the financial value of general liability losses as of January 1, 2003, for the five policy terms of 1997 through 2001. The second set of figures shows the same losses at a valuation date of January 1, 2004. The last set shows the company's general liability loss history as of January 1, 2004, for the five policy terms of 1998 through 2002.

Much of the change in the aggregate loss history from January 1, 2003, to January 1, 2004, deals with changes in the reserves that are attached to specific claims. For example, a customer falls in one of the ABC Restaurants locations and breaks her shoulder on February 25, 2000. She files a claim. The woman is sixty-three years old but in good health. At first doctors believe she will recover quickly, so a reserve of $2,500 is established for medical payments. However, after three months, the woman's shoulder has not healed properly so doctors recommend surgery. The reserve is raised to $10,500 for medical costs, and an additional amount of $10,000 is reserved for pain and suffering. The condition of the woman's shoulder worsens. At this point the total reserve is increased to $50,000. More than $12,000 has been spent on medical bills. So the total incurred loss amount for

Figure 14.1

Loss History, ABC Restaurants, as of January 1, 2003
General Liability as of 1/1/03, 1997-2001 Policy Terms

Policy Term	# Closed Claims	# Open Claims	Paid Losses	Reserved Losses	Incurred Losses	ALAE	Premium
1/1/1997-98	85	0	$124,313	$0	$124,313	$4,298	$103,000
1/1/1998-99	62	0	$97,852	$0	$97,825	$3,100	$113,000
1/1/1999-00	72	1	$107,121	$27,899	$135,020	$3,842	$98,000
1/1/2000-01	63	3	$61,010	$43,212	$104,222	$2,301	$105,100
1/1/2001-02	76	17	$27,003	$65,729	$92,732	$1,621	$99,100
Total	358	21	$417,299	$136,840	$554,112	$15,162	$518,200

Total paid	$417,299
Total reserves	$136,840
Total incurred	$554,112
Total premium	$518,200

Loss History, ABC Restaurants, as of January 1, 2004
General Liability as of 1/1/04, 1997-2001 Policy Terms

Policy Term	# Closed Claims	# Open Claims	Paid Losses	Reserved Losses	Incurred Losses	ALAE	Premium
1/1/1997-98	85	0	$124,313	$0	$124,313	$4,298	$103,000
1/1/1998-99	62	0	$97,852	$0	$97,825	$3,100	$113,000
1/1/1999-00	73	0	$117,121	$0	$117,121	$3,842	$98,000
1/1/2000-01	64	2	$81,212	$81,555	$162,767	$2,301	$105,100
1/1/2001-02	85	8	$47,003	$29,888	$76,891	$1,621	$99,100
Total	369	10	$467,501	$111,443	$578,917	$15,162	$518,200

Total paid	$467,501
Total reserves	$111,443
Total incurred	$578,917
Total premium	$518,200

Loss History, ABC Restaurants, as of January 1, 2004
General Liability as of 1/1/04, 1998-2002 Policy Terms

Policy Term	# Closed Claims	# Open Claims	Paid Losses	Reserved Losses	Incurred Losses	ALAE	Premium
1/1/1998-99	62	0	$97,852	$0	$97,825	$3,100	$113,000
1/1/1999-00	73	0	$117,121	$0	$117,121	$3,842	$98,000
1/1/2000-01	64	2	$81,212	$81,555	$162,767	$2,301	$105,100
1/1/2001-02	85	8	$47,003	$29,888	$76,891	$1,621	$99,100
1/1/2002-2003	42	15	$26,799	$59,003	$85,802	$1,255	$136,799
Total	326	25	$369,987	$170,446	$540,406	$12,119	$551,999

Total paid	$369,987
Total reserves	$170,446
Total incurred	$540,406
Total premium	$551,999

this one claim has jumped to $62,000 from an original $2,500.

In reviewing Figure 14.1, you can see where the cumulative incurred losses for the 2000-01 policy term were $92,732 as of January 1, 2003. However, a year later, the value of the cumulative incurred losses for that year had increased to $162,767. A portion of the $70,035 increase results from additional payments and reserve increases on this one shoulder claim, which remains open as of January 1, 2004.

At the opposite end of the spectrum, suppose that the woman's shoulder healed more quickly than anticipated. In that event, the claim may have been settled for the original $2,500 or even less.

Insurance companies use a business's loss experience to determine whether the account is profitable or not. Profitability can be determined by calculating a *loss ratio*. A simple loss ratio for a business can be calculated by dividing the business's insurance premium into the losses:

$$\text{Loss ratio} = \frac{\text{Incurred Losses}}{\text{Premium}}$$

Figure 14.1 illustrates how the aggregate loss history for ABC Restaurants changes in one year.

The first set of figures is how the company's loss history stands as of January 1, 2003. Incurred losses total $554,112 for the five policy years shown. The premium is $518,200. ABC's loss ratio for this five-year period as of January 1, 2003, is calculated as follows:

$$\text{Loss Ratio} = \frac{\text{Five-year Incurred Losses}}{\text{Five-year Total Premium}} = \frac{\$554,112}{\$518,200} = \frac{107\% \text{ loss}}{\text{ratio as of}} \atop 1/1/03$$

By January 1, 2004, several claims were settled at amounts lower than originally estimated. However, one of the two claims that remain open for the policy year of 2000-2001 deteriorated, so the total incurred losses for that policy year increased from $104,222 as of January 1, 2003, to $162,767. The loss ratio for this five-year period therefore deteriorated in one year:

$$\text{Loss Ratio} = \frac{\text{Five-year Incurred Losses}}{\text{Five-year Total Premium}} = \frac{\$578,917}{\$518,200} = \frac{112\% \text{ loss}}{\text{ratio as of}} \atop 1/1/04$$

Because of the debit loss ratio, the underwriter increased the general liability premium at the 2002 renewal to $136,799. The business instituted several loss

control initiatives and began to aggressively manage losses, and the investment paid off in less serious general liability claims. The combination of the increased premium and lower incurred losses gives us the following loss ratio picture for the five policy terms of 1998 through 2001 as of January 1, 2004:

$$\text{Loss Ratio} = \frac{\text{Five-year Incurred Losses}}{\text{Five-year Total Premium}} = \frac{\$540,406}{\$551,999} = \frac{98\% \text{ loss}}{\text{ratio as of}} \atop 1/1/04$$

Over a period of years, the five-year general liability loss ratio for this account could be improved dramatically by a combination of claim management and loss control initiatives. The impact of claim management is even more dramatic for businesses that participate in risk-sharing programs, such as large deductible and retrospective-rated programs, and self-insurance.

STEPS TO IMPLEMENT

Step One: Setting Up and Obtaining the Data

The first step to managing losses and their reserves is obtaining information that is not only accurate but also pertinent to the operation of the individual business. This means that the information on individual claims must be set up so that meaningful reports can be generated.

Loss data (claim description, names of involved parties, location, type of incident, reserve amounts, paid amounts, expenses, and other pertinent information) are entered into an electronic data management system by either the business's risk management department or by the insurance company's claims department. These data management systems often are referred to as *Risk Management Information Systems* or *RMIS*.

Risk Management Tip

Loss information should be readily available, regardless of whether claims are administered by an insurance company claims department, by third party administrators or claims management companies, or by internal risk management employees.

There are seemingly countless types of management information systems available. Individual insurance companies may offer their proprietary systems to their business clients. Alternatively, a risk manager may develop her own data management system or purchase one from a vendor. Regardless of where the system comes from, it is critical that the information be accurate, readily available, and meaningful to what the business wants to accomplish.

Smaller businesses may have to rely on loss runs that their insurance companies print or electronically relay to them periodically. Larger companies may be able to negotiate real-time, online access to not only loss data but also claim adjuster notes. The most sophisticated and largest business will have access to customized systems.

Regardless of the size business, the bottom line is that information provided on losses be used to monitor claims in an effort to reduce their total financial impact.

Businesses with multiple locations usually code their claims by department or location. Location or departmental codes may be established according to existing internal cost center codes, or they may be specifically designed for the purpose of sorting loss data. The value in building the data along existing internal cost center codes is the consistency such a system has with other internal management programs. Once codes are set up, each claim is tied to the code when entered into the data management system. In this way, losses may be sorted by department or location automatically.

Location coding provides risk managers, loss control specialists, and insurance underwriters with the ability to

- determine which areas within the business are experiencing the most number of claims,

- determine which areas within the business are experiencing the most serious claims,

- identify areas where loss control and safety programs should be concentrated, and

- identify processes within the business that may lead to claims.

One of the most important aspects of location coding is that it can be used to allocate the cost of claims to department or location managers. A simple location coding system showing the first nine restaurants operated by ABC Restaurants, Inc., is shown in Figure 14.2.

The first two digits of each code are derived from the company's internal accounting division numbers. The next three digits represent an individual restaurant location. The last two digits represent areas on the individual restaurant property.

Information on losses at each restaurant—and in each area of each restaurant—can be obtained by this method. The information can be used in the aggregate by the risk management department for overall claims management purposes. In addition, problem areas can be pinpointed, and specific data relayed to individual restaurant managers. Many businesses will send copies of each location's loss data to the location manager so that he may review the information and be included in the claims management process. In addition, businesses often allocate a portion of the cost of claims to individual departments or locations for use in the manager's performance evaluation.

Figure 14.2 illustrates a simple location coding system. But, despite its apparent simplicity, it permits coding of up to ninety-nine divisions, up to 999 restaurants, and up to ninety-nine areas within each location. Some data management systems may permit more than a seven-digit code field.

Step Two: Reviewing the Data

Regardless of how claims information is obtained, the critical responsibility is to review and study the information, looking for keys on how to not only decrease reserves, but also on how to prevent additional claims from happening.

The most general information that is needed is a simple list of claims with brief descriptions and financial data for paid and reserved losses, as well as expenses. This information often is provided in chronological order of claim date, sorted by policy year and location code.

The first step in reviewing the data is to be sure that all the claims belong to the insured business. When insurance company or outside adjusters handle the data, there always is the possibility that some claims will be incorrectly assigned not only to the wrong location—but even to the wrong business.

If loss information is reviewed on a regular basis—such as the first week of each quarter or the tenth day of each month—changes in the financial picture of losses can be identified. As noted in Chapter 13, an initial

Figure 14.2

Sample Location Coding System	
ABC Restaurants, Inc. Numeric Coding Using Internal Department Codes Seven-Digit Field	
Claim Code	**Claim Code**

0100000	**Restaurant Holding Company, Division #01**	0205000	Cascade Restaurant, Location #05
		0205001	Kitchen
0101000	Executive Department, Dept. #01	0205002	Restaurant Serving Area
0102000	Financial Department, Dept. #02	0205003	Bar Area
0103000	Facilities Maintenance, Dept. #03	0205004	Bathrooms
0104000	Risk Management Department, Dept. #04	0205005	Entry Areas, Inside
		0205006	Sidewalks, Outside
0200000	**Restaurants, Division #02**	0205007	Outside Parking Areas
0201000	Logan Restaurant, Location #01	0206000	Cranberry Estates Restaurant, Location #06
0201001	Kitchen	0206001	Kitchen
0201002	Restaurant Serving Area	0206002	Restaurant Serving Area
0201003	Bar Area	0206003	Bar Area
0201004	Bathrooms	0206004	Bathrooms
0201005	Entry Areas, Inside	0206005	Entry Areas, Inside
0201006	Sidewalks, Outside	0206006	Sidewalks, Outside
0201007	Outside Parking Areas	0206007	Outside Parking Areas
0202000	Kettle Run Restaurant, Location #02	0207000	Creekside Restaurant, Location #07
0202001	Kitchen	0207001	Kitchen
0202002	Restaurant Serving Area	0207002	Restaurant Serving Area
0202003	Bar Area	0207003	Bar Area
0202004	Bathrooms	0207004	Bathrooms
0202005	Entry Areas, Inside	0207005	Entry Areas, Inside
0202006	Sidewalks, Outside	0207006	Sidewalks, Outside
0202007	Outside Parking Areas	0207007	Outside Parking Areas
0203000	Chelsea Restaurant, Location #03	0208000	Standardbearer Restaurant, Location #08
0203001	Kitchen	0208001	Kitchen
0203002	Restaurant Serving Area	0208002	Restaurant Serving Area
0203003	Bar Area	0208003	Bar Area
0203004	Bathrooms	0208004	Bathrooms
0203005	Entry Areas, Inside	0208005	Entry Areas, Inside
0203006	Sidewalks, Outside	0208006	Sidewalks, Outside
0203007	Outside Parking Areas	0208007	Outside Parking Areas
0204000	Vineyard Restaurant, Location #04	0209000	Mountainview Restaurant, Location #09
0204001	Kitchen	0209001	Kitchen
0204002	Restaurant Serving Area	0209002	Restaurant Serving Area
0204003	Bar Area	0209003	Bar Area
0204004	Bathrooms	0209004	Bathrooms
0204005	Entry Areas, Inside	0209005	Entry Areas, Inside
0204006	Sidewalks, Outside	0209006	Sidewalks, Outside
0204007	Outside Parking Areas	0209007	Outside Parking Areas

First set of 2 digits = Internal Accounting Division
Second set of 3 digits = Restaurant
Last 2 digits = Location within Restaurant

reserve is established for any claim that is not immediately settled. Reserves are revised as claims age. For example, an injured employee may recover more quickly than anticipated, resulting in a reserve decrease. Conversely, a reserve may be increased if complications arise after an employee is injured, and she may be forced to extend treatment or undergo surgery. It therefore is extremely important to review loss data on a regular basis to be sure that the current reserves reflect the ultimate claim values as much as possible.

Many insurance companies and brokers are able to provide clients with specially designed management reports that are developed from loss information that is contained in the loss data or risk management information system. Some electronic systems are programmed to automatically provide some types of management reports.

Types of management reports include those that list

- all claims above a certain incurred dollar amount,

- all claims with changes in the loss reserves from one report period to another,

- all claims with changes in incurred loss amounts from one report period to another, or

- all claims that are in litigation.

Figure 14.3 illustrates a sample change report that highlights changes (increases or decreases) of $5,000 or more in the incurred loss amounts. A separate change report would be issued for each of ABC Restaurant's locations. Figure 14.3 shows the incurred loss changes in general liability claims for location 020802, the serving area of the Standardbearer Restaurant, for the policy terms of 1997 through 2002.

This type of change report highlights the claims that had the greatest activity. It helps risk managers to pinpoint claims that they should review in more detail. It recaps information that is available in more detail within the database or detail loss runs.

Step Three: Make Inquiries

Open lines of communication with adjusters are critical at this point. Adjusters should be asked to explain why reserves have been increased or de-

creased, as well as for their professional opinion of options for handling problem cases. There are times when risk managers and adjusters cannot agree on how a claim is handled, how the reserves are set, and what is spent to settle a claim.

In general, once a claim is filed with an insurance company, that insurance company has the ultimate right to adjust the claim as it sees fit. However, courts have held that insurers hold the absolute right to settle claims when only their own money is involved. Therefore, the insurer has some obligation to work with the insured business to manage claims when a risk-sharing plan—such as a retrospectively rated or large deductible program—is involved. This is because both the insurance company's and the business's money is at stake. (In a retrospectively rated program, the premium is adjusted upwards or downwards after the policy expires to reflect the value of claims.)

An example is *Transport Indemnity Company v. Dahlen Transport, Inc.,* 161 N.W. 2d 546 (Minn. 1968), in which the Minnesota Supreme Court ruled that an insurer can be forced to produce evidence that settlements were made in good faith and not as a tool to avoid responsibility for making payments under excess insurance policies that it provided. A number of other cases also discuss such responsibilities in risk-sharing arrangements; they can be found in the End Notes to Chapter 13.

Formal claim reviews may be held periodically with risk management and claims adjusting representatives. Claim reviews can be an excellent way to develop and coordinate plans to successfully handle and settle claims. An outline of the claims review process is contained in Chapter 28.

Step Four: Methods to Reduce the Financial Impact of Losses

Risk managers can take some steps that may decrease the length and ultimate cost of difficult claims. These include

- instituting claims investigation procedures that are required immediately after an incident occurs,

- being willing to pay the medical bills of individuals (such as customers) who are injured on the business premises in an effort to prevent lawsuits,

Figure 14.3

		Monthly Change Report				

Claims with Changes in Inurred Amounts of $5,000 or More
Sorted by Location

Location 0208002			Prior Month Total Incurred	Current Month Total Incurred	Change Amount	Claim Status
Claim #	Date/Loss	Claim Description				
02-41233-999	06/12/02	Customer slipped on water that had spilled on floor near cash register. Broken elbow. Claimant age: 25	17,500	27,500	10,000	Open
02-89244-898	03/05/02	Customer caught heel in carpet on stairs leading to seating area, tripped, broke nose. Claimant age: 52	5,000	15,000	10,000	Open
02-15662-298	01/27/01	Customer caught heel in carpet on stairs leading to seating area, tripped, broke ankle. Claimant age: 37	5,000	13,000	8,000	Closed
02-51223-597	06/14/00	Customer slipped on wet floor next to coat rack, hurt back. Claimant age: 47	2,500	85,000	82,500	Open
0226978-597	05/24/00	Customer slipped on wet floor next to bar, hit head, bruised shoulder. Claimant age: 62.	10,000	75,000	65,000	Litigation Open
02-56823-597	10/14/99	Customer slipped on wet floor, broke hip. Claimant age: 84	35,000	76,800	41,800	Open
02-89211-197	04/15/99	Temporary floor mat curled because of wet weather, customer tripped, broke ankle. Claimant age: 72	5,000	45,000	40,000	Closed
02-54211-197	02/19/99	Customer slipped on pen on floor, twisted foot and hit head. Claimant age: 37	7,500	2,500	(5,000)	Closed
02-79421-896	01/05/98	Customer claims that waitress embarrassed her in front of other customers by refusing to serve her more liquor. Claimant age: 53	10,000	0	(10,000)	Closed
02-61245-695	06/02/97	Child running in restaurant, fell, broke teeth, cut face. Claimant age: 4	1,000	35,000	34,000	Litigation Open

- developing return-to-work initiatives, including job modifications, so that injured employees can more quickly return to work after a work-related injury,

- following up with injured workers to let them know the company cares about them, and

- developing an atmosphere of cooperation with adjusters so that both the business and its insurance company are working toward the same end.

ADVANTAGES

There are three principal advantages to managing losses:

1. It helps to generate accurate loss reserves,

2. It helps to reduce the ultimate financial impact of claims, and

3. It facilitates improved resolution of claims.

DISADVANTAGES

The two principal disadvantages of managing loss reserves are

1. The technique requires time and resources that could be allocated elsewhere, and

2. The technique requires a commitment by senior management to want to control claim costs. Without this the technique will not be successful.

WHERE CAN I FIND OUT MORE ABOUT IT?

- Associate in Claims (AIC) designation program offered by American Institute for Chartered Property Casualty Underwriters and the Insurance Institute of America, a four-part program that covers the claims area. http://www.aicpcu.org/programs/index.htm.

- *The Risk Funding and Self-Insurance Bulletins,* National Underwriter Co. http://www.nationalunderwriter.com/nucatalog/

Additional information is readily available from insurance companies, brokers, agents, and claims consultants.

QUESTIONS AND ANSWERS

Question—How can arrangements be made so that the insurance company or third party administrator handling claims provides loss information on a regular basis in a format that is meaningful?

Answer—This is best handled before an account is placed with a specific insurance company or a third party administrator is hired.

Part of the selection process should be a requirement that specific data management capabilities are provided. Accurate and timely data are the key to successful loss management. These requirements should be built into the selection process.

Question—What steps should be taken when moving an account from one insurance company to another or from one third party administrator to another? The old company will continue to handle claims that remain open when the business is moved from them. What should be done to ensure that these claims continue to receive adequate attention from the old adjusting facility?

Answer—It is important to receive ongoing information about losses even after business has been moved from one carrier or third party administrator to another. There may be opportunities to continue to receive access to an electronic claims-management system for a fee. Other options include periodic electronic downloads of the information or hard-copy loss run reports.

Some states require that loss information be made available to both current and former clients. If problems arise in obtaining the information, there may be recourse through state regulatory agencies.

Third party administration contracts often are awarded on a *cradle-to-grave* basis. This means that the business pays the TPA a fee that covers all claim-adjusting work from the inception of claims until they are settled and closed. In such situations, the TPA is obligated to continue to handle the claims and provide information to the business until all claims are closed.

Other contracts may be based on a specific period during which the TPA is to handle claims, such as two years. If the contract has ended and some claims remain open, the TPA can be asked to provide a proposal to handle those remaining open claims until they are resolved. This is called *handling the runoff*. The new TPA or another vendor also may be solicited to handle these runoff claims.

Regardless of how the remaining open claims are handled, receiving loss information and managing reserves remain priorities.

Question—Refer to Figure 14.1. Calculate the following:

1. Change in total reserves between January 1, 2003, and January 1, 2004, for the policy years of 1997-2001.

2. Change in paid claims between January 1, 2003, and January 1, 2004, for the policy years of 1997-2001.

3. The loss ratio on general liability insurance (excluding ALAE) for ABC Restaurants as of January 1, 2003, for the policy years of 1997-2001.

4. The loss ratio on general liability insurance (excluding ALAE) for ABC Restaurants as of January 1, 2004, for the policy years of 1997-2001.

5. The loss ratio on general liability insurance (excluding ALAE) for ABC Restaurants as of January 1, 2004, for the policy years of 1998-2002.

Answer—

1. ($25,397)

2. $50,202

3. 107%

4. 112%

5. 98%

Chapter 14

GLOSSARY

Aggregate. The total or collective amount.

Aggregate loss history. The total amount of claims that an individual business has incurred over a specific number of years.

Allocated loss adjustment expenses (ALAE). Adjusting expenses that can be attached to specific, individual claims, such as special surveillance, expert witness fees, and outside legal fees.

Claim tail. A commonly used term to describe the relative length of time before various types of claims are fully adjusted and settled.

Claims management. A technique to manage losses so that their financial impact is decreased.

Incurred losses. The value of claim payments plus reserves.

Loss history. The total amount of claims that an individual business has incurred over a period of years.

Loss ratio. The ratio of a business's incurred losses to its insurance premium over the same period of time.

Paid losses. The amounts that already have been paid on claims.

Reserves. Loss or claim reserves represent the value of losses that have been estimated and set up for future payment.

Risk Management Information Systems (RMIS). Electronic data management systems that include loss data and other risk management information.

INSURANCE COMPANIES AND RISK MANAGEMENT

Insurance is one of the principal means by which a risk manager transfers the financial uncertainty of losses resulting from such risks as damage to property, employee dishonesty, or risk of liability arising out of the insured's operations. As noted in Chapter 1, the term risk management has historically been closely related to the purchase and management of insurance, which transfers insurable risk to the insurance company for financial consideration—the premium.

Increasingly, the term risk management has been used to describe techniques for dealing with a variety of commercial and financial risks that are in addition to insurable risks. Despite this, insurance remains a key component of the risk management program of many businesses.

WHAT IS IT?

Insurance is a risk-transfer mechanism. Property and casualty insurance companies can be grouped into four types:

- stock insurance companies,
- mutual insurance companies,
- reciprocal exchanges, and
- Lloyd's associations.

A fifth type of mechanism is a *risk retention group (RRG)*. RRGs are not insurance companies but, rather, corporations or other associations that have the primary goal of assuming and spreading the liability risks of its group members.

Stock and Mutual Companies

Stock and mutual companies are the most prevalent type of traditional insurance mechanism.

Stock insurance companies are owned by the stockholders and are organized as for-profit corporations. The capital for the stock insurance company comes from the stockholders, and any profits or losses from their operation are enjoyed by or borne by the stockholders.

Mutual insurance companies are owned by their policyholders. The objective of the mutual insurance company is to reduce policyholders' premiums. Profits in excess of the premiums charged are returned to the policyholders in the form of lower rates or as a *dividend*. In reality, a dividend is a return of premiums that are in excess of the amounts needed to cover losses and operating costs. In addition, policyholders of a mutual company participate in electing the board of directors.

Mutual insurance companies cannot sell shares of stock to the capital markets, as stock companies can. Therefore, it is more difficult for mutual companies to raise capital than for stock insurers. There are two basic methods available to overcome this disadvantage—*demutualization* and *merger*. Demutualization is the conversion of a mutual insurance operation to a stock insurance structure, a technique that has been used primarily by life insurance companies. Merger is the consolidation of two or more companies into a single company. Demutualization begins with a plan that is subject to state insurance department review as to its fairness to mutual company policyholders. A significant part of the demutualization process deals with valuing and fairly distributing the company's equity among its policyholders. Demutualization statutes generally permit state insurance regulators to determine the appropriate method.

Reciprocal Exchanges

In concept, *reciprocal exchanges*, which also are described as interinsurance exchanges, are unincorporated arrangements in which one policyholder agrees to participate in insuring all other policyholders. In exchange, the other policyholders insure that policyholder. In practice, a reciprocal exchange (often called a *reciprocal*) is usually managed by an attorney-in-fact who is authorized by the policyholders to collect premiums in advance, to transact reciprocal agreements with new customers, and to otherwise manage the operations of the reciprocal.

Lloyd's Associations

Lloyd's associations are yet another approach to providing insurance. Lloyd's of London, which is the most famous Lloyd's association, provided ocean marine insurance in the late seventeenth century. Lloyd's of London is not an insurance company. It provides facilities, sometimes called the *underwriting room*, where insurance can be transacted with its members. Originally, insurance was transacted by individuals known as *names* that would underwrite, for their own accounts, a small portion of others' risks. Names usually join a syndicate with other names; the syndicate transacts business on their behalf, often for specific types of risk. The names at Lloyd's are required to meet certain minimum financial requirements and are subject to unlimited liability for assessments if losses exceed premiums. Lloyd's of London has been reorganized and will now accept corporate names. Lloyd's brokers transact insurance by approaching syndicates and asking them to underwrite a percentage of particular risks. The Lloyd's broker continues around the underwriting room collecting underwriting commitments until 100 percent of the risk is placed.

Risk Retention Groups

Risk retention groups (RRGs) are organizations formed to spread the liability risks of groups of similar businesses. In 1981, Congress gave businesses the right to form RRGs to provide products and completed operations liability coverage to members of groups. In 1986, the Product Liability Risk Retention Act of 1981 was substantially expanded when Congress amended it to permit risk retention and purchasing groups to be involved in a broader range of liability coverages, including liability arising from a business's premises and operations as well as its products and completed operations. RRGs are chartered under the laws of a state or other U.S. jurisdiction and are composed of members whose business activities are similar. RRGs may not be subject to all the insurance laws and regulations that pertain to insurance companies operating in specific states. The Product Liability Risk Retention Act of 1981as amended in 1986 is reprinted in Figure 15.1 in the chapter appendix.

Purchasing groups are similar to RRGs, but they do not actually provide insurance. A purchasing group is a group that has as one of its purposes the purchase of liability insurance on a group basis.

REGULATION

Insurance companies are regulated on a state-by-state basis. Each state has an insurance department, which is headed by an insurance commissioner. The primary responsibility of insurance commissioners is to provide consumer protection by regulating and monitoring the solvency of insurance companies. State insurance departments also regulate the coverage wording and structure of insurance policies that are admitted to do business in their jurisdictions, as well as monitoring the conduct of the companies doing business there.

State insurance commissioners joined together more than 100 years ago to form the National Association of Insurance Commissioners (NAIC). Commissioners of the District of Columbia and four U.S. territories also are members of the NAIC, which coordinates the regulation of multistate insurers and facilitates the development of uniform practices and policies when appropriate. Information about some of the methods used by these regulators to monitor insurance company financial strength and solvency are contained within the section of this chapter entitled **Financial Strength.**

CHOOSING AN INSURANCE ARRANGEMENT

Several factors should be considered when judging the quality of an insurer. Among these are its

- organizational structure,
- status as an admitted or nonadmitted company if a traditional insurance company is chosen,
- financial strength,
- size,
- claims-paying philosophy, and
- risk management support services.

Organizational Structure

As noted in the introduction to this chapter, there are four basic organizational structures: stock company, mutual company, reciprocal exchange, and Lloyd's associations. Reciprocal exchanges and Lloyd's associations write a substantial amount of business in certain classes of business and geographical areas. RRGs tend to be more heavily used when rates for traditional insurance arrangements are high. They also may be used when specific types of coverage are difficult to find. These types of organization are less common than are stock and mutual insurance companies.

Admitted and Nonadmitted Insurers

Insurance companies are either *admitted* or *nonadmitted* on a state-by-state basis.

Admitted companies are licensed to conduct business within a given state and are subject to state regulation and guaranty funds. Nonadmitted companies are not licensed in particular states or territories and are not directly regulated by the states in which they are not admitted.

Companies are further classified as

- domestic insurance companies, which are domiciled and licensed in a state.

- foreign companies, which are domiciled in a state other than where the coverage is being written. If the foreign companies are licensed in a state in which they are not domiciled, they are called admitted foreign companies; if not, nonadmitted companies.

- alien insurance companies, which are domiciled in another country. If licensed in a state, they are called admitted alien insurance companies in that state; if not, they are nonadmitted alien insurance companies.

Company Classification Example

If Rock Solid Insurance Company (RSIC) is domiciled in Georgia (i.e., it was chartered in Georgia), it is a Georgia domestic company. If RSIC is also licensed in Florida, it is an admitted foreign insurer in Florida. If it is not licensed in Alabama, it is a nonadmitted insurer in Alabama.

Assume RSIC has a foreign subsidiary, Slippery Rock Limited, which is domiciled in Denmark and licensed in only one state, Georgia. In Georgia, Slippery Rock is an admitted alien insurer; in Alabama it is a nonadmitted alien insurer.

It is usually easy to locate information and ratings about admitted foreign, admitted alien, and domestic insurance companies from state insurance departments or one of the insurance company rating services. It is more difficult to locate information about nonadmitted alien insurers.

One method of gathering information is to contact the NAIC, Executive Headquarters, 2301 McGee St., Suite 800, Kansas City, MO 64108-2604, NAIC Help Desk Phone (816) 783-8500, email: help@naic.org, Web site: http://www.naic.org/help/html/helpindex.htm. According to the NAIC's Web site, its International Insurers Department (IID) tracks non-U.S. insurers that want to do business in the United States surplus or excess lines market. Alien insurers may apply to the IID for placement on its quarterly list. In some states, appearance on the IID list is the only way by which an alien insurer may become eligible to write surplus or excess lines business; in others it is just one method by which such insurers can gain eligibility. Still other states use the listing as a major element of their qualifying criteria. Maintaining an IID listing requires a continuation of minimum capital and surplus, establishment of a trust fund in favor of U.S. policyholders, and annual financial filings.[1] The fact that an insurer is on the IID list does not guarantee that it is solvent. However, it does mean that it has deposits in the United States to protect its policyholders.

Another source of information is *Best's Insurance Reports on CD-ROM - International*. A. M. Best offices are at Ambest Road, Oldwick, New Jersey 08858. Phone 908-439-2200.

State Guaranty Associations

One of the primary disadvantages of using nonadmitted companies and other alternative risk-transfer mechanisms such as RRGs is that in most cases they do not participate in *state guaranty associations*.

State guaranty associations provide mechanisms to pay for covered claims filed against insolvent insurers in an effort to avoid catastrophic financial losses by the policyholders of those insolvent insurers. Property and casualty insurance companies that are covered by guaranty associations must belong to the guaranty association of a particular state as a condition of their authority to transact business in that state. Guaranty associations assess member insurers based upon their proportion of premiums written on covered lines of business in that state compared with total premiums written in the state.

Representatives for Admitted and Nonadmitted Insurers

Agents and brokers, often referred to as retail agents or brokers because they arrange coverage between individuals or businesses and insurance companies, represent admitted carriers.

Figure 15.2

Surplus Lines Ready Reference

NOTE: The notation IPC under the "Other" column stands for "Independently Procured Coverage." The question addresses whether or not a particular state allows insureds to purchase coverage directly from insurers or surplus lines carriers without going through an agent or a broker. The notation CF under "Tax" stands for "Courtesy Filings." The question addresses whether or not a particular state allows resident surplus lines brokers to file the taxes and nonavailability certificates for nonresidents as a courtesy. Any state with an asterisk (*) after its abbreviation has a surplus lines stamping office or a Surplus Lines Association.

State	Prelicense Reqs. for Residents	Nonresident Eligible	Certificate of Non-availability	Tax	Other
AL	$50,000 Bond Must be licensed as Property Prod.	YES	Within 30 Days of Procurement	6% of Net Prem	Not for L/H; Not for Lower Rate; Notice to Insured IPC: YES
AK	Must have 2 years of experience in last 5. $200,000 Bond. Exam.	YES	Within 30 Days of Procurement	2.7% of Gross Prem plus 1% Filing Fee .75%, wet marine; CF: NO	May Use Non-Approved Comps if Coverage Not Available from Approved; Not for L/H, Work Comp, or PP Auto IPC: YES
AZ*	Licensed as Prod. or Bond; Also licenses; Exam Mexican S/L Brokers	YES	YES - 3 declinations	3% of Gross Prem; Stamping Fee of .35%	Approved Comps Only; Notice to Insured; Not For Life, Work Comp, or PP Auto; Not for better rate or form; IPC: YES
AR	Must be Licensed 3 Yrs as Agent or Broker (Producer); $50,000 Bond; Exam	YES	Yes and Kept in Broker's Office; Summary to be Filed Monthly	4% of Written Prem	Insured's Consent Required; No Use for Better Rate; Notice to Insured; Not for L/A/H, Work Comp or; Public contractor bonds IPC: YES
CA*	Must be Licensed as Broker-Agent; $50,000 Bond	Only for Purch Grps	Within 60 days of Procurement	3% of Gross Prem; .25% Stamping Fee CF: NO	Notice to Insured; No Use for Lower Rate; IPC: YES Approved comps. only
CO*	$25,000 Bond	YES	YES, Monthly	3% of Gross Prem; .2% Stamping Fee CF: YES	Notice to Insured; Not for Lower Rate; Approved Cos. Only IPC: YES
CT	P&C License $25,000 Bond Exam	Yes; Must be Licensed for P&C in Home State and CT; and Pass CT Exam	YES, Within 45 Days	4% of Gross Prem CF: YES	Not for Better Rate or Pers Auto, FAIR Plan, Work Comp; Approved Cos. Only Notice to Insured IPC: YES
DE	Licensed as Broker; (Producer) $5,000 bond	Reciprocal	Within 30 Days After Eff Date	2% of Net Prem CF: YES	Not for Better Rate or Terms; Notice to Insured; Approved Comps. Only IPC: YES

Figure 15.2 (cont'd)

DC	$20,000 Bond	YES, if Near DC	YES, Monthly	2% of Gross Prem	Not for Better Rate or Terms or Pers Auto, A&H, Life, or Work Comp; IPC: YES
FL*	60 Hrs or One Yr Exp plus Exam; $50,000 Bond; Must belong to Fla. Surplus Lines Service Office	Only for Risk Ret or Purch Grps required	Quarterly; 3 declinations	5% of Gross Prem+ .3% stamping fee	Notice to Insured; Not for L&H, W Comp, or Pers Auto; Not for rate or form; only approved comps. IPC: YES
GA	Must be Licensed Agent (Producer); $50,000 Bond	YES	Diligent effort Affidavit to be Filed Quarterly	4% of Gross Prem CF: NO	Not for Life; Notice to Insured; IPC: YES
GU	Must be Licensed as Agent or Broker; $2,000 Bond	NO	Must be Filed before Insurance is Procured	4%; plus 2% for Industrial or Commercial Liability CF: NO	Not for Better Rate or Form; Notice to Insured; IPC: YES
HI	$100,000 Bond	YES-Reciprocal	Yes, Annually	4.68% of Gross Prem CF: NO	Not for Better Rate; Notice to Insured; IPC: YES
ID*	$10,000 Bond 2 yrs exper.	YES	Within 30 Days of Procurement	2.75% of Gross Prem; 1% Stamping Fee CF: NO	Only Approved Comps May be Used; Not for Life or A&H; IPC: YES Notice to Insured Not for rate or form
IL*	Lic Producers; Exam; $20,000 Bond; Must be Member of Surplus Line Assoc	YES	Must submit policies to SLA for counter-signature; 3 declinations	3% of Gross plus 1% Fire Marshall Tax; .3% Stamping Fee	Notice to Insured; Use of Comp with Less than $15 Mill in Surplus Requires Special Warning to Insured IPC: YES
IN	Licensed Producers; $20,000 Bond	YES	Filed by 20th of Month Following Placement	2.5% of Gross Prem CF: NO	Agent May Not Charge Service Fee; Not for Life, A&H, Auto, or Work Comp; Approved Cos. Only; IPC: YES
IA	Special Lic Required; Exam	YES	File Within 30 Days of Delivery	2% of Gross Prem	Only Approved Comps; Notice to Insured; IPC: YES
KS	Must Have E&O Policy of at Least $100,000; Licensed as a P&C Agt for 3 Yrs	YES	Signed Acceptance from Insured Prior to Placement	6% of Gross Prem CF: N/A	Only P&C May be Placed in S/L; Approved Cos. Only; Notice to Insured IPC: NO
KY	Must be Licensed as Agt for 3 Yrs and Represent 3 Admitted Comps; Bond and E&O Policy	YES-Reciprocal	YES, Filed Within 60 Days after Procurement	3% of Prem plus Municipal Tax plus KY Tax of 1.5% on P&C CF: NO	Not for Better Rate; Not for Life or A&H; May Only Use Comps with $3 Mill in Surplus and in Operation for 3 Yrs; Not for rate or form; IPC: YES
LA	2 Yrs Exp; Exam; $40,000 Bond	REC	within 30 days of of binding	5% of Gross Prem	Notice to Insured Authorized comps only IPC: YES

Figure 15.2 (cont'd)

ME	Must be licensed Producer; $20,000 Bond	YES	NO, but Broker Must conduct a Diligent Search	3% of Gross Prem	Not for Better Rate or Life/A&H; Notice to Insured; IPC: YES
MD	Must be Licensed as P&C Prod.; $10,000 Bond	YES	YES, Filed Within 45 Days after Month of Procurement; 3 declinations	3% of Gross Prem	Notice to Insured Required on Policy; Not for Better Rate or Form; Not for L&H, Pers Auto, W Comp, Marine, or Railroads; IPC: YES
MA	Special Brokers License; $2,000 Bond	YES	Filed Within 20 Days of Procurement	4% of Gross Prem	Not to be Used for Life, A&H, Auto, or Work Comp; Approved comps. only
MI	Must be licensed agent; Exam	NO	YES	2% of Gross Prems plus .5% regulatory fee	Must Contain Notice to Insured; S/L Agents May Add Fee of up to $25; Only approved comps.; IPC: YES
MN	P&C License bond equal to 2% of prem min., $200	YES	Must be Kept on File by the Broker 3 declinations	3% of Gross Prem eligible cos. 2%, ineligible cos. CF: YES	Must Contain Notice to Insured; Not for Pers Auto, Work Comp, or HO Below $1,118,504; Only approved comps; IPC: YES
MS*	Must be Licensed Producer; Bond of $3,000	YES	Requires Insured's Signature; Filed Monthly	4% of Gross Prems CF: YES .5% stamping fee	Only Approved Comps; Must Contain Notice to the Insured; Not for Life or A&H; IPC: NO
MO	Must be Licensed Producer; Exam; Bond of $100,000	YES	Must be Filed Within 30 Days of Effective date	5% of Net Prems CF: NO	Only Approved Comps; Must Contain Notice to the Insured; reins., L/A&H, annuities, marine, transp. Not Eligible; IPC: YES
MT*	$10,000 Bond; Licensed 5 years	YES	Must be Filed at Time Ins is Placed 3 declinations	2.75% of Net Prems Plus 2.50% of Fire Prems; CF: NO	Not for Better Rate or Terms; IPC: YES Notice to insured IPC: YES
NE	Currently Licensed Producers; Bond of $10,000 per Licensee (up to $100,000 per Firm)	YES	NO, but Agt Must File Quarterly and Annual Reports Listing All Non-admitted Business Written Along with Forms Signed by Insured	3% Plus .75% Fire Tax CF: YES	Policy Must Contain Wording That Guaranty Fund Does Not Apply; IPC: YES
NV*	Exam; Licensed as producer at least 6 months	YES	Must be Filed Within 90 Days After Placement	3.5% of Gross Prem	Not for Better Rate or Form; Notice to Insured Approved comps only IPC: YES

Figure 15.2 (cont'd)

NH	Must Pay Fee	YES	Must be Filed Monthly by 10th of Next Month	2% of Gross Prem CF: NO	Only Approved Comps; Notice to Insured IPC: YES
NJ	Currently Licensed in P&C; Exam; $25,000 Bond	YES	NO Copy of Policy Within 90 Days	3% of Gross Prem	State has a S/L Guaranty Fund; Approved Cos. Only; Notice to insured; IPC: YES
NM*	Licensed as agent; $20,000 Bond	NO	Must be Filed with Commr Within 60 Days after Each Quarter; within 15 days with DOI Stamping Office	3% of Net Prem CF: YES	Only Approved Comps; Notice to Insured; Not for Life, A&H, PP Auto, or Work Comp IPC: YES
NY*	Licensed as Producer $15,000 Bond	YES	Must be Filed Within 45 Days of Procurement; Must Show 3 Declinations	3.6% of Gross Prems; Stamping Fee, .4% CF: NO	Notice to Insured; Not for L/H, Work Comp, Title, Annuities, or PP Auto; Approved co.'s only IPC: YES
NC*	Exam, $10,000 Bond; Must Belong to S/L Assoc	REC	Filed with Commr Within 30 Working Days of Procurement	5% of Gross Prems CF: YES	Approved carriers only; Notice to Insured; IPC: YES
ND	Exam; $5,000 bond; E&O Policy	YES	Filed with Commr 15 Days After Effective Date	P/C: 1.75% of Gross Prem; L/H: 2%	Notice to Insured Not for Life/A&H Approved Cos. Only; IPC: NO
OH	Must be Licensed as Producer for Two Years; $25,000 Bond	YES	Must be Filed with Commr within 30 days of end of quarter	5% of Gross Prems	May be Used for Rate If S/L Rate is at Least 10% Better; Notice to Insured; Approved Comps Only; Not For L/A&H or WC IPC: YES
OK	Must be Licensed as Producer; Amount of Bond Depends upon Prior Year's Gross Prem	YES	YES Filed quarterly	6% of Gross Prems CF: YES-Ret.	Only Approved Comps; Not for Better Rate; or form Not for Life, A&H Notice to Insured
OR*	Must be Licensed for prop. or cas. $50,000 Bond	YES Must Hold Oregon P or C Lic	Must be Filed Within 90 Days of Procurement	2% of Gross Prem Plus 1% Prem for Fire Tax CF: YES .35% stamping fee	Notice to Insured; Not for Reinsurance, Marine, L&H, or Annuities; IPC: NO
PA*	Must be Licensed as a Broker; Exam	YES	Must be Filed within 45 Days	3% of Gross Prem CF: NO	Notice to Insured Approved Cos. Only; Notice to Insured; IPC: YES
PR	Must be Licensed Agent or Broker; $25,000 Bond	NO	Must be Filed at Time of Procurement; Must Show at Least 5 Declinations	9% of Gross Prem	Not for Better Rate or Form; Policy Notice to Insured; Approved Cos. Only; IPC: YES

Figure 15.2 (cont'd)

RI	Must hold Producer lic. $25,000 Bond	YES	Must be Signed by Insured and Filed Within 30 Days of Procurement; 3 Declinations; Not Applicable to Industrial Insureds	3% of Gross Prem	Not for Better Rate or Form; Not for L/A&H; Approved Comps Only; Notice to Insured; IPC: NO
SC	Must be Licensed Broker (Producer); $10,000 Bond	YES	Not Required	4% of All Prems Plus 2% to S.C. Munic. Assoc.	Broker Must File Annual Report and Policy Must Contain Notice to Insured; Not for L&H, PP Auto, or Work Comp; IPC: YES
SD	Licensed producers; Bond of $2,000 Exam	YES	Must be Filed with Commr Within 30 Days of Procurement	Other than Fire: 2.5%; Fire: 3% CF: NO	Policy Must Contain Notice to the Insured; Not for Life or A&H; IPC: YES Approved Cos. Only
TN	Must be Authorized Agent	YES	Must be Filed with Commr upon Procurement; Must Show "diligent effort"	Excess WC: 4.4%; Property: 3.25%; Liability: 2.5% CF: NO	PP Auto and Work Comp Are Not Eligible; Approved Cos. Only; Notice to insured
TX*	Must be Licensed as for P&C or as an MGA; Exam; Bond of $50,000	Only for Purch Grps	Must be Filed with S/L Stamping Office within 60 Days	4.85% of Gross Premiums; Stamping Fee is .25% CF: NO	Only Approved Comps; May Not be Used to Avoid Assigned Risk Auto Plan; Policy Must Contain Notice to the Insured; IPC: YES
UT*	Must be Licensed Prod.	YES; Must Register with the Utah S/L Assoc	Within 60 Days CF: NO	4.25% of Gross Prems Plus .25% Stamping Fee	Approved Comps Only; Notice to Insured; IPC: YES
VT	Must be Licensed as Producer; $20,000 Bond; 2 yrs. exp. Exam	YES	Must File Quarterly Reports	3% of Gross Prem	Approved Comps Only; Notice to Insured; IPC: YES
VA	Must be Licensed as P&C Agent; $25,000 Bond	YES, If Licensed as Virginia Non-Res for P&C	Must be kept on file; Agt Must Show 3 Declinations	2.25% of Gross Prem Plus .05% Bureau Maintenance Assessment CF: NO	Notice to Insured; May be Used for Better Rate or Form; Approved comps.; Notice to Insured; IPC: YES
VI	Anyone with an Office in the VI and Approved by the Commr; $10,000 Bond	YES	Must be Filed Within 30 Days After Procurement; Must Show Declinations from a Majority of Comps Writing That Line of Business	5% of Gross Prems; Payable Quarterly	May Not be Used For Better Rate; Notice to Insured Approved comps. only
WA*	Must meet exp. requirements; $20,000 Tax Bond and $100,000 Surety Bond; Exam	REC	Must be Filed with Commr Within 30 Days of Procurement	2% of Gross Prems Plus .4% Stamping Fee CF: YES	Not for Better Rate Notice to Insured; IPC: YES

Figure 15.2 (cont'd)

WV	Must be Licensed Agent; Exam; 3 yrs. exp. $2,000 Bond	YES	Must be Filed with Commr, annually	4% of Gross Prems plus 1% Surcharge CF: NO	Not for Better Form, Rate, or for Work Comp; Policies Must Be Countersigned
WI	Must be Licensed $100,000 bond	YES	NO	Ocean Mar, .5%; All Other Lines, 3% of Gross Prem	Notice to Insured; If Placed with Un-approved Company, copy to Commr. IPC: NO
WY	Must be Licensed P&C Prod.; $10,000 Bond	YES	Must be Filed With the Commr Within 30 Days after Procurement	3% of Gross Prem CF: NO	Not for Rate or Form; Capital Reqs; IPC: YES Notice to Insured

Nonadmitted companies usually are represented by surplus lines brokers, which must be licensed to offer nonadmitted coverage. Surplus lines brokers may be referred to as *wholesalers* because they usually broker coverage between retail agents or brokers and nonadmitted carriers. Most states levy surplus-lines taxes on the premiums written by nonadmitted carriers. These carriers are not subject to the state guaranty funds. Therefore, in the event of insolvency, businesses that are insured by nonadmitted carriers are not able to tap the guaranty fund for protection. **Figure 15.2** is a state-by-state summary of surplus lines laws. Additional information on surplus lines laws is available from the individual state insurance departments or the National Association of Professional Surplus Lines Officers, Ltd., http://www.napslo.org/.

Financial Strength

It is critical to carefully evaluate the financial strength of insurers being considered for coverage. A number of companies publish financial strength ratings. Each of these companies has its own rating scale and publishes detailed reports in areas such as management, the use of reinsurance, the states in which they are licensed to transact insurance, and the nature of the insurers' operations.

Additional information on the availability of insurance company ratings can be obtained at the following Web sites:

A.M. Best
http://www.ambest.com/

Fitch Ratings
http://www.fitchratings.com/corporate/index.cfm

Moody's
http://www.moodys.com/moodys/cust/RatingAction/rlist.asp?busLineId=8&list=1

Standard & Poor's
http://www.standardandpoors.com

Weiss Ratings
http://www.weissratings.com/

Explanations for the rating grades of five such companies are contained in the appendix of this chapter.

There are other methods to gauge financial strength—some are subjective and others, objective. Risk managers may read trade publications and build networks of information to spot changes in insurance company operations. For example, if an insurer suddenly decided to become a large-scale reinsurer of California earthquake coverage, past ratings of that company would tend to lose their meaning.

Risk Management Tip

The financial strength of carriers is one of the most critical elements in choosing an insurance company. It is prudent to consult the financial evaluations published by more than just one rating agency before placing business with a carrier. Additional information on insurance company financial strength is available in each company's respective annual statements. These annual statements may be obtained from the applicable insurance company, state insurance departments, or the NAIC.

State insurance department and NAIC contact information is included in this chapter's appendix.

Despite the fact that insurance carrier financial strength is monitored by multiple rating organizations, some insurance company failures have not been anticipated. When insurance companies become insolvent, the claims that are the subject of their coverage policies are not paid.

Impact of State Guaranty Funds on Insolvencies

Individual states have passed legislation creating guaranty funds to protect the policyholders of insolvent companies. These guaranty associations, which also are referred to as guaranty funds, provide mechanisms to pay for covered claims filed against insolvent insurers in an effort to protect their policyholders from catastrophic financial loss. All states and territories other than New York have *created post-assessment guaranty associations*, which assess solvent insurers for funds to pay claims after an insolvency of another insurer has occurred. The New York Security Fund and certain funds that cover only workers compensation policyholders are considered *preassessment* guaranty funds, which means that assessments are made prior to a specific insolvency occurring.

Property and casualty insurance companies that are subject to guaranty association regulations must belong to the guaranty association of a particular state as a condition of their authority to transact business in that state. Guaranty associations assess member insurers based upon their proportionate share of premiums written on covered lines of business in the applicable state. The National Conference of Insurance Guaranty Funds (NCIGF) provides information on state guaranty funds at its Web site, www.ncigf.org. According to the NCIGF, New Jersey is the only state that has a surplus lines guaranty association, so businesses placing insurance with nonadmitted surplus lines carriers in states other than New Jersey are not eligible for guaranty fund payments. A summary of the NCIGF information is printed in this chapter's appendix.

Ignoring the difficult problem of evaluating an insurance company's financial strength and attempting to rely merely on the state guaranty association could be a serious mistake. As noted in the appendix, the scope of state guaranty fund coverage is limited. Even if policyholders of an insolvent insurer do fall within the scope of a state guaranty fund, a protracted delay in collecting claim payments from a fund is a problem for any policyholder. For a large corporation the often relatively small amount of coverage and the frequent presence of net

worth provisions reduce the relevancy of such funds to the entity. A guaranty fund is only a stopgap to prevent catastrophic financial losses for policyholders; a fund does not diminish the need for due diligence in studying the financial strength of individual insurance companies.

RRGs are not covered by guaranty funds, so their financial strength is even more critical.

Risk–Based Capital

During 1993 the NAIC developed what is called a *Risk-Based Capital (RBC) system* for analyzing the financial strength of both property and casualty and life insurance companies. The NAIC approach is designed to determine if an insurer has an adequate amount of capital, which is called *policyholders' surplus*. For an insurance company, policyholders' surplus is similar to what is termed owners' equity for noninsurance companies. It is the difference between the insurance company's admitted assets and its liabilities and, as such, may be tapped into to meet the insurance company's contractual obligations in the event of insolvency.

Before the RBC system was adopted, adequacy of capital was determined by comparing the ratio of written premium to surplus (owners' equity) method. Under the *written premium ratio system*, sometimes called the *Kenny Rule*, an insurer was assumed to have adequate capital if the ratio of its written premium to surplus was below some target, such as 3 to 1. However, the RBC system was developed because it was thought that the use of one standard ratio was no longer appropriate to determine the surplus needs of all insurers.

The purpose of the RBC system is not to provide ratings for companies, but rather to provide a benchmark for insurers. The system determines a desirable capital level that is based on the risk generated by each insurer's investment philosophy, book of business, and cash flow pattern. If the company fails to meet the target, it is given closer scrutiny.

There are two RBC formulas. One applies to life insurers and the other to property and casualty insurers. The risks examined for property and casualty insurers are similar to those of life insurers. They include:

1. asset risk,

2. credit risk,

3. underwriting risk, and

4. all other business risk.

Asset risk is the likelihood that the value of the insurer's investment portfolio will decline. Property and casualty credit risk is the chance that the insurer will not collect premiums, reinsurance, and other receivables. Underwriting risk is that premium rates and/or loss reserves will be inadequate to cover losses as they reach maturity. All other business risk includes items such as an unusually large guaranty fund assessment. Off-balance-sheet risks, such as excessive premium growth, guarantees of parents, and affiliate obligations also are examined.

The temptation to use only RBC to rate and rank companies should be avoided. It is only one of several techniques that may be used to judge financial strength and prospective solvency on respective insurance companies.[2]

Insurance Regulatory Information System (IRIS)

The NAIC Insurance Regulatory Information System (IRIS) represents a strengthening of the insurance regulatory process. It is part of a system designed to provide state insurance departments with an integrated approach to screening and analyzing the financial condition of insurance companies. IRIS was developed by a committee of state insurance regulators and is intended to assist state insurance departments allocate resources to the insurers in greatest need of regulatory attention. IRIS, however, is not intended to replace the indepth financial analysis and examinations that state insurance departments conduct.[3] The IRIS ratios are a series of calculations that are used to develop and gauge the acceptability of various financial measures. The adequacy of policyholders' surplus is a key indicator of an insurer's ability to absorb above-average losses, and IRIS ratios help to gauge the adequacy of policyholders' surplus.

Size

Information published by the various rating organizations includes details on the size of individual insurance companies. Size is important because it reflects the assets that are available to back the liabilities of insurance companies.

Risk Management Question

ABC Insurance Company has offered to insure the property and liability exposures of T&T Construction Company. T&T is an $85 million company. ABC Insurance has assets of $67 million. Is ABC large enough to handle the insurance for a company the size of T&T Construction? Does the financial size of an insurance company matter? How would the ABC insurance company's use of reinsurance influence your evaluation?

Claims-paying Philosophy

Some insurance companies are well known for their philosophy of erring in favor of their insureds in situations in which coverage is not clear-cut. Other insurers have a reputation for contesting claim payments whenever possible. An insurance company's claims-paying philosophy can only be measured subjectively. However, risk managers may seek opinions about how insurers treat the claims process from other risk managers, their brokers, or agents. Informal information also may be exchanged on one online discussion forum, at http://www.riskmail.org/Default.htm.

Claim Reserving Practices

Establishing realistic reserves for unpaid claims is not a simple task. But it is critical to a company's financial adequacy because they represent the amount of money that would be needed to pay all claims against the insurer. Reserves include both future estimated payments for claims that already have been filed and future estimated payments for claims that have occurred but have not yet been reported. The latter category is known as *incurred but not reported (IBNR)* claims. This refers to the fact that some injury or damage to which the policy applies has occurred, but the claim for damages has not yet been reported to the insurance company.

When claim reserves are understated, the company's surplus will be overstated. Conversely, overstated reserves diminish surplus. IRIS uses two ratios to test for the accuracy of loss reserves. They use both a one-year reserve development to policyholders' surplus ratio and a two-year reserve development to policyholders' surplus. (See Figure 15.3.) Ratios 9, 10, and 11 are used to check the historical accuracy of loss reserves.

Figure 15.3 outlines the ratio formulas and range of acceptable values. Additional information on IRIS measurements is available from the NAIC, www.naic.org.

Figure 15.3

Property and Liability		
Insurance Regulatory Information System (IRIS) Ratios		
Ratio	**Description**	**Acceptable Values**
#1 Gross Premium to Surplus Ratio =	(Gross Premium Written) ÷ (Policyholders Surplus)	Less than or equal to 900%
#1A Net Premium to Surplus Ratio =	(Net Premium Written) ÷ (Policyholders Surplus)	Less than or equal to 300%
#2 Change in Net Writings Ratio =	(Change in Net Writings)÷ (Net Premium Written [Prior Year])	Greater than -33% and less than +33%
Note: Changes in writings is equal to net premium written for current year minus the net premium written for the prior year.		
#3 Surplus Aid to Surplus Ratio =	(Surplus Aid)÷ (Policyholders' Surplus)	Less than 15%
Note: Surplus aid is equal to the ceding commissions ratio multiplied by ceded reinsurance unearned premium for nonaffiliates. The ceding commissions ratio is determined by dividing reinsurance ceded commissions by reinsurance ceded premium. Estimated surplus aid is calculated as a percentage of policyholders' surplus in order to obtain the ratio result.		
#4 Two-Year Overall Operating Ratio =	(Two-year Loss Ratio) + (Two-year Expense Ratio) - (Two-year Investment Income Ratio)	Less than 100%
Note: The two-year loss ratio is determined by adding together the total of losses, loss adjustment expenses, and policyholder dividends and dividing by net premiums earned. The expense ratio is equal to other underwriting expenses less other income divided by net premiums written. The investment income ratio is net investment income divided by net premiums earned. A two-year overall operating ratio of less than 100 percent shows an operating profit; more than 100 percent shows an operating loss.		
#5 Investment Yield Ratio =	(Net Investment Income) ÷ (Average Cash and Invested Assets [Current and Prior Year])	Greater than 4.5% and less than 10%

Figure 15.3 (cont'd)

#6

| Change in Surplus Ratio | = | $\dfrac{\text{(Change in Surplus)}}{\text{(Adjusted Surplus Prior Year)}}$ | Greater than -10% and less than +50% |

Note: Change in surplus is equal to adjusted surplus for the current year minus adjusted surplus for the prior year. Adjusted surplus is the total of policyholders' surplus plus deferred acquisition expense for either the current or prior year. Deferred acquisition expense is determined by multiplying unearned premiums reserve by the ratio of acquisition expenses to net premiums written. Acquisition expenses include commissions, taxes, licenses and fees, and half of all other underwriting expenses.

#7

| Liabilities to Liquid Assets Ratio | = | $\dfrac{\text{(Liabilities)}}{\text{(Liquid Assets)}}$ | Less than 105% |

Note: Liquid assets are equal to (1) installment premiums booked but deferred and not yet due plus (2) cash and invested assets plus accrued investment income minus (3) investments in affiliated companies minus (4) excess of real estate over 5 percent of liabilities.

#8

| Ratio of Agents' Balances to Surplus | = | $\dfrac{\text{(Agents' Balances in Course of Collection)}}{\text{(Policyholders Surplus)}}$ | Less than 40% |

#9

| One-Year Reserve Development to Prior Year's Surplus Ratio | = | $\dfrac{\text{(One Year Reserve Development)}}{\text{(Prior Year's Policyholders Surplus)}}$ | Less than 20% |

Note: One-year reserve development is equal to incurred losses for all years except current accident year minus incurred losses for all years as reported in prior year.

#10

| Two-Year Reserve Development to Policyholders Surplus | = | $\dfrac{\text{(Two-year Reserve Development)}}{\text{(Second Prior Year's Policyholders Surplus)}}$ | Less than 20% |

Note: Two-year reserve development is equal to incurred losses for all years except two prior accident years minus reserves set for those losses for all years as reported in second prior year.

#11

| Estimated Current Reserve Deficiency to Surplus | = | $\dfrac{\text{(Estimated Reserve Deficiency [redundancy])}}{\text{Policyholders Surplus}}$ | Less than 25% |

 Note: Estimated reserve deficiency (redundancy) is equal to estimated reserves required minus stated reserves for the current year. The estimated reserves required are equal to net premium earned for current year times average ratio of developed reserves to premium.[4]

Risk Management Support Services

One of the key factors in the choice of insurers is how well they can support the insured entity's risk management activities. Questions that should be considered include:

- Can the insurer provide resources such as boiler and machinery inspections, workers compensation safety training, and fire protection inspections?

- Does the insurer offer a Risk Management Information System (RMIS) for use by the insured?

- Will the insurer allow frequent communication with adjusters?

- Will the insurer agree to meet with the insured to review claims handling and reserving issues?

REINSURANCE

Reinsurance is a concept under which one insurer transfers part or all of certain risks that it has agreed to insure to one or more other insurers. Reinsurance is used by insurance companies for many reasons, including:

- stabilizing loss ratios and underwriting results,

- protecting against overwhelming financial impact from catastrophes,

- increasing policyholders' surplus,

- increasing capacity, and

- exiting a line of business.

The insurer that purchases reinsurance is called the *ceding insurer* or *ceding company*. The ceding insurer also may be called the *primary insurer*, the *direct insurer*, the *cedant*, or the *reinsured*. The insurance company that accepts the transfer of risk is called the *reinsurer, assuming insurer*, or *assuming company*.

Simple Reinsurance Example

There are many types of reinsurance arrangements. An example of one type would be ABC Property Insurance Company, which writes property insurance for commercial establishments. ABC wants to retain responsibility for only the first $25,000 of each claim on each property it insures. Therefore, ABC will enter into a treaty with Property Reinsurance Company, in which ABC *cedes* losses above $25,000 to Property Re on each of the properties it insures.

There are two basic types of reinsurance:

- treaty reinsurance, and

- facultative reinsurance.

A *treaty* is a contract governing what portion and types of risks are ceded (transferred by contract) to the reinsurer. It is negotiated between the ceding company (primary insurer) and the reinsurance company. Under a treaty, the reinsurer automatically assumes part of each risk that meets the criteria of the treaty. The reinsurance coverage becomes effective at the time that direct insurance covered by the treaty is written.

Facultative reinsurance is negotiated separately as direct insurers underwrite risks. The direct insurer is not obligated to cede any risks, and the reinsurer is not obligated to accept any risk. Facultative reinsurance may be used to permit writing a risk that is larger than the direct insurer wants to assume, even after taking the carrier's treaty reinsurance into account; to protect a treaty; to obtain more competitive pricing; or to obtain coverage for a special exposure that the primary insurer cannot cover.

Treaty Reinsurance

The automatic nature of treaty reinsurance tends to eliminate some of the reinsurer's exposure to adverse selection that may occur in connection with facultative reinsurance. This is because treaty reinsurance is automatic and does not offer the opportunity to cede only unusually difficult risks. All risks that fall within the dictates of the treaty must be ceded and accepted.

There are many types of reinsurance treaties. The general and subcategories of traditional treaty reinsurance are

1. Pro Rata (proportional)

   - Quota Share

   - Surplus Share

Figure 15.4

Quota Share Treaty

30% Retention — Treaty Limit $1,000,000 — Division of Insurance, Premiums, and Losses

Policy	Total Amount			Direct Insurer Retains			Reinsurer Assumes		
	Insurance	Premiums	Losses	Insurance	Premiums*	Losses	Insurance	Premiums	Losses
1	$1,000	$10	$20	$300	$3	$6	$700	$7	$14
2	10,000	100	200	3,000	30	60	7,000	70	140
3	100,000	1,000	100,000	30,000	300	30,000	70,000	700	70,000
4	200,000	2,000	150,000	60,000	600	45,000	140,000	1,400	105,000
5	1,800,000	3,600	180,000	800,000**	1,600	80,000	1,000,000	2,000	100,000
6	1,000,000	5,000	100	300,000	1,500	30	700,000	3,500	70

*The reinsurer would also pay a ceding commission to the direct insurer.

**For Policy Number 5, the reinsurer would assume only $1,000,000 of the coverage because of its treaty limit in that amount. The primary insurer would assume its normal 30% retention ($540,000) plus the excess of the amount of insurance ($1,800,000) over the sum of its retention ($540,000) and the treaty limit ($1,000,000), which is $260,000. The direct insurer retains a total of $800,000 of insurance.

Figure 15.5

Surplus Share Treaty

$100,000 Retention — Treaty Limit $1,000,000 — Division of Insurance, Premiums, and Losses

Policy	Total Amount			Direct Insurer Retains			Reinsurer Assumes		
	Insurance	Premiums	Losses	Insurance	Premiums***	Losses	Insurance	Premiums	Losses
1	$1,000	$10	$20	$1,000	$10	$20	*	*	*
2	10,000	100	200	10,000	100	200	*	*	*
3	100,000	1,000	100,000	100,000	1,000	100,000	*	*	*
4	200,000	2,000	150,000	100,000	1,000	75,000	100,000	1,000	75,000
5	1,800,000	3,600	180,000	800,000****	1,600	80,000	1,000,000	2,000	100,000
6	1,000,000	5,000	100	100,000	500	10	900,000	4,500	90

***The reinsurer would also pay a ceding commission to the direct insurer.

****For Policy Number 5, the direct insurer would retain its normal retention of $100,000 plus the excess of the total amount of insurance ($1,800,000) over the sum of the retention ($100,000) and the treaty limit ($1,000,000), which is $700,000. The direct insurer retains a total of $800,000 of insurance.

2. Excess of Loss (nonproportional)

   • Per Risk

   • Per Occurrence (or catastrophe)

   • Aggregate (or stop loss)

Pro Rata Treaties

The ceding insurer and reinsurer share the amount of insurance, premium, and covered losses in the same proportion. If the reinsurer assumed one-third of the amount of insurance, it gets one-third of the premium and pays one-third of each covered loss.

Quota Share Treaties

Under a quota share treaty the reinsurer participates in a fixed percentage of the premiums and losses of the ceding company. If the quota share to the reinsurer were 30 percent, the reinsurer would receive 30 percent of premiums and losses. In the case of a $25,000 loss, the reinsurer would pay 30 percent or $7,500.

Figure 15.4 illustrates a quota share treaty with a 30 percent retention and a treaty limit of $1,000,000.

Surplus Share Treaties

A surplus share treaty allows the primary insurer to underwrite the full amount of insurance it has established as a retention limit and reinsure only those amounts above the retention limit. The retention limit is called its *line*. The amount of the reinsurance available in the treaty is set as a multiple of the primary insurer's line. The primary insurer's retention is stated as a dollar amount under a surplus share treaty, rather than as a percentage.

Figure 15.5 illustrates a surplus share treaty with a $100,000 retention (line) and a treaty limit of $1,000,000. Compare it with Figure 15.4 to see how the two different types of treaties would respond to the same six types of primary insurance contracts.

Excess of Loss Treaties

Excess of loss treaties do not come into play until the amount of loss exceeds the retention. In other words, they do not contribute to losses that are below the

retention or line. In addition, the methods to calculate excess reinsurance premiums are much more complex than the simple proportionate percentage basis used in pro rata treaties. Reinsurers customarily do not pay ceding commissions to direct insurers under excess of loss reinsurance treaties.

Per Risk Treaties

Per risk or per loss excess reinsurance treaties protect the direct insurer against the financial effects of individual large losses. The reinsurer does not pay anything unless an individual claim exceeds the retention, and then it only pays the amount in excess of the retention. The premium for an excess of loss treaty is negotiated based upon the ceding company's entire book of reinsured policies. Figure 15.6 illustrates a per risk excess treaty with a $100,000 retention and a $1,000,000 treaty limit.

Figure 15.6

Per Risk Excess Treaty
$100,000 Retention
Treaty Limit $1,000,000
Division of Losses

Policy Number	Amount of Loss	Retained by Direct Insurer	Assumed by Reinsurer
1.	$20	$20	$0
2.	200	200	0
3.	100,000	100,000	0
4.	150,000	100,000	50,000
5.	180,000	100,000	80,000
6.	100	100	0
7.	1,500,000	500,000	1,000,000*

*Reinsurer's liability is limited by the treaty limit.

Per Occurrence Treaties

Per occurrence treaties are also known as *catastrophe treaties* when used in property insurance. They are similar to per risk excess treaties except that both the retention and the treaty limit apply to all losses arising from a single event, such as a hurricane, tornado, riot, or earthquake. Rate making for catastrophe treaties depends heavily on judgment of the reinsurance underwriter.

Figure 15.7

Reinsurance Contracts

Type	What Is Ceded	Large Line Capacity	Surplus Relief	Stabilizes Loss Experience	Catastrophe Protection	Retention Applies To
Proportional						
Quota Share	Insurance, premium & losses ceded proportionally	Yes	Yes	No	Peripherally	% amount of insurance
Surplus Share	Reinsurer receives same percentage of losses as it does of premium	Yes	Yes	No	No	Dollar amount of insurance
Nonproportional						
Per Risk Excess	Excess losses ceded Treaty premium negotiated	Yes	No	Yes	Yes (limited)	Dollar amount per loss Applies separately to each subject of insurance
Per Accident Excess	Excess losses ceded Treaty premium negotiated	No	No	Yes	Yes	Dollar amount per occurrence
Aggregate Excess	Excess losses ceded Treaty premium negotiated	Yes	No	Yes	Yes	Dollar amount over stated period, loss ratio over stated period, or combination of both

Aggregate Excess Treaties

Aggregate excess treaties sometimes are called *stop loss treaties.* They come into play when the aggregate losses during a specified period of time exceed the retention of the treaty. The stated period usually is twelve months but not necessarily a calendar year. The retention under an aggregate excess treaty may be stated in dollars or as a loss ratio. *Loss ratio* is the ratio of incurred losses to earned premiums. For example, an aggregate excess treaty will pay when the ceding company's loss ratio exceeds the stated amount. Aggregate excess treaties are the most effective types of treaties in limiting the ceding company's loss ratio.

Figure 15.7 illustrates the basic differences among and reasons to use the various types of proportional and excess of loss treaties.

Facultative Reinsurance

Under facultative reinsurance, the reinsurer has no obligation to accept any offered business. Facultative reinsurance is used to reinsure specific policies rather than an entire book of business. The primary reasons that direct insurers use facultative reinsurance are:

- To provide coverage for areas that are excluded in the company's treaty reinsurance,

- To protect a treaty when a direct insurer wants to write an exposure that poses higher than average risk,

- To provide coverage for limits that exceed treaty maximums,

- To provide large line capacity on a single risk,

- To provide additional stabilization of loss experience, or

- To provide a pricing advantage.

Reinsurance Pools

Reinsurance pools have been used when the potential loss of a risk exceeds any one company's ability to underwrite the risk. Under this arrangement, a number of companies combine resources and assume a percentage of the risks submitted to the pool. For example, this arrangement might be used in aviation insurance where the loss of a single passenger jetliner could produce a multimillion-dollar loss.

Areas of Impact

Reinsurance is a cost of doing business that the ceding company must pass along to its policyholders. The reinsurance company's surplus is also subject to being reduced by the impact of heavier than anticipated losses or a decline in the value of its investments. Other factors also affect reinsurers, including the fact that catastrophic losses tend to accumulate in the reinsurance market. In addition, inflation can have a larger impact on reinsurance companies than on ceding companies. For example, if a reinsurer covered only losses in excess of $100,000, its participation in a loss of $101,000 would be $1,000 without inflation. An inflation rate of 1 percent would increase the loss over time to $102,010, and the reinsurance company would be required to pay $2,010. This would increase the reinsurer's participation more than 100 percent. Another factor that could affect reinsurers that hold assets in a foreign currency is a drop in the exchange rate. This would have the effect of reducing its surplus relative to premiums written expressed in U.S. dollars.

Reinsurers can deal with adverse conditions by raising rates, restricting coverage, reducing the number of risks that they will write, and negotiating higher retentions with ceding companies. Factors such as these may sharply influence both pricing and availability of coverage in the direct market. When many of these factors deteriorate at the same time, the effect on policyholders can be dramatic.

During such periods of high prices and restricted capacity a number of offshore insurers have been created to meet the insurance needs of large corporations. After obtaining its initial seed capital such insurers may maintain a safe ratio of premiums written to surplus by requiring that new policyholders purchase an amount of the insurer's stock at least equal to the premium which its paid.

FINANCIAL SERVICES REFORM

The 1916 Federal Reserve Act (12 U.S.C.S. § 92) stated that nationally chartered banks could sell insurance in towns with fewer than 5,000 residents. However, state-chartered banks, as well as national bank offices in towns with more than 5,000 residents, were prohibited from the practice.

It should be noted that Federal Reserve Act restrictions relating to bank-owned insurance agencies did not stop the formation of holding companies that owned stock in both banks and insurance companies. Congress acted again by passing the Bank Holding Company Act (BHCA), which required that holding companies with subsidiary banks divest of either their bank or their insurance company subsidiaries by July 1,1958. The BHCA reinforced Congress' intent by requiring, in effect, that holding companies could engage in approved banking or nonbanking activities—but not both.

In 1993, a national bank—Barnett Bank of Marion County—doing business in a small Florida town purchased an insurance agency that was licensed by the state of Florida. Subsequently, the Florida insurance commissioner ordered the agency to stop selling prohibited forms of insurance. Barnett then requested that a Florida district court determine whether the Federal Reserve Act preempted the Florida statute (Fla. Stat. § 626.988) that precluded national bank subsidiaries from selling insurance in that state. The district court held that the national statute did not preempt the Florida law. In its ruling, the district court reasoned that the McCarran-Ferguson Act, 15 U.S.C.S. § 1011, provided for state regulation of insurance and that state regulation was not preempted by federal law—unless the federal statute specifically provided otherwise.

Barnett appealed the decision, and in 1996 the Supreme Court overturned the district court.[5] *Barnett* was one of the catalysts to the convergence of the financial services industry and signaled a wave of state legislation aimed at permitting state-chartered banks to sell insurance. After several years of debate, Congress passed the Gramm-Leach-Bliley Act (GLBA), which became effective on March 11, 2000. GLBA brings banking regulation full circle. The GLBA is a very detailed piece of legislation that attempts to reconcile and coordinate the regulatory history governing banking, insurance, and securities underwriting. The following discussion is a brief overview of some of the principal points of the GLBA.

Imbedded in the act are provisions allowing for the creation of a Financial Holding Company (FHC) that can own subsidiaries engaged in banking, securities underwriting and dealing, and insurance sales and underwriting. The act allows for the addition of other permitted financial companies that the Federal Reserve Board may deem to be financial in nature after consultation with the Secretary of the Treasury. The Federal Reserve Board acts as the overall regulator for both bank holding companies and financial holding companies. Existing bank holding companies (BHCs) can apply to the Federal Reserve to become a FHC. Banking subsid-

iaries will continue to be regulated by the primary bank regulators, which include the Federal Reserve Board, Federal Deposit Insurance Corporation, and the Office of the Comptroller of Currency.

The subsidiaries of the FHC continue to be regulated as they have been in the past. For example, state insurance departments still regulate insurance company activity, and the Securities Exchange Commission will regulate securities activities. However, the act preempts state laws preventing the affiliation of depository institutions or their affiliates and insurance entities. In addition, the act continues to allow national banks to engage in insurance agency operations from a location with a population of 5,000 or less.

With respect to insurance sales there are *antitying provisions*, which require that the granting of credit cannot be conditioned upon purchase of insurance. In other words, banks cannot insist that loan customers purchase insurance on the loan collateral from a bank-affiliated insurance operation. Financial institutions must also develop privacy policies concerning the sharing of customer information, and they must disclose their privacy policies to customers. GLBA requires the financial institution to inform consumers that nonpublic information about them may be shared with nonaffiliated third parties. The law allows the consumer to opt out of this information sharing.

GLBA is a complex law that has led to the issuing of even more complex regulations. Further regulatory activity has continued, with proposals to enact an optional federal charter for insurance companies and, in some cases, insurance agencies. GLBA has contributed to a change in competition within the financial services industry, and some believe that it allows financial services professionals to compete on a more even playing field. One of the favorable results of the GLBA may be the development of new risk financing tools. Regulatory activities will continue to evolve. Selected resources for additional information in this area are included at the end of this chapter in the section entitled **WHERE CAN I FIND OUT MORE ABOUT IT?**

PREMIUM AND PRICING OF INSURANCE

One of the goals of state insurance regulation is to produce rates that are adequate, reasonable, and not unfairly discriminatory. Rates must be adequate so that insurers remain solvent and have the resources to pay claims. The requirement for reasonable rates is to make insurance affordable and prevent price gouging. Insurance underwriting by its nature is discriminatory. The rate for fire insurance on a building with sprinklers would reasonably be expected to be lower than the rate for buildings without such protection. This difference in rates would not be deemed to discriminate unfairly, especially if it can be supported by previous loss statistics.

State insurance rate regulation takes a number of forms. States with *prior approval laws* require the insurer to file its rates with the insurance regulators and obtain approval before using the rates. States with *file and use laws* require the insurers to file their rates with regulators for review. Under this type of regulation the insurance company can begin to use filed rates without first obtaining approval. If, after review, the regulators do not approve the rates, they may stop their use. *Flex-rating laws* allow insurers to reflect changes in conditions by filing rates with regulators and then adjusting them up or down within a preset range without prior approval. *Open competition laws* allow insurance companies to set their own rates. Under this type of law insurers must maintain records of rating structures for review by regulators. Many states exempt very large insureds from rate regulation and allow insurers to use their judgment.

One problem for the insurance industry is to properly price its products. The use of class or manual rates has its limitations. Under the manual rate system, a rate classification is established for specific types of exposures in specific geographic territories. For actuarial purposes the classification is used to track premiums and losses for the types of insureds falling within the classification. For automobile insurance, the rate classification would include factors such as the type of vehicle, annual miles driven, use of the vehicle, and age of the driver. The applicant for insurance falling within the class is then charged a premium based upon his classification. No matter how detailed the rate classification is, however, there will be differences among the drivers within the rate grouping that cannot be recognized in the classification. For example, some drivers in the classification may drive defensively while others may drive aggressively. Even though the rate category does *not explain* everything about a given exposure, the underwriter can achieve a loss ratio close to what is expected by underwriting a large number of risks in each class.

As the scale of the policyholder activities increases, the unique factors of its operations begin to influence

the premium that should be charged. For example, no two trucking firms are exactly the same even if they operate in the same territory. The problem for the underwriter is to decide how much weight should be given to the expected losses using the class rates and how much weight shall be given to the insured's actual loss experience. The use of an insured business's own record of past losses to influence the determination of future premiums is the concept behind experience rating. Actuaries have developed a variety of *credibility tables* to assist the underwriter in determining the appropriate experience-rated premium for a particular risk. The factors in the credibility tables vary from 0.00 for very small risks to 1.00 for very large risks.

The formula for determining the experience modification (EM) to be applied to the premium for a given risk might be as simple as:

$$EM = ((A-E)/E) \times C^6$$

Credibility Example

For example, an insured has an expected loss ratio of .35. The actual loss ratio is .45. If the credibility factor were .40, the resulting experience modification would be calculated as:

$$EM = ((.45-.35)/.35) \times .40 \text{ or}$$

$$EM = +11.4\%$$

The class rated annual premium for the renewal of the policyholder's coverage would be increased by 11.4 percent to reflect the policyholder's own loss experience. For a very large insured with an applicable credibility factor approaching 1.0, the premium for its coverage is essentially self-rated.

The use of experience rating makes it important for the insured and the insurer to jointly review the claims record to be sure that there are no errors in the calculation of the modification. Similarly the insurer's workers compensation summary of loss data should be reviewed prior to its filing with the workers compensation-rating bureau.

The computation of the experience modification for workers compensation coverage is more complicated because it allows for the introduction of factors to dampen the impact of losses, favorable or unfavorable, which are sustained by smaller policyholders. Workers compensation experience rating is discussed in Chapter 18, Workers Compensation.

Another approach to pricing is to use retrospective rating to adjust the policy premium based upon losses for the current year. Under this arrangement, the policy is issued with a retrospective premium agreement that sets the parameters for determining the ultimate policy premium. The agreement sets out a standard or deposit premium, a minimum premium, and a maximum premium as well as placing a limit on the amount of losses to be included in the formula as a result of any one event. The standard or deposit premium in an incurred loss retrospective program is usually the premium that would be calculated based on manual rates. The minimum premium is the least that the insured will ultimately pay, even if losses are exceptionally low. The maximum premium is the most that the insured will ultimately pay when losses are worse than expected. For example, the minimum premium might be set at 80 percent while the maximum premium might be set at 130 percent of the deposit premium. In such an arrangement there may be a cap on the amount that the insured must pay on each claim. For instance, only the first $25,000 of loss from any one event might be included in the retrospective premium adjustment formula. The retrospective premium adjustment formula might be as simple as

Premium = (a fixed dollar charge) + [(included losses) x (a loss conversion factor)]

At policy inception the insured pays the standard or deposit premium. The insurance company adjusts and pays losses as the policy period unfolds. After the policy expires, the terms of the retrospective premium agreement are applied to actual losses to produce the final premium. The insured then is billed for any additional premium that is earned because of claims. If claims are better than expected, the insured may receive a return premium credit.

Retrospective rating is used for larger businesses that want—or are forced to—share their risks with an insurance company. Some businesses choose retrospective rating because their claims are under control and they believe they ultimately will pay less than under a guaranteed cost program. Other businesses may be forced to accept a retrospectively rated policy because their losses are not under control and insurance underwriters do not want to lose money on the account.

WHERE CAN I FIND OUT MORE ABOUT IT?

Insurance Company Structure and Accounting

- American Institute for Chartered Property Casualty Underwriters (AICPCU) and the Insurance Institute of America (IIA), http://www.aicpcu.org/.

Financial Services Convergence

- White, Michael D., *A Comprehensive Guide to Bank Insurance*, Cincinnati: The National Underwriter Company, 1998. http://www.nationalunderwriter.com/nucatalog.

- American Bankers Insurance Association (ABIA), http://www.aba.com/ABIA/default.htm.

- Corporation for American Banking (CAB), http://www.aba.com/CAB/default.htm.

- Independent Insurance Agents and Brokers of America, www.iiaba.org.

- Office of the Comptroller of the Currency, U.S. Department of the Treasury, http://www.occ.treas.gov/index.htm.

- The Council of Insurance Agents + Brokers, http://ciab.com.

- Federal Reserve Bank of San Francisco, http://frbsf.org/publications/banking/gramm/grammpg1.html.

END NOTES

[1] NAIC International Insurers Department, http://www.naic.org/1misc/aboutnaic/about/about13.htm.

[2] The National Underwriter Company, "Excess Coverage and Deductibles," *The Risk Funding & Self-Insurance Bulletins (RF&S Bulletins)*, March 2001, Ec-13 to Ec-18.

[3] NAIC, *Insurance Regulatory Information System (IRIS)*, 2001 Property/Casualty Edition, 7.

[4] The National Underwriter Company, "Property and Liability Insurance Regulatory Information System (IRIS) Ratios," *The Risk Funding & Self-Insurance Bulletins (RF&S Bulletins)*, June 2001, Eo-1 to Eo-3, compiled from information obtained from the NAIC.

[5] *Barnett Bank of Marion County, N.A., Petitioner v. Bill Nelson, Florida Insurance Commissioner*, 116 S. Ct. 1103 (1996).

[6] Where A is the actual losses, E is the expected losses, and C is the credibility factor. The calculation of the experience modification in casualty insurance is usually based upon a rolling three-year record of expected and actual losses. A-E measures the difference between actual and expected losses. By dividing this number by the expected loss (E) the difference is expressed as a percentage. How are the results of this calculation interpreted? Consider two cases. First, an individual driving one automobile may have an expected loss of $250. On average this individual would go many years without sustaining a loss. A loss of $5,000 would be twenty times his expected losses. Alternatively, consider a trucking firm with expected losses of $250,000. Expected losses of this magnitude reflect the fact that the trucking company would sustain many losses of varying sizes over the year. For the trucking company, a loss of $5,000 would only be one-fiftieth of expected losses. The trucking company's losses have an element of regularity, while the individual's losses are more random. The use of a credibility factor (C) gives more weight to the trucking company's more stable loss experience than to the individual's more random loss experience. As stated previously, the credibility factor varies from 0.0 for small insureds to 1.0 for very large insureds.

The amount of any one loss included in the insured's actual losses is limited. For example only the first $25,000 of a $100,000 might be included in the experience modification calculation.

Chapter 15

GLOSSARY

Admitted insurance carrier. Insurance companies that are licensed to conduct business within a certain state and are subject to that state's regulation and guaranty fund arrangements.

Aggregate excess treaties. A type of treaty in which the reinsurer pays when the total amount (aggregate) of loss from all claims filed within a specified period exceeds the treaty retention. Also known as a stop loss treaty.

Alien insurance companies. Insurance companies that are domiciled in a non-U.S. country.

Asset risk. The likelihood that the value of an insurance company's investment portfolio will decline.

Assuming insurer (assuming company). The insurance company that accepts the transfer of risk; also known as the reinsurer or reinsurance company.

Bank holding companies (BHC). Holding companies that can own subsidiary banking operations and with a few exceptions not more than 5 percent of the voting stock of nonbanking companies.

Catastrophe treaties. Another name for a per occurrence excess of loss treaty.

Cedant. The insurer that purchases reinsurance; also known as the primary or direct insurer.

Ceding insurer (ceding company). The insurer that purchases reinsurance; also known as the primary or direct insurer.

Credit risk. The possibility that an insurer will not collect premiums, reinsurance, and other receivables.

Demutualization. The conversion of a mutual insurance operation to a stock insurance structure.

Domestic insurance companies. Insurance companies that are domiciled and licensed in a specific state.

Excess of loss treaties. Treaties in which the reinsurer only shares in the risk when the amount of loss exceeds the amount that the ceding insurer is retaining, Types of excess of loss treaties are per risk, per occurrence, and aggregate excess.

Facultative reinsurance. A type of reinsurance that is used to transfer a specific risk or portion of a risk to a reinsurer; reinsurance that is written on a case-by-case basis and not under a treaty.

File and use laws. A type of state regulation that permits insurance companies to implement rates that have been filed with regulators for review during the review process. If the regulators do not ultimately approve the rates, they may stop their use.

Financial holding company (FHC). A holding company, as provided for in the Gramm-Leach-Bliley Act, that can own subsidiaries engaged in banking, merchant banking, securities underwriting and dealing, and insurance agencies and underwriting.

Flex-rating laws. A type of state regulation that allows insurers to reflect changes in conditions by filing rates with regulators and then adjusting them within a preset range without prior approval.

Foreign insurance companies. Insurance companies that are domiciled in a state other than where coverage is being written.

Gramm-Leach-Bliley Act (GLBA). A federal law that permits the formation of Financial Holding Companies and their operations in such activities as banking, merchant banking, insurance, and securities underwriting.

Incurred But Not Reported (IBNR) claims. Damages that have been incurred for which claims have not yet been reported to the insurance company.

Insurance commissioner. The chief officer of a state insurance department. An insurance commissioner's main responsibility is to provide consumer protection by regulating and monitoring insurance companies.

Insurance Regulatory Information System (IRIS). Part of a system that is designed to provide state insurance departments with an integrated approach to screening and analyzing the financial condition of insurance companies.

Interinsurance exchange. Another name for a reciprocal exchange.

Kenny Rule. Another name for the written premium ratio system, which was used before the Risk Based Capital system to determine adequacy of an insurance company's capital.

Line. The amount of insurance that a ceding insurer retains in-house; the retention amount in a surplus share reinsurance treaty.

Lloyd's associations. A system in which individuals, known as names, underwrite, for their own accounts, a small portion of others' risks. Names usually join a syndicate with other names to transact business for specific types of risks.

Loss ratio. The ratio of a business's incurred losses to its insurance premium over the same period of time.

Mutual insurance company. An insurance company that is organized as a for-profit company and is owned by its respective policyholders, who receive the advantage of operational profits in the form of lower rates or dividends. Some mutuals are assessable, which means that policyholders may be assessed to pay for operational losses.

Mutual insurance holding company (MIHC). A company that is formed during the demutualization process. Under the MIHC arrangement, converted stock insurers become wholly owned subsidiaries of the MIHC, which are designed to provide greater access to capital markets and an enhanced ability to diversify operations.

National Association of Insurance Commissioners (NAIC). An association of the state insurance commissioners of the fifty states, District of Columbia, and four U.S. territories. The NAIC coordinates the regulation of multistate insurers and facilitates the development of uniform policy when appropriate.

Nonadmitted insurance carrier. Insurance companies that are not licensed in a given state or territory and are not directly regulated by that state or territory.

Open competition laws. A type of rate regulation that allows insurance companies to set their rates as long as they maintain records of rating structures for regulator review.

Per occurrence excess of loss treaty. An excess of loss treaty in which the retention and treaty limit apply to all losses arising from a single event, such as a hurricane, tornado, or riot.

Per risk excess of loss treaty. An excess of loss treaty in which the reinsurer does not pay until an individual claim exceeds the amount of the retention; only losses in excess of the retention are reinsured.

Policyholders' surplus. The difference between an insurance company's admitted assets and its liabilities; similar to owner's equity for noninsurance companies.

Prior approval laws. A type of rate regulation that requires insurers to file rates with insurance regulators and obtain approval before using them.

Pro rata treaties. Reinsurance treaties in which the ceding insurer and the reinsurer share the amount of insurance, premium, and covered losses in the same proportion. Types of pro rata treaties are quota share and surplus share.

Purchasing groups. Groups that have, as one of their purposes, the purchase of liability insurance for group members.

Reciprocal exchanges. Unincorporated arrangements in which one policyholder agrees to participate in insuring all other policyholders. Also known as an interinsurance exchange.

Reinsurance. The system by which one insurer transfers all or part of the risks it has assumed to another insurance company, which is called the reinsurer or the reinsurance company.

Reserves. Loss or claim reserves represent the value of losses that have been estimated and set up for future payment.

Retail agents or brokers. Insurance agents or brokers that arrange coverage between individuals or businesses and insurance companies.

Retrospective rating. A system for rating an insurance policy in which the insured business pays a premium at the beginning of the policy term that subsequently is adjusted up or down based on the value of claims incurred during the policy term.

Risk based capital. A system developed by the NAIC to analyze the financial strength of insurance companies. The system attempts to determine if an insurer has an adequate amount of capital.

Risk retention groups (RRGs). Organizations formed to spread the liability risks of groups of similar businesses. RRGs are formed under the federal Product Liability Risk Retention Act of 1981 and its 1986 amendments.

State guaranty associations. Associations that pay a portion of covered claims filed against insolvent insurers in an effort to avoid catastrophic financial losses for the policyholders of those insolvent insurance companies. Also known as state guaranty funds.

Stock insurance company. An insurance company that is organized as a for-profit company and owned by its shareholders, who bear the result of operational profits and losses.

Surplus lines brokers. Insurance brokers that usually broker coverage between retail agents and nonadmitted insurance carriers. Also known as wholesalers.

Treaty or treaty reinsurance. A contract that governs what portion and types of risks are transferred (ceded) to a reinsurance company.

Underwriting risk. The risk that premium rates or loss reserves will not be adequate to cover losses as they mature.

Appendix

Figure 15.1

UNITED STATES CODE

TITLE 15. COMMERCE AND TRADE

LIABILITY RISK RETENTION

Section

§ 3901. Definitions

(a) As used in this chapter —

(1) "Insurance" means primary insurance, excess insurance, reinsurance, surplus lines insurance, and any other arrangement for shifting and distributing risk which is determined to be insurance under applicable State or Federal law,

(2) "liability" —

(A) means legal liability for damages (including costs of defense, legal costs and fees, and other claims expenses) because of injuries to other persons, damage to their property, or other damage or loss to such other persons resulting from or arising out of —

(i) any business (whether profit or nonprofit), trade, product, services (including professional services), premises, or operations, or

(ii) any activity of any State or local government, or any agency or
political subdivision thereof, and

(B) does not include personal risk liability and an employer's liability with respect to its employees other than legal Liability under the Federal Employers' Liability Act (45 USC 51 et seq.);

(3) "personal risk liability" means liability for damages because of injury to any peon, damage to property, or other loss or damage resulting from any personal, familial, or household responsibilities or activities, rather than from responsibilities or activities referred to in paragraphs (2)(A)and(2)(B);

(4) "risk retention group" means any corporation or other limited liability association —

(A) whose primary activity consists of assuming and spreading all, or any portion, of the liability exposure of its group members;

Figure 15.1 (cont'd)

(B) which is organized for the primary purpose of conducting the activity described under subparagraph (A);

(C) which —

(i) is chartered or licensed as a liability insurance company under the laws of a State and authorized to engage in the business of insurance under the laws of such State; or

(ii) before January 1, 1985, was chartered or licensed and authorized to engage in the business of insurance under the laws of Bermuda or Cayman Islands and, before such date, had certified to the insurance commissioner of at least one State that it satisfied the capitalization requirements of such State, except that any such group shall be considered to be a risk retention group only if it has been engaged in business continuously since such date and only for the purpose of continuing to provide insurance to cover product liability or completed operations liability (as such terms were defined in this section before the date of the enactment of the Risk Retention Act of 1986);

(D) which does not exclude any person from membership in the group solely to provide for members of such a group a competitive advantage over such a person;

(E) which —

(i) has as its owners only persons who comprise the membership of the risk retention group and who are provided insurance by such group; or

(ii) has as its sole owner an organization which has as —

(I) its members only persons who comprise the membership of the risk retention group; and

(II) its owners only persons who comprise the membership of the risk retention group and who are provided insurance by such group;

(F) whose members are engaged in businesses or activities similar or related with respect to the liability to which such members are exposed by virtue of any related, similar, or common business, trade, product, services, premises, or operations;

(G) whose activities do not include the provision of insurance other than —

(i) liability insurance for assuming and spreading all or any portion of the similar or related liability exposure of its group members; and

(ii) reinsurance with respect to the similar or related liability exposure of any other risk retention group (or any member of such other group) which is engaged in businesses or activities so that such group (or member) meets the requirement described in sub paragraph (F) for membership in the risk retention group which provides such reinsurance; and

(H) the name of which includes the phrase "Risk retention Group";

(5) "purchasing group" means any group which —

(A) has as one of its purposes the purchase of liability insurance on a group basis;

(B) purchases such insurance only for its group members and only to cover their similar or related liability exposure, as described in subparagraph (C);

Figure 15.1 (cont'd)

(C) is composed of members whose businesses or activities are similar or related with respect to the liability to which members are exposed by virtue of any related, similar, or common business, trade, product, services, premises, or operations; and

(D) is domiciled in any State;

(6) "State" means any State of the United States or the District of Columbia; and

(7) "hazardous financial condition" means that, based on its present or reasonably anticipated financial condition, a risk retention group is unlikely to be able —

(A) to meet obligations to policyholders with respect to known claims and reasonably anticipated claims; or

(B) to pay other obligations in the normal course of business.

(b) Nothing in this act [15 USCS __ 3901 et seq.] shall be construed to affect either the tort law or the law governing the interpretation of insurance contracts of any State, and the definitions of liability, personal risk liability, and insurance under any State law shall not be applied for the purposes of this act [15 USCS§§3901 et seq.], including recognition or qualification of risk retention groups or purchasing groups.

§ 3902. Risk retention group exemptions

(a) Except as provided in this section, a risk retention group is exempt from any State law, rule, regulation, or order to the extent that such law, rule, regulation, or order would —

(1) make unlawful, or regulate, directly or indirectly, the operation of a risk retention group except that the jurisdiction in which it is chartered may regulate the formation and operation of such a group and any State may require such a group to —

(A) comply with the unfair claim settlement practices law of the State;

(B) pay, on a nondiscriminatory basis, applicable premium and other taxes which are levied on admitted insurers and surplus lines insurers, brokers, or policyholders under the laws of the State;

(C) participate, on a nondiscriminatory basis, in any mechanism established or authorized under the law of the State for the equitable apportionment among insurers of liability insurance losses and expenses incurred on policies written through such mechanism;

(D) register with and designate the State insurance commissioner as its agent solely for the purpose of receiving service of legal documents or process;

(E) submit to an examination by the State insurance commissioner in any State in which the group is doing business to determine the group's financial condition, if —

(i) the commissioner of the jurisdiction in which the group is chartered has not begun or has refused to initiate an examination of the group; and

(ii) any such examination shall be coordinated to avoid unjustified duplication and unjustified repetition;

(F) comply with a lawful order issued

(i) in a delinquency proceeding commenced by the State insurance commissioner if there has been a finding of financial impairment under subparagraph (E); or

Figure 15.1 (cont'd)

(ii) in a voluntary dissolution proceeding;

(G) comply with any State law regarding deceptive, false, or fraudulent acts or practices, except that if the State seeks an injunction regarding the conduct described in this subparagraph, such injunction must be obtained from a court of competent jurisdiction;

(H) comply with an injunction issued by a court of competent jurisdiction, upon a petition by the State insurance commissioner alleging that the group is in hazardous financial condition or is financially impaired; and

(I) provide the following notice, in 10-point type, in any insurance policy issued by such group:

NOTICE

"This policy is issued by your risk retention group. Your risk retention group may not be subject to all of the insurance laws and regulations of your State. State insurance insolvency guaranty funds are not available for your risk retention group.

(b) The exemptions specified in subsection (a) of this section apply to laws governing the insurance business pertaining to —

(1) liability insurance coverage provided by a risk retention group for —

(A) such group; or

(B) any person who is a member of such group;

(2) the sale of liability insurance coverage for a risk retention group; and

(3) provision of —

(A) insurance related services;

(B) management, operations, and investment activities; or

(C) loss control and claims administration (including loss control and claims administration services for uninsured risks retained by any member of such group);

for a risk retention or any member of such group with respect to
liability for which the group provides insurance.

(c) A State may require that a person acting, or offering to act, as an agent or broker for a risk retention group obtain a license from that State, except that a State may not impose any qualification or requirement which discriminates against a nonresident agent or broker.

(d) Each risk retention group shall submit —

(1) to the insurance commissioner of the State in which it is chartered —

(A) before it may offer insurance in any State, a plan of operation or a feasibility study which includes the coverages, deductibles, coverages limits, rates, and rating classification systems for each line of insurance the group intends to offer; and

Figure 15.1 (cont'd)

(B) revisions of such plan or study if the group intends to offer any additional lines of liability insurance;

(2) to the insurance commissioner of each State in which it intends to do business, before it may offer insurance in such State —

(A) a copy of such plan or study (which shall include the name of the State in which it is chartered and its principal place of business); and

(B) a copy of any revisions to such plan or study, as provided in paragraph (l)(B) (which shall include any change in the designation of the State in which it is chartered); and

(3) to the insurance commissioner of each State in which it is doing business, a copy of the group's annual financial Statement submitted to the State in which the group is chartered as an insurance company, which statement shall be certified by an independent public accountant and contain a Statement of opinion on loss and loss adjustment expense reserves made by —

(A) a member of the American Academy of Actuaries, or

(B) a qualified loss reserve specialist.

(e) Nothing in this section shall be construed to affect the authority of any Federal or State court to enjoin —

(l) the solicitation or sale of insurance by a risk retention group to any person who is not eligible for membership in such group; or

(2) the solicitation or sale of insurance by, or operation of, a risk retention group that is in hazardous financial condition or is financially impaired.

(f)(l) Subject to the provisions of subsection (a)(l)(G) of this section (relating to injunctions)and paragraph (2), nothing in this act [15 USCS __ 3901 et seq.] shall be construed to affect the authority of any State to make use of any of its powers to enforce the laws of such State with respect to which a risk retention group is not exempt under this act [15 USCS __ 3901 et seq.].

(2) If a State seeks an injunction regarding the conduct described in paragraphs (l) and (2) of subsection (e) of this section, such injunction must be obtained from a Federal or State court of competent jurisdiction.

(g) Nothing in this act [15 USCS __ 3901 et seq.] shall affect the authority of any State to bring an action in any Federal or State court.

(h) Nothing in this act [15 USCS __ 3901 et seq.] shall be construed to affect the authority of any State to regulate or prohibit the ownership interest in a risk retention group by an insurance company in that State, other than in the case of ownership interest in a risk retention group whose members are insurance companies.

§ 3903. Purchasing group exemptions

(a) Except as provided in this section and section 3905 of this title, a purchasing group is exempt from any State law, rule, regulation, or order to the extent that such law, rule, regulation, or order
would —

(l) prohibit the establishment of a purchasing group;

(2) make it unlawful for an insurer to provide or offer to provide insurance on a basis providing, to a purchasing group or its members, advantages, based on their loss and expense experience, not afforded to other persons with respect to rates, policy forms, coverages or other matters;

Figure 15.1 (cont'd)

   (3) prohibit a purchasing group or its members from purchasing insurance on a group basis described in paragraph (2) of this subsection;

   (4) prohibit a purchasing group from obtaining insurance on a group basis because the group has not been in existence for a minimum period of time or because any member has not belonged to the group for a minimum period of time;

   (5) require that a purchasing group must have a minimum number of members, common ownership or affiliation, or a certain legal form;

   (6) require that a certain percentage of a purchasing group must obtain insurance on a group basis;

   (7) require that any insurance policy issued to a purchasing group or any members of the group be countersigned by an insurance agent or broker residing in that State; or

   (8) otherwise discriminate against a purchasing group or any of its members.

   (b) The exemptions specified in subsection (a) of this section apply to —

   (l) liability insurance, provided to —

   (A) a purchasing group; or

   (B) any person who is a member of a purchasing group; and

   (2) the provision of —

   (A) lability coverage;

   (B) insurance related services; or

   (C) management services;

       to a purchasing group of member of the group.

   (c) A State may require that a person acting, or offering to act, as an agent or broker for a purchasing group obtain a license from that State, except that a State may not impose any qualification or requirement which discriminates against a nonresident agent or broker.

   (d)(l)A purchasing group which intends to do business in any State shall furnish notice of such intention to the insurance commissioner of such State. Such notice —

   (A) shall identify the State in which such group is domiciled;

   (B) shall specify the lines and classifications of liability insurance which the purchasing group intends to purchase;

   (C) shall identify the insurance company from which the group intends to purchase insurance and the domicile of such company; and

   (D) shall identify the principal place of business of the group.

   (2) Such purchasing group shall notify the commissioner of any such State as to any subsequent changes in any of the items provided in such notice.

Figure 15.1 (cont'd)

(e) A purchasing group shall register with and designate the State insurance commissioner of each State in which it does business as its agent solely for the purpose of receiving service of legal documents or process, except that such requirement shall not apply in the case of a purchasing group —

(1) which —

(A) was domiciled before April 1, 1986; and

(B) is domiciled on and after the date of the enactment of this Act [enacted Sept. 25, 1981];

in any State of the United States;

(2) which —

(A) before the enactment of this Act [enacted Sept. 25, 1981], purchased insurance from an insurance carrier licensed in any State; and

(B) since such date of enactment, purchases its insurance from an insurance carrier licensed in any State;

(3) which was a purchasing group under the requirements of this Act [15 USCS __ 3901 et seq.] before the date of enactment of the Risk Retention Amendments of 1986 [enacted Oct. 27, 1986]; and

(4) as long as such group does not purchase insurance that was not authorized for purposes of an exemption under this Act [15 USCS __ 3901 et seq.] as in effect before the date of enactment of the Risk Retention Amendments of 1986 [enacted Oct. 27, 1986].

(f) A purchasing group may not purchase insurance from a risk retention group that is not chartered in a State or from an insurer not admitted in the State in which the purchasing group is located, unless the purchase is effeb ed through a licensed agent or broker acting pursuant to the surplus lines laws and regulations of such State.

(g) Nothing in this act [15 USCS __ 3901 et seq.] shall be construed to affect the authority of any State to make use of any of its powers to enforce the laws of such State with respect to which a purchasing group is not exempt under this act [15 USCS __ 3901 et seq.].

(h) Nothing in this act [15 USCS __ 3901 et seq.] shall affect the authority of any State to bring an action in any Federal or State court.

§ 3904. Applicability of securities laws

(a) The ownership interests of members in a risk retention group shall be —

(1) considered to be exempted securities for purposes of section 5 of the Securities Act of 1933 and for purposes of section 12 of the Securities Exchange Act of 1934; and

(2) considered to be securities for purposes of the provisions of section 17 of the Securities Act of 1933 and the provisions of section 10 of the Securities Exchange Act of 1934.

(b) A risk retention group shall not be considered to be an investment company for purposes of the Investment Company Act of 1940.

(c) The ownership interests of members in a risk retention group shall not be considered securities for purposes of any State blue sky law.

Figure 15.1 (cont'd)
§ 3905. Clarification concerning permissible state authority

(a) Nothing in this Act [15 USCS __ 3901 et seq.] shall be construed to exempt a risk retention group or purchasing group authorized under this Act [15 USCS __ 3901 et seq.] from the policy form or coverage requirements of any State motor vehicle no-fault or motor vehicle financial responsibility insurance law.

(b) The exemptions provided under this Act [15 USCS __ 3901 et seq.] shall apply only to the provision of liability insurance by a risk retention group or the purchase of liability insurance by a purchasing group, and nothing in this Act [15 USCS __ 3901 et seq.] shall be construed to permit the provision or purchase of any other line of insurance by any such group.

(c) The terms of any insurance policy provided by a risk retention group or purchased by a purchasing group shall not provide or be construed to provide insurance policy coverage prohibited generally by State statute or declared unlawful by the highest court of the State whose law applies to such policy.

(d) Subject to the provisions of section 3902(a)(4) [15 USCS __ 3902 (a)(4)] relating to discrimination, nothing in this Act [15 USCS __ 3901 et seq.] shall be construed to preempt the authority of a State to specify acceptable means of demonstrating financial responsibility where the State has required a demonstration of financial responsibility as a condition for obtaining a license or permit to undertake specified activities. Such means may include or exclude insurance coverage obtained from an admitted insurance company, an excess lines company, a risk retention group, or any other source regardless of whether coverage is obtained directly from an insurance company or through a broker, agent, purchasing group, or any other person.

§ 3906. Injunctive orders issued by United States District Courts

Any district court of the United States may issue an order enjoining a risk retention group from soliciting or selling insurance, or operating, in any State (or in all States) or in any territory or possession of the United States upon a finding of such court that such group is in hazardous financial condition. Such order shall be binding on such group, its officers, agents, and employees, and on any other person acting in active concert with any such officer, agent, or employee, if such other person has actual notice of such order.

National Conference of Insurance Guaranty Funds
2001 Summary of Property & Casualty Insurance Guaranty Association
Acts of the Various States and US Territories
Summary by Provision

Excluded Lines of Business

STATE	LIFE	A&H	FIN GUAR	MORT GUAR	DISAB	SURETY	CREDIT	TITLE	OCEAN MARINE	OTHER (1)
NAIC	X	X	X	X	X	X	X	X	X	FIDELITY, WARRANTY, GOVT
NCIGF	X	X	X	X	X	X	X	X	X	FIDELITY, WARRANTY, GOVT
AL	X	X		X		X	X	X	X	
AK	X		X	X	X	X	X	X		FIDEL,WARRANTY,GOVT,INV RISK
AZ	X			X	X	X	X	X	X	WORKERS' COMP
AR	X	X	X	X	X		X	X	X	WARRANTIES, BAIL BONDS
CA	X	X	X	X	X	X	X	X	X	GOVT OBLIGATIONS, FIDELITY
CO	X	X	X	X	X	X	X	X	X	
CT	X	X	X	X	X	X	X	X	X	FLOOD, GOVT, WARRANTY
DE	X	X	X	X	X	X	X	X	X	FIDELITY, WARRANTY, GOVT
DC	X	X	X	X	X	X	X	X	X	FIDELITY, WARRANTY,GOVT, INV RISK
FL	X	X	X	X	X	X	X	X	X	FIDELITY, WARRANTY, GOVT
FLWC	X	X	X	X	X	X	X	X	X	(30)
GA	X	X	X	X	X	X	X	X	X	FIDELITY, WARRANTY
HI	X	X	X	X	X	X	X	X	X	FIDELITY, WARRANTY
ID	X	X	X	X	X	X	X	X	X	WARRANTY
IL	X	X	X	X		X			X	FIDELITY, WARRANTY, CROP, FLOOD
IN	X	X	X	X		X	X	X	X	FIDELITY, WARRANTY, GOVT
IA	X	X	X	X	X	X	X	X	X	FIDELITY, WARRNTY
KS	X	X		X				X		CREDIT LIFE
KY	X	X		X			X	X	X	INV RISK, WARRANTY, GOVT
LA	X	X	X	X	X	X	X	X	X	FIDELITY, AUTO, BREAKDOWN
ME	X	X	X	X			X	X	WET	SURPLUS LINES COVERAGE
MD	X	X		X						SURPLUS LINES, RISK RETENTION
MA	X	X	X	X	X	X	X	X	X	WARRANTY
MI	X				X					
MN	X	X	X	X			X	X	X	ANNUITY, INV RISK, GOVT
MS	X	X	X	X	X	X	X	X	X	FIDELITY, SERVICE CONTRACT
MO	X	X		X	X	X	X	X	X	
MT	X			X	X	X	X	X	X	
NE	X	X	X	X		X	X	X	X	FIDELITY, AUTO BREAKDOWN
NV	X	X	X	X	X	X	X	X	X	WARRANTY, INV RISK GOVT, INDUS
NH	X	X		X		X	X	X	X	
NJ	X	X		X		X	X	X	X	WORKERS COMP, FIDELITY
NM	X	X	X	X	X	X	X	X	X	MOTOR CLUB COVERAGES
NY	X	X	X	X	X		X	X	X	
NC	X	X	X	X	X	X	X	X	X	WARRANTY, FIDELITY
ND	X	X	X	X	X	X	X	X	X	GOVT, WARRANTY, FIDELITY
OH	X	X	X	X	X	X	X	X	X	GOVT, WARRANTY, WC, FIDELITY
OK	X	X	X	X		X	X	X	X	WARRANTY, COL PROT
OR	X	X		X		X	X	X	WET	TRANSPORTATION INS
PA	X	X	X	X	X	X	X	X	X	WC, WARRANTY, GOVT
PAWC	X	X	X	X	X	X	X	X	X	(30)
PR	X	X	X	X	X			X	X	GUARANTEE, WARRANTY, GOVT, INV RISK
RI	X	X	X	X	X	X	X	X	X	FIDELITY,WARRANTY,XS LIABILITY ,PROT CEL
SC	X	X	X	X		X	X	X	X	FIDELITY, WARRRANTY, RETROSPECTIVE CVRGE
SD	X	X	X	X	X	X	X	X	X	FIDELITY,WARRANTY, GOVT, INV RISK
TN	X	X	X	X	X	X	X	X	X	WARRANTY, FIDELITY, COL PROT
TX	X	X	X	X		X	X	X	X	FIDELITY, CROP, FLOOD, WARRANTY
UT	X		X	X	X	X	X	X	X	WARRANTY, GOVT PROG
VT	X	X		X		X	X	X	X	
VI	X			X	X	X	X	X	X	
VA	X	X	X	X	X	X	X	X	X	FIDELITY, WARRANTY, RISK RETENTION
WA	X			X	X	X	X	X	X	WORKERS' COMPENSATION
WV	X			X	X	X	X	X	X	WORKERS' COMPENSATION
WI			X	X		X	X	X	X	FIDELITY, WARRANTY
WY	X			X	X	X	X	X	X	

	National Conference of Insurance Guaranty Funds 2001 Summary of Property & Casualty Insurance Guaranty Association Acts of the Various States and US Territories Summary by Provision ## Claim Parameters			
STATE	**DEDUCTIBLE/COVERED CLAIM**	**MAXIMUM PER CLAIM**	**WORKERS' COMP PAID IN FULL?**	**NET WORTH PROVISION**
NAIC	NONE	$300,000 / CLAIMANT	YES	YES
NCIGF	NONE	$300,000 / CLAIMANT	YES	YES
AL	$100	150,000	YES	YES $25M 1ST, 3RD
AK	NONE	500,000	YES	NONE
AZ	$100	100,000	WC NOT CVRD (4)	NONE
AR	NONE	300,000	(5)	YES $50M 1ST, 3RD
CA	$100 (3)	500,000	YES	NONE
CO	$100	100,000	YES	YES $10M 1ST, $25M 3RD
CT	$100	300,000	YES	YES $50M SUBRO
DE	NONE	300,000	YES	YES $10M 1ST, $25M SUBRO
DC	NONE	300,000	YES	YES $50M SUBRO
FL	$100	$300,000 (14)	WC NOT CVRD (9)	NONE
FLWC	NONE	NONE	YES	NONE
GA	$25 (3)	100,000	YES	YES $3M 1ST, 3RD
HI	NONE	300,000	YES	YES $25M 1st, $50M SUBRO
ID	NONE	300,000	YES	NONE
IL	NONE	300,000	YES	YES $25M 1ST, 3RD, SUBRO
IN	NONE	$100K / CLAIM; $300K / OCC.	(5)	YES $5M 1ST, $50M 3RD
IA	NONE	300,000	YES	NONE (16)
KS	$100	300,000	YES	NONE
KY	NONE	300,000	YES	YES $25M 1ST, SUBRO
LA	$100	$150K / CLAIM / $300K / OCC.	YES	YES $25M 1ST, 3RD
ME	NONE	300,000	YES	NONE
MD	$100	$300,000 / CLAIM	YES	YES $50M 1ST
MA	NONE	300,000	YES	NONE
MI	$10	.05% OF P/Y PREM	(6)	YES .1% OF AGG PREM PRCDG YR
MN	NONE	300,000	YES	YES $25M 1ST, SUBRO
MS	$100	300,000	YES	NONE
MO	$100	300,000	YES	YES $25M 1ST, 3rd
MT	$100	300,000	YES	YES $50M SUBRO
NE	$100	300,000	YES	NONE
NV	NONE	300,000	YES	YES $25M 1ST, 3RD
NH	$50	300,000	YES	NONE
NJ	NONE	$300K / CLM; $75K / AUTO CLM	WC NOT CVRD (9)	NONE
NM	$25	$100K PER CLM OR CLMNT	YES	NONE
NY	NONE	$1MM / CLM; $5MM / POL (NONRES)	WC NOT CVRD (9)	NONE
NC	$50	300,000	YES	YES $50M SUBRO
ND	NONE	300,000	(7)	YES $10M 1ST, $25M 3RD
OH	$100 (3)	300,000	(7)	YES $50M SUBRO
OK	NONE	150,000	YES	YES $50M SUBRO
OR	NONE	300,000	YES	YES $25M 1st
PA	NONE	300,000	WC NOT CVRD (9)	YES $25M 1ST, $50M SUBRO
PAWC	NONE	(29)	YES	NONE
PR	$100	150,000	(11)	NONE
RI	NONE	300,000	YES	YES $50M SUBRO
SC	$250	300,000	YES	YES $10M 1st, $25M SUBRO
SD	NONE	300,000	YES	YES $50M 1st, SUBRO
TN	$100	100,000	YES	YES $10M 1ST, $25M SUBRO
TX	NONE	300,000	YES	YES $50M SUBRO
UT	NONE	300,000	YES	YES $25M 1ST, SUBRO
VT	NONE	300,000	YES	NONE
VI	$50	50,000	(5)	NONE
VA	NONE	300,000	YES	YES $50M SUBRO
WA	$100	300,000	WC NOT CVRD (7)	NONE
WV	$100	300,000	WC NOT CVRD (7)	NONE
WI	$200	$300,000 / RISK, LOSS OR LIFE	(6)	YES, OLD MODEL SUBRO PROV
WY	$250	$150,000 / CLAIMANT	(7)	NONE

	National Conference of Insurance Guaranty Funds 2001 Summary of Property & Casualty Insurance Guaranty Association Acts of the Various States and US Territories Summary by Provision **Non-Covered Claims**			
STATE	**PRE-LIQ. FEES**	**PUNITIVE DAM**	**NON-EC LOSS**	**OTHER (2)**
NAIC		X		
NCIGF		X		
AL				
AK		X		
AZ	X			
AR	X	X		INTEREST
CA	X	X		CLAIMS COVERED BY GOV'T INS OR GUARANTY
CO				
CT				NON-U.S. CLAIMS & CLAIMS OF ALIENS
DE		X		BAD FAITH DAMAGES
DC		X		
FL				PENALTIES OR INTEREST
FLWC				PENALTIES OR INTEREST
GA		X		
HI		X		CLAIMS COVERED BY GOV'T INS OR GUARANTY
ID		X		
IL		X		
IN	X		X	INTEREST
IA	X	X		SIR, FINES, PEN. INT. POL W/LGE DED
KS				
KY				CERTAIN LEGAL EXPENSES
LA	X			PENALTIES OR INTEREST
ME		X		CLAIMS COVERED BY GOV'T INS
MD				
MA				
MI	X			INTEREST
MN				
MS		X		
MO		X	X	
MT		X		
NE	X		X	
NV	X			INTEREST
NH				
NJ		X		PENALTIES, INTEREST
NM	X			INTEREST
NY				
NC		X		CLAIMS COVERED BY GOV'T INS OR GUARANTY
ND		X		
OH		X		
OK	X	X		INT; CLAIMS CVRD BY GOV'T INS OR GUAR
OR				
PA		X		
PAWC				
PR		X		
RI		X		CLAIMS COVERED BY GOV'T INS. OR GUAR
SC		X		SELF INS RETENTION, GOV'T INS
SD		X		
TN		X	X	
TX	X	X		PENALTIES, INTEREST, BAD FAITH DAM.
UT	X	X		INTEREST
VT	X			
VI	X			INTEREST
VA		X		CLAIMS COVERED BY GOV'T INS. OR GUARANTY
WA				
WV				
WI		X		CLAIMS COVERED BY GOV'T INS. OR GUARANTY
WY	X			INTEREST

STATE	FINAL ORDER OF LIQUIDATION WITH A FINDING OF INSOLVENCY	FINDING OF INSOLVENCY ONLY	OTHER
	National Conference of Insurance Guaranty Funds 2001 Summary of Property & Casualty Insurance Guaranty Association Acts of the Various States and US Territories Summary by Provision **Guaranty Fund Trigger**		
NAIC	X		
NCIGF	X		
AL	X		
AK	X		
AZ		X	
AR		X	
CA			10
CO	X		
CT		X	
DE	X		
DC	X		
FL	X		
FLWC	X		
GA	X		
HI	X		
ID	X		
IL	X		
IN	X		
IA	X		
KS		X	
KY	X		
LA	X		(17)
ME			
MD	X		
MA		X	
MI			LIQUIDATOR APPOINTED BY FINAL ORDER
MN	X		
MS	X		
MO	X		
MT		X	
NE	X		
NV	X		(8)
NH		X	
NJ		X	
NM	X		
NY			INSOLVENCY OF INSURER
NC	X		
ND	X		
OH			(10)
OK			(10)
OR	X		
PA	X		
PAWC			FIND OF INSOLV OR LIQ. APPOINTED
PR	X		
RI	X		
SC		X	
SD	X		
TN	X		
TX		X	(12)
UT	X		
VT		X	
VI		X	
VA	X		
WA			(10)
WV			(10)
WI			FINAL ORDER OF LIQUIDATION
WY	X		

EXPLANATORY NOTES

(1) Where possible, all covered lines of business were listed.

(2) Almost without exception, each state's guaranty association act provides that: amounts due a reinsurer, insurer, insurance pool or underwriting association are not covered claims, and further that any covered claim shall be reduced by amounts covered by other insurance or another guaranty association. These provisions were not included under this section; but nonetheless are also limitations on covered claims.

(3) Claims up to deductible amount are not paid, claims over deductible amount paid in full.

(4) Worker's compensation claims of insolvent insurers paid by Arizona competitive state fund.

(5) Worker's compensation payments subject only to maximum claim amount.

(6) Worker's compensation payments subject only to deductible.

(7) Worker's compensation insurance written exclusively through monopolistic state fund.

(8) Also triggered if insurer is involved in a judicial proceeding related to the determination of solvency, rehabilitation or liquidation, and court involved in proceeding(s) has issued an order prohibiting the insurer from paying claims for more than thirty (30) days.

(9) Worker's compensation claims covered by separate worker's compensation security fund.

(10) Triggered by finding of insolvency and liquidation order.

(11) Worker's compensation payments subject to both deductible and maximum claim amount.

(12) Triggered if: (i)Insurer is placed in receivership based on a finding of insolvency, or (ii)conservatorship after being deemed by commissioner to be insolvent and an impaired insurer.

(13) Limit applies to assessments paid in 1995 and beyond, 1992 limit: 13%; 1993 limit: 11%; and 1994 limit: 13%.

(14) Limit of $100,000 per residential unit for policies covering condominium associations or homeowners associations.

(15) An additional 2% of the "All Other" account may be assessed to the extent necessary to address insolvencies related to Hurricane Andrew.

(16) Iowa does not cover claim of person whose net worth is greater than that allowed by guaranty fund law of his or her state of residence.

(17) Association also obligated to pay claims of an insurer in rehabilitation upon joint motion of association and receiver.

(18) For assessments made before January 1, 1993 - 10% per year for ten (10) successive years beginning March 1, 1996; for assessments made on or after January 1, 1993, 20% per year for the five years beginning with the calendar year following the calendar year in which assessments are paid.

(19) Total premiums shall not include medical malpractice liability premiums to which an additional charge has been applied for deposit in the New Jersey Medical Malpractice Reinsurance Recovery Fund.

(20) Association may assess worker's comp LOB 3% for assessments made on or before December 31, 1995. This provision expires January 1, 1996.

(21) Premium tax offset allowed to the extent of .05% of direct gross premium income per account involved for certificates issued prior to January 98. Unamortized amounts on such certificates may be amortized at 10% per year of unamortized portion.

(22) For assessments paid prior to April 1, 1993 and after July 27, 1997.

(23) For insolvencies after June 3, 1993.

(24) Payment by fund to workers' compensation residual market to be recouped through assessment.

(25) Effective January 1, 1997, member may offset against corporate excise tax and fire insurance premium tax but not gross premium tax.

(26) Additional assessment may be authorized for national disaster or catastropic event.

(27) Act provides for aggregate limit of $10 Million per insured per insolvency.

(28) Not specified. Left as local option.

(29) Maximum is award amount. Payment pursuant to Longshore & Harbor Workers' Compensation Act shall be made at federal or state benefit level, whichever is lower.

(30) Fund covers Workers' Compensation only.

Insurance Company Rating Definitions

A.M. Best Company

Ambest Road
Oldwick, NJ 08858
Telephone (908) 439–2200
Fax (908) 439–3363

www.ambest.com

A.M. Best Company has provided ratings for the insurance industry since 1899. Ratings can be obtained via A.M. Best's Web site, www.ambest.com. These ratings are defined as follows:

Secure Best's Ratings

A++ and A+ (Superior)

Assigned to companies that have, in our opinion, a superior ability to meet their ongoing obligations to policyholders.

A and A- (Excellent)

Assigned to companies that have, in our opinion, an excellent ability to meet their ongoing obligations to policyholders.

B++ and B+ (Very Good)

Assigned to companies that have, in our opinion, a good ability to meet their ongoing obligations to policyholders.

Vulnerable Best's Ratings

B and B- (Fair)

Assigned to companies that have, in our opinion, a fair ability to meet their current obligations to policyholders, but are financially vulnerable to adverse changes in underwriting and economic conditions.

C++ and C+ (Marginal)

Assigned to companies that have, in our opinion, a marginal ability to meet their current obligations to policyholders, but are financially vulnerable to adverse changes in underwriting and economic conditions.

C and C- (Weak)

Assigned to companies that have, in our opinion, a weak ability to meet their current obligations to policyholders, but are financially very vulnerable to adverse changes in underwriting and economic conditions.

D (Poor)

Assigned to companies that in our opinion, may not have an ability to meet their current obligations to policyholders and are financially extremely vulnerable to adverse changes in underwriting and economic conditions.

E (Under Regulatory Supervision)

Assigned to companies (and possibly their subsidiaries/affiliates) that have been placed by an insurance regulatory authority under a significant form of supervision, control or restraint whereby they are no longer allowed to conduct normal ongoing insurance operations. This would include conservatorship or rehabilitation, but does not include liquidation. It may also be assigned to companies issued cease and desist orders by regulators outside their home state or country.

F (In Liquidation)

Assigned to companies that have been placed under an order of liquidation by a court of law or whose owners have voluntarily agreed to liquidate the company. Note: Companies that voluntarily liquidate or dissolve their charters are generally not insolvent.

S (Rating Suspended)

Assigned to rated companies that have experienced sudden and significant events affecting their balance sheet strength or operating performance whose rating implications cannot be evaluated due to a lack of timely or adequate information.

"Not Rated" (NR) Categories

NR-1 (Insufficient Data)

Assigned predominately to small companies for which A.M. Best does not have sufficient financial information required to assign rating opinions. The information contained in these limited reports is obtained from several sources, which include the individual companies, the National Association of Insurance Commissioners (NAIC) and other data providers. Data received from the NAIC, in some cases, is prior to the completion of its cross-checking and validation process.

NR-2 (Insufficient Size and/or Operating Experience)

Assigned to companies that do not meet A.M. Best's minimum size and/or operating experience requirements. To be eligible for a letter rating, a company must generally have a minimum of $2 million in policyholders' surplus to assure reasonable financial stability and have sufficient operating experience to adequately evaluate its financial performance, usually two to five years. General exceptions to these requirements include: companies that have financial or strategic affiliations with Best rated companies; companies that have demonstrated long histories of financial performance; companies that have achieved significant market positions; and newly formed companies with experienced management that have acquired seasoned books of business and/or developed credible business plans.

NR-3 (Rating Procedure Inapplicable)

Assigned to companies that are not rated by A.M. Best, because our normal rating procedures do not

apply due to a company's unique or unusual business features, which include companies that: are in run-off with no active business writings, are effectively dormant, underwrite financial or mortgage guaranty insurance, or retain only a small portion of their gross premiums written. Exceptions to the assignment of the NR-3 category to run-off companies relate to those that commenced run-off plans in the current year or are inactive companies that have been structurally separated from active affiliates within group structures that pose potential credit, legal or market risks to the group's active companies.

NR-4 (Company Request)

Assigned to companies that were assigned a Best's Rating but request that their ratings not be published because the companies disagree with Best's rating conclusion. The NR-4 will be assigned at the request of the company following the dissemination by A.M. Best of the latest letter rating assignment.

NR-5 (Not Formally Followed)

Assigned to insurers that request not to be formally evaluated for the purposes of assigning a rating opinion. It is also assigned retroactively to the rating history of traditional U.S. insurers when they provide prior year(s) financial information to A.M. Best and receive a Best's Rating or another NR designation in more recent years. Finally, it is assigned currently to those companies that historically had been rated, but no longer provide financial information to A.M. Best because they have been liquidated, dissolved, or merged out of existence.

Affiliation Codes

"g" Group Rating: Assigned to the parent company of a group and is based on the consolidation of the parent company and its insurance subsidiaries where ownership or board control exceeds 50%.

The group rating is also assigned to core subsidiaries based on the consolidation of the subsidiary and the parent. To qualify, a core subsidiary must be deemed integral to the group's business strategy, generally operates under common management and/or ownership, and serves as a strategic marketing or distribution arm of its parent. A core subsidiary may be a strategic affiliate that pools a substantial portion of its net business, or reinsures a substantial portion of its excess losses above a modest retention level, with other group members.

"p" Pooled Rating: Assigned to members of an inter-company pool that effectively pool all their net business. The pooled rating is based on the consolidation of pool members and their subsidiaries. To qualify, a pool member must operate under common management and/or ownership (or substantial board control for mutual insurers) serve as a strategic affiliate to the group, and prorate all current and prior premiums, expenses and losses among the pool members in accordance with specified percentages that are comparable to the distribution of the policyholders' surplus of each member of the group.

Typically, all pool members are assigned the same group rating and Financial Size Category, based on their consolidation. NOTE: Many of these pooling arrangements do not include joint and several liability clauses between the company members.

"r" Reinsured Rating: Assigned to a company within a group that reinsures substantially all direct premiums written with an affiliated reinsurer. The rating is based on the consolidation of the company's reinsurer and its subsidiaries. To qualify, a company must operate under common management and/or ownership as its reinsurer. Typically, reinsured affiliates are assigned the same rating and Financial Size Category as their reinsurer.

Rating Modifiers

"u" Under Review: Assigned to companies whose rating is currently under review due to a recent event or abrupt change in its financial condition, which may have positive, developing, or negative rating implications.

A company's rating remains under review until A.M. Best meets with management to fully review the rating implications of the event before either affirming the rating or taking any positive or negative rating action. Generally, a company's rating is placed Under Review for less than six months.

"pd" Public Data Rating: Assigned to Canadian, UK and other European insurers, and HMOs and health insurers (United States) that do not subscribe to our interactive rating process. Best's Public Data Ratings reflect both qualitative and quantitative analysis using publicly available data and other public information.

"s" Syndicate Rating: Assigned to syndicates operating at Lloyds that meet our minimum size and operating experience requirements for a Best's Rating and subscribe to our interactive rating process.

Fitch Ratings

55 East Monroe St.
Chicago, IL 60603
(312) 368-3157
Fax (312) 263-4064

www.fitchratings.com

Fitch's Insurance Group provides ratings on over 800 insurance entities in close to thirty countries. The Insurance Group maintains three significant analytical staffing centers in Chicago, London, and New York and also coordinates local analytical resources in other parts of the world on behalf of Fitch's global office network.

Insurer Financial Strength Ratings are directed at a vast cross section of ratings users, including insurance brokers and agents, risk managers, security committees, financial planners, pension fund advisors, individual policyholders and claimants, and are used extensively in the insurance marketplace to support insurance carrier selection and placement decisions.

The IFS Rating uses the same ratings scale and symbols used by Fitch Ratings for its international ratings of long-term debt obligations and issuers. However, the definitions associated with the ratings reflect the unique aspects of the IFS Rating within an insurance industry context.

Ratings in the 'AA' through 'CCC' categories may be amended with a (+) or (-) sign to show relative standing within the major rating category. Ratings of 'BBB-' and higher are considered to be 'Secure', and those of 'BB+' and lower are considered to be 'Vulnerable'.

AAA

Exceptionally strong. Insurers assigned this highest rating are viewed as possessing exceptionally strong capacity to meet policyholder and contract obligations. For such companies, risk factors are minimal and the impact of any adverse business and economic factors is expected to be extremely small.

AA

Very strong. Insurers are viewed as possessing very strong capacity to meet policyholder and contract obligations. Risk factors are modest, and the impact of any adverse business and economic factors is expected to be very small.

A

Strong. Insurers are viewed as possessing strong capacity to meet policyholder and contract obligations. Risk factors are moderate, and the impact of any adverse business and economic factors is expected to be small.

BBB

Good. Insurers are viewed as possessing good capacity to meet policyholder and contract obligations. Risk factors are somewhat high, and the impact of any adverse business and economic factors is expected to be material, yet manageable.

BB

Moderately weak. Insurers are viewed as moderately weak with an uncertain capacity to meet policyholder and contract obligations. Though positive factors are present, overall risk factors are high, and the impact of any adverse business and economic factors is expected to be significant.

B

Weak. Insurers are viewed as weak with a poor capacity to meet policyholder and contract obligations. Risk factors are very high, and the impact of any adverse business and economic factors is expected to be very significant.

CCC, CC, C

Very weak. Insurers rated in any of these three categories are ass very weak with a very poor capacity to meet policyholder and contract obligations. Risk factors are extremely high, and the impact of any adverse business and economic factors is expected to be insurmountable. A 'CC' rating indicates that some form of insolvency or liquidity impairment appears probable. A 'C' rating signals that insolvency or liquidity impairment appears imminent.

DDD, DD, D

Distressed. These ratings are assigned to insurers that have either failed to make payments on their obligations in a timely manner, are deemed to be insolvent, or have been subjected to some form of regulatory intervention. Within the DDD-D range, those companies rated 'DDD' have the highest prospects for resumption of business operations or, if liquidated or wound down, of having a vast majority of their obligations to policyholders and contract holders ultimately paid off, though on a delayed basis (with recoveries expected in the range of 90-100%). Those rated 'DD' show a much lower likelihood of ultimately paying off material amounts of their obligations in a liquidation or wind down scenario (in a range of 50-90%). Those rated 'D' are ultimately expected to have very limited liquid assets available to fund obligations, and therefore any ultimate payoffs would be quite modest (at under 50%).

Notes: "+" or "-" may be appended to a rating to indicate the relative position of a credit within the rating category. Such suffixes are not added to ratings in the "AAA" category or to ratings below the "CCC" category.

A **Rating Outlook** indicates the direction a rating is likely to move over a one to two-year period. Outlooks may be positive, stable or negative. A positive or negative Rating Outlook does not imply a rating change is inevitable. Similarly, ratings for which outlooks are 'stable' could be upgraded or downgraded before an outlook moves to positive or negative if circumstances warrant such an action. Occasionally, Fitch Ratings may be unable to identify the fundamental trend. In these cases, the Rating Outlook may be described as evolving.

Rating Watch: Ratings are placed on Rating Watch to notify investors that there is a reasonable probability of a rating change and the likely direction of such change. These are designated as "Positive", indicating a potential upgrade, "Negative", for a potential downgrade, or "Evolving", if ratings may be raised, lowered or maintained.

Rating Watch is typically resolved over a relatively short period.

Moody's Investors Service

Church Street
New York, NY 10007
Telephone (212) 553-0300
Fax (212) 553-0010

www.moodys.com

Moody's Investors Service has been rating bonds since 1909, adding insurers' strength in 1986. Moody's looks at both quantitative and qualitative measures. It seeks to measure credit risk. Fee schedules are available upon request.

Aaa
Companies offer exceptional financial security.

Aa
Similar to Aaa, but companies face slightly higher long-term risk.

A
Good, but may be susceptible to impairment in the future.

Baa
Adequate security.

Ba
Companies are questionable.

B
Companies offer poor financial security.

Caa
Poor security, companies may be in default on their obligations.

Ca
Very poor. Companies may be in default on their obligations.

C
Extremely poor prospects of ever offering financial security.

Moody's considers Aaa through Baa to be strong companies, Ba through C to be weak.

Printed with permission of Moody's Investors Service.

STANDARD & POOR'S

55 Water Street
New York, NY 10041
Telephone: (212) 438-2400
Fax: (212) 438-7195

www.standardandpoors.com

Insurer Financial Strength Ratings

A Standard & Poor's Insurer Financial Strength Rating is a current opinion of the financial security characteristics of an insurance organization with respect to its ability to pay under its insurance policies and contracts in accordance with their terms. Insurer Financial Strength Ratings are also assigned to health maintenance organizations and similar heath plans with respect to their ability to pay under their policies and contracts in accordance with their terms.

An insurer rated 'BBB' or higher is regarded as having financial security characteristics that outweigh any vulnerabilities, and is highly likely to have the ability to meet financial commitments.

AAA An insurer rated 'AAA' has EXTREMELY STRONG financial security characteristics. 'AAA' is the highest Insurer Financial Strength Rating assigned by Standard & Poor's.

AA An insurer rated 'AA' has VERY STRONG financial security characteristics, differing only slightly from those rated higher.

A An insurer rated 'A' has STRONG financial security characteristics, but is somewhat more likely to be affected by adverse business conditions than are insurers with higher ratings.

BBB An insurer rated 'BBB' has GOOD financial security characteristics, but is more likely to be affected by adverse business conditions than are higher rated insurers.

An insurer rated 'BB' or lower is regarded as having vulnerable characteristics that may outweigh its strengths. 'BB' indicates the least degree of vulnerability within the range; 'CC' the highest.

BB An insurer rated 'BB' has MARGINAL financial security characteristics. Positive attributes exist, but adverse business conditions could lead to insufficient ability to meet financial commitments.

B An insurer rated 'B' has WEAK financial security characteristics. Adverse business conditions will likely impair its ability to meet financial commitments.

CCC An insurer rated 'CCC' has VERY WEAK financial security characteristics, and is dependent on favorable business conditions to meet financial commitments.

CC An insurer rated 'CC' has EXTREMELY WEAK financial security characteristics and is likely not to meet some of its financial commitments.

R An insurer rated 'R' has experienced a REGULATORY ACTION regarding solvency. The rating does not apply to insurers subject only to non-financial actions such as market conduct violations.

NR An insurer designated 'NR' is NOT RATED, which implies no opinion about the insurer's financial security.

Plus (+) or minus (-) signs following ratings from 'AA' to 'CCC' show relative standing within the major rating categories.

CreditWatch (*see CreditWatch definition under the general definitions*).

'pi' Ratings Ratings with a 'pi' subscript are based on an analysis of an issuer's published financial information, as well as additional information in the public domain. They do not, however, reflect in-depth meetings with an issuer's management and are therefore based on less comprehensive information than ratings without a 'pi' subscript. Ratings with a 'pi' subscript are reviewed annually based on a new year's financial statements, but may be reviewed on an interim basis if a major event occurs that may affect the issuer's credit quality.

Outlooks are not provided for ratings with a 'pi' subscript, nor are they subject to potential CreditWatch listings. Ratings with a 'pi' subscript generally are not modified with '+' or '-' designations. However, such designations may be assigned when the issuer's credit rating is constrained by sovereign risk or the credit quality of a parent company or affiliated group.

General Definitions

CreditWatch highlights an emerging situation which may materially affect the profile of a rated corporation and can be designated as positive, developing or negative. Following a full review the rating may either be affirmed or changed in the direction indicated.

A **Rating Outlook** assesses the potential direction of an issuer's long-term debt rating over the intermediate- to long-term. In determining a **Rating Outlook**, consideration is given to possible changes in the economic and/or fundamental business conditions. An Outlook is not necessarily a precursor of a rating change or future **CreditWatch** action. A 'Rating Outlook - Positive' indicates that a rating may be raised; 'Negative' means a rating may be lowered; 'Stable' indicates that ratings are not likely to change; and 'Developing' means ratings may be raised or lowered. N.M. means not meaningful, e.g. for structured or managed fund ratings.

Weiss Research

4176 Burns Road
Palm Beach Gardens, FL 33410
Telephone (561) 627–3300 or (800) 289–9222
Fax (561) 625–6685

www.WeissRatings.com

Weiss Research started publicly rating insurers in 1989. The company currently rates more than 1,700 companies and charges a fee of $15 to callers for a letter grade. Other services are available, and fees vary depending on the depth of the report requested.

The ratings are designed to predict an insurer's ability to meet its commitments, both under current conditions and in the event of economic decline or other changes.

Excellent

The company offers excellent financial security. It has maintained a conservative stance in its strategies, business operations, and underwriting commitments. While the financial position of any company is subject to change, Weiss believes that this company has the resources necessary to deal with severe economic conditions.

Good

The company offers good financial security and has the resources to deal with a variety of adverse economic conditions. It comfortably exceeds the minimum levels for all Weiss's rating criteria and is likely to remain healthy for the near future. However, in the event of a severe recession or major financial crisis, Weiss feels that this assessment should be reviewed to make sure that the firm is still maintaining adequate financial strength.

Fair

The company offers fair financial security and is currently stable. But during an economic downturn or other financial pressures, Weiss feels it may encounter difficulties in maintaining its financial stability.

Weak

The company currently demonstrates what Weiss considers to be significant weaknesses that could negatively impact policyholders. In an unfavorable economic environment, these weaknesses could be magnified.

Very Weak

The company currently demonstrates what Weiss considers to be significant weaknesses and has also failed some of the basic tests that Weiss uses to identify fiscal stability. Therefore, even in a favorable economic environment, it is Weiss's opinion that policyholders could incur significant risks.

Failed

The company has failed and is either 1) under supervision of state insurance commissioners; 2) is in the process of liquidation; or 3) has voluntarily dissolved after disciplinary or other regulatory action by state insurance commissioners.

+

The plus sign is an indication that with new data, there is a modest possibility that the company could be upgraded. The A+ rating is an exception since no higher grade exists.

-

The minus sign is an indication that, with new data, there is a modest possibility that the company could be downgraded. The E- rating is an exception.

Unrated Companies

The company is unrated for one or more of the following reasons: 1) total assets are less than $1 million; 2) premium income for the current year was less than $100,000; 3) the company functions almost exclusively as a holding company rather than as an underwriter; or 4) there is not enough information to reliably issue a rating.

Printed with the permission of Weiss Research.

Chapter 16

WORKING WITH AN AGENT OR BROKER

WHAT IS IT?

For numerous reasons—primarily because of state licensing requirements—businesses typically are not able to approach insurance companies directly. Most must use intermediaries, either licensed agents or brokers, to implement and maintain their risk management and insurance programs. In addition to arranging for the placement and servicing of insurance coverage, agents and brokers often provide many other services to clients. These services may include:

- Assisting with risk assessments,

- Drawing up specifications for needed insurance coverages,

- Marketing insurance coverages,

- Interpreting coverage,

- Advising clients about the insurance marketplace,

- Issuing insurance documents, such as certificates and binders of insurance,

- Billing and processing insurance invoices,

- Ordering or processing change endorsements,

- Analyzing losses, including developing loss projections,

- Researching technical exposure and coverage questions,

- Managing services provided by insurance carriers and other insurance-related vendors, and

- Offering creative and innovative ways to handle the business's risks.

Working effectively with an agent or broker requires that corporate risk and insurance managers provide timely, accurate information to insurance representatives, institute procedures to insure the timely submission of claims, and be willing to devote sufficient time to address relevant risk management issues.

The relationship between a corporation and its insurance intermediary should be a highly valued relationship, similar to that shared with legal and accounting professionals. Trust is an important part of it.

STEPS TO IMPLEMENT

The first step in this process is to select an agent or broker. As noted in Chapter 7, businesses may first select an intermediary, who then is asked to design and set up the insurance portion of the program. In other cases, businesses may issue requests for insurance and risk management proposals. In those situations, the agent or broker who presents the best program may be selected as the intermediary.

Once the relationship is established, coverage is placed and insurance policies are issued. During the coverage term, the intermediary should provide the level of service that was discussed during the selection process. Performance should be evaluated on a periodic basis, which is established in the evaluation procedure.

Compensation

Many agents and brokers are compensated through commissions paid by insurance companies on the policies sold. Others are compensated through a service fee. When a service fee is used, the broker or agent often commits to a specified level of service and is compensated accordingly.

ADVANTAGES AND DISADVANTAGES

Most businesses do not have a choice about using an agent or broker to market and place the insurance portion of their risk management program. Therefore, the quality of the relationship between the insured business and its intermediary is the key to the advantages and disadvantages.

As explained in Chapter 7, the type of intermediary chosen should reflect the needs of the business. Types of intermediaries include brokers, independent agents, exclusive agents, direct-writing agents, and exclusive agents. Surplus lines agents usually do not deal directly with businesses but, rather, deal through retail agents or brokers to reach the client.

TIME AND CASH COMMITMENT

Risk managers must be willing to gather and submit the information and data that an intermediary requires. Accurate information that is supplied on a timely basis is a necessity.

There is a cost associated with using an intermediary. They are compensated either through commission paid by insurers on the coverages written, or by the insured business through a service fee. Often a service contract is negotiated and executed to form the basis for the service fee.

Some businesses believe that a performance incentive should be built into the intermediary's compensation structure. Figure 16.2, a sample agent/broker review procedure, includes a provision for incentive payments.

Agent/broker reviews should be conducted at least annually. Some intermediaries present status reports on what they have accomplished, outstanding items, and strategic issues on a more frequent basis. As with any partnership, communication is a key to success.

WHERE CAN I FIND OUT MORE ABOUT IT?

- *Risk Management Best Practices.* New York: Risk and Insurance Management Society (RIMS), Inc. http://www.rims.org/content/Publications1/default.htm.

QUESTIONS AND ANSWERS

Question—A business has decided to solicit proposals for its insurance program. It invites two independent agents and one broker to present proposals. What are some of the ways in which the business can control the process?

Answer—Most insurance companies will issue only one insurance proposal for a business. Therefore, if two intermediaries approach the same insurance company with insurance specifications for the same business, only one insurance proposal

will be issued. Usually the insurer will offer its proposal to the first intermediary that submits a complete proposal.

In order to avoid overlapping submissions, businesses often choose a limited number of potential intermediaries and then assign the markets they can access. For example, ABC Restaurants is seeking insurance and risk management proposals. It agrees to let three intermediaries participate. In order to control the marketing process, ABC assigns Insurers 1, 2, and 3 to Agent I; Insurers 3, 4, and 5 to Broker II; and Insurers 6, 7, and 8 to Agent III. As part of the process, ABC Restaurants gives the three intermediaries letters authorizing them to solicit insurance proposals from each of the three companies they are assigned. In this way, the intermediaries do not overlap one another as they approach potential insurance companies.

Figure 16.1 is a sample market-appointment letter. A separate letter would be issued by ABC Restaurants for each of the nine insurance companies they assign to the three intermediaries.

Question—Is it better to be represented by one insurance intermediary (broker or agent) or more than one?

Answer—The answer to this question depends upon the size and complexity of the insured business. Smaller businesses may find that one intermediary is best because that one representative has the opportunity to better understand the entire business. This helps to ensure that there are fewer—or no gaps—in the insurance program. In addition, businesses that do not have full-time risk managers only have to deal with one intermediary.

Larger, more complex businesses may value the diverse resources that two intermediaries bring to their account. In addition, some risk managers feel more comfortable when two intermediaries are familiar with their businesses. They may desire that the two back up one another when complex exposures arise and answers are needed.

Question—What is a good way to measure an intermediary's performance?

Answer—Intermediaries should be held accountable for the service they provide, and businesses should conduct periodic reviews of agent/broker performance. Figure 16.2, which follows, is a sample broker evaluation procedure. The first part outlines the reasoning behind the process, and the second part is an evaluation form. It can be used to develop an evaluation process that is customized to a particular business.

Figure 16.1

SAMPLE MARKET-APPOINTMENT LETTER

Important: The letter should be on the client's (insured business's) stationery.

(Insured's Name)
(Insured's Address)

(Date)

(Insurer Name)
(Street Address)
(City, State, Zip)

Dear (Underwriter Name—if known):

RE: (Client Name)
    (Coverage Type, such as commercial property insurance or commercial general liability insurance)

Please be advised that, effective (date), we have authorized (Broker or Agency Name, Address) to approach your company for proposals for the above noted insurance coverages. You are authorized to provide representatives of (Broker or Agency Name) with your proposal for these lines of insurance coverage.

This letter supersedes any other letter previously issued that may assign your company to a different agent or broker for insurance marketing purposes.

Sincerely,

(Authorized Representative, Named Insured)

Figure 16.2

SAMPLE AGENT/BROKER EVALUATION PROCEDURE

I. **Purpose**

The purpose of the agent/broker review is threefold:

1. To provide a methodology for evaluating agent/broker performance,
2. To provide the basis for continuing a relationship with the agent/broker, and
3. To determine appropriate compensation based upon the quality and quantity of service.

   The objective of this program is to maximize efficiencies, increase communication between the agent/broker and client, and provide incentive for superior service.

II. **Background**

Insurance purchases are distinguished from the purchase of many other services due to the highly valued relationships involved. The agent/broker relationship to the carriers they represent can translate into premium dollars, or even coverage availability, depending upon relationships of the people involved. The client relies upon the advice of the agent/broker and, therefore, the expertise of the agent/broker must be highly credible.

The agent/broker acts as a gatekeeper of carrier services such as loss control inspections, preliminary audits, and coverage interpretations. It is important that the agent/broker understand the needs of the client in order that the services delivered are according to that need.

The agent/broker <u>also</u> benefits from this review process. The agent/broker understands the expectations of the client and is able to behave accordingly. Misunderstandings and the consultant's potential for unintentional error should decrease.

The review process will also provide a basis for "fee-based" compensation of the agent/broker. A very high aggregate score would indicate a high value being added to the insurance transaction by the agent/broker and a commensurate compensation is indicated. Fee-based compensation would permit a reward-based system of compensation for service where commissions do not.

III. **Policy**

In support of the Corporate Risk Management Policy, the Risk Management Division will foster professional relationships with competent, experienced agents and brokers that add significant value to the insurance transaction.

IV. **Scope**

This policy and procedure will be applied to all Property and Casualty Insurance broker/agent situations where the client has an ongoing business relationship.

Figure 16.2(Cont'd)

SAMPLE AGENT/BROKER EVALUATION PROCEDURE

V. Definitions

1. Agent

   A term loosely used to mean a representative of one or more insurance companies with a limited authority to bind coverage, receive premiums, and otherwise consummate insurance sales

2. Annual Compensation Fee

   See "Fee-based Compensation" below

3. Annual Review

   A complete review of agent/broker characteristics and services according to this Standard Operating Procedure.

4. Broker

   An independent businessperson (or firm) who represents the insurance buyer in an insurance purchase. A broker usually has no binding authority.

5. Commission

   Agent/broker recompense based upon a percentage of the annual premium for the coverage sold. Commissions are paid by the insuring company according to a predetermined schedule contained in the agent/broker agreement or according to a special agreement for a particular account.

6. Fee-based Compensation

   Agent/broker recompense for services based upon a negotiated, pre-determined sum instead of a percentage of the annual premium. Fees are paid directly by the insurance buyer to the agent/broker. (These broker fees should be paid on a quarterly installment basis.)

7. Incentive Bonus Compensation

   Extra compensation paid at the end of a predetermined period for meeting predetermined service performance standards. We do encourage a more aggressive performance-based fee structure and we encourage the broker to entertain an amended fee in exchange for a more beneficial bonus opportunity.

8. Independent Agent (Agent)

   A firm in the business of selling insurance, usually as a representative of several unrelated insurance companies. The independent agent represents the insurance company, not the insurance buyer.

Figure 16.2(Cont'd)

SAMPLE AGENT/BROKER EVALUATION PROCEDURE

VI. **Procedure and Requirements**

A. Types of reviews and frequency

Annual review - 60 days prior to the annual compensation renewal date established by Risk Management.

Note: Midterm reviews may be conducted at any time if deemed appropriate by the Risk Analyst.

B. Forms

The attached form entitled "Agent/broker Review" will be used for all reviews.

C. Performance

A performance chart (typically bar chart) will be developed to illustrate scoring of each major category and performance index change for previous periods.

D. Sequential Process.

1. The review form will be completed by client personnel within the time frame indicated in A above.

Note: Scoring will be determined based upon the perception of the client's Risk Management Division. Client reserves the right to make any and all scoring decisions based upon their sole judgment. Client reserves the right to change or alter scoring criteria at any time in order to improve the review process.

2. The form will be signed and dated by the Risk Analyst (originator) and copied. The form will then be submitted to the Director of Risk Management for signature. Appropriate copies will be made.

3. A meeting will then be arranged with agent/broker personnel for comments and an interactive dialogue on positive and negative aspects of the review. Although aggregate scoring for each major category can be disclosed, scores for each individual criterion should not.

4. A copy of the matrix, the associated chart of performance, and bonus check, if applicable, will be given to the agent/broker at the conclusion of the meetings. All originals will be retained in the office of the Director of Risk Management.

5. The information will be entered into a computer database to assist statistical analysis.

Figure 16.2(Cont'd)

SAMPLE AGENT/BROKER EVALUATION PROCEDURE

E. Confidentiality

The information contained on the review sheet will be treated confidentially between parties with an operational interest. However, it should be treated as a fully discoverable document.

This document should not be shared with other Agents/Brokers/Consultants, Risk Managers, insurance buyers, or other entities without the express written consent of each party.

VII. **Incentive Bonus Compensation**

Agent/broker will:

In order to align the performance of agents/brokers with the goals and mission of the Risk Management Division, an incentive bonus program has been established as a part of this review process. Agent/brokers who perform according to the table below will earn the indicated bonus payable in a lump sum at the time of the agent/broker review. The % indicated will be multiplied by the annual compensation fee negotiated annually to determine the amount of cash bonus.

Agent/brokers who do not meet the performance level for an incentive bonus will not receive any bonus compensation for the review period.

Note: A broker that prenegotiates the fee and is willing to negotiate on the advance fee in consideration for an adjusted bonus potential may actually receive a bonus that exceeds the following schedule.

Annual Review Incentive Bonus Performance Chart

Performance Chart	Bonus %
7.5 (maximum)	12
7.25 - 7.499	10
7.10 - 7.249	5
7.00 - 7.099	2
Below 7.00	0

Figure 16.2(Cont'd)

SAMPLE AGENT/BROKER EVALUATION PROCEDURE

Review Period _____   NAME OF FIRM _____

Coverage/Services provided (include expiration dates if applicable):

_____

_____

_____

_____

_____

_____

RATING POINTS

(1) unacceptable (2)

        (3) needs improvement (4)

               (5) adequate (6)

                      (7) good (8)

                             (9) excellent (10)

(For policy and procedures concerning completion of this form, refer to <u>Risk Management</u> <u>Program Policies and Procedures</u> "Agent/broker Review")

Figure 16.2(Cont'd)

SAMPLE AGENT/BROKER EVALUATION PROCEDURE

I.   <u>GENERAL</u>   <u>Score:</u>

    a.   Knowledge of insurance markets ....   _____

    b.   Knowledge of insurance products...   _____

    c.   Market impact...   _____

    d.   Knowledge of industry and Client ....   _____

    e.   Effectiveness of back-up personnel ....   _____

    f.   Overall professionalism ....   _____

    g.   Broad representation of licensed carriers
       (agency contract) ....   _____

    h.   Errors and Omissions coverage ....   _____

    I.   Staff retention ....   _____

                                         I. Subtotal ....   _____

Comments:

Figure 16.2(Cont'd)

SAMPLE AGENT/BROKER EVALUATION PROCEDURE

II. **COMPENSATION**   **Score:**

    a.   Willingness to disclose and negotiate .... _____

    b.   Willingness to compensate on fee basis .... _____

    c.   Overall value for overall compensation .... _____

                           II. Subtotal .... _____

Comments:

III. **PROFESSIONALISM**   **Score:**

    a.   Overall presentation .... _____

    b.   Information credibility .... _____

    c.   Ongoing education .... _____

    d.   Support staff education (including ARM) .... _____

    e.   Ethical considerations .... _____

                           III. Subtotal .... _____

Comments:

Figure 16.2(Cont'd)

SAMPLE AGENT/BROKER EVALUATION PROCEDURE

IV.   <u>**COMMUNICATIONS**</u>   <u>Score</u>:

    a.   Inform/new developments ....   _____

    b.   Effectiveness/listen, research, react ....   _____

    c.   Technical explanation ....   _____

    d.   Documentation appropriate ....   _____

    e.   Regular contacts (phone, meetings) ....   _____

    f.   Responsiveness ....   _____

        e.g.:   Phone calls returned in timely manner

             Deadlines for quotes and research met

                              IV. Subtotal ....   _____

Comments:

Figure 16.2(Cont'd)

SAMPLE AGENT/BROKER EVALUATION PROCEDURE

V.   POLICYHOLDER SERVICES   <u>Score:</u>

    a.   Timely delivery of policies .... _____

    b.   Accuracy of premiums and coverage
           quoted vs. policy delivery .... _____

    c.   Binders and ID card delivery .... _____

    d.   Accurate, on-time invoicing .... _____

    e.   Timely processing of endorsements .... _____

    f.   Claims processing efficiency (include use of
           draft authority when possible) .... _____

    g.   Return premium credits mailed promptly .... _____

    h.   Claim status reporting (include reserve review) .... _____

    I.   Certificate of insurance support .... _____

    j.   Quotations in writing with appropriate disclosure .... _____

    k.   Loss analysis .... _____

    l.   Loss control assistance and support .... _____

    m.   Loss control recommendations - response, advocacy .... _____

                              V. Subtotal .... _____

Comments:

Figure 16.2(Cont'd)

SAMPLE AGENT/BROKER EVALUATION PROCEDURE

VI.   **CONSULTING SERVICES**   **Score:**

    a.   Availability of In-house Consulting Services .... _____

    b.   Effectiveness/listen, research, react .... _____
             Technical expertise .... _____
             e.g.: ability to listen and understand
                  issue and the ability to deliver
                  an appropriate proposal/resolution

    d.   Documentation appropriate .... _____

    e.   Regular contacts (phone, meetings) .... _____

    f.   Responsiveness .... _____

             e.g.: Phone calls returned in timely manner

                  Deadlines for research/deliverable met

    g.   Innovation .... _____

                          IV. Subtotal .... _____

Comments:

Summary:

Signatures

(Sign) _____ (Print)_____ (Date) _____
        Originator

(Sign) _____ (Print)_____ (Date) _____
        Director, Risk Management

COMMERCIAL GENERAL LIABILITY INSURANCE

WHAT IS IT?

The commercial general liability (CGL) coverage form is an insurance policy that provides coverage for the insured's liability. Through a CGL form, the insured business chooses to transfer some of its risk exposures to an insurance company. So, if the insured has to pay for injury or damage to another person or company, the commercial general liability form requires the insurance company to pay the insured's legal obligations—up to the limits of the policy.

The coverage is *commercial* because the insured is a business entity as opposed to a person. For example, Joe Smith, as a homeowner, needs a personal liability policy, whereas Joe Smith, Inc., as a business, needs the CGL form. This is because the risk exposures of a person and a business are different and need to be handled differently.

BUSINESS USES

The CGL form is termed *general liability* because it provides coverage for the overall risk exposures of the insured. This includes the insured's risk exposures from business premises and operations, as well as from products and completed operations.

Liability Exposure Examples

Example #1, Premises Exposure

A company owns an office building. If a visitor trips and falls in the building lobby and is injured, the insured's CGL form would apply to a resulting claim. The insured, as the owner of the building, owes a duty to visitors to maintain the premises in such a way that no harm comes to them. If that duty is breached and harm results to an innocent victim, the building owner is liable to the injured person for the damages.

Example #2, Operations Exposure

A property manager owns an apartment building, and her employee is laying carpet in a hallway. While hammering the tacks into the carpet, the employee lets the hammer slip and it flies into the face of a deliveryman. The insured—through her employee's activity—is performing an operation in her building. This operation caused an injury. The CGL form would apply to a resultant claim.

Example #3, Products Exposure

A business manufactures chairs. A customer buys a set of chairs, and one collapses when he sits on it. The customer falls and breaks his arm. This is a product failure. The insured manufacturer is liable because the company made the product and offered it for sale as a safe and useful product to the general public. The product failed, which was a breach of duty. The breach caused harm, and the CGL form would apply to a claim that arose from the breach of duty.

Example #4, Completed Operations Exposure

A contractor builds a retaining wall for a customer. One month after the job is completed, the wall falls on the customer's son, causing severe internal injuries. The retaining wall is a completed operation of the contractor that injured an innocent victim. The CGL form would respond to a claim made against the insured contractor.

The key point throughout all these examples is that the insured was legally liable for the injuries. The commercial general liability form will provide insurance coverage for the insured as long as the insured is legally liable for the injury or damage. *Legal liability* means that the individual or entity causing the injury or damage to a third party has been found liable for the injury or damage and so becomes obligated by law to pay for the damages suffered by that third party. If the insured is not legally liable, the CGL form will not pay for the injured person's injury or damages.

Duty to Defend

It is important to note here that, even though the CGL form will not pay damages if the insured is not legally liable, the form will pay defense costs for the insured if sued due to the damages. This is called the *duty to defend*. The CGL form includes this duty to defend provision in addition to its duty to pay damages. The expenses paid in defense of the insured are in addition to the limits of insurance applicable to pay damages.

Why a CGL Policy May Be Valuable for Defense Purposes

A diner sued ABC Restaurants, claiming that she was seriously injured when she fell on an icy sidewalk outside one of the restaurants. The diner alleged that there had been ice on the sidewalk when she entered the restaurant and that the ice was still there when she left three hours later.

ABC was unable to settle this claim, so it went to court. ABC's CGL insurer handled the claim, appointed a lawyer, defended the ultimate lawsuit, and then paid the court judgment. The total paid was $12,963 for defense and $50,000 for settlement. The CGL insurer paid the total amount. The $12,963 was paid in addition to the policy's limit of insurance.

The duty to defend is broader than the duty to pay. For example, if the insured business is sued for allegedly causing injury to someone, the CGL form requires the insurer to defend the insured. If the insured is found not legally liable for causing the injury, there is no duty to pay damages. However, the CGL form will pay the cost to defend the insured. It is only when it is clear and certain that the CGL form does not apply to the claim against the insured—for example, if an exclusion on the form definitely and totally precludes any coverage—that the duty to defend is not applicable.

As noted above, the CGL form covers the insured's general liability exposures. However, this coverage is not absolute. There are exclusions and limitations on the CGL form that affect the scope of coverage. The exclusions will be discussed subsequently, but the limitations on the coverage can be noted now.

Coverage Limitations

One of the limitations is that the liability insurance provided by the commercial general liability form is for *bodily injury* (BI), *property damage* (PD), or *personal and advertising injury*. These are all defined terms on the

form, and, if the injury or damage claim alleged against the insured business does not match one of these definitions, the CGL form will not cover the claim.

For example, *bodily injury* on the CGL form means "bodily injury, sickness, or disease sustained by a person, including death resulting from any of these at any time." If the claim against the insured consists only of a claim for mental distress, discrimination, or breach of a contract, the CGL form will not respond because there was no BI or PD—as defined on the form. If the claimant alleges mental distress and some type of resultant bodily injury or disease, then the CGL form would respond.

If a claimant alleges a personal injury against the insured, the injury must match the definition on the CGL form. *Personal and advertising injury* is defined as injury that arises out of offenses such as malicious prosecution, false arrest, libel or slander, and copyright violation in the insured business's advertisement. It includes infringing upon another's copyright but does not include patent infringement. The CGL form therefore would not cover a patent infringement claim against the insured.

Deciding When Damage Occurs

Another limitation is that the injury or damage has to take place in the coverage territory and during the policy period. The coverage territory is defined on the standard CGL form; it is discussed later. "During the policy period" means that the injury or damage has to occur while the policy is "in force".

There can be disputes between the insured and the insurer over when an injury or damage occurred, with the result being that a CGL insurer denies coverage because the adjuster believes the damage did not occur within the coverage period.

It is not so troublesome if the claim against the insured is one for property damage. The overwhelming majority of jurisdictions around the country hold that property damage occurs at the time the damage is discovered or when it has manifested itself.

Which Policy Applies?

An insured business manufactures washing machines and has a CGL form through ABC Insurance Company with effective dates of July 1, 2001, to July 1,

2002. The insured makes a washing machine in July 2001, and a customer buys it in August 2001. On July 1, 2002, the insured switches his general liability coverage to DEF Insurance Company. If the washing machine damages the customer's clothes in December 2002, it is the CGL form that is in effect in December 2002 from DEF Company that will apply to the claim. The washing machine may have been negligently made and may have been purchased while ABC Company's policy was in force, but the property damage occurred during the policy term of DEF Company.

The timing of bodily injury is not so clear-cut. Disputes over when BI occurs usually pertain to such things as asbestos or pollution injuries that can occur over a long period of time and that can, subsequently, include a number of different insurance policies and insurers. Various courts have accepted several approaches as to when BI occurs:

- the exposure theory,

- the manifestation theory,

- the injurious process theory (also called the triple trigger or multiple trigger theory), and

- the injury-in-fact theory.

Advocates of the *exposure theory* hold that when the disease or injury manifests itself has nothing to do with when the bodily injury took place. Liability coverage is triggered (and therefore, covered by the policy in effect at the time) by the victim's exposure to the harm-causing agent, whether or not the disease or injury manifests itself during the policy period.

The *manifestation theory* states that it is the date of the actual diagnosis of the injury or, with respect to those cases in which no diagnosis was made prior to death, the date of death, that determines the date of occurrence. This idea focuses on the result rather than the cause as the element upon which the policy coverage depends.

The *injurious process theory* holds that the occurrence was a continuing process beginning with the exposure to the danger, proceeding through the damage being caused by that exposure, and ending with the manifestation of the disease or injury. So, any CGL form in effect during this continuing process would apply to the claim.

The *injury-in-fact theory* depends on when the injury actually occurs. The manifestation of the injury or expo-

sure to dangers that can cause the injury is discounted under this idea; the trigger to coverage under the CGL form has been pulled only when the injury really happens. This theory may require a very accurate medical diagnosis, but it does match quite simply the requirement of the liability insuring agreement that the bodily injury occur during the policy period. For example, if the insured is exposed to asbestos for five years, but asbestosis develops only in that fifth year, the injury in fact proponents would say only the policy in effect during that fifth year is applicable. When the disease manifests itself is not the point either. If it manifests itself two or three years after the injury occurred, this theory would still say only the fifth year policy is applicable.

The Application of Limits of Liability

Finally, there is a limitation on just how much the insurer will pay for a claim against the insured. When a business chooses to transfer its liability exposures by buying an insurance policy, the business must select the limits of insurance. These limits are the most the insurer will pay for a claim regardless of the number of insureds, claims made or lawsuits brought, or persons or organizations making the claims or bringing the lawsuits. If the amount the insured business has to pay an injured person exceeds the limits of insurance that are stated on the CGL form's declarations page, that particular part of the risk will not fall to the insurer.

There are normally four major limits of liability on a CGL form. They are the:

- each occurrence limit,

- personal and advertising liability limit,

- general aggregate limit, and

- products/completed operations aggregate limit.

There also are sublimits for damages to premises rented to the insured and medical expenses.

The *each occurrence limit* caps the amount that will be paid for damages arising from each occurrence or accident, regardless of how many claims may arise from the occurrence. The *personal and advertising liability limit* is the most the insurer will pay for all damages that arise because of personal and advertising injury sustained by any one person or organization. The *general aggregate limit* caps the amount that will be paid for all medical expenses, premises and operations claims, and personal and advertising injury during one policy term. The *products/completed operations aggregate limit* is the most the insurance company will pay for bodily injury or property damage arising from an insured's products or completed operations.

For example, the insured business chooses an *each occurrence* limit of $500,000. That business has chosen to have its liability risk exposures—up to $500,000—transferred to the insurance company. If someone is injured and the business is liable for those injuries, the business can expect the insurer to pay no more than the $500,000. Or, if six individuals are injured because of the same occurrence and six claims are filed, the total amount payable still is $500,000. If the damage amount is more than that, the insured will have to pay the excess amount itself or seek additional insurance coverage through other policies.

Occurrence Versus Claims–Made Forms

Once the insured has chosen the amount of risk exposures to transfer through the use of a liability insurance policy, the insured also needs to decide if that policy should be an *occurrence-based* or a *claims-made* form. These are the two types of commercial general liability coverage forms that are offered.

An occurrence-type CGL form simply means that, for coverage to apply, the injury or damage must occur—take place—during the policy period. The claim against the insured can be made at any time after the occurrence, even after the policy has expired. For example, if the insured's product injures someone today during the policy period of policy A, but a claim is not made against the insured until after policy A expires, that policy will still provide coverage for the insured.

How an Occurrence–based Form Applies

Consider the washing machine claim discussed previously. If the clothes had been damaged on June 25, 2001 (during ABC Insurance Company's policy), but the owner of the washing machine didn't make a claim until July 25, 2002 (during DEF Insurance Company's policy), the ABC policy's issuer would respond. This is because, with an occurrence-based form, the claim reverts to the policy in force when the damage occurred—not when the claim was filed.

A claims-made form, like the occurrence type, requires an occurrence to take place during the policy period. In addition, the claim for damages has to be made during the policy period. Using the example in the previous paragraph, after the claimant is injured, the claim has to be made against the insured before the policy expires in order for the policy to respond to the claim. If the claim is made after the policy expires, that policy will not be applicable to the claim.

There is an exception to this approach: the *extended reporting period*—a unique feature of a claims-made policy. The extended reporting period is a period of time, prescribed in the policy, that extends after the policy has expired and during which a claim can be made so that coverage applies.

The standard claims-made CGL form allows for two extended reporting periods:

- the basic period and
- the supplemental period.

These reporting periods do not extend the policy period or scope of coverage. They only extend the time during which a claim against the insured can be reported and, thus, covered by the policy.

The *basic extended reporting period* is automatically provided by the insurer without additional premium charges. It extends the reporting period for five years. This means that if an injury occurs during a policy period that expires on July 31, 2002, the insured can report the claim made against him at any time during the five-year period from July 31, 2002, to July 31, 2007, and the policy will respond. Although the occurrence that caused the injury must be reported to the insurer no later than sixty days after the end of the policy period, the actual claim has a five-year grace period in which it can be made and reported to the insurer.

The basic extended reporting period does not apply to claims that are covered under any subsequent insurance that the named insured buys. It does not apply if the amount of insurance applicable to the particular claim has been exhausted by previous claim payments. And, the extended reporting period does not reinstate or increase the declared limits of insurance.

The *supplemental extended reporting period* is of unlimited duration—that is, no set year time limit—but the insured must pay an additional premium. This provision is added to the CGL form by an endorsement. This supplemental period begins when the basic period ends, establishes its own limits of insurance, and affords insurance on an excess basis over any other valid and collectible insurance.

DESIGN FEATURES

Policy Structure

A risk manager should know what her liability policy covers and what it does not. Unfortunately, most insurance policies are long and complicated legal documents. The policy structure of the CGL form has sections dealing with insuring agreements, exclusions, supplementary payments, who is an insured, limits of insurance, conditions, and definitions.

Insuring Agreements

The *insuring agreements* are the contractual connection between the insured and the insurer. In consideration for the premium paid by the insured, the insurer agrees to pay "those sums that the insured becomes legally obligated to pay as damages." The standard CGL form has three insuring agreements:

- Coverage A—bodily injury and property damage coverage,

- Coverage B—personal and advertising injury coverage, and

- Coverage C—medical payments coverage.

The bodily injury and property damage coverage applies to damages because of BI and PD suffered by another (called a *third party)* for which the insured is liable. The insuring agreement means that the insurer will pay those sums that the insured has to pay because of those damages. For example, if the insured owns a restaurant and an employee accidentally spills hot water on a customer, burning his hands and ruining his pants, the insured is liable for the bodily injury and property damage the customer suffered. If the payment for the injuries is $5,000 and payment for the pants is $100, the insurer, through the CGL form, will pay those amounts to the claimant.

The personal and advertising injury coverage applies to damages because of personal and advertising injury for which the insured is liable. *Personal and advertising injury* is a defined term on the CGL form and includes injury arising out of offenses like false arrest, wrongful entry into a dwelling or premises, slander and libel, and infringing upon another's copyright, trade dress, or slogan in the insured's advertisements. This coverage acts as a complement to coverage A in the CGL form in that bodily injury coverage is attuned toward actual physical injury to someone, while the personal and advertising injury coverage pertains mainly to non-physical injury. For example, suppose a customer is wrongfully accused of shoplifting in the insured's store and is held against his will, waiting for the police to be called. The customer sues the insured for false arrest, claiming mental anguish and embarrassment. Since there is no claim of bodily injury here, the insured would not look for insurance protection under coverage A of the CGL form, but instead would look to coverage B.

There are two other points to note about coverage B. Coverage B does apply to some bodily injury arising out of the personal and advertising injury offenses, but the BI has to be consequential. For example, if the wrongfully accused customer's arm is broken while being held by the insured's security personnel, the bodily injury is a consequence of the false arrest. Therefore, the insured could look to coverage B to apply to a claim involving the broken arm.

The other point to consider is that coverage B applies to an *offense* that is committed by the insured, as opposed to coverage A, which applies to an *occurrence.* This difference is because the coverage B insuring agreement is meant to apply to intended actions of the insured. Occurrence means an accident, but, if the insured commits an act included in the definition of personal and advertising injury, that act is not accidental. For example, if the insured detains someone or writes an article that libels a person, those acts of detaining or writing are intentional (not accidental). Coverage A, being based on an accidental event, would not be applicable.

The coverage C insuring agreement provides premises and operations medical payments insurance. This coverage pays for medical expenses incurred by a person (other than an insured) as a result of his sustaining bodily injury arising from the insured's premises or operations. This is insurance coverage without regard to any negligence or fault on the part of the insured. For example, a child in the insured's grocery store falls in a food aisle and suffers a concussion. There is no apparent reason for the fall since the aisle was clear and dry. However, the insured wants to pay for the medical expenses to care for the child. Coverage C will do that.

Coverage C provides help to an insured in controlling his risk exposures in two ways: 1) The prompt assumption of medical bills may mean either that a liability claim will not follow the accident or, if one does, that the claim will be for a lower financial amount. 2) The medical payments coverage provides a sense of goodwill for businesses when some medical services can be provided for injured persons without question or delay. This coverage often is referred to as a *goodwill* payment.

The coverage is available without regard to fault, but the insurer does put some limitations on coverage C. The medical expenses must be incurred and reported to the insurer within one year of the date of the accident; the injured person must submit to an exam required by the insurer; the payments cannot exceed the limit of insurance chosen by the insured; and the expenses must be reasonable.

Exclusions

All of the insuring agreements on the CGL form have *exclusions*, which are specified exposures not covered by the policy. If an exclusion is applicable, the insurer will not pay the sums due, even if the insured is clearly liable for the injuries or damages.

The exclusions on the liability policy are standardized and represent those types of exposures that an insurer either cannot or does not want to insure against, or exposures that are better insured on other types of policies. For example, coverage A has an exclusion for BI or PD expected or intended from the standpoint of the insured. The coverage A insuring agreement is based on an occurrence—an accident. If the insured intended to hurt someone or damage another's property, that action would not be in accord with the intent of the insuring agreement to cover accidents.

Other examples are the workers compensation and employers liability exclusions. These exposures are better handled by a workers compensation policy in accordance with the workers compensation system established in the various states. Bodily injury or property damage arising from the escape or release of pollutants is largely excluded under a CGL form because of the specialty nature of the exposure. Property damage to personal property in the care, custody, or control of the insured, and bodily injury or property damage arising out of the use of an auto owned by the insured are all excluded. They are risk exposures that the insurer wants to cover under policies other than a general liability policy.

The personal and advertising injury liability insuring agreement does apply to intended acts of the insured, but this does not mean the coverage is without limitations. For example, coverage B will not apply to criminal acts committed by the insured. The same is true of a knowing violation of the rights of another by publishing material that the insured knows is false. And, if the insured is in the business of advertising, broadcasting, publishing, or telecasting, the personal and advertising liability coverage will not apply. These businesses need a specialty type liability policy that can specifically address their unique liability exposures.

Even the coverage C insuring agreement—the one not dependent on any fault of the insured—has some applicable exclusions. For example, coverage C does not apply to expenses for bodily injury to any insured. If the insured falls on his own premises and is injured, he must seek coverage for his medical expenses under his own health care plan (if he has one). The CGL form is not designed to care for those injuries. Another example of an exclusion is the one that applies to bodily injury to a person injured on that part of premises owned by the insured that the person normally occupies. This exclusion would apply, for instance, to a tenant of the insured's apartment building being injured in his own apartment. And, finally, expenses for bodily injury due to war are not covered by the medical payments insuring agreement because the risk exposure is too high and too difficult to assess. An adequate premium cannot be charged.

There are many exclusions listed on the CGL form. The few mentioned here are just examples to show that not all liability risk exposures can be transferred to a commercial general liability policy. For a complete listing of the policy exclusions, see the CGL forms published in the chapter appendix.

Supplementary Payments

Supplementary payments are amounts that the insurer promises to pay in addition to the limits of insurance—that is, the payments will not reduce the limits of insurance stated on the declarations page. They apply to insuring agreements A and B and are paid with respect to any claim that the insurer investigates or settles, as well as any lawsuit against the insured that the insurer defends. There are seven such payments.

The first is all the expense that the insurer incurs in investigating or settling a claim, or in defending the

Commercial General Liability Insurance

insured. The insurer agrees to pay sums that the insured is legally liable for and agrees to defend the insured in any lawsuits. So it is a logical extension of these agreements that the insurer would also pay the expenses required to accomplish these tasks.

The second is the cost of bail bonds up to $250. For this provision to apply, these bonds must be required because of accidents or traffic law violations arising out of the use of a vehicle to which the policy's bodily injury liability coverage applies. The CGL form's auto exclusion allows for some exceptions, such as for parking nonowned autos on the insured's premises, and the CGL form covers bodily injury or property damage due to the use of mobile equipment, so this requirement is not superfluous. The insurer does not have to actually furnish the bonds.

The third payment is for the cost of bonds to release attachments. An attachment is the legal act of seizing one's property in order to secure a debt or claim in the event that a judgment is rendered against the owner. For example, if the insured injures someone, the injured party goes to court and seeks an attachment on the building that the insured owns. An attachment bond is issued by the court to prevent the insured from disposing of the property before any judgment is granted in the lawsuit against the insured. This makes sure that the insured has assets available to satisfy any judgment that the injured party may gain against the insured. This attachment bond may be released if the insured posts his own bond guaranteeing to pay the entire judgment and courts costs should the court decide in favor of the injured party. This type of bond is called a release of attachment bond. The CGL form will pay for the cost of this bond but the insurer does not have to furnish the release bond.

The fourth payment is for all reasonable expenses incurred by the insured at the insurer's request to assist the insurer in investigating or defending the claim or lawsuit. This includes actual loss of earnings up to $250 a day to compensate the insured for time off from work. The insurer will pay reasonable expenses and, since that term is not a defined term on the policy, the amount paid will be subject to the insurer's agreement.

The fifth payment is for all costs imposed against the insured in the lawsuit.

The sixth payment is for prejudgment interest awarded against the insured on that part of the judgment that the insurer pays. Some courts allow prejudg-

ment interest on an award because the time that elapses between the actual injury and the final judgment may be years, and this prejudgment interest award compensates the injured claimant for the wait. As for the costs taxed against the insured, the party that loses a case often has to pay court costs (such as paper work and fees to offset court expenses). If the insured is the losing party, the insurer agrees to pay the court costs.

The final supplementary payment is for all interest on the full amount of any judgment that accrues after entry of the judgment and before the insurer has paid or offered to pay or deposited in court the part of the judgment that is within the applicable limit of insurance. This clause assures that, if the insurer decides to appeal a judgment against the insured, the insurer and not the insured will pay any accrued interest on that judgment.

Who Is An Insured

This part of the CGL form tells who is considered an insured under the terms of the policy. The current CGL form lists several classes of insureds.

The named insured is the person or entity named on the declarations page. If the named insured is an individual, he and his spouse are insureds, but only with respect to the conduct of a business of which the named insured is the sole owner. For example, Joe Smith owns a small retail store. If the named insured on the CGL form is Joe Smith, and the type of business checked on the declarations page is "individual," Smith and his wife are insureds for claims that arise out of that business. No other family members are mentioned in this provision, regardless of any possible involvement in the conduct of the business.

If the named insured is designated as a partnership or joint venture on the declarations page, the members, partners, and their spouses are insureds with respect to the conduct of the business. Using the previous example, Joe and Tom are partners in the retail store. Both of them and their respective wives are considered as insureds under the store's CGL form.

If the named insured is designated as a limited liability company, the members of the company and its managers are insureds, again with respect to the conduct of the business.

If the named insured is listed as an organization other than a partnership, joint venture, or limited liability company—in other words, a corporation—the following are considered as insureds:

- the named insured,
- executive officers and directors with respect to their duties, and
- stockholders with respect to their liability as stockholders.

This wording fits with the idea that, even though corporations are legal persons, they cannot act except through their officers, directors, and employees. So, these actual persons are given insured status under the CGL form as a matter of common sense.

Trusts and volunteer workers have been added as insureds under the most recent version of the standard CGL form. Both classes are insureds only with respect to their duties as trustees or while performing duties related to the conduct of the named insured's business as volunteers, respectively. It was possible prior to the most recent revision of the CGL form to add trustees and volunteers as insureds through the use of endorsements. But now, the status is automatic.

Employees of the named insured are insureds, but only for acts within the scope of their employment or while performing duties related to the conduct of the named insured's business. This last phrase is meant to encompass a leased employee's activities since the term *employee* is defined on the CGL form to include leased workers. Employees are considered insureds under the employer's CGL form because, as noted above, a company cannot act except through its officers and employees. However, to be considered an insured, the employee must be doing the insured's business.

When Is an Employee an Insured?

An employee working at an insured restaurant spills coffee on a customer and injures her. The employee is considered an insured for this accident. This same employee, while on his day off, spills his cup of coffee on someone at the park. He is not considered an insured under the restaurant's CGL form for this incident.

There are other instances when an employee is not an insured under the CGL form, for example, when he injures the named insured or a fellow employee, when he provides professional health care services, and when he causes property damage to the property of the named insured or a fellow employee. These instances are described more fully on the CGL forms found published in the appendix.

Also listed on the CGL forms are other groups of insureds: any person or organization acting as the real estate manager of the named insured; any person or organization having proper temporary custody of the named insured's property if he dies; any person while driving mobile equipment on a public highway with the named insured's permission; and any newly acquired or formed organization (other than a partnership, joint venture, or limited liability company) for a period of up to ninety days after the acquisition or formation.

Additional Insureds on the CGL

Additional insureds must be added to the CGL form by endorsing the policy. This method of adding other individuals or entities as insureds to the CGL form extends the coverages of the CGL form to those added and described in the endorsements.

Many additional insured endorsements are patterned to fit the insured's particular needs and the insurer's underwriting philosophy. The additional insured endorsement can be a standard form—for example, an additional insured – vendors endorsement—or the endorsement can be a *manuscript* form. A manuscript form is one that is written to fit a particular situation and is not predesigned and published by the insurance company. The endorsement can be simple, with only two sentences, or it can be more complicated and run for two pages. But, regardless of the length or format of an additional insured endorsement, an insured should realize that a decision to make another entity an additional insured on its CGL policy should not be dismissed as a simple business decision that has no real consequences. There can be legal and financial consequences—some perhaps unexpected—that arise from such a decision.

For one thing, the named insured shares its liability insurance with another entity. More often than not, the named insured pays the insurer to extend its insurance to apply to sums that the additional insured becomes legally obligated to pay as damages. Also, the insured should be aware of the fact that the limits of insurance paid out for its claims are being shared with additional insureds. For example, if the general aggregate limit of a named insured's CGL form is $500,000, that is the most the insurer will pay during one policy term regardless of the number of additional insureds that are endorsed onto the policy. So, any losses paid on behalf of the additional insured will decrease the aggregate limit available to the named insured. The endorsing of additional insureds onto a CGL policy *dilutes* the named insured's available amount of coverage because the policy limits must be shared with all the additional insureds on the policy.

An important aspect of an additional insured endorsement is the extent of the coverage. Most additional insured endorsements make the designated entity an insured "but only with respect to liability arising out of…:" (a certain activity, contract, or operation). For example, the additional insured – condominium unit owners endorsement, makes such owners additional insureds—but only with respect to liability arising out of the ownership, maintenance, or repair of that portion of the premises not reserved for that unit owner's exclusive use or occupancy. Another example is the additional insured – owners, lessees or contractors endorsement. This endorsement makes the person or organization shown in the endorsement an additional insured, but only with respect to liability arising out of the named insured's ongoing operations.

The problem, even when such wording is used, is: what does the phrase "arising out of" mean?

Some in the insurance industry would read the phrase narrowly, limiting an additional insured's role as an insured only to its vicarious liability—that is, no coverage for any negligence of the additional insured that is independent of the activities of the named insured. Put another way, the liability of the additional insured flows only from the liability of the named insured and his premises, operations, products, or completed operations.

Others would say the "arising out of" phrase deserves a broader interpretation—so broad that the additional insured's own activities could lead to liability coverage under the named insured's CGL form. Put another way, if the activities of the additional insured (instead of the named insured) cause injury to someone, the named insured's CGL form will apply to a claim as long as there is some connection between the additional insured's activities and those of the named insured.

This question is an ongoing one and is usually decided on a case-by-case basis when it goes to a court.

For an example of additional insured endorsements, see the chapter appendix.

Limits of Insurance

This part of the CGL form describes the amounts that the insurer will pay for a claim against the insured. The limits of insurance are stated on the declarations page under various categories: general aggregate limit; products-completed operations aggregate limit; personal and advertising injury limit; each occurrence limit; fire damage limit; and medical expense limit. These declared limits are the most the insurer will pay regardless of the number of insureds, claims made, or persons making the claims.

As mentioned previously, the general aggregate limit is the most the insurer will pay for the sum of coverages A for premises and operations losses, B, and C. For example, if the insured has a $500,000 general aggregate limit, that is the most the insured will pay during the policy period for all claims that involve coverages A, B, and C combined or individually. If the total amount of claims exceeds $500,000, the insured's CGL form will not respond because the limits will have been exhausted.

The products-completed operations aggregate limit is the most that the insurer will pay under coverage A for damages because of BI or PD included in the products-completed operations hazard. In other words, if the claim against the insured is based on a product or completed operation of the insured, this limit is the most the insurer will pay over the policy period. This limit is separate from the general aggregate limit.

In addition to the general and products-completed operations aggregate limits, the CGL form is subject to a per person (or per organization) limit for all personal and advertising injury payable under coverage B. Coverage B is subject to the general aggregate limit. So it is possible that a coverage B claim would not be payable, despite a declared sufficient per person limit for the claim, if previous coverage A claims had exhausted the general aggregate limit.

The CGL form is also subject to an "each occurrence" limit for coverages A and C. In other words, expenses paid under coverage C are applied to, and therefore reduce, the amount payable per occurrence under coverage A.

The fire damage limit previously was called the fire legal liability limit. This is the most the insurer will pay for damages because of property damage to any one premises while rented to the named insured or temporarily occupied by the named insured with the permission of the owner. For example, if the insured rents office space and negligently causes a fire that destroys the space, this liability limit is the amount that the insurer will pay to the owner for the damage.

The last declared limit of insurance is for coverage C, medical payments. This amount is usually a mere fraction of the liability limits because payment is not based on legal liability. The standard limit is $5,000, but the insured and the insurer can set the limit in accordance with what both parties think local medical expenses can cost. This limit is on a per person basis.

Conditions

The conditions section of the CGL form sets guidelines for the insurer and the insured to follow. The conditions are legally binding on both parties.

One of the conditions pertains to the duties of the insured in the event of a claim or lawsuit. In that event, the insured has the duty to notify the insurer as soon as possible and, if a lawsuit is filed, the insured must forward the legal paper work to the insurer as soon as practicable. If the insured receives a complaint in June of 2002, it cannot wait until May of 2003 and expect the insurer to handle the lawsuit without objecting to the delay. Lawsuits need to be investigated, attorneys hired, and defense strategy planned. It is reasonable for the insured to give notice to the insurer quickly so that all these things can be handled. If the insured delays notice to the insurer for a long time, the insurer may seek to have the insured declared in breach of the contractual agreement, thereby relieving the insurer of its duty to defend and to pay.

Another clause that could cause trouble between the insured and the insurer is the representations clause. This condition states that, by accepting the policy, the insured agrees that the statements made by him in the declarations page are accurate and complete, and that the policy was issued in reliance upon those representations. If the statements made by the insured are false, the insurer could seek to have the contract declared void or seek a correction in the terms of the policy. An example of a misrepresentation is the insured declaring that his business is a retail store but, in reality, it is a restaurant. Another example is the insured telling the insurer of only one minor loss in the last year when, in reality, the business had five serious losses during that time. In both

instances, the insurer can say it wrote the policy under false pretenses and wants to have the policy declared void. The insurer can say that it would not have covered the insured's business and would not have allowed the insured's risk exposures to be transferred to it if the insured had told the truth. The insured breached the contract, and the insurer would be within its legal and contractual rights to seek to have the contract voided.

The other conditions on the CGL form are not as potentially troublesome, but they still need to be acknowledged as contractual obligations.

One of these is the other insurance clause, which deals with the status of the CGL form when other insurance exists. The CGL insurance is either primary or excess depending on certain circumstances.

Another clause is the separation of insureds clause wherein the insurer acknowledges that each insured is a separate entity and will be treated as such. For example, one insured can make a claim against another insured under the terms of the CGL form, and the insurer must handle the claim for both sides. Or, if an employer as the named insured is sued along with his employee, who is an insured under the terms of the policy, the insurer must defend both parties and treat each party as a separate client. The limits of insurance are not increased because there are two insureds to defend, but the two parties must still be treated as separate insureds with possible separate interests that are still covered by the same policy.

Another condition is the transfer of rights clause or the *subrogation* clause. Subrogation is the right of the party that has paid for the loss of a second party to be reimbursed by a third party that is responsible for the loss. This condition says that the rights of recovery that the insured may have against a third party are transferred to the insurer. This is because the insurer is the party that has made the payments to the claimant. The insured can waive his rights to recovery before a loss occurs but not after the loss.

Finally, there is the nonrenewal clause. If the insurer decides not to renew the CGL form, it must mail or deliver to the first named insured written notice of the nonrenewal not less than thirty days before the expiration date of the policy. State laws may override this clause, but it does give the insured at least a minimum amount of time so that the coverages may be sought from some other source.

Definitions

Some of the terms used throughout the CGL form are defined on the policy itself. These definitions are important in that the applicability of insuring agreements, exclusions, and conditions might depend on how a word is defined. For example, the word *you* is defined as the named insured. When an exclusion or a condition applies to *you*, that means that only the named insured is affected; other insureds are not. As another example, *personal and advertising injury* is a defined term, and the applicability of coverage B depends on that definition being met. If an offense claimed against the insured does not match the list of offenses cited as a personal and advertising injury, the coverage B insuring agreement cannot be used by the insured to cover the offense.

There are quite a number of definitions on the CGL form, and the complete list can be seen on the forms reprinted in the chapter appendix. However, the following definitions are worth mentioning.

Advertisement means a notice that is broadcast or published to the general public, or specific market segments, about the named insured's goods, products, or services. The purpose is to attract customers or supporters. The term "advertisement" is important due to its use in coverage B, personal and advertising injury liability. For example, coverage B applies to injury arising out of the infringement of copyright, trade dress, or slogan if the infringement occurred in the named insured's advertisement. Also, coverage B applies to injury arising out of the use of another's advertising ideas in the named insured's advertisement.

Coverage territory is defined as the United States, Puerto Rico, and Canada. This is important because the occurrence or offense that triggers coverage under the CGL form must take place in the coverage territory. It should be noted that the coverage territory includes all parts of the world for injury or damages arising out of products made or sold by the named insured in the three areas named in the coverage territory. For example, a product made by the named insured in the United States but sold abroad would be covered for liability purposes, as long as the insured's liability was determined in a lawsuit on the merits brought in the U.S., Puerto Rico, or Canada. This worldwide products coverage extension does not apply to completed operations. Say, for example, that the insured's business is aircraft repair. If faulty repair of an aircraft results in injury or damage to others while the aircraft is outside the stated coverage territory, coverage will be denied. Worldwide coverage is available under the CGL form for Internet and other electronic means of communication, reflecting the global nature of the Internet; however, the insured's liability still must be determined in a lawsuit brought in the U.S., Puerto Rico, or Canada.

An *employee* is not defined on the CGL form, as it would be in a dictionary. The CGL definition simply says that an employee includes a leased worker but not a temporary worker. This is done to show that leased employees are to be considered the same as regular employees when it comes to the CGL form and its coverages.

Some definitions help describe the scope of a coverage or an exclusion. For example, the contractual coverage offered by the CGL form depends on whether the insured has assumed liability for damages in a contract or agreement that fits within the definition of an *insured contract*. As another example, the application of the *impaired property exclusion* depends on whether the definition of impaired property has been met. Also, the CGL form applies to the use of *mobile equipment*, and this term is defined so that the insured knows what is covered. The same can be said for the *products-completed operations hazard*.

The list of definitions on the CGL form is useful in determining coverage, but the insured should be aware that even defined terms are subject to varying judicial interpretations. A good example of this is the word *pollutant*. The CGL form defines pollutant as any solid, liquid, gaseous or thermal irritant or contaminant, including smoke, vapor, soot, fumes, acids, alkalis, chemicals, and waste. This is a broad definition and can be used to apply to just about anything. Yet, some courts have interpreted the word as being limited to only environmental hazards or the items listed in the EPA (Environmental Protection Agency) official list of pollutants.

OTHER BUSINESS USES

The entity seeking to transfer its liability risk exposures through the use of a CGL insurance form should analyze its exposures and decide if a CGL form is the appropriate tool to handle them.

A CGL form applies to liability exposures that an entity faces arising out of the entity's premises, operations, products, and completed operations. A CGL form is the appropriate tool to transfer risk exposures for businesses such as retail stores, offices, motels and hotels, service organizations, theaters, and clubs. These entities have no out-of-the-ordinary risk exposures, and a commercial general liability policy should be adequate. This is especially true since the CGL form is comprehensive in scope and applies to all of an insured's liability exposures unless there is an applicable exclusion, either on the form itself or on an endorsement.

For example, a retail store that sells alcohol in addition to groceries can use a CGL form to cover its risk exposures. But, the alcohol exposure is excluded on the CGL form, so the store would have to buy separate insurance or bear the liability risks by itself.

In other situations, endorsements curb the broad scope of a CGL form. An example is the Insurance Services Office (ISO) form CG 21 56, exclusion – funeral services. Without this endorsement, a CGL form would apply to liability arising out of errors or omissions in the handling, burial, cremation, or disinterment of dead bodies. Since this is an exposure that is of a professional nature and is not an ordinary business risk, a general liability insurer would not want to insure it under a general liability policy so attaches the endorsement.

Specialty-type policies or other liability policies are available for exposures that are excluded under a CGL form. For example, the retail store that sells alcohol can use a liquor liability coverage form in addition to its CGL form. This way, an insured has general liability exposures coverage and liability coverage for injuries due to the selling, servicing, or furnishing of any alcoholic beverage.

Other liability policies exist to fill the exposure gaps on the CGL form that exist due to its exclusions. For example, there are pollution liability coverage forms that offer protection for this type of liability. There is an employment-related practices liability form that applies to injuries based on things like humiliation, discrimination, and sexual harassment—all injuries that are not covered under the CGL form. And there are various professional liability policies that more properly apply to professional exposures than does the CGL form.

There also are certain risks that, while not always specifically excluded under a CGL form, should have a different liability form so that the unique exposures are properly handled. Examples of this are the owners and contractors protective liability coverage form, which applies to bodily injury or property damage arising out of operations performed for the named insured by a

contractor or the named insured's acts or omissions in connection with the general supervision of those operations; an underground storage tank policy, which applies to bodily injury or property damage arising out of a release of petroleum from an underground storage tank into water or subsurface soils; and a warehouseman's legal liability coverage policy, which applies to the insured's legal liability for loss to property while in his care, custody, or control.

Whatever liability risk exposures an entity has, if the business decision is made to manage those exposures through insurance, the risk manager of the entity must look at all the possible liability exposures and decide what type of liability policy is best suited for the purpose. A CGL form will apply to most of the liability exposures, but, as noted here, other liability policies may be needed to complete the protective circle around the insured. One size, of course, does not fit all when it comes to buying insurance. So, the specific problems, exposures, goals, and financial situation of the individual company must be determined before making an insurance-buying decision.

As part of the decision-making process, the entity should discuss its liability exposures with an experienced insurance agent or broker so that the proper types of liability policies may be purchased.

Premium

One more item that an insured and an agent or broker should discuss is the premium. The premium paid for the liability insurance should be within the range that the insured can and wants to pay to have its liability risks covered by an insurer.

Monitoring Results

Once the CGL policy (and any other liability policies) has been purchased, the insured needs to monitor the results. Questions such as the following should be considered:

- Are the liability policies applicable to the losses and claims?
- Are the limits of insurance adequate?
- Is the amount paid in premium cost effective?
- Are there any new exposures that have arisen since the liability policies became effective?

- Have any claims and lawsuits been properly handled by the insurer?

If the results of this monitoring are satisfactory, the insured can rest assured that its decision to purchase liability insurance was a wise business decision. If the results are not as expected, changes should be made.

ADVANTAGES

One advantage to buying a CGL form is that many (if not most) of the entity's liability risk exposures are transferred. The insured company does not have to worry about and plan for certain types of losses, so the time and money spent on responding to losses can be spent on other items designed to aid the profitability, continuing operations, and survival of the company. Should a loss occur or a lawsuit be filed, the company resources won't be spent paying for the loss or defense costs.

Another advantage is that the premium paid for the CGL form is a legitimate business expense that can be deducted from tax liabilities.

In addition, the insured can rely on the insurance company to handle all the legal work and other paper work after a claim or lawsuit is filed. Assuming that the insurance company is competent, the liability claims against the insured will be disposed of or paid promptly so the insured need not spend time addressing the problem.

On the preloss side, an insurance company could act as a loss control consultant to the insured so that exposures are analyzed and preventive measures put into place to prevent losses. For example, an insurer may send its loss control specialist to the insured's premises. The specialist may find something that could cause a future loss and recommends steps to prevent the loss. The insured complies and no loss occurs as a result.

DISADVANTAGES

Some of the disadvantages mirror the advantages. For example, the insured transfers its liability risks to the insurer and so, when a loss occurs, the insured does not have to spend its capital on that loss. On the other hand, the insurance coverage costs money, and the premium spent on insurance is money that the insured does not have for any of its business plans or cash flow needs.

Also, businesses may avoid the hassle of having to manage a claim or lawsuit when the insurer handles it. However, if the insurer does not handle the claim properly or is not willing to settle a claim quickly, the insured gets the bad publicity. A lawsuit that may develop because an insurance company did not properly handle a claim will involve time on the part of the insured business.

This leads to another disadvantage. The insured does not need to manage claims because the insurer will. But, the insured, through the insurance contract, has agreed to give up any control over claims management and settlement. The general liability insurer retains for itself the right to investigate and settle any claim or lawsuit without the insured having any right to either force a settlement or reject a settlement. Regardless of whether this fits the management style of the insured company or not, it is part of the CGL contract.

If an insurance company should become insolvent, the burden of management and settlement of the claim or lawsuit falls back on the insured. No court would allow an injured party to go without compensation just because the business's insurer files for bankruptcy. The insured will be forced to pay the compensation because, after all, it is the party legally liable for the injuries to the claimant.

A final disadvantage is that, while the CGL form does provide financial protection for the insured, that protection is limited by the form's exclusions and set policy limits—not all the risk exposures of the insured will be covered by the CGL form. The policy limits are finite, and the final sum for which the insured is liable may exceed those policy limits. This may leave the insured with the responsibility of paying that excess amount.

WHERE CAN I FIND OUT MORE ABOUT IT?

- *The FC&S Bulletins*, Cincinnati: The National Underwriter Company.

  http://www.nationalunderwriter.com/nucatalog/

- Malecki, Donald S., CPCU, and Arthur L. Flitner, CPCU. 2001. *Commercial General Liability Seventh Edition*. Cincinnati: The National Underwriter Company.

- American Institute for Chartered Property Casualty Underwriters and the Insurance Institute of America, which offer a variety of programs that include discussion of commercial general liability issues and coverage. http://www.aicpcu.org/programs/index.htm

- Risk and Insurance Management Society, Inc. (RIMS) http://www.rims.org/

- Liability Insurance Research Bureau, 3025 Highland Parkway Suite 800, Downers Grove, IL. 60515-1291. http://www.lirb.org/defaultnew5.html

- The Defense Research Institute, 150 North Michigan Ave., Suite 300, Chicago, IL 60601. http://www.dri.org/dri/index.cfm

QUESTIONS AND ANSWERS

Question—What are the two duties assumed by the insurer under the terms of a CGL coverage form?

Answer—The insurer agrees to pay those sums that the insured becomes legally obligated to pay as damages, and the insurer agrees to pay defense costs in the event of a lawsuit.

Question—The insured is sued for patent infringement. Will the CGL form respond to this lawsuit?

Answer—No, the current CGL form does not cover personal and advertising injury arising out of patent infringement.

Question—The insured buys a CGL form with an effective date of August 1, 2002. A claim is made against the insured for property damage that the insured allegedly caused on July 31, 2002. Will the current CGL form apply to the claim?

Answer—No, for a property damage claim to be covered by the CGL form, the damage must occur during the policy period.

Question—What is the difference between the exposure theory and the manifestation theory when it comes to bodily injury coverage under the CGL form?

Answer—The exposure theory holds that liability coverage under the CGL form is triggered by the victim's exposure to a harm-causing agent. The manifestation theory holds that liability coverage is triggered by the date of actual diagnosis of the injury caused by the harm-causing agent.

Question—The insured's CGL form has a $500,000 each occurrence limit. If there are six people injured in one occurrence, does that affect the amount paid by the insurer?

Answer—No, the limits of insurance shown on the policy's declarations page are the most the insurer will pay regardless of the number of claims made or the number of persons making claims.

Question—What are the two types of CGL coverage forms?

Answer—The occurrence type form and the claims-made type form.

Question—What is the main difference between an occurrence form and a claims-made form?

Answer—A claims-made form does require an occurrence to take place during the policy period as the occurrence form does, but the claims-made policy also requires that the claim for damages be first made against the insured during the policy period.

Question—State one way in which the basic extended reporting period on the claims-made CGL form differs from the supplemental extended reporting period?

Answer—The basic extended reporting period is automatically provided by the insurer without an additional premium. The supplemental extended reporting period is added to the policy by endorsement only after the insured has requested it and paid an extra charge for it.

Question—What are the three insuring agreements on the CGL form?

Answer—Coverage A, bodily injury and property damage liability; Coverage B, personal and advertising injury liability; and coverage C, medical payments.

Question—What are some examples of personal and advertising injury?

Answer—False arrest, wrongful entry into a dwelling or premises, slander, libel, and infringing upon another's copyright, trade dress, or slogan in the named insured's advertisement

Question—What is one important difference between the medical payments coverage and coverages A and B under the CGL form?

Answer—The medical payments coverage applies without regard to any negligence or fault on the part of the insured. Liability on the insured's part is not required for the payments to be made.

Question—How much will the insurer pay as a supplementary payment due to the insured's having to take time off from work to assist in the defense of a lawsuit?

Answer—The insurer will pay up to $250 a day for the actual loss of earnings of the insured.

Question—The named insured under the CGL form is a partnership. Who besides the named partnership is an insured?

Answer—If the named insured is a partnership, the partners and their spouses are insureds, but only with respect to the conduct of the partnership business.

Question—If the named insured is sued, can he force the insurer to settle with the claimant?

Answer—No, the insurer retains the right to settle any claim or lawsuit without the insured having any right to either force a settlement or reject a settlement.

Question—If the insurer decides not to renew the CGL form, how much notice must be given to the insured?

Answer—If the insurer decides to nonrenew the policy, it must mail or deliver to the first named insured written notice of the nonrenewal not less than thirty days before the expiration date. However, this condition is subject to state laws on time requirements for nonrenewals of insurance policies.

Figure 17.1

FORMS AND CHECKLISTS

General Liability Insurance Coverage Checklist

For most businesses, the liability exposures are the most severe and at the same time often the most complex of all the property/casualty exposures. Whereas property, business earnings, and dishonesty exposures are limited to the value of the property or income exposed, and workers compensation is limited by statute, there is no certain monetary ceiling on liability claims that might be made against an insured. A large liability claim (or claims) can put the insured out of business, so it is critically important that the survey examine with great care both the many liability exposures and the various insurance coverages that can be written to protect against them.

Commercial General Liability (CGL) Checklist

General Information

Named Insured:

D/B/A:

Address:

City, State:

Phone:

Fax:

Named Insured is a: ___Individual ___Partnership ___Corporation
___Limited Liability Corporation
___Joint Venture ___Other

General business operations:

States/territories in which insured has operations:

Location addresses:

Loss control contact name/phone:

General Considerations

____1. Does the insured have any worldwide exposures?

____2. Check insured's operations, premises owned or occupied, and payroll and sales records against the Declarations and latest audit statements of the various liability policies, using the rating manuals for reference, to determine whether: a) limits of liability are adequate for probable maximum exposure; note especially the aggregate limits; b) all premises, operations, products, and activities of the insured or on the insured's behalf are recognized and properly included in the coverage; c) rating classifications are proper for all the exposures insured; d) proper premium bases—area, payroll, sales, etc.—have been used.

____3. Obtain premium and loss information for the current experience period, including reserves for open claims. Compare this data with experience modifications, if any, under the policies. Also determine the extent to which any aggregate limits in the policy have been used up or reduced by payment of loss or by pending claims.

____4. Are all liability risks of the insured written by the same insurer? If not, can they be?

____5. Is insured large enough to be eligible for retrospective rating? For a program of self-insured retention with excess liability over the retained limits? Consider possible advantages and disadvantages for insured with each.

____6. Umbrella coverage should be considered.

____7. All liability policies should be checked to see whether they apply on an occurrence or a claims-made basis. For occurrence coverage, has any previous policy for the same coverage been on a claims-made basis? If so—as well as for all present claims-made policies—check for gaps in the continuity of coverage for undiscovered claims not covered by a present occurrence policy or, for a claims-made policy, occurring prior to the policy's retroactive date. Has extended reporting period coverage been provided to fill the gap in coverage? If not, can it be purchased?

____8. Are limits of liability adequate?

____9. Has the insured ever filed for bankruptcy?

____10. Has the insured ever been cancelled or nonrenewed?

Additional Interests

____1. Are all necessary additional insureds named in the policies? Consider such interests as parties with a contractual interest calling for insurance on their behalf, landlords or tenants, as well as affiliated or subsidiary companies, individual partners, joint ventures, etc. Are appropriate certificates of insurance provided to all additional insureds that require them?

____2. When additional interests are included, has proper endorsement been used, showing the actual interest and properly limiting the coverage to the intended interest only?

____3. Check for possible conflict between additional insured's status as an insured and as named insured's indemnitor under a hold-harmless agreement.

____4. Are there "care, custody or control" property damage liability exposures—as to premises? As to personal property?

Owners and Contractors Protective

____1. Does insured utilize independent contractors for any activities? If so, is owners and contractors protective coverage provided? Has insured obtained certificates of liability and workers compensation insurance from these independent contractors, and has proper premium credit been allowed for the evidence of insurance.

____2. If insured employs independent contractors, are there any hold harmless contracts to be considered? Any additional insureds considerations?

Products-Completed Operations

____1. Does insured need products liability coverage? Completed operations coverage?

____2. Is vendor's products coverage required for distributors of insured's product? If so, is it provided with proper limits? Are certificates of insurance required? Have they been provided?

Figure 17.1 (cont'd)

_____3. If insured depends on supplier vendor's coverage for products liability protection, are proper certificates of such insurance obtained? Is the vendor's products coverage adequate as to limits of insurance? Does insured handle other products, outside the scope of the vendor's form? Do the insured's activities include handling of the products (repackaging, relabeling, etc.)? Should insured's own products coverage be provided instead of, or in addition to, the vendor's coverage?

_____4. Do any products exposures involve unusually high potential loss or a prolonged discovery period, or both? Examples include manufacture of aircraft parts, machine tools, structural materials, drugs, toxic or hazardous chemicals, and use of radioactive materials. If so, are substantial limits of liability maintained, and does the insured have adequate records of old policies that might be called on for coverage belatedly?

_____5. Does insured have a foreign products liability exposure? If so, is the definition of policy territory broad enough to cover this exposure? (Note that under basic CGL provisions product must have been sold in the United States, its territories or possessions or Canada, and suit must also be brought there.)

_____6. Does the insured with no other obvious product liability exposures have an exposure for the miscellaneous or occasional sale of property—e.g., sale of a motor vehicle, boat, airplane, building, office or plant machinery or equipment? Is product liability coverage provided for this exposure?

Contractual Liability

_____1. Has the insured assumed liability (insured contracts) for the actions of others? Are any certificates of insurance required? Have they been furnished?

_____2. For any "hold harmless" agreements discovered, does the indemnitor provide liability insurance or only "indemnify" after other party has paid for defense and judgment?

_____3. For other parties agreeing to hold harmless, are policies or certificates of insurance required? If so, have they been furnished? Do they show coverage in accordance with the contract's requirements?

Professional Liability

_____1. Do the insured's operations include performance of any kind of professional services? On a regular or incidental basis? By employees or by others on insured's behalf? For employees or others?

_____2. Is the professional liability exposure covered by the general liability insurance or excluded? If covered, does the exposure go beyond the bodily (or personal) injury and property damage coverage provided? If so, or if excluded, is professional liability or errors and omissions insurance provided with substantial limits for those professional liability exposures found to exist?

Personal Injury

_____1. Does the liability insurance cover personal injury in addition to bodily injury?

_____2. Does insured have any advertising, broadcasting, or television personal injury exposure? Is it insured by them or on their behalf? Have they assumed advertisers' liability for others? Is this exposure insured? By whom?

_____3. Is there a potential exposure to other personal injuries—discrimination, humiliation, alienation of affections, etc.—not covered by standard personal injury insurance? Has broader coverage been provided to include any of these additional kinds of injury?

Liquor Liability

____1. Does insured have a liquor liability exposure? If so, is adequate dram shop or liquor liability insurance provided to cover this exposure? Consider in this regard the dram shop or liquor liability situation of the individual state(s) of insured's operations, to determine what coverage is appropriate.

Other Exposures

____1. Does insured sponsor sports teams or other activities involving employees or other non-employee participants? If so, does the liability insurance recognize and cover such sponsorship? Is athletic teams medical payments coverage called for?

____2. Does the insured have medical payments coverage?

____3. Partners, officers, directors, or employee benefit trustees may be exposed to liability claims by employees, other partners, officers, or directors, stockholders, or others, not covered by the general liability insurance. Is directors and officers liability or fiduciary liability coverage provided against these exposures? Do any insureds serve in a business capacity as officers, directors, or trustees of other organizations? Are they protected by that organization's D & O or fiduciary liability coverage? If not, do they or should they have individual coverage to protect against these exposures?

____4. Aircraft/watercraft: Does insured have any aircraft or watercraft exposures, even as little as occasional nonowned or hired exposures? What is done to cover such exposures?

____5. Nuclear energy: Does the insured operate any nuclear facility to which the nuclear exclusion applies? Has insured provided necessary separate coverage for this exposure? With maximum available limits?

____6. Has liability for punitive damages been considered?

____7. Is insured engaged in any gas, oil, or other underground operations?

____8. Does insured have a pollution liability exposure? Is environmental impairment liability insurance provided? Is it obtainable for this insured? With adequate limits? Can and should it be offered?

____9. Does the insured lease employees? Does the insured use volunteers?

Operating Practices

____1. Does the insured have an active and effective loss control program? If not, is the insured receptive to such a program, with help and guidance from the insurer?

____2. Has the insured established and maintained adequate records in areas affecting insurance coverage and loss control? If not, a genuine service can be rendered by including in the survey recommendations for adequate record maintenance. This is especially important for insureds with potentially long tail product or professional liability exposures that may require documentation of past coverages or practices long beyond the time that most records are normally kept.

Figure 17.2

POLICY NUMBER: _____

COMMERCIAL GENERAL LIABILITY DECLARATIONS

COMPANY NAME AREA	PRODUCER NAME AREA

NAMED INSURED: _____

MAILING ADDRESS: _____

_____

POLICY PERIOD: FROM _____ TO _____ AT 12:01 A.M. TIME AT
YOUR MAILING ADDRESS SHOWN ABOVE

IN RETURN FOR THE PAYMENT OF THE PREMIUM, AND SUBJECT TO ALL THE TERMS OF THIS POLICY, WE AGREE WITH YOU TO PROVIDE THE INSURANCE AS STATED IN THIS POLICY.

LIMITS OF INSURANCE

EACH OCCURRENCE LIMIT	$ _____	
DAMAGE TO PREMISES RENTED TO YOU LIMIT	$ _____	Any one premises
MEDICAL EXPENSE LIMIT	$ _____	Any one person
PERSONAL & ADVERTISING INJURY LIMIT	$ _____	Any one person or organization
GENERAL AGGREGATE LIMIT	$ _____	
PRODUCTS/COMPLETED OPERATIONS AGGREGATE LIMIT	$ _____	

RETROACTIVE DATE (CG 00 02 ONLY)

THIS INSURANCE DOES NOT APPLY TO "BODILY INJURY", "PROPERTY DAMAGE" OR "PERSONAL AND ADVERTISING INJURY" WHICH OCCURS BEFORE THE RETROACTIVE DATE, IF ANY, SHOWN BELOW.

RETROACTIVE DATE: _____

(ENTER DATE OR "NONE" IF NO RETROACTIVE DATE APPLIES)

DESCRIPTION OF BUSINESS

FORM OF BUSINESS:

☐ INDIVIDUAL   ☐ PARTNERSHIP   ☐ JOINT VENTURE   ☐ TRUST

☐ LIMITED LIABILITY COMPANY   ☐ ORGANIZATION, INCLUDING A CORPORATION (BUT NOT IN-CLUDING A PARTNERSHIP, JOINT VENTURE OR LIMITED LIABILITY COMPANY)

BUSINESS DESCRIPTION: _____

CG DS 01 10 01   © ISO Properties, Inc., 2000   **Page 1 of 2**

ALL PREMISES YOU OWN, RENT OR OCCUPY	
LOCATION NUMBER	ADDRESS OF ALL PREMISES YOU OWN, RENT OR OCCUPY

CLASSIFICATION AND PREMIUM

LOCATION NUMBER	CLASSIFICATION	CODE NO.	PREMIUM BASE	RATE		ADVANCE PREMIUM	
				Prem/Ops	Prod/Comp Ops	Prem/Ops	Prod/Comp Ops
			$	$	$	$	$

STATE TAX OR OTHER (if applicable) $ _____

TOTAL PREMIUM (SUBJECT TO AUDIT) $ _____

PREMIUM SHOWN IS PAYABLE:

AT INCEPTION $ _____

AT EACH ANNIVERSARY $ _____

(IF POLICY PERIOD IS MORE THAN ONE YEAR AND PREMIUM IS PAID IN ANNUAL INSTALLMENTS)

AUDIT PERIOD (IF APPLICABLE)	☐ANNUALLY	☐SEMI-ANNUALLY	☐QUARTERLY	☐MONTHLY

ENDORSEMENTS

ENDORSEMENTS ATTACHED TO THIS POLICY:

_____
_____
_____

THESE DECLARATIONS, TOGETHER WITH THE COMMON POLICY CONDITIONS AND COVERAGE FORM(S) AND ANY ENDORSEMENT(S), COMPLETE THE ABOVE NUMBERED POLICY.

Countersigned:	By:
(Date)	(Authorized Representative)

NOTE

OFFICERS' FACSIMILE SIGNATURES MAY BE INSERTED HERE, ON THE POLICY COVER OR ELSEWHERE AT THE COMPANY'S OPTION.

Figure 17.3

COMMERCIAL GENERAL LIABILITY COVERAGE FORM

Various provisions in this policy restrict coverage. Read the entire policy carefully to determine rights, duties and what is and is not covered.

Throughout this policy the words "you" and "your" refer to the Named Insured shown in the Declarations, and any other person or organization qualifying as a Named Insured under this policy. The words "we", "us" and "our" refer to the company providing this insurance.

The word "insured" means any person or organization qualifying as such under Section **II** – Who Is An Insured.

Other words and phrases that appear in quotation marks have special meaning. Refer to Section **V** – Definitions.

SECTION I – COVERAGES

COVERAGE A BODILY INJURY AND PROPERTY DAMAGE LIABILITY

1. Insuring Agreement

a. We will pay those sums that the insured becomes legally obligated to pay as damages because of "bodily injury" or "property damage" to which this insurance applies. We will have the right and duty to defend the insured against any "suit" seeking those damages. However, we will have no duty to defend the insured against any "suit" seeking damages for "bodily injury" or "property damage" to which this insurance does not apply. We may, at our discretion, investigate any "occurrence" and settle any claim or "suit" that may result. But:

(1) The amount we will pay for damages is limited as described in Section **III** – Limits Of Insurance; and

(2) Our right and duty to defend ends when we have used up the applicable limit of insurance in the payment of judgments or settlements under Coverages **A** or **B** or medical expenses under Coverage **C**.

No other obligation or liability to pay sums or perform acts or services is covered unless explicitly provided for under Supplementary Payments – Coverages **A** and **B**.

b. This insurance applies to "bodily injury" and "property damage" only if:

(1) The "bodily injury" or "property damage" is caused by an "occurrence" that takes place in the "coverage territory";

(2) The "bodily injury" or "property damage" occurs during the policy period; and

(3) Prior to the policy period, no insured listed under Paragraph **1.** of Section **II** – Who Is An Insured and no "employee" authorized by you to give or receive notice of an "occurrence" or claim, knew that the "bodily injury" or "property damage" had occurred, in whole or in part. If such a listed insured or authorized "employee" knew, prior to the policy period, that the "bodily injury" or "property damage" occurred, then any continuation, change or resumption of such "bodily injury" or "property damage" during or after the policy period will be deemed to have been known prior to the policy period.

c. "Bodily injury" or "property damage" which occurs during the policy period and was not, prior to the policy period, known to have occurred by any insured listed under Paragraph **1.** of Section **II** – Who Is An Insured or any "employee" authorized by you to give or receive notice of an "occurrence" or claim, includes any continuation, change or resumption of that "bodily injury" or "property damage" after the end of the policy period.

d. "Bodily injury" or "property damage" will be deemed to have been known to have occurred at the earliest time when any insured listed under Paragraph **1.** of Section **II** – Who Is An Insured or any "employee" authorized by you to give or receive notice of an "occurrence" or claim:

(1) Reports all, or any part, of the "bodily injury" or "property damage" to us or any other insurer;

(2) Receives a written or verbal demand or claim for damages because of the "bodily injury" or "property damage"; or

(3) Becomes aware by any other means that "bodily injury" or "property damage" has occurred or has begun to occur.

e. Damages because of "bodily injury" include damages claimed by any person or organization for care, loss of services or death resulting at any time from the "bodily injury".

2. Exclusions

This insurance does not apply to:

a. Expected Or Intended Injury

"Bodily injury" or "property damage" expected or intended from the standpoint of the insured. This exclusion does not apply to "bodily injury" resulting from the use of reasonable force to protect persons or property.

b. Contractual Liability

"Bodily injury" or "property damage" for which the insured is obligated to pay damages by reason of the assumption of liability in a contract or agreement. This exclusion does not apply to liability for damages:

(1) That the insured would have in the absence of the contract or agreement; or

(2) Assumed in a contract or agreement that is an "insured contract", provided the "bodily injury" or "property damage" occurs subsequent to the execution of the contract or agreement. Solely for the purposes of liability assumed in an "insured contract", reasonable attorney fees and necessary litigation expenses incurred by or for a party other than an insured are deemed to be damages because of "bodily injury" or "property damage", provided:

(a) Liability to such party for, or for the cost of, that party's defense has also been assumed in the same "insured contract"; and

(b) Such attorney fees and litigation expenses are for defense of that party against a civil or alternative dispute resolution proceeding in which damages to which this insurance applies are alleged.

c. Liquor Liability

"Bodily injury" or "property damage" for which any insured may be held liable by reason of:

(1) Causing or contributing to the intoxication of any person;

(2) The furnishing of alcoholic beverages to a person under the legal drinking age or under the influence of alcohol; or

(3) Any statute, ordinance or regulation relating to the sale, gift, distribution or use of alcoholic beverages.

This exclusion applies only if you are in the business of manufacturing, distributing, selling, serving or furnishing alcoholic beverages.

d. Workers' Compensation And Similar Laws

Any obligation of the insured under a workers' compensation, disability benefits or unemployment compensation law or any similar law.

e. Employer's Liability

"Bodily injury" to:

(1) An "employee" of the insured arising out of and in the course of:

(a) Employment by the insured; or

(b) Performing duties related to the conduct of the insured's business; or

(2) The spouse, child, parent, brother or sister of that "employee" as a consequence of Paragraph **(1)** above.

This exclusion applies:

(1) Whether the insured may be liable as an employer or in any other capacity; and

(2) To any obligation to share damages with or repay someone else who must pay damages because of the injury.

This exclusion does not apply to liability assumed by the insured under an "insured contract".

Commercial General Liability Insurance

Figure 17.3 (cont'd)

f. Pollution

(1) "Bodily injury" or "property damage" arising out of the actual, alleged or threatened discharge, dispersal, seepage, migration, release or escape of "pollutants":

(a) At or from any premises, site or location which is or was at any time owned or occupied by, or rented or loaned to, any insured. However, this subparagraph does not apply to:

(i) "Bodily injury" if sustained within a building and caused by smoke, fumes, vapor or soot from equipment used to heat that building;

(ii) "Bodily injury" or "property damage" for which you may be held liable, if you are a contractor and the owner or lessee of such premises, site or location has been added to your policy as an additional insured with respect to your ongoing operations performed for that additional insured at that premises, site or location and such premises, site or location is not and never was owned or occupied by, or rented or loaned to, any insured, other than that additional insured; or

(iii) "Bodily injury" or "property damage" arising out of heat, smoke or fumes from a "hostile fire";

(b) At or from any premises, site or location which is or was at any time used by or for any insured or others for the handling, storage, disposal, processing or treatment of waste;

(c) Which are or were at any time transported, handled, stored, treated, disposed of, or processed as waste by or for:

(i) Any insured; or

(ii) Any person or organization for whom you may be legally responsible; or

(d) At or from any premises, site or location on which any insured or any contractors or subcontractors working directly or indirectly on any insured's behalf are performing operations if the "pollutants" are brought on or to the premises, site or location in connection with such operations by such insured, contractor or subcontractor. However, this subparagraph does not apply to:

(i) "Bodily injury" or "property damage" arising out of the escape of fuels, lubricants or other operating fluids which are needed to perform the normal electrical, hydraulic or mechanical functions necessary for the operation of "mobile equipment" or its parts, if such fuels, lubricants or other operating fluids escape from a vehicle part designed to hold, store or receive them. This exception does not apply if the "bodily injury" or "property damage" arises out of the intentional discharge, dispersal or release of the fuels, lubricants or other operating fluids, or if such fuels, lubricants or other operating fluids are brought on or to the premises, site or location with the intent that they be discharged, dispersed or released as part of the operations being performed by such insured, contractor or subcontractor;

(ii) "Bodily injury" or "property damage" sustained within a building and caused by the release of gases, fumes or vapors from materials brought into that building in connection with operations being performed by you or on your behalf by a contractor or subcontractor; or

(iii) "Bodily injury" or "property damage" arising out of heat, smoke or fumes from a "hostile fire".

(e) At or from any premises, site or location on which any insured or any contractors or subcontractors working directly or indirectly on any insured's behalf are performing operations if the operations are to test for, monitor, clean up, remove, contain, treat, detoxify or neutralize, or in any way respond to, or assess the effects of, "pollutants".

(2) Any loss, cost or expense arising out of any:

(a) Request, demand, order or statutory or regulatory requirement that any insured or others test for, monitor, clean up, remove, contain, treat, detoxify or neutralize, or in any way respond to, or assess the effects of, "pollutants"; or

(b) Claim or "suit" by or on behalf of a governmental authority for damages because of testing for, monitoring, cleaning up, removing, containing, treating, detoxifying or neutralizing, or in any way responding to, or assessing the effects of, "pollutants".

However, this paragraph does not apply to liability for damages because of "property damage" that the insured would have in the absence of such request, demand, order or statutory or regulatory requirement, or such claim or "suit" by or on behalf of a governmental authority.

g. Aircraft, Auto Or Watercraft

"Bodily injury" or "property damage" arising out of the ownership, maintenance, use or entrustment to others of any aircraft, "auto" or watercraft owned or operated by or rented or loaned to any insured. Use includes operation and "loading or unloading".

This exclusion applies even if the claims against any insured allege negligence or other wrongdoing in the supervision, hiring, employment, training or monitoring of others by that insured, if the "occurrence" which caused the "bodily injury" or "property damage" involved the ownership, maintenance, use or entrustment to others of any aircraft, "auto" or watercraft that is owned or operated by or rented or loaned to any insured.

This exclusion does not apply to:

(1) A watercraft while ashore on premises you own or rent;

(2) A watercraft you do not own that is:

(a) Less than 26 feet long; and

(b) Not being used to carry persons or property for a charge;

(3) Parking an "auto" on, or on the ways next to, premises you own or rent, provided the "auto" is not owned by or rented or loaned to you or the insured;

(4) Liability assumed under any "insured contract" for the ownership, maintenance or use of aircraft or watercraft; or

(5) "Bodily injury" or "property damage" arising out of the operation of any of the equipment listed in Paragraph **f.(2)** or **f.(3)** of the definition of "mobile equipment".

h. Mobile Equipment

"Bodily injury" or "property damage" arising out of:

(1) The transportation of "mobile equipment" by an "auto" owned or operated by or rented or loaned to any insured; or

(2) The use of "mobile equipment" in, or while in practice for, or while being prepared for, any prearranged racing, speed, demolition, or stunting activity.

i. War

"Bodily injury" or "property damage" due to war, whether or not declared, or any act or condition incident to war. War includes civil war, insurrection, rebellion or revolution. This exclusion applies only to liability assumed under a contract or agreement.

j. Damage To Property

"Property damage" to:

(1) Property you own, rent, or occupy, including any costs or expenses incurred by you, or any other person, organization or entity, for repair, replacement, enhancement, restoration or maintenance of such property for any reason, including prevention of injury to a person or damage to another's property;

(2) Premises you sell, give away or abandon, if the "property damage" arises out of any part of those premises;

(3) Property loaned to you;

(4) Personal property in the care, custody or control of the insured;

(5) That particular part of real property on which you or any contractors or subcontractors working directly or indirectly on your behalf are performing operations, if the "property damage" arises out of those operations; or

(6) That particular part of any property that must be restored, repaired or replaced because "your work" was incorrectly performed on it.

Figure 17.3 (cont'd)

Paragraphs **(1)**, **(3)** and **(4)** of this exclusion do not apply to "property damage" (other than damage by fire) to premises, including the contents of such premises, rented to you for a period of 7 or fewer consecutive days. A separate limit of insurance applies to Damage To Premises Rented To You as described in Section **III** ñ Limits Of Insurance.

Paragraph **(2)** of this exclusion does not apply if the premises are "your work" and were never occupied, rented or held for rental by you.

Paragraphs **(3)**, **(4)**, **(5)** and **(6)** of this exclusion do not apply to liability assumed under a sidetrack agreement.

Paragraph **(6)** of this exclusion does not apply to "property damage" included in the "products-completed operations hazard".

k. Damage To Your Product

"Property damage" to "your product" arising out of it or any part of it.

l. Damage To Your Work

"Property damage" to "your work" arising out of it or any part of it and included in the "products-completed operations hazard".

This exclusion does not apply if the damaged work or the work out of which the damage arises was performed on your behalf by a subcontractor.

m. Damage To Impaired Property Or Property Not Physically Injured

"Property damage" to "impaired property" or property that has not been physically injured, arising out of:

(1) A defect, deficiency, inadequacy or dangerous condition in "your product" or "your work"; or

(2) A delay or failure by you or anyone acting on your behalf to perform a contract or agreement in accordance with its terms.

This exclusion does not apply to the loss of use of other property arising out of sudden and accidental physical injury to "your product" or "your work" after it has been put to its intended use.

n. Recall Of Products, Work Or Impaired Property

Damages claimed for any loss, cost or expense incurred by you or others for the loss of use, withdrawal, recall, inspection, repair, replacement, adjustment, removal or disposal of:

(1) "Your product";

(2) "Your work"; or

(3) "Impaired property";

if such product, work, or property is withdrawn or recalled from the market or from use by any person or organization because of a known or suspected defect, deficiency, inadequacy or dangerous condition in it.

o. Personal And Advertising Injury

"Bodily injury" arising out of "personal and advertising injury".

Exclusions **c.** through **n.** do not apply to damage by fire to premises while rented to you or temporarily occupied by you with permission of the owner. A separate limit of insurance applies to this coverage as described in Section **III** – Limits Of Insurance.

COVERAGE B PERSONAL AND ADVERTISING INJURY LIABILITY

1. Insuring Agreement

a. We will pay those sums that the insured becomes legally obligated to pay as damages because of "personal and advertising injury" to which this insurance applies. We will have the right and duty to defend the insured against any "suit" seeking those damages. However, we will have no duty to defend the insured against any "suit" seeking damages for "personal and advertising injury" to which this insurance does not apply. We may, at our discretion, investigate any offense and settle any claim or "suit" that may result. But:

(1) The amount we will pay for damages is limited as described in Section **III** ñ Limits Of Insurance ; and

(2) Our right and duty to defend end when we have used up the applicable limit of insurance in the payment of judgments or settlements under Coverages **A** or **B** or medical expenses under Coverage **C**.

No other obligation or liability to pay sums or perform acts or services is covered unless explicitly provided for under Supplementary Payments ñ Coverages **A** and **B.**

b. This insurance applies to "personal and advertising injury" caused by an offense arising out of your business but only if the offense was committed in the "coverage territory" during the policy period.

2. **Exclusions**

This insurance does not apply to:

a. **Knowing Violation Of Rights Of Another**

"Personal and advertising injury" caused by or at the direction of the insured with the knowledge that the act would violate the rights of another and would inflict "personal and advertising injury".

b. **Material Published With Knowledge Of Falsity**

"Personal and advertising injury" arising out of oral or written publication of material, if done by or at the direction of the insured with knowledge of its falsity.

c. **Material Published Prior To Policy Period**

"Personal and advertising injury" arising out of oral or written publication of material whose first publication took place before the beginning of the policy period.

d. **Criminal Acts**

"Personal and advertising injury" arising out of a criminal act committed by or at the direction of the insured.

e. **Contractual Liability**

"Personal and advertising injury" for which the insured has assumed liability in a contract or agreement. This exclusion does not apply to liability for damages that the insured would have in the absence of the contract or agreement.

f. **Breach Of Contract**

"Personal and advertising injury" arising out of a breach of contract, except an implied contract to use another's advertising idea in your "advertisement".

g. **Quality Or Performance Of Goods – Failure To Conform To Statements**

"Personal and advertising injury" arising out of the failure of goods, products or services to conform with any statement of quality or performance made in your "advertisement".

h. **Wrong Description Of Prices**

"Personal and advertising injury" arising out of the wrong description of the price of goods, products or services stated in your "advertisement".

i. **Infringement Of Copyright, Patent, Trademark Or Trade Secret**

"Personal and advertising injury" arising out of the infringement of copyright, patent, trademark, trade secret or other intellectual property rights.

However, this exclusion does not apply to infringement, in your "advertisement", of copyright, trade dress or slogan.

j. **Insureds In Media And Internet Type Businesses**

"Personal and advertising injury" committed by an insured whose business is:

(1) Advertising, broadcasting, publishing or telecasting;

(2) Designing or determining content of websites for others; or

(3) An Internet search, access, content or service provider.

However, this exclusion does not apply to Paragraphs **14.a., b.** and **c.** of "personal and advertising injury" under the Definitions Section.

For the purposes of this exclusion, the placing of frames, borders or links, or advertising, for you or others anywhere on the Internet, is not by itself, considered the business of advertising, broadcasting, publishing or telecasting.

k. **Electronic Chatrooms Or Bulletin Boards**

"Personal and advertising injury" arising out of an electronic chatroom or bulletin board the insured hosts, owns, or over which the insured exercises control.

Figure 17.3 (cont'd)

l. Unauthorized Use Of Another's Name Or Product

"Personal and advertising injury" arising out of the unauthorized use of another's name or product in your e-mail address, domain name or metatag, or any other similar tactics to mislead another's potential customers.

m. Pollution

"Personal and advertising injury" arising out of the actual, alleged or threatened discharge, dispersal, seepage, migration, release or escape of "pollutants" at any time.

n. Pollution-Related

Any loss, cost or expense arising out of any:

(1) Request, demand or order that any insured or others test for, monitor, clean up, remove, contain, treat, detoxify or neutralize, or in any way respond to, or assess the effects of, "pollutants"; or

(2) Claim or suit by or on behalf of a governmental authority for damages because of testing for, monitoring, cleaning up, removing, containing, treating, detoxifying or neutralizing, or in any way responding to, or assessing the effects of, "pollutants".

COVERAGE C MEDICAL PAYMENTS

1. Insuring Agreement

a. We will pay medical expenses as described below for "bodily injury" caused by an accident:

(1) On premises you own or rent;

(2) On ways next to premises you own or rent; or

(3) Because of your operations;

provided that:

(1) The accident takes place in the "coverage territory" and during the policy period;

(2) The expenses are incurred and reported to us within one year of the date of the accident; and

(3) The injured person submits to examination, at our expense, by physicians of our choice as often as we reasonably require.

b. We will make these payments regardless of fault. These payments will not exceed the applicable limit of insurance. We will pay reasonable expenses for:

(1) First aid administered at the time of an accident;

(2) Necessary medical, surgical, x-ray and dental services, including prosthetic devices; and

(3) Necessary ambulance, hospital, professional nursing and funeral services.

2. Exclusions

We will not pay expenses for "bodily injury":

a. Any Insured

To any insured, except "volunteer workers".

b. Hired Person

To a person hired to do work for or on behalf of any insured or a tenant of any insured.

c. Injury On Normally Occupied Premises

To a person injured on that part of premises you own or rent that the person normally occupies.

d. Workers Compensation And Similar Laws

To a person, whether or not an "employee" of any insured, if benefits for the "bodily injury" are payable or must be provided under a workers' compensation or disability benefits law or a similar law.

e. Athletics Activities

To a person injured while taking part in athletics.

f. Products-Completed Operations Hazard

Included within the "products-completed operations hazard".

g. Coverage A Exclusions

Excluded under Coverage **A.**

h. War

Due to war, whether or not declared, or any act or condition incident to war. War includes civil war, insurrection, rebellion or revolution.

SUPPLEMENTARY PAYMENTS – COVERAGES A AND B

1. We will pay, with respect to any claim we investigate or settle, or any "suit" against an insured we defend:

a. All expenses we incur.

CG 00 01 10 01 | © ISO Properties, Inc., 2000 | **Page 7 of 16**

b. Up to $250 for cost of bail bonds required because of accidents or traffic law violations arising out of the use of any vehicle to which the Bodily Injury Liability Coverage applies. We do not have to furnish these bonds.

c. The cost of bonds to release attachments, but only for bond amounts within the applicable limit of insurance. We do not have to furnish these bonds.

d. All reasonable expenses incurred by the insured at our request to assist us in the investigation or defense of the claim or "suit", including actual loss of earnings up to $250 a day because of time off from work.

e. All costs taxed against the insured in the "suit".

f. Prejudgment interest awarded against the insured on that part of the judgment we pay. If we make an offer to pay the applicable limit of insurance, we will not pay any prejudgment interest based on that period of time after the offer.

g. All interest on the full amount of any judgment that accrues after entry of the judgment and before we have paid, offered to pay, or deposited in court the part of the judgment that is within the applicable limit of insurance.

These payments will not reduce the limits of insurance.

2. If we defend an insured against a "suit" and an indemnitee of the insured is also named as a party to the "suit", we will defend that indemnitee if all of the following conditions are met:

a. The "suit" against the indemnitee seeks damages for which the insured has assumed the liability of the indemnitee in a contract or agreement that is an "insured contract";

b. This insurance applies to such liability assumed by the insured;

c. The obligation to defend, or the cost of the defense of, that indemnitee, has also been assumed by the insured in the same "insured contract";

d. The allegations in the "suit" and the information we know about the "occurrence" are such that no conflict appears to exist between the interests of the insured and the interests of the indemnitee;

e. The indemnitee and the insured ask us to conduct and control the defense of that indemnitee against such "suit" and agree that we can assign the same counsel to defend the insured and the indemnitee; and

f. The indemnitee:

(1) Agrees in writing to:

(a) Cooperate with us in the investigation, settlement or defense of the "suit";

(b) Immediately send us copies of any demands, notices, summonses or legal papers received in connection with the "suit";

(c) Notify any other insurer whose coverage is available to the indemnitee; and

(d) Cooperate with us with respect to coordinating other applicable insurance available to the indemnitee; and

(2) Provides us with written authorization to:

(a) Obtain records and other information related to the "suit"; and

(b) Conduct and control the defense of the indemnitee in such "suit".

So long as the above conditions are met, attorneys' fees incurred by us in the defense of that indemnitee, necessary litigation expenses incurred by us and necessary litigation expenses incurred by the indemnitee at our request will be paid as Supplementary Payments. Notwithstanding the provisions of Paragraph **2.b.(2)** of Section **I** – Coverage **A** – Bodily Injury And Property Damage Liability, such payments will not be deemed to be damages for "bodily injury" and "property damage" and will not reduce the limits of insurance.

Our obligation to defend an insured's indemnitee and to pay for attorneys' fees and necessary litigation expenses as Supplementary Payments ends when:

a. We have used up the applicable limit of insurance in the payment of judgments or settlements; or

b. The conditions set forth above, or the terms of the agreement described in Paragraph **f.** above, are no longer met.

Figure 17.3 (cont'd)

SECTION II – WHO IS AN INSURED

1. If you are designated in the Declarations as:

   a. An individual, you and your spouse are insureds, but only with respect to the conduct of a business of which you are the sole owner.

   b. A partnership or joint venture, you are an insured. Your members, your partners, and their spouses are also insureds, but only with respect to the conduct of your business.

   c. A limited liability company, you are an insured. Your members are also insureds, but only with respect to the conduct of your business. Your managers are insureds, but only with respect to their duties as your managers.

   d. An organization other than a partnership, joint venture or limited liability company, you are an insured. Your "executive officers" and directors are insureds, but only with respect to their duties as your officers or directors. Your stockholders are also insureds, but only with respect to their liability as stockholders.

   e. A trust, you are an insured. Your trustees are also insureds, but only with respect to their duties as trustees.

2. Each of the following is also an insured:

   a. Your "volunteer workers" only while performing duties related to the conduct of your business, or your "employees", other than either your "executive officers" (if you are an organization other than a partnership, joint venture or limited liability company) or your managers (if you are a limited liability company), but only for acts within the scope of their employment by you or while performing duties related to the conduct of your business. However, none of these "employees" or "volunteer workers" are insureds for:

      (1) "Bodily injury" or "personal and advertising injury":

         (a) To you, to your partners or members (if you are a partnership or joint venture), to your members (if you are a limited liability company), to a co-"employee" while in the course of his or her employment or performing duties related to the conduct of your business, or to your other "volunteer workers" while performing duties related to the conduct of your business;

         (b) To the spouse, child, parent, brother or sister of that co-"employee" or "volunteer worker" as a consequence of Paragraph (1)(a) above;

         (c) For which there is any obligation to share damages with or repay someone else who must pay damages because of the injury described in Paragraphs (1)(a) or (b) above; or

         (d) Arising out of his or her providing or failing to provide professional health care services.

      (2) "Property damage" to property:

         (a) Owned, occupied or used by,

         (b) Rented to, in the care, custody or control of, or over which physical control is being exercised for any purpose by

         you, any of your "employees", "volunteer workers", any partner or member (if you are a partnership or joint venture), or any member (if you are a limited liability company).

   b. Any person (other than your "employee" or "volunteer worker"), or any organization while acting as your real estate manager.

   c. Any person or organization having proper temporary custody of your property if you die, but only:

      (1) With respect to liability arising out of the maintenance or use of that property; and

      (2) Until your legal representative has been appointed.

   d. Your legal representative if you die, but only with respect to duties as such. That representative will have all your rights and duties under this Coverage Part.

3. With respect to "mobile equipment" registered in your name under any motor vehicle registration law, any person is an insured while driving such equipment along a public highway with your permission. Any other person or organization responsible for the conduct of such person is also an insured, but only with respect to liability arising out of the operation of the equipment, and only if no other insurance of any kind is available to that person or organization for this liability. However, no person or organization is an insured with respect to:

   a. "Bodily injury" to a co-"employee" of the person driving the equipment; or

   b. "Property damage" to property owned by, rented to, in the charge of or occupied by you or the employer of any person who is an insured under this provision.

4. Any organization you newly acquire or form, other than a partnership, joint venture or limited liability company, and over which you maintain ownership or majority interest, will qualify as a Named Insured if there is no other similar insurance available to that organization. However:

   a. Coverage under this provision is afforded only until the 90th day after you acquire or form the organization or the end of the policy period, whichever is earlier;

   b. Coverage A does not apply to "bodily injury" or "property damage" that occurred before you acquired or formed the organization; and

   c. Coverage B does not apply to "personal and advertising injury" arising out of an offense committed before you acquired or formed the organization.

No person or organization is an insured with respect to the conduct of any current or past partnership, joint venture or limited liability company that is not shown as a Named Insured in the Declarations.

SECTION III – LIMITS OF INSURANCE

1. The Limits of Insurance shown in the Declarations and the rules below fix the most we will pay regardless of the number of:

   a. Insureds;

   b. Claims made or "suits" brought; or

   c. Persons or organizations making claims or bringing "suits".

2. The General Aggregate Limit is the most we will pay for the sum of:

   a. Medical expenses under Coverage C;

   b. Damages under Coverage A, except damages because of "bodily injury" or "property damage" included in the "products-completed operations hazard"; and

   c. Damages under Coverage B.

3. The Products-Completed Operations Aggregate Limit is the most we will pay under Coverage A for damages because of "bodily injury" and "property damage" included in the "products-completed operations hazard".

4. Subject to 2. above, the Personal and Advertising Injury Limit is the most we will pay under Coverage B for the sum of all damages because of all "personal and advertising injury" sustained by any one person or organization.

5. Subject to 2. or 3. above, whichever applies, the Each Occurrence Limit is the most we will pay for the sum of:

   a. Damages under Coverage A; and

   b. Medical expenses under Coverage C

   because of all "bodily injury" and "property damage" arising out of any one "occurrence".

6. Subject to 5. above, the Damage To Premises Rented To You Limit is the most we will pay under Coverage A for damages because of "property damage" to any one premises, while rented to you, or in the case of damage by fire, while rented to you or temporarily occupied by you with permission of the owner.

7. Subject to 5. above, the Medical Expense Limit is the most we will pay under Coverage C for all medical expenses because of "bodily injury" sustained by any one person.

The Limits of Insurance of this Coverage Part apply separately to each consecutive annual period and to any remaining period of less than 12 months, starting with the beginning of the policy period shown in the Declarations, unless the policy period is extended after issuance for an additional period of less than 12 months. In that case, the additional period will be deemed part of the last preceding period for purposes of determining the Limits of Insurance.

SECTION IV – COMMERCIAL GENERAL LIABILITY CONDITIONS

1. **Bankruptcy**

   Bankruptcy or insolvency of the insured or of the insured's estate will not relieve us of our obligations under this Coverage Part.

2. **Duties In The Event Of Occurrence, Offense, Claim Or Suit**

   a. You must see to it that we are notified as soon as practicable of an "occurrence" or an offense which may result in a claim. To the extent possible, notice should include:

      (1) How, when and where the "occurrence" or offense took place;

      (2) The names and addresses of any injured persons and witnesses; and

      (3) The nature and location of any injury or damage arising out of the "occurrence" or offense.

Figure 17.3 (cont'd)

b. If a claim is made or "suit" is brought against any insured, you must:

(1) Immediately record the specifics of the claim or "suit" and the date received; and

(2) Notify us as soon as practicable.

You must see to it that we receive written notice of the claim or "suit" as soon as practicable.

c. You and any other involved insured must:

(1) Immediately send us copies of any demands, notices, summonses or legal papers received in connection with the claim or "suit";

(2) Authorize us to obtain records and other information;

(3) Cooperate with us in the investigation or settlement of the claim or defense against the "suit"; and

(4) Assist us, upon our request, in the enforcement of any right against any person or organization which may be liable to the insured because of injury or damage to which this insurance may also apply.

d. No insured will, except at that insured's own cost, voluntarily make a payment, assume any obligation, or incur any expense, other than for first aid, without our consent.

3. Legal Action Against Us

No person or organization has a right under this Coverage Part:

a. To join us as a party or otherwise bring us into a "suit" asking for damages from an insured; or

b. To sue us on this Coverage Part unless all of its terms have been fully complied with.

A person or organization may sue us to recover on an agreed settlement or on a final judgment against an insured; but we will not be liable for damages that are not payable under the terms of this Coverage Part or that are in excess of the applicable limit of insurance. An agreed settlement means a settlement and release of liability signed by us, the insured and the claimant or the claimant's legal representative.

4. Other Insurance

If other valid and collectible insurance is available to the insured for a loss we cover under Coverages **A** or **B** of this Coverage Part, our obligations are limited as follows:

a. Primary Insurance

This insurance is primary except when **b.** below applies. If this insurance is primary, our obligations are not affected unless any of the other insurance is also primary. Then, we will share with all that other insurance by the method described in **c.** below.

b. Excess Insurance

This insurance is excess over:

(1) Any of the other insurance, whether primary, excess, contingent or on any other basis:

(a) That is Fire, Extended Coverage, Builder's Risk, Installation Risk or similar coverage for "your work";

(b) That is Fire insurance for premises rented to you or temporarily occupied by you with permission of the owner;

(c) That is insurance purchased by you to cover your liability as a tenant for "property damage" to premises rented to you or temporarily occupied by you with permission of the owner; or

(d) If the loss arises out of the maintenance or use of aircraft, "autos" or watercraft to the extent not subject to Exclusion **g.** of Section **I** – Coverage **A** – Bodily Injury And Property Damage Liability.

(2) Any other primary insurance available to you covering liability for damages arising out of the premises or operations for which you have been added as an additional insured by attachment of an endorsement.

When this insurance is excess, we will have no duty under Coverages **A** or **B** to defend the insured against any "suit" if any other insurer has a duty to defend the insured against that "suit". If no other insurer defends, we will undertake to do so, but we will be entitled to the insured's rights against all those other insurers.

When this insurance is excess over other insurance, we will pay only our share of the amount of the loss, if any, that exceeds the sum of:

(1) The total amount that all such other insurance would pay for the loss in the absence of this insurance; and

(2) The total of all deductible and self-insured amounts under all that other insurance.

We will share the remaining loss, if any, with any other insurance that is not described in this Excess Insurance provision and was not bought specifically to apply in excess of the Limits of Insurance shown in the Declarations of this Coverage Part.

c. Method Of Sharing

If all of the other insurance permits contribution by equal shares, we will follow this method also. Under this approach each insurer contributes equal amounts until it has paid its applicable limit of insurance or none of the loss remains, whichever comes first.

If any of the other insurance does not permit contribution by equal shares, we will contribute by limits. Under this method, each insurer's share is based on the ratio of its applicable limit of insurance to the total applicable limits of insurance of all insurers.

5. Premium Audit

a. We will compute all premiums for this Coverage Part in accordance with our rules and rates.

b. Premium shown in this Coverage Part as advance premium is a deposit premium only. At the close of each audit period we will compute the earned premium for that period and send notice to the first Named Insured. The due date for audit and retrospective premiums is the date shown as the due date on the bill. If the sum of the advance and audit premiums paid for the policy period is greater than the earned premium, we will return the excess to the first Named Insured.

c. The first Named Insured must keep records of the information we need for premium computation, and send us copies at such times as we may request.

6. Representations

By accepting this policy, you agree:

a. The statements in the Declarations are accurate and complete;

b. Those statements are based upon representations you made to us; and

c. We have issued this policy in reliance upon your representations.

7. Separation Of Insureds

Except with respect to the Limits of Insurance, and any rights or duties specifically assigned in this Coverage Part to the first Named Insured, this insurance applies:

a. As if each Named Insured were the only Named Insured; and

b. Separately to each insured against whom claim is made or "suit" is brought.

8. Transfer Of Rights Of Recovery Against Others To Us

If the insured has rights to recover all or part of any payment we have made under this Coverage Part, those rights are transferred to us. The insured must do nothing after loss to impair them. At our request, the insured will bring "suit" or transfer those rights to us and help us enforce them.

9. When We Do Not Renew

If we decide not to renew this Coverage Part, we will mail or deliver to the first Named Insured shown in the Declarations written notice of the nonrenewal not less than 30 days before the expiration date.

If notice is mailed, proof of mailing will be sufficient proof of notice.

SECTION V – DEFINITIONS

1. "Advertisement" means a notice that is broadcast or published to the general public or specific market segments about your goods, products or services for the purpose of attracting customers or supporters. For the purposes of this definition:

a. Notices that are published include material placed on the Internet or on similar electronic means of communication; and

b. Regarding web-sites, only that part of a website that is about your goods, products or services for the purposes of attracting customers or supporters is considered an advertisement.

2. "Auto" means a land motor vehicle, trailer or semitrailer designed for travel on public roads, including any attached machinery or equipment. But "auto" does not include "mobile equipment".

Figure 17.3 (cont'd)

3. "Bodily injury" means bodily injury, sickness or disease sustained by a person, including death resulting from any of these at any time.

4. "Coverage territory" means:

   a. The United States of America (including its territories and possessions), Puerto Rico and Canada;

   b. International waters or airspace, but only if the injury or damage occurs in the course of travel or transportation between any places included in **a.** above; or

   c. All other parts of the world if the injury or damage arises out of:

      (1) Goods or products made or sold by you in the territory described in **a.** above;

      (2) The activities of a person whose home is in the territory described in **a.** above, but is away for a short time on your business; or

      (3) "Personal and advertising injury" offenses that take place through the Internet or similar electronic means of communication

   provided the insured's responsibility to pay damages is determined in a "suit" on the merits, in the territory described in **a.** above or in a settlement we agree to.

5. "Employee" includes a "leased worker". "Employee" does not include a "temporary worker".

6. "Executive officer" means a person holding any of the officer positions created by your charter, constitution, by-laws or any other similar governing document.

7. "Hostile fire" means one which becomes uncontrollable or breaks out from where it was intended to be.

8. "Impaired property" means tangible property, other than "your product" or "your work", that cannot be used or is less useful because:

   a. It incorporates "your product" or "your work" that is known or thought to be defective, deficient, inadequate or dangerous; or

   b. You have failed to fulfill the terms of a contract or agreement;

   if such property can be restored to use by:

   a. The repair, replacement, adjustment or removal of "your product" or "your work"; or

   b. Your fulfilling the terms of the contract or agreement.

9. "Insured contract" means:

   a. A contract for a lease of premises. However, that portion of the contract for a lease of premises that indemnifies any person or organization for damage by fire to premises while rented to you or temporarily occupied by you with permission of the owner is not an "insured contract";

   b. A sidetrack agreement;

   c. Any easement or license agreement, except in connection with construction or demolition operations on or within 50 feet of a railroad;

   d. An obligation, as required by ordinance, to indemnify a municipality, except in connection with work for a municipality;

   e. An elevator maintenance agreement;

   f. That part of any other contract or agreement pertaining to your business (including an indemnification of a municipality in connection with work performed for a municipality) under which you assume the tort liability of another party to pay for "bodily injury" or "property damage" to a third person or organization. Tort liability means a liability that would be imposed by law in the absence of any contract or agreement.

   Paragraph **f.** does not include that part of any contract or agreement:

   (1) That indemnifies a railroad for "bodily injury" or "property damage" arising out of construction or demolition operations, within 50 feet of any railroad property and affecting any railroad bridge or trestle, tracks, road-beds, tunnel, underpass or crossing;

   (2) That indemnifies an architect, engineer or surveyor for injury or damage arising out of:

      (a) Preparing, approving, or failing to prepare or approve, maps, shop drawings, opinions, reports, surveys, field orders, change orders or drawings and specifications; or

      (b) Giving directions or instructions, or failing to give them, if that is the primary cause of the injury or damage; or

   (3) Under which the insured, if an architect, engineer or surveyor, assumes liability for an injury or damage arising out of the insured's rendering or failure to render professional services, including those listed in **(2)** above and supervisory, inspection, architectural or engineering activities.

10. "Leased worker" means a person leased to you by a labor leasing firm under an agreement between you and the labor leasing firm, to perform duties related to the conduct of your business. "Leased worker" does not include a "temporary worker".

11. "Loading or unloading" means the handling of property:

    a. After it is moved from the place where it is accepted for movement into or onto an aircraft, watercraft or "auto";

    b. While it is in or on an aircraft, watercraft or "auto"; or

    c. While it is being moved from an aircraft, watercraft or "auto" to the place where it is finally delivered;

    but "loading or unloading" does not include the movement of property by means of a mechanical device, other than a hand truck, that is not attached to the aircraft, watercraft or "auto".

12. "Mobile equipment" means any of the following types of land vehicles, including any attached machinery or equipment:

    a. Bulldozers, farm machinery, forklifts and other vehicles designed for use principally off public roads;

    b. Vehicles maintained for use solely on or next to premises you own or rent;

    c. Vehicles that travel on crawler treads;

    d. Vehicles, whether self-propelled or not, maintained primarily to provide mobility to permanently mounted:

       (1) Power cranes, shovels, loaders, diggers or drills; or

       (2) Road construction or resurfacing equipment such as graders, scrapers or rollers;

    e. Vehicles not described in a., b., c. or d. above that are not self-propelled and are maintained primarily to provide mobility to permanently attached equipment of the following types:

       (1) Air compressors, pumps and generators, including spraying, welding, building cleaning, geophysical exploration, lighting and well servicing equipment; or

       (2) Cherry pickers and similar devices used to raise or lower workers;

    f. Vehicles not described in a., b., c. or d. above maintained primarily for purposes other than the transportation of persons or cargo.

       However, self-propelled vehicles with the following types of permanently attached equipment are not "mobile equipment" but will be considered "autos":

       (1) Equipment designed primarily for:

           (a) Snow removal;

           (b) Road maintenance, but not construction or resurfacing; or

           (c) Street cleaning;

       (2) Cherry pickers and similar devices mounted on automobile or truck chassis and used to raise or lower workers; and

       (3) Air compressors, pumps and generators, including spraying, welding, building cleaning, geophysical exploration, lighting and well servicing equipment.

13. "Occurrence" means an accident, including continuous or repeated exposure to substantially the same general harmful conditions.

14. "Personal and advertising injury" means injury, including consequential "bodily injury", arising out of one or more of the following offenses:

    a. False arrest, detention or imprisonment;

    b. Malicious prosecution;

    c. The wrongful eviction from, wrongful entry into, or invasion of the right of private occupancy of a room, dwelling or premises that a person occupies, committed by or on behalf of its owner, landlord or lessor;

    d. Oral or written publication, in any manner, of material that slanders or libels a person or organization or disparages a person's or organization's goods, products or services;

    e. Oral or written publication, in any manner, of material that violates a person's right of privacy;

    f. The use of another's advertising idea in your "advertisement"; or

    g. Infringing upon another's copyright, trade dress or slogan in your "advertisement".

Figure 17.3 (cont'd)

15. "Pollutants" mean any solid, liquid, gaseous or thermal irritant or contaminant, including smoke, vapor, soot, fumes, acids, alkalis, chemicals and waste. Waste includes materials to be recycled, reconditioned or reclaimed.

16. "Products-completed operations hazard":

   a. Includes all "bodily injury" and "property damage" occurring away from premises you own or rent and arising out of "your product" or "your work" except:

      (1) Products that are still in your physical possession; or

      (2) Work that has not yet been completed or abandoned. However, "your work" will be deemed completed at the earliest of the following times:

         (a) When all of the work called for in your contract has been completed.

         (b) When all of the work to be done at the job site has been completed if your contract calls for work at more than one job site.

         (c) When that part of the work done at a job site has been put to its intended use by any person or organization other than another contractor or subcontractor working on the same project.

         Work that may need service, maintenance, correction, repair or replacement, but which is otherwise complete, will be treated as completed.

   b. Does not include "bodily injury" or "property damage" arising out of:

      (1) The transportation of property, unless the injury or damage arises out of a condition in or on a vehicle not owned or operated by you, and that condition was created by the "loading or unloading" of that vehicle by any insured;

      (2) The existence of tools, uninstalled equipment or abandoned or unused materials; or

      (3) Products or operations for which the classification, listed in the Declarations or in a policy schedule, states that products-completed operations are subject to the General Aggregate Limit.

17. "Property damage" means:

   a. Physical injury to tangible property, including all resulting loss of use of that property. All such loss of use shall be deemed to occur at the time of the physical injury that caused it; or

   b. Loss of use of tangible property that is not physically injured. All such loss of use shall be deemed to occur at the time of the "occurrence" that caused it.

   For the purposes of this insurance, electronic data is not tangible property.

   As used in this definition, electronic data means information, facts or programs stored as or on, created or used on, or transmitted to or from computer software, including systems and applications software, hard or floppy disks, CD-ROMS, tapes, drives, cells, data processing devices or any other media which are used with electronically controlled equipment.

18. "Suit" means a civil proceeding in which damages because of "bodily injury", "property damage" or "personal and advertising injury" to which this insurance applies are alleged. "Suit" includes:

   a. An arbitration proceeding in which such damages are claimed and to which the insured must submit or does submit with our consent; or

   b. Any other alternative dispute resolution proceeding in which such damages are claimed and to which the insured submits with our consent.

19. "Temporary worker" means a person who is furnished to you to substitute for a permanent "employee" on leave or to meet seasonal or short-term workload conditions.

20. "Volunteer worker" means a person who is not your "employee", and who donates his or her work and acts at the direction of and within the scope of duties determined by you, and is not paid a fee, salary or other compensation by you or anyone else for their work performed for you.

21. "Your product":

   a. Means:

      (1) Any goods or products, other than real property, manufactured, sold, handled, distributed or disposed of by:

         (a) You;

         (b) Others trading under your name; or

         (c) A person or organization whose business or assets you have acquired; and

      (2) Containers (other than vehicles), materials, parts or equipment furnished in connection with such goods or products.

b. Includes

   (1) Warranties or representations made at any time with respect to the fitness, quality, durability, performance or use of "your product"; and

   (2) The providing of or failure to provide warnings or instructions.

c. Does not include vending machines or other property rented to or located for the use of others but not sold.

22. "Your work":

  a. Means:

   (1) Work or operations performed by you or on your behalf; and

   (2) Materials, parts or equipment furnished in connection with such work or operations.

  b. Includes

   (1) Warranties or representations made at any time with respect to the fitness, quality, durability, performance or use of "your work", and

   (2) The providing of or failure to provide warnings or instructions.

CG 00 01 10 01

Figure 17.4

POLICY NUMBER:

COMMERCIAL GENERAL LIABILITY
CG 20 10 10 01

THIS ENDORSEMENT CHANGES THE POLICY. PLEASE READ IT CAREFULLY.

ADDITIONAL INSURED – OWNERS, LESSEES OR CONTRACTORS – SCHEDULED PERSON OR ORGANIZATION

This endorsement modifies insurance provided under the following:

COMMERCIAL GENERAL LIABILITY COVERAGE PART

SCHEDULE

Name of Person or Organization:

(If no entry appears above, information required to complete this endorsement will be shown in the Declarations as applicable to this endorsement.)

A. **Section II – Who Is An Insured** is amended to include as an insured the person or organization shown in the Schedule, but only with respect to liability arising out of your ongoing operations performed for that insured.

B. With respect to the insurance afforded to these additional insureds, the following exclusion is added:

　2. Exclusions

　　This insurance does not apply to "bodily injury" or "property damage" occurring after:

(1) All work, including materials, parts or equipment furnished in connection with such work, on the project (other than service, maintenance or repairs) to be performed by or on behalf of the additional insured(s) at the site of the covered operations has been completed; or

(2) That portion of "your work" out of which the injury or damage arises has been put to its intended use by any person or organization other than another contractor or subcontractor engaged in performing operations for a principal as a part of the same project.

CG 20 10 10 01　　　© ISO Properties, Inc., 2000　　　**Page 1 of 1**

Chapter 17

GLOSSARY

Additional insured. An entity or individual who is granted insured status under the CGL policy of another entity or individual.

Advertisement. As provided in the CGL policy, a notice that is broadcast or published to the general public about the named insured's goods, products, or services for the purpose of attracting customers or supporters.

Advertising injury. Claim arising out of slander, libel, copyright infringement, or misappropriation of advertising ideas as defined on the CGL policy. Advertising injury is included in the definition of *personal and advertising injury* on the CGL form.

Basic extended reporting period. A provision of claims-made coverage forms that extends the reporting period for claims for a designated amount of time past policy expiration. The accidents from which claims arise must have occurred during the policy period.

Bodily injury. Physical injury, sickness, disease, including resulting death.

Claims-made coverage form. A type of general liability insurance that responds only to claims for injury or damage that are first made (to the insurer) during the policy period (or during a designated extended reporting period beyond expiration).

Completed operations exposures. The liability exposures of business entities, such as contractors, that arise from operations or services they have completed.

Conditions. A section of the CGL form (and other types of coverage forms) that sets legally binding guidelines for the insured and the insurer concerning policy usage.

Coverage territory. The geographic area in which an insurance policy applies.

Declarations page. Usually the first page of an insurance policy that lists details of what is included in the policy.

Duty to defend. One of the duties provided for in a CGL policy. The insurer will pay for an insured's defense against a lawsuit for damages that potentially may be covered by the policy.

Employee. A person who works for another, usually for wages or salary.

Endorsement. An amendment to a policy form.

Exclusion. A provision in an insurance policy that limits or voids coverage for a particular situation, event, or property.

Exposure theory. A theory that bodily injury occurs when the victim is exposed to a harm-causing agent. The date the injury or disease manifests itself does not matter.

General liability. The general type of liability exposures that a business or individual is subject to during its normal operation.

Injurious process theory. A theory that an occurrence is a continuing process, beginning with the exposure to damage, through damage being caused by that danger, and ending with the manifestation of the disease or injury.

Injury-in-fact theory. A theory that reasons that an occurrence happens when injury actually happens.

Insured contract. Types of contractual liability that are insured under a CGL policy.

Leased worker. A worker leased from another organization on a long-term basis.

Limit of liability. The cap on payments that will be made under various insurance coverage agreements.

Manifestation theory. A theory that bodily injury occurs when there is an actual diagnosis of the injury or the date of death. Focuses on the result rather than the cause of the injury.

Occurrence. An event that triggers coverage under an insurance policy.

Occurrence-based coverage form. Such a policy covers injury or damage that occurs during the policy period even if claim is brought months or even years after the policy has expired

Offense. Under the personal and advertising sections of the CGL policy, an offense is an intentional action of an insured that results in injury or damage.

Operations exposures. The liability exposures of business entities to third parties (customers, guests, and passersby) who may become injured or have property damaged because of the negligent acts of the business owners, their agents, or employees

Personal injury. Injury inflicted by way of false arrest, invasion of privacy, malicious prosecution, and other offenses as defined on the CGL policy. Personal injury is included in the definition of *personal and advertising injury* on the CGL form.

Premises exposures. The liability exposure of business entities to third parties who may become injured or have property damaged because of a condition on the insured's property.

Products exposures. The liability exposures of manufacturers or distributors whose malfunctioning products may cause injury or property damage to third parties.

Property damage. Physical damage to tangible property, including loss of its use, and loss of use of tangible property that is not physically damaged.

Supplemental extended reporting period. A provision in a claims-made CGL policy that provides an unlimited period of time past policy expiration in which to report claims. An additional premium is charged, and the accidents from which the claims arise must have happened during the policy period.

Third party. A person or entity who is injured or whose property is damaged because of the actions of another party.

Chapter 18

THE WORKERS COMPENSATION SYSTEM

WHAT IS IT?

The workers compensation system is a statutorily imposed mechanism that provides for the payment of specific levels of benefits to employees who suffer employment-related injuries. In return, injured employees relinquish the right to sue their employers for damages arising from such injuries.

Each state has adopted legislation and regulations that spell out when the system applies and the level of benefits that are payable for various types of injury. In general, employees who are injured because of work-related exposures or accidents are entitled to compensation for medical treatment and a portion of wages that are lost or reduced. In the event that a worker dies as the result of an employment-related exposure, the worker's spouse and dependent children are entitled to ongoing benefits as scheduled by the respective state.

The District of Columbia and all states except Texas have adopted *compulsory* workers compensation laws. These compulsory laws require employers that fall within the scope of a respective state's law to accept its provisions and be responsible for the benefits it dictates. Texas has an *elective* system. This means that employers in Texas may elect to either adopt or reject the provisions of the state workers compensation law. If a Texas employer decides to reject coverage under the law, its employees retain the right to sue the employer for a work-related injury. In addition, the employer loses certain common law defenses, such as assumption of risk, contributory negligence, and fellow employee negligence. Note that states may revise their workers compensation laws and regulations over time.

Common Law Defenses

Various common law defenses may be available to defendants to lawsuits. Briefly, in the context of workers compensation, these include: *Assumption of risk*—when an employee willingly and voluntarily agrees to expose herself to a known danger, such as volunteering to enter a chamber that is unstable and very likely to collapse. Under this theory, a person who willingly works in such an area or job assumes the risks of injury.

Contributory negligence—when an employee has failed to take ordinary care while working, which contributes with the employer's negligence to cause that employee to be injured. This might pertain to a situation in which an employee removes a machine guard and subsequently is injured; this worker would be considered to have contributed to the injury.

Fellow employee negligence—when an employer can claim that the actions of one employee caused or contributed to the injury of another employee, such as when one worker removes a machine guard and another worker—who didn't realize the guard was missing—is injured.

Workers compensation benefits are funded, for the most part, by insurance policies that employers purchase from insurance companies or from state-operated workers compensation funds. (State-operated workers compensation funds often are called *state funds.*) With limited exceptions, an employer that falls within the scope of its state workers compensation law must either purchase an insurance policy or become a *qualified self-insurer* for its workers compensation exposure. A qualified self-insurer is a business that meets certain criteria established by the individual states in which it operates; self-insurance is regulated by individual states, just as are insured workers compensation programs.

Need for Self-insurance Approval

Worker injuries can be quite complex, and recovery often stretches out for months or even years. Since workers compensation benefits are *statutorily imposed* and benefit payments are required, states want to be sure that businesses that self-insure will be able to fund benefit payments into the future. Therefore, employers may not just arbitrarily decide to operate without workers compensation insurance. Those that desire to become self-insured must meet stringent requirements that are designed to ensure that businesses will be able to pay benefits into the future.

Since the goal is that employees receive adequate medical treatment and compensation for their injuries, states usually consider the following types of information when deciding whether to approve a plan of self-insurance:

- financial stability
- whether the business is large enough to support self-insurance
- previous employee loss experience
- evidence of appropriate safety initiatives
- claims management expertise
- ability to manage a self-insurance program, whether with internal staff or outside vendors

Penalties May Be Assessed

If an employer does not purchase workers compensation coverage and is not a qualified self-insurer, the company runs the risk of being fined—and still has to pay the benefits that are set by law when an employee is injured. Some states may impose even stiffer penalties for habitually failing to participate in an approved workers compensation system, such as imprisonment or an injunction prohibiting the employer from operating in the state.

The U.S. territories of Guam, Puerto Rico, and the U.S. Virgin Islands, as well as the provinces of Canada, also have enacted workers compensation statutes and regulations that operate similarly to those of the fifty United States and the District of Columbia. Various federal laws dictate the potential sources of recovery for federal employees who are injured in connection with their employment.

BUSINESS USES

There is perhaps no other type of insurance that universally affects the American population as much as workers compensation. The workers compensation system is designed to provide prompt, equitable relief to employees who sustain work-related injury regardless of whether the employee, the employer, or no one was *at fault* for the injury. It also protects employers from lawsuits by their employees so that, at least theoretically, benefits are provided immediately without the need to prove responsibility for an accident. In other words, even when an employee is

responsible for his own injury, the workers compensation system usually responds—as long as the injury is related to employment.

In the Course of Employment

Bodily injury to an employee must arise *out of and in the course of employment* in order for workers compensation benefits to apply. Since neither the workers compensation insurance policy nor the state workers compensation statutes defines this term, case law must be considered.

In general, courts have ruled that a causal connection must exist between the injury and the employment in order for workers compensation to apply. In *Bralley v. Daugherty*, 401 N.E. 2d 448 (Ohio 1980), the Ohio Supreme Court stated that, while compensability is not necessarily limited to injuries that actually happen on an employer's premises, there must be a causal connection between the injury and the employment. The *Bralley* court stated that "the test of the right to participate in the Workers' Compensation Fund is not whether there was any fault or neglect on the part of the employer or his employees, but whether a 'causal connection' existed between an employee's injury and his employment either through the activities, the conditions, or the environment of the employment." The *Bralley* case involved an employee who was injured in a car accident while on the way to work, and the Ohio Supreme Court ruled that the accident did not fall within the workers compensation system.

Another example of this type of situation—but with the opposite result—was the case of the *Appeal of Griffin*, 671 A. 2d 541 (N.H. 1996). In this case, an employee was injured in a fight with coworkers and filed for benefits. The fight occurred as Griffin was driving coworkers back to a motel in which they were staying during an out-of-town business trip. The New Hampshire Compensation Appeals Board denied the claim because the injuries did not arise in the course of employment. However, the New Hampshire Supreme Court reversed the decision, ruling that the driving was related to work and the injury was compensable because the argument was about the driving.

Based on these and other cases, it is generally held that, if a case can be made for a causal connection between work and the injury, workers compensation applies.

Relationship to Employment

Often, employees engage in activities that may or may not be related to their employment. For example, many companies sponsor picnics, sports, and other recreational activities that may raise a question about whether they are related to employment. Questions also may arise when alcohol or drug consumption, or horseplay, is involved in the injury.

Each of these may present different fact patterns that affect whether injuries arising from them are covered by workers compensation or not. However, in general, activities that are paid for and supervised by an employer in an effort to promote business goals (such as team building or employee morale and loyalty) appear to be related to employment. Therefore, employee injuries that arise from them probably fall within the workers compensation system.

The circumstances involving injuries that arise during horseplay or fights usually dictate whether they fall within the system or not. Usually, the instigator of a fight, or the individual engaging in the horseplay, would not be eligible for workers compensation benefits. However, if another employee were injured as a result, she probably would be eligible.

Some states have enacted statutes that dictate if and when alcohol or drug use defeats a claim for workers compensation. However, absent specific legislation, an employee who is incapable of doing a job because of alcohol or drug consumption probably is not eligible for benefits if he is injured while incapacitated. However, if the employee is still able to do the job—despite alcohol or drug consumption—she probably would be eligible for benefits if injured.

Exclusive Remedy

This idea that the workers compensation system is the only source of recovery for employees injured on the job is called the doctrine of *exclusive remedy*. Exclusive remedy provides that injured workers are eligible for scheduled (preset by state regulation) medical and wage-loss benefits in exchange for giving up the right to sue the employer. Under the doctrine of exclusive remedy, the only recovery option for injured employees is that which is provided under the state's workers compensation statute and regulations, so employers are not at risk for large judicial awards that may result from employee lawsuits. The sole benefits that are available to injured workers usually are funded through a workers compen-

sation insurance policy, which is automatically tapped—with limited exceptions—for benefits once the injuries are considered to be *compensable.*

The word *compensable* is a very important word for those dealing with workers compensation insurance. Once an injury or disease is deemed to be compensable, the workers compensation insurance program is triggered and benefits are paid. This continues until the employee is completely healed and back to work. If insurance is not available because the business failed to purchase it, the employer is responsible for the benefits.

There are, of course, some exceptions to this general rule that workers compensation is the exclusive remedy for employee injuries. Various legal doctrines have eroded the concept and the seemingly clear-cut insurance arrangement. In addition, some types of employments do not fall under the state workers compensation statutes.

Exceptions to Exclusive Remedy

There are several legal doctrines that have arisen over the years to erode the exclusive remedy theory. These include the doctrines of:

- dual capacity,

- intentional tort, and

- third-party-over.

Dual Capacity

The doctrine of dual capacity holds that an employer that is normally shielded from lawsuits by the exclusive remedy rule may be liable for damages that arise from a wrongful act that is not related to the role of employer. In such a situation, the employer is judged to occupy a second, or *dual*, capacity in which the exposure is common to the public in general.

For example, ABC Widget Manufacturer may employ an individual, Mark Jones, to install widgets in retail store air-conditioning systems. While installing these widgets, Mr. Jones is considered an ABC employee operating in the course of employment. If he is injured during the installation, his sole recourse (exclusive remedy) against ABC is workers compensation. However, if a widget were defective and blew up in Mr. Jones' face after he installed it, his injuries may be considered to be the result of ABC's product as well as his employment. In other words, the widget that blew up could have injured anyone in the store. The test of this doctrine is whether the second capacity as widget manufacturer generates obligations that are unrelated to those of the first, that of an employer.

Many courts have rejected this doctrine, and some states have limited the possibility of dual capacity lawsuits by passing laws that forbid or limit it application. However, the theory may come into play in some circumstances.

Intentional Tort

Many jurisdictions have ruled that injuries caused by an employer's intentional actions do not arise out of the course of employment and, therefore, are not protected by the exclusive remedy rule. In addition, it would be against public policy to provide immunity to employers that intentionally injure or harm employees.

Willful, intentional, and even violent acts of employers against employees—such as sexual assault and harassment—usually would not be considered protected by the exclusive remedy rule. For example, in *Pursell v. Pizza Inn, Inc.*, 786 P.2d 716 (Okla. Ct. App. 1990), the Oklahoma court quoted from another case, stating:

> This court, like those before us, determines that the worker's compensation statutes were designed to provide the exclusive remedy for *accidental* injuries sustained during the course and scope of a worker's employment. The [worker's compensation] statutes *were not* designed to shield employers or co-employees from *willful, intentional or even violent conduct.*

Other examples of situations in which the exclusive remedy doctrine might be abrogated because of intentional harm by the employer include those involving the cleanup of hazardous materials without appropriate protective clothing, gross negligence, and directives to employees that almost certainly will cause injury. As with the doctrine of dual capacity, states and courts have varied on when it should be applied.

Third–Party–Over Actions

Third-party-over actions are somewhat complicated situations in which an injured employee sues a third

party, and the third party subsequently is able to bring an action against the employer. This situation may develop when an employer contractually assumes the obligations and liabilities of the third party.

Third–Party–Over Example

For example, assume that Riverside Steel Company hires B&B Electrical Contractors to do electrical maintenance work at a Riverside plant. B&B agrees to hold Riverside harmless and to indemnify it for injury to B&B employees. A B&B employee is injured when one of Riverside's overhead cranes malfunctions and runs into the scaffolding on which he is standing. The B&B employee files for workers compensation benefits with B&B's workers compensation insurer. In addition, he sues Riverside for negligence in operating the crane. Riverside turns the lawsuit over to B&B because the contractor had contractually agreed to indemnify Riverside. In this situation, B&B's insurance companies may end up paying workers compensation benefits, defending the lawsuit, and then paying the settlement.

In this type of third-party-over action, two insurance policies may be triggered. B&B's workers compensation policy would be tapped to pay the employee benefits that are dictated by the workers compensation regulations. Since B&B assumed this liability in an insured contract, B&B's commercial liability policy probably would be tapped to defend the lawsuit against Riverside and to pay any settlement against the steel company.

Types of Employments Not Covered by Workers Compensation

The majority of U.S. companies are required to purchase insurance that will respond to employee claims for injury. Certain types of employments, however, may not fall within the scope of a state workers compensation law. These include:

- small businesses that employ fewer than a specified number of workers. (The statute often legislates that a business must have more than a minimum number of workers—perhaps three or five—before the act becomes compulsory.)

- businesses that employ only casual, farm, or domestic workers.

- partners in a partnership or sole proprietors.

- employees or volunteers to certain religious organizations.

- a specified number of corporate officers.

Individual state statutes outline such exceptions.

Injury by Disease

In addition to paying benefits that are due because of workplace accidents, the workers compensation system addresses injuries that employees suffer from *bodily injury by disease.* This type of injury is commonly referred to as *occupational disease* or *OD.* It refers to health impairments that are caused by continued exposure to hazards that are inherent in an employee's occupation and compensable under most workers compensation laws. One example of an occupational disease is pneumoconiosis, or black lung disease, which afflicts coal miners.

Keep in mind that workers compensation is regulated on a state level. However, there are exceptions to this general rule. Although occupational disease benefits are payable through a workers compensation policy that has been properly endorsed, the statutes and regulations that dictate compensability and benefits levels may be adopted at the federal level. For example, black lung benefits are regulated on a federal level through the Federal Coal Mine Health and Safety Act of 1969 and its amendments (30 U.S.C. §§931-942). However, some or all of the benefits may be payable through a state workers compensation program funded by a workers compensation insurance policy.

Mental Injury

Situations involving employees who claim mental injuries that are employment-related may present difficult situations of compensability. There are three general categories of mental injury that commonly arise:

- physical trauma that results in mental injury (physical/mental)

- mental stress or stimulus that results in physical injury (mental/physical)

- mental stress or stimulus that results in mental injury (mental/mental)

In general, the first two categories of injury—physical/mental and mental/physical—are considered compensable. This is because a physical manifestation of injury is present, and the workers compensation system provides for bodily injury. However, when only mental injury is claimed, the compensability situation varies from state to state.

For example, courts in many states—including Illinois and Mississippi—have ruled that pure mental injuries are compensable. However, courts in other jurisdictions, such as Kansas and Wisconsin, have denied workers compensation benefits for pure mental injuries. The main reason for this difficulty lies in the fact that mental injuries are intangible and vague. Some believe that mental disabilities may be simulated by the claimant. In addition, an objective method to value such claims is difficult to set. Therefore, many states have determined that they are not compensable.

Examples of Mental-related Claims

Physical/mental—an example is a back injury that is difficult to treat and causes much pain, which ultimately results in serious depression.

Mental/physical—an example is a nervous condition that is brought on by unreasonable pressure to work long hours, which ultimately leads to a stomach ulcer.

Mental/mental—an example is a nervous condition that is brought on by unreasonable pressure to work long hours, which leads to serious depression.

ADVANTAGES

Employee Advantages

- Injured workers are provided with immediate medical treatment and lost-wage benefits without having to resort to a lawsuit to receive compensation. Once an employee establishes that an injury is compensable, she is entitled to benefits until the injury has healed and she is back to work.

- Workers compensation benefits may provide broader benefits than standard health insurance, especially in the area of medical rehabilitation services such as physical and occupational therapy. Individuals with permanent injuries—whether they cause total or partial disability—often are eligible for lump sum payments that are designed to help compensate for the permanent injury. Individual states have adopted payment schedules that apply to specific types of permanent disabilities.

- Employees who are permanently injured may be eligible for retraining services so that they can develop new skills that will allow them to return to gainful employment. Since lost wages are paid through the system, there is a built-in incentive to keep people working.

- Workers compensation provides a continuing stream of income to workers who otherwise may not receive any while not working.

Employer Advantages

- Employers are shielded from employee lawsuits for work-related injuries. Although there are some exceptions to this general rule, which were introduced previously in this chapter, an employer is not exposed to defense and settlement costs that could drain resources of time and money.

- Employers are able to purchase insurance to fund their liabilities under the workers compensation statute of the state(s) in which they operate. Insurance usually is available from a selection of insurance companies. However, each state also provides avenues to obtain coverage if it is not available on the open marketplace through either a *state fund* or an *assigned risk pool*. State funds are operated directly by the individual state to provide the coverage. Assigned risk programs or pools entail the assignment of a business to a company that writes workers compensation insurance in the state. The company cannot refuse to write the insurance once the assignment has been made, even if the company declined to write the business in the open marketplace.

- Employers that participate in the system and purchase coverage do not risk fines and penal-

ties for failing to comply with state law. Employers may be able to tap into safety resources, such as safety trainers and loss control inspectors, that are available through their workers compensation insurance company but would be too expensive for the employer to provide on its own.

Societal Advantage

- The workers compensation system is a statutorily imposed program that has as its main goal the equitable treatment of injured employees. Workers compensation insurance is designed to provide the funds that are needed to fulfill this purpose.

DISADVANTAGES

Employee Disadvantages

- Employees trade the right to sue their employers for damages arising from employment-related activities for the protection of the workers compensation system. Some may believe that this trade-off benefits employers more than employees. Employees who pursue workers compensation claims must act within the system, which often dictates the medical facilities and professionals that may be used and always sets the wage-loss benefit levels.

- While all medical bills theoretically are paid on compensable claims, employees may be forced to use medical professionals that are chosen by the employer or the workers compensation insurance company—at least during the beginning stages of their claims. Some employees may believe that other facilities would be better suited to their needs and resent having to see a "company doctor."

- Benefits may be terminated if employees refuse to follow the medical advice of treating professionals. They also may be required to submit to independent medical examinations when the degree of injury is questionable.

- The level of benefit payments for lost wages is calculated as a percentage of the average wage that the employee received before being injured. For example, a state may pay 66.6 percent of the employee's pre-injury wage, subject to a minimum of $130 and maximum of $750. Under this type of schedule, a low-paid worker—such as a convenience store clerk who clears $125 a week—may make more on workers compensation than when working. However, a high-paid employee who clears $950 a week suffers.

- Each state has a waiting period before wage-loss benefits are started. This ranges from one to seven days. Therefore, an employee who suffers a minor injury at work and is off work for only one day probably will not be able to draw wage-loss benefits. Medical bills, however, are paid from day one on.

Employer Disadvantages

- Most employers are required to either purchase workers compensation insurance or become qualified self-insurers, regardless of whether they have ever had any employee injuries or not. Even when sales are slow, the workers compensation premium must be paid.

- In addition to paying an insurance premium, most employers are assessed additional money after claims are paid through what is called *experience rating*. Experience rating is explained subsequently in this chapter under the section entitled **Design Features.** In essence, however, employers with fewer claims than other businesses in their peer group pay lower premiums than those with more claims than their peers. Therefore, in addition to paying an insurance premium, businesses also are assessed more if they use the insurance.

- Businesses that have a lot—or some serious—workers compensation claims may need to hire people specifically to manage the workers compensation program. In addition to this cost burden, a good deal of time may be spent working with insurance company adjusters and injured employees in an effort to have them return to work.

- The workers compensation process tends to be highly regulated and paper intensive. Employers must adhere to the regulations for reporting claims and filing necessary paperwork, which may create an administrative burden even when an insur-

ance company adjuster does most of the work. In addition, some state regulations provide that benefits must be paid even when the compensability of a claim is in question.

- Some employers may feel that benefits may be allowed to continue beyond a normal period of recovery if an employee chooses to malinger.

Societal Disadvantage

- A great deal of time may be spent debating the level of benefits, regulations and filing requirements, and premium rates that should be charged for coverage. This often polarizes support into pro-labor and pro-business camps.

Advantage and Disadvantage

- Employers may develop modified work positions in an effort to return injured employees to work more quickly. For example, an employee may injure his shoulder at work, and the treating physician may determine that the individual should not lift more than ten pounds. The employer may design a modified position that involves lifting no more than ten pounds so the employee can return to work before being completely healed. This is a valuable benefit to both the employer and employee because it returns workers to productivity sooner and often helps an employee ease back into work without a danger of being reinjured.

  However, such positions may be difficult to establish when the economy is slow or when a labor union represents the employees. Some workers may feel that employees on modified duty are getting preferential treatment and circumventing seniority systems. In fact, some seniority systems may prohibit such return-to-work programs.

DESIGN FEATURES

As stated previously, businesses that fall within the scope of their state workers compensation statutes must either purchase an insurance policy or become qualified self-insurers. Some basic information about the goals of qualifying self-insurers is mentioned in the first part of this chapter. However, for design purposes, the rest of this discussion focuses on workers compensation programs that are funded by insurance.

The Insurance Policy

Most workers compensation policies are virtually identical to one another, even though different insurance companies may issue them. Most states require that workers compensation and employers liability policy forms be filed with their respective insurance departments for approval. The National Council on Compensation Insurance, Inc. (NCCI), files forms on behalf of its member states. In other states, independent bureaus—such as the Pennsylvania Compensation Rating Bureau—file coverage forms on behalf of their members. There also are five monopolistic states in which workers compensation insurance must be written through a state insurance fund.

Monopolistic States

Monopolistic states are those that require that workers compensation coverage be purchased from a state fund. Independent insurance companies are not permitted to offer workers compensation insurance in these states.

The five monopolistic states are North Dakota, Ohio, Washington, West Virginia, and Wyoming.

Regardless of these differences, the workers compensation policy is essentially the same from state to state. A sample NCCI form is reprinted at the end of this chapter.

The policy contains three separate and distinct coverage parts:

- Part One: Workers Compensation

- Part Two: Employers Liability

- Part Three: Other States Insurance

There also are sections dealing with duties and premium.

Part One, Workers Compensation Insurance

This is the workers compensation section, which provides for the payment of benefits as they are im-

posed by the workers compensation laws of the state(s) listed on the information page. For example, a business that has operations in Michigan and Minnesota will list those states on the policy information page as follows:

3. A. Workers Compensation Insurance: Part One of the policy applies to the Workers Compensation Law of the states listed here: *Michigan, Minnesota.*

This means that the policy adheres to the requirements that are set by the workers compensation laws of those two states. Companies should list every state in which they have operations in that section. An operation is considered any location at which employees are regularly located and from which they work. For example, a company may have just one salesperson in a state, and that salesperson may work from her home office. That state should be listed in item 3.A. of Part One so that the workers compensation law of that state is included for insurance purposes.

Workers Compensation Coverage Part

This part promises to promptly pay the benefits that are required in the states that are listed. As noted previously, states in which the insured has operations as of the inception date of the policy must be noted on the information page under item 3.A. in order for this coverage to apply.

This promise to pay the benefits that are required under the applicable workers compensation statute is the essence of the policy—and of the entire system. If an insured business had failed to list the appropriate states and a compensable claim occurs, the business still would be responsible to pay them. In addition to paying benefits, the policy also promises to assume the costs to defend the insured against claims or suits for benefits that are brought against the insured.

It is important to note that the policy clearly states that it will not fund any payments that the insured becomes responsible for in excess of the benefits stipulated by the applicable workers compensation law. For example, businesses that employ minors in hazardous occupations in violation of state law will be assessed multiple damages and possibly other penalties if such a minor is injured in a work-related accident. The workers compensation policy will pay only the normal workers compensation benefits that are required under state law to the injured minor. Any excess benefits or damages must be borne by the employer.

Part Two, Employers Liability Insurance

This is the employers liability section, which provides protection for the insured against liability imposed by law for injury to employees in the course of employment that is not compensable under Part One. This coverage corresponds to the liability coverage that is found on other types of policies. It may be tapped when workers compensation coverage is not compulsory for the employer, when workers compensation coverage is elective, when the state workers compensation law permits lawsuits by the spouses or dependents of workers who are injured on the job, when a lawsuit is permitted as a third-party-over action, or when an on-the-job injury is not considered compensable but the employee still wants to hold the employer responsible.

Employers liability coverage dovetails with coverage provided by the commercial general liability policy. The employers liability section specifically provides that damages claimed against the insured in a capacity other than as an employer may be paid through its provisions. The standard commercial general liability policy specifically excludes bodily injury to an employee—regardless of whether the insured is liable as an employer or in another capacity. Therefore, the forms dovetail to make it clear that employee injuries should be covered under the workers compensation and employers liability policy and not the general liability policy.

Part Three, Other States Insurance

This section provides coverage in states that are not listed on the information page for Part One coverage (item 3.A. illustrated previously). States must be specifically listed in order for coverage to apply there.

This part is important in several situations. The most common need is for operations that are begun in a state that is not listed for Part One coverage *after* the effective date of the policy. For example, ABC Restaurants has locations in six states when its workers compensation and employers liability policy is issued for the period of January 1, 2003-04. Those six states are listed in item 3.A. of the information page for Part One coverage. On May 15, 2003, ABC opens a new location in a seventh state, which is not listed under item 3.A. ABC should notify its workers compensation insurer before the restaurant is opened so that state can be added for Part One coverage. However, if ABC neglects to do so, and the state has been listed for Part Three coverage, the policy applies as if the state were listed under Part One.

Because of this benefit of Other States Insurance, many businesses request that the words "All states other than those listed in item 3.A." be noted for Part Three coverage. However, this may create a problem because the five monopolistic states (North Dakota, Ohio, Washington, West Virginia, and Wyoming) require that workers compensation insurance be purchased from their state funds. Independent carriers are not permitted to provide coverage within their boundaries. Therefore, even if the words "All states other than those listed in item 3.A." were noted under Part Three, a restaurant that was opened in, say, Ohio, would not be accorded coverage.

Part Three also provides coverage for employees who are temporarily working in a state not listed for Part One coverage.

Notice Requirement

Part Three does include a notice requirement, which states that the insured business should notify the insurance carrier if work is begun in a state that is listed under the Other States Insurance coverage part. No penalties are listed in this section, however, but reporting changes in workers compensation exposures still is important.

Underwriting Concerns

This notice requirement, as well as the fact that automatic coverage for new operations cannot in all cases be assumed, points out the need to always report entry into new states to the workers compensation insurer. The underwriter or the insurance agent or broker may have to arrange for separate coverage under certain circumstances. In addition, the insurer may want to inspect the new location.

Other states insurance also provides for the reimbursement of benefit payments that an insured business must make to a claimant if the insurance company is not permitted to pay the benefits directly to the claimant.

Part Four, Your Duties if Injury Occurs

Part Four of the policy lists the insured's duties if injury occurs. Included are the duties of providing prompt medical treatment to injured employees, reporting the names and addresses of injured workers and witnesses, promptly giving notice of all demands and legal actions, cooperating with the insurance company in investigating and adjusting the claim, not interfering with the insurer's rights to recover payments, and not voluntarily making payments except at the business's own expense.

In general, the insurance policy will adjust and pay compensable claims in the states in which coverage applies. However, if an insured business violates one of its duties, the insurer may refuse to pay benefits.

Late Notice May Be a Problem

For example, an employer is injured at work and files a workers compensation notice with her employer. She does not immediately miss any work but does have some medical bills. Instead of notifying the workers compensation carrier of the claim, the business simply pays the injured worker's medical bills. However, the injury—a back injury that eventually is determined to be a ruptured disc—becomes more serious, and the employee now needs surgery. When surgery begins to be discussed, the business reports the claim to the workers compensation insurance company. At that point, the insurer tries to deny responsibility for paying benefits because of late notice. If such a declination is upheld and the injury is compensable, the employer will shoulder the responsibility.

Part Five, Premium

Part Five of the workers compensation and employers liability policy deals with premium.

This section states that all premium for the policy is determined by the insurer's manuals of rules, rates, rating plans, and classifications. The insurer's manuals are based on those filed by the same rating agencies (NCCI and independent state rating bureaus) that file workers compensation policy forms. The insured can affect the size of the premium by risk management efforts, managing its losses, assuming some deductibles, and other methods, but it is the insurer that determines the premium at the inception of the policy.

The following section discusses how premium is developed and factors that affect how much a business may pay for workers compensation coverage.

Classifying the Operations

Classifications are categories that are used to gauge the risks of workers compensation losses that the business will face over the policy period. The classification is based on information supplied mainly by the insured.

In addition to issuing policy forms as discussed at the beginning of this chapter, the NCCI and other independent bureaus establish the rules for classification and premium determination. These rating bureaus also develop experience rating, retrospective rating, and other rating information. Information in this chapter is based primarily on NCCI rules, but there may be variations by state. This is an overview of the process, and individual state rating manuals should be consulted for specific situations.

Classification of Exposures

In general, the idea of classifying workers is to group employers by the type of work they do. The business of the employer is classified, not the individual types of operations within the business. This is called the *governing classification*. After the governing basic classification is assigned, secondary classifications may be assigned when:

- The state manual requires that certain operations or employees be separately rated.

- The insured engages in operations—such as construction, farm, repair, or mercantile—that require additional basic classifications.

- The insured operates more than one business in a state.

All employees are assigned to the principal business classification if its rate is the same or higher than that of the secondary business classification that applies to the employees. However, the secondary business classification is used if it is higher.

The NCCI rules state that in addition to the basic business classification, there are standard exception and general exclusion operations that are classified separately. The standard exception classifications are clerical office; clerical or drafting telecommuter; drafting; drivers, chauffeurs, and their helpers; and outside salespersons, collectors, or messengers.

General exclusions are aircraft operations, new construction or alterations, stevedoring, sawmill operations, and employer-operated daycare services. These types of work are classified separately unless specifically included in the basic classification wording.

Classification Example

A retail supermarket is classified as a supermarket at, perhaps, a rate of $5.00 or more per $100 of payroll. This is the basic business classification. A clerical office rate—which is a standard exception classification—in this company's state of domicile is less than $.75 per $100 of payroll. Because of this, the supermarket owner may try to classify managers and service desk workers as clerical rather than supermarket employees. The reasoning is that the managers do not physically work in the supermarket operation. They do clerical tasks and manage the operation.

However, in order to qualify for the lower rated clerical office classification, the clerical work area must be *separated and distinguishable* from all other areas and hazards of the supermarket by floors, walls, partitions, counters, or other physical barriers. Based on this description, managers who spend part of their time in a partitioned office but also walk through the store—even on rare occasions—probably cannot be classified as clerical. The reason for this is that such individuals are subject to the same exposures (armed robbery, slipping and falling on loose produce, items falling from shelves, etc.) as a cashier or stocking clerk.

The NCCI and independent rating bureaus publish classification tables and descriptions for various types of operations. These must be followed by the insured business and the insurance company that issues the policy. When classification disputes between an insured and insurer arise, either may request a classification audit by the applicable rating bureau. Once such an audit is completed, it becomes more difficult to reassign payroll to a different classification.

A Sample page from the NCCI classification manual is shown in Figure 18.1.

Premium Basis

The premium basis for the vast majority of classifications is *remuneration*, which in essence means payroll. However, compensation that is not monetary—such as the value of meals that is considered a part of an employee's

pay—is included in remuneration. Most states include the regular pay portion of overtime pay, bonuses, and items such as store merchandise as remuneration. The key to assigning payroll lies in keeping accurate and valid payroll records by class. There are some exceptions to the use of remuneration, such as when domestic workers are classified on a per capita basis.

Payroll Limitations

Many states include executive officers under their workers compensation laws. In some states, executive officers may opt out of the system. When executive officers are included for coverage, their payroll is limited for reporting purposes. Each state sets minimum and maximum executive payroll reporting thresholds. For example, the minimum payroll for an executive officer that must be used in establishing the premium may be $100 a week—even if he does not draw any salary. The maximum may be $1,000 a week, even though she actually is paid much more than $52,000 a year. Individual classifications in state manuals should be reviewed to see if the payroll is limited.

Another aspect of payroll reporting that may cause confusion is wages for time not worked. For example, a company may require that employees work seven hours a day, five days a week. But they are paid for eight hours a day because of a paid lunch hour. The entire amount of wages paid for this idle time must be reported to the carrier.

Rates

There are two basic types of authorized rates. They are *manual rates* and rates developed by carriers that use *advisory loss costs or rates* as the basis. Individual states must approve the authorized rates that are used in their jurisdictions.

In states that authorize only *manual rates*, a set of rates is approved by the state insurance regulatory authority and must be used by each insurance carrier as a starting point. The standard or manual premium for each insured is the same, regardless of which carrier quotes the coverage. However, variations in premium are developed when the insurance company applies credits or debits to the manual premium. Carriers also may offer various types of *financial plans*—such as dividend plans or retrospectively rated programs—that serve to change the ultimate premium. These are explained later in this chapter.

Figure 18.1

2841	**Handle Mfg.** Applies only to the sawing, molding, or turning of backs or handles with no assembling.
2836	**Mfg. NOC.** Includes assembling and sawing, molding, or turning of backs and handles.
4557	**BUFFING OR POLISHING COMPOUNDS MFG.** Effective 01 Jul 2002

BUILDING MATERIAL Effective 01 Jul 2001

Dealer—New Materials Only:

8058 ♦	**Store Employees**
8232 ♦	**All Other Employees & Yard, Warehouse, Drivers**
8204 ♦	**Yard & Local Managers, Drivers.** Applies to a dealer in used, or new and used, building materials. Wrecking or salvage operations to be separately rated.
4283	**BUILDING OR ROOFING PAPER OR FELT PREPARATION—NO INSTALLATION** Effective 01 Jul 2001 Not applicable to asphalt or tar distillation or refining plants that include the saturating of paper or felt as part of their operations. Paper or felt mfg. to be separately rated.
5703 ●	**BUILDING RAISING OR MOVING & DRIVERS** Effective 01 Jul 2001 Includes incidental shoring and removal or rebuilding of walls, foundations, columns, or piers.

BUILDING —OPERATION Effective 01 Jul 2001

9015	**By Contractors.** Includes window cleaning. Painting, maintenance, or repair at any location where such contractor does not also perform janitorial services to be separately rated.
9012	**By Owner, Lessee, or Real Estate Management Firm: Professional Employees, Property Managers and Leasing Agents & Clerical, Salespersons.** The professional employments included are property managers, leasing agents, model home hosts,clerical staff and outside salespersons; no actual maintenance performed. Not applicable to an owner or lessee of a building who occupies the entire or principal portion of the premises for mfg. or mercantile purposes or to a business described by a standardexception classification. Shall not be assigned to an employee engaged in operations described by another classification.
9014	**By Owner, Lessee or Real Estate Management Firm: All Other Employees.** Not applicable to an owner or lessee of a building who occupies the entire or principal portion of the premises for mfg. or mercantile purposes. Maintenance or repair work at any location where such owner or lessee does not also perform janitorial services, operation, or maintenance of amusement devices to be separately rated.
7605 ●	**BURGLAR ALARM INSTALLATION OR REPAIR & DRIVERS** Effective 01 Jul 2001
9522	**BURIAL GARMENT MFG. AND CASKET OR COFFIN UPHOLSTERING** Effective 01 Jul 2001

BUS. CO. Effective 01 Jul 2001

8385	**Garage Employees**
7382	**All Other Employees & Drivers**
2081	**BUTCHERING** Effective 01 Jul 2001 Includes the handling of livestock, preparation of dressed meat, rendering, washing of casings, salting of hides, or cooking of offal. Codes 2081 and 2089—Packing house shall not be assigned to the same risk unless the operations described by these classifications are conducted as separate and distinct businesses.
2070	**BUTTER OR CHEESE MFG. & ROUTE SUPERVISORS, DRIVERS** Effective 01 Jul 2001
4717	**BUTTER SUBSTITUTE MFG.** Effective 01 Jul 2001 Codes 4717 and 2089—Packing house shall not be assigned to the same risk unless the operations described by these classifications are conducted as separate and distinct businesses.
3131	**BUTTON OR FASTENER MFG.—METAL** Effective 01 Jul 2001
4484	**BUTTON MFG. NOC** Effective 01 Jul 2001
2883	**CABINET MFG. FOR AUDIO OR VIDEO DEVICE** Effective 01 Jul 2001 Includes installation of components.

● = Construction Classification   ■ = Farm Classification   ♦ = Mercantile Classification

© 2000 National Council on Compensation Insurance, Inc.

The Workers Compensation System

In other states, regulators approve *individual advisory loss costs* for each workers compensation classification. The advisory loss cost is the portion of the rate that represents expected losses per $100 of payroll for that class. These loss costs are developed based on statistical information that is collected from all employers in the state for each classification. Individual insurance companies then develop final rates by loading their expenses onto the advisory loss rates.

Other Factors

Many other factors may affect premium levels. They include:

- expense constants,
- minimum premium thresholds,
- premium discounts,
- experience modifications,
- employer liability limits of liability, and
- audits.

Most states also authorize the use of an *expense constant*, which is a charge to cover expenses that are common to all workers compensation policies regardless of size. The amount of the expense constant varies by state, but it usually falls within the range of $100-200 per policy. If an insured's policy covers more than one state, only one expense constant is used—the highest from all the applicable states.

There also is a *minimum premium* that is set on a state-by-state basis. It is the lowest premium required to provide coverage under a standard policy.

The next factor to be considered is called the *premium discount*. The relative expense of issuing and servicing a policy that has a large premium is lower than for policies that develop a smaller premium. This is because of an economy of scale; it takes the same amount of time and money to issue a policy regardless of how much premium is charged. The premium discount is a percentage credit that floats with the premium size. In other words, policies with higher premiums are given higher premium discounts than those with lower premiums. The applicable state rating bureaus issue tables that list the ascending premium discount percentages.

There are a number of discount tables, depending upon the type of carrier and policy being issued, which

are available from the NCCI or other independent rating agency. A general range of discounts is from 0 percent to 16.3 percent, depending on the premium size. The appropriate discount percentage is subtracted from the total policy premium.

Policies also may be subject to an *experience modifier*, which is a factor that compares the individual business with its peer group. Businesses that have better loss experience than peers develop a credit experience modifier. Those with poorer loss experience than peers earn a debit experience modifier. Experience rating and experience modifiers are discussed in more detail later in this chapter.

Limits of Coverage

There is no limit of liability listed in Part One of the standard workers compensation policy because it provides statutory benefits that are set by the state in which the coverage applies. However, there is a limit of liability for Part Two, Employers Liability.

The standard employers liability limits are

Bodily injury by accident	$100,000 each accident
Bodily injury by disease	$500,000 policy limit
Bodily injury by disease	$100,000 each employee

Situations that may call for employers liability coverage were introduced previously, under the section entitled **Part Two, Employers Liability,** of this chapter. Some businesses may need higher employers liability limits to satisfy the requirements of a commercial umbrella policy, a lender, or a party with whom they are contracting. Employers liability limits of up to $10,000,000 are available for additional premium.

In Figure 18.2, there are only two classifications: outside salespeople and clerical employees. As shown by the difference in the rates for the two classifications ($1.17 for outside sales versus $.42 for office employees), the exposure for traveling salespeople is greater than for employees who work within the office and are not exposed to the public or auto accidents. This business needs more than the standard employers liability limits of coverage, so there is a 1.9 percent charge for that increase. The company has slightly poorer loss experience than businesses in its peer group, which generates a debit experience modifier of 1.05 percent. The premium discount is taken from tables from the appropriate rating bureau.

Figure 18.2

Sample Premium Calculation

This sample premium calculation illustrates how the various items that affect premium are shown on a policy. This is a fictitious insured, and the rates that are shown are for illustration purposes only.

Extension of Information Page

Item 4

Classification	Code Number	Premium Basis Total Estimated Annual Remuneration	Rate per $100 of Remuneration	Estimated Annual Premium
Salerspersons - Outside	8742	$985,000	1.17	$ 11,525
Clerical Office Employees NOC	8810	$3,100,000	.42	$ 13,020

Increased Limits Part Two 1.9%	$ 466
Total Estimated Standard premium	$ 25,011
Experience Modification 1.05	$ 1,251
Estimated Modified Premium	$ 26,262
Premium Discount	-$ 1,943
Expense Constant	$ 200
Estimated Annual Premium	$ 24,519

The insurance company will audit the $24,519 premium after the policy expires. If remuneration for either class differs or if additional classifications are determined, the business will either be billed for additional premium or receive a return premium check from the insurance company.

Since the amount of remuneration often changes during the policy period, an adequate premium charge is more properly figured at the end of the policy period. In all cases, however, the minimum premium required in the state will be the lowest premium that ultimately is collected.

If the insurance company cancels the policy before it normally would end, the final premium is calculated on a *pro rata* basis This means that the amount of premium will be based on the proportion of time the policy was in force. If the insured cancels the policy, the final premium is based on the time the policy was in force **plus** a cancellation penalty. Note that a final premium figured on the basis of an insured-cancelled policy will be more than one figured on an insurer-cancelled basis because of this penalty, which is called the *short-rate cancellation penalty*.

The short-rate penalty does not apply if the insured retires from all business covered by the policy, sells the business, or completes all work covered by the policy.

Audit

The insured business must keep payroll records and make them available to the insurance companies for audit purposes. When the policy expires, the insurance company may send an auditor to the business to review these records and pick up the actual remuneration amounts. Based on the actual payrolls, the business either is billed for additional premium or sent a return premium. In some cases—especially in the case of smaller businesses—insurance companies may request self-audits from the insured. This is a request that actual payrolls be submitted to the insurer, without an individual being sent to review the physical records.

EXPERIENCE RATING

Experience rating embodies a simple goal within a complex process. It is designed to encourage safe working conditions by providing businesses with a financial incentive to reduce worker injuries. Companies that have safer working conditions and fewer worker injuries are financially rewarded through a lower than average experience modification. Businesses that fail to do so are penalized with a higher than average modification. Experience rating directly affects a company's competitive economic stance.

The Figure 18.2 sample premium calculation illustrates a company with an experience modification of 1.05. This means that the company is paying 5 percent more than average among its peers for workers compensation insurance based on previous loss experience.

Experience rating is mandatory for all eligible insureds. Businesses may not cancel, rewrite, or extend a workers compensation policy in an attempt to avoid experience rating or qualify for or avoid a change in their experience modifications. Eligibility for experience rating is determined by the amount of qualifying premium that an insured generates. Specific information on the qualifying premium is available from the NCCI or other applicable independent rating organizations.

This discussion centers on the NCCI experience rating plan, which provides a framework for understanding the process. It is important, however, to check state regulations for differences.

General Points

There are several general items to consider about experience rating:

- A company's previous loss data is used to adjust future premiums; that is, experience rating is prospective.

- Experience modifications generally are developed on an annual basis and are effective for a period of twelve months.

- Only one experience modification is applied to a risk at any one time. That experience modification applies to all of the company's operations. This is true regardless of whether one or more insurance policies are used to insure them. For example, a dairy operation may own 100 percent of a separate company to haul its milk. For various reasons, the dairy may buy one policy for the general dairy

business and a separate policy to cover the trucking operation. The losses (claims) that are paid by each policy will be compiled and used to generate one experience modification for the entire company. That modifier will be used in developing the premium on each policy.

- A company's past losses are compared to the expected losses for all businesses in its class of operations. For example, the expected losses for a specific manufacturer would be compared with the expected losses for all manufacturers in the state.

- Experience rating can substantially affect the amount of workers compensation premium that a business must pay. It provides a direct correlation between claims history and premium.

The Modifier

Under the NCCI plan, an experience modification factor, which often is referred to as the *experience mod* or *mod*, of less than 1.0 means that the firm will get a credit on its premium. A mod greater than 1.0 means that a debit will apply. A 1.0 mod is referred to as a *unity* modification.

For example, a mod of 1.21 indicates that the company will pay 21 percent more in premium than the average firm in its class because of its poor loss experience. A mod of .85 means that the company will get a 15 percent reduction from the standard because it has generated better-than-average loss experience.

Comparing Modifiers

Company A has an estimated standard premium of $50,000 and a mod of 1.20. It pays an additional $10,000 a year for workers compensation insurance because of poor loss experience. The 1.20 mod generates an annual premium for company A of $60,000.

One of its direct competitors, Company B, has a modifier of .87. Company B, again with a standard premium of $50,000, pays only $43,500 for workers compensation coverage. *Company B's premium is $16,500 less than what Company A has to pay.* A business has to sell a lot of loaves of bread or manufacture hundreds of widgets to make up $16,500 in bottom line costs to its competitor.

A mod is based on three years of the company's loss history. The most current year is omitted from the calculation. To illustrate, assume that a company purchases an experience-rated workers compensation policy with an inception date of January 10, 2003. Also assume that it purchased annual policies for the previous four years on January 10 of each year. The mod that is effective January 10, 2003, is based on the premium and losses for policy years January 10, 2001-2002; January 10, 2000-2001; and January 10, 1999-2000. Experience from the January 10, 2002-2003, policy year does not enter the calculation the January 10, 2004, mod is calculated, at which time the 1999-2000 year drops out of the calculation.

While three years of experience normally is used, up to three and three-fourths years of experience can be used in certain situations. There also are situations in which a newly organized business may apply for experience rating after being in business for only two years.

Anniversary Rating Date

The normal *anniversary rating date* is the effective month and day when experience modification and rate changes take effect. The anniversary rating date usually corresponds to policy inception date. However, it may differ if prior policy years were longer or shorter than twelve months in duration. Experience mods usually are effective for twelve months and cannot be used longer than fifteen months.

An insured cannot cancel an existing workers compensation policy before its normal expiration date in order to take advantage of a decrease in compensation rates or experience modification. Even if the policy were canceled and rewritten midterm, the lower rates and experience modification would not apply to the new policy until the insured's normal anniversary rating date.

Two Cases of Changing an Anniversary Rating Date

Meridian Manufacturers

In this example, Meridian Manufacturers has an experience modification that is effective April 1, 2003. It applies to a policy with an effective date of April 1, 2003 or to any policy with an effective date of up to

July 1, 2003 because of the fifteen-month rule. If Meridian decides to change its policy renewal date from April 1 to July 1, so that it coincides with its fiscal year, the April 1 anniversary rating date is used for the entire fifteen months. At the end of the fifteen months (July 1, 2004), a new experience modification applies and the normal anniversary rating date changes to July 1.

In addition, rates that were in effect for the policy on April 1 will apply until July 1, 2004.

Riverside Steel

In this case, Riverside Steel's experience modification is effective from February 1, 2003-2004. Its normal anniversary rating date is February 1. It wants to change the policy renewal date to July 1 so that premium payments coincide with its fiscal year. To accomplish this, Riverside cancels it February policy on July 1, 2003, and has its carrier rewrite the coverage for a term of July 1, 2003-2004. The February 1, 2003, modification applies until February 1, 2004. A new modification applies from February 1, 2004 until July 1, 2004. The new normal anniversary rating date begins July 1, 2004, when another new modification and rates also apply. In this case, the short-rate cancellation charge would not apply because the insured is staying with the same insurance company and is canceling the policy merely to change its normal anniversary rating date.

However, Riverside cannot take advantage of a lower experience mod or lower state-approved rates until July 1, 2004.

Why is this important? Credit and debit modifications can greatly affect the amount of workers compensation premium that a business has to pay. The experience rating procedure is designed so that a company cannot unfairly escape poor loss experience. It promotes safe workplaces by offering a financial incentive to companies that prevent worker injuries.

The Mod Formula

It is beyond the scope of this book to go into detail on the actual mod calculation. So only a basic overview is presented based on the NCCI calculation formula. Most states follow it or similar formulas.

Formula					
Actual Primary Losses +	Ballast Value +	Weighting Value Times Actual Excess Losses +	(1-Weighting Value) Times Expected Excess Losses =	Total A
Expected Primary Losses +	Ballast Value +	Weighting Value Times Expected Excess Losses +	(1-Weighting Value) Times Expected Excess Losses =	Total B

Total A, which represents the specific company being rated, is divided by Total B, which represents expected experience for the class. The mod is rounded to two places.

Unit Statistical Plan

How is information about individual businesses gathered? The mod calculation starts with the filing of *unit statistical reports*, sometimes called *unit stat reports*, by carriers on each of the businesses they write that are subject to experience rating. The reports relay premium and loss information to the appropriate rating bureau. Details are contained in the NCCI statistical plan manual, but general familiarity with how the reporting works is important for risk managers and agents because of timing issues.

The unit stat report presents a snapshot of premium and loss information at eighteen months after policy expiration and at annual intervals thereafter until three reports have been filed. Claim values on these dates are used in the mod calculation. It therefore is important to review claims *prior to the report dates* to determine whether claim reserves can be reduced and to determine other management procedures that might reduce the financial value of claims. Additional information on managing claims is contained in Chapter 13, Claims Management.

For example, a worker may hurt his back and leg at work. In the first few months of the injury, the insurance company pays medical bills of $20,000, pays lost-time wages of $8,500, sets medical reserves at $45,000, and sets lost-time reserves at $52,000. The carrier believes the employee will be off work for at least a year. However, initial treatment is successful, and he returns to work much earlier than expected. It is important for the reserved amounts to be reduced to reflect this earlier-than-anticipated return to work *before* the unit statistical report is filed. More information on claims management is contained in Chapters 13 and 14.

Making the Calculation

Upon receiving the statistical data about a risk, the NCCI calculates and issues the modification, which is effective on the normal anniversary rating date as outlined previously in this chapter. The mod is issued based on the rating bureau formula outlined previously. Risk managers should review the experience modification worksheet to be sure that the information used matches its data.

As explained previously, the modifier will increase the policy premium if it is a debit mod and decrease the policy premium if it is a credit mod. Once the modified premium is calculated, it is adjusted for credits, assigned risk surcharges, premium discounts, and expense concepts, as illustrated in Figure 18.2.

Recalculation and Revisions

A classification of a business may be revised as the result of a change in risk operations. The experience modification is recalculated when this happens, with past payrolls reassigned to the revised classification. This could result in either a higher or lower mod, depending on the premium rate of the new classification.

Sometimes a company's loss history is revised after the mod is calculated. When this happens, the mod also may be revised—but only in very limited types of situations. Changes in an experience modifier may be requested if:

1. there is a clerical error in the original unit statistical plan card;
2. there is an uncontested recovery from a third party;
3. a claim turns out not to be compensable, or
4. there is a recovery from a special fund, such as a second injury fund.

Modifications cannot be retroactively changed simply because reserves were set too high when they were initially calculated.

When a recalculation results in a lower modification, the change is made retroactively to the policy inception date or anniversary rating date. The application of a higher recalculated modification varies depending on how long a policy has been in effect or the length of time since the anniversary rating date. However, a higher recalculated mod is applied retroactively to the inception date if the recalculation is caused by:

- the employer failing to comply with audits or because of other faults caused by an agent or employer;

- retroactive reclassification of a risk; or

- change in ownership.

One Risk or Two?

Company mergers and acquisitions present special situations for experience rating. After a merger, the acquired business's historical loss experience usually is transferred to the acquiring owner and excluded from the experience of the prior owner.

Merger Example

For example, Riverside Steel purchases Meridian Manufacturers, a five-year-old company that has a modification of 1.28 because of poor claims experience. Riverside has had better than average loss experience and is benefiting from a modification of .85. Meridian's experience is reassigned to Riverside. The combination of Riverside's good experience and Meridian's poor experience results in a new modification of 1.08. The revised modification must be applied to all of Riverside's operations, even though the types of operations differ from one another.

What if Riverside doesn't want to be penalized for Meridian's poor losses? Can Meridian be kept as a separate operation to avoid a combined modification?

The NCCI experience rating plan, as well as those of other jurisdictions, in most instances requires that only one modification be used for all operations of a risk. A risk is defined as either a single entity or two or more entities that qualify for combination under the plan. Two or more entities are to be combined if:

1. the same person, group of persons, or corporation owns more than 50 percent of each entity; or

2. an entity owns a majority interest in another entity, which in turn owns a major interest in a third entity. In this case, all the entities are combined regardless of how many there are.

Therefore, if Riverside's owners, or the corporation itself, own more than 50 percent of Meridian, only one modification is used. Changes of ownership also may result from:

- sale or transfer of all or a portion or an entity's ownership interests;

- sale or transfer of an entity's physical assets to another firm that takes over the business;

- formation of a new entity after an existing entity is dissolved; or

- voluntary or court-mandated establishment of a trustee or receiver.

In these cases, the experience of the prior business usually transfers to the surviving or new business. However, the prior business's loss experience may not be transferred to the new owner if 1) there is a completely new owner, 2) there is a change in operation that results in a reclassification of the governing code, or 3) the material change in ownership includes a change in the process and hazard of the operation.

When ownership changes, the insurer reports the details of the change to the appropriate rating organization. The information may be submitted in narrative form on the insured's letterhead and signed by an officer of the company. Or, the information may be reported by using a form entitled the Confidential Request for Information (ERM-14). Often carriers request a completed ERM-14 form from insureds when there is a question of whether entities should be combined for experience purposes. A copy of this form is reproduced as Figure 18.3.

SCHEDULE RATING

Schedule rating may be used in addition to experience rating. The NCCI or other appropriate rating bureaus administer the schedule rating plans. This discussion focuses on the NCCI model.

Figure 18.3

INSTRUCTIONS FOR COMPLETING AN ERM-14 FORM

I. PURPOSE AND EFFECTIVE DATE OF CHANGE

    A.   COMBINATION OF SEPARATE ENTITIES

        1. Two or more entities sharing common ownership (more than 50% common ownership in each entity).

        2. Entities may be combined for experience rating if two or more entities wish to be written on one policy.

      Note: Include the date interest was acquired in each entity.

    B.   CHANGE OF OWNERSHIP- Necessary if there has been a change in the name of the entity, governing board or ownership.

      Note: Include the date the change occurred.

    C.   MERGER OR CONSOLIDATION

        1. Merger - When two or more entities are merged into one surviving entity.

        2. Consolidation - When two or more entities are combined into an entirely new entity.

      Note: Include the date the merger or consolidation occurred.

II. INFORMATION

    A.   NAME AND LOCATION OF ENTITY- Furnish both name and location of each entity before and after the change occurred.

    B.   POLICY NUMBER - List the carrier, policy number and effective date if available.

    C.   RATING ID NO. - List the rating ID number (Bureau file number) if available.

    D.   LEGAL STATUS - List the type of entity for each column.

III. OWNERSHIP INFORMATION

    A.   When listing ownership for each entity, remember:

        1. List all names of owners and their individual ownership (each spouseís individual ownership must be listed).

        2. If it is a partnership, list all general partnersí names and their percentage of ownership.

        3. If it is a corporation, list owners and their percentages of 5% or more voting stock.

        4. If an entity is other than a sole proprietor, partnership or corporation, list the governing board of each entity.

        5. List the total shares of stock issued at the bottom of each column.

    B.   COMBINATION - Enter each entity to be combined in each of the columns. List complete ownership for all entities. Include the date ownership was acquired for each entity. Use as many columns or additional sheets as necessary. Complete back of form regarding employee retention.

    C.   CHANGE OF NAME/OWNERSHIP - In Column A list the name of the entity ownership before the change. In Column B list the name of the entity and ownership after the change. Complete back of form regarding employee retention.

    D.   MERGER/CONSOLIDATION - In Columns A and B enter the names of the entities and the ownership of each entity involved. In Column C, list the name and ownership of the remaining entity. Complete back of form regarding employee retention.

IV. SIGNATURE

    The signature of the sole proprietor, partner or executive officer must be included on the form. Please state title.

Figure 18.3 (cont'd)

The following confidential ownership statements may be used only in establishing premiums for your insurance coverages. It is extremely important that all questions be answered completely. Your workers compensation policy requires that you report ownership changes, and other changes as detailed below, to your insurance carrier in writing within 90 days of the change. If you have questions, contact your agent, insurance company, or the appropriate rating organization. Submit the completed form to the rating organization.

PURPOSE (Check One)

_____ **Name change only**
    Complete column A for former entity and column B for newly named entity
    Complete only questions 1, 2 and 3 on page 2
_____ **Combination of separate entities**
    Complete a separate column for each entity related through common ownership (attach additional forms if necessary)
_____ **Sale, Transfer or conveyance of ownership interest**
    Complete column A for ownership before the change and column B for ownership after the change
_____ **Merger or consolidation (attach copy of agreement)**
    Complete columns A and B for the former entities and column C for the surviving entity
_____ **Formation of a new entity**
    Complete column A
_____ **Sale, Transfer or conveyance of an entityís physical assets to another entity which takes over its operations**
    Complete column A for the former entity and column B for the acquiring entity
_____ **Voluntary or court-mandated establishment of a trustee or receiver, excluding a debtor in possession, a trustee under a revocable trust or a franchisor**
    Complete column A for ownership prior to the change, and column B for the trustee or receiver established

INFORMATION **A**		**B**	**C**
Name and Street Address of Entity (P.O. Box Numbers are not acceptable)			
Legal Status of Entity (Corporation, Partnership, Sole Proprietor, Trustee, Receiver, Individual, Other)			
Ownership **Corporations** - List names of owners of 5% or more of voting stock and number of shares owned.* (Submit shareholder proposal if transaction involved exchange of stock.) **Partnerships** - List each general partner and appropriate share in the profits. (If limited partnership, list name of general partner.) **Other** - If no voting stock, list members of board of directors or comparable governing body.			
* Total shares of voting stock issued.			
Date of Ownership Change, Acquisition, or Combinability			
Carrier, Policy Number and Effective Date			
Experience Rating Identification Number (Carrier Use only)			

ERM-14 (Rev. 7/91)
© 1992 National Council on Compenation Insurance

NC790 (TA00121)

Figure 18.3 (cont'd)

CONFIDENTIAL REQUEST FOR INFORMATION   Page 2 of 2

1.   Has this entity operated under another name in the last four years? _____

2.   Is the entity **currently** related through common majority ownership to any entity not listed on the front of the form? _____

3.   Has the entity been **previously** related through common majority ownership to any other entities in the last four years? _____

If you answered yes to 1, 2, or 3 above, please provide the following information:

Name of Business	Principal Location	Carrier and Policy Number	Effective Date

4.   Were the assets and/or ownership interest (all or a portion) of this entity acquired from a previously existing business?_____
If yes, you must provide complete ownership information on the prior owner in Column A and ownership information on the new owner in Column B on the reverse side of this form.

5.   If this is a partial sale, transfer, or conveyance of an existing business (i.e., sale of one or more plants or locations):

a.   Explain what portion or location of the entire operation was sold, transferred, or conveyed. _____
_____

b.   Was this entity insured under a separate policy from the remaining portion? _____ If not, specify the entities with
which it was combined: _____
_____

6.   If this entity has operations in Delaware or Pennsylvania, provide the number of employees from each of these states retained from
the prior ownership _____ out of _____. Indicate the percentage or number retained out of the total from each of these states _____ %
_____state.

NOTE: If your business has changed significantly to result in a change to the primary (governing) classification and the process and hazard
of the operation have also changed, contact your agent, insurance company or rating organization for additional information.

This is to certify that the information contained on this form is complete and correct.

Name of Insured: _____

Name of person completing form: _____

Date this ownership change was reported in writing to your insurance carrier: _____

Signature of Owner, Partner or Executive Officer	Title	Carrier
Print name of above signature	Date	Carrier Address

ERM-14 (Rev. 7/91)
© 1992 National Council on Compenation Insurance   NC790 (TA00121)

Schedule rating credits or debits are applied after the experience modification. The maximum credit or debit is 25 percent. The goal of schedule rating is to reflect characteristics of a particular company that are not reflected in experience rating.

Schedule credits or debits are assigned for reasons such as:

- drug free workplaces;

- management cooperation;

- safety devices and equipment;

- safe work environments;

- active employee safety committees;

- on-premises emergency medical facilities or personnel;

- selection, training, experience, controls motivation, and supervision of employees;

- classification peculiarities caused by technology, employee distribution, or assignment.

Schedule credits and debits that are applied to an account must be backed up by evidence contained in the insurance company's file on the account. For example, some state rating bureaus may permit a 5 or 10 percent premium credit for an approved safety committee that is operated within and by the insured business. The business will submit evidence that an active safety committee is in place, and the credit may be approved. Conversely, a debit may be applied if the insurer believes appropriate safety activity is not in place. If an insured corrects a situation that led to a debit to the insurer's satisfaction, it may be removed effective with the date that correction documentation was received by the insurer.

Thus, in addition to the effect of an experience modification, an insured's workers compensation premium may be subject to a 25 percent increase or decrease based on schedule credits.

Why Is This Important?

Even though rates start out as either fixed manual rates or established loss costs, businesses can directly control their premiums by preventing and managing claims to earn a lower experience mod. In addition, they can institute safety and employee training programs that enable them to qualify for schedule rating, another source of potentially lower premiums.

The opposite also is true. Both experience and schedule rating penalize businesses that fail to institute programs to prevent and manage claims. These businesses are forced to pay higher premiums for coverage that is mandated by law.

PART TWO

FINANCIAL PLANS

Up to this point we have discussed how workers compensation policies are set up and how rates and premiums are developed. In addition to the initial rates and premiums, many workers compensation programs have what are called *front* and *back ends*. The front end is the cost at the start of the policy term, which is what has been discussed so far. The back end is the way in which claims affect the ultimate cost. Both the front and back ends must be considered when choosing a financial plan.

The initial premium was discussed previously. It is the starting point in determining the cost of a workers compensation policy. The standard premium is amended by application of the experience modification factor, which results in what is called the modified standard premium. The estimated modified standard premium may be paid in a lump sum (annual premium) or in installments over the term of the policy.

Some workers compensation programs start and end with the modified standard premium. In these, there is no back end. The insured merely pays the premium, the policy is issued, claims are turned into the insurance company, and no more money changes hands unless audited payrolls differ from the estimated payrolls used at policy inception. The entire risk of the workers compensation exposure is transferred to the insurance company. Such programs are called fully insured or *guaranteed cost* plans. Only a change in payrolls or a revision in the experience modifier can generate a change in premium.

The far extreme from guaranteed cost workers compensation is *self-insurance*. With self-insurance, the standard premium also is the starting point. The insured self-finances the workers compensation exposure instead of buying a policy. In other words, the insured takes on the entire risk of worker injuries. Some insureds that become qualified self-insurers cap their exposure through the use of *excess loss* or *stop loss* insurance. Excess or stop loss insurance limits the dollar value of claims for which the self-insured business is responsible. The insurance company that provides the excess coverage pays costs above the excess or stop loss point. However, for practical purposes, the exposure remains with the client. Most states require that businesses either purchase a workers compensation insurance policy or become qualified self-insurers. They cannot simply choose to operate without insurance.

Another way to view this is to look at *fixed costs* versus *variable costs*. Fixed costs are those costs that do not change unless the payroll changes. Under a guaranteed cost program, the entire premium is fixed; there is no variable cost. The insured pays the premium and does not risk having to pay more if claims are worse than expected. Conversely, the insured does not have the opportunity to receive a premium return from the insurance company if claims are better than expected.

In a self-insured program, the fixed costs are much lower than in a guaranteed cost program. The bulk of the costs are variable. Variable costs are comprised mainly of the cost of claims—both for adjusting and paying them. The ultimate cost of a self-insured program can be much different than predicted at inception because of the impact of claims.

Types of Financial Plans Available

Market conditions, account size, and account claims history affect the type of financial plans available. When the market is soft and insurance is readily available from a number of insurance companies, a greater variety of financial plans are offered. When the market hardens, however, fewer options are offered and an individual company's loss history may have a greater impact on the type of financial plan available. In addition, smaller companies may not be eligible for certain types of financial plans.

Between the two extremes of guaranteed cost and self-insurance are a number of other methods of financing the workers compensation exposure. They can be examined in terms of:

- amount of insurance purchased;

- cash flow arrangements;

- amount of fixed costs;

- amount of risk transferred to insurance company; and

- amount of collateral required.

The types of financial plans that we will discuss are:

- guaranteed cost,

- standard dividend,

- sliding scale dividend,

- incurred loss retrospective rating,

- paid loss retrospective rating, and

- deductibles.

Self-insurance and captive plans will not be discussed because they are individually designed and beyond the scope of this chapter. The appendix to this chapter provides an Option Evaluation Form, which highlights the major differences among the various types of financial plans.

Choosing a Plan

Many workers compensation experts use premium size guidelines when deciding what type of financial plan a business should seek. Very small businesses with workers compensation premiums of $25,000 or less may not be offered any choice other than a guaranteed cost or dividend plan. Since there is no downside to a dividend plan for the insured, it is attractive to small businesses. Adverse market conditions may cause insurers to refrain from offering dividend plans to all but the best accounts, however, so businesses may be forced to purchase a guaranteed cost program.

As businesses grow in size and sophistication, the types of financial plans they are offered also become more complex. There is a trade-off between risk and cash flow between the various types of plans.

The progression of risk across the various types of plans is shown in Figure 18.4. This chart shows various factors on a scale to illustrate the amount of insurance, cash flow, fixed costs, risk, and collateral requirements. Guaranteed cost programs generally include the most insurance and least risk. Cash flow management is low or nonexistent. Self-insurance features the least insurance, best cash flow management, and lowest fixed costs. In exchange for these pluses, a self-insured company takes on the most risk and highest collateral requirement. Of course, the fixed cost structures of each program vary depending upon market conditions.

In addition to risk, the qualitative and quantitative aspects of a program should be studied when choosing a plan. The quantitative aspects are the actual dollars that are expected to be needed to resolve worker injuries. Qualitatively, a company may desire a specific financial program because it provides a greater opportunity for the company to influence loss control and claim adjusting. An insurer usually is more likely to coordinate these activities with the insured that is retaining more risk.

The way in which worker injuries are managed can greatly impact both current and future workers compensation costs. Information on managing claims is included in chapters 13, 14, and 28.

Guaranteed Cost Plans

A workers compensation policy with a fixed or guaranteed cost premium is the most conservative and the easiest to understand. Such programs are stable in regard to cost. A company that chooses a guaranteed cost plan knows what worker injuries will cost at policy inception because the policy premium *is* the cost. The premium varies only as a factor of payroll and experience modifier, if applicable. It does not vary directly as the result of loss experience and cannot be increased if claims are serious.

The guaranteed cost premium is the manual, or standard, premium. If an account qualifies for an experience modifier, it is applied to the standard premium. Figure 18.2 shows the premium for a guaranteed cost program. Even though it is the easiest to understand, it may not be the most desirable—or even available in the marketplace. In periods when insurance companies have lost money writing workers compensation, many of them will not offer guaranteed cost programs. These insurers will only offer programs in which the insured business shares in the risk of claims.

Dividend Plans

These plans are designed so that an insured may receive a *dividend* if worker injuries are less expensive than anticipated. They are designed to reward

Figure 18.4

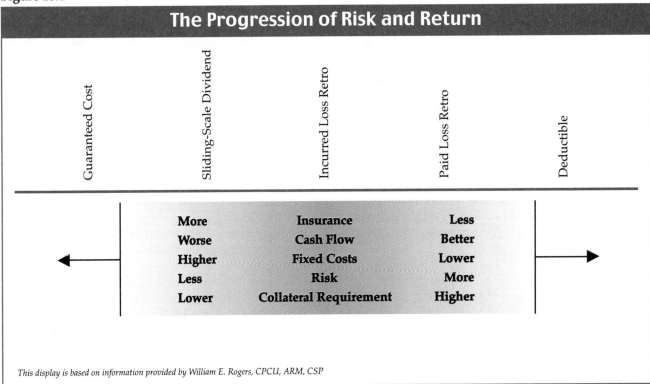

This display is based on information provided by William E. Rogers, CPCU, ARM, CSP

companies that do a good job in preventing and managing worker injury. The dividend may be based on the loss experience of a particular group to which the insured belongs or of the individual insured. In group dividend plans, the claims experience of the entire group is compiled. If the insurer has made a profit on the group, a dividend may be paid. In like fashion, individual dividends are determined based on the amount of losses an individual company, which has been written by a particular insurance company, incurs.

Dividends are never guaranteed. They are payable only upon declaration of the insurer's board of directors. The details on how and when the dividend is due should be provided before policy inception. In addition, policies with back-end dividend plans are subject to experience rating.

Standard Dividend Plans

A *standard* or *flat dividend*, if declared, is paid a year or more after a policy expires. They are most often used with affinity or group workers compensation programs. Affinity programs are designed around a type of business. For example, a trade group of manufacturers, grocery stores, schools, or other business type may develop a workers compensation group program that is open to association members. Since the group represents a large amount of premium, insurers may be willing to offer a dividend plan to the members. Even though an insured receives the benefit of a possible dividend, the insured normally will not have to pay additional premium—aside from additional premium that may be developed in the payroll audit.

Dividend plans work because insureds are rewarded when the insurance company makes an underwriting profit on a homogeneous group of accounts. Since the insured does not risk having to pay more premium in the event of bad losses, the potential return is lower than in riskier plans. There is a trade-off between risk and potential benefit, again, as shown in Figure 18.4.

Group Dividend Example

For example, an association of manufacturers applies for coverage from one carrier. Individual group members are reviewed and underwritten

separately, and the amount of premium for each is examined in total to provide the insurer with an incentive to write the coverage. Individual workers compensation policies are issued to each group member, and each pays its own premium. After the policies expire, the claims experience of all members is combined to determine whether an underwriting profit was made. If so, the insurer may declare a dividend. However, if claims costs are higher than a predetermined threshold, a dividend is not possible.

Group or affinity programs often are used when coverage is hard to obtain, especially when the workers compensation premium of individual group members is relatively low. An insurance company may not be interested in taking the risk of insuring a small retail store, which generates only $8,500 of premium but has the potential of thousands of dollars of losses. However, if a number of small companies solicit coverage as a group, the combined premium often is large enough to interest several insurers. A group of fifty retailers, each with $8,500 or premium, adds up to a total premium of $425,000—a number that could be much more attractive to one or even several insurance companies.

There are times when insurance companies will offer a group dividend to the entire group, which is computed based on the experience of the group as a whole, as well as individual dividends to members, which are computed on the experience of the member. In these types of programs, a group member is eligible to receive two dividends.

Sliding Scale Dividends

The next type of dividend plan is tied directly to the underwriting results of individual insured businesses. Instead of relying on group experience, an individual company stands on its own claims experience for purposes of dividend calculation. These are called *sliding scale dividend plans*. They start with the expectations of a particular *loss ratio*. A loss ratio is the ratio of a business's incurred losses to its insurance premium over the same period of time. When offering a sliding scale dividend plan, the insurance company calculates what loss ratio would generate a profitable piece of business. Insured businesses that develop a lower loss ratio may be rewarded with a dividend. Those who develop a higher than expected loss ratio lose the dividend opportunity.

Sliding Scale Dividend Example

For example, a plan might assume that the incurred loss ratio for a manufacturer will be 60 percent. The incurred loss ratio is determined by dividing incurred losses by the earned premium. If the loss ratio is less than 60 percent, a dividend may be declared. If the loss ratio is higher than 60 percent, the insured is not responsible to pay more premium. The insurance company has to absorb the excess losses. However, the company forfeits the dividend. This type of plan provides a financial incentive to prevent worker injuries and to manage the claims that do occur.

In a one-year sliding scale dividend plan, losses are valued as of a predetermined date, such as at twelve or eighteen months after policy expiration. If the loss ratio is less than a predetermined threshold, a dividend may be paid. The amount of the dividend *slides* with the loss ratio, subject to a maximum possible dividend. For example, a sliding scale plan could be written so that the insured gets 75 percent of the savings if the account's loss ratio is less than the expected 60 percent but greater than or equal to 35 percent. If the loss ratio is less than 35 percent, it is treated as if the loss ratio were 35 percent.

Situation #1: In the first example, ABC Company has $100,000 of losses, which translates into a 50 percent loss ratio ($100,000 of incurred losses divided by $200,000 premium). With $100,000 of losses, ABC earns a dividend of $15,000, which is 75 percent times the difference between the expected loss ratio of 60 percent ($120,000 in losses) and the actual loss ratio of 50 percent ($100,000 in losses), times the premium.

The formula is 75 percent x (60 percent - 50 percent) x $200,000, which equals a dividend of $15,000.

Situation #2: In the second example, ABC has $125,000 in losses or more than a 60 percent loss ratio. Since the loss ratio is more than 60 percent, no dividend is earned.

Sliding Scale Dividend Plan for ABC Company

The formula for this plan would be
    Dividend   =   .75 x (.60 - actual loss ratio) x Premium

The actual loss ratio used can be no lower than 35 percent.

Consider three cases. All three are based on the following assumptions:

1. A one-year sliding scale dividend plan is used.
2. The audited premium is $200,000.
3. The expected loss ratio is 60 percent (the insurer expects $120,000 in losses).
4. The dividend is based on 75 percent of the savings subject to a minimum usable loss ratio of 35 percent.

Estimated Dividend Display
Audited Premium of $100,000

Loss Ratio	Losses	Dividend	Net Premium
60%	$120,000	$ 0	$200,000
55%	$110,000	$ 7,500	$192,500
50%	$100,000	$15,000	$185,000
45%	$ 90,000	$22,500	$177,500
40%	$ 80,000	$30,000	$170,000
35%	$ 70,000	$37,500	$162,500
Less than 35%	Less than $70,000	$37,500	$162,500

As shown, the maximum dividend possible with a $200,000 premium is $37,500.

Situation #3: In the third example, ABC has $60,000 in losses, which is a 30 percent loss ratio. The formula for ABC's dividend would be

Dividend = 75 percent x

(60 percent - 30 percent) x $200,000

Dividend = $45,000

However, since the lowest loss ratio that can be used in this plan is 35 percent, ABC only receives a dividend of $37,500. The 35 percent loss ratio must be used in place of the actual 30 percent earned, for a calculation as follows:

Dividend = 75 percent x

(60 percent - 35 percent) x $200,000

Dividend = $37,500

Sliding scale plans are not often available to insureds with poor or fluctuating loss histories because there is only an opportunity to gain and no risk of paying additional premium. Keep Figure 18.4 in mind. A sliding scale dividend plan is to the right of a guaranteed cost plan because the insured is beginning to take on financial responsibility for preventing and managing its own claims.

Retrospective Rating Plans

Retrospective rating encompasses plans in which the insured business pays a policy premium to the insurance company. After the policy expires, the insured is billed additional premium if losses are higher than originally expected. The insured receives a return premium if losses are less than originally expected.

Retrospective rating rewards companies that have below average losses and penalizes those with above average losses. The premium for expired policies is adjusted as claims develop and mature. Workers compensation claims often have *long tails*, which means that it often takes a long time for them to be completely settled. An accident may occur during the policy term and remain open for several years—until the worker is completely healed and back to work or she is placed in some type of permanent disability program.

There are two basic types of retro plans:

- incurred loss retrospective rating plans
- paid loss retrospective rating plans

There are any number of hybrid or combination plans. However, only these two types will be discussed in this chapter. The information on incurred loss retro rating is based on the NCCI retro rating system. States that do not belong to the NCCI issue their own retro regulations. In addition, the discussion will focus on the NCCI one-year incurred loss retro plan, even though other types of plans, notably three-year and multiple lines plans, also are available.

Another name for a retrospectively rated insurance plan is a *retro plan.*

A retro plan utilizes a simple concept. When considering this type of plan, remember that there are two types of costs in workers compensation insurance. They are:

- fixed costs, and
- variable costs.

Fixed costs are the portion of the premium that is needed to issue the policy and operate the program. They include items such as insurance charges, underwriting costs, and agent commissions. Variable costs are the costs that fluctuate based on the number and severity of claims. They include items such as claim adjusting, benefit payments, settlement, and legal costs.

Under a retro plan, insureds pay premiums during the policy term. The premium is used to issue the policy and operate the program, as well as to pay for claims adjusting and benefits. Starting at six months after policy expiration, claims are reviewed. If the program operating (fixed) costs and claims (variable) costs are lower than the amount paid in, the insured receives a retrospective return premium. If they are higher than the amount paid in, the insured is billed a retrospective additional premium. Retro plans are evaluated six months after the end of the policy period (eighteen months from inception) and in twelve-month intervals thereafter. For an annual policy, the evaluation dates would be eighteen, thirty, forty-two, fifty-four months, etc., after policy inception.

Terminology Refresher

Incurred losses include the value of claim payments plus reserves.

Paid losses represent the amounts that already have been paid on claims.

Reserves or **reserved losses** represent the value of losses that have been estimated and set up for future payment.

In an incurred loss plan, both paid and reserved losses are included when the retro premium is calculated. Because of this, the insured is ultimately responsible for its own claims. Insureds may seek an incurred loss plan because it offers an opportunity to lower the ultimate premium substantially when claim costs are controlled.

Conversely, insurers may be willing to offer only a retro plan to insureds with poor claims experience for the same reason: the insured ultimately is charged for its losses. The possible gain of a lower premium is balanced against the risk that claims will be bad.

Companies qualify for a one-year retrospective rating plan if their estimated modified standard premium is at least $25,000. This estimated standard premium may include workers compensation and other casualty insurance lines. However, when a combined lines retro is used, the Insurance Services Office (ISO) retrospective rating plan should be consulted.

Even though a minimum $25,000 of modified standard premium is the NCCI threshold, many companies require a higher premium.

Retrospective Rating Formula

The retrospective rating premium formula is as follows:

Retrospective Premium = [(Basic Factor x Standard Premium) + (Losses x Loss Conversion Factor)] x Tax Multiplier

The retro premium is limited by minimum and maximum premiums.

The *basic factor (BF)* is the percentage standard premium that is needed to issue the policy and operate the program. It includes insurer underwriting expenses; producer commission, if applicable; insurance charges; and profit. The basic factor usually ranges from .15 to .35, depending upon the size of the risk, the amount of insurance being provided, and other factors in the plan. The basic factor multiplied by the standard premium develops the *basic premium*.

The *loss conversion factor (LCF)* is a percentage that represents the cost to adjust claims. Adjusting claims is the process through which claims are reviewed, managed, defended, and/or settled. The LCF usually ranges from .08 to .15 of losses. At times, adjusting costs are represented by a dollar figure per type of claim instead of a percentage. For purposes of this discussion, a percentage LCF is used. The LCF is added to the total value of claims, which then are referred to as *converted losses*. The LCF reflects general claims adjusting costs. Unusual adjusting costs—such as special surveillance and expert witness testimony—may be allocated to specific claims. These are called *allocated loss adjusting expenses (ALAE)*. ALAE are added to the converted losses, but they are not subject to the LCF.

The *tax multiplier (TM)* is the average of the taxes, fees, and assessments that apply to the account. In general, tax multipliers fall in the range of 1.04 to 1.06.

Retrospective premiums are limited by *minimum* and *maximum* premiums. The retro premium can never fall below the minimum premium, regardless of how good the loss experience is. This is because the insurance company must be able to recover its program costs. The maximum premium ensures that the risk is not subject to unlimited losses. The insured may also buy coverage that limits the amount of each individual loss that goes into the retro formula. For example, a business may decide that it wants to cap the amount of individual claim payments that are included in the retro calculation to $100,000. In that case, the business will have to pay a charge for this added protection. This is called purchasing a *loss limitation* or *loss limit*. It is discussed in more detail later in this chapter, under the heading of *Excess Loss Premium*.

Retro plans are not eligible for insurer premium discounts, which were discussed previously in the section on *Premium Calculation*. This is because premium discounts are used to lower the expense portion of the guaranteed cost premium. Since retro plan operating expenses are covered by the basic premium, operating costs are, in theory, already minimized.

The basic and loss conversion factors, as well as the minimum and maximum premiums, are set through negotiation between the insured and insurer. Therefore, there can be major differences in the final amount of the retro premium among insurance companies. It is important to monitor the financial implications of a retro plan through the entire time it remains open.

Excess Loss Premium

If the standard premium that is subject to retro rating is at least $100,000, insureds may elect to purchase *excess loss coverage*. Excess loss coverage limits the amount of incurred loss arising from one accident that will be included in the retro premium calculation. Excess loss coverage also is referred to as buying a *loss limit* or *loss limitation*.

For example, a retro plan may incorporate only the first $100,000 in cost of each worker accident in the claims portion of the retro formula. This type of plan caps losses at $100,000 per accident. Only the first $100,000 of incurred loss from each accident is used in the retro premium formula.

How a Retro Works

The following illustrates the way in which a retro works by discussing four policies, all of which are written on one-year retrospective plans. Each of the policies has:

- modified standard premium of $100,000;

- maximum premium of $140,000; and

- minimum premium of $70,000.

Figure 18.5 illustrates how the first adjustment of each policy, made at six months after expiration, generates different results for each policy.

Figure 18.5

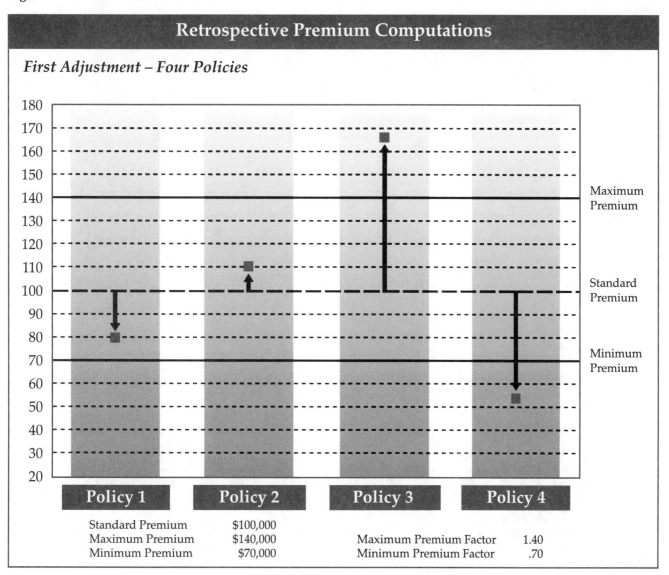

In these policies, the entire modified standard premium of $100,000 was paid to the insurance company during the policy term. Thus, retro adjustments were made on the basis of a premium pay-in of $100,000.

As discussed previously, workers compensation claims often take a significant amount of time to mature and develop to maximum potential. Over a period of years a claim may increase or decrease in value as the worker undergoes continuing treatment or goes back to work. Consequently, the losses that are used in annual retro calculations may differ significantly from those used at the first adjustment.

As shown in Figure 18.5, the first adjustment for Policy 1 resulted in a retro premium of $80,000. There-

fore, $20,000 was returned to the insured. The first adjustment for Policy 2 produced a retro premium of $110,000, so the insured was billed $10,000 additional premium. Policy 3 generated a premium of $166,000 at the first adjustment because of several large claims. Since the program includes a maximum premium of $140,000, the insured was billed only $40,000. Policy 4 would generate a return premium of $45,000 if there were no minimum premium. Lower than expected claims produced a retrospectively adjusted premium of only $55,000. The insured only received a return premium of $30,000 because $70,000 is the minimum premium.

However, the premium for each of these policies continues to be adjusted annually based in the development of losses. To illustrate this refer to Figure

Figure 18.6

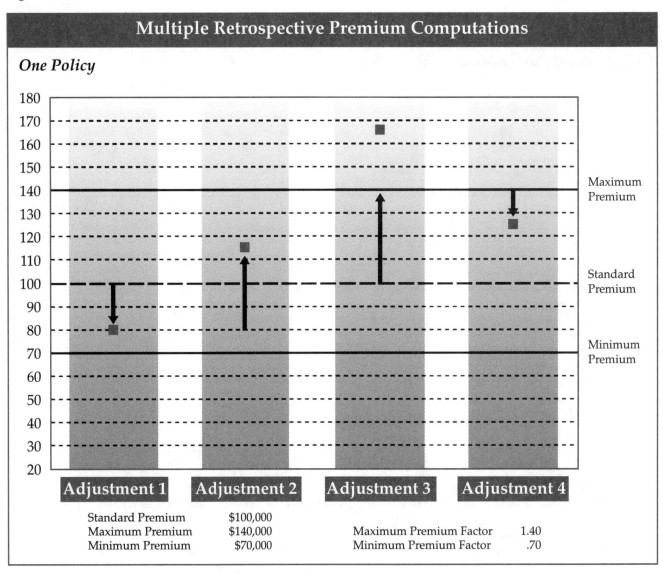

370

18.6, which charts the first four retro adjustments on Policy 1, which are issued at intervals of eighteen, thirty, forty-two, and fifty-four months after policy inception.

Policy 1 generated a $20,000 return premium at the first adjustment. At the end of thirty months (second adjustment), the retro premium was recalculated at $115,000 because several injured employees did not respond to treatment as originally anticipated, and their claim costs increased. The insured is not only required to pay the difference between the standard premium ($100,000) and the retro premium ($115,000), but it also must *repay* the $20,000 return it received at the first adjustment. Thus, the premium billing at thirty months is for $35,000. At the end of forty-two months, claims continue to deteriorate, and the retro premium increases to $165,000. The insured is billed $25,000 (the difference between $140,000 and the $115,000 paid in previously) because the $165,000 exceeds the maximum $140,000 premium. The fourth computation produces a retro premium of $125,000, because several claims were finally resolved at costs lower than anticipated. The insured therefore is returned $15,000 ($125,000 less $140,000 paid to date).

These adjustments continue until all claims are closed or the insured and insurer mutually agree to close the plan. It is not unusual for retro programs to remain open for five or more years, especially in long-term exposures such as workers compensation.

Audit versus Retro Calculation

The terms *premium audit* and *premium calculation and adjustment* often are confused, but they are decidedly different calculations. The premium audit always precedes the retro premium computation and adjustment.

For example, assume that a workers compensation risk is being retrospectively rated. The rate is applied to each $100 of payroll. The standard premium is equal to payroll divided by 100, multiplied by the manual rate and experience modification factor. The initial premium is merely an estimate, but it is the amount paid to the insurance company as premium either before or during the policy term. At policy expiration, the insurance company audits the payrolls. If the payroll is more than estimated, an additional premium is charged. If less, a refund is made. This *audited modified standard premium* then is used as the pay-in amount at the first retro adjustment.

The retro premium calculations and adjustments then are made at annual intervals and are based on the amount of incurred losses at each adjustment date.

Retro Policy Cancellation

Insured businesses may have to pay a penalty if they cancel a retro plan before it normally would end. The rules for cancellation are available from either the NCCI or other independent rating bureaus.

Retrospective Rating Forms

Insureds must sign an election form indicating that they are aware of selecting a retro rating plan. An election form usually contains information such as name of insured; date plan takes effect; formula factors (basic premium factor, minimum premium factor, maximum premium factor, loss conversion factor, tax multiplier, and retrospective development factor if applicable); loss limitations and excess loss premium factor if applicable; signature of insured; date election form signed; and policies covered under the plan. A retrospective rating endorsement is attached to the actual workers compensation insurance policy.

Incurred Loss versus Paid Loss Plans

The main difference between an incurred loss and paid loss plan is the type of claims included in the calculations.

In a paid loss plan, the insured pays the insurer a deposit premium and sets up a claims fund at the beginning of the year. The *deposit premium* is similar to the *basic premium* in an incurred loss plan. It is designed to cover insurer expenses and profit. The claims fund is established so that the insurer can pay claims as they come due. The insured is required to replenish the claims fund as the insurance company uses it to pay claims. The difference between this *pay-in amount* and the estimated standard premium usually must be posted in *collateral*. For the purposes of a paid loss retro plan, the insurance company usually requires that collateral be in the form of a fairly liquid asset that it may draw upon if, for some reason, the insured business is unable to pay claims. Typical types of collateral that insurance companies accept are irrevocable letters of credit, certificates of deposit, or first rights to an escrow account.

The Workers Compensation System

It can take many years for a paid loss plan to close. Therefore, the insured is expected to pay claims long after a policy has expired. Collateral is required as a financial guarantee that future claims will be paid.

At regular intervals, incurred losses are reviewed and an incurred loss retrospective premium is calculated. The paid-in premium and paid losses are subtracted from the incurred loss premium. This difference is used to determine whether the required collateral should be adjusted to guarantee the payment of future claim bills. Thus, the collateral may be adjusted at the date of the annual retrospective rating calculations.

Deductible Plans

Deductibles are used in some states for workers compensation and employers liability policies. For workers compensation, deductibles may be applicable to medical payments, indemnity payments, or both. Under a deductible plan, the insurance company usually pays claims and then seeks reimbursement from the insured. The insured's credit worthiness is checked thoroughly before a workers compensation deductible plan is offered.

Deductible plans are similar to self-insured retention plans, in that both require the insured business to pay the first portion of claim benefits. However, there are some differences in regard to how the payments flow between the insured and insurer to the claimant. However, both types of plans operate in a fairly similar fashion.

There are state-specific guidelines for deductible programs, so individual state regulations should be reviewed for specific information.

Deductibles can serve two purposes. Small deductibles are used to eliminate insurance companies having to deal with nuisance claims. Large deductibles are designed to offer the insured a method for increasing the amount of risk it assumes without incurring unlimited liability and without having to handle claims, as it would under a self-insured retention. Many insurers sell large deductible plans to large companies. The deductible usually ranges from $100,000 to $1,000,000 per accident. Aggregate coverage for losses falling within the deductible layer usually is available.

The set-up of a large deductible plan is similar to the paid loss retrospective rating plan discussed previously.

The insured pays a deductible premium and sets up an escrow account with funds adequate to pay the deductible portion of expected claims for a sixty to ninety-day period. Additionally, the insured is billed every month for actual payments that fall within the deductible layer. The amount of collateral required is based on estimated losses and the insured's financial condition.

As with the paid loss retro plan, the initial pay-in is substantially less than the full estimated standard premium, which is collected up-front in an incurred loss retro program.

WHERE CAN I FIND OUT ABOUT IT?

There are many resources available for more information on workers compensation. Among them are:

- U.S. Chamber of Commerce Statistics and Research Center, *Analysis of Workers' Compensation Laws*, updated annually. http://www.uschamber.com/Research+and+Statistics/Publications/Workers+Comp.htm.

- The National Council on Compensation Insurance, Inc., 901 Peninsula Corporate Circle, Boca Raton, FL 33487. Phone (561) 893-1000. www.ncci.com.

- State Workers Compensation Administrators, which are listed in the chapter appendix.

QUESTIONS AND ANSWERS

Question—My company has been unable to find workers compensation insurance from an insurance company. What options do we have for coverage?

Answer—Each state has made provisions for coverage, either through a state workers compensation fund or an assigned risk pool. Your broker or agent should be able to access a program for you.

Question—Do workers compensation losses that fall under the voluntary compensation endorsement (WC 00 03 11A) go into the calculation for a workers compensation experience modifier? Also, the voluntary compensation endorsement includes information about workers compensation benefits *and* suits against the employer. How does this endorsement apply?

Answer—Any losses that occur under this endorsement are chargeable to the workers compensation modifier, just as regular part one or part two losses on the workers compensation policy. They also would apply to any financial program calculations, such as retrospective rating adjustments or deductible calculations, unless the financial agreement states otherwise.

In regard to how the endorsement works, it permits employers to offer workers or volunteers who are normally exempt from workers compensation the statutory workers' compensation benefits of the state(s) designated on the endorsement. The classes of workers to which the employer wants to offer benefits must be listed on the endorsement.

However, the injured employee does not *have* to accept the workers compensation statutory benefit. He or she can sue the employer. That suit would fall under the employers liability section of the voluntary compensation endorsement. The fact that the employee or volunteer can accept or decline the statutory benefits is why both workers compensation and employers liability provisions are included in the endorsement.

Question—What does the "last injurious exposure rule" mean in regard to workers compensation coverage?

Answer—The last injurious exposure rule consists of two main, complementing parts. First, the rule holds that the last employer of a claimant with an accepted claim relating to a specific body part bears the burden of proving that an injury to the claimant at a subsequent employment was new, was not caused by the prior incident, and independently contributed to a worsening of the claimant's underlying condition.

Second, when an employee sustains a subsequent injury that is found, in fact, to be a new injury, the liability for all awards is placed on th e insurer of the risk at the time of the second injury. This absolves the insurer at the time of the first injury of liability for compensation payments.

For example, assume that an employee is injured on the job today. A dispute arises between the previous employer and the current employer over whether the injury is new or simply an aggravation of an injury that the employee suffered while at the previous job. Under the last injurious exposure rule, the previous employer has the duty to show that the injury is a new one. If that is accomplished, the current employer (or, as is more likely, the current employer's workers compensation insurer) must make relevant compensation payments. If that is not accomplished, the previous employer (or its insurer) may end up paying the compensation or splitting the payments, depending on how and to whom the workers compensation board apportions the injury.

Under the last injurious exposure rule, if the current employer is ordered to make all the compensation payments, neither the employer nor its insurer is allowed to pursue the previous employer or its insurer for any contribution to the payment unless state law permits such a course of action. It is important for businesses to keep accurate, up-to-date workers compensation records that may be reviewed in the event of such a dispute.

FORMS AND CHECKLISTS

APPENDIX A: WORKERS COMPENSATION STATE ADMINISTRATIVE OFFICES

State–by–State Office Listings

The function of administering the workers compensation laws of each of the various states is the responsibility of a state board or commission. The principal location of these administrative offices for each state, American Samoa, the District of Columbia, Guam, and Puerto Rico, and a federal program are listed below.

ALABAMA
Workers Compensation Division
Department of Industrial Relations
649 Monroe St.
Montgomery AL 36131
WATS: (800) 528-5166
(334) 242-2868
FAX: (334) 261-3143
Fraud: (800) 923-2533
Ombudsman: (800) 528-5166
http://www.dir.state.al.us/wc.htm

ALASKA
Department of Labor
Workers Compensation Division
P.O. Box 25512
Juneau AK 99802
(907) 465-2790
FAX: (907) 465-2797
http://www.labor.state.ak.us/wc/wc.htm

AMERICAN SAMOA
Workers Compensation Commission
Office of the Governor
American Samoa Government
Pago Pago AS 96799
http://members.aol.com/pologa/welcome.html

ARIZONA
The Industrial Commission of Arizona
800 W. Washington St.
Phoenix AZ 85007
(602) 542-4411
FAX: (602) 542-7889
Ombudsman: (602) 542-4538
http://www.ica.state.az.us

ARKANSAS
Workers Compensation Commission
Fourth & Spring Sts.
P.O. Box 950
Little Rock AR 72203
(501) 682-3930
WATS: (800) 622-4472
FAX: (501) 682-2777
http://www.awcc.state.ar.us

CALIFORNIA
Division of Workers Compensation
Department of Industrial Relations
Commission on Health and Safety and Workers Compensation (CHSWC)
455 Golden Gate Ave., 10th Fl.
San Francisco CA 94102
(415) 703-4600
FAX: (415) 703-3971
http://www.dir.ca.gov

COLORADO
Division of Workers Compensation
1515 Arapahoe St.
Denver CO 80202-2117
(303) 318-8700
(888) 390-7936
FAX: (303) 318-8710
http://workerscomp.cdle.state.co.us

CONNECTICUT
Workers Compensation Commission
21 Oak St., 4th Fl.
Hartford CT 06106
(860) 493-1500
FAX: (860) 247-1361
http://www.state.ct.us

DELAWARE
Dept. of Labor
Office of Workers Compensation
4425 North Market St.
Wilmington DE 19802
(302) 761-8200
http://www.delawareworks.com/divisions/
industaffairs/diaindex.html

DISTRICT OF COLUMBIA
Office of Workers Compensation
1200 Upshur St. N.W.
Washington DC 20011
(202) 576-6265
FAX: (201) 541-3595
http://www.ci.washington.dc.us

FLORIDA
Dept. of Labor and Employment Security
Div. of Workers Compensation
301 Forrest Bldg.
2728 Centerview Dr.
Tallahassee FL 32399
(850) 488-2514
FAX: (850) 922-6779
http://www2.myflorida.com/les/wc

GEORGIA
State Board of Workers Compensation
270 Peachtree St. N.W.
Atlanta GA 30303
(404) 656-2058
WATS: (800) 533-0682
FAX: (404) 656-7768
http://www.ganet.org/sbwc

GUAM
Workers Compensation Commission
Department of Labor
Government of Guam
P.O. Box 9970
Tamuning GU 96911
(671) 647-4205
FAX: (671) 649-4922
http://www.gov.gu

HAWAII
Disability Compensation Division
Dept. of Labor & Industrial Relations
830 Punchbowl St., Rm. 209
Honolulu HI 96813
(808) 586-9174
FAX: (808) 586-9219
http://dlir.state.hi.us

IDAHO
Industrial Commission
P.O. Box 83720
Boise ID 83720
(208) 334-6000
WATS: (800) 950-2110
FAX: (208) 334-2321
http://www.state.id.us/iic

ILLINOIS
Industrial Commission of Illinois
100 W. Randolph St., Ste. 8-200
Chicago IL 60601
(312) 814-6611
http://www.state.il.us/agency/iic

INDIANA
Workers Compensation Board
402 W. Washington St., Rm. W-196
Indianapolis IN 46204
(317) 232-3809
FAX: (317) 233-5493
http://www.state.in.us/wkcomp

IOWA
Iowa Division of Workers Compensation
1000 E. Grand Ave.
Des Moines IA 50319
(515) 281-5387
WATS: (800) JOB-IOWA
FAX: (515) 281-6501
http://www.state.ia.us/iwd/wc

KANSAS
Div. of Workers Compensation
Dept. of Human Resources
800 S.W. Jackson, Ste. 600
Topeka KS 66612
(785) 296-3441
FAX: (785) 296-0839
http://www.hr.state.ks.us/wc/html/htm

KENTUCKY
Workers Compensation Board
301 E. Main St., 7th Fl.

Lexington KY 40507
(859) 246-2773
FAX: (859) 246-2779

Dept. of Workers Claims
1270 Louisville Rd.
Perimeter Park West
Frankfort KY 40601
(502) 564-5550
FAX: (502) 564-8250
http://dwc.state.ky.us

LOUISIANA
Dept. of Labor
Office of Workers Compensation Administration
P.O. Box 94040
Baton Rouge LA 70804
(504) 342-7555
WATS: (800) 824-4592
FAX: (504) 342-5665
http://www.ldol.state.la.us

MAINE
Workers Compensation Board
Deering Bldg., State House Station 27
Augusta ME 04333-0027
(207) 287-3751
FAX: (207) 287-7198
http://state.me.us/wcb

MARYLAND
Workers Compensation Commission
10 E. Baltimore St.
Baltimore MD 21202
(410) 864-5100
WATS: (800) 492-0479
FAX: (410) 864-5101
http://www.charm.net/wcc

MASSACHUSETTS
Dept. of Industrial Accidents
600 Washington St., 7th Fl.
Boston MA 02111
(617) 727-4900
WATS:(800) 323-3249
FAX: (617) 727-6477
http://www.state.ma.us/dia

MICHIGAN
Bureau of Workers Disability Compensation
Dept. of Labor
P.O. Box 30016
Lansing MI 48909

(517) 322-1296
FAX: (517) 322-1808
http://www.cis.state.mi.us/wkrcomp/bwdc/
home.htm

MINNESOTA
Workers Compensation Div.
Dept. of Labor and Industry
443 Lafayette Rd.
St. Paul MN 55155
(612) 296-6107
WATS: (800) DIAL-DLI
FAX: (612) 296-6107
http://www.doli.state.mm.us

MISSISSIPPI
Workers Compensation Commission
1428 Lakeland Dr.
P.O. Box 5300
Jackson MS 39296
(601) 987-4200
http://www.mwcc.state.ms.us

MISSOURI
Div. of Workers Compensation
P.O. Box 58
Jefferson City MO 65102
(573) 751-4231
FAX: (573) 751-2012
http://www.dolir.state.mo.us/wc/index.htm

MONTANA
State Compensation Fund
5 S. Last Chance Gulch
Helena MT 59604
(406) 444-6500
FAX: (406) 444-7796
http://stfund.state.mt.us

NEBRASKA
Workers Compensation Court
129 N. 10th St., #300
Lincoln NE 68508
(402) 471-6468
WATS: (800) 599-5155
FAX: (402) 471-2700
http://www.nol.org/home/wc

NEVADA
Division of Industrial Relations
400 W. King St., #400
Carson City NV 89703

(775) 684-7260
FAX: (702) 687-6305
http://dirweb.state.nv.us/index.htm

NEW HAMPSHIRE
Dept. of Labor
Div. of Workers Compensation
State Office Park South
95 Pleasant St.
Concord NH 03301
(603) 271-3174
http://www.state.nh.us/dol/wc/index.html

NEW JERSEY
Div. of Workers Compensation
Dept. of Labor, CN 381
Trenton NJ 08625-0381
(609) 292-2515
FAX: (609) 984-2515
http://www.state.nj.us/labor/wc

NEW MEXICO
Workers Compensation Administration
P.O. Box 27198
Albuquerque NM 87125
(505) 841-6000
WATS: (800) 255-7965
http://www.state.nm.us/wca

NEW YORK
Workers Compensation Board
100 Broadway-Menands
Albany NY 12241
(518) 474-6670
FAX: (518) 473-1415
http://www.wcb.state.ny.us

NORTH CAROLINA
Industrial Commission
4319 Mail Service Center
Raleigh NC 27699
(919) 733-4820
FAX: (919) 715-0282
http://www.comp.state.nc.us

NORTH DAKOTA
Workers Compensation Bureau
500 E. Front Ave.
Bismarck ND 58504
(701) 328-3800
FAX: (701) 328-3750
http://www.ndworkerscomp.com

OHIO
Bureau of Workers Compensation
30 W. Spring St.
Columbus OH 43215
(614) 466-1320
WATS: (800) OHIOBWC
FAX: (877) 520-OHIO
http://www.bwc.state.oh.us

OKLAHOMA
Workers Compensation Division
4001 N. Lincoln Blvd.
Oklahoma City OK 73105
(405) 528-1500
FAX: (405) 528-5751
http://www.oklaosf.state.ok.us

OREGON
Workers Compensation Department
350 Winter St. N.E., Rm. 21
Salem OR 97310
(503) 947-7810
WATS: (800) 452-0288
FAX: (503) 947-7514
http://www.cbs.state.or.us/wcd

PENNSYLVANIA
Bureau of Workers Compensation
Department of Labor and Industry
1171 S. Cameron St., Rm. 103
Harrisburg PA 17104
(717) 772-3702
WATS: (800) 482-2383
http://www.dli.state.pa.us

PUERTO RICO
Industrial Commissioner's Office
G.P.O. Box 364446
San Juan PR 00936-4466
(787) 783-3808
FAX: (787) 783-5610
http://fortaleza.govpr.org/ingles/govwel.htm

RHODE ISLAND
Workers Compensation Unit
One Dorance Plz.
Providence RI 02903
(401) 277-3097
FAX: (401) 421-3123
http://www.state.ri.us

SOUTH CAROLINA
Workers Compensation Commissioner

1612 Marion St.
P.O. Box 1715
Columbia SC 29202
(803) 737-5700
FAX: (803) 737-5768
http://www.wcc.state.sc.us

SOUTH DAKOTA
Div. of Labor and Management
Dept. of Labor
700 Governors Dr.
Pierre SD 57501-2291
(605) 773-3101
FAX: (605) 773-4211
http://www.state.sd.us/dol/dol.htm

TENNESSEE
Workers Compensation Div.
Dept. of Labor
Gateway Plz., 2nd Fl.
710 James Robertson Pkwy.
Nashville TN 37243
(615) 532-4812
WATS: (800) 332-2667
FAX: (615) 532-1468
http://www.state.tn.us/labor/wcomp.html

TEXAS
Workers Compensation Commission
4000 S. I-35, MS 20
Austin TX 78704
(512) 440-5690
FAX: (512) 440-3552
http://www.twcc.state.tx.us/commission

UTAH
Industrial Accidents Div.
P.O. Box 146610
Salt Lake City UT 84114
(801) 530-6800
FAX: (801) 530-6804
http://www.labor.state.ut.us/indacc

VERMONT
Workers Compensation Div.
National Life Bldg., Drawer 20
Montpelier VT 05620
(802) 828-2288
FAX: (802) 828-2195
http://www.state.vt.us/labind

VIRGINIA
Workers Compensation Commission

1000 DMV Dr.
Richmond VA 23220
(804) 367-8600
FAX: (804) 367-9740
http://www.vwc.state.va.us

WASHINGTON
Dept. of Labor and Industries
P.O. Box 44851
Olympia WA 98504
(360) 902-5799
FAX: (360) 902-5792
http://www.wa.gov/lni

WEST VIRGINIA
Workers Compensation Div.
4700 Maccorkle Ave. S.E.
Charleston WV 25304
(304) 926-5048
WATS: (800) 628-4265
FAX: (304) 926-5372
http://www.state.wv.us/bep/wc

WISCONSIN
Dept. of Industry, Labor and Human Relations
Workers Compensation Div.

201 E. Washington Ave., Rm. 161
P.O. Box 7901
Madison WI 53707
(608) 266-1340
FAX: (608) 267-0394
http://www.dwd.state.wi.us/notespub/wcadvcou

WYOMING
Workers Compensation Div.
State Treasurer's Office
Herschler Bldg., 2nd Fl., East Wing
122 W. 25th St.
Cheyenne WY 82002
(307) 777-7159
FAX: (307) 777-6552
http://wydoe.state.wy.us/wscd

UNITED STATES—FEDERAL PLANS
Dept. of Labor
Employment Standards Administration
200 Constitution Ave. N.W.
Washington DC 20210
(202) 219-6191
FAX: (202) 219-8457
http://www.dol.gov/dol/esa

Advisory loss costs. The portion of a workers compensation premium rate that represents expected losses per $100 of payroll for that classification.

Anniversary rating date. The effective date of when experience modification and state rate changes take effect. Often coincides with workers compensation policy inception date.

Classifications. Categories used in the workers compensation system to gauge the risk of workers compensation losses that the business will face over the policy period.

Collateral. An asset that is pledged to back up future workers compensation claim payments.

Compensable. A determination that an employee's injury or disease arose out of and in the course of employment and are eligible for benefits provided under a specific state's workers compensation system.

Compulsory workers compensation law. A law that requires employers that fall within the scope of a respective state's workers compensation law to accept its provisions and be responsible for the benefits it dictates.

Dual capacity. A legal doctrine that holds that an employer that normally is shielded from lawsuits through the exclusive remedy rule of workers compensation may be liable for damages that arise from a wrongful act that is not related to the role of employer. The exposure is common to the public in general as well as to the business's employees.

Elective workers compensation law. A law that permits employers that fall within the scope of a respective state's workers compensation law to either accept or reject its provisions.

Employers liability. The liability of a business for injury to its employees that arise in the course of employment but that are not compensable under that state's applicable workers compensation statute.

Excess loss insurance. Sometimes referred to as stop loss insurance, this type of coverage is used to cap a business's exposure to claim payments at a predetermined limit. Excess loss insurance can be purchased to *stop losses* on either a per claim or per occurrence basis.

Exclusive remedy. The doctrine that workers compensation is the sole source of recovery for employee work-related injuries.

Experience modifier or **experience modification.** A factor that compares an individual business's workers compensation loss experience with the loss experience of other companies in the same peer group. Sometimes referred to as an *experience mod* or *mod*.

Experience rating. Using a business's workers compensation loss experience as a factor in developing a policy premium.

Fixed costs. The workers compensation costs that are fixed at policy inception. They include items such as insurance charges, agent commission, underwriting costs, and policy issuance costs.

Guaranteed cost workers compensation policy. A workers compensation policy that is fully insured. The business pays a policy premium to an insurance company, which adjusts and pays employee-injury claims. Once the premium is paid, the insured business is not assessed for claim costs.

In the course of employment. A causal connection between a worker's injury and her employment.

Intentional tort. Committing an intentional harm to another party, such as an employer intentionally causing injury to an employee.

Manual rates. One type of authorized workers compensation rates. Manual rates are developed by state rating agencies and approved by the state insurance regulatory authority. In a manual-rate state, insurance companies use the manual rates as a starting point in developing a policy premium.

Monopolistic states. States that require that workers compensation coverage be purchased from their state funds. The five monopolistic states are North Dakota, Ohio, Washington, West Virginia, and Wyoming.

NCCI. An abbreviation for National Council on Compensation Insurance, Inc. See definition of National Council on Compensation Insurance, Inc.

National Council on Compensation Insurance, Inc. A rating and statistical bureau that files forms, develops rates, and collects data from workers compensation programs in its member states.

OD. An abbreviation for occupational disease. See definitional for occupational disease.

Occupational disease. A health impairment that is caused by continued exposure to hazards that are inherent in an employee's occupation.

Premium calculation and adjustment. The periodic adjustments in premium that are made in retrospective rating plans. The amount of premium that has been paid to date is compared with the fixed insurance charges and the amount of money spent and reserved for claim payments. The retrospective premium is then adjusted on the basis of this comparison.

Premium discount. A percentage credit that floats with the workers compensation premium size and is applied to equalize the cost of issuing a policy among various sizes and types of businesses.

Pro rata cancellation. Calculating the premium that a business should pay based on the amount of time the policy was in effect before it was cancelled; there is no cancellation penalty.

Qualified self-insurer. A business that meets criteria that is established by an individual state and is approved to self-insure its workers compensation exposure.

Remuneration. The premium basis for most workers compensation policies. Remuneration includes payroll and nonmonetary employee compensation, such as the value of meals and lodging that is considered a part of an employee's pay.

Retrospective rating plan. A workers compensation financial plan in which an insured business's policy premium is adjusted after the policy expires based on claims experience. Retrospective rating rewards companies that have better than expected loss experience with return premiums and penalizes companies that have worse than expected loss experience by charging additional premiums. Often referred to as a retro plan or retro.

Schedule rating. The application of credits or debits to a workers compensation premium to reflect positive or negative characteristics of an individual company for workers compensation purposes.

Self-insurance. A workers compensation plan in which an insured business is approved to self-finance its workers compensation exposure.

Short-rate cancellation penalty. A premium charge for a cancelled policy that includes an amount based on the proportion of time the policy was in force plus a cancellation penalty. Short-rate cancellation tables are used when insureds cancel policies without an acceptable reason.

Sliding scale dividend plan. A workers compensation financial plan that may reward an insured business that manages claim costs by paying a dividend. The dividend fluctuates, or slides up and down, based on the insured business's loss ratio. Dividends cannot be guaranteed and are payable only upon declaration by the insurance company board of directors.

Standard dividend plan. A workers compensation financial plan that may reward an insured business that manages claim costs by paying a dividend. Dividends cannot be guaranteed and are payable only upon declaration by the insurance company board of directors.

State funds. For the purposes of workers compensation programs, state funds are state-operated workers compensation funds that fund workers compensation programs.

Third-party-over action. A situation in which a third party is able to bring an action against an employer after that employer's worker is injured on the job. These actions usually stem from an employer contractually assuming the obligations and liabilities of the third party.

Unit statistical report. A report that insurance carriers submit to state workers compensation rating bureaus. The report includes premium and loss information on an individual business's workers compensation experience and is used to develop the business's experience modification.

Unity modification. An experience modification of 1.0, which indicates average workers compensation loss experience.

Variable costs. The portion of workers compensation costs that fluctuates with the level of claims. Variable costs include items such as benefit payments, defense costs, and adjusting costs.

Figure 18.7

Option Evaluation Form

Evaluation Questions	Guaranteed Cost Plan	Standard Dividend Plan	Sliding Scale Dividend Plan	Incurred Loss Retrospective Rating Plan	Paid Loss Retrospective Rating Plan	Large Deductible Plan	Self-insured Retention Plan
1 Is this type of plan auditable?	Yes	Yes	Yes	Yes	Yes	Yes	Yes
Cash Flow							
2 Can costs other than audit results be fixed in advance?	Yes	Yes	Yes	No	No	No	No
3 If losses are good, do I get money back?	No	Yes	Yes	Yes	Possible/collateral	Possible/collateral	Possible/collateral
4 If losses are bad, do I have to pay more money?	No	No	No	Yes	Yes	Yes	Yes
5 Are all program costs paid in the first year of the program?	Yes	Yes	Yes	No	No	No	No
6 Are calculations made on an incurred loss or paid loss basis?	N/A	Incurred	Incurred	Incurred	Paid	Variable	Variable
7 Who earns interest income?	Insurer	Insurer	Insurer	Insurer	Negotiable	Negotiable	Negotiable
8 Can any of the program costs be deferred?	Possible	Possible	Possible	Yes	Yes	Yes	Yes
9 Is additional up-front cash required to set up program?	No	No	No	No	Yes, loss fund	Yes, loss fund	Yes, loss fund
Rating							
10 Is there potential for a dividend payment?	No	Yes	Yes	N/A	N/A	N/A	N/A
11 Is price subject to negotiation?	No	No	No	Yes	Yes	Yes	Yes
12 Is program easy to understand?	Yes	No	Yes	May be difficult	May be difficult	May be difficult	May be difficult
13 Does an expense discount apply?	Yes	Yes	Yes	No	No	Yes	Yes
14 Is composite rating possible?	Yes	Yes	Yes	Yes	Yes	Yes	Yes
15 Is a compensating balance arrangement possible?	N/A	N/A	N/A	N/A	Yes	Yes	Yes
Taxes & Assessments							
16 Does insured pay full premium taxes?	Yes	Yes	Yes	Yes	Yes	Y/STR	Y/STR
17 Are costs tax deductible?	Yes	Yes	Yes	Yes	Yes/STR	Y/STR	Y/STR
18 Are residual market loadings avoided?	No	No	No	No	No	May be reduced	May be reduced
19 Are there other assessments?	Incl. in premium	Incl. in premium	Incl. in premium	Incl. in premium	Incl. in premium	May be reduced	May be reduced
Losses							
20 Does insured share risk with insurer?	No	No	No	Yes	Yes	Yes	Yes
21 Are loss limitations available?	N/A	N/A	N/A	Yes	Yes	Yes	Yes
22 How important is loss reserving?	Not important	Somewhat	Somewhat	Extremely important	Very important	Very important	Very important
Services							
23 How much control do I have over how the program is managed?	No control	No control	No control	Fair control	Fair control	Good control	Good control
24 Who has the final say on how claims are managed?	Insurer	Insurer	Insurer	Consultative/Insurer	Consultative/Insurer	Consultative/Insurer	Consultative/Insurer
25 How easy will it be for me to customize loss control efforts?	Difficult	Difficult	Difficult	Negotiable	Negotiable	Negotiable	Negotiable
26 Can services be unbundled?	No	No	No	Sometimes	Sometimes	Sometimes	Usually
27 Will I need an internal staff to manage the program?	No	No	No	Possible	Possible	Possible	Possible
28 Is additional record keeping needed?	No	No	No	Yes	Yes	Yes	Yes
General Considerations							
29 How much do market conditions impact this program?	Great impact	Great impact	Great impact	Minimal impact	Minimal impact	Minimal impact	Minimal impact
30 Does the program provide a buffer between my company and third parties?	Yes	Yes	Yes	Yes	Yes	Yes	Yes
31 In general, how flexible is the plan?	Inflexible	Inflexible	Inflexible	Minimally flexible	Fairly flexible	Fairly flexible	Fairly flexible
32 Does the plan encourage loss control?	No	Minimally	Minimally	Yes	Yes	Yes	Yes
33 Is firm's credit worthiness an important factor?	No	No	No	Possibly	Yes	Yes	Yes
34 How hard is it to move away from this type of program?	Easy	Easy	Easy	Difficult	Difficult	Difficult	Difficult

WC 00 00 00 A   **WORKERS COMPENSATION AND EMPLOYERS LIABILITY INSURANCE POLICY**

Standard   *Effective April 1, 1992*   **1st Reprint**

WORKERS COMPENSATION AND EMPLOYERS LIABILITY INSURANCE POLICY

In return for the payment of the premium and subject to all terms of this policy, we agree with you as follows:

GENERAL SECTION

A. The Policy

This policy includes at its effective date the Information Page and all endorsements and schedules listed there. It is a contract of insurance between you (the employer named in Item 1 of the Information Page) and us (the insurer named on the Information Page). The only agreements relating to this insurance are stated in this policy. The terms of this policy may not be changed or waived except by endorsement issued by us to be part of this policy.

B. Who Is Insured

You are insured if you are an employer named in Item 1 of the Information Page. If that employer is a partnership, and if you are one of its partners, you are insured, but only in your capacity as an employer of the partnership's employees.

C. Workers Compensation Law

Workers Compensation Law means the workers or workmen's compensation law and occupational disease law of each state or territory named in Item 3.A. of the Information Page. It includes any amendments to that law which are in effect during the policy period. It does not include any federal workers or workmen's compensation law, any federal occupational disease law or the provisions of any law that provide nonoccupational disability benefits.

D. State

State means any state of the United States of America, and the District of Columbia.

E. Locations

This policy covers all of your workplaces listed in Items 1 or 4 of the Information Page; and it covers all other workplaces in Item 3.A. states unless you have other insurance or are self-insured for such workplaces.

PART ONE
WORKERS COMPENSATION INSURANCE

A. How This Insurance Applies

This workers compensation insurance applies to bodily injury by accident or bodily injury by disease. Bodily injury includes resulting death.
1. Bodily injury by accident must occur during the policy period.
2. Bodily injury by disease must be caused or aggravated by the conditions of your employment. The employee's last day of last exposure to the conditions causing or aggravating such bodily injury by disease must occur during the policy period.

B. We Will Pay

We will pay promptly when due the benefits required of you by the workers compensation law.

C. We Will Defend

We have the right and duty to defend at our expense any claim, proceeding or suit against you for benefits payable by this insurance. We have the right to investigate and settle these claims, proceedings or suits.

We have no duty to defend a claim, proceeding or suit that is not covered by this insurance.

D. We Will Also Pay

We will also pay these costs, in addition to other amounts payable under this insurance, as part of any claim, proceeding or suit we defend:
1. reasonable expenses incurred at our request, but not loss of earnings;
2. premiums for bonds to release attachments and for appeal bonds in bond amounts up to the amount payable under this insurance;
3. litigation costs taxed against you;
4. interest on a judgment as required by law until we offer the amount due under this insurance; and
5. expenses we incur.

E. Other Insurance

We will not pay more than our share of benefits and costs covered by this insurance and other insurance

WORKERS COMPENSATION AND EMPLOYERS LIABILITY INSURANCE POLICY   WC 00 00 00 A

1st Reprint   *Effective April 1, 1992*   **Standard**

or self-insurance. Subject to any limits of liability that may apply, all shares will be equal until the loss is paid. If any insurance or self-insurance is exhausted, the shares of all remaining insurance will be equal until the loss is paid.

F. **Payments You Must Make**

You are responsible for any payments in excess of the benefits regularly provided by the workers compensation law including those required because:
1. of your serious and willful misconduct;
2. you knowingly employ an employee in violation of law;
3. you fail to comply with a health or safety law or regulation; or
4. you discharge, coerce or otherwise discriminate against any employee in violation of the workers compensation law.

If we make any payments in excess of the benefits regularly provided by the workers compensation law on your behalf, you will reimburse us promptly.

G. **Recovery From Others**

We have your rights, and the rights of persons entitled to the benefits of this insurance, to recover our payments from anyone liable for the injury. You will do everything necessary to protect those rights for us and to help us enforce them.

H. **Statutory Provisions**

These statements apply where they are required by law.
1. As between an injured worker and us, we have notice of the injury when you have notice.
2. Your default or the bankruptcy or insolvency of you or your estate will not relieve us of our duties under this insurance after an injury occurs.
3. We are directly and primarily liable to any person entitled to the benefits payable by this insurance. Those persons may enforce our duties; so may an agency authorized by law. Enforcement may be against us or against you and us.
4. Jurisdiction over you is jurisdiction over us for purposes of the workers compensation law. We are bound by decisions against you under that law, subject to the provisions of this policy that are not in conflict with that law.
5. This insurance conforms to the parts of the

workers compensation law that apply to:
a. benefits payable by this insurance;
b. special taxes, payments into security or other special funds, and assessments payable by us under that law.
6. Terms of this insurance that conflict with the workers compensation law are changed by this statement to conform to that law.

Nothing in these paragraphs relieves you of your duties under this policy.

PART TWO
EMPLOYERS LIABILITY INSURANCE

A. **How This Insurance Applies**

This employers liability insurance applies to bodily injury by accident or bodily injury by disease. Bodily injury includes resulting death.
1. The bodily injury must arise out of and in the course of the injured employee's employment by you.
2. The employment must be necessary or incidental to your work in a state or territory listed in Item 3.A. of the Information Page.
3. Bodily injury by accident must occur during the policy period.
4. Bodily injury by disease must be caused or aggravated by the conditions of your employment. The employee's last day of last exposure to the conditions causing or aggravating such bodily injury by disease must occur during the policy period.
5. If you are sued, the original suit and any related legal actions for damages for bodily injury by accident or by disease must be brought in the United States of America, its territories or possessions, or Canada.

B. **We Will Pay**

We will pay all sums you legally must pay as damages because of bodily injury to your employees, provided the bodily injury is covered by this Employers Liability Insurance.

The damages we will pay, where recovery is permitted by law, include damages:
1. for which you are liable to a third party by reason of a claim or suit against you by that third party to recover the damages claimed against such

WC 00 00 00 A **WORKERS COMPENSATION AND EMPLOYERS LIABILITY INSURANCE POLICY**

Standard *Effective April 1, 1992* **1st Reprint**

third party as a result of injury to your employee;

2. for care and loss of services; and

3. for consequential bodily injury to a spouse, child, parent, brother or sister of the injured employee;

provided that these damages are the direct consequence of bodily injury that arises out of and in the course of the injured employee's employment by you; and

4. because of bodily injury to your employee that arises out of and in the course of employment, claimed against you in a capacity other than as employer.

C. Exclusions

This insurance does not cover:

1. liability assumed under a contract. This exclusion does not apply to a warranty that your work will be done in a workmanlike manner;

2. punitive or exemplary damages because of bodily injury to an employee employed in violation of law;

3. bodily injury to an employee while employed in violation of law with your actual knowledge or the actual knowledge of any of your executive officers;

4. any obligation imposed by a workers compensation, occupational disease, unemployment compensation, or disability benefits law, or any similar law;

5. bodily injury intentionally caused or aggravated by you;

6. bodily injury occurring outside the United States of America, its territories or possessions, and Canada. This exclusion does not apply to bodily injury to a citizen or resident of the United States of America or Canada who is temporarily outside these countries;

7. damages arising out of coercion, criticism, demotion, evaluation, reassignment, discipline, defamation, harassment, humiliation, discrimination against or termination of any employee, or any personnel practices, policies, acts or omissions;

8. bodily injury to any person in work subject to the Longshore and Harbor Workers' Compensation Act (33 USC Sections 901-950), the Nonappropriated Fund Instrumentalities Act (5 USC Sections 8171-8173), the Outer Continental Shelf Lands Act (43 USC Sections 1331-1356), the

Defense Base Act (42 USC Sections 1651-1654), the Federal Coal Mine Health and Safety Act of 1969 (30 USC Sections 901-942), any other federal workers or workmen's compensation law or other federal occupational disease law, or any amendments to these laws;

9. bodily injury to any person in work subject to the Federal Employers' Liability Act (45 USC Sections 51-60), any other federal laws obligating an employer to pay damages to an employee due to bodily injury arising out of or in the course of employment, or any amendments to those laws;

10. bodily injury to a master or member of the crew of any vessel;

11. fines or penalties imposed for violation of federal or state law; and

12. damages payable under the Migrant and Seasonal Agricultural Worker Protection Act (29 USC Sections 1801-1872) and under any other federal law awarding damages for violation of those laws or regulations issued thereunder, and any amendments to those laws.

D. We Will Defend

We have the right and duty to defend, at our expense, any claim, proceeding or suit against you for damages payable by this insurance. We have the right to investigate and settle these claims, proceedings and suits.

We have no duty to defend a claim, proceeding or suit that is not covered by this insurance. We have no duty to defend or continue defending after we have paid our applicable limit of liability under this insurance.

E. We Will Also Pay

We will also pay these costs, in addition to other amounts payable under this insurance, as part of any claim, proceeding, or suit we defend:

1. reasonable expenses incurred at our request, but not loss of earnings;

2. premiums for bonds to release attachments and for appeal bonds in bond amounts up to the limit of our liability under this insurance;

3. litigation costs taxed against you;

4. interest on a judgment as required by law until we offer the amount due under this insurance; and

5. expenses we incur.

© 1991 National Council on Compensation Insurance

F. Other Insurance

We will not pay more than our share of damages and costs covered by this insurance and other insurance or self-insurance. Subject to any limits of liability that apply, all shares will be equal until the loss is paid. If any insurance or self-insurance is exhausted, the shares of all remaining insurance and self-insurance will be equal until the loss is paid.

G. Limits of Liability

Our liability to pay for damages is limited. Our limits of liability are shown in Item 3.B. of the Information Page. They apply as explained below.

1. Bodily Injury by Accident. The limit shown for "bodily injury by accident—each accident" is the most we will pay for all damages covered by this insurance because of bodily injury to one or more employees in any one accident. A disease is not bodily injury by accident unless it results directly from bodily injury by accident.
2. Bodily Injury by Disease. The limit shown for "bodily injury by disease—policy limit" is the most we will pay for all damages covered by this insurance and arising out of bodily injury by disease, regardless of the number of employees who sustain bodily injury by disease. The limit shown for "bodily injury by disease—each employee" is the most we will pay for all damages because of bodily injury by disease to any one employee. Bodily injury by disease does not include disease that results directly from a bodily injury by accident.
3. We will not pay any claims for damages after we have paid the applicable limit of our liability under this insurance.

H. Recovery From Others

We have your rights to recover our payment from anyone liable for an injury covered by this insurance. You will do everything necessary to protect those rights for us and to help us enforce them.

I. Actions Against Us

There will be no right of action against us under this insurance unless:
1. You have complied with all the terms of this policy; and

2. The amount you owe has been determined with our consent or by actual trial and final judgment.

This insurance does not give anyone the right to add us as a defendant in an action against you to determine your liability. The bankruptcy or insolvency of you or your estate will not relieve us of our obligations under this Part.

PART THREE
OTHER STATES INSURANCE

A. How This Insurance Applies

1. This other states insurance applies only if one or more states are shown in Item 3.C. of the Information Page.
2. If you begin work in any one of those states after the effective date of this policy and are not insured or are not self-insured for such work, all provisions of the policy will apply as though that state were listed in Item 3.A. of the Information Page.
3. We will reimburse you for the benefits required by the workers compensation law of that state if we are not permitted to pay the benefits directly to persons entitled to them.
4. If you have work on the effective date of this policy in any state not listed in Item 3.A. of the Information Page, coverage will not be afforded for that state unless we are notified within thirty days.

B. Notice

Tell us at once if you begin work in any state listed in Item 3.C. of the Information Page.

PART FOUR
YOUR DUTIES IF INJURY OCCURS

Tell us at once if injury occurs that may be covered by this policy. Your other duties are listed here.

1. Provide for immediate medical and other services required by the workers compensation law.
2. Give us or our agent the names and addresses of the injured persons and of witnesses, and other information we may need.
3. Promptly give us all notices, demands and legal

papers related to the injury, claim, proceeding or suit.

4. Cooperate with us and assist us, as we may request, in the investigation, settlement or defense of any claim, proceeding or suit.

5. Do nothing after an injury occurs that would interfere with our right to recover from others.

6. Do not voluntarily make payments, assume obligations or incur expenses, except at your own cost.

PART FIVE—PREMIUM

A. Our Manuals2

All premium for this policy will be determined by our manuals of rules, rates, rating plans and classifications. We may change our manuals and apply the changes to this policy if authorized by law or a governmental agency regulating this insurance.

B. Classifications

Item 4 of the Information Page shows the rate and premium basis for certain business or work classifications. These classifications were assigned based on an estimate of the exposures you would have during the policy period. If your actual exposures are not properly described by those classifications, we will assign proper classifications, rates and premium basis by endorsement to this policy.

C. Remuneration

Premium for each work classification is determined by multiplying a rate times a premium basis. Remuneration is the most common premium basis. This premium basis includes payroll and all other remuneration paid or payable during the policy period for the services of:

1. all your officers and employees engaged in work covered by this policy; and

2. all other persons engaged in work that could make us liable under Part One (Workers Compensation Insurance) of this policy. If you do not have payroll records for these persons, the contract price for their services and materials may be used as the premium basis. This paragraph 2 will not apply if you give us proof that the employers of these persons lawfully secured their workers compensation obligations.

D. Premium Payments

You will pay all premium when due. You will pay the premium even if part or all of a workers compensation law is not valid.

E. Final Premium

The premium shown on the Information Page, schedules, and endorsements is an estimate. The final premium will be determined after this policy ends by using the actual, not the estimated, premium basis and the proper classifications and rates that lawfully apply to the business and work covered by this policy. If the final premium is more than the premium you paid to us, you must pay us the balance. If it is less, we will refund the balance to you. The final premium will not be less than the highest minimum premium for the classifications covered by this policy.

If this policy is canceled, final premium will be determined in the following way unless our manuals provide otherwise:

1. If we cancel, final premium will be calculated pro rata based on the time this policy was in force. Final premium will not be less than the pro rata share of the minimum premium.

2. If you cancel, final premium will be more than pro rata; it will be based on the time this policy was in force, and increased by our short-rate cancelation table and procedure. Final premium will not be less than the minimum premium.

F. Records

You will keep records of information needed to compute premium. You will provide us with copies of those records when we ask for them.

G. Audit

You will let us examine and audit all your records that relate to this policy. These records include ledgers, journals, registers, vouchers, contracts, tax reports, payroll and disbursement records, and programs for storing and retrieving data. We may conduct the audits during regular business hours during the policy period and within three years after the policy period ends. Information developed by audit will be used to determine final premium. Insurance rate service organizations have the same rights we have under this provision.

© **1991 National Council on Compensation Insurance**

WORKERS COMPENSATION AND EMPLOYERS LIABILITY INSURANCE POLICY   WC 00 00 00 A

1st Reprint   *Effective April 1, 1992*   **Standard**

PART SIX—CONDITIONS

A. **Inspection**

We have the right, but are not obliged to inspect your workplaces at any time. Our inspections are not safety inspections. They relate only to the insurability of the workplaces and the premiums to be charged. We may give you reports on the conditions we find. We may also recommend changes. While they may help reduce losses, we do not undertake to perform the duty of any person to provide for the health or safety of your employees or the public. We do not warrant that your workplaces are safe or healthful or that they comply with laws, regulations, codes or standards. Insurance rate service organizations have the same rights we have under this provision.

B. **Long Term Policy**

If the policy period is longer than one year and sixteen days, all provisions of this policy will apply as though a new policy were issued on each annual anniversary that this policy is in force.

C. **Transfer of Your Rights and Duties**

Your rights or duties under this policy may not be transferred without our written consent.

If you die and we receive notice within thirty days after your death, we will cover your legal representative as insured.

D. **Cancelation**
1. You may cancel this policy. You must mail or deliver advance written notice to us stating when the cancelation is to take effect.
2. We may cancel this policy. We must mail or deliver to you not less than ten days advance written notice stating when the cancelation is to take effect. Mailing that notice to you at your mailing address shown in Item 1 of the Information Page will be sufficient to prove notice.
3. The policy period will end on the day and hour stated in the cancelation notice.
4. Any of these provisions that conflict with a law that controls the cancelation of the insurance in this policy is changed by this statement to comply with the law.

E. **Sole Representative**

The insured first named in Item 1 of the Information Page will act on behalf of all insureds to change this policy, receive return premium, and give or receive notice of cancelation.

Chapter 19

COMMERCIAL PROPERTY INSURANCE

WHAT IS IT?

Commercial property insurance is one of the most widely used and convenient of the risk transfer tools. The insured pays a relatively small dollar amount in exchange for the insurer's promise to pay the greater dollar expenses arising from a loss to some type of property. The insured receives a contract—an insurance policy—outlining what is covered, what is not, what the insurer will do in event of a loss, and what the insured must do in order to receive the benefits of the contract.

The term *commercial property insurance* refers to the many types of policy forms that businesses or not-for-profit organizations may use. The most common forms cover buildings and personal property used in the business, boiler and machinery equipment, business income (loss of income because of a property loss), and crime exposures. At times there is a need for a coverage called *inland marine insurance*, which may cover such items as a contractor's heavy equipment or goods while they are being transported. Additional types of commercial property insurance include coverage for condominium associations, buildings under construction, and flood damage.

BUSINESS USES

Commercial property insurance will pay to repair or replace damaged property. If the property is not replaced, the policy usually will pay for its *actual cash value*. (In insurance terms, actual cash value connotes the replacement cost of property less depreciation.) Property insurance is considered *first-party* insurance coverage because it normally benefits the party who owns the property that has been damaged or destroyed. It can be a valuable source of recovery after, for example, a fire damages or destroys a covered building and its contents. If the insured business had to rebuild the property without the benefit of insurance, the cost could seriously constrain the business's cash flow.

In addition, many lenders require that insurance be carried on property that is used as collateral for a mort-

gage or loan. In these transactions, the mortgage holder or lender often requires that the property be insured. This protects the lender's financial interest in it. In many cases, the financing of high-valued properties is not completed until evidence of satisfactory property insurance is provided.

Many insurance companies that provide commercial property insurance offer property loss control services in addition to the insurance policy. These services usually are available for higher valued properties and include such services as analysis of the adequacy of fire-suppression systems and inspections of boilers and machinery to comply with governmentally required certifications.

ADVANTAGES AND DISADVANTAGES

Risk managers must weigh the advantages and disadvantages of transferring any risk to an insurer. For example, the risk manager for a medium-sized manufacturing business might decide the best course of action is to obtain insurance for every exposure presented—building, contents, computers, boilers and machinery, shipped cargo, and ornamental landscaping. But is this really feasible? Coverage for landscaping, although available, is normally extremely expensive. Therefore, the possibility of loss to the landscaping is something the business may decide to retain. Other risk management techniques—such as avoidance or contractual transfer of risks—also might be more appropriate.

ADVANTAGES

However, in analyzing exposures, the advantages of insurance must be considered. In the area of commercial property insurance, advantages include:

- Peace of mind and a sense of security that money will be available to repair or replace damaged property.

- Loss control services (many insurers provide these) that may decrease the chance of loss.

- Standardized coverage forms, which have been interpreted in the courts.

- The opportunity to pay small dollar amounts for possible large recoveries.

- The opportunity to take advantage of the greater financial resources of insurers.

- The ability to eliminate potential loss of revenue.

- Eliminating a reduction in property value because of unrepaired damage.

- The fact that commercial property insurance is provided by an industry that is regulated by state departments of insurance.

DISADVANTAGES

But, of course, there are disadvantages to be weighed, including:

- The cost of insurance—premium dollars tied up.

- Desired coverage may not be available.

- It may be difficult to identify exposures.

- It may be difficult to establish the appropriate amount of insurance.

- The amount of loss may exceed the insurance that is in place.

- An insurer may become insolvent and unable to pay claims.

- Loss may not be covered because of policy exclusions or limitations.

- An insurance policy might be cancelled or nonrenewed for a number of reasons.

DESIGN FEATURES

The design features of the most common commercial property coverage forms are discussed in this chapter, beginning with the commercial building and personal property coverage form.

Building and Personal Property Coverage

The common coverage forms in use are those from the *Insurance Services Office* (ISO) and *American Association of Insurance Services* (AAIS). These organizations provide forms, collect information on claims, and provide many other services to the insurance industry. Both the ISO and AAIS forms cover buildings and contents; other structures that are not buildings, such as outdoor fixtures; and personal business property that may not, strictly speaking, be *contents* of the building. For example, business personal property in the open (or in a vehicle) within one hundred feet of the described premises is covered on both.

For larger commercial risks, the selected form may be combined with a commercial general liability form (CGL), business auto form, workers compensation and employers liability form, boiler and machinery form, crime coverage, and perhaps inland marine coverage to make a complete insurance package. For smaller risks— a mom-and-pop grocery, perhaps—a businessowners form, which provides some of these coverages in one policy, may be all that is necessary. Very large properties with high values may be insured on stand-alone property forms that are endorsed (amended) to provide specialized coverage enhancements.

Methods of Insuring Commercial Property

There are two methods of insuring commercial property. The first is to assign a separate limit to each building or each class of property that is to be insured. This is called *specific insurance*. For example, an insured might have a limit of $200,000 on a building at 100 Canal Street and a limit of $50,000 on its contents.

The other method is to *blanket* insure the same property. Under this method, one limit of $250,000 will apply to building and contents located at 100 Canal Street.

Or, the insured business might own three buildings at different locations. He might elect to purchase $1,000,000 of insurance that would apply to the three buildings, exclusive of their contents. Under blanket insurance, there is no per-building limit. The advantage of blanket insurance is that, in general, there should be enough insurance to cover a loss at any one building. If a loss to the building at 100 Canal Street exceeded $200,000, the entire $1,000,000 of coverage typically would be available to settle the claim.

Policy Structure

The commercial property policy is formed by attaching a *causes of loss form* and the *commercial property conditions* to the *coverage form*. The coverage form tells what is covered (buildings, contents, other structures); the causes of loss form lists the *perils* (potential causes of loss, such as fire or windstorm) that will apply; and the conditions form provides information on the insurer's right to cancel, who pays the premium, and what will happen if the named insured dies.

What's Covered

Buildings

The building and personal property form (the *coverage form)* covers the building or structure described in the policy *Declarations*. (The declarations page usually is the first page of an insurance policy, which identifies the insurance company, the effective period of coverage or policy term, forms and endorsements that are attached, the named insured, and the limits of coverage.) Included within the meaning of *building* are completed additions and, under certain conditions, additions in the course of construction, and fixtures, including outdoor fixtures. *Fixtures* could be bookcases or they could be partitions that have been attached to the walls. In the case of *outdoor fixtures*, signs or even a metal tent frame attached to a concrete patio would qualify. Also included within the meaning of building are permanently installed machinery and equipment, which could include a furnace or central air conditioning system mounted on the roof.

Personal property that the insured owns and uses to maintain or service the building or premises is also covered as part of the *building*. This property could include appliances such as refrigerators and stoves, floor coverings, and fire extinguishing equipment.

An entity that owns a building and leases or rents it to others might purchase coverage for the building only.

Business Personal Property

The next category of covered property is *business personal property*. Many items are included in this category; among them furniture and (once again) fixtures, machinery, leased property the insured has a contractual responsibility to insure, other personal property

used in the business, and labor and materials the insured uses to perform work on personal property of others. For example, the insured's business may be processing jams and jellies for another company. The insured's business personal property will therefore be the jars, lids, and labels, while the contents that come from the other company would belong to the other company.

The term *fixtures* as used in the context of personal property is generally held to mean property that may be removed by a tenant, such as shelving or counters. This is different from *improvements and betterments*, which also are covered as business personal property. Improvements and betterments are items installed by the tenant that become part of the realty and are not removable, such as a storefront plate glass window. Here, the policy responds to a covered loss by paying the insured's *use interest* in the property; that is, the policy either pays the value of the items if the insured replaces them or the value of the items prorated over the remaining time of the lease.

The use of *fixtures* in both the building and personal property coverages has led to much confusion, however, and there is no clear-cut answer. For example, building fixtures might be cubicle walls that are bolted into the walls, but cubicle walls might also be viewed as business personal property fixtures because they are removable.

Business personal property includes the insured's *stock*, which means merchandise held in storage or for sale, raw materials and in-process or finished products, and any packing or shipping materials. The final category of covered property is for personal property of others.

An organization that does not own the building in which it is located would probably need to purchase coverage for business personal property only. (Of course, situations vary. The building owner might require, as a condition of the lease, that the tenant purchase insurance on the building.)

Property Not Covered

Although the coverage forms appear to be quite broad, there are many types of property that have limited coverage or no coverage at all. Some types of property are better insured elsewhere, such as autos or vehicles licensed for use on public roads; others are considered uninsurable, such as land and contraband. Other examples of property that is not covered are: bills and currency; bridges, roadways, and other paved surfaces; personal property while air- or waterborne; and underground pipes and foundations below the lowest basement floor. This is not an all-inclusive list, however. Property coverage forms must be consulted on a regular basis for a complete listing.

Why the Category of Property Is Important

The difference between the various categories of property—building, personal property, stock, etc.—can be critical when a loss occurs. If coverage is placed incorrectly, sufficient insurance proceeds may not be available at the time of loss.

Property Category Problems

Situation #1: A tenant moves into a completed office suite so did not pay to have the improvements and betterments (e.g., cubicles and partitions) installed. This tenant purchases only business personal property insurance, even though the lease requires that he replace the improvements and betterments if they are destroyed by fire. Unfortunately a fire does occur, and the tenant files a claim on the partitions and cubicles. The insurance adjuster denies that part of the claim because the cubicles and partitions cannot be considered business personal property. Since they are part of the building and the tenant did not originally pay for them, the policy requires that they be covered under *buildings*. Since the tenant does not carry building insurance, the tenant must absorb the cost of replacing the improvements and betterments.

Situation #2: A company occupies a building that it owns. It carries $1,000,000 of specific insurance on the building and $300,000 of specific insurance on its business personal property. After the building and its contents are destroyed by a hurricane, it is discovered that the true value of the building is $700,000 and that there is $600,000 of business personal property. Even though the total amount of insurance ($1,000,000 building and $300,000 business personal property—$1,300,000 total) is the same as the actual amount of property ($700,000 building and $600,000 business personal property—$1,300,000 total), there will not be enough insurance proceeds to replace all the business personal property. Only $300,000 of coverage (or less)

will be available to replace business personal property. This is true even though the building was over-insured by $300,000.

Additional Coverages

The commercial property forms contain *additional coverages,* which are in addition to that discussed previously. These coverages are: 1) expense to remove debris of covered property that has been damaged or destroyed by a covered peril, 2) fire department service charge, 3) limited expense to clean up pollutants from land or water at the described premises, 4) additional cost to repair or replace a damaged building because of an ordinance or law (if the insured has purchased replacement cost coverage on buildings, discussed below), and 5) limited coverage to restore lost or damaged electronic data. All of these have dollar caps on what will be paid, but they are in addition to the limits of liability shown on the declarations page.

Coverage Extensions

The coverage forms also contain *coverage extensions.* These extensions provide additional amounts of insurance for the designated property. For example, a newly-acquired building or a building in the course of construction on the insured premises will be covered for up to $250,000 and newly-acquired business personal property is covered up to $100,000 for up to thirty days. Insurers typically offer a number of other coverage extensions, which usually offer capped limits of insurance.

But, in order to make a claim under any of these, the declarations page must show a *coinsurance* percentage of at least 80 percent or more or a *value reporting* symbol.

Coinsurance is a means of enforcing *insurance to value,* which means purchasing enough insurance to match the value of the covered property. Because the majority of property losses are partial (only part of a structure is damaged), many persons may be enticed to purchase only minimum limits of coverage, believing that they would never need more. An insurer would therefore be in the position of paying many small claims yet never recouping enough premium dollars to pay all losses and expenses. The *coinsurance clause* on a property policy requires that the insured purchase an amount of insurance equal to a specified percentage of the value of the insured property. The insured gets a reduced rate, and the insurer collects enough premium.

Common coinsurance percentages are 80, 90, or 100 percent of the property value. If the insured does not maintain the required percentage of insurance, claim payments are reduced, and the insured is penalized for not carrying enough insurance. The coinsurance formula works like this:

$$\frac{\text{Limit of Insurance}}{\text{Value of Covered Property}} \times \text{Coinsurance Penalty} \times \frac{\text{Total Amount of Covered Loss} \quad \text{Minus the Deductible}}{} = \frac{\text{Amount Insured Can Collect}}{}$$

This is commonly referred to as:

$$\frac{\text{Did}}{\text{Should}} \times \text{Loss} \quad \text{Minus the Deductible} = \text{Amount Payable}$$

Value reporting is used with business personal property. It means that a limit of insurance is set high enough to cover the maximum value of property the insured expects to have on hand at any time during the policy period. Actual values of this property are reported on a periodic basis, such as monthly or quarterly. If values are accurately reported, then the insurer will pay the full amount of a covered loss—subject to the limit selected—even if the amount of the loss is greater than the value last reported. Value reporting is particularly useful when amounts of merchandise or product on hand fluctuate. Think, for example, of the amount of merchandise in a toy store before the holidays as opposed to in January.

How Losses Are Settled

Limit of Insurance

A commercial property policy will pay up to the limit of insurance that is shown in the declarations for any one occurrence. In general, an *occurrence* is an event that triggers coverage under a policy, such as a fire, windstorm, or hail storm. Additional limits of insurance may be paid for ancillary property, such as signs and the property covered under the extensions and additional coverages.

Deductibles

This policy section tells how a deductible is applied to a loss. A *deductible* is the amount of a loss that the insured agrees to assume. Although deductibles typically are stated as dollar amounts, they may be percentages. For example, in earthquake coverage, a percentage is applied to the amount of loss. Insureds may select different deductibles to apply to different property covered on

the same policy. A policy might cover three apartment buildings at the same location, with a different deductible applying to each one and another deductible applying to business personal property.

Applying the Deductible

It is common practice to apply the deductible to the total loss, which works to the benefit of the insured. For example, an apartment building that is insured for $100,000 is completely destroyed. (Assume no coinsurance applies.) The insured carries a $1,000 deductible, so he collects $99,000. But if the building were actually worth $110,000, the insured would collect $100,000— the $110,000 building value minus $1,000 equals $109,000. However, the limit of insurance, which is the most the insured can collect, is $100,000.

Valuation

Valuation means how a property is financially valued at the time of loss. Commercial property policies typically offer a choice of three valuation systems:

- replacement cost,
- agreed value, or
- actual cash value.

Replacement Cost

Replacement cost typically means the cost to repair or replace damaged property. If the insured has purchased replacement cost coverage, covered loss or damage to insured property is settled on the basis of the *least of* 1) the limit of insurance that applies, 2) the cost to replace the property with other property of like kind and quality and used for the same purpose, or 3) the amount the insured actually had to spend to repair or replace the property.

An insured can decide to rebuild elsewhere in the event of a total covered loss, but, in that case, she will not receive a greater payment than would have been received if rebuilding at the insured location.

Since the coinsurance condition applies to the replacement cost, the insured should carry a higher limit of insurance to avoid being penalized by the condition.

Many insurers, however, charge lower rates for higher coinsurance percentages. For example, an insured who carries, say, $90,000 coverage on a building valued at $100,000 (90 percent coinsurance) will find that he is paying proportionately less than if he carried only $70,000 (70 percent coinsurance).

The replacement cost optional coverage states that the cost of repair or replacement does not include any increased cost because of enforcement of a law or ordinance governing rebuilding or repair. *Replacement* entails restoring the insured to a preloss condition. Even though the insured's old property is replaced with new, it is not the intent to give unlimited upgrade coverage for items that might be required by a building ordinance or law.

For example, an insured's 1960s three-story office building is destroyed. *Replacement cost coverage* will pay to restore the building to a preloss condition using new materials. What the coverage will not do, however, is pay the total cost to widen hallways, build ramps, or make washrooms wheelchair accessible in accordance with the Americans with Disabilities Act (ADA). That is a function of the ordinance or law additional coverage, which is typically included in commercial property policies that offer replacement cost coverage. Coverage is limited under the ordinance and law additional coverage to the lesser of 5 percent of the limit of insurance applicable to the building or $10,000 in the ISO commercial property form. This is not a lot of coverage, so it is prudent to purchase additional coverage limits.

Agreed Value

An insured may elect to have losses settled on an *agreed value basis.* The insured and insurer agree, before a loss occurs, that the value shown for a covered item is its insured value for loss settlement purposes. When this option is chosen, the coinsurance condition will not apply in event of a covered loss—even a partial loss. The insured must submit a statement of values—either for full actual cash value or full replacement cost—to the insurer in order to qualify for the optional coverage.

The drawback to this arrangement is that the agreed value provisions are effective for a year, after which they expire and the coinsurance clause will be reinstated. In addition, some insurers may require that the insured pay for a property appraisal, which establishes property values, before agreed value coverage is provided.

Actual Cash Value

If the insured has not selected replacement cost or agreed value coverage, then most covered losses to insured property are settled on an actual cash value basis. *Actual cash value* is commonly defined as replacement cost minus depreciation. So, for example, if an insured's 1960s office building burns to the ground, he will receive the depreciated value of the building, depending upon whether the coinsurance condition was met.

However, not all property loss is settled on an actual cash value basis. If the coinsurance condition for a damaged building is met and the cost to repair or replace does not exceed $2,500, the cost to repair or replace will be paid. (As in replacement cost coverage, the cost to repair or replace does not include any increased costs because of enforcement of any law or ordinance governing building.) Under this provision, though, loss to certain types of property, such as floor coverings, is settled at actual cash value, even if the property is attached to the building.

Other types of property are not settled on an actual cash value basis. Glass losses are settled with safety glazing material if the law requires this. Stock that has been sold but not delivered—that is, the insured's product, including raw materials and materials for shipping—is valued at selling price less discounts and expenses the insured would have had had the loss not occurred.

Valuable papers and records, including those on electronic media, are replaced at the cost of blank materials and the labor to transcribe or copy the records if there is a duplicate.

If the insured rents premises and has made improvements or betterments to the property, loss settlement may take one of three options. First, the insurer pays nothing if others, such as the owner of the premises, pay for the repairs or replacement. Second, the insurer will pay actual cash value if repairs are made *promptly,* which is not defined and therefore subject to interpretation. Third, if repairs are not made promptly, the insurer will pay only for the tenant's remaining use interest in them.

Perils Insured Against

The business and personal property forms tell what kinds of property are covered and how losses will be settled. These forms alone will not provide coverage. *Causes of loss* forms must be attached. These forms list the perils (causes of loss such as fire or hail) that the property will be protected against. All of the causes of loss forms state that they cover direct *physical* loss. That is, physical, rather than consequential, loss is covered by the forms. Consequential losses are those that may result from a property loss. For example, because a warehouse is destroyed, a business grinds to a halt and loses income. The loss of income is a consequential loss. Or, two of an insured's fleet of seven tractor-trailers burn. The loss of the trucks is a *physical* loss; the loss of their use is a *consequential* loss.

There are three causes of loss forms: *basic, broad,* and *special.* The basic and broad forms are structured to state which causes of loss are covered. The number of covered causes of loss in the basic form is eleven and in the broad, fourteen. The special form covers any cause of loss that is not specifically excluded. In addition, the broad and special forms provide coverages not found in the basic form.

Figure 19.1 compares the causes of loss that are covered on the basic and broad forms.

The special form does not list all of the above causes of loss, because a loss is covered unless specifically excluded.

Additional Coverages: Collapse and Fungus Cleanup

The broad form provides two additional coverages. The first of these is for direct physical loss or damage to covered property caused by *collapse* of an insured building or part of an insured building. Therefore, the coverage applies to the building or to the property contained within it. Prior to the current ISO form's definition of *collapse*—which essentially meaning falling down to a heap of rubble—various legal jurisdictions interpreted *collapse* as either reduced to rubble or simply structurally impaired. Therefore, it is important to refer to the form in use to see whether a definition of *collapse* appears. (Other commercial property forms may not define collapse.)

Coverage for collapse is limited on the ISO commercial property form. It is covered only if caused by one of the perils listed on either the basic or broad forms; by hidden decay or insect or vermin damage; by weight of people, personal property, or rain collected on a roof; or by defective materials or construction methods if the collapse occurs during construction, remodeling, or renovation. There are also restrictions on certain types of property. Coverage for collapse is included within the limit applying to the property.

The current broad form also provides limited coverage ($15,000) for clean up of fungus, which includes all forms of mold, wet or dry rot, and bacteria. The event

Figure 19.1

Causes of Loss	
Basic Form	**Broad Form**
fire	fire
lightning	lightning
explosion	explosion
windstorm or hail	windstorm or hail
smoke	smoke
aircraft or vehicles	aircraft or vehicles
riot, civil commotion	riot, civil commotion
vandalism	vandalism
sprinkler leakage	sprinkler leakage
sinkhole collapse	sinkhole collapse
volcanic action	volcanic action
falling objects	weight of snow, ice, sleet
	water damage from a plumbing device

triggering the coverage must be one of the causes of loss listed for the broad form other than fire or lightning. If the insured has purchased flood coverage (we will discuss this later in the chapter), the mold remediation coverage will also respond. However, this coverage is included within the limit of liability applying to the insured property. This is the most that will be paid no matter what causes the mold damage.

The current special form provides collapse and mold remediation, and adds three coverage extensions. These are for: property in transit; water damage, other liquids, powder or molten material damage; and glass. The details of these coverages are described in the special form.

Coverage Limitations and Exclusions

All policies of insurance contain limitations and exclusions. That is, coverage for some types of property is limited, and there is no coverage at all for other types of property. There are reasons for this. For one, many insureds do not need and would not be willing to pay for extensive coverage on property such as heavy equipment, for example. Then, some exposures are uninsurable (such as war) or that are better insured elsewhere (such as flood, which is often insured through the federal government).

It is not the purpose here to review each and every nuance of the limitations and exclusions. Policy forms should be consulted for specifics. Therefore, when reading this section, remember that it is not intended to be all-encompassing.

All of the causes of loss forms contain exclusions. However, because the special form covers anything not otherwise excluded, it actually contains more exclusions than do the other forms. All of the standard forms exclude the following:

- *Ordinance or law.* This exclusion precludes coverage for increased costs incurred to comply with any ordinance or law when damaged property is being rebuilt or replaced. (However, the ISO coverage form gives $10,000 additional coverage for ordinance or law provided the insured has selected replacement cost.)

- *Earth movement.* There is no coverage for landslide, mine subsidence, or earth shifting. However, if the earth movement results in fire or explosion, that resulting damage is covered.

- *Governmental action.* There is no coverage for seizure or destruction of property by order of a governmental authority, but there is coverage if the property is destroyed to prevent a fire's spreading

- *Nuclear hazard.* Although closely allied with the *war* exclusion, it need not be the same. Remember Three Mile Island and the nuclear damage that arose because of the reactor's malfunction.

- *Utility services.* If a power or other utility failure occurs off the insured premises, there is no coverage for the resulting loss unless the failure results in a covered cause of loss on the insured premises.

- *War and military action.* Although not included in the exclusions, acts of terrorism, including biological or nuclear action, are now frequently excluded by endorsement. Some terrorism exclusions give limited coverage (fire resulting from the act is covered) but many are absolute (no coverage whatsoever).

- *Water.* Although some water damage is covered, most is excluded.

Doctrine of Concurrent Causation

All of the above exclusions are preceded by language intended to prevent operation of the *doctrine of concurrent causation.* This doctrine holds that if any covered cause of loss contributes to an otherwise excluded loss, the entire loss must be covered. For example, if human negligence (not specifically excluded) causes a utility failure, the doctrine of concurrent causation would operate to provide coverage. The exclusions just discussed are prefaced with language stating that there is no coverage—no matter what other cause or event contributes "concurrently or in any sequence" (ISO's language) to the loss. Therefore, these exclusions apply no matter what other factors are involved.

Coverage for some of these exposures may be purchased—notably earthquake, flood, ordinance and law, and failure of utility service.

Other Exclusions

The next list of exclusions contains many that are not absolute. For example, a loss that is confined to the subject of the exclusion may not be covered, but resulting damage to other property may well be covered.

They appear in all the causes of loss forms.

- Artificially generated electric current. But if the current results in a fire, the fire damage is covered.

- Explosion of steam boilers, pipes, or engines owned by, leased by, or under the control of the insured. But if explosion results in fire or combustion explosion, the resulting damage is covered.

- Mechanical breakdown. But if a covered cause of loss results (such as a fire or sprinkler leakage) that damage is covered.

- Neglect. If the insured does not use all reasonable means to preserve or protect covered property from further damage at the time of a loss, the resulting damage is not covered.

Remember, each causes of loss form covers progressively more perils that may result in a loss, until the special form covers anything that is not otherwise excluded. So, gradually coverage is expanded.

In the special form, no perils are named, only the applicable exclusions. The special form, therefore, excludes loss caused by such things as wear and tear, rust, smog, smudging, or smoke from industrial operations, settling, nesting or infestation of insects, birds, rodents or other animals, and delay or loss of use or market—as well as a number of causes of loss that are either uninsurable or better insured on another coverage form.

Business Income Coverage

The amount of business income coverage any given organization will need is something that cannot be left to chance. Sound business planning—based on a worst-case scenario—must take place prior to a loss occurring. Even an unprofitable business may have on-going expenses, so business income coverage should be included as part of an insurance package even when it would appear to be unnecessary.

Many questions must be addressed during this exercise, among them

- Will the company remain in business following a total loss?

- *Should* the business attempt to remain in business?

- How long would it take to restore the business to where it was before a loss occurs?

- Is there a business recovery plan in place, or are we relying on loss prevention?

Risk managers must determine values of buildings—including what it would cost to replace them as well as increased costs of construction because of ordinance or law—and the cost to replace personal business property. They might also consider whether additional equipment would be necessary to operate on an emergency basis. Bottom line, the amount of business income coverage purchased should be enough to allow the business to reestablish itself on a preloss basis.

Various insurance forms may be used to respond to business income losses. There are two main standard forms that are issued by ISO. However, many insurers have their own forms and there may be differences. One of the ISO forms covers business income without extra expense, and the other covers business income with extra expense. We will discuss the *extra expense* coverage below.

The business income forms provide coverage for the net profit or loss before income taxes that would have been earned had there been no loss, plus continuing normal operating expenses, including payroll. A covered cause of loss must be the cause of the loss of income. For example, *flood* is excluded on standard policies, so if a flood damages the insured premises, forcing the business to stop operations, there is no coverage for business income. It is possible for an insured to sustain a business income loss without direct loss to his own insured property. For example, if the insured leases part of a building, and a fire occurs in another part of the building that forces the insured to temporarily close, the loss is covered even though there is no direct physical damage to the insured's property.

Rental value may be included in the coverage. *Rental value*, as the name implies, is net profit or loss the insured would earn as rental income from property he owns or rents to others, and the fair rental value of any part of that premises the insured occupies himself.

Both ISO business income forms contain additional coverages and extensions. These are

- **Civil authority**. If access to the premises is prohibited by civil authority because of a direct physical loss of property by a covered cause of loss at other than the insured premises, coverage is provided for loss of business income for up to three weeks.

- **Alterations and new buildings**. Loss or damage to new buildings or structures caused by a covered cause of loss resulting in business interruption triggers coverage.

- **Extended business income**. When a business cannot operate for a time and then resumes operations, there is a gap between when production begins and market share is recaptured. This coverage gives the insured time to get operations back up to speed.

- **Interruption of computer operations**. The forms provide $2,500 for all loss because of interruption of computer operations when caused by a covered cause of loss. Given the complex nature of modern business operations, this amount probably is inadequate, and businesses should consider arranging more coverage.

- **Newly acquired locations**. A maximum of $100,000 is available for covered business interruption at a newly acquired location.

- **Expenses to reduce loss.** This coverage is found only on the business income (without extra expense) form. This coverage extension responds to necessary expenses incurred—but only to the extent they reduce the total business income loss. For example, a business income loss is $250,000. The insured rents other equipment for $25,000 and reduces the business income loss to $100,000. He collects $125,000. But if the equipment costs $125,000 and he reduces the loss only to $200,000, he only can collect $250,000 and will be out $75,000. This coverage is sometimes confused with extra expense coverage.

Extra expense coverage, distinguished from expenses to reduce loss, will pay costs the insured incurs that would not have been necessary had there not been a covered loss. It may be included on the business income coverage form, or it may be purchased as a separate type of coverage. Extra expense coverage could be used for renting replacement equipment, hiring extra workers, or paying the expense of relocating the business to another premises. It also might include the cost to subcontract work to complete a project that the insured, because of the loss, cannot. The coverage also may pay to repair or replace property to the extent it reduces the business income loss.

For example, say the insured does not have enough personal property coverage to replace all damaged items, such as stock, computers, and desks. In order to get the business functioning in a timely manner, the extra expense coverage will respond provided the insured has selected a sufficient amount of coverage.

There are a few more things to note about business income coverage. A time deductible usually applies. Coverage for business income will not begin until seventy-two hours after the time of the direct physical loss, and it ends on the earlier of the date when the property should be (*should be*, not *is*) restored, repaired, or rebuilt at the described premises or the date business resumes at a new permanent location. A coinsurance percentage, if the insured has chosen one, applies. Finally, various exclusions do apply.

It is frequently necessary to tailor business income coverage, and several coverage endorsements are available to do that.

One of the most commonly used endorsements covers business income caused by damage at a *dependent property*. A dependent property is one on which the insured depends for customers, supplies, or distribution of its product. Think of a manufacturer. The organization purchases supplies from a supplier (point A), processes them (point B—the manufacturer), and then sells the finished product through a distributor or retail store (point C). What happens to the manufacturer's business income if either point A or point C is damaged and closes down? Unendorsed forms will not respond because there has been no direct physical loss at point B. Or, point B may be a store located in a mall. Point B relies on points A and C, large anchor stores, to attract customers to its own store.

Loss of business income also can be arranged for when a covered cause of loss that occurs to the off-premises utility forces the insured business to suspend operations.

Another of the exclusions on the property coverage form precludes coverage, except for the limited additional coverage, for loss arising out of ordinance or law. If the period of restoration is prolonged because of an ordinance or law governing rebuilding or repair, business income coverage for that period of time may be added.

Educational institutions—colleges, universities, or prep schools—face a business income exposure that is unique. Say, for example, a college has a fire at its main administration building during the summer break. Even if the building can be rebuilt in time for the autumn semester, many of the planned-for students will decide to enroll elsewhere. Coverage for the loss in tuition and fees can be added to the business income coverage.

Common Commercial Property Endorsements

Like most lines of insurance, commercial property coverage can be tailored to suit the insured's needs. In the following section, we briefly discuss some of the more common endorsements.

It is possible to arrange coverage so that when a covered cause of loss causes an interruption to utility service, there will be coverage for loss or damage to insured property that might otherwise not be covered. For example, a loss in power might cause an expensive piece of equipment to come to a halt, damaging its bearings. Mechanical breakdown is otherwise excluded unless this endorsement is attached. Or, loss of water might cause a cooling unit to seize, damaging it. The endorsement covers the loss.

And, if the cooling unit contains refrigerated property that spoils as a result, that is a consequential loss that would not be covered unless coverage for spoilage is arranged.

Noted previously as well was the exclusion for coverage, except on a limited basis, for increased costs because of enforcement of any ordinance or law. Coverage can be arranged to respond to costs to demolish an undamaged portion of a building, the increased costs associated with repair or replacement, or loss to an undamaged portion of a building.

Earth movement is an excluded cause of loss. Coverage for loss caused by earthquake or volcanic eruption may be added.

Flood, likewise, is an excluded cause of loss. We discuss the National Flood Insurance Program later in this chapter. However, it is possible to arrange coverage in addition to that provided under the federal plan. Many insurers include flood coverage on policies intended for large commercial clients.

Boiler and Machinery

Manufacturing operations rely on machinery to process goods. Even businesses not engaged in manufac-

turing have some kinds of equipment, such as furnaces, air conditioners, or computers that can break down. Coverage for these exposures is limited under the building and personal property forms, so special coverage is needed.

The current coverage forms can include coverage for loss or damage to the covered equipment as well as consequential losses, such as for spoilage or loss of business income. For example, if the insured leases the premises, she will not own the boiler but might still be legally liable for damages arising out of an explosion.

Although computer breakdown is a part of the coverage, loss caused by a computer error or virus is not covered. There are specialty lines of insurance that provide coverage for loss arising from hacking, denial of service, or misuse of data, among others.

As is typical in property insurance, there are exclusions that affect coverage. Therefore, coverage forms should be reviewed with care.

Builders Risk

Buildings under construction present unique exposures in that, as buildings go up, their values change. Owners, contractors, and subcontractors may all have insurable interests to protect. Coverage is necessary to protect not only the building itself, but also the materials and supplies used in construction.

There are two common types of forms used. The first, which is the standard commercial property form, is often adequate for smaller projects. Because collapse during the course of construction is a very real possibility, coverage should be added by endorsement. The form provides limited coverage for materials and supplies that are owned by others; located in, on, or within one hundred feet of the premises, in the care of the insured; and intended to become a permanent part of the building.

The other form falls into the category of *inland marine* insurance. Inland marine is a term that was first applied to "instrumentalities of transport," such as bridges, or communication structures such as radio and television towers. Coverage under this type of form is generally much broader than that of the standard forms. For example, these forms generally cover collapse of a building while in the course of construction, while the standard forms do not. The forms often cover property in transit to the building site, boiler explosion, and property of others. Coverage for flood, earthquake, and *soft costs* may usually be added. Soft costs are those that arise when a covered loss occurs. They may include additional cost to refinance a lease on leased equipment, additional interest on a new loan necessitated by a loss, or additional architect fees.

Condominium Association

Condominium buildings are owned in common by those persons owning units within the building. The coverage form for this type of structure is similar to the business and personal property form. A causes of loss form and the commercial property conditions forms are then attached along with any endorsements.

The condominium form adds another category of covered property, for property contained in the individual units. Covered property consists of appliances, such as dishwashers and refrigerators, and fixtures, improvements, and alterations that are a part of the building or structures if the condominium association agreement requires it.

Flood Insurance

The federal government reinsures most flood coverage. Flood insurance is available either directly from the government or through private insurers who participate in the "Write Your Own" program. Larger commercial risks may be able to purchase flood insurance as a part of their property coverage programs. This approach probably will result in broader coverage than that available from the National Flood Insurance Program (NFIP).

There are three forms in use through the federal program:

- the dwelling form,
- the general property form, and
- the residential condominium building association policy.

The general property form is the one used for nonresidential risks, including commercial condos. The form may be used to cover both building and personal property, which, under this form, includes stock.

The forms cover direct physical loss caused by flood as defined in the policy. *Flood* can include run-off of surface waters, mudflow (also defined in the form), and

collapse or subsidence of land along the shore of a lake or similar body of water if the result of a flood. Consequential losses, such as loss of use of the property or business income, are not covered. The exclusions and the types of property not covered vary substantially from the building and personal property forms.

Federal flood coverage is not unlimited. A maximum of $500,000 per building and $500,000 for contents is currently available for nonresidential risks. Property cannot be insured on a blanket basis, so separate amounts of coverage must be indicated for building and contents. Deductibles apply separately to each loss. For example, if an insured has a building loss of $20,000 and a contents loss of $15,000, with a $1,000 deductible, the most he or she will collect is ($35,000 - $2,000) = $33,000. Losses under this form are settled on an actual cash value basis.

Prudent building practice would preclude building in harm's way, unless the insured was prepared to implement strict loss control measures and self-insure in the case of a large risk. Flood coverage forms do not cover much property in a basement, which includes any sunken room or portion of a room having its floor below ground level on all sides. Because many manufacturing operations have heavy equipment on a ground floor or in a basement, a flood could cause great harm. And, because flood is an excluded cause of loss on many property forms, business income coverage, which is triggered by a covered cause of loss, would not be available unless specifically endorsed.

The residential condominium building association policy is used for, as the name implies, condominium buildings in which at least 75 percent of the floor area is occupied for residential purposes. (Either the dwelling or the general property form is used to insure a unit within the condo building.) The form covers the building and contents owned in common. An amount of insurance equal to $250,000 times the number of units may be purchased.

For access to the federal flood insurance plan, go to the FEMA Web site: http://www.fema.gov/nfip/.

Inland Marine

We touched briefly on inland marine coverage in connection with builders' risk coverage. The forms available in this class of coverage may be used to insure property from **A** (accounts receivable) to **Z**ip codes (well, mail anyway).

In keeping with inland marine's transportation origins, most of the forms provide coverage for property in transit. Broad coverage is common, although some forms provide more limited coverage. Lost or damaged property may be valued on an actual cash value basis, replacement cost basis, or, in the case of property in transit between buyer and seller, on an invoice basis.

Commonly used forms are those for musical instruments, cameras, signs, film (used for commercial film production), mail, physicians and dentists' equipment, and jewelry (coverage for a commercial jewelry establishment is referred to as a jeweler's block policy). When these forms are used, they are attached to a general commercial conditions form, an inland marine conditions form, and a declarations page.

Although the coverage is extremely broad (for example, flood is not excluded), loss resulting from war, governmental action, and the nuclear hazard are not covered.

Inland marine coverage may also be arranged to insure transportation exposures. A risk manager for any manufacturer that ships products should carefully analyze this process. Does the manufacturer use its own tractor-trailers? If not, whose? Common carrier (services are offered to the general public), or contract carrier (contracts solely with the manufacturer)? Or will goods be shipped by air or by water? A combination? What types of loss could each shipping method be susceptible to? Are goods shipped overseas?

Often the manufacturer (or other entity) will elect to insure the possible loss. Although many transporters provide insurance on the goods they ship, many times coverage is limited.

Businessowners

Finally, a brief description of businessowners insurance. Businessowners insurance is generally used for a smaller business for which the commercial property form would be too costly. The eligibility requirements include a cap on annual gross sales and a limit on the business's total floor area. Examples of the classes of business suited to the program are apartment buildings, office buildings, wholesale or mercantile operations, and small contractors. Restaurants meeting eligibility requirements may be written.

Unlike the building and personal property form, the businessowners form automatically includes coverage for loss of business income and accounts receivable. The insured may also include, for additional premium, coverage for money and securities, employee dishonesty, and mechanical breakdown (boiler and machinery coverage).

Under the current program, liability coverage is included. The liability coverage is similar in nature to that of the commercial general liability form, discussed elsewhere.

WHERE CAN I FIND OUT MORE ABOUT IT?

- Federal Emergency Management Agency (FEMA) http://www.fema.gov/nfip/.

- *The FC&S Bulletins*, Cincinnati: The National Underwriter Company http://www.national underwriter.com/nucatalog/

- Hillman, Bruce, and Michael K. McCracken. 2001. *Commercial Property Coverage Guide, Second Edition*. Cincinnati: The National Underwriter Company.

- American Institute for Chartered Property Casualty Underwriters and the Insurance Institute of America, including courses in the Associate in Claims (AIC) and Chartered Property Casualty Underwriter (CPCU) courses of study. http://www.aicpcu.org/programs/index.htm

QUESTIONS AND ANSWERS

Question—A fire at the power plant that supplies a business causes a power failure. Refrigeration equipment at the insured business (a food wholesaler) does not work and the food spoils. What special arrangements would have to be made to have this type of claim covered?

Answer—This loss would not be not covered unless special endorsements were attached to the food wholesaler's commercial property policy. This is because food spoilage is a consequential loss, not a direct physical loss. The food wholesaler should consider purchasing an endorsement, which is entitled Spoilage Coverage, which would provide coverage.

If the details of the incident were slightly different, the wholesaler might have coverage. For example, if the power failure causes a piece of equipment to spark and start a fire on the wholesaler's premises, that fire loss is covered even without the spoilage endorsement.

Question—Riverside Holding Company owns a number of manufacturing plants in six different locations. All the facilities are located in the United States, but none are located closer than 100 miles from each other. The total insurable values (TIV) of all the facilities are $500 million. The insurance premium to cover $500 million in property values is far more than Riverside wants to spend on insurance. What methods could Riverside use to decrease the cost of its commercial property insurance?

Answer—Riverside could employ a number of methods to lower the cost of its commercial property insurance. It would be impossible to list all the possibilities, but some examples would include reviewing the cost savings for assuming a higher deductible on the coverage and reviewing the maximum probable loss and purchasing a loss limit policy that would insure that figure. Instituting property loss control systems also could help.

As noted in Chapter 3, the concepts of maximum probable and maximum possible loss can be important in quantifying loss exposures and then insuring them. *Maximum probable loss* defines the maximum amount of loss that a structure will sustain given the facts of its construction, occupancy, protection, and exposure (COPE) data. For example, a heavy timber, mill-constructed building that is filled with machinery may have a maximum probable loss of 30 percent of its total value. A ten-story, sprinklered, fire-resistive office building located in any major metropolitan area may have a maximum probable loss of approximately three stories (again, 30 percent). The construction, occupancy, and protection—as well as the surrounding exposures, such as the types of buildings that surround the facilities—of these structures will affect what *probably* would be the maximum loss from any one incident, such as fire, windstorm, or explosion.

However, the expression *maximum possible loss* has assumed far greater importance since the terrorist attacks of September 11, 2001. As the term implies, maximum possible loss describes the absolute maximum amount of value considered to be at risk. In the above examples, if the buildings' values were $10 million each, the maximum *probable* loss might be pegged at $3 million. Each of the buildings' maximum *possible* loss, however, would be their total value, or $10 million each. Prior to September 11, 2001, using maximum possible loss to describe the value-at-risk was rarely done, but experience with the World Trade Center incident may have changed that. However, there still is value in using maximum probable loss calculations especially when facilities are situated at a distance from one another.

In the case of Riverside Holding Company, each of its facilities is situated miles from one another. It would be impossible for the same fire, for example, to destroy a facility in California and one in Illinois. Therefore, the maximum probable loss by fire for these two facilities would be the value of either of them. Businesses may consider arranging property coverage based on the maximum probable loss. Obviously, there must be agreement between the insured and the insurer about the TIV (total insurable values), as well as the maximum probable and maximum possible values. The policy then could be written without coinsurance with a limit that reflects the maximum exposure at any one facility.

Chapter 19

GLOSSARY

Actual cash value. A valuation provision in which property losses are adjusted on the basis of the property's replacement cost minus depreciation. The market value of an item may be used to help determine its actual cash value.

Agreed value clause. A valuation provision in which the insured and the insurer agree on the value of insured property. When agreed value is selected, the coinsurance clause is suspended.

American Association of Insurance Services (AAIS). An association of insurance companies providing filing and other technical services on behalf of its member companies.

Blanket property insurance. A means of insuring various items of property under one limit of liability. Contrast with specific insurance.

Builders risk insurance. Property insurance that applies to buildings while they are under construction.

Building. Another term for real property, such as buildings and other structures. Items that are considered for coverage under the building section of a property policy are listed on the policy.

Business income coverage. Insurance coverage for net profit and continuing expenses that a business might have earned if there had not been physical damage to property.

Business personal property. Business property that usually is removable from the real property.

Businessowners policy. A package insurance policy that is designed for small to mid-sized businesses.

Civil authority business income insurance. Business income insurance that is activated when access is denied by a governmental or quasi-governmental authority because of physical damage to other properties or parts of property.

Coinsurance. A means of enforcing insurance to value. Purchasing insurance in an amount that equals a percentage of the property value as stated in the policy.

Commercial property insurance. The type of insurance that businesses or not-for-profit organizations may purchase to cover the various types of property they own.

Deductible. The amount of loss that an insured agrees to assume.

Doctrine of concurrent causation. A legal doctrine holding that if any covered cause of loss contributes to an otherwise excluded loss, the entire loss must be covered.

Exclusions. Provisions that void or limit coverage for a particular type of property or a cause of loss.

Extra expense insurance. Insurance that pays extra costs an insured business incurs as the result of direct physical damage from a covered cause of loss (peril).

Fixtures. Items of personal property that have become annexed to real property so that they are considered to be part of it.

Fortuitous losses. Losses that happen by chance; accidents.

Improvements and betterments. For purposes of commercial property insurance, items installed at the tenant's expense that become part of the realty and are not removable.

Inland marine coverage. A type of insurance that is used to cover property that is exposed to perils of transportation or kept at locations other than the insured's customary premises.

Installation floater. A type of builders risk insurance that applies to property being transported to or installed into a building that already exists.

Insurance Services Office (ISO). An organization that provides statistical information, actuarial analyses, policy language, and related services for the insurance industry.

Monoline policy. An insurance policy that is comprised of only one coverage part, such as a property policy or a commercial general liability policy.

Package policy. An insurance policy that is comprised of various coverage parts, such as property, general liability, auto, and umbrella.

Peril. A potential cause of loss.

Rental value. Net profit or loss a business would earn as rental income from property owned, as well as the fair rental value of any part of the premises that an insured occupies.

Replacement cost. A property valuation method in which the property losses are adjusted on the basis of full replacement cost without deduction for depreciation, subject to the terms of the coinsurance clause.

Specific insurance. An insurance policy that covers property specifically described in the policy and for which a specific limit of coverage is assigned. Contrast with blanket property insurance.

Stock. Merchandise held in storage or for sale, raw materials, in-process or finished goods, and packing or shipping materials.

Value reporting. A limit of insurance is set to cover the maximum value of property that is expected to be on hand at any time during the policy period. The actual value of the property is then reported to the insurer periodically (on a monthly or quarterly basis) throughout the policy term.

Chapter 20

DIRECTORS AND OFFICERS LIABILITY INSURANCE

WHAT IS IT?

Directors and officers (D&O) liability insurance is a coverage developed to protect individuals who serve as directors and officers of corporations. The policy responds primarily to financial loss arising from wrongful acts committed or alleged against these individuals. Its original scope has been expanded, however, beyond solely insuring such personal liabilities. Some D&O policies now offer coverage for certain types of loss arising from wrongful acts claimed against the entity itself.

D&O policy forms differ from insurer to insurer. In fact, insurance companies may even offer different forms of coverage from within their own organizations. Because of this, D&O policies cannot be measured against a standard format, but, rather, must be compared one-to-one against each other. It can be said in general, however, that D&O policies are written to respond to financial loss and not bodily injury or property damage claims, which are more appropriately insured by other types of liability policies.

There are certain attributes and coverage areas that are of particular importance when reviewing D&O coverage. This chapter will highlight those in order to give risk managers and insurance professionals a road map by which to evaluate a particular insurance company's D&O program—and whether it is appropriate for the exposures involved.

Types of Entities Needing D&O Coverage

Many types of organizations have boards of directors. These include

- publicly traded corporations,
- privately or closely held companies, and
- not-for-profit organizations.

Publicly traded corporations are those whose shares are traded publicly on a stock exchange. *Privately held companies* are companies that are owned by one or a small group of individuals—or a family. These companies do not offer ownership of company shares to the general public. *Closely held companies* are typically owned by a small group of individuals. Members of the group may trade or sell shares among themselves or select individuals, but they do not offer ownership in the company to the general public. *Not-for-profit* organizations (which may be erroneously referred to as non-profit organizations) are organized for a purpose other than that of making a profit, although not-for-profit organizations are permitted to realize a profit from their operations. Such organizations usually are organized to serve a community, charitable, or fraternal purpose. (See the National Underwriter Company book, *Tools and Techniques of Charitable Planning*, for more information.)

For the sake of simplicity in this chapter, the terms *entity*, *organization*, and *corporation* are used in their broadest generic sense. In general, the terms are used interchangeably to include publicly traded, private, and not-for-profit organizations. Chapter sections that deal with D&O insurance that is designed solely and specifically for one type of organization will clearly state how the discussion is limited.

Responsibilities of Directors and Officers

Directors are elected by an entity's shareholders or membership to govern the entity. Collectively, these individuals are referred to as the board of directors. Most directors are recruited from outside the entity and may be community leaders, experts in a particular area such as accounting, or officers of noncompetitor companies that are engaged in similar types of operations. A director may also be a corporate officer. For example, the president or chief executive officer of a corporation may also be a member of the board of directors.

Directors who do not serve as corporate officers are not involved in the day-to-day operation and management of the entity. Rather, they are charged with overseeing long-range strategic matters. They do this through areas such as the appointment and removal of executive officers, the declaring of dividends, the monitoring of financial data, and the overseeing of merger and acquisition activity. There may be a conflict of interest—or at least the appearance of a conflict—when a director who also is a corporate officer must take action that affects her position with the company.

General Categories of Exposures

In general, shareholder suits are the most frequent and serious exposure for directors and officers of publicly traded companies. Shareholder suits usually are filed as *derivative suits*, which are brought by shareholders on behalf of the corporation. The shareholders normally must demand that the corporation file suit against the alleged wrongdoing of directors and officers, and the corporation usually must decline to do so, before a derivative suit is allowed. Such shareholder suits may be brought for various reasons, but they are frequently seen when the price of the corporation's stock drops and the shareholders allege that the actions of the directors and officers caused the loss in value.

Shareholder suits obviously are not a common problem for privately held and not-for-profit organizations because there are no outside shareholders in those types of business organizations. That may lead some directors and officers—especially those that serve privately held entities—to falsely believe that they are insulated from legal action. However, minority shareholder suits are always possible, even in family-owned businesses, and all types of organizations—public, private, and not-for-profit—are exposed to claims from a variety of sources other than shareholders. These include claims filed by the corporation, itself, or by its employees, customers, competitors, financial backers, or the government.

Varieties of Shareholder and Corporate Claims

Fiduciary Duty

Directors and officers of all three types of organizations have a *fiduciary duty* to the corporation and its shareholders; they must put the interests of the corporation above their own. Owing a fiduciary duty also means that the directors owe the organization—and its shareholders in a publicly traded organization—a high degree of good faith, candor, and loyalty. Directors may face personal liability if they are found to have breached this fiduciary duty in their dealings as board members.

For example, a group of directors may try to stop shareholder efforts to change the makeup of the board, executive management, or majority ownership. These directors may be sued for blocking such a change. In defending their attempts to impede the change, the directors may have to prove that they were acting in the best interest of the corporation—and not out of self-interest—in order to avoid a finding that they breached their fiduciary duty.

Negligence

In addition to having a fiduciary duty to the entity, directors and officers may be liable for losses that arise from negligence in their actions as board members. Many states have tempered this potential liability by adopting what is called the *business judgment rule*. The business judgment rule provides a shield against liability for those who act in good faith in making business decisions that subsequently prove faulty or detrimental to the organization. The business judgment rule, however, would not shield a director or officer who was grossly negligent or took action that was outside his duty as a director.

Bad Faith

The third general type of liability faced by directors is bad faith, sometimes called unauthorized conduct. Directors and officers are not shielded by the business judgment rule when they engage in bad faith actions or fraud, or when they operate outside the activities permitted by the company's articles of incorporation and bylaws. For example, a developer filed bankruptcy before completing a planned community that included a marina. The developer and the homeowners' association agreed on an allocation of expenses between the marina and the residential units that was voted on by board members who owned residential units. The marina club sued to invalidate the allocation, claiming that it was unreasonable. The bankruptcy court held that the business judgment rule did not protect the allocation, which was unreasonable, and substituted another allocation. On appeal, the court found that the board members' conflict of interest negated application of the business judgment rule because the board's action was unreasonable and in bad faith.[1]

Other Categories of Claims

Employee Claims

Employee claims of employment discrimination and/or wrongful discharge against directors and officers have skyrocketed in recent decades. Directors and officers frequently are targeted when such actions are filed with state or federal equal employment commissions or in the courts. The basis of many such claims is discrimination that arises from the employee's membership in a *protected group*. In general, state and federal employment laws prohibit employers from making employment decisions on the basis of an individual's

- race,
- gender,
- religion or creed,
- national origin,
- age, or
- disability.

These six categories often are referred to as *protected groups*. Employers that fall within the scope of such employment laws—which usually is determined by the number of employees—are precluded from discriminating against employees because of their membership in one of the groups. Individual states may add protected categories. For example, in Kentucky, employers are prohibited from discriminating against employees on the basis of tobacco usage.

In response to the escalating number and severity of such claims, a special type of insurance coverage—employment-related practices liability (ERPL) insurance—was developed. Many D&O policies include coverage for ERPL claims against directors and officers within their forms. Others extend that coverage to managers who are not directors and officers and to claims against the organization (the entity) by attaching an ERPL endorsement. At times, a separate ERPL insurance policy may be more appropriate.

Risk Management Tip

Employment-related practices liability may arise from failure to hire, failure to promote, wrongful discharge, and similar employment-related practices. Directors and officers often find coverage for such allegations in their D&O insurance policies. However, managers and supervisors within an organization would not be covered for such allegations in a D&O insurance policy unless it is endorsed to provide broader ERPL coverage. It is important to keep in mind, however, that when the D&O policy is expanded to provide coverage to managers, supervisors, and the entity, the limit of insurance that is available to the directors and officers is diluted. In other words, the entire limit conceivably could be exhausted in a class action employment-related lawsuit and no coverage left for other claims against the directors and officers.

Employment-related claims are probably the biggest source of legal action against directors and officers, other than shareholder claims in publicly traded companies.

Claims from Those Outside the Organization

Customers, vendors, and competitors may allege that corporate officers or directors are personally liable for financial damages they incurred because the directors or officers were directly involved in an action. In other words, if a corporation decides to terminate a lease or draw up plans, an individual officer may be held personally liable if she was directly involved in the activity that led to the claimant's financial loss.

Competitors also may be the source of claims alleging personal liability. For example, corporate officers who control the day-to-day operations of an organization may be held personally liable for direct involvement in activities that involve unfair competition, stealing trade secrets, or patent infringement.

Various governmental agencies may be able to file actions against individual directors and officers for violation of certain laws if the individuals are directly involved in the alleged violations. Included among these would be violations of the Employee Retirement Income Security Act of 1974 (ERISA) and various federal environmental laws. For example, a corporate officer may be held liable for pollution violations if the officer was involved in the day-to-day operation of waste disposal that resulted in a violation.

Another situation in which directors and officers may be held personally liability, which has received increasing attention in recent years, is the theory of *deepening insolvency*. Deepening insolvency describes a process in which directors and officers may keep a business alive in the face of deepening financial problems, which leads to further extensions of credit. Instead of deciding to end the business, the executives are accused of failing to take reasonable action to cease operations. Keeping the business going and masking financial problems may lead creditors to become more deeply entrenched with the company. Directors and officers may face allegations of mismanagement and/or misrepresentation about the state of the business's finances.

BUSINESS USES

There are various methods that may help to pay for losses that involve a director's or officer's personal liability for business decisions.

Corporate Indemnification

Corporate indemnification is one method of protecting directors and officers from their liability exposure from business management decisions. Most states have passed statutes that permit corporations to indemnify (secure against financial damage) directors and officers for their business decisions. The statutes are aimed at encouraging capable individuals to serve on corporate boards without fearing that their personal assets could be tapped to pay for liability arising from their good-faith business decisions.

There are two types of corporate indemnification:

- mandatory, and
- permissive.

Mandatory indemnification can be defined as an absolute statutory requirement that directors and officers be indemnified for their expenses to defend proceedings brought against them, as well as for settlements or judgments arising from such actions. *Permissive indemnification* involves situations in which a corporation is permitted, but not required, to indemnify directors and officers in situations where the individual is not entitled to mandatory indemnification. An example of permissive indemnification would be a proceeding in which a claim is settled before final judgment, with the claim being settled even though the executive acted in good faith. Since each state's laws vary as to mandatory and permissive indemnification, individual statutes should be reviewed for particular situations. In addition, corporate bylaws should be reviewed to determine whether

they take full advantage of indemnification possibilities.

Corporate indemnification is important because it is the first line of protection available to directors and officers. It permits corporations to pay for the costs of defending suits against directors and officers for their good-faith actions, along with paying for judgments and settlements against them.

So Why Buy D&O Insurance?

If corporate indemnification is available to directors and officers, why should an organization spend the money to purchase a D&O liability policy?

In general, D&O policies fund the personal liability exposures of individuals serving as officers and directors, as well as paying the corporation's expenses to indemnify those individuals. A D&O policy might not be necessary if corporate indemnification were assured. But, even in cases in which mandatory indemnification is required, the organization may not have sufficient funds to pay for the defense and settlement. And there are situations in which corporate indemnification is not required.

D&O insurance is necessary *in addition to* corporate indemnification provisions. It is just as valuable as the more common types of liability insurance—such as commercial general and auto liability policies—because it responds to claims for pure financial loss. In contrast, general and auto liability policies only respond to damages that arise from bodily injury, property damage, or personal liability. In fact, most D&O policies exclude coverage for damages arising from bodily injury, property damage, or personal injury since these types of losses are more appropriately insured on the other types of liability insurance policies. Risk managers also should be aware that most personal umbrella policies will not respond to business claims against directors and officers who serve on for-profit boards of directors.

Terminology Refresher

Bodily injury means direct injury, sickness, disease, or death.

Financial loss means financial damages, settlements, judgment, and defense costs but does not usually include civil or criminal fines and taxes.

Property damage means physical injury to tangible property, along with loss of use of the property that is not physically injured.

And defending or settling a claim for financial loss may cost just as much—or even more—than defending a claim for bodily injury. Since the personal assets of directors and officers may be exposed by their service on an organization's board, most require that D&O insurance be provided before they will serve.

ADVANTAGES

There are many advantages to using D&O insurance as a tool to protect directors and officers. They include the following:

- D&O insurance may be required before individuals from outside of an organization will serve as directors. The insurance therefore facilitates the recruitment of outside directors.

- D&O insurance may be the only protection that directors and officers have in the event of an organization's insolvency. If there are no funds available, there will be no corporate indemnification.

- D&O insurance protects the assets of the corporation that otherwise would be needed to indemnify officers and directors for defense and settlement costs. Such lawsuits could unduly strain the organization financially.

- Organizations that are organized as not-for-profit entities simply may not have enough funds available to defend a lawsuit against the board members and executives.

- The cost of D&O insurance premiums could be miniscule when compared with the cost of defense and settlement of a serious claim.

- Some D&O insurers may be able to offer or recommend resources—such as risk management consultants or legal firms that specialize in director and officer claims—of which an organization might not otherwise be aware.

DISADVANTAGES

Disadvantages to purchasing D&O liability insurance include the following:

- Although the premium for a D&O insurance policy may be very small when compared with the potential exposures, the coverage usually is called upon much less frequently that the more standard liability policies. Some may question the wisdom of investing in an insurance policy that is rarely used.

- A great deal of time may be required to accurately complete a D&O insurance policy application, and those who sign the application must warrant that the information is correct. In signing the application *warranty*, the officer pledges that the information supplied is true and complete.

- There are no standard D&O policies. So risk managers must take time to review the coverage being provided on a specific form. Comparing various D&O insurance proposals may present an additional burden.

- D&O insurance is a specialized practice area, and it is important to obtain information about the coverage from agents, brokers, and underwriters who are experienced in the area.

- The cost of defense is included within the limit of liability on D&O policies. Other liability policies provide defense costs in addition to the limit of liability. Therefore, the D&O limit may have to be stretched to cover both defense and judgment or settlement costs.

- D&O policies will not respond to all claims against directors and officers, and some may misunderstand the scope of what is covered.

ADVANTAGES AND DISADVANTAGES

There are some areas that could be considered both advantages and disadvantages, depending on the details of the situation. For example:

- Most D&O policies provide that the insured organization will control the defense of claims. This means that the organization must engage legal counsel and direct the defense of its directors and officers—with assistance from the D&O insurer. This is an advantage in that the personal reputations and assets of the directors and officers are on the line, and they probably will want to play a prominent role in their own defense. However, it also means that organizational resources will be tied up in the defense. In other words, the organization will not be able to just turn a claim over to the insurer and let it handle everything.

- The lengthy process of correctly completing a coverage application may lead to risk management initiatives that otherwise would be overlooked.

DESIGN FEATURES

There are three types of D&O policies that will be introduced in this chapter. They are those designed for private or closely held corporations, not-for-profit organizations, and publicly traded companies. We first discuss attributes that are common to all three types of policy, even though there would be variations in specific wording between different forms and insurance companies. We then discuss attributes that may apply to only one type of policy.

It is important to keep in mind that variations of these three types of policies are available. For example, schools and universities may purchase an educators legal liability (ELL) policy in lieu of a D&O policy. An ELL policy may provide additional coverage that is specifically designed for educational organizations.

It also is important to remember that D&O policies differ from insurer to insurer, and even within individual insurance companies. Therefore, the attributes discussed in this chapter apply in a general fashion to most forms. Individual coverage forms must be consulted, however, for specific details.

General Attributes of Most D&O Policies

Coverage Grants

Most policies provide at least two insuring agreements:

- Coverage A *(Side A Coverage)*, which provides coverage to directors and officers for losses that are not subject to corporate indemnification, and

- Coverage B *(Side B Coverage)*, which funds claims that are subject to corporate indemnification.

There usually is no *retention* or *deductible*, or a very small one, attached to Side A because that coverage applies to individual directors and officers for claims that do not qualify for corporate indemnification. A *retention* or *deductible* is the amount that the insured pays before the insurance policy begins to pay. The deductible for Side B may range from a thousand dollars upwards to tens or hundreds of thousands of dollars.

When a claim is received, the D&O insurer is put on notice. If the organization has amended its bylaws to maximize corporation indemnification, and if the claim involves allegations that fall within the scope of that indemnification, Side B will be triggered. However, if corporate indemnification is not permissible in the situation being claimed, Side A will be triggered. It should be noted, however, that most policies are written to state that Side B will be used for all claims that are *subject to the broadest application of the jurisdiction's corporate indemnification statutes, regardless of whether the corporation chooses to indemnify or not.* Therefore, Side B is the most common insuring agreement that comes into play.

Aggregate Limit of Liability

There is an aggregate limit of liability, which is the most that will be paid in any policy period—including defense costs—for all claims from both Side A and Side B. Defense costs are included within the limit of liability, and risk managers should consider the possible cost of defense when choosing a coverage limit. In addition, claims arising from any extensions of coverage, such as endorsements that provide extended employment-related practices liability coverage, also will erode this aggregate limit. So determining the amount of coverage that should be purchased is a crucial exercise. Many organizations that need a high limit of liability will increase the retention or deductible in order to achieve a more reasonable premium. Individual insurers establish D&O coverage rates; there are no published class rates. Underwriter discretion is frequently permitted, and the interaction of limit and retention may be an important factor.

Once the aggregate limit is exhausted, a new policy must be purchased. Of course, if an aggregate limit is ever completely used up, underwriters will be more wary of the potential for claims and will correspondingly increase the premium or decrease the amount of coverage that is offered.

Claims-made Coverage

D&O policies are almost universally written on a claims-made basis. This means that the policy applies to claims (to which coverage applies) that are made against an insured *and* reported to the insurer during the policy or discovery period. The *discovery period* is a period of time after the policy is canceled or nonrenewed (either because the company didn't renew it or the insurer refused to renew it) that the insured is given to discover claims that arise from wrongful acts (occurrences) that happened during the policy period. The insured is charged additional premium to purchase extended discovery periods.

Claims-made and reported coverage differs slightly. It specifies that the claim must be made against the insured and *must be reported to the insurance company* during the policy period.

Claims-made coverage may be contrasted to occurrence-based coverage, which is common in many other types of liability policies. With occurrence-based coverage, the policy that applied to the occurrence that caused the damage will respond regardless of when the claim is filed.

Claims-made versus Occurrence Comparison

The ABC Steel Company is a publicly traded corporation with claims-made directors and officers liability insurance policies that run from January 1 through December 31 of each year. On December 1, 2001, the board of directors reviewed a proposal to sell one division, which produced a specialty type of steel that had limited application. The board voted not to sell the division on December 15, 2001, but directed management to monitor the sales situation.

Within the next year, sales of the specialty product fell drastically. The media publicized the company's

problems, and, on December 12, 2002, ABC's stock price plummeted. Shareholders took legal action on February 20, 2003, against the corporation and its directors and officers, alleging that a sale of the division should have been executed when the opportunity arose and that the board's failure to act led to the plummeting stock price.

ABC received notice of the legal action on February 21, 2003, and notified its D&O carrier on February 23, 2003. If the D&O coverage was written on a claims-made basis, the policy that was in effect for the term of January 1-December 31, 2003, would apply to the claim because the *claim was received by the insured and reported to the insurance company* within that policy term. This is true even though the decision that is alleged to have caused the loss—the board decision not to sell the division—happened during the policy term of January 1-December 31, 2001.

Discovery Period Purchased

If ABC had nonrenewed its D&O policy on December 31, 2002—or the insurer had refused to renew the policy—ABC may have purchased a one- or two-year *discovery period*. If the situation arose under this scenario, the claim would be received during the discovery period of the January 1-December 31, 2002, policy. The claim would be handled under that policy because it was received during that policy's discovery period.

No Discovery Period Purchased

If ABC had nonrenewed its D&O policy—or if the carrier nonrenewed it—and ABC did not purchase a replacement policy or a discovery period, what would the situation be? If the claim came in on February 21, 2003, (after the expiration of the last policy on December 31, 2002), there would be no coverage.

Occurrence-based Option

If the coverage had been written on an occurrence basis, the policy that applied would be the one that was in effect when the occurrence that led to the claim happened. That would be the January 1-December 31, 2001, policy, which applied when the vote not to recall the parts was held.

Directors and Officers Liability Insurance

Claim-reporting Requirements

The policy's *Notice* or *Claim Reporting* provisions are an important part of the policy. In general, these clauses require that the insured organization or individual insured director or officer notify the insurer in writing of any claim within a certain timeframe from when the claim is received. Many policies specify that the claim must be reported "as soon as practicable." Others give a specific time period. Regardless of the amount of time given to report the claim, it must be reported before the end of the policy or discovery period (if a discovery period is applicable). A grace period of thirty or more days after policy expiration may be provided for claims that are received within the last few days of the policy period.

For example, ABC Steel's current policy is due to expire on December 31, 2003. Its policy requires that claims be reported to the insurer as soon as practicable but no later than the policy expiration date (December 31, 2003). ABC receives a D&O claim against two directors and the company president at 2 p.m. December 31, 2003. It would be impossible to file this claim *in writing* with the insurer before the policy expires. Because of such possible situations, many insurers have included a thirty-day grace period for claim reporting. These grace periods state that claims received within, say, the final thirty days of the policy period, must be reported in writing to the insurer within thirty days after the policy expires. Again, individual policies should be reviewed for the time periods and reporting provision requirements.

Circumstances That May Result in a Claim

There also is a requirement that insureds notify the insurer when they become aware of any occurrence or circumstance that may reasonably be expected to result in a claim. The insured must notify the insurer in writing of the expectation, including the reasons for expecting it. Any claim that subsequently is received based on the reported circumstances will be considered to have been made when the notice of occurrence was given.

This type of requirement is common in claims-made policy forms. It is designed to make underwriters more aware of possible claim payments that will be needed so subsequent policies can be priced effectively. In addition, it serves to allocate claims to the most appropriate policy period. It must be noted, however, that insurers will not accept nonspecific information about circumstances that just might result in a claim. Most forms clearly state that insureds must provide specific information and details about the incident, along with why they believe that a claim may follow.

Definitions

The definitions section is very important, especially since forms differ so greatly from one to another. They play a critical role as coverage evolves and different insurers expand or contract policy provisions. It is impossible to discuss every conceivable definition in this chapter, but certain ones are introduced because they traditionally have a great impact on how coverage may apply. They are:

- claim,
- director or officer,
- insured,
- loss, and
- wrongful act.

Particular attention should be paid to these five definitions when reviewing a coverage form. However, risk managers should familiarize themselves with all the definitions on their organization's D&O policy in order to interpret the coverage correctly.

Claim

The definition of claim originally included written demands for monetary relief or nonmonetary relief and civil, criminal, or arbitration proceedings for monetary or nonmonetary relief . Current definitions, however, usually go much further and may add situations such as written demands for injunctive relief, regulatory proceedings, and civil, administrative, criminal, or regulatory investigations. Again, specific wording differs from form to form.

Director or Officer

The definition of director or officer may fall under terms such as *insured persons, executive, individual insured,* or similar wording. In essence, the individual directors and officers category usually includes past, present, and future directors, officers, trustees, or governors of the organization, and past, present, and future members of management committees or management boards. With such general wording, individual directors and officers do not need to be named on the policy in order for coverage to apply.

Insured

The definition of insured may reference the individual directors and officers as explained previously. However, *insured* often is defined to include individual insureds and the organization—sometimes referred to as the *entity.*

Loss

The definition of loss varies among insurance companies. In general, however, *loss* includes damages, settlements, judgments, interest on judgments, and defense costs that arise from a situation to which the policy applies. Loss usually specifically excludes items such as fines and penalties, taxes, punitive damages (additional damages levied as a punishment), exemplary damages (additional damages levied to set an example), the multiplied portion of multiplied damages (awards that the court chooses to increase, or *multiply,* because the action was particularly onerous), amounts the insured is not financially liable for, and items that are considered uninsurable by law. Some forms exclude employment-related benefits and stock options from the definition of loss. As a general rule, items that the insured would have to pay regardless of the claim—such as wages or benefits—and items that are levied to punish the insured—such as punitive damages and fines—are excluded from the definition of loss.

This definition is important because it qualifies what types of costs and damages the policy will provide to covered insureds.

Wrongful Act

The definition of wrongful act is one of the most critical portions of the policy. Keep in mind that the policy responds to *loss* that arises from a *claim* against an *insured* for a *wrongful act* that the insured committed. Respective definitions of wrongful act can be quite lengthy. In essence, however, they include actions such as breach of duty, neglect, errors, mistakes, misstatements, misleading statements, and acts or omissions

that insureds may commit in their capacities as directors, officers, or other insureds.

Exclusions

The exclusions sections of policies are always must-reads. The D&O policy is no exception. It is critical that all insureds—including the individual directors and officers—understand how the exclusion defines what is covered.

In addition to reviewing the section that is subtitled *Exclusions,* risk managers must keep in mind that exclusionary language may be included in other parts of the policy. For example, as noted previously, the definition of *loss* states what is *excluded* in addition to what is *included* in the meaning of loss.

Within the exclusions section of most policies are two basic types of exclusions: those that deal with corporate governance and those that are either uninsurable or better insured elsewhere. For example, good corporate governance standards would imply that those charged with governing an organization should not be entitled to gain profit or advantage from their positions if they are not legally entitled to it. Following this standard, there is an exclusion on nearly all D&O policies that voids coverage for claims arising from or attributable to the "gaining in fact of any profit or advantage to which the **Insured** was not legally entitled."[2]

Other common corporate governance exclusions include those that void coverage for payments to a director or officer without previous approval of the shareholders or members of the organization, deliberate criminal or fraudulent acts of an insured, profits to which the organization or an insured was not legally entitled, service as members of other boards unless specifically endorsed onto the policy, claims brought by one insured against the other(s), and the public offering of securities by privately held or not-for-profit organizations.

In regard to claims that are either uninsurable or better insured on other policies, most D&O forms include exclusions for bodily injury, property damage, and personal injury claims because they are better insured by other types of liability policies. There also frequently are exclusions for pollution liability, litigation or claims that were instigated before continuous D&O coverage was begun, and for violations of the Employment Retirement Income Security Act of 1974 and similar laws. All of these are either not insurable or better insured elsewhere.

Limit of Liability

A noted previously, the coverage limit includes defense costs, which differs from many liability policies that offer defense costs in addition to the limit of liability. Most policies highlight this provision in the policy and, possibly, in the application form.

There also is an aggregate limit, which caps the amount that the insurer will pay for all claims—including defense costs—within the policy period.

Control of Defense

The insured, and not the insurance company, controls the defense of claims. The insurance company usually *has no duty to defend any insured* although it may end up paying for all or part of the defense. This means that insureds must defend themselves and contest claims that are made against them. However, the policy requires that insureds not admit or assume liability for any claims without approval from the insurer, and it also specifies that insureds must notify the insurance company of all claims and obtain written consent from the insurer before incurring defense costs. This is because, even though the insureds control and are responsible for their defense, the insurance company may ultimately pay these costs. Notifying the insurer of the claim and how the defense is being handled keeps the insurance company appraised of developments and aware of how serious the claim actually is. In addition, the D&O insurer will want to monitor the defense and may elect to participate in it and in settlement negotiations, especially if its money ultimately will be used.

Risk managers may require that the insurer include a provision stating that it will advance defense costs once the deductible or retention is satisfied, and many policies include such wording in their forms.

Panel Counsel

Some D&O insurers require that defense attorneys for certain types of claims be chosen from preapproved lists, called *panel counsel* lists, that are attached to and form part of the policy. For example, an insurance company may have a panel counsel list of attorneys that

are to be used in securities cases or in employment-related practices claims. If insureds choose attorneys that are not on the list, the insurer must preapprove them. These lists are made up of specialists in particular areas of law. In addition, their fee schedules have been negotiated in advance with the insurer. The use of panel counsel, according to some D&O underwriters, provides insureds with legal specialists at fee levels that are reasonable and set in advance.

Discovery Provisions

As noted in the section entitled **Claims-made Coverage,** D&O policies often have a built-in provision that allows the insured to extend the period for filing claims after policies have been nonrenewed by either the insured or the insurer. For example, the policy may provide that, for a preset percentage of the expiring premium, an insured may buy an extended discovery period of one or more years if the policy is not renewed. This is important because of the claims-made and reported aspect of the coverage, which means that the policy responds to claims that are made and reported to the insurer within the policy period. If a policy is not renewed, claims that are received after the policy expires as a result of actions taken by board members during the policy period would not be covered. There are two types of discovery clauses:

- unilateral discovery, and
- bilateral discovery.

When a unilateral discovery clause is provided in the policy, an extended discovery period is guaranteed to be available *only if* the policy is nonrenewed by the insurance company. Under a bilateral discovery clause, the extended discovery period is available if either the insured or the insurer nonrenew the policy. Most policies include the percentage of expiring premium that will be charged for various discovery period lengths.

Changing Carriers

The discovery clause may be important to insureds that, for one reason or another, decide to change D&O carriers. There are many reasons for such a change, including premium pricing considerations and the breadth or limit of coverage that is offered by a replacement insurer compared with that being offered by the expiring carrier.

If an insured decides to change insurers, the new carrier should be asked to provide *prior acts coverage.* Prior acts coverage means that the new policy will cover claims that arise from wrongful acts that were committed before the new policy began. When prior acts coverage is provided on the new policy, the insured should not need to purchase an extended discovery period on the nonrenewed policy.

However, the replacement carrier may attach a *retroactive date.* When a retroactive date is attached to the replacement policy, the insuring agreements will respond to claims that are filed against the insured that arise from *wrongful acts that occurred between the retroactive date and the policy expiration date.* This means that there would be no coverage for a claim that is filed between the retroactive and policy expiration dates if the claim arose from board action that was taken prior to the retroactive date on the new policy. The insured would have to purchase the extended discovery period to cover such a possibility.

One Danger When Changing Carriers

ABC Steel is reviewing D&O proposals from several insurance companies because its policy is scheduled to renew on January 1, 2003. ABC's current insurer—X Insurance Company—has increased the renewal premium and decreased the amount of coverage it is offering for the renewal. In contrast, Z Insurance Company will renew the coverage at the same premium and with the same coverage as on the expiring policy.

Scenario #1: Z Insurance Company offers full prior acts coverage, so ABC Steel will not have to buy an extended discovery period from its expiring insurer. Z's policy will state that it will cover claims that are made against ABC Steel and reported to the insurance company within the policy period.

Scenario #2: Z Insurance Company wants to limit its coverage, so it proposes attaching a retroactive date of January 1, 2003—the same date as the inception date of its policy. Under this situation, the policy will specify that it applies to claims that are made against ABC Steel and reported to the insurance company within the policy period *as long as they arise from wrongful acts that occurred between the retroactive date and policy expiration.* In this situation, a claim that was made on March 3, 2003, but arose from board action of Sept. 10, 2002, would not be covered because the

wrongful act (the board decision) that gave rise to the claim happened prior to the retroactive date of January 1, 2003.

Changes in the Organization

In general, major changes in an organization—such as a merger or acquisition—should be reported to the D&O insurer as soon as possible. In the event of a merger or company sale, the policy may be invalidated upon completion of the deal, depending upon which party takes control of the newly formed organization. And most directors and officers want to be sure that claims received after the deal is completed—but based on their decision to merge—are covered by insurance. There often is automatic coverage for subsidiaries that are added to the organization, as long as the assets of the subsidiary are no more than 10-25 percent (as specified in the policy) of the total assets of the combined organization.

It always is a good risk management policy, however, to notify the D&O insurer when merger, consolidation, acquisition, or sale plans are gaining momentum.

Other Insuring Agreements

A somewhat recent development in the D&O insurance arena is that of offering coverage for the entity itself. One of the most common insuring agreements that may be offered in addition to Coverage A and B is Coverage C *(Side C)*, Organizational Entity Coverage.

Not-for-Profit Entity Coverage

Entity coverage often is provided on insurance policies designed for not-for-profit entities. The theory behind this is that not-for-profit organizations may lack the financial assets to successfully defend a suit seeking financial damages that is filed against the organization. In addition to offering the coverage for the not-for-profit entity, these insuring agreements also may agree to advance defense costs for the organization.

Publicly Traded Entity Coverage

Side C entity coverage also may be included on policies designed for publicly traded companies. In this case, the coverage usually is restricted to entity coverage for *securities claims* only. A securities claim will be defined on the policy but generally would include claims alleging the violation of regulations or statutes regulating securities, including their purchase and sale. Securities claims often involve a drop in stock price or allegations of misleading information that encouraged the purchase or sale of that stock. Forms differ on how they handle administrative or regulatory proceedings involving securities. Some may provide coverage for such proceedings against the entity only if an insured director or officer also is named; others may exclude such regulatory proceedings entirely; and others may offer it regardless of whether an individual also is named in the suit. There also may be other significant limitations on the entity coverage for securities claims.

The Allocation Issue

The presence or absence of entity coverage is important because of the allocation issue, which arises when part of a claim is covered and part is not. Defense and settlement costs must be allocated between the covered portion of the claim and the part that is not covered. In D&O insurance, there are two types of covered/uncovered situations:

- claims that involve covered and uncovered parties, and

- claims that involve covered and uncovered allegations.

The covered parties in D&O insurance usually are the directors and officers; the uncovered parties are the corporation or organization (the entity) and/or employees. This differs from other forms of liability insurance, in which the corporation is the named insured. In those policies, directors, officers, and employees also are insureds for coverage purposes. However, with D&O insurance, the directors and officers are the insureds, and there is no auxiliary coverage for the entity—unless it is specifically added to the policy, such as by adding a Coverage C, Entity, insuring agreeing.

Therefore, when a claim is made against directors, officers, and the corporation for wrongful acts alleged against all of them, there has to be a decision as to how much coverage will be allocated to the individual insureds and how much will be allocated to the entity. There also has to be an allocation of defense costs.

Allocation Example

Consider the case of ABC Steel and its board decision not to sell the division. Assume that the claim is filed within the current policy period, and the allegations in the claim are essentially covered by the D&O policy. However, in addition to naming the seven directors and the executive officers, the claim also names the organization—ABC Steel Company. The relative fault of the covered parties (directors and officers) must be assessed against the relative fault of the uncovered party (ABC Steel). Some D&O policies may state that the insured and insurer agree to use their "best efforts" to arrive at a reasonable allocation of both defense and settlement costs. In some cases, a court may determine that the entire burden should be assigned to the directors and officers. ABC's policy would have to be reviewed to determine its stated position on the issue.

However, if ABC had purchased Coverage C, Entity Coverage, for securities claims, the allocation of costs and settlement may not be an issue.

It must be remembered, however, that entity coverage for publicly traded companies usually does not extend beyond securities claims. So other types of claims may trigger an allocation issue, even if Coverage C has been purchased.

Entity coverage also is often available for employment-related practices liability claims if a special ERPL endorsement is added to the policy. However, absent that endorsement, an allocation issue may arise if an ERPL claim is filed against both directors and the entity.

The same situation may result if a claim involves some allegations that are covered, and others that are not covered.

Other Enhancements

The variety and breadth of D&O policy enhancements sometimes appears to be nearly unlimited. These enhancements may be found in differing wording of definitions, exclusions, and even insuring agreements. However, in addition to entity coverage and ERPL coverage, there are several enhancements that commonly are available. They include:

- outside directorship coverage, and

- spousal extensions.

Outside Directorship

Outside directorship coverage extends the corporate D&O policy to cover the activities of individuals who serve on outside not-for-profit boards at the direction of their employer. The coverage is usually excess of any insurance coverage available from the not-for-profit organization and that organization's indemnification of the director. In addition, the D&O policy usually requires that the board service that is included be listed on the policy and that the service be fulfilled at the request of the corporation. For example, ABC Steel wants to encourage community service among its employees. As a way of setting an example, ABC asks its executive officers to volunteer as directors of various charitable organizations, such as the local not-for-profit hospital, the Red Cross, or a youth organization. These not-for-profit entities may indemnify these individuals for claims arising from such service, and they may purchase D&O insurance. However, ABC also has its D&O policy amended to extend coverage to settlements against their representatives that exceed the funds available from the not-for-profit group and its insurance.

Spousal Extensions

Some policies also may include an extension to cover the inclusion of a spouse (or a spouse's interest in property) in a claim that is made against an insured person. For example, some executives may jointly own personal property with their spouses. Since personal assets may be tapped to pay for D&O judgments, a spouse may be named in the suit. The D&O spousal extension would then provide coverage for the inclusion of the spouse. This coverage only applies, however, when a spouse is named as the result of actions by an insured person (director or officer). Direct claims against the spouse, which arise from actions of that spouse that do not relate to a corporate decision, are not covered.

Coverage for Claims Arising from Initial Public Offerings (IPOs)

Private companies, as explained in the introductory section of this chapter, do not offer shares of their companies to the general public. However, a private company may decide to offer shares to the public in an effort to raise money or broaden its scope of operations. This first offering of stock is called an initial public offering. Companies that already have "gone public" may decide to offer additional shares of stock, which is called a secondary offering. Such stock offerings offer rich fodder for future claims, especially if the stock's value does not rise as much or as quickly as originally anticipated.

Private company D&O policies usually exclude coverage for IPOs. This is because the D&O underwriter wants to review and analyze the information that is developed to sell these initial shares. Most of the information about the IPO that the underwriter needs to review is contained in the prospectus, which is a document that describes the enterprise and is distributed to prospective investors. If the underwriter is not satisfied with how the offering is being made, he may decline to provide D&O coverage for it and the publicly traded operation. Some private company D&O policies may offer what is called securities coverage. In essence, this provides limited coverage for claims arising from certain types of securities. In addition, and perhaps most importantly, this policy provision states that the underwriter must offer a coverage proposal for the IPO as long as the private company notifies the underwriter of the IPO in advance, provides appropriate details, and pays the premium charged. The advance notice must be given to the underwriter at least thirty days (or some other preset number of days) before the IPO is scheduled. This is an important feature because it guarantees that coverage will be offered if the insured complies with the notification terms.

The Application

The application for coverage is an integral part of the D&O policy. It actually is attached to, and becomes a part of, the policy. Therefore, representations that are made in the application form the basis for coverage, and material misrepresentations may void coverage. Because of this, extreme care must be taken when completing the application.

A duly authorized officer of the organization must sign the application. In doing so, the officer warrants that the information is true and correct.

What happens if an officer warrants the application information and it later is determined that some material information was incorrect? If the officer knew of the information and falsely warranted the information, coverage probably will be voided for that individual. However, coverage for innocent insureds probably would not be voided. If the officer was not aware of the information—and had made reasonable efforts to fully complete the application—coverage probably would not be voided for him. However, the details of each situation would have to be reviewed to determine when coverage could be voided.

Some risk managers poll the board members, asking them to review the application to be sure material information is not omitted, in an effort to avoid a faulty application.

WHERE CAN I FIND OUT MORE ABOUT IT?

Corporate Governance in General

- Organization for Economic Cooperation and Development (OECD) and the OECD Principles of Corporate Governance, www.oecd.org.

Directors & Officers Liability Exposures and Insurance

- The Professional Liability Underwriting Society (PLUS), 4248 Park Glen Road, Minneapolis, MN 55416, Phone (952) 928-4644, http://plusweb.org/.

- Hagglund, Clarance E., J.D., and Britton D. Weimer, J.D., and Joseph P. Monteleone, Esq. 1999. *D&O: Guide to Risk Exposures & Coverage.* Cincinnati: The National Underwriter Co. http://nationalunderwriter.com/nucatalog

- *D&O MAPS (Market Information, Analysis of Policies, and Policy Service).* Dallas: International Risk Management Institute.

- *The D&O Book: A Comparison Guide to Directors & Officers Liability Insurance Policies.* 1993. Newport Beach, CA: Griffin Communications, Inc.

- Leimberg, Stephan R., et al. 2001. *The Tools & Techniques of Charitable Planning.* Cincinnati: The National Underwriter Company.

QUESTIONS AND ANSWERS

Question—What is the difference between the terms "claims-made" and "claims-made and reported" in regard to D&O policies?

Answer—A claims-made form will specify that it covers claims made against the insureds within the policy period or any applicable discovery period. A claims-made and reported form specifies that the claim must be made against the insured *and reported to the insurance company* during the policy period or any applicable discovery period.

Question—At one time, D&O policies included a *retroactive date.* There is little reference to retroactive dates now, but a new "date" has been introduced— a continuity date. Do they serve the same purpose?

Answer—Retroactive dates usually apply to all coverage grants on the policy. In order for coverage to apply, the wrongful act must occur between the retroactive and policy expiration dates, and the claim would have to be received during the policy period. In general, current D&O policies no longer have a retroactive date. Some have introduced *continuity dates.* Continuity dates usually apply to coverage agreements that have been added to the policy in more recent years and may not apply to all provisions of the policy. In some situations, litigation, proceedings, or investigations that an insured person knew about prior to the continuity date are excluded from coverage. In other situations, the continuity date acts like a retroactive date for a specific type of coverage and excludes claims that arise from wrong acts that an insured person knew about prior to the date.

For example, ABC Steel adds entity coverage for securities claims on January 1, 2002. At the time, the directors know about a securities claim. The insurer would affix a continuity date of January 1, 2002, to the entity coverage insuring agreement. This would exclude coverage for any possible costs or settlements arising from that particular securities claim.

Question—Is it always best to buy the broadest D&O coverage available and add provisions such as entity coverage, employment-related practices liability coverage, outside directorship, etc., to it?

Answer—Yes and no. Most risk managers and business owners are accustomed to looking for the broadest coverage at a certain premium level. However, it is important to keep in mind that D&O insurance is well named—it was designed primarily to protect the directors and officers. So every time coverage extensions are added, such as when entity or ERPL coverage is added, the amount of insurance available to the directors and officers is diluted. This is because the policies include an aggregate limit of liability and because defense costs are included within that aggregate. One way to get the best of both worlds might be to purchase a broad policy with many coverage extensions that would provide a certain limit of coverage—such as $10 million—and then add an additional tower of limits that is available for the individual directors and officers only.

Exercise

Three directors and officers liability coverage forms, which are written by members of the American International Group of companies, are reproduced in this chapter's appendix. They are the:

- Not-for-Profit Protector℠—designed for not-for-profit companies,

- Private Collection℠ Management Liability Coverage for Private Companies—designed for mid-

sized private companies with up to 1,000 employees,

- Executive and Organization Liability Insurance Policy—designed for publicly traded companies.

Compare the insuring agreements (stated as Coverage A, Coverage B, Coverage C, etc.) that are included in each of the policies to determine how the coverage is crafted for the unique exposures of that type of company. How are the same? Are Coverage A and Coverage B identical in all four of them?

Review the definitions and exclusions to discern the major differences.

Section One of the Private Collection℠ policy provides coverage for individual insureds (directors and officers) and the company. Section Two provides Employment Practices Liability coverage. How do the definitions of *claim* and *wrongful act* differ between the two sections?

END NOTES

[1]   *Croton River Club, Inc., v. Half Moon Bay Homeowners Association, Inc., et al.*, 52 F. 3d 41(2d Cir. 1995).

[2]   American International Group, Executive and Organization Liability Insurance Policy exclusion 4. (a), Form 75879 (3/00).

GLOSSARY

Aggregate limit of liability. The most that will be paid by an insurance policy in one policy term for all claims.

Allocation issue. In D&O insurance (as well as possibly other types) defense and settlement costs must be allocated between the covered portion of the claim and the part that is not covered.

Bilateral discovery. A provision under which an extended discovery period must be guaranteed to be available if either the insured or the insurance company cancels or nonrenews a claims-made policy.

Business judgment rule. A legal premise that directors are immune from liability for ordinary negligence if they act in good faith in making business decisions.

Claims-made basis. A type of insurance policy that applies to claims to which the policy applies that are made against an insured within the policy period or discovery period if applicable.

Claims-made and reported basis. A type of insurance policy that applies to claims to which the policy applies that are made and reported to the insurance company within the policy period or discovery period, if applicable.

Closely held companies. Companies that are owned by a small group of individuals. Members may trade or sell shares among themselves or with select others, but the shares are not traded publicly on a stock exchange.

Continuity date. A date that defines the extent of coverage in regard to time under claims-made liability policies. In some situations, litigation, proceedings, or investigations that an insured person knew about prior to the continuity date are excluded from coverage. In other situations, the continuity date acts like a retroactive date for a specific type of coverage and excludes claims that arise from wrongful acts that an insured person knew about prior to the date.

Corporate indemnification. A provision by which an entity may indemnify (make whole) a director or officer for liabilities arising from their service to the entity.

Corporate officer. An individual who holds an office within a corporation or organization that is established by the group's bylaws.

Coverage A, D&O Insurance. Coverage A, also known as Side A coverage, responds to losses directors and officers incur that are not subject to corporate indemnification.

Coverage B, D&O Insurance. Coverage B, also known as Side B coverage, responds to losses that are subject to corporate indemnification.

Coverage C, Entity Coverage, D&O Insurance. Coverage C, also known as Side C coverage, responds to certain types of claims that are filed directly against the entity (corporation).

Deepening insolvency. A process in which directors and officers downplay the company's financial situation and keep it going in the face of deepening financial problems, which leads to further extensions of credit.

Derivative suits. Lawsuits that are filed by shareholders on behalf of the corporation in which they hold stock.

Directors. Individuals who are elected by an entity's shareholders or members to govern the organization.

Discovery period. A period of time after a claims-made policy is canceled or nonrenewed during which the insured can discover and file claims with the insurance company. The claims must arise from wrongful acts committed within the policy period.

Educators legal liability. A specialized form of D&O insurance that is tailored to educational entities, such as schools and colleges.

Employee Income Security Act of 1974 (ERISA). The federal law that governs various employee benefits, such as pensions, health care, and disability payments.

Employment related practices. Practices taken in the normal employer-employee relationship.

Employment related practices liability (ERPL) insurance. A special form of insurance that responds to claims of employment related practices that allegedly were made on the basis of an individual's membership in a protected group.

Entity. A corporate body.

Fiduciary duty. The duty that directors and officers owe to the organization they serve to put the organization's interests above their own. Includes a high degree of good faith, candor, and loyalty.

Initial public offering (IPO). The first offering of stock to the public by a private corporation.

Mandatory indemnification. An absolute statutory requirement that directors and officers be indemnified for expenses to defend proceedings and resulting settlements brought against them as a result of their business decisions.

Material misrepresentation. A misrepresentation that makes a meaningful difference. In insurance terms, a material misrepresentation by an insured usually will cause the insurance company to agree to offer coverage that it would not ordinarily provide absent the misinformation.

Not-for-profit organizations. Organizations that are formed for a purpose (often community, charitable, or fraternal) other than making a profit, although these organizations may realize a profit. Sometimes referred to as non-profit organizations.

Notice provisions. The clause in an insurance policy that dictates how and when an insurance company should be notified of an occurrence, wrongful act, or claim.

Occurrence-based coverage. The policy form that was in effect when the occurrence happened will respond to a claim for damages, regardless of when the claim is filed.

Outside directorship coverage. An extension of D&O insurance to cover the activities of corporate officers who serve on outside not-for-profit boards of directors at the request of their corporation.

Panel counsel. A list of attorneys who are specialists in a particular field and whose rates are acceptable by the insurance company. D&O insureds are encouraged to use attorneys from the panel counsel list in defending claims filed against them.

Permissive indemnification. Situations in which an entity is permitted by law, but not required, to indemnify directors and officers for expenses to defend proceedings and resulting settlements brought against them as a result of their business decisions.

Prior acts coverage. A provision under which a policy that replaces an expired claims-made form will cover claims that arise from wrongful acts that were committed before the replacement policy began.

Privately held companies. Corporations that are owned by one or a small group of individuals. Ownership of shares in these types of companies are not offered to the general public.

Protected group. The categories of individuals that are protected by various federal and state antidiscrimination laws.

Publicly traded corporations. Corporations whose shares are traded publicly on a stock exchange.

Retroactive date. A date that defines the extent of coverage in regard to time under claims-made liability policies. Claims resulting from wrongful acts that occurred prior to the policy's stated retroactive date are excluded.

Securities claims. In regard to a D&O policy, securities claims in general include claims alleging the violations of regulations or statutes regulating securities, including their sale and purchase.

Spousal extension of coverage. An extension of coverage on a D&O policy that covers the inclusion of a spouse or a spouse's interest in property in a claim made against an insured individual.

Unilateral discovery. A provision under which an extended discovery period must be guaranteed to be available if the insurance company cancels or nonrenews a claims-made policy.

Warrants or warranty. A guarantee or pledge that information is correct.

Wrongful act. In general, wrongful act is defined as actions such as mistakes, errors, omissions, neglect, breach of duty, and misleading statements that individuals may commit in their capacities as insureds.

Appendix

AMERICAN INTERNATIONAL COMPANIES®

NOT-FOR-PROFIT INDIVIDUAL AND ORGANIZATION INSURANCE POLICY
INCLUDING EMPLOYMENT PRACTICES LIABILITY INSURANCE

NOT-FOR-PROFIT PROTECTOR^{sm}

In consideration of the payment of the premium, and in reliance upon the statements made to the Insurer by application forming a part hereof and its attachments and the material incorporated therein, the insurance company designated in Item 8 of the Declarations, herein called the "Insurer", agrees as follows:

1. **INSURING AGREEMENTS**

   COVERAGE A: INDIVIDUAL INSURED INSURANCE

   This policy shall pay on behalf of each and every Individual Insured Loss arising from a Claim first made against such Individual Insured during the Policy Period or the Discovery Period (if applicable) and reported to the Insurer pursuant to the terms of this policy for any actual or alleged Wrongful Act in his/her respective capacities as an Individual Insured of the Organization, except when and to the extent that the Organization has indemnified the Individual Insured. The Insurer shall, in accordance with and subject to Clause 8, advance Defense Costs of such Claim prior to its final disposition.

   COVERAGE B: ORGANIZATION INDEMNIFICATION
   REIMBURSEMENT INSURANCE

   This policy shall pay on behalf of the Organization Loss arising from a Claim first made against an Individual Insured during the Policy Period or the Discovery Period (if applicable) and reported to the Insurer pursuant to the terms of this policy for any actual or alleged Wrongful Act in his/her respective capacities as an Individual Insured of the Organization, but only when and to the extent that the Organization has indemnified such Individual Insured for such Loss pursuant to law, common or statutory, or contract, or the Charter or By-laws of the Organization duly effective under such law which determines and defines such rights of indemnity. The Insurer shall, in accordance with and subject to Clause 8, advance Defense Costs of such Claim prior to its final disposition.

68467 (8/97)   1

COVERAGE C: ORGANIZATION ENTITY COVERAGE

This policy shall pay on behalf of the Organization Loss arising from a Claim first made against the Organization during the Policy Period or the Discovery Period (if applicable) and reported to the Insurer pursuant to the terms of this policy for any actual or alleged Wrongful Act of the Organization. The Insurer shall, in accordance with and subject to Clause 8, advance Defense Costs of such Claim prior to its final disposition.

DEFENSE PROVISIONS

The Insurer does not assume any duty to defend; provided, however, the Named Organization may at its sole option, and in accordance with Clause 8, tender to the Insurer the defense of a Claim for which coverage is provided by this policy. Regardless of whether the defense is so tendered, the Insurer shall advance Defense Costs (excess of the Retention amount) of such Claim prior to its final disposition. Selection of counsel to defend a "Class Action Claim", as defined in Clause 9, shall be made in accordance with Clause 9 of the policy.

2. **DEFINITIONS**

   (a) "Affiliate" shall mean any not for profit organization other than a Subsidiary which:

      (1) the Named Organization or any Subsidiary controls or otherwise has the ability to direct the financial or managerial decisions of such entity, whether through the operation of law, contract or agreement, stock ownership or membership, charter, articles of incorporation, or by-law provisions; or

      (2) is granted by contract the right to control the financial or managerial decisions of the Organization or any Subsidiary.

      Provided, however that such coverage as is provided by sections (1) and (2) above shall be limited solely to Wrongful Acts occurring in the course of the exercise of such control of financial or managerial decisions.

   (b) "Claim" means:

      (1) a written demand for monetary relief; or

68467 (8/97)   2

(2) a civil, criminal, regulatory or administrative proceeding for monetary or non-monetary relief which is commenced by:
(i) service of a complaint or similar pleading; or
(ii) return of an indictment (in the case of a criminal proceeding); or
(iii) receipt or filing of a notice of charges; or

(3) any request to toll or waive any statute of limitations.

The term "Claim" shall include an Employment Practices Claim, provided however, that in no event shall the term "Claim" include any labor or grievance proceeding which is subject to a collective bargaining agreement.

(c) "Continuity Date" means the date set forth in:

    (1) Item 6A of the Declarations with respect to all coverages other than Coverage C; or

    (2) Item 6B of the Declarations with respect to Coverage C only.

(d) "Defense Costs" means reasonable and necessary fees, costs and expenses consented to by the Insurer (including premiums for any appeal bond, attachment bond or similar bond, but without any obligation to apply for or furnish any such bond) resulting solely from the investigation, adjustment, defense and appeal of a Claim against the Insureds, but excluding salaries of Individual Insureds.

(e) "Employee(s)" means any past, present or future employee of the Organization, whether such employee is in a supervisory, co-worker or subordinate position or otherwise, including any full-time, part-time, seasonal and temporary Employee of the Organization in his or her capacity as such.

(f) "Employment Practices Claim" means a Claim alleging an Employment Practices Violation.

(g) Employment Practices Violation(s) means any actual or alleged:

    (1) wrongful dismissal, discharge or termination (either actual or constructive) of employment, including breach of an implied contract;

68467 (8/97)   3

(2)   harassment (including sexual harassment whether "quid pro quo", hostile work environment or otherwise);

(3)   discrimination (including but not limited to discrimination based upon age, gender, race, color, national origin, religion, sexual orientation or preference, pregnancy, or disability);

(4)   Retaliation (including lockouts);

(5)   employment-related misrepresentation(s) to an Employee or applicant for employment with the Organization;

(6)   employment-related libel, slander, humiliation, defamation or invasion of privacy;

(7)   wrongful failure to employ or promote;

(8)   wrongful deprivation of career opportunity, wrongful demotion or negligent Employee evaluation, including the giving of negative or defamatory statements in connection with an employee reference;

(9)   wrongful discipline;

(10)   failure to grant tenure or practice privileges;

(11)   failure to provide or enforce adequate or consistent organization policies or procedures relating to any Employment Practices Violation;

(12)   violation of an individual's civil rights relating to any of the above, but only if the Employment Practices Violation relates to an Individual Insured, or applicant for employment, with the Organization or an Outside Entity, whether direct, indirect, intentional or unintentional.

(h)   "Financial Insolvency" means: (1) entering into proceedings in bankruptcy or (2) becoming a debtor in possession; or (3) the taking of control, the supervision of, or the managing or liquidating the financial affairs of such entities by a receiver, conservator, liquidator, trustee, rehabilitator, or similar official.

(i)   "Individual Insured(s)" means a past, present or future duly elected or appointed director, officer, trustee, trustee emeritus, executive director, department head, committee member (of a duly constituted committee of the Organization), staff or faculty member (salaried or non-salaried), Employee or volunteer of the Organization. Coverage will automatically apply to all new persons who become Individual Insureds after the inception date of this policy.

(j) "Insured(s)" means the Organization and all Individual Insureds.

(k) "Loss" means damages (including back pay and front pay), judgments, settlements, pre- and post-judgment interest, the multiple or liquidated damages awards under the Age Discrimination in Employment Act and the Equal Pay Act and Defense Costs; however, Loss shall not include: (1) any amount for which the Insureds are not financially liable or which are without legal recourse to the Insureds; (2) employment-related benefits, stock options, perquisites, deferred compensation or any other type of compensation other than salary, wages or bonus compensation; (3) any liability or costs incurred by any Insured to modify any building or property in order to make said building or property more accessible or accommodating to any disabled person, or any liability or costs incurred in connection with any educational, sensitivity or other corporate program, policy or seminar relating to an Employment Practices Claim; or (4) matters which may be deemed uninsurable under the law pursuant to which this policy shall be construed.

If an additional premium is stated in Item 7B of the Declarations page, then Loss shall specifically include, (subject to the policyís other terms, conditions and exclusions) punitive, exemplary and multiple damages. It is further understood and agreed that the enforceability of the foregoing coverage shall be governed by such applicable law which most favors coverage for punitive, exemplary and multiple damages. If an additional premium is not stated in Item 7B of the Declarations, then Loss shall not include punitive, exemplary damages or the multiplied portion of multiple damages. In all events, coverage shall not be provided to any particular Insured who has been adjudicated to have obtained a profit or advantage or committed a fraudulent or dishonest act or a willful violation of any statute, rule or law.

(l) "No Liability" means: (1) a final judgment of no liability obtained prior to trial, in favor of all Insureds, by reason of a motion to dismiss or a motion for summary judgment, after the exhaustion of all appeals; or (2) a final judgment of no liability obtained after trial, in favor of all Insureds, after the exhaustion of all appeals. In no event shall the term "No Liability" apply to a Claim made against an Insured for which a settlement has occurred.

(m) "Non-Employment Discrimination" means any actual or alleged sexual harassment or unlawful discrimination, as described in paragraphs (2) and (3) of the definition of Employment Practices Violation, or the violation of the civil rights of a person relating to such sexual harassment or discrimination, when such acts are alleged to be committed against anyone other than an Individual Insured, or applicant for employment with the Organization or an Outside Entity, including, but not limited to: students, patients, members, customers and suppliers.

(n)   The "Organization" means: (1) the Named Organization designated in Item 1 of the Declarations; (2) any Subsidiary thereof; and (3) any Affiliate thereof listed by endorsement to this policy.

(o)   "Outside Entity" means a not-for-profit organization, other than a Subsidiary or listed Affiliate, on which an Individual Insured serves, at the specific written request of the Organization, as a director, trustee, trustee emeritus or governor. Such coverage as is provided by this policy shall be specifically excess of any insurance in force as respects such Outside Entity and any indemnification provided by such Outside Entity.

(p)   "Policy Period" means the period of time from the inception date shown in Item 3 of the Declarations to the earlier of the expiration date shown in Item 3 of the Declarations or the effective date of cancellation of this policy.

(q)   "Policy Year" means a period of one year, within the Policy Period, commencing each year on the day and hour first named in Item 3. of the Declarations, or if the time between the effective date or anniversary and termination of the Policy is less than one year, then such lesser period.

(r)   "Related Wrongful Acts" shall mean Wrongful Acts which are the same, related or continuous, or Wrongful Acts which arise from a common nucleus of facts. Claims can allege Related Wrongful Acts regardless of whether such Claims involve the same or different claimants, Insureds or legal causes of action.

(s)   "Retaliation" means a Wrongful Act of an Insured relating to or alleged to be in response to any of the following activities: (1) the disclosure or threat of disclosure by an Employee to a superior or to any governmental agency of any act by an Insured which is alleged to be a violation of any federal, state, local or foreign law, common or statutory, or any rule or regulation promulgated thereunder; (2) the actual or attempted exercise by an Employee of any right that such Employee has under law, including rights under worker's compensation laws, the Family and Medical Leave Act, the Americans with Disabilities Act or any other law relating to employee rights; (3) the filing of any claim under the Federal False Claims Act or any other federal, state, local or foreign "whistle-blower" law; or (4) Employee strikes.

(t)   "Subsidiary" means:

68467 (8/97)   6

a) any organization which, on or before the inception of the Policy Period, the Organization owns more than fifty percent (50%) of the voting interest, either directly, or indirectly through one or more of its Subsidiaries, or has, on or before the inception of the Policy Period, the right to elect or appoint more than fifty percent (50%) of the voting directors, or trustees, either directly or indirectly through one or more of its Subsidiaries;

b) automatically any not for profit organization which becomes a Subsidiary during the Policy Period and where the book value of such entity's assets determined in accordance with Generally Accepted Accounting Principles ("GAAP") totals less than 30% of the similarly calculated assets of the Named Organization as of the inception date of the Policy Period; or

c) any for profit organization which becomes a Subsidiary during the Policy Period and where the book value of such entity's assets determined in accordance with "GAAP" totals less than 20% of the similarly calculated assets of the Named Organization as of the inception date of the Policy Period.

With regard to paragraphs b) and c) above, the Named Organization shall provide the Insurer with full particulars of the Subsidiary before the end of the Policy Period.

Any organization which becomes a Subsidiary during the Policy Period but exceeds the asset limitations stated in b) or c) above, (hereinafter "New Subsidiary") shall be provided coverage under this policy, but only upon the condition that within 90 days after the date of its becoming a Subsidiary, the Named Organization shall have provided the Insurer with full particulars of the New Subsidiary and agreed to any additional premium or amendment of the provisions of this policy required by the Insurer relating to such New Subsidiary. Further, such coverage as shall be afforded to the New Subsidiary is conditioned upon the Named Organization paying when due any additional premium required by the Insurer relating to such New Subsidiary.

An organization becomes a Subsidiary when the Named Organization owns more than fifty percent (50%) of the voting interest, either directly, or indirectly through one or more of its Subsidiaries, or has, on or before the inception of the Policy Period, the right to elect or appoint more than fifty percent (50%) of the voting directors, or trustees, either directly or indirectly through one or more of its Subsidiaries.

68467 (8/97)   7

In all events, such coverage as is afforded under this policy with respect to a Claim made against any Subsidiary, or any Individual Insured of a Subsidiary, shall only apply for Wrongful Acts committed or allegedly committed after the effective time that such Subsidiary became a Subsidiary and prior to the time that such Subsidiary ceased to be a Subsidiary.

(u) "Wrongful Act" means:

(1) with respect to Individual Insureds, any breach of duty, neglect, error, misstatement, misleading statement, omission or act by such Insureds in his/her respective capacities as such, or any matter claimed against such Individual Insured solely by reason of his/her status as Individual Insureds of the Organization;

(2) with respect to the Organization under Coverage C, any breach of duty, neglect, error, misstatement, misleading statement, omission or act by or on behalf of the Organization;

(3) with respect to service on an Outside Entity, any matter claimed against such Individual Insureds arising out of such Insured serving as a director, trustee, trustee emeritus or governor of an Outside Entity in such capacity, but only if such service is at the specific written request or direction of the Organization;

(4) with respect to both the Individual Insureds and the Organization and subject to paragraphs 1,2 and 3 above, "Wrongful Act" shall specifically include:

> (a) Employment Practices Claims;
> (b) Non-Employment Discrimination;
> (c) violation of the Sherman Antitrust Act or similar federal, state or local statutes or rules;
> (d) libel, slander, defamation or publication or utterance in violation of an individualís right of privacy;
> (e) wrongful entry or eviction or other invasion of the right of occupancy;
> (f) false arrest or wrongful detention;
> (g) plagiarism; and
> (h) infringement of copyright or trademark or unauthorized use of title.

3. EXTENSIONS

68467 (8/97)   8

Subject otherwise to the terms hereof, this policy shall cover Loss arising from any Claims made against the estates, heirs, or legal representatives of deceased Individual Insureds, and the legal representatives of Individual Insureds in the event of an Individual Insured's incompetency, insolvency or bankruptcy, who were Individual Insureds at the time the Wrongful Acts upon which such Claims are based were committed.

Subject otherwise to the terms hereof, this policy shall cover Loss arising from all Claims made against the lawful spouse (whether such status is derived by reason of statutory law, common law or otherwise of any applicable jurisdiction in the world) of an Individual Insured for all Claims arising solely out of his or her status as the spouse of an Individual Insured, including a Claim that seeks damages recoverable from marital community property, property jointly held by the Individual Insured and the spouse, or property transferred from the Individual Insured to the spouse; provided, however, that this extension shall not afford coverage for any Claim for any actual or alleged Wrongful Act of the spouse, but shall apply only to Claims arising out of any actual or alleged Wrongful Acts of an Individual Insured, subject to the policy's terms, conditions and exclusions.

4. **EXCLUSIONS**

The Insurer shall not be liable to make any payment for Loss in connection with a Claim made against an Insured:

(a)   arising out of, based upon or attributable to the gaining in fact of any profit or advantage to which an Insured was not legally entitled;

(b)   arising out of, based upon or attributable to the committing in fact of any criminal, or deliberate fraudulent act;

[The Wrongful Act of an Insured shall not be imputed to any other Insured for the purpose of determining the applicability of exclusions 4(a) through 4(b).]

(c)   alleging, arising out of, based upon or attributable to the facts alleged, or to the same or Related Wrongful Act alleged or contained in any Claim which has been reported, or in any circumstances of which notice has been given, under any policy of which this policy is a renewal or replacement or which it may succeed in time;

(d)   alleging, arising out of, based upon or attributable to as of the Continuity Date, any pending or prior: (1) litigation; or (2) administrative or regulatory proceeding or investigation; or the alleging of any Wrongful Act which is the

68467 (8/97)   9

same or a Related Wrongful Act to that alleged in such pending or prior litigation or administrative or regulatory proceeding or investigation;

(e)   alleging, arising out of, based upon or attributable to any actual or alleged act or omission of an Individual Insured serving in any capacity, other than with the Organization or as a director, trustee, trustee emeritus or governor of an Outside Entity;

(f)   which is brought by or on behalf of the Organization against any Individual Insured; provided however, this exclusion shall not apply to any derivative Claim made on behalf of the Organization by a member, an attorney general or any other such representative party if such action is brought and maintained independently of and without the solicitation of or assistance of, or active participation of or intervention of any Individual Insured or the Organization or any Affiliate thereof;

(g)   for any Wrongful Act arising out of an Individual Insured serving as a director, trustee, trustee emeritus or governor of an Outside Entity if such Claim is brought by the Outside Entity or by any director, trustee, trustee emeritus or governor thereof;

(h)   for bodily injury, sickness, disease, or death of any person, or damage to or destruction of any tangible property, including the loss of use thereof;

(i)   alleging, arising out of, based upon, attributable to, or in any way involving, directly or indirectly:

(1)   the actual, alleged or threatened discharge, dispersal, release or escape of pollutants; or

(2)   any direction or request to test for, monitor, clean up, remove, contain, treat, detoxify or neutralize pollutants,

including but not limited to a Claim alleging damage to the Organization or its members.

Pollutants include (but are not limited to) any solid, liquid, gaseous or thermal irritant or contaminant, including smoke, vapor, soot, fumes, acids, alkalis, chemicals and waste. Waste includes (but is not limited to) materials to be recycled, reconditioned or reclaimed;

(j)   for violation(s) of any of the responsibilities, obligations or duties imposed by the Employee Retirement Income Security Act of 1974, the Fair Labor Standards Act (except the Equal Pay Act), the National Labor Relations Act, the Worker Adjustment and Retraining Notification Act, the Consolidated Omnibus Budget Reconciliation Act, the Occupational Safety and Health Act, any rules or regulations of the foregoing promulgated thereunder, and amendments thereto or any similar provisions of any federal, state or local statutory law or common law; provided , however, that this exclusion shall not apply to Loss arising from a Claim for Retaliation;

(k) alleging, arising out of, based upon or attributable to any actual or alleged contractual liability of an Insured under any express contract or agreement; provided, however, that this exclusion shall not apply to liability which would have attached in the absence of such express contract or agreement;

(l) for any civil or criminal fines imposed by law and any taxes (whether imposed by federal, state, local or other governmental authority);

(m) alleging, arising out of, or in any way relating to any purchase or sale of securities by the Named Organization, Subsidiary or Affiliate or Claims brought by securities holders of the Organization in their capacity as such; provided, however, this exclusion shall not apply to the issuance by the Organization of tax exempt bond debt or Claims brought by tax exempt bond debt holders.

5. LIMIT OF LIABILITY (FOR ALL LOSS - INCLUDING DEFENSE COSTS)

The Limit of Liability stated in Item 4 of the Declarations is the limit of the Insurer's liability for all Loss, under Coverage A, Coverage B and Coverage C combined, arising out of all Claims first made against the Insureds during a Policy Year or the Discovery Period (if applicable); however, the Limit of Liability for the Discovery Period shall be part of, and not in addition to, the Limit of Liability for the Policy Year in which the Discovery Period is elected. Further, any Claim which is made subsequent to a Policy Year or the Discovery Period (if applicable) which, pursuant to Clause 7(b) or 7(c) is considered made during the Policy Year or Discovery Period shall also be subject to the one applicable aggregate Limit of Liability stated in Item 4 of the Declarations.

Defense Costs are not payable by the Insurer in addition to the Limit of Liability. Defense Costs are part of Loss and as such are subject to the Limit of Liability for Loss.

This policy provides one aggregate Limit of Liability for each Policy Year. In no event shall the Limit of Liability for any one Policy Year exceed the aggregate Limit of Liability as stated in Item 4 of the Declarations.

6. RETENTION CLAUSE

The Insurer shall only be liable for the amount of Loss arising from a Claim which is in excess of the Retention amount stated in Item 5(B) of the Declarations, such Retention amount to be borne by the Organization and shall remain uninsured, with regard to all Loss for which the Organization has indemnified or is permitted or required to indemnify the Individual Insureds ("Indemnifiable Loss") and Loss under Coverage C. A single Retention amount shall apply to Loss arising from all Claims alleging the same Wrongful Act or Related Wrongful Acts.

Except as hereinafter stated, no Retention shall apply to a Claim in the event of the Financial Insolvency of the Named Organization and all Subsidiaries or Affiliates which are permitted or required to indemnify the Individual Insured with regard to such Claim. Provided, however, the Organization hereby agrees to indemnify the Insureds to the fullest extent permitted by law taking all steps necessary in furtherance thereto, including the making in good faith of any required application for court approval and the passing of any required corporate resolution or the execution of any contract. The Named Organization and all Subsidiaries and Affiliates will be conclusively deemed to have indemnified the Individual Insureds to the extent that the Organization is permitted or required to indemnify them pursuant to law, common or statutory, or contract, or the charter or by-laws of the Organization.

Further, no Retention shall apply to all coverages for any Claim which is in the form of a civil litigation for monetary relief, and the Insurer shall thereupon reimburse the Defense Costs paid by the Insured, in the event of:

(1) a determination of No Liability of all Insureds; or

(2) a dismissal or a stipulation to dismiss the civil litigation Claim without prejudice and without the payment of any consideration by any Insured;

provided, however, that in the case of (2) above, such reimbursement shall occur one hundred twenty (120) days after the date of dismissal or stipulation as long as the Claim is not re-brought (or any other Claim which is subject to the same single retention by virtue of Clause 6 is not brought) within ninety (90) days from the time

68467 (8/97) 12

of such dismissal or stipulation, and further subject to an undertaking by the Organization in a form acceptable to the Insurer that such reimbursement shall be paid back by the Organization to the Insurer in the event the Claim (or any other Claim which is subject to the same single retention by virtue of Clause 6) is brought after such 90 day period and before the expiration of the statute of limitations for such Claim.

7.   NOTICE/CLAIM REPORTING PROVISIONS

Notice hereunder shall be given in writing to the Insurer named in Item 8 of the Declarations at the address indicated in Item 8 of the Declarations. If mailed, the date of mailing shall constitute the date that such notice was given and proof of mailing shall be sufficient proof of notice.   A Claim shall be considered to have been first made against an Insured when written notice of such Claim is received by any Insured, by the Named Organization on the behalf of any Insured or by the Insurer, whichever comes first.

(a)   The Insureds shall, as a condition precedent to the obligations of the Insurer under this policy, give written notice to the Insurer of any Claim made against an Insured as soon as practicable and either:

  (1)   anytime during the Policy Year or during the Discovery Period (if applicable); or

  (2)   within 30 days after the end of the Policy Year or the Discovery Period (if applicable), as long as such Claim is reported no later than 30 days after the date such Claim was first made against an Insured.

(b)   If written notice of a Claim has been given to the Insurer pursuant to Clause 7(a) above, then any Claim which is subsequently made against the Insureds and reported to the Insurer alleging, arising out of, based upon or attributable to the facts alleged in the Claim for which such notice has been given, or alleging any Wrongful Act which is the same as or related to any Wrongful Act alleged in the Claim of which such notice has been given, shall be considered made at the time such notice was given.

(c)   If during the Policy Period or during the Discovery Period (if applicable) the Insureds shall become aware of any circumstances which may reasonably be expected to give rise to a Claim being made against the Insureds and shall give written notice to the Insurer of the circumstances and the reasons for anticipating such a Claim, with full particulars as to dates, persons and entities involved, then any Claim which is subsequently made against the Insureds and reported to the Insurer alleging, arising out of, based upon or attributable to such circumstances or alleging any Wrongful Act which is the same as or related to any Wrongful Act alleged or contained in such circumstances, shall be considered made at the time such notice of such circumstances was given.

8. DEFENSE COSTS, SETTLEMENTS, JUDGMENTS (INCLUDING THE ADVANCEMENT OF DEFENSE COSTS)

The Insurer does not assume any duty to defend. The Insureds shall defend and contest any Claim made against them.

Notwithstanding the foregoing, the Insureds shall have the right to tender the defense of any Claim to the Insurer, which right shall be exercised in writing by the Named Organization on behalf of all Insureds to the Insurer pursuant to Clause 7 of this policy. This right shall terminate if not exercised within 30 days of the date the Claim is first made against an Insured, pursuant to Clause 7 of the policy. Further, from the date the Claim is first made against the Insureds to the date when the Insurer accepts the tender of the defense of such Claim, the Insureds shall take no action, or fail to take any required action, that prejudices the rights of the Insureds or the Insurer with respect to such Claim. Provided that the Insureds have complied with the foregoing, the Insurer shall be obligated to assume the defense of the Claim, even if such Claim is groundless, false or fraudulent. The assumption of the defense of the Claim shall be effective upon written confirmation thereof sent by the Insurer to the Named Organization. Once the defense has been so tendered, the Insured shall have the right to effectively associate with the Insurer in the defense of such Claim, including, but not limited to, negotiating a settlement, subject to the provisions of this Clause 8. However, the Insurer shall not be obligated to defend such Claim after the Limit of Liability has been exhausted, or after an Insured's rejection of a Settlement Opportunity as described in this Clause 8.

When the Insurer has not assumed the defense of a Claim pursuant to Clause 8, the Insurer shall advance nevertheless, at the written request of the Insured, Defense Costs prior to the final disposition of a Claim. Such advanced payments by the Insurer shall be repaid to the Insurer by the Insureds, severally according to their respective interests, in the event and to the extent that the Insureds shall not be entitled under the terms and conditions of this policy to payment of such Loss.

The Insureds shall not admit or assume any liability, enter into any settlement agreement, stipulate to any judgment, or incur any Defense Costs without the prior written consent of the Insurer. Only those settlements, stipulated judgments and Defense Costs which have been consented to by the Insurer shall be recoverable as Loss under the terms of this policy. The Insurer's consent

68467 (8/97)   14

shall not be unreasonably withheld, provided that the Insurer, when it has not assumed the defense of a Claim pursuant to this Clause 8, shall be entitled to effectively associate in the defense and the negotiation of any settlement of any Claim, and provided further that in all events the Insurer may withhold consent to any settlement, stipulated judgment or Defense Costs, or any portion thereof, to the extent such Loss is not covered under the terms of this policy.

The Insurer shall have the right to effectively associate with the Insureds in the defense of any Claim that appears reasonably likely to involve the Insurer, including but not limited to negotiating a settlement. The Insureds shall give the Insurer full cooperation and such information as it may reasonably require.

If the Insurer recommends a settlement within the policy's applicable Limit of Liability which is acceptable to the claimant (a "Settlement Opportunity"), and the Insureds consent to such settlement, then the Organization's applicable Retention amount shall be retroactively reduced by ten percent (10%) for such Loss. It shall be a condition to such reduction that the Insureds must consent to such settlement within thirty (30) days of the date the Insureds are first made aware of the Settlement Opportunity, or in the case of a Settlement Opportunity which arises from a settlement offer by the claimant, then within the time permitted by the claimant to accept such settlement offer, but in all events no later than thirty (30) days after the settlement offer was made.

However, if a Settlement Opportunity arises and the Insureds do not consent to the settlement within the time prescribed above, the Retention amount shall remain the applicable amount set forth in Item 5 of the Declarations even if consent is given to a subsequent Settlement Opportunity.

Furthermore, in the event the Insureds do not consent to the first Settlement Opportunity within the time prescribed, then, the Insurer's liability for all Loss on account of such Claim shall not exceed: (1) the amount for which the Insurer could have settled such Claim plus Defense Costs incurred as of the date such settlement was proposed in writing by the Insurer, ("Settlement Opportunity Amount") plus (2) 50% of covered Loss in excess of such Settlement Opportunity Amount subject to the policy's Limit of Liability. Notwithstanding the foregoing, this paragraph shall not apply until the Settlement Opportunity Amount exceeds the Retention amount stated in Item 5 of the Declarations.

9. **PRE-AUTHORIZED CLASS ACTION DEFENSE ATTORNEYS**

This clause applies only to a Claim filed as a class action (hereinafter referred to as a "Class Action Claim").

Affixed as Appendix A hereto and made a part of this policy is a list of Panel Counsel law firms ("Panel Counsel Firms") from which a selection of legal counsel may be made to conduct the defense of any Class Action Claim against an Insured pursuant to the terms set forth below.

In the event the Insurer has assumed the defense pursuant to Clause 8 of this policy, then the Insurer shall be obligated to select a Panel Counsel Firm to defend the Insureds. In the event the Insureds are already defending a Class Action Claim, then the Insureds may at their option select a Panel Counsel firm to defend the Insureds. If the Insured does not select a Panel Counsel firm, such non-Panel Counsel firm selection shall be subject to the Insurer's consent, which consent shall not be unreasonably withheld.

The selection of the Panel Counsel Firm, when done by the Insurer, shall be from the jurisdiction in which the Class Action Claim is brought.

The list of Panel Counsel Firms may be amended from time to time by the Insurer. However, no change shall be made to the specific list attached to this policy during the Policy Period without the consent of the Named Organization.

10. DISCOVERY CLAUSE

Except as indicated below, if the Named Organization shall cancel or the Insurer or the Named Organization shall refuse to renew this policy, the Named Organization, upon payment of the respective "Additional Premium Amount" described below, shall have the right to a period of one, two or three years after the effective date of such cancellation or nonrenewal (herein referred to as the "Discovery Period") in which to give to the Insurer written notice of Claims first made against the Insureds during the selected period for any Wrongful Act occurring prior to the end of the Policy Period and otherwise covered by this policy. The rights contained in this paragraph shall terminate, however, unless written notice of such election together with the additional premium due is received by the Insurer within 30 days of the effective date of cancellation or nonrenewal. The Additional Premium Amount for the Discovery Period shall be fully earned at the inception of the Discovery Period. The Discovery Period is not cancelable. This clause and the rights contained herein shall not apply to any cancellation resulting from non-payment of premium.

The Additional Premium Amount for: (1) one year shall be 40% of the "full annual premium"; (2) two years shall be 75% of the "full annual premium";(3) three years shall be 100% of the "full annual premium". As used herein, "full annual premium" means the premium level in effect immediately prior to the end of the Policy Period.

In the event of a Transaction, as defined in Clause 12, the Named Organization shall have the right, within 30 days before the end of the Policy Period, to request an offer from the Insurer of a Discovery Period (with respect to Wrongful Acts occurring prior to the effective time of the Transaction) for a period of no less than six years or for such longer or shorter period as the Named Organization may request. The Insurer shall offer such Discovery Period pursuant to such terms, conditions and premium as the Insurer may reasonably decide. In the event of a Transaction, the right to a Discovery Period shall not otherwise exist except as indicated in this paragraph.

11. CANCELLATION CLAUSE

This policy may be canceled by the Named Organization only by mailing written prior notice to the Insurer or by surrender of this policy to the Insurer or its authorized agent. If this policy is canceled by the Named Organization, the Insurer shall retain the customary short rate proportion of the premium herein. However, if the Policy Period as designated in Item 3 of the Declarations is more than one year, this policy may not be cancelled by the Named Organization.

This policy may be canceled by or on the behalf of the Insurer only in the event of nonpayment of premium by the Named Organization. In the event of non-payment of premium by the Named Organization, the Insurer may cancel this policy by delivering to the Named Organization or by mailing to the Named Organization, by registered, certified, or other first class mail, at the Named Organization's address as shown in Item 1 of the Declarations, written notice stating when, not less than 30 days thereafter, the cancellation shall be effective. The mailing of such notice as aforesaid shall be sufficient proof of notice. The Policy Period terminates at the date and hour specified in such notice, or at the date and time of surrender. The Insurer shall have the right to the premium amount for the portion of the Policy Year during which the policy was in effect.

If the period of limitation relating to the giving of notice is prohibited or made void by any law controlling the construction thereof, such period shall be deemed to be amended so as to be equal to the minimum period of limitation permitted by such law.

12. CHANGE IN CONTROL OF NAMED ORGANIZATION

If during the Policy Period:

a.   the Named Organization shall consolidate with or merge into, or sell all or substantially all of its assets to, any other person or entity, or group of persons or entities acting in concert;

68467 (8/97)   17

b. · any person or entity, or group of persons or entities, acting in concert shall acquire an amount of the voting interest representing more than fifty percent (50%) of the voting power for the election or appointment of directors or trustees of the Named Organization, or acquires the voting rights of such an amount of such interest; or

c. the Named Organization shall change from not-for-profit to for-profit status;

(any of the above events herein referred to as the "Transaction")

then this policy shall continue in full force and effect as to Wrongful Acts occurring prior to the effective time of the Transaction, but there shall be no coverage afforded by any provision of this policy for any actual or alleged Wrongful Act occurring after the effective time of the Transaction. This policy may not be canceled after the effective time of the Transaction and the entire premium for this policy shall be deemed earned as of such time. The Named Organization shall also have the right to an offer by the Insurer of a Discovery Period described in Clause 10 of the policy.

The Named Organization shall give the Insurer written notice of the Transaction as soon as practicable, but not later than thirty (30) days after the effective date of the Transaction.

13. SUBROGATION

In the event of any payment under this policy, the Insurer shall be subrogated to the extent of such payment to all the Insureds' rights of recovery thereof, and the Insureds shall execute all papers required and shall do everything that may be necessary to secure such rights including the execution of such documents necessary to enable the Insurer to effectively bring suit in the name of any Insureds. In no event, however, shall the Insurer exercise its rights of subrogation against an Insured under this policy unless such Insured has been convicted of a criminal act, or been determined to have committed a dishonest or fraudulent act, or obtained any profit or advantage to which such Insured was not legally entitled.

14. OTHER INSURANCE AND INDEMNIFICATION

Such insurance as is provided by this policy shall apply only as excess over any valid and collectible insurance. This policy shall be specifically excess of any other policy pursuant to which any other insurer has a duty to defend a Claim for which this policy may be obligated to pay Loss.

In the event of a Claim against a director, trustee, trustees emeritus or governor arising out of his or her service as a director, trustee, trustees emeritus or governor of

68467 (8/97)   18

an Outside Entity, coverage as is afforded by this policy shall be specifically excess of indemnification provided by such Outside Entity and any insurance provided to such Outside Entity with respect to its directors, trustees, trustees emeriti or governors.

Further, in the event such other insurance is provided to an Outside Entity by the Insurer or any member company of American International Group, Inc. (AIG) (or would be provided but for the application of the retention amount, exhaustion of the Limit of Liability or failure to submit a notice of a Claim) then the Insurer's maximum aggregate Limit of Liability for all Losses combined in connection with a Claim covered, in part of in whole, by this policy and such other insurance policy issued by AIG shall not exceed the greater of the Limit of Liability of this policy or the limit of liability of such other AIG insurance policy.

15. NOTICE AND AUTHORITY

It is agreed that the Named Organization shall act on behalf of the Subsidiaries and all Insureds with respect to the giving of notice of Claim or giving and receiving notice of cancellation, the payment of premiums and the receiving of any return premiums that may become due under this policy, the receipt and acceptance of any endorsements issued to form a part of this policy, the exercising or declining to tender the defense of a Class Action Claim to the Insurer and the exercising or declining of any right to a Discovery Period.

16. ASSIGNMENT

This policy and any and all rights hereunder are not assignable without the written consent of the Insurer.

17. ACTION AGAINST INSURER

No action shall lie against the Insurer unless, as a condition precedent thereto, there shall have been full compliance with all of the terms of this policy, nor until the amount of the Insureds' obligation to pay shall have been finally determined either by judgment against the Insureds after actual trial or by written agreement of the Insureds, the claimant and the Insurer.

Any person or organization or the legal representative thereof who has secured such judgment or written agreement shall thereafter be entitled to recover under this policy to the extent of the insurance afforded by this policy. No person or organization shall have any right under this policy to join the Insurer as a party to any action against the Insureds to determine the Insureds' liability, nor shall the Insurer be impleaded by the

68467 (8/97)   19

Insureds or their legal representatives. Bankruptcy or insolvency of the Insureds or of their estates shall not relieve the Insurer of any of its obligations hereunder.

18. REPRESENTATIONS AND SEVERABILITY

In granting coverage under this policy, it is agreed that the Insurer has relied upon the statements and representations contained in the application for this policy (including materials submitted thereto and, if this is a renewal application, all such previous policy applications for which this policy is a renewal) as being accurate and complete. All such statements and representations shall be deemed to be material to the risk assumed by the Insurer, are the basis of this policy and are to be considered as incorporated into this policy.

With respect to such statements and representations, no knowledge or information possessed by any Individual Insured shall be imputed to any other Individual Insured. If any person who executed the application knew that such statement or representation was inaccurate or incomplete, such statement shall not be imputed to any trustee, trustee emeritus or governor other than such signator and any other Individual Insureds who knew such statement or representation was inaccurate or incomplete.

19. HEADINGS

The descriptions in the headings of this policy are solely for convenience, and form no part of the terms and conditions of coverage.

20. WORLDWIDE TERRITORY

This policy shall apply to Claims made against an Insured anywhere in the world.

AMERICAN INTERNATIONAL COMPANIES®

PRIVATE COLLECTION^SM

**Management Liability Coverage
for Private Companies**

Policy Number:
Renewal of Policy Number:

AIU Insurance Company	Granite State Insurance Company
American Home Assurance Company	Illinois National Insurance Company
American International Pacific Insurance Company	National Union Fire Insurance Company of Pittsburgh, Pa.
American International South Insurance Company	National Union Fire Insurance Company of Louisiana
Birmingham Fire Insurance Company of Pennsylvania	New Hampshire Insurance Company

(each of the above being a capital stock company)

NOTICE: EXCEPT TO SUCH EXTENT AS MAY OTHERWISE BE PROVIDED HEREIN, THE COVERAGE OF THIS POLICY IS GENERALLY LIMITED TO LIABILITY FOR ONLY THOSE CLAIMS THAT ARE FIRST MADE AGAINST THE INSUREDS DURING THE POLICY PERIOD AND REPORTED IN WRITING TO THE INSURER PURSUANT TO THE TERMS HEREIN. VARIOUS PROVISIONS IN THIS POLICY RESTRICT COVERAGE. PLEASE READ THE ENTIRE POLICY CAREFULLY AND DISCUSS THE COVERAGE HEREUNDER WITH YOUR INSURANCE AGENT OR BROKER TO DETERMINE RIGHTS, DUTIES AND WHAT IS AND IS NOT COVERED.

NOTICE: THE LIMIT OF LIABILITY AVAILABLE TO PAY JUDGMENTS OR SETTLEMENTS SHALL BE REDUCED BY AMOUNTS INCURRED FOR LEGAL DEFENSE. AMOUNTS INCURRED FOR LEGAL DEFENSE SHALL BE APPLIED AGAINST THE RETENTION AMOUNT.

NOTICE: THE INSURER DOES NOT ASSUME ANY DUTY TO DEFEND. HOWEVER THE INSUREDS MAY UNDER CERTAIN CONDITIONS TENDER THE DEFENSE OF A CLAIM. IN ALL EVENTS, THE INSURER MUST ADVANCE DEFENSE COST PAYMENTS PURSUANT TO THE TERMS HEREIN PRIOR TO THE FINAL DISPOSITION OF A CLAIM.

DECLARATIONS

ITEMS		
1	**NAMED ENTITY**:	(herein "**Named Entity**")
1(a)	MAILING ADDRESS:	
1(b)	State of Incorporation or State of Formation of the Named Entity:	
2	**POLICY PERIOD**: From: To: 12:01 A.M. standard time at the address stated in Item 1(a)	

76171 (6/00)   1   Order by 77152 (8/00)

ITEMS (continued)	
3	**COVERAGE SECTIONS PURCHASED:** **D&O and Corporate Liability ("D&O")** Yes No **Employment Practices Liability ("EPL")** Yes No
4	**LIMIT OF LIABILITY** A. $_____ **AGGREGATE LIMIT OF LIABILITY** (herein "Aggregate Limit of Liability") for all Loss combined under this policy, including Defense Costs B. $_____ Separate Limit of Liability for all Loss combined under the D&O Coverage Section, including Defense Costs C. $_____ Separate Limit of Liability for all Loss combined under the EPL Coverage Section, including Defense Costs The Separate Limits of Liability shall be part of and not in addition to the Aggregate Limit of Liability.
5	**RETENTION:** **D&O COVERAGE:**

NON-INDEMNIFIABLE LOSS: Judgments, Settlements and Defense Costs: $ None	**INDEMNIFIABLE LOSS**: Judgments, Settlements and Defense Costs : $_____ *	**COMPANY LOSS:** Judgments, Settlements and Defense Costs: $_____ *

EPL COVERAGE:

ALL CLAIMS: $_____ *

- The Retention applies for Loss arising from Claims alleging the same Wrongful Act or Related Wrongful Acts.

76171 (6/   2

	ITEMS (continued)				
6	**CONTINUITY DATE** (herein "**Continuity Date**"):				
6(a)	D&O Coverage, other than **Outside Entity Executive** Coverage:	_____	**6(b)**	**Outside Entity Executive** Coverage:	The date on which the **Individual Insured** first served as an **Outside Entity Executive** of such **Outside Entity**.
6(c)	EPL Coverage:	_____			
7	**PREMIUM:**	$			
8	**NAME AND ADDRESS OF INSURER** (herein "**Insurer**"): This policy is issued only by the insurance company indicated in this Item 8.				

IN WITNESS WHEREOF, the Insurer has caused this policy to be signed on the Declarations by its President, a Secretary and a duly authorized representative of the Insurer.

_____   _____
PRESIDENT   SECRETARY

_____
AUTHORIZED REPRESENTATIVE

_____   _____
COUNTERSIGNATURE DATE   COUNTERSIGNED AT

SPECIMEN

76171 (6/00)   4

PRIVATE COLLECTION^{SM}

GENERAL TERMS AND CONDITIONS

In consideration of the payment of the premium, and in reliance upon the statements made to the Insurer by application, including its attachments and the material incorporated therein, which form a part of this policy, the Insurer agrees as follows:

1. TERMS AND CONDITIONS

These General Terms and Conditions shall be applicable to all Coverage Sections, unless otherwise stated to the contrary. The terms and conditions of each coverage section shall only apply to that particular coverage section and shall in no way be construed to apply to any other coverage section of this policy.

2. DEFINITIONS

(a) "Affiliate" means: (i) any person or entity that directly, or indirectly through one or more intermediaries, controls or is controlled by, or is in common control with, another person or entity; or (ii) any person or entity that directly, or indirectly through one or more intermediaries, is a successor in interest to another person or entity.

(b) "Bodily Injury" means physical injury, sickness, or disease (other than emotional distress and mental anguish), including death resulting therefrom.

(c) "Company" means the Named Entity and any Subsidiary thereof.

(d) "Continuity Date" means the date set forth in Item 6 of the Declarations with respect to each coverage.

(e) "Defense Costs" means reasonable and necessary fees, costs and expenses consented to by the Insurer (including premiums for any appeal bond, attachment bond, bonds to release property used to secure a legal obligation, or similar bond arising out of a covered judgment, but without any obligation to apply for or furnish any such bond), resulting solely from the investigation, adjustment, defense and appeal of a Claim against the Insureds, but excluding salaries of officers or Employees of the Company.

76174 (6/00)   1

(f)   "Director(s) or Officer(s)" means:

   (1) past, present or future duly elected or appointed directors, officers, management committee members, and members of the Board of Managers of the Company (or equivalent position); and

   (2) with respect to operations of the Company in a jurisdiction other than the United States, its possessions and territories, such past, present or future persons in duly elected or appointed positions of the Company that is equivalent to an executive position listed in Definition (f)(1),

but only in their respective capacities as such. Coverage will automatically apply to all new Director(s) and Officer(s) after the inception date of this policy.

(g)   "Employee(s)" means any past, present or future employee, whether such employee is in a supervisory, co-worker or subordinate position or otherwise, including any part-time, seasonal and temporary employee in his or her capacity as such. Independent contractors and individuals who are leased to the Company are not Employees; however, with respect to Coverage Section Two only, Insureds are covered for Loss arising from Wrongful Acts of independent contractors and such leased individuals.

(h)   "Indemnifiable Loss" means Loss for which the Company has indemnified or is permitted or required to indemnify any Individual Insured(s).

(i)   "Individual Insured(s)" means an individual Insured, as that term is defined within each Coverage Section.

(j)   "Insured(s)" means an Insured, as that term is defined within each Coverage Section.

(k)   "Loss" means Loss, as that term is defined within each Coverage Section.

(l)   "Named Entity" shall mean the entity listed in Item 1 of the Declarations.

(m)   "Outside Entity" means any: (1) not-for-profit organization; or (2) other entity listed as an "Outside Entity" in an endorsement attached to this policy.

(n) "Outside Entity Executive" means any: (1) Director(s) or Officer(s) of the Company who is or was acting at the specific written request or direction of the Company as a Director(s) or Officer(s) of an Outside Entity; or (2) any other person listed as an Outside Entity Executive in an endorsement attached to this policy.

(o) "Policy Period" means the period of time from the inception date shown in Item 2 of the Declarations to the earlier of the expiration date shown in Item 2 of the Declarations or the effective date of cancellation of this policy.

(p) "Property Damage" means physical injury to, or destruction of tangible or intangible property, including the loss of use thereof, or the loss of use of tangible or intangible property, which has not been physically injured or destroyed.

(q) "Related Wrongful Acts" means Wrongful Acts, which are the same, related or continuous, or Wrongful Acts, which arise from a common nucleus of facts. Claims can allege Related Wrongful Acts regardless of whether such Claims involve the same or different claimants, Insureds or legal causes of action.

(r) "Subsidiary" means:

   (1) any for-profit organization, whose securities are not publicly traded, which on or before the inception of the Policy Period is more than 50% owned by the Named Entity, either directly, or indirectly through one or more of its Subsidiaries;

   (2) automatically any for-profit organization, whose securities are not publicly traded and whose assets total less than 25% of the total consolidated assets of the Company as of the inception date of this policy, which organization becomes a Subsidiary during the Policy Period. The Named Entity shall provide the Insurer with full particulars of the new Subsidiary before the end of the Policy Period; and

   (3) automatically any for-profit organization, whose securities are not publicly traded and whose assets total 25% or more than the total consolidated assets of the Company as of the inception date of this policy, but such entity shall be a Subsidiary only: (i) for a period of ninety (90) days from the date the organization became a Subsidiary; or (ii) until the end of the Policy Period, whichever ends or occurs first (hereinafter "Auto-Subsidiary Period");

provided that the Named Entity or any other Insured shall report such Subsidiary to the Insurer, in writing, prior to the end of the Policy Period.

76174 (6/00)   3

The Insurer shall extend coverage for any Subsidiary described in (r)(3) above, and any Individual Insured thereof, beyond its respective Auto-Subsidiary Period if during such Auto-Subsidiary Period, the Named Entity shall have provided the Insurer with full particulars of the new Subsidiary and agreed to any additional premium and amendment of the provisions of this policy required by the Insurer relating to such Subsidiary. Further, coverage as shall be afforded to any Subsidiary and any Individual Insured thereof is conditioned upon the Named Entity paying when due any additional premium required by the Insurer relating to such Subsidiary.

An organization becomes a Subsidiary when the Named Entity owns more than a 50% ownership interest in such Subsidiary, either directly, or indirectly through one or more of its Subsidiaries. An organization ceases to be a Subsidiary when the Named Entity ceases to own more than 50% ownership interest in such Subsidiary, either directly, or indirectly through one or more of its Subsidiaries.

In all events, coverage as is afforded under this policy with respect to a Claim made against Individual Insureds of any Subsidiary, or any Subsidiary shall only apply for Wrongful Acts committed or allegedly committed after the effective time that such Subsidiary became a Subsidiary and prior to the time that such Subsidiary ceased to be a Subsidiary.

(s) "Wrongful Act" means a Wrongful Act, as that term is defined within each Coverage Section.

3. EXTENSIONS

Subject otherwise to the terms hereof, this policy shall cover Loss arising from any Claims made against the estates, heirs, or legal representatives of deceased Individual Insureds, and the legal representatives of Individual Insureds in the event of incompetency, insolvency or bankruptcy, who were Individual Insureds at the time the Wrongful Acts upon which such Claims are based were committed.

Subject otherwise to the terms hereof, this policy shall cover Loss arising from all Claims made against the lawful spouse (whether such status is derived by reason of statutory law, common law or otherwise of any applicable jurisdiction in the world) of an Individual Insured for all Claims arising solely out of his or her status as the spouse of an Individual Insured, including a Claim that seeks damages recoverable from marital community property, property jointly held by the Individual Insured and the spouse, or property transferred from the Individual Insured to the spouse; provided, however, that this extension shall not afford coverage for any Claim for

76174 (6/00) 4

any actual or alleged Wrongful Act of the spouse, but shall apply only to Claims arising out of any actual or alleged Wrongful Acts of an Individual Insured, subject to the policy's terms, conditions and exclusions.

4. EXCLUSIONS

The Insurer shall not be liable to make any payment for Loss in connection with any Claim made against an Insured:

(a) arising out of, based upon or attributable to the gaining in fact of any profit or advantage to which an Insured was not legally entitled;

(b) alleging, arising out of, based upon or attributable to the facts alleged, or to the same or Related Wrongful Act alleged or contained in any claim which has been reported, or in any circumstances of which notice has been given, under any policy of which this policy is a renewal or replacement or which it may succeed in time;

(c) alleging, arising out of, based upon or attributable to as of the Continuity Date, any pending or prior: (1) litigation; or (2) administrative or regulatory proceeding or investigation of which an Insured had notice, or alleging any Wrongful Act which is the same or Related Wrongful Act to that alleged in such pending or prior litigation or administrative or regulatory proceeding or investigation;

(d) for any actual, alleged or threatened discharge, dispersal, release or escape of pollutants; or for any direction or request to test, monitor, clean up, remove, contain, treat, detoxify or neutralize pollutants; provided, however, that with respect to the D&O Coverage Section only, that this exclusion shall not apply to any Claim brought by a securities holder of the Company in its capacity as such;

Pollutants include (but are not limited to) any solid, liquid, gaseous or thermal irritant or contaminant, including smoke, vapor, soot, fumes, acids, alkalis, chemicals and waste. Waste includes (but is not limited to) materials to be recycled, reconditioned or reclaimed;

(e) alleging, arising out of, based upon or attributable to, or in any way involving, directly or indirectly, Bodily Injury or Property Damage; provided, however, that with respect to the D&O Coverage Section only, that this exclusion shall not apply to any Securities Claim;

(f) for violation(s) of any of the responsibilities, obligations or duties imposed by the Employee Retirement Income Security Act of 1974, the Fair Labor Standards

Act, the National Labor Relations Act, the Worker Adjustment and Retraining Notification Act, the Consolidated Omnibus Budget Reconciliation Act, the Occupational Safety and Health Act, any rules or regulations of the foregoing promulgated thereunder, and amendments thereto or any similar provisions of any federal, state, local or foreign statutory law or common law; provided, however, that with respect to the EPL Coverage Section only, this exclusion shall not apply to:

    (i) the Equal Pay Act; or

    (j) Loss arising from a Claim for Retaliation;

(g) alleging, arising out of, based upon or attributable to any obligation pursuant to any worker's compensation, disability benefits, or unemployment compensation, unemployment insurance, retirement benefits, social security benefits or similar law; provided, however, that with respect to the EPL Coverage Section only, this exclusion shall not apply to Loss arising from a Claim for Retaliation.

For the purpose of determining the applicability of the foregoing Exclusions 4(a), (d), (e) (f) and (g): (1) the facts pertaining to and knowledge possessed by any Insured shall not be imputed to any other Individual Insured; and (2) only facts pertaining to and knowledge possessed by any past, present or future chairman of the board, president, chief executive officer, chief operating officer, chief financial officer (or equivalent position) of the Company shall be imputed to the Company.

5. LIMIT OF LIABILITY

AGGREGATE LIMIT OF LIABILITY (FOR ALL LOSS UNDER THIS POLICY COMBINED - INCLUDING DEFENSE COSTS)

The Aggregate Limit of Liability stated in Item 4A of the Declarations is the maximum limit of the Insurer's liability for all Loss under all coverages combined, arising out of all Claims first made against the Insureds during the Policy Period and the Discovery Period (if applicable); however, the Aggregate Limit of Liability for the Discovery Period shall be part of, and not in addition to, the Aggregate Limit of Liability for the Policy Period. Further, a Claim which is made subsequent to the Policy Period or Discovery Period (if applicable) which pursuant to Clause 7(b) or 7(c) is considered made during the Policy Period or Discovery Period shall also be subject to the Aggregate Limit of Liability stated in Item 4A of the Declarations and subject to the applicable Separate Limits of Liability, if any.

If Separate Limits of Liability are stated in Items 4B and 4C of the Declarations, each such Separate Limit of Liability shall be the maximum limit of the Insurer's liability

76174 (6/00)   6

for all Loss, arising out of all Claims first made against the Insureds during the Policy Period and the Discovery Period (if applicable) with respect to the Coverage Section for which it is shown; however, the Separate Limit of Liability for the Discovery Period shall be part of, and not in addition to, the Separate Limit of Liability for the Policy Period. The Separate Limits of Liability shall be part of and not in addition to the Aggregate Limit of Liability for all Loss under this policy as stated in Item 4A of the Declarations and in no way shall serve to increase the Insurer's Limit of Liability as therein stated.

Defense Costs are not payable by the Insurer in addition to the Aggregate Limit of Liability or Separate Limit of Liability, if any. Defense Costs are part of Loss and as such are subject to the Aggregate Limit of Liability for Loss and the applicable Separate Limit of Liability, if any. Amounts incurred for Defense Costs shall be applied against the Retention amount.

6. RETENTION CLAUSE

The Insurer shall only be liable for the amount of Loss arising from a Claim which is in excess of the applicable Retention amount stated in Item 5 of the Declarations, such Retention amount to be borne by the Company and/or the Insureds and shall remain uninsured, with regard to: (i) all Indemnifiable Loss; and (ii) Loss of the Company. A single Retention amount shall apply to Loss arising from all Claims alleging the same Wrongful Act or Related Wrongful Acts. In the event a Claim triggers more than one amount stated in Item 5 of the Declarations, only the highest such amount shall apply, which amount shall apply to all Loss under such Claim.

7. NOTICE/CLAIM REPORTING PROVISIONS

Notice hereunder shall be given in writing to the Insurer named in Item 8 of the Declarations at the address indicated in Item 8 of the Declarations. If mailed, the date of mailing shall constitute the date that such notice was given and proof of mailing shall be sufficient proof of notice. A Claim shall be considered to have been first made against an Insured when written notice of such Claim is received by any Insured, by the Company on the behalf of any Insured or by the Insurer, whichever comes first.

(a)   The Company or the Insureds shall, as a condition precedent to the obligations of the Insurer under this policy, give written notice to the Insurer of any Claim made against an Insured as soon as practicable and either:

   (1)   anytime during the Policy Period or during the Discovery Period (if applicable); or

(2) within 30 days after the end of the Policy Period or the Discovery Period (if applicable), as long as such Claim was first made against an Insured within the final 30 days of the Policy Period or the Discovery Period (if applicable).

(b) If written notice of a Claim has been given to the Insurer pursuant to Clause 7(a) above, then any Claim which is subsequently made against the Insureds and reported to the Insurer alleging a Related Wrongful Act to the Claim for which such notice has been given shall be considered made at the time such notice was given.

(c) If during the Policy Period or during the Discovery Period (if applicable), the Company or the Insureds shall become aware of any circumstances which may reasonably be expected to give rise to a Claim being made against the Insureds and shall give written notice to the Insurer of the circumstances and the reasons for anticipating such a Claim, with full particulars as to dates, persons and entities involved, then any Claim which is subsequently made against the Insureds and reported to the Insurer alleging, arising out of, based upon or attributable to such circumstances or alleging any Related Wrongful Act to such circumstances, shall be considered made at the time such notice of such circumstances was given.

(d) All Claims asserted in a Class Action Suit will be treated as arising out of the same or Related Wrongful Act.

8. DEFENSE COSTS, SETTLEMENTS, JUDGMENTS (INCLUDING THE ADVANCEMENT OF DEFENSE COSTS)

The Insurer does not assume any duty to defend. The Insureds shall defend and contest any Claim made against them.

Notwithstanding the foregoing, the Insureds shall have the right to tender the defense of the Claim to the Insurer, which right shall be exercised in writing by the Named Entity on behalf of all Insureds to the Insurer pursuant to the notice provisions of Clause 7 of these General Terms and Conditions. This right shall terminate if not exercised within 30 days of the date the Claim is first made against an Insured, pursuant to Clause 7 of these General Terms and Conditions. Further, from the date the Claim is first made against the Insureds to the date when the Insurer accepts the tender of the defense of such Claim, the Insureds shall take no action, or fail to take any required action, that prejudices the rights of the Insureds or the Insurer with respect to such Claim. Provided that the Insureds have complied with the foregoing, the Insurer shall be obligated to assume the defense of the Claim, even if such Claim is groundless, false or fraudulent. The assumption of the defense of the Claim shall be effective upon written confirmation sent thereof by the Insurer to the Named Entity.

Once the defense has been so tendered, the Insured shall have the right to effectively associate with the Insurer in the defense and negotiation of any settlement of any Claim, subject to the provisions of this Clause 8. However, the Insurer shall not be obligated to defend such Claim after the applicable Limit of Liability has been exhausted, or after an Insured's rejection of a Settlement Opportunity as defined in this Clause 8.

When the Insurer has not assumed the defense of a Claim pursuant to this Clause 8, the Insurer shall advance nevertheless, at the written request of the Insured, Defense Costs prior to the final disposition of a Claim. Such advanced payments by the Insurer shall be repaid to the Insurer by the Insureds or the Company, severally according to their respective interests, in the event and to the extent that the Insureds or the Company shall not be entitled under the terms and conditions of this policy to payment of such Loss.

The Insureds shall not admit or assume any liability, enter into any settlement agreement, stipulate to any judgment, or incur any Defense Costs without the prior written consent of the Insurer. Only those settlements, stipulated judgments and Defense Costs, which have been consented to by the Insurer, in writing, shall be recoverable as Loss under the terms of this policy. The Insurer's consent shall not be unreasonably withheld, provided that the Insurer, when it has not assumed the defense of a Claim pursuant to this Clause 8, shall be entitled to effectively associate in the defense and negotiation of any settlement of any Claim, and provided further that in all events the Insurer may withhold consent to any settlement, stipulated judgment or Defense Costs, or any portion thereof, to the extent such loss is not covered under the terms of this policy.

The Insurer shall have the right to effectively associate with the Company in the defense of any Claim that appears reasonably likely to involve the Insurer, including but not limited to negotiating a settlement. The Company and the Insureds shall give the Insurer full cooperation and such information as it may reasonably require.

If the Insurer recommends a settlement within the policy's applicable Limit of Liability which is acceptable to the claimant (a "Settlement Opportunity"), and the Insureds consent to such settlement, then the Insured's applicable retention amount shall be retroactively reduced by ten percent (10%) for such Loss. It shall be a condition to such reduction that the Insureds must consent to such settlement within thirty (30) days of the date the Insureds are first made aware of the Settlement Opportunity, or in the case of a Settlement Opportunity which arises from a settlement offer by the claimants, then within the time permitted by the claimant to accept such settlement offer, but in all events no later than thirty (30) days after the settlement offer was made.

However, if a Settlement Opportunity arises and the Insureds do not consent to the settlement within the time prescribed above, the retention amount shall remain the

76174 (6/00)   9

applicable amount set forth in Item 5 of the Declarations even if consent is given to a subsequent Settlement Opportunity.

Furthermore, in the event the Insureds do not consent to the first Settlement Opportunity within the time prescribed, then, subject to the applicable limit of liability, the Insurerís liability for all Loss on account of such Claim shall not exceed: (1) the amount for which the Insurer could have settled such Claim, plus Defense Costs incurred as of the date such settlement was proposed in writing by the Insurer, ("Settlement Opportunity Amount"), plus (2) 50% of covered Loss in excess of such Settlement Opportunity Amount, it being a condition of this insurance that the remaining 50% of such Loss excess of the Settlement Opportunity Amount shall be carried by the Company and the Insureds at their own risk and be uninsured. Notwithstanding the foregoing, this paragraph shall not apply until the Settlement Opportunity Amount exceeds the Retention amount stated in Item 5 of the Declarations.

9. PRE-AUTHORIZED DEFENSE ATTORNEYS

This clause applies to all Claims under this policy. Affixed as Appendix A hereto and made a part of this policy is a list or lists of Panel Counsel law firms (herein "Panel Counsel Firms") from which a selection of legal counsel shall be made to conduct the defense of any Claim(s) against any Insured(s) pursuant to the terms set forth below.

In the event the Insurer has assumed the defense pursuant to Clause 8 of these General Terms and Conditions, then the Insurer shall select a Panel Counsel Firm to defend the Insureds. In the event the Insureds are already defending a Claim, then the Insureds shall select a Panel Counsel Firm to defend the Insureds.

The selection of the Panel Counsel Firm, whether done by the Insurer or the Insureds, shall be from the list of Panel Counsel Firms designated for the type of Claim and be from the jurisdiction in which the Claim is brought. In the event a Claim is brought in a jurisdiction not included on the appropriate list, the selection shall be made from a listed jurisdiction which is the nearest geographic jurisdiction to either where the Claim is maintained or where the corporate headquarters or state of formation of the Named Entity is located. In such instance, however, the Insurer shall, at the written request of the Named Entity assign a non-Panel Counsel Firm of the Insurer's choice in the jurisdiction in which the Claim is brought to function as "local counsel" on the Claim to assist the Panel Counsel Firm, which will function as "lead counsel" in conducting the defense of the Claim.

With the express prior written consent of the Insurer, an Insured may select (in the case of the Insured defending the Claim), or cause the Insurer to select (in the case of the Insurer defending the Claim), a Panel Counsel Firm different from that selected by other Insured defendants if such selection is required due to an actual conflict of interest or is otherwise reasonably justifiable.

76174 (6/00)   10

The list of Panel Counsel Firms may be amended from time to time by the Insurer. However, no change shall be made to the specific list attached to this policy during the Policy Period without the consent of the Named Entity.

10. DISCOVERY CLAUSE

Except as indicated below, if the Named Entity shall cancel or the Named Entity or the Insurer shall refuse to renew this policy, the Named Entity shall have the right to a period of either one, two or three years following the effective date of such cancellation or nonrenewal upon payment of the respective "Additional Premium Amount" described below (herein referred to as the "Discovery Period") in which to give to the Insurer written notice of Claims first made against the Insureds during said Discovery Period for any Wrongful Act occurring prior to the end of the Policy Period and otherwise covered by this policy. The rights contained in this paragraph shall terminate, however, unless written notice of such election together with the additional premium due is received by the Insurer within 30 days of the effective date of cancellation or nonrenewal.

Notwithstanding the first paragraph of Clause 5 of these General Terms and Conditions, if the Named Entity gives notice of its intention to cancel or the Named Entity or the Insurer non-renew this policy, then the Named Entity shall also have the right, within 60 days before the end of the Policy Period, to request an offer from the Insurer of a Discovery Period (with respect to Wrongful Acts occurring prior to the end of the Policy Period) for a period of one, two or three years with an aggregate limit of liability applicable to Claims made against the Insured during such Discovery Period which is in addition to, and not part of, the Aggregate Limit of Liability set forth in Item 4A of the Declarations. The Insurer shall quote such a Discovery Period pursuant to such terms, conditions, exclusions and additional premium, as it deems appropriate in its' sole and absolute discretion.

The Additional Premium Amount for: (1) one year shall be 75% of the "full annual premium"; (2) two years shall be 150% of the "full annual premium"; and (3) three years shall be a reasonable premium amount to be mutually agreed upon by the Named Entity and the Insurer. As used herein, "full annual premium" means the premium level in effect immediately prior to the end of the Policy Period.

In the event of a Transaction, as defined in Clause 12 of these General Terms and Conditions, the Named Entity shall have the right, within 30 days before the end of the Policy Period, to request an offer from the Insurer of a Discovery Period (with respect to Wrongful Acts occurring prior to the effective time of the Transaction) for a period of no less than three years or for such longer or shorter period as the Named Entity may request. The Insurer shall offer such Discovery Period pursuant to such terms, conditions and premium as the Insurer may reasonably decide. In the event of

76174 (6/00)   11

a Transaction, the right to a Discovery Period shall not otherwise exist except as indicated in this paragraph.

The Additional Premium for the Discovery Period shall be fully earned at the inception of the Discovery Period. The Discovery Period is not cancelable, except for non-payment of premium. This clause and the rights contained herein shall not apply to any cancellation resulting from non-payment of premium.

11. CANCELLATION CLAUSE

This policy may be canceled by the Named Entity at any time only by mailing written prior notice to the Insurer or by surrender of this policy to the Insurer or its authorized agent; provided, however, that the Named Entity may not cancel this policy if the Policy Period as set forth in Item 2 of the Declarations is twenty-four (24) months or longer.

This policy may be canceled by or on the behalf of the Insurer only in the event of nonpayment of premium by the Named Entity. In the event of non-payment of premium by the Named Entity, the Insurer may cancel this policy by delivering to the Named Entity or by mailing to the Named Entity, by registered, certified, or other first class mail, at the Named Entity's address as shown in Item 1(a) of the Declarations, written notice stating when, not less than 30 days thereafter, the cancellation shall be effective. The mailing of such notice as aforesaid shall be sufficient proof of notice. The Policy Period terminates at the date and hour specified in such notice, or at the date and time of surrender. The Insurer shall have the right to the premium amount for the portion of the Policy Period during which the policy was in effect.

If this policy shall be canceled by the Named Entity, the Insurer shall retain the customary short rate proportion of the premium herein.

If the period of limitation relating to the giving of notice as set forth above is also set forth in any law controlling the construction thereof, the period set forth above shall be deemed to be amended so as to be equal to the minimum period of limitation set forth in the controlling law.

12. CHANGE IN CONTROL OF NAMED ENTITY

If during the Policy Period:

    a.   the Named Entity shall consolidate with or merge into, or sell all or substantially all of its assets to any other person or entity or group of persons or entities acting in concert; or

76174 (6/00)   12

b. any person or entity or group of persons or entities acting in concert shall acquire an amount of the outstanding securities representing more than 50% of the voting power for the election of directors of the Named Entity, or acquires the voting rights of such an amount of such securities;

(either of the above events herein referred to as the "Transaction"),

then this policy shall continue in full force and effect as to Wrongful Acts occurring prior to the effective time of the Transaction, but there shall be no coverage afforded by any provision of this policy for any actual or alleged Wrongful Act occurring after the effective time of the Transaction. This policy may not be canceled after the effective time of the Transaction and the entire premium for this policy shall be deemed earned as of such time. The Named Entity shall also have the right to an offer by the Insurer of a Discovery Period described in Clause 10 of these General Terms and Conditions.

The Named Entity shall give the Insurer written notice of the Transaction as soon as practicable, but not later than 30 days after the effective date of the Transaction.

13. SUBROGATION

In the event of any payment under this policy, the Insurer shall be subrogated to the extent of such payment to all the Insureds' rights of recovery thereof, and the Insureds shall execute all papers required and shall do everything that may be necessary to secure such rights, including the execution of such documents necessary to enable the Insurer to effectively bring suit in the name of the Insureds. In no event, however, shall subrogation be had against any Insured under this policy, unless such Insured has been convicted of a criminal act, or been determined to have committed a dishonest, fraudulent act or willful violation of any statute, rule or law, or obtained any profit or advantage to which such Insured was not legally entitled.

14. OTHER INSURANCE

Such insurance as is provided by this policy shall apply only as excess over any other valid and collectible insurance. This policy specifically shall be excess of any other policy pursuant to which any other insurer has a duty to defend a Claim for which this policy may be obligated to pay Loss.

In the event of a Claim against an Insured arising out of his or her service as an Outside Entity Executive; or a Claim against an Insured for the Insured's liability with respect to a leased Employee as described in definition (g) of these General Terms and Conditions, coverage as is afforded by this policy shall be specifically

76174 (6/00)   13

excess of indemnification provided by such Outside Entity or such leasing company and any insurance provided to such Outside Entity or such leasing company.

Further, in the event other insurance is provided to the Outside Entity or leasing company referenced in the above paragraph, or is provided under any pension trust or employee benefit plan fiduciary liability insurance policy, and such other insurance is provided by the Insurer or any member company of American International Group, Inc. (AIG) (or would be provided but for the application of the retention amount, exhaustion of the limit of liability or failure to submit a notice of a Claim), then the Insurerís maximum aggregate Limit of Liability for all Losses combined in connection with a Claim covered, in part or in whole, by this policy and such other insurance policy issued by AIG shall not exceed the greater of the Limit of Liability of this policy or the limit of liability of such other AIG insurance policy.

15. NOTICE AND AUTHORITY

It is agreed that the Named Entity shall act on behalf of its Subsidiaries and all Insureds with respect to the giving of notice of a Claim, the giving and receiving of notice of cancellation, the payment of premiums and the receiving of any return premiums that may become due under this policy, the receipt and acceptance of any endorsements issued to form a part of this policy, the exercising or declining of the right to tender the defense of a Claim to the Insurer and the exercising or declining to exercise any right to a Discovery Period.

16. ASSIGNMENT

This policy and any and all rights hereunder are not assignable without the prior written consent of the Insurer.

17. DISPUTE RESOLUTION PROCESS

The Insured shall have the option, in its sole discretion, to submit all disputes or differences which may arise under or in connection with this policy, whether arising before or after termination of this policy, including any determination of the amount of Loss, to the alternative dispute resolution process ("ADR") set forth in this clause.

The Insureds may elect the type of ADR discussed below. The Insurer agrees to submit to the ADR process chosen by the Insured. Once elected, the ADR cannot be terminated prior to a determination without consent of the Insured and the Insurer.

There shall be two choices of ADR: (1) non-binding mediation administered by the American Arbitration Association, in which the Insurer and Insureds shall try in good faith to settle the dispute by mediation under or in accordance with its then-prevailing Commercial Mediation Rules; or (2) arbitration submitted to the American Arbitration Association under or in accordance with its then-prevailing Commercial Arbitration Rules, in which the arbitration panel shall be composed of three disinterested individuals. In either mediation or arbitration, the mediator(s) or arbitrators shall have knowledge of the legal, corporate management, or insurance issues relevant to the matters in dispute. The mediator(s) or arbitrators shall also give due consideration to the general principles of the law of the state where the Named Entity is incorporated or formed in the construction or interpretation of the provisions of this policy; provided, however, that the terms, conditions, provisions and exclusions of this policy are to be construed in an even-handed fashion in the manner most consistent with the relevant terms, conditions, provisions or exclusions of the policy. In the event of arbitration, the decision of the arbitrators shall be final and binding and provided to both parties, and the arbitrators' award shall not include attorney's fees or other costs. In the event of mediation, either party shall have the right to commence a judicial proceeding; provided, however, that no such judicial proceeding shall be commenced until the mediation shall have been terminated and at least 120 days shall have elapsed from the date of the termination of the mediation. In all events, each party shall share equally the expenses of the ADR.

Either choice of ADR may be commenced in either New York, New York; Atlanta, Georgia; Chicago, Illinois; Denver, Colorado; or in the state indicated in Item 1(a) of the Declarations as the mailing address for the Named Entity. The Named Entity shall act on behalf of all Insureds in deciding to proceed with ADR under this clause.

18. ACTION AGAINST INSURER

Except as provided in Clause 17 above, no action shall lie against the Insurer unless, as a condition precedent thereto, there shall have been full compliance with all of the terms of this policy, not until the amount of the Insureds' obligation to pay shall have been finally determined either by judgment against the Insureds after actual trial or by written agreement of the Insureds, the claimant and the Insurer.

Any person or organization or the legal representative thereof who has secured such judgment or written agreement shall thereafter be entitled to recover under this policy to the extent of the insurance afforded by this policy. No person or organization shall have any right under this policy to join the Insurer as a party to any action against the Insureds or the Company to determine the Insureds' liability, nor shall the Insurer be impleaded by the Insureds or the Company or their legal representatives. Bankruptcy or insolvency of the Company or the Insureds or of their estates shall not relieve the Insurer of any of its obligations hereunder.

19. WORLDWIDE TERRITORY

Where legally permissible, this policy shall apply to Claims for Wrongful Acts made against an Insured anywhere in the world.

76174 (6/00)   15

20. HEADINGS

The descriptions in the headings of this policy are solely for convenience, and form no part of the terms and conditions of coverage.

76174 (6/00)

16

PRIVATE COLLECTION^{SM}

AIG

DIRECTORS, OFFICERS AND PRIVATE COMPANY LIABILITY COVERAGE SECTION ONE

In consideration of the payment of the premium, and in reliance upon the statements made to the Insurer by application, including its attachments and the material incorporated therein, which form a part of this policy, the Insurer agrees as follows:

1. INSURING AGREEMENTS

COVERAGE A: INDIVIDUAL INSURED INSURANCE

This policy shall pay the Loss of each and every Director, Officer, Outside Entity Executive and Employee of the Company arising from a Claim first made against such Individual Insureds during the Policy Period or the Discovery Period (if applicable) and reported to the Insurer pursuant to the terms of this policy for any actual or alleged Wrongful Act in their respective capacities as Directors, Officers, Outside Entity Executives and Employees of the Company, except when and to the extent that the Company has indemnified such Individual Insureds.   The Insurer shall, in accordance with Clause 8 of the General Terms and Conditions, advance Defense Costs of such Claim prior to its final disposition.

COVERAGE B: PRIVATE COMPANY INSURANCE

This policy shall pay the Loss of the Company arising from a:

    (i)   Claim first made against the Company, or

    (ii) Claim first made against an Individual Insured,

during the Policy Period or the Discovery Period (if applicable) and reported to the Insurer pursuant to the terms of this policy for any actual or alleged Wrongful Act, but, in the case of (ii) above, only when and to the extent that the Company has indemnified the Individual Insured for such Loss pursuant to law, common or statutory, or contract, or the charter or by-laws of the Company duly effective under such law which determines and defines such rights of indemnity. The Insurer shall, in accordance with Clause 8 of the General Terms and Conditions, advance Defense Costs of such Claim prior to its final disposition.

76177 (6/00)   1

2. DEFINITIONS

(a) "Claim" means:

    (1) a written demand for monetary, non-monetary or injunctive relief (including any request to toll or waive any statute of limitations); or

    (2) a civil, criminal, administrative, regulatory or arbitration proceeding for monetary, non-monetary or injunctive relief which is commenced by:

        (i) service of a complaint or similar pleading; or

        (ii) return of an indictment, information or similar document (in the case of a criminal proceeding); or

        (iii) receipt or filing of a notice of charges.

The term "Claim" shall include a Securities Claim.

(b) "Individual Insured(s)" means any:

    (1) Director(s) or Officer(s);

    (2) Employees of the Company; and

    (3) Outside Entity Executive.

(c) "Insured(s)" means:

    (1) an Individual Insured(s); and

    (2) the Company.

(d) "Loss" means damages, judgments, settlements, pre-judgment and post-judgment interest on that part of any judgment paid under this Coverage Section, and Defense Costs; however, Loss shall not include: (1) civil or criminal fines or penalties; (2) punitive or exemplary damages; (3) the multiplied portion of multiplied damages; (4) taxes; (5) any amount for which the Insureds are not financially liable or which are without legal recourse to the Insureds; and (6) matters which may be deemed uninsurable under the law pursuant to which this policy shall be construed.

(e) "Securities Claim" means a Claim made against any Insured:

(1) alleging a violation of any federal, state, local or foreign regulation, rule or statute regulating securities (including but not limited to the purchase or sale or offer or solicitation of an offer to purchase or sell securities) which is:

(i) brought by any person or entity alleging, arising out of, based upon or attributable to the purchase or sale or offer or solicitation of an offer to purchase or sell any securities of the Company; or

(ii) brought by a security holder of the Company with respect to such security holder's interest in securities of the Company; or

(2) brought derivatively on the behalf of the Company by a security holder of the Company.

(f) "Wrongful Act" means any actual or alleged breach of duty, neglect, error, misstatement, misleading statement, omission or act:

(1) with respect to Individual Insureds, by such Individual Insureds in his or her capacity as such, or any matter claimed against such Individual Insured solely by reason of his or her status as Directors, Officers, Outside Entity Executives or Employees of the Company;

(2) with respect to Coverage B(i), by the Company.

3. EXCLUSIONS

The Insurer shall not be liable to make any payment for Loss in connection with a Claim made against an Insured:

(a) arising out of, based upon or attributable to the committing in fact of any criminal, fraudulent or dishonest act;

(b) arising out of, based upon or attributable to: (1) profits in fact made from the purchase or sale by an Insured of securities of the Company within the meaning of Section 16(b) of the Securities Exchange Act of 1934 and amendments thereto or similar provisions of any state statutory law; or (2) payments to an Insured of any remuneration without the previous approval of the stockholders of the Company, which payment without such previous approval shall be held to have been illegal;

(c) alleging, arising out of, based upon, or attributable to, directly or indirectly resulting from, in consequence of, or in any way involving, employment of any

76177 (6/00) 3

individual or any employment practice (including but not limited to wrongful dismissal, discharge or termination, discrimination, harassment, retaliation or other employment-related claim);

(d) alleging, arising out of, based upon or attributable to any actual or alleged act or omission of an Insured serving in any capacity, other than as a Director, Officer, Outside Entity Executive or Employee of the Company;

(e) for any Wrongful Act arising out of an Individual Insured serving in a capacity as an Outside Entity Executive, if such Claim is brought by the Outside Entity or a director, officer, trustee or governor thereof;

(f) alleging, arising out of, based upon or attributable to the purchase by the Company of securities of a "publicly traded entity" in a transaction which resulted, or would result, in such entity becoming an Affiliate or Subsidiary of the Company; provided, however, this exclusion shall not apply in the event that within 30 days prior to it becoming an Affiliate or Subsidiary, the Named Entity gives written notice of the transaction to the Insurer together with full particulars and underwriting information required and agrees to any additional premium or amendment of the provisions of this policy required by the Insurer relating to the transaction. Further, coverage as shall be afforded to the transaction is conditioned upon the Named Entity paying when due any additional premium required by the Insurer relating to the transaction. An entity is a "publicly traded entity" if any securities of such entity have previously been subject to a public offering;

(g) with respect to Coverage B(i) only:

(1) for any actual or alleged plagiarism, misappropriation, infringement or violation of copyright, patent, trademark, trade secret or any other intellectual property rights;

(2) for any actual or alleged violation of any law, whether statutory, regulatory or common law, respecting any of the following activities: anti-trust, business competition, unfair trade practices or tortious interference in another's business or contractual relationships;

(3) alleging, arising out of, based upon or attributable to any actual or alleged contractual liability of any Insured under any contract or agreement (either oral or written);

(4) seeking fines or penalties or non-monetary relief against the Company;

(5) for the rendering or failure to render any service to a customer or client of the Insured;

Provided, however, that exclusions (g)(4) and (g)(5) shall not apply to any Securities Claim.

(h) for emotional distress, or for injury from libel or slander, or defamation or disparagement, or for injury from a violation of a person's right of privacy; provided, however, that this exclusion shall not apply to any Securities Claim;

(i) which is brought by any Insured; or which is brought by any security holder of the Company, whether directly or derivatively, unless such security holder's Claim is instigated and continued totally independent of, and totally without the solicitation of, or assistance of, or active participation of, or intervention of, any Insured. This exclusion, however, shall not apply to any Claim brought by an Individual Insured where such Claim is in the form of a cross-claim or third-party claim for contribution or indemnity which is part of and results directly from a Claim which is not otherwise excluded by the terms of this policy;

(j) alleging, arising out of, based upon or attributable to any public offering of securities by the Company, an Outside Entity or an Affiliate or alleging a purchase or sale of such securities subsequent to such public offering;

provided, however, that this exclusion shall not apply to:

(1) any purchase or sale of securities exempted pursuant to section 3(b) of the Securities Act of 1933. Coverage for such purchase or sale transaction shall not be conditioned upon payment of any additional premium; however, the Named Entity shall give the Insurer written notice of any public offering exempted pursuant to section 3(b), together with full particulars and as soon as practicable, but not later than 30 days after the effective date of the public offering;

(2) any public offering of securities (other than a public offering described in paragraph (1) above), as well as any purchase or sale of such securities subsequent to such public offering, in the event that within thirty (30) days prior to the effective time of such public offering: (i) the Named Entity shall give the Insurer written notice of such public offering together with full particulars and underwriting information required thereto and (ii) the Named Entity accepts such terms, conditions and additional premium required by the Insurer for such coverage. Such coverage is also subject to the Named Entity paying when due any such additional premium. In the event the Company gives written notice with full particulars and underwriting information pursuant to (i) above, then the Insurer must offer a quote for coverage under this paragraph.

76177 (6/00)   5

For the purpose of determining the applicability of the foregoing Exclusions, other than exclusion (i): (1) the facts pertaining to and knowledge possessed by any Insured shall not be imputed to any other Individual Insured; and (2) only facts pertaining to and knowledge possessed by any past, present or future chairman of the board, president, chief executive officer, chief operating officer, chief financial officer (or equivalent positions) of the Company shall be imputed to the Company.

76177 (6/00)   6

PRIVATE COLLECTION^{SM}

EMPLOYMENT PRACTICES LIABILITY
COVERAGE SECTION TWO

In consideration of the payment of the premium, and in reliance upon the statements made to the Insurer by application, including its attachments and the material incorporated therein, which form a part of this policy, the Insurer agrees as follows:

1. INSURING AGREEMENT

This policy shall pay the Loss of each and every Insured arising from a Claim first made against such Insured during the Policy Period or the Discovery Period (if applicable) and reported to the Insurer pursuant to the terms of this policy for any actual or alleged Wrongful Act against an Employee(s) of the Company. The Insurer shall, in accordance with Clause 8 of the General Terms and Conditions advance Defense Costs of such Claim prior to its final disposition.

2. DEFINITIONS

(a) "Claim" means:

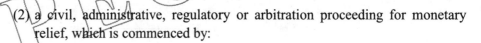

(1) a written demand for monetary relief; or

(2) a civil, administrative, regulatory or arbitration proceeding for monetary relief, which is commenced by:

(i) service of a complaint or similar pleading; or

(ii) receipt or filing of a notice of charges.

The term Claim shall include an Equal Employment Opportunity Commission ("EEOC"), Department of Labor ("DOL") or Office of Federal Contract Compliance Program ("OFCCP") (or similar federal, state or local agency) proceeding or investigation commenced by the filing of a notice of charges, service of a complaint or similar document of which notice has been given to the Insured.

However, in no event, shall the term Claim include any labor or grievance proceeding, which is subject to a collective bargaining agreement.

(b) "Class Action Suit" means any suit seeking certification or that is certified as a class action by a federal or state court.

76180 (6/00)   1

(c) "Individual Insured(s)" means any Director, Officer or Employee of the Company.

(d) "Insured(s)" means:

(1) an Individual Insured; and

(2) the Company.

(e) "Loss" means damages (including front pay and back pay), judgments, settlements, pre-judgment and post-judgment interest on that part of any judgment paid under this Coverage Section, statutory attorneys fees and Defense Costs; however, Loss shall not include: (1) civil or criminal fines or penalties imposed by law; (2) punitive or exemplary damages; (3) the multiplied portion of multiplied damages; (4) taxes; (5) any amount for which the Insureds are not financially liable or which are without legal recourse to the Insureds; (6) employment-related benefits, stock options, perquisites, deferred compensation or any other type of compensation other than salary, wages or bonus compensation; or (7) matters which may be deemed uninsurable under the law pursuant to which this policy shall be construed.

(f) "Retaliation" means a Wrongful Act of an Insured alleged to be in response to, the actual or attempted exercise by an Employee of any right that such Employee has under the law. Provided, however, Retaliation shall not include the Wrongful Act of an Insured alleged to be in response to the threat of or the actual filing of any claim or litigation under the Federal False Claims Act or any other federal state, local or foreign Whistleblower Law.

(g) "Whistleblower Law" means a statute, rule or regulation, which protects an employee against discrimination from his or her employer, if the employee discloses or threatens to disclose to a superior or any governmental agency, or who gives testimony relating to, any action with respect to the employer's operations, which may be a violation of public policy as reflected in legislation, administrative rules, regulations or decisions, judicial decisions and professional codes of ethics.

(h) "Wrongful Act(s)" means any actual or alleged:

1. wrongful dismissal, discharge or termination (either actual or constructive), including breach of an implied contract;

2. harassment (including sexual harassment, whether "quid pro quo", hostile work environment or otherwise);

76180 (6/00)   2

3. discrimination (including but not limited to discrimination based upon age, gender, race, color, national origin, religion, sexual orientation or preference, pregnancy, or disability);

4. Retaliation (including lockouts);

5. employment-related misrepresentation(s) to an Employee or applicant for employment with the Company;

6. wrongful failure to employ or promote;

7. employment-related libel, slander, humiliation, defamation or invasion of privacy;

8. wrongful deprivation of career opportunity, wrongful demotion or negligent Employee evaluation, including the giving of negative or defamatory statements in connection with an Employee reference;

9. wrongful discipline;

10. failure to grant tenure;

11. With respect to any of the foregoing items (1) through (10) of this definition: negligent hiring, retention, training or supervision, infliction of emotional distress, mental anguish, failure to provide or enforce adequate or consistent corporate policies and procedures, or violation of an individual's civil rights.

3. EXCLUSIONS

The Insurer shall not be liable to make any payment for Loss in connection with a Claim made against an Insured:

(a) arising out of, based upon or attributable to the committing in fact of any dishonest, fraudulent, criminal, or malicious act;

(b) alleging, arising out of, based upon or attributable to any actual or alleged contractual liability of any Insured under any express contract or agreement. This exclusion, however, shall not apply to:

(i) the extent any liability does not arise under such express contract or agreement;

(ii) Loss constituting Defense Costs;

(c) which is brought by any Insured. This exclusion, however, shall not apply to a Claim brought by an Employee of the Company, other than an Employee who is or was a Director of the Company;

(d) seeking any non-monetary relief, including but not limited to: (1) injunctive relief; (2) declaratory relief; (3) disgorgement; (4) job reinstatement; (5) costs or expenses incurred in accommodating any disabled person, pursuant to the Americans with Disabilities Act of 1990 (ADA), including amendments to that law or similar federal, state or local statutory or common law; (6) any liability or costs incurred in connection with any educational, sensitivity or other corporate program, policy or seminar relating to a Claim alleging a Wrongful Act(s); and (7) other equitable remedies, including as to all of the above, the cost of compliance therewith; provided, however, if such request for non-monetary relief is part of an otherwise covered Claim, the Insurer will not seek to allocate Defense Costs for the portion of the Claim seeking non-monetary relief;

(e) alleging, arising out of, based upon or attributable to any actual or alleged act or omission of an Insured serving in any capacity, other than as a Director, Officer or Employee of the Company;

(f) alleging, arising out of, based upon or attributable to any offering of securities or alleging a purchase or sale of such securities subsequent to such offering.

For the purpose of determining the applicability of the foregoing Exclusions, other than exclusion (c): (1) the facts pertaining to and knowledge possessed by any Insured shall not be imputed to any other Individual Insured; and (2) only facts pertaining to and knowledge possessed by any past, present or future chairman of the board, president, chief executive officer, chief operating officer, chief financial officer (or equivalent positions) of the Company shall be imputed to the Company.

AIG AMERICAN INTERNATIONAL COMPANIES®

AIU Insurance Company	Granite State Insurance Company
American Home Assurance Company	Illinois National Insurance Co.
American International Pacific Insurance Company	National Union Fire Insurance Company of Pittsburgh, Pa.
American International South Insurance Company	National Union Fire Insurance Company of Louisiana
Birmingham Fire Insurance Company of Pennsylvania	New Hampshire Insurance Company

(each of the above being a capital stock company)

EXECUTIVE AND ORGANIZATION LIABILITY INSURANCE POLICY

NOTICE: COVERAGES A, B AND C ARE CLAIMS MADE. THE COVERAGE OF THIS POLICY IS GENERALLY LIMITED TO LIABILITY FOR CLAIMS THAT ARE FIRST MADE AGAINST THE INSUREDS AND CRISIS FIRST OCCURRING DURING THE POLICY PERIOD AND REPORTED IN WRITING TO THE INSURER PURSUANT TO THE TERMS HEREIN. PLEASE READ THIS POLICY CAREFULLY AND REVIEW ITS COVERAGE WITH YOUR INSURANCE AGENT OR BROKER.

NOTICE: AMOUNTS INCURRED FOR LEGAL DEFENSE SHALL REDUCE THE LIMIT OF LIABILITY AVAILABLE TO PAY JUDGMENTS OR SETTLEMENTS, AND SHALL BE APPLIED AGAINST THE RETENTION AMOUNT.

NOTICE: THE INSURER DOES NOT ASSUME ANY DUTY TO DEFEND. THE INSURER MUST ADVANCE DEFENSE COSTS, EXCESS OF THE APPLICABLE RETENTION, PURSUANT TO THE TERMS HEREIN PRIOR TO THE FINAL DISPOSITION OF A CLAIM.

NOTICE: TERMS APPEARING IN BOLD FACE TYPE HAVE SPECIAL MEANING. SEE CLAUSE 2 OF THE POLICY.

DECLARATIONS

ITEMS		
1	**NAMED ENTITY:**	(herein "**Named Entity**")
1(a)	MAILING ADDRESS:	
1(b)	STATE OF INCORPORATION/FORMATION:	
2	**POLICY PERIOD:** From: To: 12:01 A.M. standard time at the address stated in Item 1(a)	
3	**POLICY AGGREGATE LIMIT OF LIABILITY** (herein "**Limit of Liability**") For all **Loss**, in the aggregate, under this policy including **Defense Costs**:	$
4	**RETENTION:** Not applicable to **Non-Indemnifiable Loss** and certain **Defense Costs** - (See Clause 6 for details.)	
4(a)	**Securities Claims** - (**Defense Costs** only): $	4(b) **Employment Practices Claims**: $
4(c)	All other **Claims**: $	

75010(2/00)   1   Order by 75879 (3/00)

ITEMS (continued)					
5	**CONTINUITY DATE** (herein **"Continuity Date"**):				
5(a)	Coverages A and B, other than **Outside Entity Executive** coverage: _____		5(b)	**Outside Entity Executive** coverage, including Coverage C:	The date on which the **Insured Person** first served as an **Outside Entity Executive** of such **Outside Entity**
5(c)	Coverage D: _____				
6	**PREMIUM:**				$
7	**CRISISFUND**SM limit:				
7(a)	**Crisis Loss:**	$	7(b)	Additional **CRISISFUND**SM for **Delisting Crisis Loss**:	$
8	**NAME AND ADDRESS OF INSURER** (herein **"Insurer"**): This policy is issued only by the insurance company indicated in this Item 8.				

IN WITNESS WHEREOF, the **Insurer** has caused this policy to be signed on the Declarations by its President, a Secretary and its duly authorized representative.

_____   _____
PRESIDENT   SECRETARY

_____
AUTHORIZED REPRESENTATIVE

_____   _____   _____
COUNTERSIGNATURE   DATE   COUNTERSIGNED AT

75010(2/00)   2   Order by 75879 (3/00)

AIG   **EXECUTIVE AND ORGANIZATION LIABILITY INSURANCE POLICY**

In consideration of the payment of the premium, and in reliance upon the **Application** and the statements therein, which form a part of this policy, the **Insurer** agrees as follows:

1. INSURING AGREEMENTS

With respect to Coverage A, B and C, solely with respect to **Claims** first made against an **Insured** during the **Policy Period** or the **Discovery Period** (if applicable) and reported to the **Insurer** pursuant to the terms of this policy, and subject to the other terms, conditions and limitations of this policy, this policy affords the following coverage:

COVERAGE A: EXECUTIVE LIABILITY INSURANCE

This policy shall pay the **Loss** of any **Insured Person** arising from a **Claim** made against such **Insured Person** for any **Wrongful Act** of such **Insured Person**, except when and to the extent that an **Organization** has indemnified such **Insured Person**. Coverage A shall not apply to **Loss** arising from a **Claim** made against an **Outside Entity Executive**.

COVERAGE B: ORGANIZATION INSURANCE

(i) *Organization Liability*: This policy shall pay the **Loss** of any **Organization** arising from a **Securities Claim** made against such **Organization** for any **Wrongful Act** of such **Organization**.

(ii) *Indemnification of an Insured Person*: This policy shall pay the **Loss** of an **Organization** arising from a **Claim** made against an **Insured Person** (including an **Outside Entity Executive**) for any **Wrongful Act** of such **Insured Person**, but only to the extent that such **Organization** has indemnified such **Insured Person**.

COVERAGE C: OUTSIDE ENTITY EXECUTIVE LIABILITY INSURANCE

This policy shall pay the **Loss** of any **Outside Entity Executive** arising from a **Claim** made against such **Outside Entity Executive** for any **Wrongful Act** of such **Outside Entity Executive** but only excess of any indemnification provided by an **Outside Entity** and any insurance coverage afforded to an **Outside Entity** or its **Executives** applicable to such **Claim**, except when and to the extent that an **Organization** has indemnified such **Outside Entity Executive**.

COVERAGE D: CRISISFUND^{SM} INSURANCE

This policy shall pay the **Crisis Loss** (including **Delisting Crisis Loss**) of an **Organization** solely with respect to a **Crisis** (including a **Delisting Crisis**) occurring during the **Policy Period** or the **Discovery Period** (if applicable) and reported to the **Insurer** pursuant to the terms of this policy, up to the amount of the respective **CrisisFund**^{SM}, from first dollar; provided that payment of any **Crisis Loss** under this policy shall not waive any of the **Insurer's** rights under this policy or at law. This Coverage D shall apply regardless of whether a **Claim** is ever made against an **Insured** arising from such **Crisis** and, in the case where a **Claim** is made, regardless of whether the amount is incurred prior to or subsequent to the making of the **Claim**.

2. DEFINITIONS

(a) **"Application"** means each and every signed application, any attachments to such applications, other materials submitted therewith or incorporated therein and any other documents submitted in connection with the underwriting of this policy or the underwriting of any other directors and officers (or equivalent) liability policy issued by the **Insurer**, or any of its affiliates, of which this policy is a renewal, replacement or which it succeeds in time, and any public documents filed by an **Organization** with any federal, state, local or foreign regulatory agency (including but not limited to the Securities and Exchange Commission (SEC)).

(b) **"Claim"** means:

(1) a written demand for monetary, non-monetary or injunctive relief;

(2) a civil, criminal, administrative, regulatory or arbitration proceeding for monetary or non-monetary relief which is commenced by: (i) service of a complaint or similar pleading; (ii) return of an indictment, information or similar document (in the case of a criminal proceeding); or (iii) receipt or filing of a notice of charges; or

(3) a civil, criminal, administrative or regulatory investigation of an **Insured Person**:

(i) once such **Insured Person** is identified in writing by such investigating authority as a person against whom a proceeding described in Definition (b)(2) may be commenced; or

(ii) in the case of an investigation by the SEC or a similar state or foreign government authority, after the service of a subpoena upon such **Insured Person**.

The term **"Claim"** shall include any **Securities Claim** and any **Employment Practices Claim**.

(c) **"Crisis"** has the meaning as defined in Appendix B attached to this policy.

(d) **"CrisisFund^{SM}"** means:

(1) in the case of all **Crisis Loss**, other than **Delisting Crisis Loss**, the dollar amount set forth in Item 7(a) of the Declarations; and

(2) in the case of **Delisting Crisis Loss** the dollar amount set forth in Item 7(a) of the Declarations plus the additional dollar amount set forth in Item 7(b) of the Declarations, combined.

(e) **"Crisis Loss"** has the meaning as defined in Appendix B attached to this policy. **"Delisting Crisis Loss"** means a **Crisis Loss** resulting solely from a **Delisting Crisis** (as defined in Appendix B).

(f) **"Defense Costs"** means reasonable and necessary fees, costs and expenses consented to by the **Insurer** (including premiums for any appeal bond, attachment bond or similar bond arising out of a covered judgment, but without any obligation to apply for or furnish any such bond) resulting solely from the investigation, adjustment, defense and/or appeal of a **Claim** against an **Insured**, but excluding any compensation of any **Insured Person** or any **Employee** of an **Organization**.

(g) **"Employee"** means any past, present or future employee, other than an **Executive** of an **Organization**, whether such employee is in a supervisory, co-worker or subordinate position or otherwise, including any full-time, part-time, seasonal and temporary employee.

(h) **"Employment Practices Claim"** means a **Claim** alleging any **Employment Practices Violation**.

(i) "**Employment Practices Violation**" means any actual or alleged:

    (1)   wrongful dismissal, discharge or termination, either actual or constructive, of employment;

    (2)   harassment (including but not limited to sexual harassment);

    (3)   discrimination;

    (4)   retaliation;

    (5)   employment-related misrepresentation;

    (6)   employment-related libel, slander, humiliation, defamation or invasion of privacy;

    (7)   wrongful failure to employ or promote;

    (8)   wrongful deprivation of career opportunity, wrongful demotion or negligent **Employee** evaluation;

    (9)   wrongful discipline;

    (10) failure to grant tenure; or

    (11) with respect to any of the foregoing items (1) through (10) of this definition: negligent hiring, retention, training or supervision, infliction of emotional distress, failure to provide or enforce adequate or consistent corporate policies and procedures, or violation of an individual's civil rights,

but only if such act, error or omission relates to an **Executive** of, an **Employee** of or an applicant for employment with an **Organization** or an **Outside Entity**, whether committed directly, indirectly, intentionally or unintentionally. In addition, with respect to any natural person customer or client, "**Employment Practices Violation**" shall mean only actual or alleged discrimination, sexual harassment or violation of an individual's civil rights relating to such discrimination or sexual harassment, whether committed directly, indirectly, intentionally or unintentionally.

(j) "**Executive**" means any:

    (1) past, present and future duly elected or appointed director, officer, trustee or governor of a corporation, management committee member of a joint venture and member of the management board of a limited liability company (or equivalent position);

    (2) past, present and future person in a duly elected or appointed position in an entity organized and operated in a **Foreign Jurisdiction** that is equivalent to an executive position listed in Definition (j)(1); or

    (3) past, present and future General Counsel and Risk Manager (or equivalent position) of the **Named Entity**.

(k) "**Foreign Jurisdiction**" means any jurisdiction, other than the United States or any of its territories or possessions.

(l) "**Foreign Policy**" means the **Insurer's** or any other member company of American International Group, Inc.'s (AIG) standard executive managerial liability policy (including all mandatory endorsements, if any) approved by AIG to be sold within a **Foreign Jurisdiction** that provides coverage substantially similar to the coverage afforded under this policy. If more than one such policy exists, then "**Foreign Policy**" means such standard policy most recently registered in the local language of the **Foreign Jurisdiction**, or if no such policy has been registered, then the policy most recently registered in that **Foreign Jurisdiction**. The term "**Foreign Policy**" shall not include any partnership managerial, pension trust or professional liability coverage.

(m) "**Indemnifiable Loss**" means **Loss** for which an **Organization** has indemnified or is permitted or required to indemnify an **Insured Person** pursuant to law or contract or the charter, bylaws, operating agreement or similar documents of an **Organization**.

(n) "**Insured**" means any:

    (1) **Insured Person**; or

    (2) **Organization**, but only with respect to a **Securities Claim**.

(o) **"Insured Person"** means any:

    (1) **Executive** of an **Organization**;
    (2) **Employee** of an **Organization**; or
    (3) **Outside Entity Executive**.

(p) **"Loss"** means damages, settlements, judgments (including pre/post-judgment interest on a covered judgment), **Defense Costs** and **Crisis Loss**; however, **"Loss"** (other than **Defense Costs**) shall not include: (1) civil or criminal fines or penalties; (2) taxes; (3) punitive or exemplary damages; (4) the multiplied portion of multiplied damages; (5) any amounts for which an **Insured** is not financially liable or which are without legal recourse to an **Insured**; and (6) matters which may be deemed uninsurable under the law pursuant to which this policy shall be construed.

Notwithstanding the foregoing paragraph, **Loss** shall specifically include (subject to this policy's other terms, conditions and limitations, including but not limited to exclusions relating to profit or advantage, deliberate fraud or deliberate criminal acts): (1) civil penalties assessed against any **Insured Person** pursuant to Section 2(g) (2)(C) of the Foreign Corrupt Practices Act, 15 U.S.C. §78dd-2(g)(2)(C); and (2) solely with respect to **Securities Claims**, punitive, exemplary and multiplied damages. Enforceability of this paragraph shall be governed by such applicable law that most favors coverage for such penalties and punitive, exemplary and multiple damages.

In the event of a **Claim** alleging that the price or consideration paid or proposed to be paid for the acquisition or completion of the acquisition of all or substantially all the ownership interest in or assets of an entity is inadequate, **Loss** with respect to such **Claim** shall not include any amount of any judgment or settlement representing the amount by which such price or consideration is effectively increased; provided, however, that this paragraph shall not apply to **Defense Costs** or to any **Non-Indemnifiable Loss** in connection therewith.

(q) **"Management Control"** means: (1) owning interests representing more than 50% of the voting, appointment or designation power for the selection of a majority of: the Board of Directors of a corporation; the management committee members of a joint venture; or the members of the management board of a limited liability company; or (2) having the right, pursuant to written contract or the by-laws, charter, operating agreement or similar documents of an **Organization**, to elect, appoint or designate a majority of: the Board of Directors of a corporation; the management committee of a joint venture; or the management board of a limited liability company.

(r) **"No Liability"** means a final judgment of no liability obtained: (1) prior to trial, in favor of each and every **Insured** named in the **Claim**, by reason of a motion to dismiss or a motion for summary judgment, after the exhaustion of all appeals; or (2) after trial and after the exhaustion of all appeals, in favor of each and every **Insured** named in the **Claim**. In no event shall the term **"No Liability"** apply to a **Claim** made against an **Insured** for which a settlement has occurred.

(s) **"Non-Indemnifiable Loss"** means **Loss** for which an **Organization** has neither indemnified nor is permitted or required to indemnify an **Insured Person** pursuant to law or contract or the charter, bylaws, operating agreement or similar documents of an **Organization**.

(t) "**Organization**" means:

(1) the **Named Entity**;
(2) each **Subsidiary**; and
(3) in the event a bankruptcy proceeding shall be instituted by or against the foregoing entities, the resulting debtor-in-possession (or equivalent status outside the United States), if any.

(u) "**Outside Entity**" means any: (1) not-for-profit entity; or (2) other entity listed as an "**Outside Entity**" in an endorsement attached to this policy.

(v) "**Outside Entity Executive**" means any: (1) **Executive** of an **Organization** who is or was acting at the specific written request or direction of an **Organization** as an **Executive** of an **Outside Entity**; or (2) any other person listed as an **Outside Entity Executive** in an endorsement attached to this policy.

(w) "**Policy Period**" means the period of time from the inception date shown in Item 2 of the Declarations to the earlier of the expiration date shown in such Item 2 or the effective date of cancellation of this policy.

(x) "**Securities Claim**" means a **Claim**, other than an administrative or regulatory proceeding against, or investigation of an **Organization**, made against any **Insured**:

(1) alleging a violation of any federal, state, local or foreign regulation, rule or statute regulating securities (including but not limited to the purchase or sale or offer or solicitation of an offer to purchase or sell securities) which is:
   (a) brought by any person or entity alleging, arising out of, based upon or attributable to the purchase or sale or offer or solicitation of an offer to purchase or sell any securities of an **Organization**; or
   (b) brought by a security holder of an **Organization** with respect to such security holder's interest in securities of such **Organization**; or
(2) brought derivatively on the behalf of an **Organization** by a security holder of such **Organization**.

Notwithstanding the foregoing, the term "**Securities Claim**" shall include an administrative or regulatory proceeding against an **Organization**, but only if and only during the time that such proceeding is also commenced and continuously maintained against an **Insured Person**.

(y) "**Subsidiary**" means: (1) any for-profit entity that is not formed as a partnership of which the **Named Entity** has **Management Control** ("**Controlled Entity**") on or before the inception of the **Policy Period** either directly or indirectly through one or more other **Controlled Entities**; and (2) any not-for-profit entity under section 501(c)(3) of the Internal Revenue Code of 1986 (as amended) sponsored exclusively by an **Organization**.

(z) "**Wrongful Act**" means:

(1) any actual or alleged breach of duty, neglect, error, misstatement, misleading statement, omission or act or any actual or alleged **Employment Practices Violation**:
   (i) with respect to any **Executive** of an **Organization**, by such **Executive** in his or her capacity as such or any matter claimed against such **Executive** solely by reason of his or her status as such;
   (ii) with respect to any **Employee** of an **Organization**, by such **Employee** in his or her capacity as such, but solely in regard to any: (a) **Securities Claim**; or (b) other **Claim** so long as such other **Claim** is also made and continuously maintained against an **Executive** of an **Organization**; or
   (iii) with respect to any **Outside Entity Executive**, by such **Outside Entity Executive** in his or her capacity as such or any matter claimed against such **Outside Entity Executive** solely by reason of his or her status as such; or
(2) with respect to an **Organization**, any actual or alleged breach of duty, neglect, error, misstatement, misleading statement, omission or act by such **Organization**, but solely in regard to a **Securities Claim**.

3. WORLDWIDE EXTENSION

Where legally permissible, this policy shall apply to any **Claim** made against any **Insured** anywhere in the world.

In regard to **Claims** brought and maintained solely in a **Foreign Jurisdiction** against an **Organization** formed and operating in such **Foreign Jurisdiction** or an **Insured Person** thereof for **Wrongful Acts** committed in such **Foreign Jurisdiction**, the **Insurer** shall apply to such **Claim(s)** those terms and conditions (and related provisions) of the **Foreign Policy** registered with the appropriate regulatory body in such **Foreign Jurisdiction** that are more favorable to such **Insured** than the terms and conditions of this policy. However, this paragraph shall apply only to Clauses 1-4, 9-13, 15, 16, 18, 20 and 21 of this policy and the comparable provisions of the **Foreign Policy**. In addition, this paragraph shall not apply to the non-renewal or claims made and reported provisions of any policy.

All premiums, limits, retentions, **Loss** and other amounts under this Policy are expressed and payable in the currency of the United States of America. If judgment is rendered, settlement is denominated or other elements of **Loss** are stated or incurred in a currency other than United States of America dollars, payment of covered **Loss** due under this policy (subject to the terms, conditions and limitations of this policy) will be made either in such other currency (at the option of the **Insurer** and if agreeable to the **Named Entity**) or, in United States of America dollars, at the rate of exchange published in The Wall Street Journal on the date the Insurerês obligation to pay such **Loss** is established (or if not published on such date the next publication date of The Wall Street Journal).

4. EXCLUSIONS

The **Insurer** shall not be liable to make any payment for **Loss** in connection with any **Claim** made against an **Insured**:

(a) arising out of, based upon or attributable to the gaining in fact of any profit or advantage to which the **Insured** was not legally entitled;

(b) arising out of, based upon or attributable to payments to an **Insured** of any remuneration without the previous approval of the stockholders or members of an **Organization**, which payment without such previous approval shall be held to have been illegal;

(c) arising out of, based upon or attributable to the committing in fact of any deliberate criminal or deliberate fraudulent act by the **Insured**;

(d) alleging, arising out of, based upon or attributable to the facts alleged, or to the same or related **Wrongful Acts** alleged or contained in any **Claim** which has been reported, or in any circumstances of which notice has been given, under any policy of which this policy is a renewal or replacement or which it may succeed in time;

(e) alleging, arising out of, based upon or attributable to, as of the **Continuity Date**, any pending or prior: (1) litigation; or (2) administrative or regulatory proceeding or investigation of which an **Insured** had notice, or alleging or derived from the same or essentially the same facts as alleged in such pending or prior litigation or administrative or regulatory proceeding or investigation;

(f) with respect to any **Outside Entity Executive**, for any **Wrongful Act** occurring prior to the **Continuity Date** if any **Insured**, as of such **Continuity Date**, knew or could have reasonably foreseen that such **Wrongful Act** could lead to a **Claim** under this policy;

(g) alleging, arising out of, based upon or attributable to any actual or alleged act or omission of an **Insured Person** serving in his or her capacity as an **Executive** or an **Employee** of any entity that is not an **Organization** or an **Outside Entity**, or by reason of his or her status as an **Executive** or an **Employee** of such other entity;

(h) for bodily injury (other than emotional distress or mental anguish), sickness, disease, or death of any person, or damage to or destruction of any tangible property, including the loss of use thereof;

75011(2/00)   6   Order by 75879 (3/00)

(i) which is brought by or on behalf of any **Insured Person**, other than an **Employee** of an **Organization**, or an **Organization**; or which is brought by any security holder or member of an **Organization**, whether directly or derivatively, unless such security holder's or member's **Claim** is instigated and continued totally independent of, and totally without the solicitation of, or assistance of, or active participation of, or intervention of, any **Executive** of an **Organization** or an **Organization**; provided, however, this exclusion shall not apply to:

(1) any **Claim** brought by an **Insured Person** in the form of a cross-claim or third-party claim for contribution or indemnity which is part of, and results directly from, a **Claim** that is covered by this policy;

(2) any **Employment Practices Claim** brought by an **Insured Person,** other than an **Insured Person** who is or was a member of the Board of Directors (or equivalent governing body) of an **Organization**;

(3) in any bankruptcy proceeding by or against an **Organization**, any **Claim** brought by the examiner, trustee, receiver, liquidator or rehabilitator (or any assignee thereof) of such **Organization**, if any;

(4) any **Claim** brought by any past **Executive** of an **Organization** who has not served as a duly elected or appointed director, officer, trustee, governor, management committee member, member of the management board, General Counsel or Risk Manager (or equivalent position) of or consultant for an **Organization** for at least four (4) years prior to such **Claim** being first made against any person; or

(5) any **Claim** brought by an **Executive** of an **Organization** formed and operating in a **Foreign Jurisdiction** brought and maintained outside the United States, Canada or any other common law country (including any territories thereof);

(j) for any **Wrongful Act** arising out of the **Insured Person** serving as an **Executive** of an **Outside Entity** if such **Claim** is brought by the **Outside Entity** or by any **Executive** thereof; or which is brought by any security holder of the **Outside Entity**, whether directly or derivatively, unless such security holder's **Claim** is instigated and continued totally independent of, and totally without the solicitation of, or assistance of, or active participation of, or intervention of the **Outside Entity**, any **Executive** of the **Outside Entity** or an **Organization** or any **Executive** of an **Organization**;

(k) alleging, arising out of, based upon or attributable to, directly or indirectly: (i) the actual, alleged or threatened discharge, dispersal, release or escape of **Pollutants**; or (ii) any direction or request to test for, monitor, clean up, remove, contain, treat, detoxify or neutralize **Pollutants**, (including but not limited to a **Claim** alleging damage to an **Organization** or its securities holders); provided, however, that this exclusion shall not apply to **Non-Indemnifiable Loss**;

The term "**Pollutants**" includes (but is not limited to) any solid, liquid, gaseous or thermal irritant or contaminant, including smoke, vapor, soot, fumes, acids, alkalis, chemicals and **Waste**. "**Waste**" includes (but is not limited to) materials to be recycled, reconditioned or reclaimed;

(l) for emotional distress of any person, or for injury from libel, slander, defamation or disparagement, or for injury from a violation of a person's right of privacy; provided, however, this exclusion shall not apply to an **Employment Practices Claim**; and

(m) for violation(s) of any of the responsibilities, obligations or duties imposed upon fiduciaries by the Employee Retirement Income Security Act of 1974 or amendments thereto, or any similar provisions of any state, local or foreign statutory or common law.

For the purpose of determining the applicability of the foregoing Exclusions 4(a) through 4(c) and Exclusion 4(f): (1) the facts pertaining to and knowledge possessed by any **Insured** shall not be imputed to any other **Insured Person**; and (2) only facts pertaining to and knowledge possessed by any past, present or future chairman of the board, president, chief executive officer, chief operating officer, chief financial officer or General Counsel (or equivalent position) of an **Organization** shall be imputed to an **Organization**.

This Clause 4, Exclusions, shall not be applicable to **Crisis Loss**.

5. LIMIT OF LIABILITY (FOR ALL LOSS - INCLUDING DEFENSE COSTS)

The **Limit of Liability** stated in Item 3 of the Declarations is the aggregate limit of the **Insurer's** liability for all **Loss**, under Coverages A, B, C and D combined, arising out of all **Claims** first made against each and every **Insured**, and all **Crisis Loss** occurring, during the **Policy Period** and the **Discovery Period** (if applicable). The **Limit of Liability** for the **Discovery Period** and the **CrisisFund**^{SM} shall be part of, and not in addition to, the **Limit of Liability** for the **Policy Period**. Further, a **Claim** which is made subsequent to the **Policy Period** or **Discovery Period** (if applicable) which pursuant to Clause 7(b) or 7(c) is considered made during the **Policy Period** or **Discovery Period** shall also be subject to the one aggregate **Limit of Liability** stated in Item 3 of the Declarations. The limit of the **Insurer's** liability for **Crisis Loss** and **Delisting Crisis Loss** arising from all **Crises** occurring during the **Policy Period**, in the aggregate, shall be the amounts set forth as the **CrisisFund**^{SM}. The **CrisisFund**^{SM} shall be the aggregate limit of the **Insurer's** liability for all **Crises** under this policy regardless of the number of **Crises** occurring during the **Policy Period**.

Defense Costs are not payable by the Insurer in addition to the Limit of Liability. Defense Costs are part of Loss and as such are subject to the Limit of Liability for Loss.

6. RETENTION CLAUSE

For each **Claim**, the **Insurer** shall only be liable for the amount of **Loss** arising from a **Claim** which is in excess of the applicable Retention amounts stated in Items 4(a), 4(b) and 4(c) of the Declarations, such Retention amounts to be borne by an **Organization** and/or the **Insured Person** and remain uninsured, with regard to all **Loss** other than **Non-Indemnifiable Loss**. The Retention amount specified in:

(i) Item 4(a) applies to **Defense Costs** that arise out of a **Securities Claim**;
(ii) Item 4(b) applies to **Loss** that arises out of an **Employment Practices Claim**; and
(iii) Item 4(c) applies to **Loss** that arises out of any **Claim** other than a **Securities Claim** or an **Employment Practices Claim**.

A single Retention amount shall apply to **Loss** arising from all **Claims** alleging the same **Wrongful Act** or related **Wrongful Acts**.

In the event a **Claim** triggers more than one of the Retention amounts stated in Items 4(a), 4(b) and 4(c) of the Declarations, then, as to that **Claim**, the highest of such Retention amounts shall be deemed the Retention amount applicable to **Loss** (to which a Retention is applicable pursuant to the terms of this policy) arising from such **Claim**.

Further, with respect to all **Claims**, other than **Employment Practices Claims**, no Retention shall apply to **Loss** arising from such **Claims** and the **Insurer** shall reimburse **Defense Costs** otherwise covered hereunder and paid by the **Insured**, in the event of: (1) a determination of **No Liability** of each and every **Insured** against whom the same **Claim** or related **Claims** have been made; or (2) a dismissal or a stipulation to dismiss each and every **Insured** against whom the same **Claim** or related **Claims** have been made without prejudice and without the payment of any consideration by or on behalf of any **Insured**. However, in the case of (2) above, such reimbursement shall occur 90 days after the date of dismissal or stipulation as long as such **Claim** is not brought (or any other **Claim** which is subject to the same single retention by virtue of Clause 6 is not pending or brought) again within that time, and further subject to an undertaking by an **Organization** in a form acceptable to the **Insurer** that such reimbursement shall be paid back by such **Organization** to the **Insurer** in the event the **Claim** (or any other **Claim** which is subject to the same single retention by virtue of Clause 6) is brought after such 90-day period.

No Retention amount is applicable to **Crisis Loss** or **Non-Indemnifiable Loss**.

7. NOTICE/CLAIM REPORTING PROVISIONS

Notice hereunder shall be given in writing to the Insurer named in Item 8 of the Declarations at the address indicated in Item 8 of the Declarations. If mailed, the date of mailing shall constitute the date that such notice was given and proof of mailing shall be sufficient proof of notice.

(a) An **Organization** or an **Insured** shall, as a condition precedent to the obligations of the **Insurer** under this policy, give written notice to the **Insurer** of a **Claim** made against an **Insured** or a **Crisis** as soon as practicable: (i) after the **Named Entity's** Risk Manager or General Counsel (or equivalent position) first becomes aware of the **Claim**; or (ii) the **Crisis** commences, but in all events no later than either:

   (1) the end of the **Policy Period** or the **Discovery Period** (if applicable); or
   (2) within 30 days after the end of the **Policy Period** or the **Discovery Period** (if applicable), as long as such **Claim** was first made against an **Insured** within the final 30 days of the **Policy Period** or the **Discovery Period** (if applicable).

(b) If written notice of a **Claim** has been given to the **Insurer** pursuant to Clause 7(a) above, then a **Claim** which is subsequently made against an **Insured** and reported to the **Insurer** alleging, arising out of, based upon or attributable to the facts alleged in the **Claim** for which such notice has been given, or alleging any **Wrongful Act** which is the same as or related to any **Wrongful Act** alleged in the **Claim** of which such notice has been given, shall be considered related to the first **Claim** and made at the time such notice was given.

(c) If during the **Policy Period** or during the **Discovery Period** (if applicable) an **Organization** or an **Insured** shall become aware of any circumstances which may reasonably be expected to give rise to a **Claim** being made against an **Insured** and shall give written notice to the **Insurer** of the circumstances, the **Wrongful Act** allegations anticipated and the reasons for anticipating such a **Claim**, with full particulars as to dates, persons and entities involved, then a **Claim** which is subsequently made against such **Insured** and reported to the **Insurer** alleging, arising out of, based upon or attributable to such circumstances or alleging any **Wrongful Act** which is the same as or related to any **Wrongful Act** alleged or contained in such circumstances, shall be considered made at the time such notice of such circumstances was given.

8. DEFENSE COSTS, SETTLEMENTS, JUDGMENTS (INCLUDING THE ADVANCEMENT OF DEFENSE COSTS)

Under Coverages A, B and C of this policy, except as hereinafter stated, the **Insurer** shall advance, excess of any applicable retention amount, covered **Defense Costs** no later than ninety (90) days after the receipt by the **Insurer** of such defense bills. Such advance payments by the **Insurer** shall be repaid to the **Insurer** by each and every **Insured** or **Organization**, severally according to their respective interests, in the event and to the extent that any such **Insured** or **Organization** shall not be entitled under this policy to payment of such **Loss**.

*The **Insurer** does not, however, under this policy, assume any duty to defend. The **Insureds** shall defend and contest any **Claim** made against them. The **Insureds** shall not admit or assume any liability, enter into any settlement agreement, stipulate to any judgment, or incur any **Defense Costs** without the prior written consent of the **Insurer**. Only those settlements, stipulated judgments and **Defense Costs** which have been consented to by the **Insurer** shall be recoverable as **Loss** under the terms of this policy. The **Insurer's** consent shall not be unreasonably withheld, provided that the Insurer shall be entitled to effectively associate in the defense, the prosecution and the negotiation of any settlement of any **Claim** that involves or appears reasonably likely to involve the **Insurer**.*

75011(2/00)   9   Order by 75879 (3/00)

The **Insurer** shall have the right to effectively associate with each and every **Organization** and **Insured Person** in the defense and prosecution of any **Claim** that involves, or appears reasonably likely to involve, the **Insurer**, including but not limited to negotiating a settlement. Each and every **Organization** and **Insured Person** shall give the **Insurer** full cooperation and such information as it may reasonably require.

Notwithstanding any of the foregoing, if all **Insured** defendants are able to dispose of all **Claims** which are subject to one retention amount (inclusive of **Defense Costs**) for an amount not exceeding any applicable retention amount, then the **Insurer's** consent shall not be required for such disposition.

No **Organization** is covered in any respect under Coverage A or Coverage C. An **Organization** is covered, subject to the policy's terms, conditions and limitations only with respect to: (1) its indemnification of its **Insured Persons** under Coverage B(ii) as respects a **Claim** against such **Insured Persons**; and (2) under Coverage B(i) for a **Securities Claim**. Accordingly, the **Insurer** has no obligation under this policy for covered **Defense Costs** incurred by, judgments against or settlements by an **Organization** arising out of a **Claim** made against an **Organization** other than a covered **Securities Claim**, or any obligation to pay **Loss** arising out of any legal liability that an **Organization** has to a claimant, except as respects a covered **Securities Claim** against such **Organization**.

With respect to: (i) **Defense Costs** jointly incurred by; (ii) any joint settlement entered into by; and/or (iii) any judgment of joint and several liability against any **Organization** and any **Insured** in connection with any **Claim** other than a **Securities Claim**, any such **Organization** and any such **Insured** and the **Insurer** agree to use their best efforts to determine a fair and proper allocation of the amounts as between any such **Organization**, any such **Insured** and the **Insurer**, taking into account the relative legal and financial exposures, and the relative benefits obtained by any such **Insured** and any such **Organization**. In the event that a determination as to the amount of **Defense Costs** to be advanced under the policy cannot be agreed to, then the **Insurer** shall advance **Defense Costs** excess of any applicable retention amount which the **Insurer** states to be fair and proper until a different amount shall be agreed upon or determined pursuant to the provisions of this policy and applicable law.

This Clause 8 shall not be applicable to **Crisis Loss**. Nevertheless the **Insurer** does not, under this policy, assume any duty to defend.

9. PRE-AUTHORIZED SECURITIES DEFENSE ATTORNEYS

Affixed as Appendix A hereto and made a part of this policy is a list of Panel Counsel law firms ("**Panel Counsel Firms**"). The list provides the **Insureds** with a choice of law firms from which a selection of legal counsel shall be made to conduct the defense of any **Securities Claim** made against such **Insureds**.

The **Insureds** shall select a **Panel Counsel Firm** to defend the **Securities Claim** made against the **Insureds** in the jurisdiction in which the **Securities Claim** is brought. In the event the **Claim** is brought in a jurisdiction not included on the list, the **Insureds** shall select a **Panel Counsel Firm** in the listed jurisdiction which is the nearest geographic jurisdiction to either where the **Securities Claim** is brought or where the corporate headquarters of the **Named Entity** is located. In such instance the **Insureds** also may, with the express prior written consent of the **Insurer**, which consent shall not be unreasonably withheld, select a non-**Panel Counsel Firm** in the jurisdiction in which the **Securities Claim** is brought to function as "local counsel" on the **Claim** to assist the **Panel Counsel Firm** which will function as "lead counsel" in conducting the defense of the **Securities Claim**.

With the express prior written consent of the **Insurer**, an **Insured** may select a **Panel Counsel Firm** different from that selected by another **Insured** defendant if such selection is required due to an actual conflict of interest or is otherwise reasonably justifiable. The list of **Panel Counsel Firms** may be amended from time to time by the **Insurer**. However, no firm shall be removed from the specific list attached to this policy during the **Policy Period**, without the consent of the **Named Entity**.

10. DISCOVERY CLAUSE

Except as indicated below, if the **Named Entity** shall cancel or the **Named Entity** or the **Insurer** shall refuse to renew this policy, the **Named Entity** shall have the right to a period of either one, two or three years following the effective date of such cancellation or nonrenewal (the "**Discovery Period**") upon payment of the respective "**Additional Premium Amount**" described below in which to give to the **Insurer** written notice pursuant to Clause 7(a) and 7(c) of the policy of: (i) **Claims** first made against an **Insured**; and (ii) circumstances of which an **Organization** or an **Insured** shall become aware, in either case during said **Discovery Period** and solely with respect to a **Wrongful Act** occurring prior to the end of the **Policy Period** and otherwise covered by this policy.

The **Additional Premium Amount** for: (1) one year shall be no more than 75% of the **Full Annual Premium**; (2) two years shall be no more than 150% of the **Full Annual Premium**; and (3) three years shall be no more than 225% of the **Full Annual Premium**. As used herein, "**Full Annual Premium**" means the premium level in effect immediately prior to the end of the **Policy Period**.

Notwithstanding the first paragraph of Clause 5, if the **Named Entity** shall cancel or the **Insurer** or the **Named Entity** shall refuse to renew this policy, then the **Named Entity** shall also have the right, to request an offer from the **Insurer** of a **Discovery Period** (with respect to **Wrongful Acts** occurring prior to the end of the **Policy Period**) with an aggregate limit of liability applicable to **Claims** made against the **Insured** during such **Discovery Period** which is in addition to, and not part of, the applicable **Limit of Liability** set forth in Item 3 of the Declarations. The **Insurer** shall quote such a **Discovery Period** pursuant to such terms, conditions, exclusions and additional premium as it deems appropriate in its sole and absolute discretion.

In the event of a **Transaction** as defined in Clause 12(a), the **Named Entity** shall have the right to request an offer from the **Insurer** of a **Discovery Period** (with respect to **Wrongful Acts** occurring prior to the effective time of the **Transaction**). The **Insurer** shall offer such **Discovery Period** pursuant to such terms, conditions, exclusions and additional premium as the **Insurer** may reasonably decide. In the event of a **Transaction**, the right to a **Discovery Period** shall not otherwise exist except as indicated in this paragraph.

The **Discovery Period** is not cancelable and the additional premium charged shall be fully earned at inception. This Clause 10 shall not apply to any cancellation resulting from non-payment of premium. The rights contained in this Clause 10 shall terminate unless written notice of election of a **Discovery Period** together with any additional premium due is received by the **Insurer** no later than thirty (30) subsequent to the effective date of the cancellation, nonrenewal or **Transaction**.

11. CANCELLATION CLAUSE

This policy may be canceled by the **Named Entity** at any time only by mailing written prior notice to the **Insurer** or by surrender of this policy to the **Insurer** or its authorized agent. This policy may only be canceled by or on behalf of the **Insurer** in the event of non-payment of premium by the **Named Entity**. In the event of non-payment of premium by the **Named Entity**, the **Insurer** may cancel this policy by delivering to the **Named Entity** or by mailing to the **Named Entity**, by registered, certified, or other first class mail, at the **Named Entity's** address as shown in Item 1(a) of the Declarations, written notice stating when, not less than 15 days thereafter, the cancellation shall be effective. The mailing of such notice as aforesaid shall be sufficient proof of notice. The **Policy Period** terminates at the date and hour specified in such notice, or at the date and time of surrender. The **Insurer** shall have the right to the premium amount for the portion of the **Policy Period** during which the policy was in effect.

If this policy shall be canceled by the **Named Entity**, the **Insurer** shall retain the customary short rate proportion of the premium herein. If the period of limitation relating to the giving of notice as set forth in this Clause 11 is also set forth in any law controlling the construction thereof, then such period shall be deemed to be amended so as to be equal to the minimum period of limitation set forth in the controlling law.

12. ORGANIZATIONAL CHANGES

(a) If during the **Policy Period**:

    (1) the **Named Entity** shall consolidate with, merge into, or sell all or substantially all of its assets to any other person or entity or group of persons or entities acting in concert; or

    (2) any person or entity or group of persons or entities acting in concert shall acquire **Management Control** of the **Named Entity**;

(any of such events being a "**Transaction**"), then this policy shall continue in full force and effect as to **Wrongful Acts** occurring prior to the effective time of the **Transaction**, but there shall be no coverage afforded by any provision of this policy for any actual or alleged **Wrongful Act** occurring after the effective time of the **Transaction**. This policy may not be canceled after the effective time of the **Transaction** and the entire premium for this policy shall be deemed earned as of such time. The **Named Entity** shall also have the right to an offer by the **Insurer** of a **Discovery Period** described in the fourth paragraph of Clause 10 of this policy.

(b) *Subsidiary Additions*: "**Subsidiary**" also means any for-profit entity that is not formed as a partnership of which the **Named Entity** first had **Management Control** during the **Policy Period**, whether directly or indirectly through one or more other **Subsidiaries**, and:

    (i) whose assets total less than 25% of the total consolidated assets of each and every **Organization** as of the inception date of this policy; or

    (ii) whose assets total 25% or more than the total consolidated assets of each and every **Organization** as of the inception date of this policy, but such entity shall be a "**Subsidiary**" only: (1) for a period of sixty (60) days from the date the **Named Entity** first had **Management Control** of such entity; or (2) until the end of the **Policy Period**, which ever ends or occurs first (hereinafter "**Auto-Subsidiary Period**");

provided that the **Named Entity** or any other **Insured** shall report such **Subsidiary** to the **Insurer**, in writing, prior to the end of the **Policy Period**.

The **Insurer** shall extend coverage for any **Subsidiary** described in 12(b)(ii) above, and any **Insured Person** thereof, beyond its respective **Auto-Subsidiary Period** if during such **Auto-Subsidiary Period**, the **Named Entity** shall have provided the **Insurer** with full particulars of the new **Subsidiary** and agreed to any additional premium and amendment of the provisions of this policy required by the **Insurer** relating to such **Subsidiary**. Further, coverage as shall be afforded to any **Subsidiary** and any **Insured Person** thereof is conditioned upon the **Named Entity** paying when due any additional premium required by the **Insurer** relating to such **Subsidiary**.

(c) *Insured Persons and Outside Entity Executives*: Coverage will automatically apply to all new **Insured Persons** and **Outside Entity Executives** following the inception date of this policy.

(d) *Other Organizational Changes*: In all events, coverage as is afforded under this policy with respect to a **Claim** made against any **Organization** and/or any **Insured Person** thereof shall only apply for **Wrongful Acts** committed or allegedly committed after the effective time such **Organization** became an **Organization** and such **Insured Person** became an **Insured Person**, and prior to the effective time that such **Organization** ceases to be an **Organization** or such **Insured Person** ceases to be an **Insured Person**. An **Organization** ceases to be an **Organization** when the **Named Entity** no longer maintains **Management Control** of an **Organization** either directly or indirectly through one or more of its **Subsidiaries**.

13. SUBROGATION

In the event of any payment under this policy, the **Insurer** shall be subrogated to the extent of such payment to all of each and every **Organization's** and **Insured's** rights of recovery thereof, and each such **Organization** and **Insured** shall execute all papers required and shall do everything that may be necessary to secure such rights including the execution of any and all documents necessary to enable the **Insurer** effectively to bring suit in the name of each such **Organization** and each such **Insured**. In no event, however, shall the **Insurer** exercise its rights of subrogation against an **Insured** under this policy unless such **Insured** has been convicted of a deliberate criminal act, or been determined to have in fact committed a deliberate fraudulent act, or determined to have in fact obtained any profit or advantage to which such **Insured** was not legally entitled.

14. OTHER INSURANCE AND INDEMNIFICATION

Such insurance as is provided by this policy shall apply only as excess over any other valid and collectible insurance, unless such other insurance is written only as specific excess insurance over the **Limit of Liability** provided by this policy. This policy shall specifically be excess of any other valid and collectible insurance pursuant to which any other insurer has a duty to defend a **Claim** for which this policy may be obligated to pay **Loss**.

In the event of a **Claim** made against an **Outside Entity Executive**, coverage as is afforded by this policy, whether under Coverage B(ii) or Coverage C, shall be specifically excess of: (1) any indemnification provided by an **Outside Entity**; and (2) any insurance coverage afforded to an **Outside Entity** or its **Executives** applicable to such **Claim**. Further, in the event such other **Outside Entity** insurance is provided by the **Insurer** or any other member company of American International Group, Inc. (AIG) (or would be provided but for the application of the retention amount, exhaustion of the limit of liability or failure to submit a notice of a claim as required) then the **Insurer's** maximum aggregate **Limit of Liability** for all **Loss** under this policy, as respects any such **Claim**, shall be reduced by the amount of the limit of liability (as set forth on the Declarations) of the other AIG insurance provided to such **Outside Entity**.

15. NOTICE AND AUTHORITY

It is agreed that the **Named Entity** shall act on behalf of its **Subsidiaries** and each and every **Insured** with respect to the giving of notice of **Claim**, the giving and receiving of notice of cancellation, the payment of premiums and the receiving of any return premiums that may become due under this policy, the receipt and acceptance of any endorsements issued to form a part of this policy and the exercising or declining of any right to a **Discovery Period**.

16. ASSIGNMENT

This policy and any and all rights hereunder are not assignable without the written consent of the **Insurer**.

17. ALTERNATIVE DISPUTE RESOLUTION PROCESS

It is hereby understood and agreed that all disputes or differences which may arise under or in connection with this policy, whether arising before or after termination of this policy, including any determination of the amount of **Loss**, shall be submitted to the alternative dispute resolution ("**ADR**") process set forth in this clause.

Either the **Insurer** or an **Insured** may elect the type of **ADR** process discussed below; provided, however, that such **Insured** shall have the right to reject the **Insurer's** choice of the type of **ADR** process at any time prior to its commencement, in which case such **Insured's** choice of **ADR** process shall control.

The **Insurer** and each and every **Insured** agrees that there shall be two choices of **ADR** process: (1) non-binding mediation administered by the American Arbitration Association, in which the **Insurer** and any such **Insured** shall try in good faith to settle the dispute by mediation under or in accordance with its then-prevailing Commercial Mediation Rules; or (2) arbitration submitted to the American Arbitration Association in accordance with its then-prevailing Commercial Arbitration Rules, in which the arbitration panel shall consist of three disinterested individuals. In either mediation or arbitration, the mediator or arbitrators shall have knowledge of the legal, corporate management, or insurance issues relevant to the matters in dispute. The mediator or arbitrators shall also give due consideration to the general principles of the law of the state where the **Named Entity** is incorporated in the construction or interpretation of the provisions of this policy. In the event of arbitration, the decision of the arbitrators shall be final and binding and provided to both parties, and the arbitrators' award shall not include attorneys fees or other costs. In the event of mediation, either party shall have the right to commence a judicial proceeding; provided, however, that no such judicial proceeding shall be commenced until the mediation shall have been terminated and at least 120 days shall have elapsed from the date of the termination of the mediation. In all events, each party shall share equally the expenses of the **ADR** process.

Either choice of **ADR** process may be commenced in New York, New York; Atlanta, Georgia; Chicago, Illinois; Denver, Colorado; or in the state indicated in Item 1(a) of the Declarations as the mailing address for the **Named Entity**. The **Named Entity** shall act on behalf of each and every **Insured** in deciding to proceed with an **ADR** process under this clause.

18. ACTION AGAINST INSURER

Except as provided in Clause 17 of the policy, no action shall lie against the **Insurer** unless, as a condition precedent thereto, there shall have been full compliance with all of the terms of this policy, or until the amount of the **Insured's** obligation to pay shall have been finally determined either by judgment against such **Insured** after actual trial or by written agreement of the **Insured**, the claimant and the **Insurer**.

Any person or organization or the legal representative thereof who has secured such judgment or written agreement shall thereafter be entitled to recover under this policy to the extent of the insurance afforded by this policy. No person or organization shall have any right under this policy to join the **Insurer** as a party to any action against any **Insured or Organization** to determine the **Insured's** liability, nor shall the **Insurer** be impleaded by any **Insured Person**, their spouse, any **Organization** or any legal representative of the foregoing.

19. BANKRUPTCY

Bankruptcy or insolvency of any **Organization** or any **Insured Person** shall not relieve the **Insurer** of any of its obligations hereunder.

It is further understood and agreed that the coverage provided under this policy is intended to protect and benefit the **Insured Persons**. Further, if a liquidation or reorganization proceeding is commenced by the **Named Entity** and/or any other **Organization** (whether voluntarily or involuntarily) under Title 11 of the United States Code (as amended), or any similar state, local or foreign law (collectively "**Bankruptcy Law**") then, in regard to a covered **Claim** under this policy, the **Insureds** hereby:

(a) waive and release any automatic stay or injunction to the extent it may apply in such proceeding to the proceeds of this policy under such **Bankruptcy Law**; and
(b) agree not to oppose or object to any efforts by the **Insurer** or any **Insured** to obtain relief from any stay or injunction applicable to the proceeds of this policy as a result of the commencement of such liquidation or reorganization proceeding.

20. SPOUSAL AND LEGAL REPRESENTATIVE EXTENSION

If a **Claim** against an **Insured Person** includes a **Claim** against: (i) the lawful spouse of such **Insured Person**; or (ii) a property interest of such spouse, and such **Claim** arises from any actual or alleged **Wrongful Act** of such **Insured Person**, this policy shall cover **Loss** arising from the **Claim** made against that spouse or the property of that spouse to the extent that such **Loss** does not arise from a **Claim** for any actual or alleged act, error or omission of such spouse. This policy shall cover **Loss** arising from a **Claim** made against the estates, heirs, or legal representatives of any deceased **Insured Person**, and the legal representatives of any **Insured Person**, in the event of incompetency, insolvency or bankruptcy, who was an **Insured Person** at the time the **Wrongful Acts** upon which such **Claim** is based were committed.

21. RENEWAL APPLICATION PROCEDURE

If this policy is a renewal of, a replacement of, or succeeds in time any policy (providing similar coverage) issued by the **Insurer**, or any of its affiliates, then in granting coverage under this policy it is agreed that the **Insurer** has relied upon the **Application** as being accurate and complete in underwriting this policy. This Clause 21 together with the **Application** constitute the complete **Application** that is the basis of this policy and form a part hereof, and is material to the risk assumed by the **Insurer**. No written renewal application form need be completed by the **Named Entity** in order to receive a renewal quote from the **Insurer**, although the **Insurer** reserves the right to require specific information upon renewal.

22. ORDER OF PAYMENTS

In the event of **Loss** arising from a covered **Claim** for which payment is due under the provisions of this policy, then the **Insurer** shall in all events:

(a) first, pay **Loss** for which coverage is provided under Coverage A and Coverage C of this policy; then

(b) only after payment of **Loss** has been made pursuant to Clause 22(a) above, with respect to whatever remaining amount of the **Limit of Liability** is available after such payment, at the written request of the chief executive officer of the **Named Entity**, either pay or withhold payment of such other **Loss** for which coverage is provided under Coverage B(ii) of this policy; and then

(c) only after payment of **Loss** has been made pursuant to Clause 22(a) and Clause 22(b) above, with respect to whatever remaining amount of the **Limit of Liability** is available after such payment, at the written request of the chief executive officer of the **Named Entity**, either pay or withhold payment of such other **Loss** for which coverage is provided under Coverage B(i) of this policy.

In the event the **Insurer** withholds payment pursuant to Clause 22(b) and/or Clause 22(c) above, then the **Insurer** shall at such time and in such manner as shall be set forth in written instructions of the chief executive officer of the **Named Entity** remit such payment to an **Organization** or directly to or on behalf of an **Insured Person**.

The bankruptcy or insolvency of any **Organization** or any **Insured Person** shall not relieve the **Insurer** of any of its obligations to prioritize payment of covered **Loss** under this policy pursuant to this Clause 22.

23. HEADINGS

The descriptions in the headings of this policy are solely for convenience, and form no part of the terms and conditions of coverage.

Chapter 21

EMPLOYMENT–RELATED PRACTICES LIABILITY INSURANCE

WHAT IS IT?

Employment-related practices liability (ERPL) insurance is a specialized coverage that protects employers from allegations of employment discrimination. The allegations typically arise from employer decisions on who to hire and who to fire, which employees are promoted and which are demoted, and whether a discriminatory work environment or wage scale is fostered or even permitted.

Federal and state discrimination laws restrict employers from basing such employment decisions on an employee's membership in certain groups. These groups are called *protected classes* or *protected groups*. The protected classes vary from state-to-state, based on provisions in respective state laws that may broaden the types and number of protected groups. However, in general, the protected classes established by federal statute are

- sex (gender)
- age,
- disability,
- national origin
- race, and
- creed (religion).

You may remember these as SADNORC. Actions also may be based on other factors, such as pregnancy.

Federal statutes upon which ERPL claims frequently are based include Title VII of the Civil Rights Act of 1964 and its amendments (42 U.S.C. §2000); the Civil Rights Act of 1991; the Age Discrimination in Employment Act (ADEA); and the Americans with Disabilities Act (ADA). Title VII deals with employment discrimination based on race, color, religion, sex, and national origin. The Civil Rights Act of 1991 was enacted to grant additional monetary damages and to overturn several Supreme Court decisions. The ADEA added age to the list of protected classifications, and the ADA added disability as a basis.

Many states have enacted legislation that further expands the protected classes. For example, some states have enacted legislation to prevent discrimination based on such items as tobacco use, marital status, sexual orientation, size, or ancestry. In addition, common law may give rise to employment-related actions such as breach of contract, infliction of emotional distress, defamation, and misrepresentation. Figure 21.1 outlines state-specific protected classes and the sizes of business to which the individual state laws apply. The chart also outlines the time requirement for bringing a complaint and the damages that are permitted by state.

However, since Title VII serves as a backdrop to employment-related laws prohibiting discrimination, this chapter uses that law as its focal point.

The Equal Employment Opportunity Commission (EEOC)

The Equal Employment Opportunity Commission (EEOC), which is an independent agency, administers Title VII. Potential violations of Title VII are brought before the EEOC through its own investigation and compliance activity, as well as by individuals who make complaints. The law specifically outlines how complaints are to be filed. In general, however, charges may be filed with either the EEOC or a state or local agency. The EEOC first notifies the business that it is the subject of a complaint; the EEOC then investigates. If the complaint is found to be valid, the EEOC attempts to resolve the issues. If reconciliation is not possible, the EEOC may bring a civil action in United States district court.

If the EEOC finds no cause of action, or if there has not been a reconciliation or action filed with 180 days of the complaint, the EEOC notifies the complainant of a "right to sue." The complainant then has ninety days in which to bring a civil action in federal district court. The laws outline the damages and relief that may be awarded in successful actions.

BUSINESS USES

ERPL coverage was born in response to the expansion of employment-discrimination legislation and the escalating number and severity of employment-related practices claims. Most provisions of federal discrimination laws apply to businesses with fifteen or more employees; the ADEA applies to businesses with twenty or more employees. In addition, many state laws lower the threshold for the number of employees. Therefore, nearly all but the very smallest of businesses may need employment-related practices liability insurance.

As noted in Chapter 20, many directors and officers (D&O) liability policies include coverage for ERPL claims against directors and officers. Other endorsements on D&O policies may extend that coverage to managers who are not directors and officers and to claims against the organization (the entity or corporation). However, a separate ERPL insurance policy may be more appropriate in many instances.

Why a Separate ERPL Policy May Be Desirable

A separate ERPL insurance policy—apart from the D&O policy—may be desirable for several reasons:

- A separate policy will protect the D&O limits from being used—and perhaps exhausted—by employment-related claims that are made against supervisors and managers who are not directors or officers.

- A separate policy may offer more extensive coverage than an endorsement to the D&O policy.

- A separate policy will offer limits of coverage that are dedicated solely to defense of, judgments entered, and settlements made on ERPL claims. Based on the circumstances of the discriminatory action, ERPL lawsuits can include a large group of employees across the entire organization.

Risk Management Tip

Employment-related practices liability may arise from failure to hire, failure to promote, wrongful discharge, and similar employment-related practices. Directors and officers often find coverage for such allegations in their D&O insurance policies. However, managers and supervisors would not be covered for such allegations in a D&O insurance policy unless it is endorsed to provide that type of specific coverage. In addition, the entire limit of an ERPL policy conceivably could be needed in a class action employment-related lawsuit.

Commercial general liability (CGL) policies typically will not respond to employment-related practices claims. There are several reasons for this, including the following:

- The standard, unendorsed CGL policy requires that damages arising from bodily injury, property damage, personal injury, or advertising injury be alleged before coverage is triggered. Most ERPL claims do not allege these types of injuries. However, some may contain elements of personal injury allegations, such as libel, slander, defamation, or violation of privacy by an employee. In such instances, the CGL policy may respond—but only to the allegations that fall within the definition of personal injury.

- ERPL claims often allege only financial injury, which CGL policies typically do not encompass.

- The bodily injury and property damage coverage section of the CGL policy excludes coverage for bodily injury (a defined term that implies injury to a person's body, including sickness and resulting death) to employees that arise out of their employment.

- Insurance companies may attach an exclusionary endorsement on their CGL policies to eliminate possible coverage for damages arising from wrongful termination and other employment-related practices. Such endorsements typically exclude potential coverage from both the bodily injury/property damage coverage grant and the personal injury coverage grant. In general, these endorsements state that bodily injury or personal injury (including libel, slander, defamation, etc.) arising from a refusal to employ or a decision to terminate employment—as well as demotion, harassment, discrimination, or other employment-related practices—is excluded on the CGL form to which they are attached.

ADVANTAGES

The main advantage of purchasing stand-alone ERPL coverage is that it is designed specifically to address the risks associated with employment-related practices. No other policy is designed solely for that exposure. Even when other policies, such as the D&O insurance, are endorsed to provide the coverage, the stand-alone coverage offers limits of coverage for defense and settlement that are dedicated solely to the exposure.

Some insurers that offer ERPL insurance also make other risk management resources available to their insureds. For example, some may make loss control consultants and resources available to businesses that purchase the coverage.

DISADVANTAGES

One of the main disadvantages is that there is no standard ERPL policy. The coverage originated with individual insurance companies, which drafted their own policy language independent of one another. In 1998 the Insurance Services Office (ISO) introduced a standardized form. While some companies may choose to use the ISO ERPL product, the insurers who introduced the coverage prior to ISO continue to offer their own formats. Therefore, any ERPL policy should be reviewed carefully because coverage nuances, exclusions, and limitations will differ from carrier to carrier.

Since ERPL insurance is a relative newcomer to the risk management and insurance arena, some businesses may question the need for the coverage. It may be difficult for a business owner to justify the expense of this insurance until it is too late—after an employment-related practices action is filed.

The limit of coverage includes the cost of defense and settlements. This is the same as with a D&O policy but differs from other types of liability policies (such as CGL and auto liability) in which defense costs are paid *in addition to* the limit of liability.

DESIGN FEATURES

Covered Wrongful Acts

In contrast with D&O policies, ERPL insurance typically lists the types of wrongful acts to which the coverage applies. Wrongful acts are defined on the individual policy, and substantial differences may be found in these definitions when comparing one insurer's ERPL policy against that issued by a different insurer. Many policies address wrongful acts such as wrongful termination,

harassment, discrimination, dismissal, retaliation, failure to employ or promote, wrongful deprivation of career opportunity, and refusal to employ. The scope of covered wrongful acts is the primary key to the coverage.

Common Exclusions

Again, there is no one set of exclusions that appears on individual policies offered by different insurers. However, there typically are exclusions that void coverage for all or some intentional acts, contractual liability claims, criminal or fraudulent activity, and statutory benefits that are offered under workers compensation and other employee benefit laws.

Copayments

ERPL policies may include a *copayment provision*. A copayment provision states that the insured will share in claim defense costs and damage assessments. Copayments may be expressed as a dollar amount deductible or as a percentage. When a percentage is shown, the insured must pay that percentage of claim costs (defense and settlement).

Claims-made Structure

ERPL policies are almost universally written on a claims-made basis. In most cases this means that the policy applies to claims that are made against an insured *and* reported to the insurer during the policy or *extended reporting* or *discovery* period. The *extended reporting* or *discovery period* is a period of time after the policy is canceled or nonrenewed that the insured is given to discover claims that arise from wrongful acts (occurrences) that happened during the policy period.

Claims-made coverage may be contrasted to occurrence-based coverage, which is common in many other types of liability policies. With occurrence-based coverage, the policy that applied to the occurrence that caused the damage will respond regardless of when the claim is filed.

It is important, therefore, to report ERPL claims to the insurer as soon as they are received. In addition, many claims-made policies require that insureds notify the insurance company when they become aware of an incident that may result in injury, even though a claim has not yet been made.

Who Is an Insured

The "who is an insured" section of an ERPL policy should be reviewed to determine how the policy would react to allegations made against different individuals. Included as insureds may be the business or corporation, executive officers and directors, and managerial and supervisory employees.

Limit of Insurance

As noted previously, the limit of insurance typically applies to both defense and settlement costs (judgments). It is wise to consider that defending a class-action lawsuit may use up a substantial amount of money when selecting a limit of coverage.

Control Issues

ERPL insurers may require that businesses enact certain loss control measures before writing the coverage. For example, many insurers require that businesses develop and enforce a sexual harassment policy and that they develop and formally adopt an employee handbook. Some carriers may audit a business's enforcement of such policies.

WHERE CAN I FIND OUT MORE ABOUT IT?

- A number of insurance companies specialize in ERPL coverage. These carriers may offer resources to their insured businesses, such as access to employment-practices law firms and risk management books. Large insurance brokers, as well as risk management consultants, also may offer valuable information.

- Employment law is a specialized discipline. The services of an attorney who specializes in this area of the law may provide information that could be used to successfully manage many aspects of the exposure.

- Hagglund, Clarance E., and Britton D. Weimer, T. Michael Speidel, and Andrew F. Whitman. 1998. *Employment Practices Liability: Guide to Risk Exposures & Coverage.* Cincinnati: The National Underwriter Company, http://www.nationalunderwriter.com/nucatalog/.

- Labor & Employment Law Practice Group of Dinsmore & Shohl, LLP. 2001. *The HR Survival Guide to Labor & Employment Law.* Cincinnati: The National Underwriter Company, http://www.nationalunderwriter.com/nucatalog/.

- Professional Liability Underwriting Society (PLUS), http://plusweb.org/.

- Society for Human Resources Management (SHRM), http://www.shrm.org/pegs/.

QUESTIONS AND ANSWERS

Question—The state in which your business is located has a law that prohibits employment discrimination. It applies to businesses with five or more employees. The federal laws that prohibit employment discrimination apply to businesses of fifteen or more employees. Your company has ten employees. Which law(s) applies?

Answer—State statutes take precedence. However, a state statute must be at least as restrictive as the comparable federal statute; it cannot be more lenient than federal law. Therefore, absent other factors, the state law would apply to the business with ten employees. In some cases, state and federal laws may conflict with one another. In those situations, preemption comes into play only if the state statute conflicts with the federal statute or if there is language in the federal law that dictates preemption.

Question—Many states are categorized as *employment at will* states. This means that employers may terminate employees whenever they want to. Does this conflict with state and federal antidiscrimination-in-employment statutes?

Answer—Employment *at will* means that the employment relationship may be terminated at any time by either party—employer or employee—for any legal reason. Limitations on an employer's right to fire an employee may be found when employment contracts or statutes have been violated or when the termination has been done with improper communication.

For example, a union collective-bargaining agreement may dictate the acceptable reasons for and procedures that must be followed when terminating an employee. Federal and state employment laws also state that employees may not be terminated because of factors such as inclusion in a protected group, complaining about wage-related matters, union activities, or filing a health or safety complaint.

In addition, employers may be the subject of legal action if they disclose inaccurate information about an employee's misconduct or termination.

In other words, employers may terminate an employment relationship for any reason in an *at will* state, but they are not free to violate contracts or statutes, and they are not allowed to defame an employee or invade her privacy. (An employee may be terminated for a good reason or for no reason—but not for the "wrong" reason.) Some actions that arise from allegations that an employer breached any of these duties may be covered by an ERPL policy, and some may not be covered. The individual policy should be reviewed for details of coverage applicability.

Question—What is the difference between *disparate treatment* discrimination in employment and *disparate impact* discrimination in employment?

Answer—Disparate treatment typically is an intentional action that leads to discrimination. An example is a policy stating that only males may work in a certain area of a company. This is an employment policy that intentionally discriminates against some workers based on their gender.

Disparate impact (or *adverse impact*) discrimination occurs when a policy that appears to be neutral has a discriminatory impact. For example, a company may require that individuals pass a certain test in order to be promoted. If the test is proven to prevent certain minorities from advancing and does not meet a bona fide employment purpose, it may be said to have a disparate impact. Even though all employees are subject to the same test before promotion, use of the test results in discrimination.

END NOTES

[1]   Rothstein, Mark A., and Lance Liebman. 1994. *Cases and Materials on Employment Law, Third Edition.* Westbury, NY: The Foundation Press, Inc.

Figure 21.1

Additional protected classes, Lower business size limits, Time limit for filing a complaint, and Potential awards by state

ALABAMA
Additional protected classes: none
Lower business size limits: n/a
**Time limit for filing a complaint **: n/a
Potential awards *: n/a

ALASKA
Additional protected classes: changes in marital status and pregnancy or parenthood
Lower business size limits: one or more
Time limit for filing a complaint: within 180 days
Potential awards*: back pay, attorney fees, and costs

ARIZONA
Additional protected classes: genetic test results and tobacco use for state employees
Lower business size limits: one or more for sexual harassment allegations, otherwise fifteen or more
Time limit for filing a complaint: within 180 days
Potential awards*: back pay (two years maximum) and attorney fees

ARKANSAS
Additional protected classes: ancestry
Lower business size limits: nine or more
Time limit for filing a complaint: within one year
Potential awards*: (in court): back pay with interest (two years maximum), attorney fees, and compensatory and punitive damages with the following limits:

Number of Employees	Limit
< 15	$15,000
15-100	$50,000
101-200	$100,000
201-500	$200,000
500 +	$300,000

CALIFORNIA
Additional protected classes: ancestry, medical condition, marital status, sexual orientation, and pregnancy, childbirth, or related medical condition
Lower business size limits: five or more
Time limit for filing a complaint: within one year
Potential awards*: back pay and actual damages (not to exceed $150,000, including emotional pain, suffering, inconvenience, mental anguish, and loss of enjoyment of life)

COLORADO
Additional protected classes: ancestry, marriage to or plans to marry another employee, and sexual orientation
Lower business size limits: n/a
Time limit for filing a complaint: within six months
Potential awards*: back pay

CONNECTICUT

Additional protected classes: marital status, genetic information, ancestry, sexual orientation, and tobacco use*

Lower business size limits: three or more

Time limit for filing a complaint:** within 180 days

Potential awards*:** attorney fees and costs

DELAWARE

Additional protected classes: marital status and genetic information

Lower business size limits: four or more

Time limit for filing a complaint:** within ninety days or within 120 days of discovery of discrimination

Potential awards*:** back pay

DISTRICT OF COLUMBIA

Additional protected classes: marital status, personal appearance, sexual orientation, family responsibility, matriculation, political affiliation, pregnancy or childbirth, and tobacco use*

Lower business size limits: one or more

Time limit for filing a complaint:** within one year

Potential awards*:** back pay, compensatory damages, attorney fees, and costs

FLORIDA

Additional protected classes: marital status, HIV status, and sickle-cell trait

Lower business size limits: fifteen or more

Time limit for filing a complaint:** within one year

Potential awards*:** back pay (two years maximum), attorney fees, and costs

GEORGIA

Additional protected classes: none

Lower business size limits: n/a

Time limit for filing a complaint:** within 180 days

Potential awards*:** a Special Master may award back pay (two years maximum) and actual damages

HAWAII

Additional protected classes: sexual orientation, ancestry, marital status, and arrest and court records

Lower business size limits: n/a

Time limit for filing a complaint:** within 180 days

Potential awards*:** back pay (two years maximum), damages, attorney fees, expert witness fees, and costs

IDAHO

Additional protected classes: none

Lower business size limits: five or more

Time limit for filing a complaint:** within ninety days (in district court)

Potential awards*:** actual damages (including back pay [two years maximum] and benefits) and punitive damages (up to $1,000 per violation)

ILLINOIS

Additional protected classes: citizenship status, ancestry, marital status, military status, unfavorable discharge from military service; expunged, sealed, or impounded arrest or criminal record, and use of lawful products off of employer's premises during nonworking hours

Lower business size limits: one or more in cases of handicap discrimination, otherwise fifteen or more

Time limit for filing a complaint:** within 180 days

Potential awards*:** actual damages, back pay, fringe benefits, attorney fees, and costs

Figure 21.1 (cont'd)

INDIANA
Additional protected classes: ancestry and tobacco use*
Lower business size limits: six or more
Time limit for filing a complaint:** within 180 days
Potential awards*:** lost wages, salaries, and commissions

IOWA
Additional protected classes: HIV status
Lower business size limits: n/a
Time limit for filing a complaint:** within 180 days
Potential awards*:** back pay, actual damages, costs, and attorney fees

KANSAS
Additional protected classes: ancestry and HIV status
Lower business size limits: four or more
Time limit for filing a complaint:** within six months
Potential awards*:** back pay and damages for pain, suffering, and humiliation ($2,000 limit)

KENTUCKY
Additional protected classes: familial status, tobacco use*, and HIV status
Lower business size limits: fifteen or more for disability claims, otherwise, eight or more
Time limit for filing a complaint:** within 180 days
Potential awards*:** back pay, damages for humiliation and embarrassment, and costs

LOUISIANA
Additional protected classes: pregnancy, childbirth, and related medical conditions, sickle-cell trait, and tobacco use*
Lower business size limits: twenty-five or more for pregnancy, childbirth, or related medical condition
Time limit for filing a complaint:** within 180 days
Potential awards*:** back pay, compensation for humiliation and embarrassment, and costs

MAINE
Additional protected classes: ancestry, sexual orientation, and tobacco use*
Lower business size limits: n/a
Time limit for filing a complaint:** within six months
Potential awards*:** (in court) back pay and compensatory and punitive damages with the following limits (many specific conditions apply):

Number of Employees	Limits
15-100	$50,000
101-200	$100,000
201-500	$200,000
500+	$300,000

MARYLAND
Additional protected classes: marital status, sexual orientation, and genetic information
Lower business size limits: n/a
Time limit for filing a complaint:** within six months
Potential awards*:** many different provisions grouped by county

MASSACHUSETTS
Additional protected classes: ancestry and sexual orientation (excluding pedophilia)
Lower business size limits: n/a
Time limit for filing a complaint**: within six months
Potential awards***: back pay, attorney fees, and costs

MICHIGAN
Additional protected classes: height, weight, marital status, and arrest records
Lower business size limits: one or more
Time limit for filing a complaint**: n/a
Potential awards***: back pay, actual damages, costs, attorney fees, and expert witness fees

MINNESOTA
Additional protected classes: marital status, status with regard to public assistance, sexual orientation, and tobacco use*
Lower business size limits: one or more
Time limit for filing a complaint**: within one year
Potential awards***: litigation and hearing costs, attorney fees, expert witness fees, and compensatory and punitive damages

MISSISSIPPI
Additional protected classes: none
Lower business size limits: n/a
Time limit for filing a complaint**: n/a
Potential awards***: n/a

MISSOURI
Additional protected classes: ancestry and tobacco use*
Lower business size limits: six or more
Time limit for filing a complaint**: within 180 days
Potential awards***: actual damages

MONTANA
Additional protected classes: marital status and tobacco use*
Lower business size limits: one or more
Time limit for filing a complaint**: within 180 days
Potential awards***: reasonable measures to rectify any harm, pecuniary or otherwise and (in court) attorney fees

NEBRASKA
Additional protected classes: marital status and HIV status
Lower business size limits: n/a
Time limit for filing a complaint**: within 300 days
Potential awards***: back pay (two years maximum) and (in court) attorney fees and costs

NEVADA
Additional protected classes: sexual orientation, legal use of consumable goods during nonworking hours and off the employer's premises, genetic information, and tobacco use*
Lower business size limits: n/a
Time limit for filing a complaint**: within 180 days
Potential awards***: back pay with interest (two years maximum), fringe benefits

Figure 21.1 (cont'd)

NEW HAMPSHIRE
Additional protected classes: marital status, sexual orientation, and tobacco use*
Lower business size limits: six or more
Time limit for filing a complaint**: within 180 days
Potential awards***: back pay and compensatory damages

NEW JERSEY
Additional protected classes: marital status, genetic information, ancestry, affectional or sexual orientation, atypical or hereditary cellular or blood trait, genetic information, service in Armed Forces, familial status, and tobacco use*
Lower business size limits: n/a
Time limit for filing a complaint**: within 180 days
Potential awards***: back pay and attorney fees

NEW MEXICO
Additional protected classes: marital affiliation, ancestry, and tobacco use*
Lower business size limits: fifty or more for marital affiliation, otherwise four or more
Time limit for filing a complaint**: within 180 days
Potential awards***: actual damages and attorney fees

NEW YORK
Additional protected classes: engagement in recreational activities, political activities, and legal use of consumable products during nonworking hours and off of employer's premises, genetic predisposition or carrier status, and marital or familial status
Lower business size limits: four or more
Time limit for filing a complaint**: within one year
Potential awards***: back pay, compensatory damages, and payment to state of any profits obtained through unlawful discrimination

NORTH CAROLINA
Additional protected classes: tobacco use*, HIV status, sickle-cell trait, and hemoglobin c trait
Lower business size limits: n/a
Time limit for filing a complaint**: within 180 days
Potential awards***: court costs, attorney fees, and compensatory damages

NORTH DAKOTA
Additional protected classes: marital status, public assistance status, and participation in lawful activity off of employer's premises during nonworking hours
Lower business size limits: n/a
Time limit for filing a complaint**: within 300 days
Potential awards***: back pay (two years maximum), attorney fees, and costs

OHIO
Additional protected classes: ancestry and pregnancy, childbirth, or related medical condition
Lower business size limits: four or more
Time limit for filing a complaint**: within six months
Potential awards***: back pay, punitive damages, and attorney fees

OKLAHOMA
Additional protected classes: tobacco use*
Lower business size limits: n/a
Time limit for filing a complaint**: within 180 days
Potential awards***: back pay, costs, and attorney fees

OREGON

Additional protected classes: marital status, juvenile record that has been expunged, genetic disorders, employment of another family member, pregnancy, childbirth, or related medical condition, and tobacco use*

Lower business size limits: one or more

Time limit for filing a complaint**: within one year

Potential awards***: (in court) back pay (two years maximum) and compensatory and punitive damages

PENNSYLVANIA

Additional protected classes: ancestry, GED recipients, and refusal to perform an abortion or sterilization

Lower business size limits: four or more

Time limit for filing a complaint**: within 180 days

Potential awards***: back pay and actual damages (including humiliation and embarrassment)

RHODE ISLAND

Additional protected classes: sexual orientation, gender identity or expression, ancestry, pregnancy, childbirth, or related medical condition, HIV status, and tobacco use*

Lower business size limits: four or more

Time limit for filing a complaint**: within one year

Potential awards***: back pay with interest, attorney fees, expert fees, and compensatory damages

SOUTH CAROLINA

Additional protected classes: tobacco use*

Lower business size limits: n/a

Time limit for filing a complaint**: within 180 days

Potential awards***: back pay (two years maximum)

SOUTH DAKOTA

Additional protected classes: ancestry and tobacco use*

Lower business size limits: one or more

Time limit for filing a complaint**: within 180 days

Potential awards***: back pay, compensation, costs, and attorney fees

TENNESSEE

Additional protected classes: none

Lower business size limits: eight or more

Time limit for filing a complaint**: within 180 days

Potential awards***: back pay, damages for humiliation and embarrassment, attorney fees, and costs

TEXAS

Additional protected classes: genetic test results

Lower business size limits: n/a

Time limit for filing a complaint**: within 180 days

Potential awards***: back pay (two years maximum), costs, compensatory and punitive damages, and attorney fees

UTAH

Additional protected classes: pregnancy, childbirth, or related medical condition

Lower business size limits: n/a

Time limit for filing a complaint**: within 180 days

Potential awards***: back pay and benefits, attorney fees, and costs

Figure 21.1 (cont'd)

VERMONT
Additional protected classes: ancestry, sexual orientation, HIV status, and place of birth
Lower business size limits: one or more
Time limit for filing a complaint: n/a
Potential awards*: back pay and benefits, costs, attorney fees, and compensatory and punitive damages

VIRGINIA
Additional protected classes: pregnancy, childbirth, or related medical condition, and marital status
Lower business size limits: n/a
Time limit for filing a complaint: within 180 days
Potential awards*: (in court): back pay with interest (one year maximum), and attorney fees (no more than 25 percent of back pay award)

WASHINGTON
Additional protected classes: marital status and HIV status
Lower business size limits: eight or more
Time limit for filing a complaint: within six months
Potential awards*: back pay and damages for humiliation and suffering (up to $10,000)

WEST VIRGINIA
Additional protected classes: ancestry and tobacco use*
Lower business size limits: twelve or more
Time limit for filing a complaint: within one year
Potential awards*: back pay, costs, and attorney fees

WISCONSIN
Additional protected classes: marital status, ancestry, sexual orientation, arrest or conviction record, service in Armed Forces, genetic test results, use or nonuse of legal product off of employer's premises during nonworking hours, pregnancy, childbirth, or related medical condition, and honesty test results
Lower business size limits: n/a
Time limit for filing a complaint: within 300 days
Potential awards*: back pay (two years maximum) and compensation in lieu of reinstatement

WYOMING
Additional protected classes: ancestry and tobacco use*
Lower business size limits: two or more
Time limit for filing a complaint: within ninety days
Potential awards*: back pay

*In compliance with company smoking policies.

**The time is from the date the discriminatory act occurred or from the date of the last act in a pattern of discriminatory acts.

***These awards are by Civil Rights Commissions, unless otherwise indicated.

Chapter 21

GLOSSARY

Age Discrimination in Employment Act (ADEA). The federal law that prohibits employment discrimination based on age.

Americans with Disabilities Act (ADA). The federal law that prohibits discrimination based on disability.

Copayment provision. A provision in an insurance policy that provides for the insured to share in defense costs and damage assessments that are covered by the policy.

Directors & officers liability policy (D&O policy). An insurance policy that covers damages arising from wrongful acts committed by directors and officers of the organization.

Disparate impact. Also known as *adverse impact*. A situation in which an employment policy appears to be neutral on its face but, in reality, results in discrimination.

Disparate treatment. An intentional action that leads to discrimination.

Employment at will. A term that means that an employment relationship may be terminated at any time by either party—employer or employee—for any legal reason.

Equal Employment Opportunity Commission (EEOC). An independent agency that administers Title VII.

Extended reporting period or discovery period. A period of time after a claims-made policy expires that the insured is given to uncover and file claims to which the policy applies.

Protected classes or protected groups. The groups of individuals that are given legal protection from discrimination through federal, state, or local laws and regulations.

Title VII. A shortened name for Title VII of the Civil Rights Act of 1964, which provides protection from employment discrimination based on race, color, religion, sex, and national origin.

Wrongful acts. The types of actions that are covered by certain insurance policies, including employment-related practices liability and directors and officers liability policies.

BUSINESS AUTOMOBILE INSURANCE

WHAT IS IT?

Business automobile insurance is a tool used to insure against losses due to *property damage* and *bodily injury* caused by commercial autos. It is designed to cover risks associated with vehicles driven on public roads. Coverage may be purchased for *owned, nonowned,* and *hired* autos.

Owned autos are autos that the insured owns or acquires during the policy period. Nonowned autos are those that are used in connection with the insured's business but are not owned, leased, hired, rented, or borrowed by the named insured. Hired autos are those that the named insured leases, hires, rents, or borrows.

A business auto policy (BAP) may be used to cover owned or nonowned vehicles such as private passenger autos, service vehicles, trucks, tractor trailers, and trailers—almost any type of vehicle used in a business. However, trucking companies, garages, and motor carriers need coverages that are not provided by a business auto policy. So they must be insured on more specialized forms.

Terminology Refresher

Property damage: damage to or loss of use of tangible property, along with loss of use of the property that is not physically injured.

Bodily injury: direct injury, sickness, or disease sustained by a person, including resulting death.

Business auto policies primarily offer two types of protection:

- Liability
- Physical Damage

Liability Protection

Liability insurance generally pays for damages that the insured becomes legally obligated to pay because of property damage or bodily injury that she causes. Liability claims always involve a *third party*. A third party is another entity involved in the loss in addition to the insured and the insurer. For example, an employee driving a company-owned car on the way to a sales call runs a red light and hits another car. The driver of the other car, a third party, suffers whiplash and extensive damage to his vehicle. The employee who caused the accident is responsible for the resulting damages. Liability insurance would respond by covering the monetary damages incurred to treat the injured driver's whiplash and to repair the damage to his car, up to the policy limits. The insurer would also owe the insured a *duty to defend* if the injured driver filed a lawsuit against the employee who caused the accident.

The duty to defend is broader than the duty to indemnify. The insured does not need to prove that coverage exists in order for the insurer to have a duty to defend. The possibility that the claims of a third party might be covered under a policy is enough to trigger the duty to defend.

Physical Damage Protection

Physical damage protection covers actual damage to the covered auto. The damage may result from a variety of covered causes, such as collision, fire, theft, or hail. Other causes, such as pollution or war, may result in damage but may be excluded.

BUSINESS USES

Business auto insurance may be used either as a *monoline* policy or as one coverage part in a *multiline* or *package* policy. Autos owned by sole proprietors, partnerships, corporations, unincorporated associations, individuals, not-for-profit organizations, or government agencies may be insured by a business auto policy. As mentioned previously, business auto coverage may also be purchased for nonowned, hired, leased, or rented autos.

Monoline policy: an insurance policy that covers a single line of insurance, such as business auto, or part of a single line, such as business auto liability.

Multiline or *package policy*: an insurance policy that covers more than one line of insurance, such as business auto and workers compensation combined.

Sole proprietors (a business owned by an individual who has not formed a corporation) and partnerships (a business owned by two or more individuals or companies that have joined formally to operate the business) may have only one or two autos that are used for business purposes, while corporations may own a fleet of vehicles. However, both may benefit from business auto insurance because it covers losses that are usually excluded under an individual's personal auto policy.

The policy is used to cover the costs of losses incurred by business owners and their employees that are caused by the use of a business auto. The policy also allows business to comply with compulsory auto insurance laws imposed by states (which are discussed later in this chapter).

ADVANTAGES

There are many advantages to using business auto insurance as a tool to protect companies that use autos in the course of business activities. They include the following:

- As mentioned earlier, the business auto policy allows businesses to comply with proof of financial responsibility or other compulsory auto insurance laws enacted in each state.

- For auto loans and leases, financial institutions usually require that the vehicle be insured. Business auto insurance can meet that requirement.

- Business auto insurance protects the assets of the business that otherwise would be needed for defense and settlement costs in third-party auto liability claims.

- Business auto insurance offers indemnity for not-for-profit organizations that may not have funds available for defense and settlement costs.

- Insurers will handle any claims, so the business's personnel are free from those duties.

- The cost of business auto premiums may be lower than the cost to defend or settle a lawsuit.

- Business auto premiums are legitimate deductible business expenses.

DISADVANTAGES

Business auto insurance does have some disadvantages. These include:

- Many exclusions and limitations apply to the business auto policy. So not all losses will be covered. Reserves must still be set aside in the event of uncovered losses.

- Policy limits are finite. So any losses that exceed the limits must be paid by the insured.

- Premiums must be paid for business auto insurance whether or not any claims are ever made.

- The insured loses the control of handling and management of its own defense or claims.

DESIGN FEATURES

The Insurance Services Office, Inc. (ISO) offers a standard business auto coverage form that will be discussed in this section. (ISO is an organization that provides statistical information, actuarial analysis, policy language, and related services for the insurance industry. http://www.iso.com/) Keep in mind that many insurance companies use their own policy forms that may contain features that differ from the ISO standard form.

Policy Structure

The BAP is comprised of the following parts:

1. Declarations Form

2. Liability Coverage

3. Physical Damage Coverage

4. Conditions

5. Definitions

Declarations Form

The business auto declarations form is attached to the auto coverage form to provide basic information about the insured and the type of coverage bought by the insured, to indicate what *endorsements* are attached to the policy, and to show the amount of premium paid for the exposures insured.

> *Endorsement*: an amendment to a policy form that adds or removes specified coverages or amends existing coverages.

The form lists the named insured, mailing address, and policy period. The type of business is specified as well. One of the keys to the design of the business auto policy is the use of *symbols* to designate what types of autos are covered by the liability and physical damage sections of the policy. The declarations form includes a column for the insured to show the symbols for the

covered autos. There are nine such symbols. Figure 22.1 lists the symbols and their meanings.

If, for example, the insured wants liability coverage for any auto, symbol 1 is placed in the column next to the liability coverage; if the insured wants collision coverage for specifically described autos only, symbol 7 goes in the column next to the physical damage-collision coverage. Because coverage under the BAP is for covered autos, the insurance carrier must enter the proper symbol on the declarations form to make sure that the correct types of autos are provided the desired coverage. If the correct symbol is not entered, the insured may not receive the coverage intended.

Figure 22.1

Business Auto Policy Coverage Symbols

Symbol	Description Of Covered Auto Designation Symbols	
1	Any "Auto"	
2	Owned "Autos" Only	Only those "autos" you own (and for Liability Coverage any "trailers" you don't own while attached to power units you own). This includes those "autos" you acquire ownership of after the policy begins.
3	Owned Private Passenger "Autos" Only	Only the private passenger "autos" you own. This includes those private passenger "autos" you acquire ownership of after the policy begins.
4	Owned "Autos" Other Than Private Passenger "Autos" Only	Only those "autos" you own that are not of the private passenger type (and for Liability Coverage any "trailers" you don't own while attached to power units you own). This includes those "autos" not of the private passenger type you acquire ownership of after the policy begins.
5	Owned "Autos" Subject To No-Fault	Only those "autos" you own that are required to have No-Fault benefits in the state where they are licensed or principally garaged. This includes those "autos" you acquire ownership of after the policy begins provided they are required to have No-Fault benefits in the state where they are licensed or principally garaged.
6	Owned "Autos" Subject To A Compulsory Uninsured Motorists Law	Only those "autos" you own that because of the law in the state where they are licensed or principally garaged are required to have and cannot reject Uninsured Motorists Coverage. This includes those "autos" you acquire ownership of after the policy begins provided they are subject to the same state uninsured motorists requirement.
7	Specifically Described "Autos"	Only those "autos" described in Item Three of the Declarations for which a premium charge is shown (and for Liability Coverage any "trailers" you don't own while attached to any power unit described in Item Three).
8	Hired "Autos" Only	Only those "autos" you lease, hire, rent or borrow. This does not include any "auto" you lease, hire, rent, or borrow from any of your "employees", partners (if you are a partnership), members (if you are a limited liability company) or members of their households.
9	Nonowned "Autos" Only	Only those "autos" you do not own, lease, hire, rent or borrow that are used in connection with your business. This includes "autos" owned by your "employees", partners (if you are a partnership), members (if you are a limited liability company), or members of their households but only while used in your business or your personal affairs.

- Insuring Agreement
- A Description of Who Is an Insured
- Coverage Extensions
- Exclusions
- Limit of Insurance

The insuring agreement is the heart of the contract between the insurer and the insured. The agreement states what the insurer will cover in the event of a loss. The BAP liability insuring agreement consists of three parts: (1) coverage for bodily injury and property damage resulting from an accident caused by a covered auto; (2) coverage for pollution costs and expenses resulting from an accident caused by a covered auto; and (3) the insurer's duty and right to defend the insured in a lawsuit seeking damages when such accidents occur.

The insuring agreement also defines who is considered an insured under the policy. Those considered insureds under the policy include the *named insured*; anyone using a covered auto owned, borrowed, or hired by the named insured with the named insured's permission (with exceptions); and anyone liable for the conduct of a described insured, but only to the extent of that liability.

Terminology Refresher

A named insured on a BAP is the party specifically named as the insured on the policy's declarations page. Others may have claim on the coverage through internal provisions, but any such right is provided by agreement between the named insured and the insurance company.

Coverage extensions included in the insuring agreement consist of *supplementary payments* and *out-of-state coverage extensions*. These extensions provide coverage in addition to the limit of insurance. For instance, the policy allows up to $2,000 in additional payments for bail bonds that are required due to a covered accident. *Supplementary payments* are payments to supplement the coverage and are in addition to the limit of insurance. Through the *out-of-state coverage extension*, the insurance company agrees to increase the limit of insurance for liability coverage to meet those required by a compulsory or financial responsibility law of the jurisdiction where the covered auto is being used. In other words, if an auto titled and insured in one state is involved in an accident in a different state, the BAP automatically will meet the compulsory insurance requirements of the state where the accident happened.

Risk Management Tip

Symbol 1 is the broadest symbol available because it stands for "any auto;" it is usually reserved for use under the liability coverage section of the policy. Symbol 2 stands for "owned 'autos' only." It often is considered the broadest symbol that is used for physical damage coverage. Many risk managers and business owners request that symbol 1 be used for liability coverage and symbol 2 for physical damage so that their companies are provided with the broadest coverage available. However, while many underwriters may agree to such requests, some may want to limit coverage by using more restrictive coverage symbols, such as symbol 7, "specifically described 'autos'," for physical damage coverage. If a symbol 7 is used, only those vehicles that are specifically listed on the policy are covered.

Because of this, careful review of the coverage symbols used is critical to understanding and confirming the breadth of coverage provided.

The declarations form also contains a schedule of coverages and covered autos. In order to obtain insurance, the insured must supply—among other information—a description of each owned auto, the cost of each, the city and state where each is principally kept, and a classification of each auto's use—private passenger or service, retail, or commercial for truck-type vehicles.

Private passenger autos are used by a business's by employees or owners as part of their business activities. *Service* vehicles are those used for transporting the insured's personnel, equipment, and incidental supplies to or from a job location. *Retail* vehicles are used to pick up property or deliver property to individual locations. *Commercial* vehicles are defined as those used to transport property other than vehicles that fall within the service or retail categories.

A summary of premiums, limits, and deductibles for each auto and each coverage is offered. Schedules for hired or borrowed covered auto coverage and nonownership liability are also found on the declarations form, as well as other information used for rating purposes, such as the number of employees or partners in the company.

Liability Coverage

The liability coverage part of the BAP consists of several sections:

Exclusions

The insuring agreement contains *exclusions* that curtail the liability coverage. An exclusion eliminates coverage for specified loss exposures. The policy should be read carefully to determine which exclusions apply and in what circumstances. The BAP contains exclusions for a variety of exposures, such as injuries that are expected or intended by the insured.

Of particular interest in the BAP is the *fellow employee* exclusion. A fellow employee, for the purposes of auto coverage, is a coworker of an insured who is injured during the course of employment. The exclusion precludes coverage for bodily injury to a fellow employee of the insured that occurs in the course of employment or while performing business-related activities. Workers compensation and employers liability insurance are the proper methods for compensating these types of injuries. For example, an employee of the insured business is driving a covered auto on a business trip. Two coworkers of the driver are in the car. The car is involved in an accident for which the driver is legally liable. The exclusion voids coverage under the business auto policy for a claim that the injured coworkers (fellow employees) might file against the negligent employee-driver.

While the BAP does not define what constitutes actions that occur "in the course of employment," many courts have addressed the meaning of that phrase. For instance, the Ohio Supreme Court said that "a causal connection must exist between an employee's injury and his employment either through the activities, the conditions, or the environment of the employment" in *Bralley v. Daugherty*, 401 N.E.2d 448 (Ohio 1980).

Note that the BAP is not intended to insure autos involved in professional racing or demolition contests or autos while being prepared for such contests or activities.

Limits

The next part of the liability insuring agreement is the limit of insurance section. This part states the most that the insurer will pay in various situations. If, for example, property damage occurs due to repeated exposure to the same conditions, the damage will be considered the result of one accident. The policy also says that, regardless of the number of covered insureds, autos, premiums paid, claims made, or vehicles involved in the accident, the most the insurer will pay is the limit of insurance shown on the declarations page.

How Limits Apply

Kelly Consulting, Inc. owns three vehicles that are involved in the same accident. All of the vehicles are insured on Kelly's business auto policy. Kelly is entitled to only the declared limits of liability, not three times the liability limit. However, if each of the covered vehicles were involved in *separate* accidents, each accident would qualify for coverage up to the liability limit shown.

Physical Damage Coverage

The physical damage section of the BAP is made up of the following:

- Coverage Agreements
- Coverage Extension
- Exclusions
- Limit of Insurance
- Deductible Provision

The BAP specifies three different ways that the insurer may agree to pay for physical damage to a covered auto or its equipment: *comprehensive coverage*, *specified causes of loss coverage*, or *collision coverage*.

Comprehensive coverage is the insurer's promise to pay for loss to a covered auto or its equipment that results from any cause other than collision with another object or if the auto overturns. For example, hail damage and fire damage are considered under comprehensive coverage. *Specified causes of loss coverage* provides coverage for causes that are explicitly listed in the policy. *Collision coverage* applies only to the covered auto's loss due to a collision with another object or if the auto overturns. An auto designation symbol (see Figure 22.1) must be written in the proper item on the declarations form to activate coverage. Figure 22.2 contains a reprint of the policy declarations on which chosen coverage is indicated.

If an insured wants to select comprehensive coverage for all autos, a "1" would be placed on the appropriate line on the declarations form. If an insured wants to select collision coverage for hired autos only, an "8" would be placed in the appropriate line on the declarations form:

Figure 22.2

POLICY NUMBER: _____

ITEM TWO

SCHEDULE OF COVERAGES AND COVERED AUTOS

This policy provides only those coverages where a charge is shown in the premium column below. Each of these coverages will apply only to those "autos" shown as covered "autos". "Autos" are shown as covered "autos" for a particular coverage by the entry of one or more of the symbols from the Covered Autos Section of the Business Auto Coverage Form next to the name of the coverage.

COVERAGES	COVERED AUTOS (Entry of one or more of the symbols from the Covered Autos Section of the Business Auto Coverage Form shows which autos are covered autos.)	LIMIT THE MOST WE WILL PAY FOR ANY ONE ACCIDENT OR LOSS	PREMIUM
LIABILITY		$	$
PERSONAL INJURY PROTECTION (or equivalent No-fault Coverage)		SEPARATELY STATED IN EACH P.I.P. ENDORSEMENT MINUS $ DED.	$
ADDED PERSONAL INJURY PROTECTION (or equivalent added No-fault Coverage)		SEPARATELY STATED IN EACH ADDED P.I.P. ENDORSEMENT.	$
PROPERTY PROTECTION INSURANCE (Michigan only)		SEPARATELY STATED IN THE P.P.I. ENDORSEMENT MINUS $ DED. FOR EACH ACCIDENT.	$
AUTO MEDICAL PAYMENTS		$	$
UNINSURED MOTORISTS		$	$
UNDERINSURED MOTORISTS (When not included in Uninsured Motorists Coverage)		$	$
PHYSICAL DAMAGE COMPREHENSIVE COVERAGE		ACTUAL CASH VALUE OR COST OF REPAIR, WHICHEVER IS LESS, MINUS $ DED. FOR EACH COVERED AUTO, BUT NO DEDUCTIBLE APPLIES TO LOSS CAUSED BY FIRE OR LIGHTNING. See ITEM FOUR For Hired Or Borrowed "Autos".	$
PHYSICAL DAMAGE SPECIFIED CAUSES OF LOSS COVERAGE		ACTUAL CASH VALUE OR COST OF REPAIR, WHICHEVER IS LESS, MINUS $ DED. FOR EACH COVERED AUTO FOR LOSS CAUSED BY MISCHIEF OR VANDALISM. See ITEM FOUR For Hired Or Borrowed "Autos".	$
PHYSICAL DAMAGE COLLISION COVERAGE		ACTUAL CASH VALUE OR COST OF REPAIR, WHICHEVER IS LESS, MINUS $ DED. FOR EACH COVERED AUTO. See ITEM FOUR For Hired Or Borrowed "Autos".	$
PHYSICAL DAMAGE TOWING AND LABOR		$ For Each Disablement Of A Private Passenger "Auto".	$
			$
		PREMIUM FOR ENDORSEMENTS	$
		*ESTIMATED TOTAL PREMIUM	$

*This policy may be subject to final audit.

© ISO Properties, Inc., 2000
CA DS 03 10 01

Although specified causes of loss are listed in the policy, questions may arise regarding the difference between a comprehensive loss and a collision loss. *Collision* is not defined in the policy, but the following examples illustrate some examples of collisions:

- A bicyclist running into an auto parked on the street

- An auto suffering damage from contact with a large hole in the road

- An auto striking a tree

All involve a covered auto colliding with another object.

The object that collides with the auto does not need to be another auto or in motion. Because the term is not defined in the policy, some confusion exists at where the line is drawn between comprehensive causes of loss and collision. Since an insurance policy is a *contract of adhesion*, any ambiguities in the policy will be decided in favor of the insured.

Terminology Refresher

Contract of adhesion: one party selects the terms and language of the agreement and offers it to the other party on a take-it-or-leave-it basis. Ambiguities in such contracts are interpreted against the party that drafted it. In the case of a business auto insurance policy, the insurer usually offers the policy "as is" to the insured business, which has little opportunity to change the wording of the form.

Under comprehensive coverage, the insured is also covered for glass breakage, loss caused by hitting a bird or animal, and loss caused by falling objects or missiles. Coverage extensions are offered for transportation expenses and loss of use expenses for hired auto physical damage, both on a per diem basis with a maximum amount allowed.

Another part of the physical damage coverage agreement is the insurer's offer to pay for towing and labor costs incurred each time a covered private passenger auto is disabled. However, only labor performed at the place of disablement is covered. Suppose an insured parks his covered auto in a customer's parking lot. The car fails to start and the insured calls for a tow. When the truck arrives, the driver states that the car's battery needs a jump, so it will not need to be towed to a garage.

The cost of the jump would be covered because the labor was performed at the place of disablement.

The physical damage section, like the liability section, contains exclusions and limit of insurance provisions.

Conditions

The BAP conditions section includes *loss conditions* and *general conditions*. The loss conditions spell out the procedure for getting an appraisal if the parties disagree on the amount of loss; the duties of both the insured and the insurer when an accident, claim, suit, or loss occurs; when a legal action may be brought against the insurer; options from which the insurer may chose to pay for losses; and the terms for transfer of rights of recovery from others to the insurer.

General conditions describes several situations, such as the insurer's obligation if the insured declares bankruptcy or becomes insolvent, how other insurance works in conjunction with the policy, and what the policy period and coverage territory are.

The ISO business auto program also includes a separate form of *common policy conditions* that must be attached to the policy. These conditions outline what is necessary to cancel the policy, how changes can be made to the policy, the rules governing the insurer's examination of the insured's books, who is responsible for paying premiums, and the transferring of rights and duties under the policy.

Definitions

The BAP uses words throughout the form that are in quotation marks. These words have special definitions that are located at the end of the policy. The applicability of insuring agreements, exclusions, and conditions often depends on a word's definition. When a term is undefined in a policy, or if the meaning of defined words is unclear, many insureds turn to the courts for an interpretation.

For example, this is the policy's definition of *accident*: "includes continuous or repeated exposure to the same conditions resulting in 'bodily injury' or 'property damage.'" Some may agree that an accident could include continuous and repeated exposure to the same conditions but would also argue that an accident is usually considered a sudden occurrence. A court might turn to the accepted, common, dictionary definition of the word: "an unforeseen and an unplanned event; something happening by chance rather than by design."

The important point to understand is that policy definitions may contain meanings for terms that are specific to the contract and not necessarily the everyday meaning of the word.

Endorsements

Endorsements can be used in several ways to modify the BAP. Additional insureds can be added to the policy, exclusions can be added or modified, or existing coverages can be redefined. For instance, *auto medical payments coverage* and *uninsured/ underinsured motorists coverage* may be added to the BAP by endorsement. Auto medical payments coverage offers payment to insureds for medical services that are needed because of an auto accident. No liability is required on the part of the insured. Many insureds purchase this coverage for good will purposes so that the insured can get the cost of medical services paid quickly. Many purchase the coverage because state compulsory auto laws require it.

Uninsured and underinsured motorists coverage provides coverage for injuries (and sometimes damage to their property) incurred as the result of an accident with an uninsured or underinsured motorist. An uninsured motorist is one who does not carry the amount of liability insurance required by the state in which the vehicle is titled. An underinsured motorist is one who carries less liability insurance than the innocent party who is injured.

LEGAL ASPECTS

Fiscal Responsibility and Compulsory Insurance Laws

All states have laws that assure compensation for victims of automobile accidents. Business auto insurance will satisfy the requirements for compulsory insurance in most states. Companies should be aware of the victims compensation laws in states where they do business. Figure 22.3 lists the financial responsibility requirements for each state and the District of Columbia.

Five types of statutes address victim compensation:

- Financial responsibility laws
- Compulsory automobile liability insurance
- Unsatisfied judgment fund laws
- Laws requiring uninsured motorists coverage
- No-fault automobile laws

While statutes vary considerably among states, the purpose of all victim compensation laws is to require owners and operators of automobiles to maintain a degree of solvency to compensate those they may injure by motor vehicles.

In general, the basic elements of these laws in various combinations relate to accidents, to convictions for certain offenses, and to judgments arising out of use of an automobile. Because there are as many variations as there are laws, the operation and objectives of these statutes will be discussed generally.

Financial Responsibility Laws

The term *financial responsibility law* refers to the statutes in some states that do not require proof of insurance or other responsibility until after a driver's first accident or until conviction of certain offenses, such as driving under the influence.

Compulsory Insurance Laws

Compulsory insurance laws require that every person who registers a motor vehicle in a given state prove or certify that liability insurance is carried equal to at least the state minimum requirements. The enforcement of these laws can be handled in six different ways. Some states use only one method of enforcement; others use a combination.

- Self-certification: when applying for new or renewal license plates, the driver must sign a sworn statement that he has liability insurance in force and will not operate a motor vehicle in the state without such insurance.

- Proof of insurance: some states require proof of insurance when registering a car.

- At time of motor vehicle inspection: some states require an annual safety inspection of all vehicles registered.

512

- Verification by the police: often, motorists must prove to a policeman at the time of an accident or ticket that they have insurance.

- Cancellation of insurance policy: some states require insurers to report auto policy cancellations to the department of motor vehicles.

- Random verification by state: some states require random checking of a given percentage of registrations for proof of financial responsibility.

Unsatisfied Judgments

Several states have established a fund out of which benefits are paid to the victim of an accident involving a driver not meeting the financial responsibility requirements or an unknown motor vehicle (the victim for one reason or another does not have access to uninsured motorists coverage and recoveries). These funds are created with contributions from motor vehicle registrants, insurance companies, or both. When an accident occurs and the negligent party cannot pay the damages, the injured party may seek recovery from the unsatisfied judgment fund. There are unsatisfied judgment funds in several states but their continued existence is always subject to the political currents and financial conditions that arise in those states.

Generally, the rules for the submission of a claim under the unsatisfied judgment fund are similar to the requirements for asserting a claim under standard uninsured motorists coverage. However, since this fund is an entity created by state law, any recovery may be limited by law to the amount required by the individual state's financial responsibility limits. The fund is not considered the insurer of the driver responsible for the accident.

Judgments and the Laws

Under these financial responsibility and compulsory insurance laws, treatment of judgments arising out of auto accidents differs from treatment of accidents. The party against whom a judgment is returned may have to pay it before license and registration are restored and may also have to supply proof of financial responsibility as to future accidents. This treatment could apply to judgments in any state, not merely to judgments where the debtor is licensed. Judgments are deemed satisfied, regardless of amounts involved, when amounts equivalent to required liability limits per person and per accident have been paid.

There are exceptions to the rule that judgments must be paid before reinstatement of driving and registration privileges, but proof of financial responsibility for the future, where required, is not waived. In some states, if the person to whom the judgment is payable consents, driving privileges may be restored, but proof must be given as a prerequisite to restoration.

Uninsured Motorists Coverage Laws

When an insured or his passengers are involved in an accident where the at-fault driver has no auto liability insurance, *uninsured motorists coverage* steps in to fill the gap. Coverage is usually to the extent of limits required by state auto financial responsibility laws. State laws vary. Some require auto policies to include uninsured motorists coverage. Others allow the coverage to be rejected. Some states have also enacted uninsured motorists coverage laws concerning hit-and-run vehicles. Risk managers should be aware of the specific uninsured motorists laws in the states where the company is located, in states where the company does business, and in states where autos are principally garaged. (See Figure 22.3 at the end of this chapter for a state-by-state comparison of auto financial responsibility laws, including uninsured motorists coverage requirements.)

Some of the states' uninsured motorists coverage laws also apply to *underinsured motorists coverage*. Underinsured motorists coverage is necessary when the at-fault driver in an accident has auto liability insurance with lesser limits than the insured's. This coverage lies atop uninsured motorists coverage or atop the at-fault driver's low limit automobile liability insurance and provides the insured and passengers with protection equal (usually) to the insured's own automobile liability cover.

Important Concepts

Uninsured motorists coverage: Fills the gap when an insured or his passengers are involved in an accident where the at-fault driver has no auto liability insurance. Coverage is usually to the extent of limits required by state auto financial responsibility laws.

Underinsured motorists coverage. This coverage is used when the at-fault driver in an accident has auto liability insurance with lesser limits than the insured's. It lies atop uninsured motorists coverage or atop the at-fault driver's low limit automobile liability insurance and provides the insured and passengers with protection equal (usually) to the insured's own automobile liability cover.

No–Fault Automobile Laws

No-fault automobile insurance describes a system under which a person injured in an automobile accident receives compensation for his economic losses caused by the injuries from his own auto insurer. His insurer pays even when another person might be demonstrably at fault and responsible for payment under the liability system.

There are three types of no-fault systems: pure no-fault, add-on plans, and modified no-fault plans. Under a pure no-fault plan, the injured person cannot sue for damages at all and collects damages from his own insurer. Add-on plans pay certain benefits to the injured person without regard to fault. Under modified no-fault plans, the injured person may choose to sue for damages if the claim exceeds a certain monetary or verbal threshold.

Insurance Policies and the Laws

The failure of an insurer to pay the damages caused by its insured does not mean suspension of the license to drive. In fact, insurance policies do not serve as anything more than documents through which a driver can prove his required financial responsibility—whether the insurance policy applies to the accident and subsequent claim is not relevant in this case. All that matters is that the driver has a policy with limits of liability equal to or greater than the state-mandated minimum limits.

Auto insurance coverage forms do take note of victim compensation laws. The business auto coverage form states that the declared limits will increase automatically to provide higher limits if such limits are required by compulsory or financial responsibility laws of the particular jurisdiction where the covered auto is being used. Furthermore, the form will provide at least the minimum amounts and types of coverages that are required by law whenever a covered auto is used outside the state in which the auto is principally garaged.

WHERE CAN I FIND OUT MORE ABOUT IT?

- *Commercial Auto Insurance*. Dallas: International Risk Management Institute.

- *Fire, Casualty & Surety Bulletins*. Cincinnati: The National Underwriter Company.

- Thamann, David. 1998. *Business Auto Coverage Guide: Interpretation and Analysis*. Cincinnati: The National Underwriter Company.

QUESTIONS AND ANSWERS

Question—What is the difference between *owned*, *nonowned*, and *hired* autos?

Answer—An owned auto is an auto owned or acquired by the insured during the policy period. A nonowned auto is used in connection with the insured's business but is not owned, rented, leased, hired, or rented by the named insured. A hired auto is one leased, rented, borrowed, or hired by the named insured.

Question—Explain when the insurer has the duty to defend its insured under the BAP.

Answer—The insurer has a duty to defend when a possibility exists for coverage to apply. The insured need not prove that the loss is covered.

Question—What is the difference between *liability protection* and *physical damage protection* as it applies to the BAP?

Answer—Liability protection generally pays for damages that the insured becomes legally obligated to pay to a third party because of property damage or bodily injury that he causes. Physical damage protection covers the actual damage to the covered auto.

For example, take an accident in which an insured pickup truck causes an accident. The pickup is badly damaged and declared a total loss. In addition, the car the pickup hit was totaled, and the driver required hospital treatment. Both vehicles were pushed by the force of the collision through a plate glass window in a supermarket. The damage to the pickup falls under the auto physical damage protection. The rest of the injuries and damage—to the other driver, the other car, and supermarket—are subject to liability coverage.

Question—Name the five parts that make up the BAP.

Answer—The BAP consists of a declarations form, liability coverage, physical damage coverage, conditions, and definitions.

Question—What is the difference between *comprehensive coverage* and *collision coverage*?

Answer—Comprehensive coverage is the insurer's promise to pay for loss to a covered auto or its equipment that results from any cause other than collision with another object or if the auto overturns. Collision coverage applies only to the covered auto's loss due to a collision with another object or if the auto overturns. A collision does not have to be with another vehicle or a moving object.

Question—What is a *compulsory insurance law*?

Answer—A compulsory insurance law requires that every person who registers a motor vehicle in a given state prove or certify that he carries liability insurance equal to at least the state minimum requirements.

FORMS AND CHECKLISTS

Business Auto Checklist

Date: _____

Named Insured: _____

Address: _____

City/State/Zip: _____

Phone: _____

Insured is: _____ individual _____ corporation

_____ partnership _____ limited liability company

_____ joint venture

Business type: _____

Expiration date: _____

Deductible: _____

Coverages and Covered Auto Symbols: _____

Liability Coverage: _____

Physical Damage Coverage: _____

Symbol 1—Any Auto

Symbol 2—Owned Autos Only

Symbol 3—Owned Private Passenger Autos

Symbol 4—Owned Autos Other Than Private Passenger Autos Only

Symbol 5—Owned Autos Subject to No-Fault

Symbol 6—Owned Autos Subject to A Compulsory U.M. Law

Symbol 7—Specifically Described Autos

Symbol 8—Hired Autos Only

Symbol 9—Nonowned Autos Only

Exposure Considerations

Auto med pay? .... _____Yes   _____No

Auto leasing or rental? .... _____Yes   _____No

Drive other car? .... _____Yes   _____No

Hired/nonowned auto? .... _____Yes   _____No

Hired car PD? .... _____Yes   _____No

No-fault/PIP? .... _____Yes   _____No

UM/UIM? .... _____Yes   _____No

Out-of-state coverage concerns? .... _____Yes   _____No

Contractual (insured contracts)? .... _____Yes   _____No

Pollution exposure? .... _____Yes   _____No

Additional insureds? .... _____Yes   _____No

Physical damage—comprehensive? .... _____Yes   _____No

Physical damage—specified causes of loss? .... _____Yes   _____No

Physical damage—collision? .... _____Yes   _____No

Physical damage deductible? .... _____Yes   _____No

Towing coverage? .... _____Yes   _____No

Higher transportation expenses? .... _____Yes   _____No

Higher loss of use expenses? .... _____Yes   _____No

Tapes, records, and discs coverage? .... _____Yes   _____No

Audio, visual, and data equipment coverage? .... _____Yes   _____No

Any loss payees? .... _____Yes   _____No

Employees as insureds? .... _____Yes   _____No

Garagekeepers liability exposure? .... _____Yes   _____No

Any Mexican or other foreign travel exposure? .... _____Yes   _____No

Delete fellow employee exclusion? .... _____Yes   _____No

Special Considerations

Are limits of liability adequate? .... _____Yes   _____No

Does insured have other insurance? .... _____Yes   _____No

Are certificates of insurance needed? .... _____Yes   _____No

Does insured have or need any manuscripted endorsements? .... _____Yes   _____No

Has the insured ever filed for bankruptcy? .... _____Yes   _____No

Has insured ever been cancelled or nonrenewed? .... _____Yes   _____No

Does insured have an active and effective loss control program? .... _____Yes   _____No

Check driving records of drivers? .... _____Yes   _____No

Are auto carrier and general liability carrier the same? .... _____Yes   _____No

Any trailers used? .... _____Yes   _____No

Figure 22.3

Required Compulsory Auto Insurance Limits and Uninsured Motorist Requirements by State

State	Required Limits	UM Required?	Rejection Allowed?	Must UM=BI?	Sign-off Required for Lower Limits?	UIM Seperate from UM?	Must UMPD Be	Stacking Allowed?
AL	20/40/10 or 50	Yes	Yes	No	N/A	No	No	Yes (Limited)
AK	50/100/25 or 125	Yes	Yes	No	Yes	No	Included	No
AZ	15/30/10 or 40	No	Yes	Yes	Yes	Yes	No	No
AR	25/50/25	Yes	Yes	No	N/A	N/A	Yes	No
CA	15/30/5	Yes	Yes	Yes	Yes	No	No	No
CO	25/50/15	Yes	Yes	Yes	Yes	No	Yes	Yes (Limited)
CT	20/40/10	Yes	No	Yes	Yes	No	No	No
DE	15/30/10	Yes	Yes	No	No	Yes*	Yes	No
DC	25/50/10	Yes	No	No	No	Yes	Yes	No
FL	10/20/10 or 30	Yes	Yes	Yes	Yes	No	N/A	Optional
GA	25/50/25	Yes	Yes	No	No	No	Yes	Yes (Limited)
HI	25/40/10	Yes	Yes	No	N/A	Yes	No	Optional
ID	25/50/15	Yes	Yes	No	N/A	Yes	N/A	No
IL	20/40/15	Yes	No	Yes	Yes	Yes	Yes	No
IN	25/50/10	Yes	Yes	Yes	Yes	Yes	No	Yes***
IA	20/40/15	Yes	Yes	No	No	Yes	Yes	Optional
KS	25/50/10	Yes	No	Yes	Yes	No	N/A	No
KY	25/50/10 or 60	Yes	Yes	No	N/A	Yes	N/A	No
LA	10/20/10	Yes	Yes	Yes	Yes	No	Yes	No
ME	50/100/25	Yes	No	Yes	Yes	No	N/A	No
MD	20/40/15	Yes	No	Yes	Yes	No	Yes	No
MA	15/30/5	Yes	No	No	N/A	Yes	N/A	No
MI	20/40/10	No	Yes	No	N/A	Yes	N/A	N/A
MN	30/60/10	Yes	No	No	N/A	No	No	No
MS	10/20/5	Yes	Yes	No	N/A	No	Yes	Yes
MO	25/50/10	Yes	No	No	N/A	Yes	No	Yes
MT	25/50/10	Yes	Yes	No	N/A	N/A	N/A	No
NE	25/50/25	Yes	Yes	No	N/A	No	No	No
NV	15/30/10	Yes	Yes	Yes	Yes	No	N/A	No
NH	25/50/25	Yes	No	Yes	Yes	No	Yes	No
NJ	15/30/5	Yes	No	No	N/A	No	Yes	No
NM	25/50/10	Yes	Yes	No	N/A	No	Included	Yes
NY	25/50/10*	Yes	No	No	Yes	No	No	No
NC	30/60/25	Yes	Yes	No	Yes	No	Yes	No
ND	25/50/25	Yes	No	No	N/A	Yes	No	No
OH	12.5/25/7.5	No	Yes	No	No	Yes	No	No
OK	10/20/10	Yes	Yes	No	Yes	No	N/A	Optional
OR	25/50/10	Yes	No	Yes	Yes	No	Yes	No
PA	15/30/5	Yes	Yes	Yes	Yes	Yes	N/A	Optional
RI	25/50/25	Yes	No	Yes	Yes	No	Yes	Yes
SC	15/30/10	Yes	No	No	N/A	Yes	Included	Yes (Limited)
SD	25/50/25	Yes	No	Yes	N/A	No	N/A	No
TN	25/50/10	Yes	Yes	Yes	Yes	No	Yes	No
TX	20/40/15	Yes	Yes	No	No	No	Included	No
UT	25/50/15	Yes	Yes	Yes	Yes	No	Yes	No
VT	25/50/10	Yes	No	Yes	N/A	No	Yes	Yes
VA	25/50/20	Yes	No	Yes	Yes	No	Yes	Yes
WA	25/50/10	Yes	Yes	Yes	Yes	No	Yes	No
WV	20/40/10	Yes	No	No	No	Yes	Included	No
WI	25/50/10	Yes	No	No	No	Yes	N/A	No
WY	25/50/20	Yes	Yes	No	N/A	No	N/A	No

* UIM applies only if UM is purchased above the minimum   ** 50/100 wrongful death   *** insurer may insert nonstacking language

KEY

UM = Uninsured Motorist Coverage
UIM = Underinsured Motorist Coverage

BI = Bodily Injury
UMPD = Uninsured Motorist Property Damage
Limited = Certain restrictions apply

Optional = Policies containing stacking provisions may be purchased by the insured

Chapter 22

GLOSSARY

Bodily injury. Direct injury, sickness, or disease sustained by a person, including resulting death.

Collision coverage. Collision coverage applies only to the covered auto's loss due to a collision with another object or if the auto overturns. A collision does not have to be with another vehicle or moving object.

Comprehensive coverage. Comprehensive coverage is the insurer's promise to pay for loss to a covered auto or its equipment that results from any cause other than collision with another object or overturning of the auto.

Compulsory insurance laws. Compulsory insurance laws require that every person who registers a motor vehicle in a given state prove or certify that she carries liability insurance equal to at least the state minimum requirements.

Contract of adhesion. One party selects the terms and language of the agreement and offers it to the other party on a take-it-or-leave-it basis. Ambiguities in such contracts are interpreted against the party that drafted it.

Duty to defend. The duty to defend is broader than the duty to indemnify. The insured does not need to prove that coverage exists in order for the insurer to have a duty to defend. The possibility that the claims of a third party might be covered under a policy is enough to trigger the duty to defend.

Endorsement. An amendment to a policy form that adds or removes specified coverages or amends existing coverages.

Exclusion. An exclusion eliminates coverage for specified loss exposures.

Financial responsibility laws. Refers to the statutes in some states that do not require proof of insurance or other responsibility until after a driver's first accident or until conviction of certain offenses, such as driving under the influence.

General conditions. General conditions in the BAP describe several situations, such as the insurer's obligation if the insured declares bankruptcy or becomes insolvent, how other insurance works in conjunction with the policy, and what the policy period and coverage territory are.

Hired auto. Hired autos are those that the named insured leases, hires, rents, or borrows.

Liability insurance. Liability insurance generally pays for sums that the insured becomes legally obligated to pay as damages due to property damage or bodily injury that he causes to third parties.

Loss conditions. Loss conditions in the BAP spell out the procedure for getting an appraisal if the parties disagree on the amount of loss; the duties of both the insured and the insurer when an accident, claim, suit, or loss occurs; when a legal action may be brought against the insurer; options from which the insurer may choose to pay for losses; and the terms for transfer of rights of recovery from others to the insurer.

Monoline policy. A monoline policy is an insurance policy that covers a single line of insurance, such as business auto, or part of a single line, such as business auto liability.

Multiline or package policy. A mulitline policy is an insurance policy that covers more than one line of insurance, such as business auto, property, and general liability combined on one policy.

Nonowned auto. Nonowned autos are those that are used in connection with the insured's business that are not owned, leased, hired, rented, or borrowed by the named insured.

Out-of-state coverage extension. The insurer agrees to increase the limit of insurance for liability coverage to meet limits specified by a compulsory or financial responsibility law of the jurisdiction where the covered auto is being used.

Owned auto. Owned autos are autos that the insured owns or acquires during the policy period.

Physical damage protection. Physical damage protection covers the actual damage to the covered auto. The damage may result from a variety of covered causes, such as collision, fire, theft, or hail. Other causes may result in damage but may be excluded, such as pollution or war.

Property damage. Damage to or loss of use of tangible property, along with loss of use of the property that is not physically injured.

Specified causes of loss coverage. Specified causes of loss coverage provides coverage for causes that are explicitly listed in the policy.

Supplementary payments. Payments that are made by the insurer for extended coverage in addition to the limit of insurance.

Third party. In regard to BAP coverage, a third party is another entity involved in the loss in addition to the insured and the insurer.

Underinsured motorists coverage. This coverage is necessary when the at-fault driver in an accident has auto liability insurance with lesser limits than the insured's. This coverage lies atop uninsured motorists coverage or atop the at-fault driver's low limit automobile liability insurance and provides the insured and passengers with protection equal (usually) to the insured's own automobile liability cover.

Uninsured motorists coverage. Fills the gap when an insured or her passengers are involved in an accident where the at-fault driver has no auto liability insurance. Coverage is usually to the extent of limits required by state auto financial responsibility laws.

Unsatisfied judgment fund. When an accident occurs and the negligent party cannot pay the damages, the injured party may seek recovery from the unsatisfied judgment fund. There are unsatisfied judgment funds in several states, but their continued existence is always subject to the political currents and financial conditions that arise in those states.

Chapter 23

CRIME INSURANCE

WHAT IS IT?

Crime insurance is designed to cover the risk of losing money and securities because of fraudulent acts that commercial organizations face in carrying out their operations. It also typically covers the theft of money, securities, and other types of property by their employees.

Crime insurance is needed because commercial property forms usually exclude or limit coverage for:

- money and documents that represent money or debt to the business,

- securities the business owns, and

- dishonest or criminal acts of employees against their employer.

For example, the standard commercial property form states that covered property does not include "accounts, bills, currency, deeds, food stamps or other evidences of debt, money, notes or securities. . ." In addition, most commercial property forms exclude dishonest and criminal acts by individuals who are insured under the policy, including employees. These types of exposures are better insured elsewhere—in this case, on a crime policy.

Among the types of dishonest acts typically covered by crime insurance are

- employee dishonesty or theft;

- forgery or alteration of checks and other written promises of payment that are drawn upon the insured businesses;

- theft of money and securities from inside the business premises;

- robbery or safe burglary of other property from inside the insured premises;

- theft of money, securities, or other properties from company representatives when they are away from the premises;

- computer fraud;

- fraudulently-ordered transfer of funds; and

- loss arising from money orders or counterfeit paper currency.

Each of these types of losses is defined on the crime insurance policies.

In addition, crime policies may be extended to cover other types of crime. For example, they may be endorsed (amended) to *exclude* or *limit* coverage for certain classifications of people or for specific individuals. They also may be endorsed to *add* coverage for certain types of people—such as agents who are not employees—or to cover additional causes of loss, such as vandalism and the forgery of business credit or debit cards.

BUSINESS USES

Businesses purchase crime insurance to cover their loss of money and securities, as well as losses caused by the dishonesty of employees. Cash regularly flows through many types of businesses, especially retail sales establishments such as grocery and convenience stores, and their need for crime coverage is readily apparent. The *2001 National Retail Security Survey* report, issued by the University of Florida, (www.soc.ufl.edu/srp.htm) states that retail establishments alone lost $15.24 billion in 2001 through employee theft. The fact that banks and other financial institutions need crime coverage also is obvious. Perhaps less apparent are crime exposures such as employee schemes to embezzle money over a period of time, theft of payroll or corporate checks that then are forged and cashed, and the robbery of messengers (such as the armed robbery of employees while on the way to the bank to deposit business proceeds).

In addition, employee benefit plans that are subject to the federal Employee Retirement Income Security Act of 1974 (ERISA) may be insured under a crime policy. The trustee, employee, or administrator who handles funds under an ERISA-regulated plan also may be insured. When considering potential coverage for ERISA plans, it is important to note that crime policies do not apply to poor investment returns. Coverage is restricted to criminal acts (such as theft or embezzlement) that an ERISA-plan trustee or administrator may commit, and not for errors in judgment in regard to investing or plan operation.

In other cases, certain public officials may be required by law or regulation to be insured against their dishonesty. This is called *employee bonding* or being *bonded*. Individuals who have custody and control of other people's money—such as a municipal treasurer or tax collector—may be required to be bonded. In such situations, the law will set the amount of bond required for the position. For example, a school district or village treasurer may be required to carry a bond of a specific amount, such as $100,000, or for a percentage of the money collected, such as a bond for 10 percent of taxes collected in a year. Since requirements vary from position to position, the individual law must be reviewed for details.

Similar requirements are in place for employees of banks, who must be bonded according to banking regulations.

ADVANTAGES AND DISADVANTAGES

The main advantage of purchasing crime insurance is that it provides coverage for risks that typically are excluded on other types of insurance policies. In addition, coverage may be required to meet certain regulations, such as those requiring that financial institutions carry crime insurance on their employees.

Under the employee dishonesty insuring agreement, limits may be arranged to apply either on a per loss or a per employee basis. The per loss arrangement means that the limit of employee dishonesty (theft) coverage is the most that will be paid for loss arising from any one scheme, regardless of how many employees are involved. The per employee limit provides that the coverage will be paid for each employee's actions. This provides a business with some flexibility in arranging coverage and negotiating premiums.

However, businesses may be forced to adopt certain loss control procedures in order to qualify for the coverage. For example, a crime underwriter may require that a business hire an armored car company to pick up bank deposits, instead of permitting a manager to take the money to the bank. Underwriters frequently require internal controls to guard against employee theft. For example, an underwriter may

require that bookkeepers take at least five consecutive days of vacation each year in an effort to detect potential employee dishonesty schemes. While these procedures may result in a reduction in crime losses, they often cost money that a business owner might prefer to invest elsewhere.

It also is important to realize that standard employee dishonesty coverage forms exclude dishonest acts committed by partners in a partnership or members of a limited liability company. Therefore, if a partner embezzles funds, there would be no coverage unless the crime policy had been endorsed to provide coverage for individual partners. This could leave the innocent partners in the operation without coverage for a potentially large loss.

DESIGN FEATURES

Crime coverage most often is provided on standardized forms that are developed by either the Surety Association of America (SAA), www.surety.org, or the Insurance Services Office, Inc. (ISO), www.iso.com. The SAA is an organization of member companies that underwrite bonds in the United States. It also serves as a statistical agent for reporting loss experience on *fidelity* (employee dishonesty) and *surety* (e.g., performance and payment bonds) business. ISO is an organization that provides statistical information, actuarial analyses, policy language, and related services for the insurance industry. Since most crime coverage forms are based on either SAA or ISO formats, the coverage tends to be written on fairly consistent forms.

However, as with all insurance policies, any crime form can be amended through the use of endorsements. Endorsements either broaden, exclude, or limit coverage for certain exposures and causes of loss. Some may refer to endorsements as *riders*, especially when referring to fidelity bonds.

This discussion focuses on concepts that affect crime insurance in broad terms rather than the details of specific crime forms.

Two Areas of Coverage

There are two main categories of crime coverage. They respond to either

- dishonest acts of employees or

- dishonest acts of individuals not affiliated with the insured business.

Coverage that applies to dishonest acts of employees often is referred to as *employee dishonesty, employee theft,* or *fidelity* coverage. Dishonest acts of outside individuals are insured by coverages known as forgery or alteration, robbery, burglary, and passing of counterfeit currency. Each of these specialized types of coverage is provided on crime insurance forms through individual *insuring agreements.* Insuring agreements are provisions that state what the policy will pay. For example, a typical ISO commercial crime insuring agreement for employee theft states that the insurer "will pay for loss of or damage to 'money', 'securities' and 'other property' resulting directly from 'theft' committed by an 'employee', whether identified or not, acting alone or in collusion with other persons." Each of the words in quotation marks is defined on the policy. So, for example, the term "employee" is defined on the policy in an effort to avoid controversy about how the coverage applies.

Similar wording is provided under each insuring agreement on a crime form.

Coverage Forms

In general, there are two types of coverage forms. They are the

- loss sustained form and
- discovery form.

The *loss sustained form* applies to crime losses that arise because of acts committed or events that occur during the policy period and that are discovered by the insured during the policy period or extended discovery period. The *extended discovery period* is a period of time that the insured is given in which to uncover losses that happened during the policy period. (The loss sustained form may cover losses that are suffered during prior coverage periods, but only under certain conditions.)

The *discovery form* applies to losses that are sustained at any time but *discovered* during the policy period or the extended discovery period.

The extended discovery period is especially important when a company cancels or decides not to renew crime coverage because it provides for additional time in which losses may be found. For example, a company may have been the victim of an employee scheme to take

a small amount of money each week from the cash drawer. Since the weekly loss is small, it may be overlooked for a long period of time. However, an audit may uncover the cumulative loss after a substantial period of time elapses, perhaps after the crime policy expires.

Loss Sustained vs. Discovery Forms

The difference between the two forms lies primarily with when the actual crime must occur in order to trigger coverage. For example, the accounts receivable manager for ABC Restaurants steals $50,000 on March 25, 2002, but the business does not uncover the loss until the following August. The restaurant chain did not purchase crime (employee dishonesty) coverage until July 1, 2003.

If the policy purchased on July 1, 2003, is written on a *loss sustained form,* it would not pay the $50,000 loss. This is because the actual theft occurred (on March 25, 2002) before the policy period began (July 1, 2003), so it does not meet the requirement that the loss be sustained during the policy period.

However, if the policy that was purchased on July 1, 2003, were written on a discovery form, the loss probably would be covered. This is because a discovery form applies to losses that occur *at any time* as long as they are discovered during the policy period or extended reporting period.

It must be noted that there probably would be no coverage under even the discovery form if ABC Restaurants knew about the March 25, 2002, theft but misrepresented the fact in its application for its first crime policy. A failure to list such an occurrence on the application—if the business knows about it—probably would result in a denial of coverage because the insured misrepresented the facts when applying for the insurance.

Blanket vs. Schedule Coverage

Some types of employee dishonesty coverage permit *blanket* or *schedule* coverage. Blanket employee dishonesty coverage means that all employees are covered; individual names or individual positions do not have to be listed on the policy. Schedule coverage, however, requires that either the names of covered employees or the titles of covered positions be listed in order for coverage to apply to them. Therefore, schedule coverage requires that changes in either employees or titles of positions be submitted to the insurer. Some employee dishonesty forms have done away with these options, but many such forms remain in use.

Endorsements

As noted previously, there are a number of endorsements that may be used to amend coverage. Therefore, risk managers should review their crime policies, especially the exclusions sections. If coverage that is needed is not in place, the underwriter should be asked whether an endorsement might be attached to address the exposure.

Select Exclusions

Certain types of exclusions that appear on most crime forms often are the subject of confusion. It is impossible to address each of them in this chapter. However, several of the more common exclusions are discussed next.

Acts Committed by the Insured, Partners, or Members

Crime insurance is not meant to cover criminal acts that are committed by business owners against their own interests. Therefore, most crime policies exclude loss that results from dishonest acts of the owner, partners in an insured partnership, and members of a limited liability company. This exclusion typically applies regardless of whether the owners are acting alone or in concert with people outside the company. Endorsements may be available to offer additional coverage in this area.

Indirect Losses

A large percentage of property and casualty insurance is designed to cover direct losses. The same is true of crime coverage. Therefore, indirect losses, such as an inability to gain income and costs associated with proving a loss, are excluded on many crime forms.

Employee Cancelled under Prior Insurance

Coverage for employees who commit dishonest acts is automatically cancelled. Once coverage for such an employee has been cancelled, prospective (future) coverage for them also is eliminated. Therefore, if an insured business discovers that an employee has stolen from the business, coverage for that employee is automatically cancelled for possible future acts. Coverage for that employee must be affirmatively reinstated by an insurer in order for future coverage to apply, even if two different insurance companies are involved.

For example, the accounts receivable manager for ABC Restaurants steals from the company. That theft is covered by Ajax Insurance, which writes crime insurance for the restaurant chain. As soon as the theft is discovered, however, employee dishonesty coverage for possible future dishonest acts of the accounts receivable manager is automatically cancelled. So, if the manager is kept on and commits another theft, there would be no coverage under the Ajax Insurance policy. When ABC Restaurants' crime policy expires, the company switches from Ajax Insurance to High-Rate Insurance. Even though a new policy is written with a new insurance company, the accounts receivable manager still is excluded from the coverage. Her coverage would have to be affirmatively reinstated by High-Rate in order for coverage to apply.

Inventory Shortages

Mere inventory shortages typically are not covered. There must be additional evidence of loss in order for the policy to be triggered.

Voluntary Parting With

Businesses at times may voluntarily give another party items of value. For example, ABC Restaurants hires a contractor to replace a roof. ABC might be duped into sending payment to the contractor before the job is started. If the contractor never does the work, the crime policy probably would not respond to the loss of money because the restaurant chain *voluntarily* paid the money.

This exclusion does not apply to the employee dishonesty section of coverage. Therefore, if an employee conspired with an outsider to defraud the business by voluntarily making bogus payments, coverage may be triggered, depending upon the details of the situation.

Coverage for Financial Institutions

Specialized crime coverage is available for financial institutions, such as banks and securities firms. Fidelity and crime insurers should be consulted for information on these specialized forms.

WHERE CAN I FIND OUT MORE ABOUT IT?

- *Commercial Property Insurance.* Dallas: International Risk Management Institute. www.irmi.com.

- *Commercial Property Risk Management and Insurance.* Malvern: The American Institute for CPCU and the Insurance Institute of America, www.aicpcu.org.

- *Fire, Casualty, & Surety (FC&S) Bulletins.* Cincinnati: The National Underwriter Company, www.nationalunderwriter.com/nucatalog/.

- Slep, Gary M. and Roger A. Haynes. *Bank Insurance & Risk Management.* Boston: Standard Publishing Corp. www.standardpublishingcorp.com.

- The Surety Association of America, www.surety.org.

QUESTIONS AND ANSWERS

Question—Many companies provide services (such as home healthcare services) through which subcontractors enter the homes of clients. If such a company carries employee dishonesty insurance, would the coverage extend to the theft of property or money from client homes?

Answer—No. Employee dishonesty or theft insurance applies only to losses that an employer experiences because of the dishonesty of its own employees. In this case, a client—not the employer—was the theft victim. In addition, the individuals who are being sent to client homes are subcontractors, and employee theft insurance would not apply to them. However, the service agency may be able to purchase other types of coverage to address this need.

For example, the agency could purchase a *surety bond* that would provide that subcontractors pay the service agency for stolen client property. Surety bonds are discussed in Chapter 27. Another method might be to amend the definition of covered property on the agency's commercial crime policy to include client property away from the insured business's premises. This type of coverage could reimburse the service agency for money it pays to clients for the stolen property. A third method might be to require that subcontractors extend the coverage on *their* property insurance to include client property away from their premises. Each of these methods should be discussed with an insurance professional before selecting one of them to be sure that both parties understand how the potential coverage would apply.

Question—A store accepts a check from an individual. When the store tries to redeem the check through its bank, it turns out that the check is forged. The store carries crime coverage for forgery or alteration. How does that coverage apply to this type of loss?

Answer—Forgery or alteration coverage typically would not cover this type of situation. This is because the crime policy's forgery/alteration coverage protects insured businesses against the forging of checks or other instruments that are drawn on its own account. For example, if payroll checks were stolen, forged, and cashed, the store's forgery or alteration insurance probably would cover the loss. Or, a business may be sued if its checks are forged and it refuses to honor them. The policy also would provide the costs for defending this type of suit.

Question—A business hires a payroll service company to issue payroll checks, file taxes, issue W-2 forms, etc. The payroll service company gets into financial trouble and begins to use the clients' tax fund to cover its own expenses. The payroll company then files bankruptcy. Shortly after this, it is discovered that the business's taxes were not paid, and the IRS has asked for back payments and penalties, even though the business did transfer the money to the payroll service company. What type of crime coverage would apply?

Answer—The business's employee dishonesty or employee theft insurance could be endorsed to amend the definition of *employee* to include *designated agents.* This type of endorsement expands the definition of employee to include agents—persons, partnerships, or corporations—that the insured business appoints in writing to act as its agent in a specific capacity. The agent and the capacity in which they represent the insured business must be shown on the endorsement.

Question—A payroll clerk for a home goods store steals money from her company by inflating her own payroll checks. She doubles the amount of money she should be earning. The thievery is not discovered for almost a year, when the store's auditors discover it. Is this type of employee dishonesty covered by the typical employee theft coverage?

Answer—This type of loss may or may not be covered—depending on what type of employee dishonesty coverage form has been written. The difference lies in the form's definition of employee dishonesty or employee theft.

For example, one version of the coverage specifies that an employee must act dishonestly with a manifest intent to cause the employer to sustain loss and to obtain financial benefit *other than* employee benefits earned in the normal course of employment, including: salaries, commissions, fees, bonuses, promotions, awards, profit sharing or pensions.

Various courts have addressed the question of whether wages or commissions that are fraudulently obtained qualify for coverage. The court in *Hartford Accident & Indemnity Ins. Co. v. Washington National Ins. Co.*, 638 F. Supp. 78 (N.D. Ill. 1986) quoted an earlier court that dealt with this definition by saying: "The comprehensive crime insurance policy clearly and unambiguously excludes from coverage the acts of an employee who fraudulently or dishonestly obtains salary or commission."

Other courts that have taken the same stance are *Auburn Ford Lincoln Mercury, Inc. v. Universal Underwriters Ins. Co.*, 967 F. Supp. 475 (M.D. Ala. 1997), *Benchmark Crafters, Inc. v. Northwestern National Ins. Co. of Milwaukee*, 363 N.W.2d 89 (Minn. Ct. App. 1985), and *Berger v. Fireman's American Loss Control Co.*, (Slip Op., Md. Ct. Spec. App. 1982).

However, another version of coverage, which uses employee theft as the title for employee-caused losses, has dropped this exclusionary language for wages and other employee benefits. Therefore, the definitions on the form being used must be considered when answering this question.

Chapter 23

GLOSSARY

Blanket employee dishonesty coverage. Employee dishonesty coverage that applies to all employees.

Bonded. Also known as *employee bonding.* When an employee carries employee dishonesty coverage.

Discovery form. Crime coverage that applies to losses that are sustained at any time but are discovered during the policy period or extended reporting period.

Employee Retirement Income Security Act of 1974 (ERISA). The federal law that regulates certain employee benefits, especially retirement plans.

Endorsements. Policy or bond amendments that exclude, limit, or broaden coverage.

Fidelity coverage. Coverage that responds to employee dishonesty.

Indirect loss. Loss that indirectly results from an act that is covered by an insurance policy.

Insuring agreement. The part of an insurance policy that states what the policy covers.

Loss sustained form. Crime coverage that applies to losses that arise from acts that are committed during the policy period and are discovered during the policy period or extended reporting period.

Riders. Another name for policy or bond amendments or endorsements. Documents that are attached to bonds or insurance policies to amend coverage.

Schedule employee dishonesty coverage. Employee dishonesty coverage in which the names of individuals or titles of positions must be listed in order for coverage to apply.

Securities. As defined on typical crime policies, securities are negotiable and nonnegotiable instruments or contracts that represent money or other property.

Chapter 24

CAPITAL MARKETS RISK TRANSFER TOOLS

WHAT IS IT?

Transferring risk directly into the capital markets is a relatively new phenomenon. Prior to 1995 the only way risk was transferred into the capital markets was through direct equity investment in insurance and reinsurance companies. For example, an institutional investor may own shares in a publicly traded insurer. Because the insurer uses the funds raised through the sale of its stock to finance risk, the investor indirectly funds the risk. Today, there are additional ways for insurance and reinsurance companies to fund risk in the capital markets, primarily through the issuance of debt securities. These include *catastrophe bonds* and *insurance derivatives*.

DESIGN FEATURES OF CATASTROPHE BONDS

A catastrophe bond is a structured debt security issued by insurers and reinsurers designed to transfer catastrophic loss caused by natural disasters—such as hurricanes and earthquakes—into the capital markets. The bonds are priced based on a risk-free rate such as LIBOR (London Interbank Offered Rate), plus a spread. To date, each issue has been a private placement, meaning that qualified investors are identified prior to the bond's issuance. Each bond is structured to cover certain perils, for example, windstorm, within specified geographic boundaries. The bonds can be issued for one-year or multiyear periods and are usually rated by the various debt-rating agencies, such as Moody's or Standard & Poor's. Catastrophe bonds may be issued in a single tranche (risk layer) or multiple tranches. Each tranche is assigned its own debt rating based on its level of risk. Tranches with investment grade ratings (A or better) carry less risk of default (insurance loss) and subsequently offer lower investment yields than do tranches with greater risk and non-investment grade ratings. For example, Moody's might rate tranche A "Bbb" (noninvestment grade), and tranche B, "Aaa." Accordingly, tranche A might yield 700 basis points above LIBOR while tranche B would only yield 400 basis points above LIBOR.

Catastrophe bonds require the issuer to utilize a special purpose vehicle (SPV).

Loss Triggers

Catastrophe bonds, similar to insurance, have loss triggers. A loss trigger is defined as an event that causes an insurance policy to pay a loss. Insurance loss triggers are known as *indemnification* triggers. When a loss occurs, the insured is indemnified based on the amount of the loss and the amount of in-force insurance coverage. Indemnification triggers are *dollar-amount* triggers. Many catastrophe bonds also utilize indemnification triggers; however, there are two additional trigger types used by catastrophe bonds. These are

1. parametric triggers and

2. special index triggers.

The term parametric means *event*. A parametric trigger is an event—such as an earthquake—that causes a loss. A special index is a set of property loss data against which actual losses are measured.

Expected Losses and Loss Modeling

Catastrophe bond pricing is, in part, based on the expected losses associated with the insured peril, similar to insurance and reinsurance. Because there is usually no credible loss frequency associated with catastrophic natural disasters, loss models are used to estimate the probability of a loss event. Catastrophe loss models are highly sophisticated computer-based calculations using hundreds of years of historical data. Loss expectations are expressed as a percentage chance of the occurrence of a loss (bond default). Most catastrophe bonds carry expected loss probabilities from .5 percent to 2 percent.

ADVANTAGES AND DISADVANTAGES OF CATASTROPHE BONDS

Catastrophe bonds can be effective tools for transferring risk into the capital markets. However, they are very expensive when compared to traditional reinsurance, even when reinsurance rates are not considered inadequate. Unlike reinsurance, they are not standardized; each catastrophe bond is considered a "one-off" deal, which contributes to their high costs. In addition, catastrophe bonds take, on average, about six months to create and execute. A typical traditional reinsurance transaction can take a little as several weeks to several days, depending on the circumstances. In spite of these impediments, many insurers and reinsurers consider catastrophe bonds a worthy investment of time and money, since they represent an important diversification tool in an ever-changing risk transfer environment. Investors also find value in catastrophe bonds because they do not correlate with any other investment, thus providing effective portfolio diversification. Also, catastrophe bonds have typically offered excellent yields as compared to other investments, especially when the equities markets are losing value.

Figure 24.1 illustrates how a typical catastrophe bonds operates. Investors purchase bonds from the special purpose vehicle and receive interest. The SPV deposits the proceeds into a trust. The issuer (insurance or reinsurance company) pays a premium to the SPV and in return receives reinsurance equal to the amount of the bond proceeds.

Figure 24.1

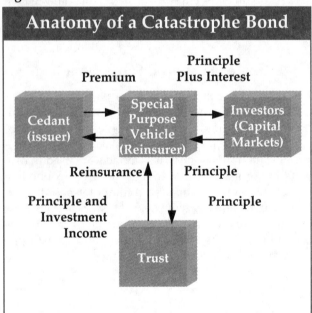

DESIGN FEATURES OF INSURANCE DERIVATIVES

Derivatives are investments whose value is derived from another asset, commonly known as the *underlying asset*. While derivatives have been used as purely specu-

lative investments, their primary use is to hedge against (to counteract) price movements in the underlying asset. Derivatives are traded on organized exchanges like the New York and American Stock Exchanges and the Chicago Board of Trade (CBOT).

For example, manufacturers that sell globally are exposed to potential loss simply as a result of movements in the value of currency. Assume a U.S. company sells a machine in Germany, and the payment is expressed in German Deutche marks (DM). The contract is completed on December 1, but payment is not due until January 1. The deal is closed based on the December 1 exchange rate of $1.00 equaling DM2.00. During the month of December the dollar gains significant value against the mark, and the rate on January 1 becomes $1.00 equals DM3.00. This means that it takes *one third* more marks to equal the dollar value of the transaction. Since the contract's price was based on the December 1 exchange rate, the U.S. manufacturer will lose one third of the contract price. An FX (foreign exchange) derivative can hedge against losses due to exchange rate fluctuations by setting a price floor (known as the *strike price*) beneath which the derivative will pay if rates fall below that level. Similar to insurance, the derivative is sold for a premium, but the cost is far less than the potential loss.

Figure 24.2

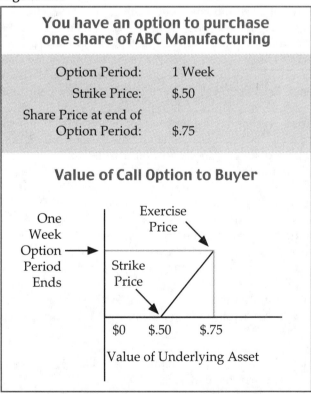

Figure 24.2 illustrates a derivative option to purchase one share of stock.

Options

An option allows the holder the right (but not the obligation) to buy or sell an asset, for example, a commodity or an equity, at a predetermined price within a defined period of time for a premium paid by the purchaser to the seller. In this example, the purchaser (holder) buys a *call option* to purchase one share of ABC Manufacturing stock. The *option period* is one week; if the option is not exercised within this timeframe, it expires without value.

The *strike price* is the value at which the share of stock may be purchased. The example assumes that the share price rises from $.50 to $.75 by the end of the option period, meaning that the option is *in-the-money*.

If the option holder then purchases the share of stock at the $.50 strike price and immediately sells it at the market price of $.75, he earns $.25. The holder could also buy a *put option* with the same strike price on this share of stock. This would mean that if the stock's market value falls *below* $.50, the option holder can *sell* the stock at the strike price to avoid the loss of share value as reflected by the market.

Figure 24.3 illustrates a technique using call options with different strike prices to create insurance

Figure 24.3

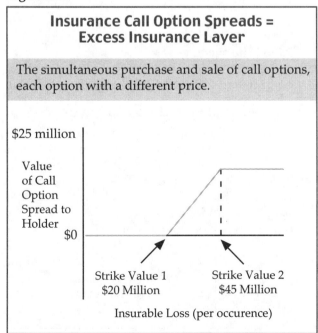

Insurance Call Option Spreads = Excess Insurance Layer

The simultaneous purchase and sale of call options, each option with a different price.

$25 million

Value of Call Option Spread to Holder

$0

Strike Value 1
$20 Million

Strike Value 2
$45 Million

Insurable Loss (per occurence)

capacity for insurers and reinsurers. The total maximum value of the call option spreads to the holder is $25 million of loss, attaching at $20 million (the first strike price), and ending at $45 million (the second strike price). Losses under the first strike value are paid by the holder as a retention, and losses above the second strike value are uninsured or covered under a traditional reinsurance program. Insurance derivatives similar to this one were traded on the Chicago Board of Trade (CBOT) from 1995 through 2000; trading ceased on January 1, 2001. Another exchange, the Bermuda Commodities Options Exchange (BCOE) was a short-lived experiment trading exclusively in insurance derivatives. The BCOE was closed within a year. As of this writing there are no formally traded insurance derivatives.

What killed the exchanges? *Basis risk.* Each exchange used a proprietary index of industry property losses to determine the settlement values of their options, similar to that which is used in some catastrophe bonds. And while the catastrophe bond issuer assumes the basis risk in those deals, neither party to an exchange-traded contract could tolerate basis risk because of the lack of *transparency.* All exchange-traded securities must be transparent; that is, only the trading activity can affect the prices (not unknown or tangential risk factors). Basis risk rendered the exchange-traded derivatives untenable because basis risk is tantamount to underwriting risk, which is anything *but* transparent.

Catastrophe Equity Put

Another form of derivatives contract is the catastrophe equity put. It is a form of postloss financing in that the funds to pay the loss are not raised until after the loss occurs. It functions similar to a put option, where the holder has the right to exercise the option at any time during the option period.

In this case, however, the option's holder is a publicly traded corporation and the seller (also known as the writer) is an insurance or reinsurance company. In a catastrophe equity put the holder (a publicly traded company) is entitled to sell a quantity of its stock to the insurer or reinsurer (the option's seller) when a loss meets or exceeds the option's strike value. For example, assume ABC Corporation purchases such an option from ZYX Re. The strike value is $5 million, and a $6 million covered loss occurs. ABC would exercise the option and issue $1 million worth of stock to XYZ Re. XYZ Re would then pay $1 million for the stock. This is a unique way to fund excess losses leveraging the company's market value. However, because the equity sale is from treasury stock (stock the company owns) it also has the effect of diluting the number of outstanding shares of stock.

ADVANTAGES AND DISADVANTAGES OF INSURANCE DERIVATIVES

While there have been two failed experiments trading insurance derivatives on open exchanges, the success of catastrophe bonds and other customized one-off deals such as the catastrophe equity put suggests that the capital markets will play an ever-increasing role in the management and financing of event risk. Until the basis risk problem is solved, it is doubtful that any new exchange traded insurance derivative products will appear. However, it is probably only a matter of time before this issue is resolved.

WHERE CAN I FIND OUT MORE ABOUT IT?

* Bawcutt, P.A. 1997. *Captive Insurance Companies: Establishment, Operation and Management, Fourth Edition*. London: Witherby Publishers of UK.

* *Financing Risk & Reinsurance*. Dallas: International Risk Management Institute (IRMI).

* *Risk Financing* (Reference Service). Dallas: International Risk Management Institute (IRMI).

QUESTIONS AND ANSWERS

Question—What role does a *special purpose vehicle* have in regards to catastrophe bonds?

Answer— Catastrophe bonds require the issuer to utilize a special purpose vehicle (SPV). Special purpose vehicles are non-owned single-purpose companies from which the bond is actually issued. SPVs are established offshore in places like Grand Cayman and Bermuda by the issuer's investment bank in the form of a trust. Since every trust must have a beneficiary, a local charity is named. When the bond term expires, the charity receives whatever proceeds remain in the trust (usually a small amount of cash). SPVs are established offshore in order to

avoid U.S. state insurance regulation and to preserve insurance accounting and taxation. Once the SPV has sold the security, it then reinsures the issuer (the insurer or reinsurer) on a dollar for dollar basis. For example, XYZ Re forms (through its investment banker) ABC Limited, a Grand Cayman special purpose vehicle. ABC Limited is empowered to sell catastrophe bonds to qualified investors and raises $50 million. ABC Limited then acts as a reinsurer to XYZ Re, and sells XYZ Re $50 million in reinsurance limits.

This transaction, unlike the insurance transaction, is *not* leveraged. The SPV must be fully collateralized for every dollar of reinsurance it sells to the issuer (XYZ Re). Insurance, on the other hand, is a highly leveraged mechanism since a relatively small premium is used to purchase a relatively large amount of protection. (For example, a $1 million umbrella policy may cost only $10,000 in premium.)

Question—When discussing catastrophe bonds, what is the difference between a *parametric loss trigger* and a *special index trigger*?

Answer—A parametric trigger is when an event causes a loss. The most prevalent parametric trigger used in catastrophe bonds is the earthquake. Instead of a specific dollar amount of loss, a bond with a parametric trigger covering earthquake is triggered by a predetermined earthquake event as measured on, for example, the Richter scale. For example, a bond with such a parametric loss trigger might pay a loss only if the earthquake in the covered geographic region equals or exceeds 7.0 on the Richter scale. Even if the earthquake causes major financial loss, the bond would not be triggered unless the 7.0 threshold is reached.

An *index* is a collection of data against which an average, or representational value, may be derived. A good example of an index is the Dow Jones Industrial Averages (the *Dow*). The Dow is a collection of industrial stocks traded on the New York Stock Exchange. Its collective value is used as an index to represent the value of the market traded on the exchange. The index's value rises and falls in response to changing stock prices. For example, if the index loses 150 points, it is safe to assume that more stocks lost value than gained value during that trading day. Of course, not every stock reflects the movement of the index, but that is the risk inherent in indexes. Some catastrophe bonds rely on special indexes comprised of property loss data. These indexes can include the issuer's overall annual loss experience, total industry loss experience, or the loss experience of a combination of each. Similar to the Dow, however, a special index will rarely (if ever) equate to the bond issuer's actual losses. The difference between the issuer's actual losses and the settlement value of an index is called *basis risk*. Another term for basis risk is *underwriting risk.* Because the issuer is an insurance or reinsurance company, it is able to absorb the basis risk associated with special index triggers.

Chapter 24

GLOSSARY

Basis risk. The difference between a bond issuer's actual losses and the settlement value of an index that is used to represent overall loss experience. Also known as underwriting risk.

Catastrophe bond. A structured debt security issued by insurers and reinsurers that is designed to transfer catastrophic loss cause by natural disasters into the capital markets.

Derivative. Investments whose value is derived from another asset.

Hedge. An action that is undertaken to counteract the effects of another action; to counteract price movements in an underlying asset, such as the foreign exchange rate.

Index. A collection of data against which an average, or representational value, may be derived.

In the money. Profitable.

Loss trigger. An event that causes an insurance policy to pay.

Option. The ability (but not the obligation) to buy or sell an asset at a predetermined price within a defined period of time.

Parametric. An event. A parametric loss trigger is an event (such as an earthquake or flood) that causes a loss.

Portfolio diversification. When individual investments that form an investment portfolio operate independently of one another and do not correlate with one another.

Put option. The option to sell an asset at a predetermined price if the stock falls below that (strike) price.

Special purpose vehicle (SPV). A company that is formed for a single purpose, i.e., to issue catastrophe bonds.

Strike price. An agreed-upon price at which an option contract can be exercised; a price floor beneath which a derivative will pay.

Tranche. A risk layer of a catastrophe bond.

Chapter 25

LOSS CONTROL TOOLS

OVERVIEW

The purpose of this chapter is to describe and present in a logical fashion some of the common loss control tools available to risk managers. There are three loss control approaches that risk managers can take to mitigate hazards:

- Avoidance

- Prevention

- Reduction

All individual loss control activities can be organized under these three basic tools.

The purpose of avoidance is to reduce the probability of loss to zero. The purpose of prevention is to decrease the probability of loss to an acceptable level. The purpose of reduction is to decrease the severity of losses to an acceptable amount.

Prevention and reduction are not mutually exclusive; risk managers may apply both solutions simultaneously to various hazards. Entire books have been written about many of the tools discussed here. This chapter, which is organized around avoidance, prevention, and reduction as they relate to different types of exposures, provides a brief introduction to such tools. Figure 25.6 in the appendix lists the exposures and tools in chart form.

BUSINESS USES

Avoidance

The ultimate loss control tool is avoidance. However, this is regarded as an extreme solution because, by avoiding the risk, its potential return also is lost. The essence of business is to take acceptable risks in exchange for prospective returns. Avoidance is acceptable and appropriate only when the return does not justify assuming the risk.

There are two ways to use avoidance: *proactively* and *reactively*.

Proactive avoidance. A risk manager can decide not to adopt a risky project. By not engaging in the activity, there is no chance of having a loss. In other words, the probability of loss is zero. For example, if the marketing department suggests selling a new product that, in the risk manager's opinion, is too risky from a product liability perspective, the firm may decide not to sell the product. By not selling it, the probability of a product liability suit drops to zero. Of course, there's a cost to eliminating the risk entirely. The certainty of loss avoidance equates to the certainty of not obtaining gain—so the firm will not make a profit on a product it is not willing to sell. It's ample justification for the phrase, "no risk, no reward!"

Reactive avoidance. If a firm is already engaged in a risky behavior, the risk manager may recommend reactive avoidance to stop the behavior. While the possibility of claims arising as a result of past behavior still lingers, the chance of new future losses arising from the activity has been eliminated through stopping the problematic behavior. With complete termination of the loss-causing behavior, the probability of future claims is zero.

For example, if the firm had manufactured a product that proved to be defective, the company may decide to halt production. Claims may still come in from past sales, but since sales of new products have been halted, the stream of claims has been interrupted.

Of course, in business, it is neither possible nor advisable to avoid all risk. When avoidance is not the appropriate solution, the risk manager turns to prevention and reduction. Prevention and reduction tools differ for the diverse types of exposures. We've separated them by exposure class:

- Assets

- Liabilities

- Human resources

Consequential losses can be sustained within each of these three exposure classes. Therefore, consequential loss control tools are discussed within each class.

Despite the differences among the types of exposure, acronyms may help risk managers remember the option details. Examples are COPE (construction, occupancy, protection, and environment), SOAP (specialization, organization, activities, and physical), and ITIM (information management, transfers, inspections, and mandates).

Note that property specialists frequently refer to the E in COPE as exposure. This chapter modifies that to environment.

Risk Management Tip

Ways to remember optional tools:

COPE means Construction, Occupancy, Protection, Environment.

SOAP means Specialization, Organization, Activities, and Physical.

ITIM means Information Management, Transfers, Inspections, and Mandates.

ASSET LOSS CONTROL

Asset Loss Prevention

Common sense tells us that prevention is an effective way to decrease asset losses. Property exposures face a myriad of hazards, and loss control engineers have developed two acronyms to help risk managers remember some of them: COPE and ITIM, which were previously introduced. Each is briefly analyzed here in the context of property loss prevention.

COPE: *Construction*: When building a new structure or designing a new facility, the method of construction and the materials used are key determinants of asset safety. For example, a risk manager can decrease the probability of the structure burning by assuring it is constructed with fire resistant materials.

Figure 25.1 illustrates classifications of construction and their relative fire resistance.

Buildings of mixed construction generally are coded as the predominant construction class. For example, a building that is 40 percent fire-resistive and 60 percent modified fire-resistive would be classified as modified fire-resistive.

Figure 25.1

Construction Classifications in Ascending Order of Fire Resistance	
Frame	Walls and interior in whole or part of wood or other combustible materials, including brick veneer, stucco on wood frame, and corrugated iron no wood frame.
Joisted Masonry	Combustible floors and roofs with exterior walls constructed of masonry materials like brick, concrete, or adobe.
Noncombustible	Exterior walls, floors, and roofs constructed with and supported by metal or other noncombustible material.
Modified Fire-resistive	Masonry or reinforced concrete walls, floors, and roofs with a minimum fire-resistance rating of one hour on structural parts.
Fire-resistive	Structural members of approved fire-resistive materials with a rating of not less than two hours for walls, floors, and roofs. Approved masonry or reinforced concrete exterior and interior bearing walls.

COPE: *Occupancy:* The activities inside a building also affect the probability of loss. Occupancy deals with both the operations being performed and the material used in those operations. All else held equal, a fireworks factory has a greater probability of explosion loss than a water bottling plant. A risk manager may restrict the occupancy of certain buildings to modify the probability (as well as the severity) of loss.

It may be impossible to change the actual operations because of their impact on the core business. However, it is likely that less hazardous materials could be used in an effort to prevent losses to assets. For example, painting may be an integral part of a production process. A company may establish standards limiting the flammability of painting materials being used in order to prevent fire losses. An even more stringent loss control measure would be to outsource the painting to a subcontractor or to move the painting process to a separate and special building designed to prevent or limit fire damage.

COPE: *Protection:* While protective devices primarily are loss reduction tools, if used effectively and creatively, their presence will also encourage prevention. For instance, a security alarm may do double duty: it may reduce the severity of burglary losses, and also, because of prominent notices that a premises is protected by such an alarm, decrease the probability of burglaries.

COPE: *Environment:* Maintaining safe surroundings will decrease the chance of asset losses. For example, removing debris or keeping lawns mowed will decrease the likelihood of fires. Unkempt premises are visual cues that security is lacking and serve as invitations to burglars and vandals. Likewise, businesses that lease their premises may be able to prevent losses by considering the occupancies of neighboring buildings or the types of neighboring tenants. For example, businesses may decide not to locate in a particular building because politically volatile organizations already lease space there.

ITIM: *Information management:* The actual sharing of information about prevention activities promotes loss prevention. Posting large and highly visible signs that night watchmen monitor a premise will discourage vandals. Notices that state "No more than $100 in cash on premises" will decrease the probability of crime.

However, sometimes not sharing information with others will also decrease the probability of crime. For example, randomly changing a money messenger's deposit times and routes will confuse and discourage potential robbers. Some companies may not post their names on their buildings to discourage politically motivated vandalism.

ITIM: *Transfers:* A well-established method to decrease the chance of asset losses is to transfer the responsibility for losses to others. It is common for a building owner to transfer the obligation to pay for property losses to the tenant-lessee. Often, the lessee is required to purchase property insurance to finance this transfer. Chapter 6 discusses in detail the contractual transfer of risk as a loss control activity.

ITIM: *Inspections:* A visual examination of assets is a good way to uncover potential loss causes. Inspections will decrease the probability of loss because the firm will be alerted to hazardous conditions and may take preventative actions before losses occur.

Property walk-throughs should be scheduled on a rotating basis to ensure that all assets are inspected at least annually. Inspections may be conducted by internal personnel, by external loss control specialists, or, if the property is insured, by insurance company loss control engineers. Recommendations that result from inspections should be prioritized and tracked by management through completion. Organizations may decide that some recommendations are too costly to implement after a quantitative analysis is completed (see Chapter 10 for information on methods to compute the value of loss control initiatives). The value of a loss control project is a function of many attributes, and setting priorities of which projects to initiate is a difficult decision for businesses.

ITIM: *Mandates:* Government requirements to implement loss control projects decrease the chance of asset losses. Schools and other public buildings, for example, are required to install certain lighting. This safety measure also provides benefits by decreasing the chance of vandalism and malicious mischief.

Fleet Safety—Proper vehicle maintenance is a key preventative activity for firms with fleets. activities such as rotating tires and changing oil will preserve the value of these assets. Keeping the interiors clean will discourage drivers from trashing the vehicles. Keeping the exteriors clean will discourage graffiti artists.

Crime—Prevention is the risk manager's primary tool for decreasing crime losses. Maintaining well-lit facilities with proper fencing and security guards will decrease many property losses. Proper building maintenance, such as a good roof or fresh paint, will help to prevent vandalism. Both show that someone cares about the building and that someone is around to catch vandals.

Intangibles—Controlling intangible assets such as patents, trademarks, Internet sites, and databases require special attention to loss prevention. While original documents can be copied and reproduced, it is usually more cost effective to protect the originals. Keeping them in a fireproof safe or safe-deposit box is an inexpensive way to decrease the probability of loss. Putting bold and prominent trademark notices and user announcements on Internet materials or software will decrease the likelihood that users will steal software or make unlicensed copies.

Asset Loss Reduction

Risk managers can decrease the severity of losses by implementing loss reduction plans that decrease the response time and the cost of losses. As in asset loss prevention, the elements of COPE can reduce asset losses.

COPE: *Construction:* Building fire walls and other barriers will limit the spread of fire, smoke, and other perils. Thus they are effective tools to decrease the severity of losses. Information on construction types and fire protection can be found in the section entitled **Asset Loss Prevention.**

COPE: *Occupancy:* Separation of occupancies is a major loss reduction tool. Dividing and separating operations into separate locations will limit the severity of losses, and restricting the use of buildings to certain activities will decrease the potential loss amounts. For example, putting a painting operation in a building that is separate from the inventory may decrease the severity of loss.

COPE: *Protection:* Fire protection is divided into public and private protection. Public protection involves the degree of prevention, detection, and extinguishment of fire capability in communities. Private fire protection involves efforts by individual organizations to prevent, detect, and extinguish fires on their own premises. Private fire protection involves the use of fire extinguishers, smoke alarms, central station alarms, and sprinkler systems on an organization's premises. But protection involves more than the danger of fire. For example, alarm systems protect against theft, and insurers provide premium discounts for buildings and vehicles with security alarms.

COPE: *Environment:* Proper housekeeping and maintenance are vital in decreasing the severity of property losses. By keeping flammable materials stored in proper receptacles and keeping lawns trimmed and grounds free of debris, the risk manager can reduce the spread of fire and related property perils. In addition, the adjacent buildings and their contents may affect the severity of loss. While the risk manager is limited in the responses to this hazard, she should be aware of the environment and other properties surrounding their buildings.

Consequential Loss Reduction

As a consequence of a direct property loss, a firm likely will incur down time and a loss of revenues or additional expenses. These consequential asset losses can be prevented or reduced by having contingency plans in place prior to any losses. For example, having spare parts on hand will allow the firm to minimize down time and lost sales. In addition, it may be more cost effective to store the spare parts than to have to special order them, at premium prices, after a loss. Replacing parts for older or obsolete equipment may pose special consequential loss problems, especially for manufacturing organizations. Sources of parts for such equipment should be identified, or difficult-to-obtain spare parts purchased, prior to any loss in order to reduce the possibility of extended down time.

Other Loss Reduction Tools

In addition to COPE and consequential loss reduction tools, there are four basic loss reduction tools. You may want to think of them as SDCS:

- Separation
- Duplication
- Contractual Transfer
- Salvage

Risk Management Tip

Ways to remember optional tools:

SDCS means Separation, Duplication, Contractual Transfer, and Salvage.

SDCS: *Separation:* Dividing an asset into parts and keeping the parts physically separated may reduce the likelihood of a total

loss through a single event. "Don't put all your eggs into one basket" is a familiar adage with practical applications in business. "Don't put all your inventory in one warehouse" is one loss reduction tool. Another is to keep back-up computer disks offsite and to back up information on a daily or more frequent basis.

Organizations with large fleets may want to consider the concentration of parked vehicles in specific locations. Separating fleets of parked vehicles may reduce losses from common hazards, such as vandalism, hail, or wind storms.

SDCS: *Duplication:* Any computer user knows the value of making back-up copies. Data losses happen frequently, and prudent risk managers will implement a systematic policy of off-site backup. Likewise, operation managers know that having replacement parts on hand can get production lines up and running quickly after a loss, thus reducing the total loss of revenues.

SDCS: *Contractual Transfers:* While transfers are an effective loss prevention tool, they also play an important role in loss reduction. Typical examples are leases, inventory control, and exculpatory contracts, many of which are discussed in Chapter 6. Two difficult, yet practical issues are 1) being sure that contracts are circulated to the risk management department, and 2) being sure that hazardous projects are reviewed by risk management before they're begun. Some organizations may use a dollar threshold before involving the risk manager. However, lower cost projects may also be very hazardous.

Leases: A risk manager decreases the severity of losses for a firm by leasing rather than owning assets. This transfers at least part of the loss to the owner. The lessee's loss severity is decreased because the owner is now bearing the risk of losses.

Inventory control: The risk manager

should review purchase orders and shipping contracts to make sure the ownership of goods is not accepted until the firm can cost effectively control losses. Just-in-time inventory is one tool to decrease loss severity (as well as reduce storage costs). Warehouse-to-warehouse shipping contracts usually transfer losses to the shipper until the goods reach the purchaser's premises.

Hold harmless and *indemnity* contracts are familiar tools to decrease loss potential. By transferring the legal responsibility for assets to others, the cost of losses can also be transferred.

SDC<u>S</u>: *Salvage:* Claims management is important to decreasing loss severity. By acting after losses occur, the risk manager can minimize further damage. One aspect of claims management is salvage. Selling partially damaged assets for scrap can help diminish the total cost of a loss.

LIABILITY LOSS CONTROL

Liability Loss Prevention

Liability losses primarily arise from alleged damage to third parties, which often result in lawsuits. Risk managers have several tools available to decrease the probability of being sued. But there are challenges in managing the source and amount of third-party suits. Some basic loss control measures are available.

Information management—The responses taken to potential liability suits can greatly impact their severity. Firms that cooperate and attempt to quickly settle problems may find potential plaintiffs willing to settle for significantly lesser dollar amounts. In some cases lawsuits can be totally avoided by apologies and relatively inexpensive measures. A visit by the risk manager or other senior company official to the hospital room of an injured party demonstrates humanitarian concern and may also reduce the liability award that is demanded. Adopting a corporate loss control policy statement in this area may be an effective tool. A sample policy provided in Figure 25.2.

Figure 25.2

Sample Accident/Claim Process Management Statement

(Applicable at Individual Company Locations)

❏ Treat injured persons as you would like to be treated. Be polite and courteous.

❏ Fully complete all accident reports. Do not give the report to the injured person to complete. Show that you want to be as helpful as possible.

❏ Keep all accident information confidential. Refer requests for accident information to the risk management department.

❏ Forward all accident reports immediately to the risk management department.

❏ Note general conditions of the accident area as completely as possible on the accident report. Take pictures of the area when possible.

❏ Apologize for any inconvenience but do not accept or admit responsibility or liability for the accident. Do not promise that any payment will be made.

❏ Refer requests for additional information from the injured party to the risk management department.

❏ Notify the risk management department or its designee of any developments.

Transfers—Contractual transfers, such as hold harmless and indemnity agreements, attempt to shift liability to others. Typical examples are found on tickets for parking lots, amusement parks, or sports arenas, as well as in property and equipment leases and injury waivers. Each will usually contain a statement that the owner is not responsible for any losses to the visitor or lessee or to their property.

The wording of these agreements differs according to purpose. In addition, legal counsel should be asked to review purchase orders for the applicability of similar wording. The risk manager may not be an attorney and may not be qualified to give legal advice.

Figure 25.3 includes sample wording for several types of hold harmless and indemnity agreements. *Wording for specific situations should be carefully worked out between risk managers and legal counsel.*

Figure 25.3

Facility Usage

ABC Companies, its heirs, and assigns, voluntarily agree to release, waive, discharge, hold harmless, defend and indemnify XYZ Company, its owners, agents, officers, and employees from any and all claims, actions, or losses for bodily injury, property damage, wrongful death, loss or services, or otherwise that may arise of out the use of _____ equipment and facilities. ABC Companies releases, discharges, and waives any claims or actions that may arise in the present or future for the negligent acts or other conduct by the owners, agents, officers, and employees of XYZ Company.

* * * *

Garage Waiver

Owner and company agree. All claimed damage or loss must be reported and itemized by customer to attendant in writing before car is taken from park, after loss occurs and if not so made is waived. Company has option to make repairs at its own expense of any claimed damage within 48 hours after filing a claim. In all court actions burden of proof to establish claim remains with customer. Court actions by customer for any claims must be filed within 90 days from date of parking, in court of jurisdiction where claimed loss occurs. Company not responsible for

damage by fire, or defective brakes, or parts, or for articles left in car unless separately checked with attendant, charge being $.25 per article. Total liability of company limited to $250 for all damage or loss to customer. Company not responsible for loss of use. Company not responsible for cars after closing time. Customer must set emergency brake before leaving car. This is the entire contract and no employee can modify it. It is not assignable. Customer waives all laws in conflict with the foregoing.

When you park car in unoccupied stall, you agree that it is at your sole risk, that you will lock same, and that possession and control of your car are yours.

* * * *

Property Rental

Lessee shall indemnify and agree to indemnify and save lessor, its successors, and assigns, harmless from any and all liability, damages, or loss, including reasonable legal fees, arising out of the ownership, selection, possession, leasing, renting, operation, control, use, condition (including but not limited to latent or other defects whether or not discoverable by the lessee), maintenance, delivery, and return of the equipment or in the event that the lessee shall be in default hereunder arising out of the condition of any item of equipment sold or disposed of after use by the lessee.

* * * *

Employee Use of Fitness Room

In condition of _____ Company's sponsorship of certain nonemployment-related recreational activities, including the company health and fitness center, I, _____ (an employee) of _____ Company agree for myself and my successors, assigns, heirs, executors, and administrators to indemnify and hold harmless _____ Company, its subsidiaries, divisions, affiliates, and their respective directors, officers, employees, agents from and against any and all claims, actions, causes of action, damages, suits, liabilities, and demands whatsoever in the event of any injury, loss, or damage I may sustain while participating in any company-sponsored sports or recreational activity, including the health and fitness center.

I understand the nature and purpose of the health and fitness center and am aware that any strenuous physical activity involves certain risks. It is my responsibility to consult with my doctor before beginning a physical exercise program. I am a voluntary participant in _____Company's health and fitness center and hereby assume the risk of any and all accidents or injuries of any kind that may be sustained by me by reason of or in connection with my participation in activities at the health and fitness center. I agree for myself and my successors, assigns, heirs, executors, and administrators to hereby release, discharge, and absolve _____Company, its subsidiaries, divisions, affiliates, and their respective directors, officers, employees, and agents from and against any and all claims, actions, causes of action, damages, suits, liabilities, and demands whatsoever in the event of any injury, loss, or damage I may sustain while participating in activities at the health and fitness center.

Fleet safety—Risk managers can decrease the probability of liability suits resulting from operating fleets by using two basics tools. First, Motor Vehicle Records (MVRs) should be run on all prospective and current drivers. Drivers with poor records or suspended licenses should not be allowed to drive company vehicles. A point system may be adopted for driver acceptability. Figure 25.4 shows an example of such a point system. Employers total the points for each driver and create a set of thresholds for employment. Figure 25.5 shows one example of driver employment guidelines.

Figure 25.4

Violation	Points
Speeding	2
Reckless driving	2
Careless driving (accident)	3
Driving Under the Influence	5
Other minor violations	1

The Driver's Privacy Protection Act of 1994 (DPPA), 18 U.S.C.S. §§2721-2725, outlines under which circumstances state motor vehicle departments should refrain from disclosing personal information on individuals that is contained in their motor vehicle records. Individual states also may have adopted regulations that regulate the release of such information.

Second, driver-training programs help prevent accidents and lawsuits. There are many sources for driver-training programs, including insurance company loss control department and outside vendo

Accident kits also may be included in company vehicles. Such kits, which are available from a number of sources, contain items such as instructions for handling an accident, flares, contact phone numbers, and insurance information.

Products—Product liability is a major concern for firms that manufacture or sell goods. To decrease the probability of lawsuits, the products should include proper labeling and packaging. Instructions for using the product should be clear and unambiguous. Risk managers have learned that even innocuous products such as hot coffee should have adequate warning labels. The risk manager should not rely upon the consumer's common sense but instead should work with the company's legal counsel to create package labels and product use instructions.

Common sense may not be enough!

Many risk managers recall the incident in which significant damages were assessed against McDonald's™ after a woman was burned when a cup of hot coffee spilled in her lap after she exited the drive-through restaurant. This demonstrates that assumptions of product use may not be enough protection against lawsuits.

Environmental—One of the most challenging liabilities for risk managers is the environmental liability exposure.

Being a good corporate citizen and having a pro-environment reputation are vital to ward off lawsuits. However, pollution abatement programs are very expensive, and risk managers must consider if proactive treatment of contaminants is justified.

Liability Loss Reduction

Risk managers should proactively manage all claims or possible lawsuits that are received. Several tools are available, and each has the potential to decrease the severity of liability losses. Refer to Chapter 13, Claims Management, for additional information on this subject.

Figure 25.5

Number of points	Applicants	Existing employees
More than 5 points	Do not hire	Terminate driving duties
3 to 5 points	Do not hire	Place on probation
1 to 2 points	Hire on probation	Issue warning
0 points	Hire	Issue commendation

Mediation—Allowing an unbiased third party to conduct nonbinding mediation can decrease the severity of liability claims. Mediation is also an effective prevention tool if used as soon as the firm becomes aware of a potential suit. A related tool is arbitration. While this tool legally binds the parties to a settlement, the total cost is usually significantly less than courtroom costs.

Jurisdiction—If mediation or arbitration is not used, risk managers may reduce the severity of liability losses by selecting the venue for litigation. Some areas, such as California and New York, are considered more favorable to plaintiffs than other jurisdictions. When negotiating contracts, risk managers should consider the jurisdictions that are noted for resolution of disagreements.

Legal Counsel—Risk managers who proactively retain counsel decrease their long-term loss costs. Having a lawyer as part of the claims management team will help assure the organization that proper legal procedures are followed and claimants are treated fairly.

Political Action—Although controversial, many firms and trade associations take proactive steps to promote liability reform and favorable governmental mandates. These often involve attempts to decrease the severity of lawsuits by placing statutory caps or limits on certain classes of suits.

Transfers—Contractual transfers are effective in decreasing liability losses. Two examples are incorporation and exculpatory contracts.

Incorporation or LLP—Many firms use the legal structure of incorporation or a Limited Liability Partnership (LLP), to protect the assets of owners. In the corporate structure, shareholders' losses are limited to their investment; liability losses are transferred to society. In an LLP, the partner's liability to third parties is similarly limited to their capital contribution.

Exculpatory Contracts—Contractual loss-financing transfers may decrease the impact of liability losses on a firm. One common transfer technique is to require vendors to name the owner as an additional insured on their general liability insurance and to furnish certificates of insurance evidencing coverage and the additional insured status. Another common transfer tool is to require subcontractors to assume liability for their activities and to hold the general contractor or owner harmless. These tools may reduce losses by limiting the firm's liability to an excess basis over their subcontractors.

Services may be provided without written contracts, often through purchase orders. One tool that may be used for these situations is to include hold harmless and/or indemnification wording on all purchase orders and require that vendors acknowledge it by signature. Risk managers should seek the opinion of their legal counsel when drafting such language.

Medical payments coverage—Many risk managers purchase commercial general liability policies that include medical payments coverage. Medical payments coverage provides a capped amount of coverage for medical bills arising from injury on the insured's premises, regardless of fault. Some risk managers believe that the use of medical payments results in fewer liability lawsuits because injured parties are less likely to sue if their expenses are paid.

HUMAN RESOURCE LOSS CONTROL

Human Resource Loss Prevention

Prevention is a wise course of action for human resource managers. Life-safety engineers, epidemiologists, and many other specialties have developed to assure the organization's most valuable assets—its people—are protected.

Below is a brief description of some of the tools used to prevent injury. The acronym SOAP helps keep a clean operation.

SOAP: *Specialization:* Allowing employees to become experts in their field gives them more experience and knowledge in a specific job function. Their specialized skills serve to prevent accidents and injuries. Training programs are valid tools in this area.

S**O**AP: *Organization:* By creating the appropriate business structure and interdepartmental relationships, the organization can decrease the chance that people will be harmed. Knowing the appropriate chains of command may prevent people from assuming duties outside their areas of expertise.

SO**A**P: *Activities:* Restricting the employee's activities to those for which they are trained will decrease the chance that people will be hurt while on the job. For example, permitting only certain employees into electrical closets will decrease the probability of electrical injury. Allowing only trained cutters to use saws or other cutting tools may decrease the chance of injury. Training and rigidly enforced rules about confined space entry are other examples of this tool.

SOA**P**: *Physical:* The demographic characteristics of employees can affect their chance of loss. Younger employees may be more prone to vehicle accidents. Employees with muscular builds may be more suited to lifting and carrying duties without injuring themselves. While a risk manager should legally discriminate among employee attributes to decrease the likelihood that an employee will be injured, the risk manager should simultaneously be aware of illegal discrimination. These concerns are codified in various state and federal codes. The **Where Can I Find Out More About It?** section at the end of this chapter provides some sources for these codes.

Human Factors—Understanding the interaction of people and machines helps risk managers select machines, people, and operations to prevent accidents. Ergonomics is the study of creating safe interactions of people with tools and equipment. Although its cost effectiveness is controversial, ergonomic standards have proven to decrease the likelihood of many work-related injuries. Installing properly engineered workstations, for example, will decrease the chance of many types of injuries.

Industrial Engineering—Workplace design is not only effective at decreasing the chance of worker injuries; it also decreases the chance of employer liability suits. OSHA engineers will work with firms to create safe operating environments that protect workers' safety.

Background checks—Risk managers should carefully check references and past employment histories before hiring new workers. Employees with a history of claims may increase the firm's chance of future workers compensation claims. However, the risk manager must be very careful to comply with hiring laws and regulations to avoid discrimination and employment practices liability.

Physical examinations—An effective tool to decrease the chance of worker injuries is to match the physiological abilities of workers with tasks. Asking a ninety-pound employee to lift one-hundred-pound bags is asking for injuries. Testing workers' physical skills will provide useful information to determine where that person may be best used. Full descriptions of all jobs should be written to include physical requirements. The risk manager should be sure the physical requirements match the applicant's abilities and that no employment or anti-discrimination laws are broken.

Psychological testing—Some employees are better suited to stressful jobs; some prefer inside jobs; some work best alone. Understanding the optimal utilization of human resources is an effective loss prevention tool. Psychological testing provides the risk manager with this information. Once again, the risk manager is cautioned that psychological testing must be job/skill related and cannot be illegally discriminatory.

Behavior modification—Many tools are available to modify worker behavior; a key tool is education. Educating workers about the theories and reasons for safety helps workers understand how modifying their behavior will improve their personal safety. It will also motivate them to behave in less risky ways and decrease the probability of personnel losses.

Safety training—Once workers are educated about why they should behave safely, risk managers can begin to teach them specific tools to decrease the chance of losses. Prevention tools, such as wellness programs and proper operating techniques, help prevent injuries.

Incentive programs—Safety incentive programs are a controversial yet effective tool for risk managers. These programs reward workers for working safely and not getting injured. However, for a variety of reasons, especially to enhance a team's chances of winning the incentive premium, some injuries may not be reported. It is possible the frequency of loss may decrease while simultaneously increasing the severity of loss.

Human Resource Loss Reduction

Risk managers should plan ahead for losses and react quickly to them. These tools will help to decrease the severity of personnel losses.

Physical fitness programs—One tool to decrease loss severity is to keep workers in top physical condition. A healthy body heals much faster than one that is out of shape. Closely related are wellness programs. Helping employees to quit smoking or to maintain healthy diets promotes health and safety.

Separation—Many large firms have travel policies that forbid senior executives from flying together on the same plane or driving together in the same car. By separating key employees, losses will have a lesser impact on the firm.

Duplication—Some firms have one key employee upon whom the firm's success depends. The loss of that worker may have catastrophic effects. A vital formula, recipe, or production technique may be lost with the loss of that employee. Therefore, risk managers need to encourage the cross-training of employees so they can quickly take over for lost employees. Cross-training also motivates workers to higher productivity levels.

Loss monitoring tools—Effective claims management has proven to decrease the severity of losses. By keeping on top of claims, risk managers can make sure medical bills and workers compensation claims are reasonable and justified. Many third-party administrators are available to assist risk managers in using risk management information systems (RMIS) and to monitor claims.

Return-to-work tools—Another tool to help decrease the total cost of personnel losses is to adopt return-to-work programs. Partial disabilities may prevent workers from doing their primary jobs, but the worker still may be able to contribute to the firm's productivity. Most workers want to contribute and feel a sense of pride in being part of a prosperous team. Allowing them to return to work and perform light-duty jobs will decrease the total cost of loss and encourage a positive organizational culture. It is important that full job descriptions be written, including physical requirements, before a return-to-work program is initiated.

WHERE CAN I FIND OUT MORE ABOUT IT?

Asset Loss Control Resources

http://www.nfpa.org/Home/AboutNFPA/index.asp

http://www.iso.com/

http://www.iso.com/site_search_process.cfm

Liability Loss Control Resources

Lange, Scott K., et al. *e-risk: Liabilities in a Wired World,* Cincinnati: The National Underwriter Company, 2000.

ABS Consulting. www.govinst.com for information on CFRs and environmental loss control.

http://www.rims.org/template.cfm?Template=/Search/SearchDisplay.cfm

http://www.adtsweb.com/

Human Resource Loss Control Resources

ABS Consulting. www.govinst.com for information on CFRs and ADA compliance.

QUESTIONS AND ANSWERS

Question—What is the best way to set up a property inspection program?

Answer—First, the risk manager should be familiar with the organization's mission and risk philosophy. Next, the risk manager should create a schedule of all of the organization's properties. Ask several other managers to review this schedule to be sure that no properties were omitted. Next, become familiar with the different types of construction and protection. Only now is the risk manager ready to go out into the field. Each real property asset should be measured and photographed. Make notes about any unusual physical features. Record the physical condition of the property. For business personal property the method of inspection depends on the type of property. But, in general, an inspection should include measurements, photos, and descriptions.

Question—We have a high incidence of employee injuries in the warehouse. What is the best way to attack this problem?

Answer—First, make sure the organization mission and strategies are understood. A large number of small injuries may be an acceptable loss for a large, aggressive company. However, a large number of serious injuries is almost always unacceptable.

In these cases, the risk manager should be sure to have a good record of the severity and frequency of injuries. Next, a fault tree analysis or hazard analysis may be used to try to understand the causes of the losses and the conditions or events that precipitated the losses. The risk manager should not try to place blame but instead should try to understand the hazards that increased the probability and/or severity of losses. By focusing on the hazard, the risk manager is more effective in correcting future incidents.

Question—We are very careful to have all large contracts reviewed by legal counsel and the risk manager. However, we recently were involved in a serious accident that was caused by a subcontractor. The dollar amount of the contract with the subcontractor was relatively low, so no one considered having the arrangement reviewed.

As a consequence, the subcontractor does not have sufficient insurance to pay for the damage, and our company is not even an additional insured on the subcontractor's insurance. How could we have better handled this situation?

Answer—Contract analysis is a critical responsibility of risk managers. <u>All</u> contracts should be reviewed or passed on to legal counsel. The small amount of time required to do the job right the first time is much smaller than the amount of time a defendant spends in the courtroom. Using "additional insured" endorsements on insurance contracts is a good way to transfer the financing of risk.

Question—We are setting up guidelines on the use of company vehicles by employees. What types of items should we consider in this?

Answer—First the risk manager must consider the organization's goals and risk philosophy. If the firm wants to decrease the probability of losses, then the vehicles must be maintained in good working order. Second, all drivers must be screened and their driving records reviewed on a regular basis. Letting the drivers know that the risk manager is actively working on driver and fleet safety with alert the drivers to the program.

Figure 25.6

	FORMS AND CHECKLISTS		

Categories of Tools

	Assets	Liabilities	Human Resources
Loss Prevention	Construction	Information Management	Specialization
	Occupancy	Contractual Transfers	Organization
	Protection	Fleet Safety	Activities
	Environment	Products	Physical
	Information Management	Environmental	Human Factors
	Contractual Transfers		Industrial Engineering
	Inspections		Background Checks
	Mandates		Physical Exams
	Fleet Safety		Background Checks
	Crime Prevention		Behavior Modification
	Intangibles		Safety Training
			Incentive Programs
Loss Reduction	Separation	Arbitration	Physical Fitness
	Duplication	Mediation	Separation
	Contractual Transfers	Jurisdiction	Duplication
	Salvage	Legal Counsel	Return-to-Work
	Construction	Political Action	
	Occupancy	Transfers	
	Protection	Medical Payments	
	Environment		

Chapter 25

GLOSSARY

Arbitration. Referring a dispute to an impartial third party. The parties in dispute agree in advance to abide by the arbitrator's decision, which is issued after the positions of both parties are heard.

Hold harmless agreement. A contractual arrangement in which one party assumes the liability inherent in a situation, thereby relieving the other party of responsibility.

Indemnity agreement. A contractual arrangement in which one party (indemnitor) agrees to restore the other party (indemnitee) in whole or in part for loss or damage arising from some contemplated act or responsibility assumed by the indemnitee or from a claim or demand of a third person.

Mediation. The act of a third person intervening between two contending parties with the intent of persuading them to adjust or settle a dispute or attempting to settle a dispute through the action of a neutral intermediary. Mediation usually is not legally binding.

Chapter 26

THE CERTIFICATE OF INSURANCE

WHAT IS IT?

Certificates of insurance provide evidence that risks of loss have been transferred to an insurance company. This accomplishes the risk management technique of *transfer*, in which the financial consequence of risk is transferred to another party.

Refresher

Remember that there are insurance and noninsurance transfers. Buying liability insurance is an insurance transfer—the risk of financial loss is transferred to the insurer. Conversely, entering into a *hold harmless agreement* with another party, through which that party agrees to assume your liability, is an example of a noninsurance transfer.

The insurance certificate is a document that is provided by a contractor, business, or other entity to document that it has insurance coverage. Sample blank ACORD (Association for Cooperative Operations Research and Development) forms are included in the appendix to this chapter.

Insurance certificates are frequently and widely used in risk management. A business will want to know—and in many cases will even require—that entities it does business with have appropriate and adequate insurance coverage. The insurance certificate provides this assurance. To illustrate, a company hires temporary workers through a professional employer organization (PEO). The contract between the PEO and the hiring firm requires that the PEO provide workers compensation coverage for the temporary employees. The employer—who may have a liability exposure for injury to the temp employees—wants to be sure that, indeed, the required coverage is in place. The hiring firm requests, and the PEO provides (probably through its insurance agent or broker) the insurance certificate, stating the existence and terms of the required insurance.

Terminology Tip

Certificate holder is another term for the business that requests that a certificate of insurance be issued to it by a contractor or vendor (literally, the party holding the certificate). As seen in the sample Certificates of Insurance reprinted in the chapter appendix, the *certificate holder* is entered in the block at the bottom left of the form. This indicates the name of the entity that required the evidence of coverage.

BUSINESS USES

Note that the insurance certificate is only evidence of a risk transfer. It is not a risk transfer in itself. The certificate is a statement that insurance is in place, but it is not an insurance policy. Therefore, if there is any discrepancy between what is stated on the certificate and the coverage that the policy actually provides, the policy takes precedence. For example, a property owner is constructing a building. The owner will want to be sure that contractors, subcontractors, vendors, and suppliers on the project are appropriately insured, at least for the liability that may attach to the property owner. In fact, the property owner will have adopted insurance requirements for contractors and vendors that spell out what kinds and how much insurance coverage is required. Additional information on this is found in the section entitled **Step One: Drafting Insurance Requirements.**

Instead of the property owner arranging the required insurance, a certificate of insurance is requested from each contractor or vendor. Certificates of insurance are generally issued by the contractor's or vendor's agent or broker to show the coverage in place at the time the certificate is issued. See the sections entitled **Advantages** and **Disadvantages** for more on this.

The vast majority of insurance certificates are issued using standard forms. These standard forms are produced by the Association for Cooperative Operations Research and Development. ACORD serves the industry by developing standards that enable industry information sharing. ACORD has the support and participation of more than 1,000 insurance carriers and groups, 25,000 agencies, the major providers of software and services to the industry, and nonprofit associations including agency information-system user groups, national producer associations, and the Certified Property and Casualty Underwriters (CPCU) Society.

Annually, ACORD issues more than six million certificates, with at least twenty million more being issued by agents and brokers through onsite computers licensed by ACORD. Note, however, that while ACORD forms are the predominant standard used, they are not exclusively employed. Some brokers, carriers, or corporations may use nonstandard or manuscript forms. Additionally, many municipalities have developed their own forms that incorporate additional contractual terms and conditions. Contracting and bargaining power of the entity that requests the certificate will dictate whether variations will be accepted by its contractors and suppliers—as well as their insurance carriers.

There are times when risk managers will request a revision in the standard wording that is found on an ACORD certificate. Some businesses may require that their subcontractors and vendors use nonstandard certificate forms. Since the insurance industry has generally adopted the standardized ACORD forms, any deviations from them must be approved by the insurance companies whose coverage they represent. Therefore, the insurance carrier(s) that are represented on them must approve changes in wording and substitute formats.

The purpose of insurance certificates can be contrasted to the purpose of *additional insured* status under another business's insurance policy. Additional insured status is generally implemented by endorsement to a business's insurance policy. This endorsement designates that a party other than the insured business is *an additional insured* under the policy. This brings the additional insured under the protection of the policy. This is a direct transfer of risk; the additional insured party now has the benefits of being an insured under the policy. But gaining additional insured status—while necessary in some situations—is not always practical, efficient, or even possible.

The insurance certificate, in contrast, does not convey any rights under the insurance policies it represents. It merely provides evidence that the business party has the required insurance in place.

Certificates of insurance are crucial to the transacting of business, and are used in a multitude of situations. Among the uses of certificates of insurance might be (but by no means limited to)

- a volunteer showing a local charity that she has personal auto coverage;

- a major international manufacturer assuring distributors that product liability coverage is in force;

- a one person accounting firm complying with a 500-square-foot office lease;

- a 1,000 store retail chain complying with shopping mall leases in every state;

- a sole proprietor contractor replacing the front door on your home;

- a 5,000 employee international contractor building a fifty-story-office building;

- professional liability exposure for doctors, engineers, insurance agents, and other E&O situations

There are many types of certificate of insurance forms, such as the ACORD-25 (Certificate of Liability Insurance), ACORD 24 (Certificate of Property Insurance), and ACORD 27 (Evidence of Property Insurance). Their individual attributes are discussed further in the **Design Features** section of this chapter.

STEPS TO IMPLEMENT

Step One: Drafting Insurance Requirements

Businesses must establish the insurance requirements for entities doing business with it. Prudent risk managers will require that all contractors, independent contractors, subcontractors, vendors, and other suppliers that do business with their firms have adequate and appropriate insurance coverage. Since the insurance certificate is evidence of proper coverage, all such contractors and vendors should be required to meet minimum insurance requirements before their employees, equipment, or products are used. In fact, risk managers should adopt a policy that no contractor or supplier be allowed to start performing its work before submitting an insurance certificate showing full compliance with the risk manager's insurance standards.

A business can generally create insurance standards that fit the majority of cases but can be adjusted for particular situations. Insurance requirements usually are included in contracts between the enterprise and any other entity performing work for or supplying goods to the business. Some businesses may include their insurance requirements even on purchase orders.

One company's insurance requirements policy reads:

Insurance Coverage	Limits
Commercial general liability: The coverage must include blanket contractual liability and personal injury with the contractual exclusion deleted.	The minimum acceptable limit is $1,000,000 each occurrence on a combined single limit basis for bodily injury and property damage, $1,000,000 personal and advertising injury limit, and $2,000,000 general and products/completed operations aggregate limits.
Business autombile: To include coverage for owned, hired, and nonowned vehicles.	The minimum acceptable limit is $1,000,000 per occurrence on a combined single limit basis for bodily injury and property damage.
Workers compensation: Should provide the benefits as mandated by the state workers compensation statutes.	The minimum acceptable employers liability limit is $500,000 for bodily injury by accident and $500,000 for bodily injury by disease.
Commercial Umbrella	The minimum acceptable limit is $5,000,000 per occurrence with $5,000,000 aggregate. The umbrella shall cover over the primary emloyers liability limits.
Professional Liability (if applicable)	The minimum acceptable limit is $1,000,000 per occurrence with a $1,000,000 aggregate.

Note that the requirements above only contemplate liability coverage. Financial institutions, lessors, landlords, and other entities with interest in property that is to be insured by another business will also require property insurance. They will require that the other party carry direct property damage insurance for buildings, equipment, improvements and betterments, stock, and miscellaneous property for replacement cost with sufficient limits to avoid coinsurance penalties. The requirement may also call for business income coverage for loss of profits and extra expense coverage. Further, the perils required to be insured against must be spelled out.

Step Two: Tracking Contracts

Each contract the business enters into must be reviewed with insurance standards in mind. Are the insurance requirements spelled out adequately? Is the contract clear that insurance certificates need to be supplied prior to any work being done, materials supplied, or contracting employees allowed on premises? A system should be in place for review of contractor or supplier contracts by the risk manager. Even boilerplate documents, such as purchase orders, should be re-

viewed to be sure that the contracting entity's insurance standards are clear.

Step Three: Collecting Insurance Certificates

The collection of insurance certificates is a Herculean task full of detail, but it is extremely important. In major corporations, there are literally tens of thousands of contracts to monitor and insurance certificates to track. Generally, upon entering into a contract with a vendor or contractor, the hiring party will send an initial request letter (generally a prepared form letter) restating the insurance requirements and requesting the certificate. Figure 26.1 is a sample certificate request letter.

Some companies request the insurance certificate within a certain number of days of receipt of the initial request; others simply state it is needed as soon as possible. However, it is generally prudent to be sure that certificates are on file prior to allowing work to begin, product to be delivered, or the contractor's employees to be allowed on premises. Usually, the contractor's or vendor's insurance agent or broker will respond to the request for insurance certificates.

Figure 26.1

INITIAL REQUEST LETTER

NAME OF CONTRACTOR

City, State, ZIP

INSURANCE REQUIREMENTS

Dear Sir:

Please note that your Certificate of Insurance must be issued complying with the following requirements:

1.   The Entity is named as an Additional Insured as respects this project.

2.   The General Liability and Automobile Liability limits must be:

   a.   Combined single limits $1,000,000 per occurrence and $2,000,000 aggregate (Commercial General Liability)

   b.   Combined single limit $1,000,000 (Automobile)

1.   The Umbrella limits must be a minimum of $5,000,000 per occurrence/$5,000,000 aggregate and must apply over employers liability.

2.   The General Liability policy must evidence these coverages:

   a.   "Occurrence" coverage

   b.   Contractual liability

   c.   Personal injury

   d.   Explosion, collapse, and underground coverage (if applicable)

   e.   Premisis/operations and products/completed operations

1.   Thirty (30) day notice of cancellation, nonrenewal or coverage/limit reduction.

2.   Cancellation wording on the certificate shall be as follows:

   "Should any of the above described policies be cancelled, nonrenewed, reduced in coverage or limits before the expiration date, the issuing company will provide thirty (30) days written notice to the Entity.

3.   Best Rating should be A- or above with a policy holder surplus of $100,000,000.

Please forward your certificate of insurance as soon as possible.

Sincerely,

Entity

Step Four: Ensuring Compliance

The next step is ensuring that the certificate is received and complies with the insurance requirements stated in the contract or purchase order. Each certificate should be reviewed against the contract to see that the coverage required is the same as that carried. A sample certificate of insurance checklist (Figure 26.2) is helpful for this. If the certificate does not comply with the insurance requirements, a form noncompliance letter may be sent (see Figure 26.3).

Step Five: Monitoring

Insurance policies expire, limits are depleted or exhausted, and conditions change. So it is incumbent upon the risk manager to implement a tracking system. Here is an example of a monitoring policy that is derived from one corporation's risk management manual:

Certificate of Insurance Monitoring Policy

Requesting and maintaining certificates of insurance is an important function for all entities, whether public or private.

This procedure is to be adopted by all entities under the direction of ABC Holding Company.

In order for the procedure to function properly, each subsidiary should:

- Incorporate the minimum insurance requirements into all applicable contracts.

- Assign one individual the responsibility of maintaining the certificates in each department. [**Note:** in some corporations, the risk management department has responsibility for insurance certificates corporate-wide.]

- Log the names, expiration dates, and a brief description of the vendor supplying the certificate into a computer or manual file.

- Records may be kept by type of vendor, for example, road, demolition, and painting, but they should also be kept by year.

- The person responsible for certificates at the subsidiary will also be responsible for obtaining new certificates as existing ones expire.

[**Note: a separate master log of certificate expiration dates may prove helpful.**]

- Exceptions for higher/lower limits or incomplete certificates require management approval with copies of the exception forwarded to the corporate risk management department.

ADVANTAGES

The advantages of ensuring that all contractors and suppliers are insured for appropriate amounts include:

- peace of mind

- reduction of the chance of unanticipated expense arising from loss or litigation involving the acts or products of contractors and suppliers

- evidence that the subcontractor or vendor has taken steps to treat its own exposures and is appropriately insured itself

- compliance with sound risk management principles

- in some cases a reduction in premium rates when substantial amounts of work are done by subcontractors

DISADVANTAGES

There are several disadvantages to using certificates of insurance as a risk management tool. The following are among them.

- Certificates are for information purposes only. As printed right at the top of the ACORD forms, a certificate is "...issued as a matter of information only and confers no rights upon the certificate holder. . ." Contrast this to additional insured status under a liability policy, where the additional insured does actually have coverage under the other party's policy. An insurance certificate is evidence of coverage, but it is not coverage itself.

- There has to be a trust relationship between the certificate holder and the entity providing the certificate. If, for example, the entity proffering

Figure 26.2

CERTIFICATE OF INSURANCE CHECKLIST

Contractor_____

Type of Contract - Construction/Professional/Service

A.	Coverage	Carrier	Best Rating
1.	General Liability		
2.	Workers Compensation		
3.	Automobile		
4.	Umbrella/Excess		

B.	Coverage	Policy Limits	Contract Limits
1.	General Liability		
2.	Employers Liability (E.L.)		
3.	Automobile		
4.	Umbrella/Excess		

C. <u>General Liability</u>

   1. Occurrence Form

   2. Blanket Contractual Liability

   3. Personal Injury

   4. Completed Operations/Products

   5. Independent Contractors

   6. The Entity is named as an Additional Insured

C. <u>Automobile</u>

   1. Owned

   2. Nonowned

   3. Hired

C. <u>Cancellation Provisions</u>

   1. Thirty-day notice

   2. "Endeavor" deleted

   3. Expanded to nonrenewal/reduction in coverages or limits

Date_____Reviewed by_____

Figure 26.3

NONCOMPLIANCE LETTER

NAME OF CONTRACTOR
City, State, ZIP

CERTIFICATES OF INSURANCE

Dear Sir:

We have reviewed the certificate of insurance submitted by your company. Please make these changes on the certificate and resubmit the certificate:

( )   Failure to list the Entity as an additional insured.

( )   Improper notice of cancellation wording. The wording shall be as follows:

   "Should any of the above described policies be cancelled, nonrenewed, reduced in coverage or limits, the issuing company will provide thirty (30) days written notice to the Entity.

( )   The General Liability policy does not indicate "occurrence" coverage.

( )   The General Liability limits are not "Combined Single Limit" $1,000,000 / $2,000,000 Aggregate

( )   Automobile Liability limits are not "combined Single Limit $1,000,000"

( )   No coverage is evidenced for these policies

   ( )   General Liability
   ( )   Automobile Liability
   ( )   Workers Compensation and Employers Liability
   ( )   Umbrella Policy

( )   The General Liability does not evidence coverage for
   ( )   Contractual liability
   ( )   Personal injury
   ( )   Explosion, collapse, and underground hazards
   ( )   Products / completed operations

( )   The Automobile Liability does not evidence coverage for:
   ( )   Hired vehicles
   ( )   Owned vehicles
   ( )   Nonowned vehicles
   ( )   The following insurance company(ies) do(es) not have an A- or better Best Rating, or a policyholder surplus in excess of $100,000,000:

   1.   _____
   2.   _____
   3.   _____
   4.   _____

the certificate cancels the policy the day after the certificate is issued, the certificate holder will have no recourse against the insurance company in the event of a loss.

- Other language that is preprinted on certain insurance certificates is also relevant here. The coverages section of the ACORD 24 certificate is introduced with the following: "This is to certify that the policies of insurance listed below have been issued to the insured named above for the policy period indicated. Notwithstanding any requirement, term or condition of any contract of other document with respect to which this certificate may be issued or may pertain, the insurance afforded by the policies described herein is subject to all the terms, exclusions, and conditions of such policies. Limits shown may have been reduced by paid claims." The ACORD 25 has substantially the same information. This reiterates the certificates' information-only status. Although coverage is in place in the amount required, limits may be less than adequate due to previous claims made against the policies listed.

- Another area of concern regarding the use of some ACORD forms involves the matter of cancellation of the insured's coverage. The certificate states, "Should any of the above described policies be cancelled before the expiration date thereof, the issuing company will endeavor to mail _____ days written notice to the certificate holder named. But failure to mail such notice shall impose no obligation or liability of any kind upon the company, its agents or representatives."

The challenge for risk managers is obvious: the insurance company's only obligation is *to endeavor* to mail cancellation notices to certificate holders. Although some insurance companies have cancellation notice processes in place, others do not even attempt to provide notice of cancellation to certificate holders. There is no recourse to the certificate holder (against the insurance company) in the event such notice is overlooked and the insured's coverage is cancelled after issuance of the certificate.

In 1974, the federal appeals court ruled in *US Pipe & Foundry Co. v. USF&G*, 505 F. 2d 88, that a certificate is not a contract between the certificate holder and the insurer. It only provides information to an interested third party that insurance is in force at the time of issuance. The court stated, "The provision regarding notification in the event of cancellation is a mere promise, unsupported by any consideration."

- On occasion, risk managers are dissatisfied with the information-only nature of the certificate of insurance and attempt to fashion their own forms to create legal obligations beyond the evidence-only nature of the certificate. Or they may attempt to create an actual obligation on the insurer's part to provide notice of cancellation. Although there are some corporations with the clout to enforce the use of these modifications, they are outside the industry standard and are generally resisted by underwriters, insurance agents, and other representatives of insurers.

In addition, most state insurance regulators will not permit modifications to printed text in certificates unless the modified certificates are filed with them—an impractical task.

DESIGN

Three standard forms of insurance certificates are promulgated by ACORD. In 1996, ACORD printed and distributed more than sixty-five million of its more than 300 forms. Although only three of ACORD's more than 300 forms are certificates of insurance, they represent more than 10 percent—or twenty-five million—of the printed forms.

Samples of the three forms are reprinted in the chapter appendix. They are: the certificate of liability insurance ACORD 25 (Figure 26.4); certificate of property insurance ACORD 24 (Figure 26.5); and the evidence of property insurance ACORD 27 (Figure 26.6). Each has its own use.

The **ACORD 25** evidences casualty (liability) coverage and is used to show the type and limits of liability coverage that are in place for the insured business. For example, a building owner who needs to verify coverage of a contractor prior to the contractor beginning remodeling or renovation work may request the ACORD 25.

The **ACORD 24** is the property version of the ACORD 25. It is used to evidence that appropriate or required property coverage is in place. Form 24 is used to show that a building tenant maintains property coverage on leased premises.

ACORD 27, as opposed to ACORD 25 and ACORD 24, is used when the certificate holder has an interest in the covered property, such as through being a lien holder or mortgagee. This form—the Evidence of Property Insurance—provides an assurance for mortgagees, additional insureds, and loss payees that property is insured as required by the lender. The American Bankers Association, Mortgage Bankers Association of America, the Home Loan Bank Board, and the Federal National Mortgage Association provided input in the development of this form.

A very substantial difference between the ACORD 27 and ACORD forms 24 and 25 exists. Whereas forms 24 and 25 convey no rights under the insurance policy to the certificate holder, the ACORD 27 does convey policy rights. This includes the right to notice of cancellation.

WHERE CAN I FIND OUT MORE ABOUT IT?

Selected Case Law

There are a few law cases illustrating points involving insurance certificates that may be of interest to risk managers:

US Pipe v. USF&G (505 F. 2d 88 (1974) is the defining court decision with respect to the concept that an insurance policy is a contract between an insurer and an insured, and no one else. Certificates in and of themselves do not alter the insurance contract, and are not part of the policy (contract) in any event. Therefore they are basically informational.

Criterion Leasing vs. Gulf Coast, 582 So.2d 799 (Fla. Dist. Ct. App. 1991) illustrates the difference in the court's opinion *when the certificate is issued by the insurer itself.* The reason why the court found that the insurer should pay the claim was the fact that the insurer made a promise when it issued the certificate.

Dunmenic vs. Union Oil, 606 N.E. 2d 230 (Ill. App. Ct. 1992) illustrates situations in which the agent is representing the company because the agent had the authority to do so (apparent authority).

Other Resources

Risk and Insurance Management Society. 1999. *Certificates of Insurance: A Manual Prepared by the RIMS Research Committee.* New York: Risk and Insurance Management Society.

National Underwriter Company. November 1999. "Certificates of Insurance", *The Fire, Casualty and Surety Bulletins (FC&S),* Personal Lines Volume, General section, C-1 to 12.

Marsh, James P. June 2002. "Certificates Of Insurance in Construction Accident Coverage Litigation: The Disclaimer Language Is Effective", *DCBA Brief Online (Journal of the DuPage County Bar Assn.)* (http://www.dcba.org/brief/junissue/2002/art40602.htm)

FAQs About Certificates o-f Insurance, Office of General Counsel, Maricopa Community College, http://www.dist.maricopa.edu/legal/dp/inbrief/1FAQins.htm

Appendix

Figure 26.4

ACORD™ **CERTIFICATE OF LIABILITY INSURANCE**		DATE (MM/DD/YYYY)

PRODUCER	THIS CERTIFICATE IS ISSUED AS A MATTER OF INFORMATION ONLY AND CONFERS NO RIGHTS UPON THE CERTIFICATE HOLDER. THIS CERTIFICATE DOES NOT AMEND, EXTEND OR ALTER THE COVERAGE AFFORDED BY THE POLICIES BELOW.		
	INSURERS AFFORDING COVERAGE		**NAIC #**
INSURED	INSURER A:		
	INSURER B:		
	INSURER C:		
	INSURER D:		
	INSURER E:		

COVERAGES

THE POLICIES OF INSURANCE LISTED BELOW HAVE BEEN ISSUED TO THE INSURED NAMED ABOVE FOR THE POLICY PERIOD INDICATED. NOTWITHSTANDING ANY REQUIREMENT, TERM OR CONDITION OF ANY CONTRACT OR OTHER DOCUMENT WITH RESPECT TO WHICH THIS CERTIFICATE MAY BE ISSUED OR MAY PERTAIN, THE INSURANCE AFFORDED BY THE POLICIES DESCRIBED HEREIN IS SUBJECT TO ALL THE TERMS, EXCLUSIONS AND CONDITIONS OF SUCH POLICIES. AGGREGATE LIMITS SHOWN MAY HAVE BEEN REDUCED BY PAID CLAIMS.

INSR LTR	ADD'L INSRD	TYPE OF INSURANCE	POLICY NUMBER	POLICY EFFECTIVE DATE (MM/DD/YY)	POLICY EXPIRATION DATE (MM/DD/YY)	LIMITS	
		GENERAL LIABILITY				EACH OCCURRENCE	$
		COMMERCIAL GENERAL LIABILITY				DAMAGE TO RENTED PREMISES (Ea occurence)	$
		☐ CLAIMS MADE ☐ OCCUR				MED EXP (Any one person)	$
						PERSONAL & ADV INJURY	$
						GENERAL AGGREGATE	$
		GEN'L AGGREGATE LIMIT APPLIES PER: ☐ POLICY ☐ PRO-JECT ☐ LOC				PRODUCTS - COMP/OP AGG	$
		AUTOMOBILE LIABILITY				COMBINED SINGLE LIMIT (Ea accident)	$
		ANY AUTO					
		ALL OWNED AUTOS				BODILY INJURY (Per person)	$
		SCHEDULED AUTOS					
		HIRED AUTOS				BODILY INJURY (Per accident)	$
		NON-OWNED AUTOS					
						PROPERTY DAMAGE (Per accident)	$
		GARAGE LIABILITY				AUTO ONLY - EA ACCIDENT	$
		ANY AUTO				OTHER THAN AUTO ONLY: EA ACC	$
						AGG	$
		EXCESS/UMBRELLA LIABILITY				EACH OCCURRENCE	$
		☐ OCCUR ☐ CLAIMS MADE				AGGREGATE	$
							$
		☐ DEDUCTIBLE					$
		☐ RETENTION $					$
		WORKERS COMPENSATION AND EMPLOYERS' LIABILITY				☐ WC STATU-TORY LIMITS ☐ OTH-ER	
		ANY PROPRIETOR/PARTNER/EXECUTIVE OFFICER/MEMBER EXCLUDED? If yes, describe under SPECIAL PROVISIONS below				E.L. EACH ACCIDENT	$
						E.L. DISEASE - EA EMPLOYEE	$
						E.L. DISEASE - POLICY LIMIT	$
		OTHER					

DESCRIPTION OF OPERATIONS / LOCATIONS / VEHICLES / EXCLUSIONS ADDED BY ENDORSEMENT / SPECIAL PROVISIONS

CERTIFICATE HOLDER	CANCELLATION
	SHOULD ANY OF THE ABOVE DESCRIBED POLICIES BE CANCELLED BEFORE THE EXPIRATION DATE THEREOF, THE ISSUING INSURER WILL ENDEAVOR TO MAIL _____ DAYS WRITTEN NOTICE TO THE CERTIFICATE HOLDER NAMED TO THE LEFT, BUT FAILURE TO DO SO SHALL IMPOSE NO OBLIGATION OR LIABILITY OF ANY KIND UPON THE INSURER, ITS AGENTS OR REPRESENTATIVES.
	AUTHORIZED REPRESENTATIVE

ACORD 25 (2001/08)   © ACORD CORPORATION 1988

Figure 26.4 (cont'd)

IMPORTANT

If the certificate holder is an ADDITIONAL INSURED, the policy(ies) must be endorsed. A statement on this certificate does not confer rights to the certificate holder in lieu of such endorsement(s).

If SUBROGATION IS WAIVED, subject to the terms and conditions of the policy, certain policies may require an endorsement. A statement on this certificate does not confer rights to the certificate holder in lieu of such endorsement(s).

DISCLAIMER

The Certificate of Insurance on the reverse side of this form does not constitute a contract between the issuing insurer(s), authorized representative or producer, and the certificate holder, nor does it affirmatively or negatively amend, extend or alter the coverage afforded by the policies listed thereon.

SPECIMEN

ACORD 25 (2001/08)

Figure 26.5

ACORD™ CERTIFICATE OF PROPERTY INSURANCE		DATE	

PRODUCER

THIS CERTIFICATE IS ISSUED AS A MATTER OF INFORMATION ONLY AND CONFERS NO RIGHTS UPON THE CERTIFICATE HOLDER. THIS CERTIFICATE DOES NOT AMEND, EXTEND OR ALTER THE COVERAGE AFFORDED BY THE POLICIES BELOW.

COMPANIES AFFORDING COVERAGE

COMPANY **A**

INSURED

COMPANY **B**

COMPANY **C**

COMPANY **D**

COVERAGES

THIS IS TO CERTIFY THAT THE POLICIES OF INSURANCE LISTED BELOW HAVE BEEN ISSUED TO THE INSURED NAMED ABOVE FOR THE POLICY PERIOD INDICATED, NOTWITHSTANDING ANY REQUIREMENT, TERM OR CONDITION OF ANY CONTRACT OR OTHER DOCUMENT WITH RESPECT TO WHICH THIS CERTIFICATE MAY BE ISSUED OR MAY PERTAIN, THE INSURANCE AFFORDED BY THE POLICIES DESCRIBED HEREIN IS SUBJECT TO ALL THE TERMS, EXCLUSIONS AND CONDITIONS OF SUCH POLICIES. LIMITS SHOWN MAY HAVE BEEN REDUCED BY PAID CLAIMS.

CO LTR	TYPE OF INSURANCE	POLICY NUMBER	POLICY EFFECTIVE DATE (MM/DD/YY)	POLICY EXPIRATION DATE (MM/DD/YY)	COVERED PROPERTY	LIMITS
	PROPERTY				BUILDING	$
	CAUSES OF LOSS				PERSONAL PROPERTY	$
	BASIC				BUSINESS INCOME	$
	BROAD				EXTRA EXPENSE	$
	SPECIAL				BLANKET BUILDING	$
	EARTHQUAKE				BLANKET PERS PROP	$
	FLOOD				BLANKET BLDG & PP	$
						$
	INLAND MARINE					$
	TYPE OF POLICY					$
						$
	CAUSES OF LOSS					$
	NAMED PERILS					$
	OTHER					$
	CRIME					$
	TYPE OF POLICY					$
						$
	BOILER & MACHINERY					$
						$
	OTHER					

LOCATION OF PREMISES/DESCRIPTION OF PROPERTY

SPECIAL CONDITIONS/OTHER COVERAGES

CERTIFICATE HOLDER	**CANCELLATION**
	SHOULD ANY OF THE ABOVE DESCRIBED POLICIES BE CANCELLED BEFORE THE EXPIRATION DATE THEREOF, THE ISSUING COMPANY WILL ENDEAVOR TO MAIL _____ DAYS WRITTEN NOTICE TO THE CERTIFICATE HOLDER NAMED TO THE LEFT, BUT FAILURE TO MAIL SUCH NOTICE SHALL IMPOSE NO OBLIGATION OR LIABILITY OF ANY KIND UPON THE COMPANY, ITS AGENTS OR REPRESENTATIVES.
	AUTHORIZED REPRESENTATIVE

ACORD 24 (1/95)   © ACORD CORPORATION 1995

Figure 26.6

ACORD™ **EVIDENCE OF PROPERTY INSURANCE**		DATE

THIS IS EVIDENCE THAT INSURANCE AS IDENTIFIED BELOW HAS BEEN ISSUED, IS IN FORCE, AND CONVEYS ALL THE RIGHTS AND PRIVILEGES AFFORDED UNDER THE POLICY.

PRODUCER	PHONE (A/C, No. Ext):	COMPANY

CODE:	SUB CODE:

AGENCY CUSTOMER ID #:

INSURED

LOAN NUMBER	POLICY NUMBER

EFFECTIVE DATE	EXPIRATION DATE	CONTINUED UNTIL TERMINATED IF CHECKED

THIS REPLACES PRIOR EVIDENCE DATED:

PROPERTY INFORMATION

LOCATION/DESCRIPTION

COVERAGE INFORMATION

COVERAGE/PERILS/FORMS	AMOUNT OF INSURANCE	DEDUCTIBLE

SPECIMEN

REMARKS (Including Special Conditions)

CANCELLATION

THE POLICY IS SUBJECT TO THE PREMIUMS, FORMS, AND RULES IN EFFECT FOR EACH POLICY PERIOD. SHOULD THE POLICY BE TERMINATED, THE COMPANY WILL GIVE THE ADDITIONAL INTEREST IDENTIFIED BELOW _____ DAYS WRITTEN NOTICE, AND WILL SEND NOTIFICATION OF ANY CHANGES TO THE POLICY THAT WOULD AFFECT THAT INTEREST, IN ACCORDANCE WITH THE POLICY PROVISIONS OR AS REQUIRED BY LAW.

ADDITIONAL INTEREST

NAME AND ADDRESS	MORTGAGEE	ADDITIONAL INSURED
	LOSS PAYEE	
	LOAN #	
	AUTHORIZED REPRESENTATIVE	

ACORD 27 (3/93) © ACORD CORPORATION 1993

Chapter 27

SURETY BONDS

WHAT IS IT?

Surety bonds are three-party contracts that guarantee the performance of one party to a second party. The independent third party that guarantees the performance is called the *surety*. The first party—the entity that is to perform the work—is called the *principal* or *obligor*. The second party—for whom the work is to be done—is called the *obligee.*

Surety bonding may be compared to insurance in several ways, including:

- Surety bonds involve three parties: principal, obligee, and surety. Insurance involves two parties: the insured and the insurer.

- Surety bonds are not for the benefit of the entity or individual that obtained the bond. They are written for the benefit of the obligee (second party).

- Surety bonds often may not be cancelled, even if the premium is not collected.

- The premiums for surety bonds primarily are service fees, which are paid for the use of the surety company's financial backing and guarantee. Surety companies do not *expect* to pay bond losses, whereas insurance premiums are collected to create a pool of money from which claims may be paid.

- State insurance commissioners regulate both the surety and the insurance business.

- Both insurance and surety provide for financial loss.

- The emphasis in surety underwriting is prequalifying principals as to their ability to perform a job or provide a service. Insurance underwriting is aimed at spreading risk.

The Three Parties in Surety

Principal—the party that undertakes to perform the work, such as a contractor undertaking a building project or a vendor contracting to supply materials or services.

Obligee—the entity or individual for whom the work is to be done; the party that receives the benefit of the bond.

Surety—the entity that guarantees that a job will be performed.

BUSINESS USES

Surety bonding often is required on public works projects. According to the Surety Association of America (SAA), www.surety.org, the federal government and every state government requires that prime contractors on public works projects over a certain value provide a *performance* and *payment* bond.[1] A performance bond guarantees to the obligee (project owner) that the contractor will complete the project according to specifications, on time, and within budget. A payment bond guarantees to the obligee that subcontractors and other suppliers will be paid. Another type of bond, a *bid bond*, frequently is required when a contractor submits a proposal and bids on a project. The bid bond guarantees that, if the contractor is awarded the contract, the contractor will enter into it and provide the necessary performance and payment bonds.

In addition to public works projects, governmental bodies (federal, state, and/or local) often require that individuals or entities dealing in certain professions post surety bonds. Included are real estate brokers, insurance agents, motor vehicle dealers, and surplus lines insurance brokers. Most of these types of bonds guarantee that the bonded entity or individual will comply with the rules and regulations of the authority that governs them.

Other types of commercial surety bonds are those that guarantee that other types of obligations will be performed. Examples are bonds required of qualified workers compensation self-insurers to guarantee the payment of claims; public official bonds that guarantee the officials will faithfully perform their duties; and bonds required of parties in judicial proceedings to either appear at later proceedings or pay money that is assessed.

Nongovernmental owners and financial institutions often require that bonds be posted on private projects. For example, a bank or a real estate developer may require that a general contractor post surety bonds before awarding a contract to build a large commercial structure or residential development.

ADVANTAGES

Surety bonds facilitate the construction of much of the infrastructure of the United States and the rest of the world. They serve to reduce uncertainty about the completion of large projects and business transactions.

One of the main advantages of surety bonding is the underwriting process. Sureties gauge the following three attributes when underwriting a company or individual seeking a bond:

- *Financial capital.* The surety prequalifies an entity's financial ability to successfully complete a project or fulfill a contract according to specifications.

- *Capacity.* The surety prequalifies an entity's ability to complete a project successfully. For example, does the company have enough skilled workers to complete the project? Does the company have the right type and amount of equipment to complete the project?

- *Character.* Does the entity's record show enough experience and character to complete the project as promised?

Therefore, the underwriting process evaluates prospective candidates in regard to their ability to complete projects on time and within budget. This process weeds out entities that likely would not be able to fulfill a project and provides owners and governmental authorities with a pool of qualified candidates.

When a surety writes a bond and the principal defaults, the surety guarantees that the obligation will be completed. For example, a contractor posts performance and payment bonds on a construction project. Halfway through the project, the contractor encounters unforeseen financial difficulties on another project and finds himself unable to complete the job as promised and unable to pay subcontractors. The surety may lend the

contractor funds to complete the job, hire another contractor to complete the project, or pay the project penalty. These options help to assure that the job will be completed.

Sureties also review the contract documents on projects for which they are asked to post bonds. This overview provides potential contractors with an objective opinion on unusual or difficult contract provisions. The surety also runs credit checks on prospective obligees. This is done to further guarantee that the bonded contractor will be paid on a timely basis.

DISADVANTAGES

The surety underwriting process requires a lot of information and time. Entities or individuals that need a surety bond must be willing to share confidential financial information, as well as reputation information, with the surety underwriter. And surety underwriters continue to monitor the bonded entity throughout the length of the bond.

Surety bonds often cannot be cancelled, depending upon the type of bond involved. Therefore, a surety company typically must continue a bond until the job is completed—even if the principal has failed to pay the premium or has defaulted on the contract.

The cost and availability of surety bonds rises and falls with the underwriting profile of the prospective principal. Some may say that only the cleanest companies with the best financial records are able to obtain surety bonds. Companies that do not meet the stringent underwriting guidelines will not be able to obtain bonds and will lose the ability to participate in large contracts. The general economy also may impact cost and availability.

Owners of privately or closely held companies might not want to personally indemnify the surety for possible default. However, it may be impossible for some companies to obtain surety bonding with personal indemnification. (See the section on **Design Features** for additional information on personal indemnification.)

DESIGN FEATURES

As discussed in the chapter introduction, surety bonds are three-party contracts and involve the principal, obligee, and surety. There are various surety bond formats.

Some of the most common in the construction area are those published by the American Institute of Architects (AIA), www.aia.org. The obligee on the project—whether a governmental authority or a private owner/financier—typically specifies the type of bond form that should be used. Sureties may not accept certain bond wording that an obligee requests, especially if they believe it is particularly onerous for either the principal or surety.

The obligee also may establish guidelines on the financial strength of the surety companies it will accept. This is done in an effort to guarantee that all parties to the bond will be able to perform as promised.

Underwriting Submission

The underwriting process is a key to the surety bonding process. A typical underwriting submission includes the following types of information:

- Several years of audited fiscal year-end financial statements. Most sureties require three years of financial information, along with interim current financial information.

- Background information on the prospective principal, including a detailed list of previously completed large contracts.

- References from business associates and/or project owners.

- Copies of bank note and security agreements if a bank line of credit is in place.

- Current personal financial statements of major stockholders, owners, or indemnitors.

- Certificates of the insurance coverage the principal carries.

- Schedule of work in progress for each of the year-end financial statements, along with a current work in progress report.

- Information about the business's continuity plan, including key-man life insurance, buy-sell agreements, and résumés of owners and key employees.

Surety underwriters frequently meet personally with the owners or key managers of prospective principals to discuss their underwriting needs, ask questions, and assess the abilities of the entity.

Indemnity Agreements

If a principal should default on the obligations that fall under terms of the surety bond, the surety must see that the contract is fulfilled or pay damages. When a principal defaults, however, the principal must reimburse the surety for any payments made or obligations assumed; the principal must *indemnify* (make whole) the surety. This right is granted by common law. However, many sureties require that this right to be indemnified be expressed in the bond application. In addition, the owners in a closely held or private corporation often must *personally indemnify* the surety before a bond is issued. This means that the private owners must agree to reimburse the surety from their personal assets if the entity is unable to do so.

Bond Limit

The *bond limit* or *bond penalty* is the amount for which the bond is written. The bond penalty typically is the highest amount to which a surety is obligated. However, the principal may have obligations that exceed the bond penalty.

Other Types of Surety Bonds

There are many types of surety bonds in addition to those discussed previously. Among them are the following:

- *Maintenance bonds*, which guarantee that faulty work will be corrected or defective materials replaced.

- *Subdivision bonds*, which back up a real estate developer's promise to install public improvements—such as streets and curbs—when developing a tract of land.

- *Supply bonds*, which guarantee that materials or supplies will be furnished and delivered according to contract provisions.

- *License and permit bonds*, which hold public entities harmless for damages arising from a licensee's compliance with statutes and regulations.

- *Public official bonds*, which guarantee that public officers will perform the duties of office in good faith and will account for and turn over funds to their successors. These often are referred to as guaranteeing both the *honesty* and *faithful performance* of a public official.

- *Fiduciary bonds,* which guarantee that individuals who are entrusted with property or money belonging to others will exercise those duties faithfully, account for property received, and reimburse any deficiencies for which a court holds them accountable.

WHERE CAN I FIND OUT MORE ABOUT IT?

Surety companies and surety underwriters are a rich source of information about surety bonding. Additional information may be obtained from:

- American Institute of Architects (AIA), www.aia.org.
- National Association of Surety Bond Producers (NASBP), www.nasbp.org.
- Small Business Administration (SBA), Office of Surety Guarantees (OSG), www.sba.gov/osg.
- Surety Association of America (SAA), www.surety.org.
- Surety Information Office (SIO), www.sio.org.

QUESTIONS AND ANSWERS

Question—A construction company wants to bid on a large construction project but has not been able to obtain a bid bond. What options does this company have?

Answer—There are a number of options that may help this contractor. Among them is the possibility of posting another form of guarantee, such as a letter of credit, to guarantee completion of the project. (A letter of credit is issued by a bank and certifies that the person or company named in it is entitled to draw on the writer's credit up to a certain limit.) Some project owners may accept a letter of credit in place of a surety bond.

The contractor also may approach the *secondary bond market* through a surety bond broker that specializes in hard-to-place bonds. The contractor will have to undergo a rigorous underwriting process, and the bond premium will be higher than that in the standard bond market. However, there may be an opportunity to obtain the necessary bonding from this type of facility.

The contractor may appeal to his professional association or an organization such as the federal Small Business Administration (SBA), which might have surety programs in place that some companies may find of assistance.

Question—The subject of surety bonding became a hot topic shortly after the bankruptcy filing of energy giant Enron Corporation. What type of surety bonds did Enron have, and what are the implications of those issues on bonding in general?

Answer—The jury was still out in regard to the status of Enron's surety bonds when this chapter was completed, and the actual terms were not available because of ongoing litigation. However, the company is said to have bought surety bonds to guarantee its performance of fuel-delivery contracts. When the gas marketing company defaulted, JPMorgan Chase Bank sued the sureties for payment of over $1 billion under six bonds that guaranteed the obligations of Enron-related companies.

The bank filed a lawsuit, alleging that, under express terms of the bonds, the sureties' obligation to pay was immediate and unconditional. The surety companies defended the suit by stating that the bonds were obtained as part of a fraudulent scheme in which loans by a predecessor bank (Chase Manhattan Bank, predecessor to JPMorgan Chase Bank) to Enron were disguised as the sale of assets. The net effect, according to the sureties' defense position, was that the arrangement resulted in a series of "loans" from the bank to Enron. Since the "loans" were disguised as the sale of assets, Enron could book them as revenue, and the bank could induce sureties to issue bonds that would guarantee their repayment. The surety companies contended that they were forbidden to make such guarantees under New York law. They also sought relief from paying the bond amounts with the contention that they were the product of fraudulent inducement and concealment.

The Enron situation points out the importance of the underwriting process to surety bonding. In addition, the Enron bankruptcy and issues surrounding the Enron bonds seem to have made surety companies far more cautious when underwriting new bonds.

Kmart, one of the country's leading retailers, used surety bonds to back up payment of self-insured workers compensation claims and other liabilities. The company also posted surety bonds as required of entities that sell alcohol and firearms. After the Enron failure, it was reported that Kmart's sureties required it to post substantial amounts of new security to back up its bonds. Kmart had a hard time committing the additional money to its bonding program, which was reported to be one of the factors that forced the company to file bankruptcy.

END NOTES

[1] *Protecting Consumers and the Public Treasury: Surplus Lines Broker Bonds*, Surety Association of America, July 13, 2001, www.surety.org.

GLOSSARY

Bid bond. A bond that guarantees that, if an entity is awarded the contract, the company will enter into it and provide the necessary performance and payment bonds.

Bond penalty. The bond limit; the amount for which a bond is written.

Faithful performance. A guarantee that a principal will perform her duties in good faith.

Indemnify. To compensate another party for damages; to make whole.

Obligee. The second party in a surety bond; the entity or individual for whom work is to be done.

Payment bond. A bond that guarantees that subcontractors and other suppliers will be paid.

Performance bond. A bond that guarantees that the contractor (principal) will complete a project according to specifications, on time, and within budget.

Personal indemnification. Formal agreement by owners of privately held companies or principal shareholders in closely held companies to pledge their personal assets to indemnify another party for damages it incurs.

Principal. The first party in a surety bond; the party that undertakes to perform work. Also called the *obligor*.

Surety. The third party to a surety bond; the party that guarantees that a job will be performed.

Chapter 28

CLAIM REVIEWS

WHAT ARE THEY?

Claim reviews are formal discussions about the status of a business's claims. The purpose is to help businesses develop and enact initiatives to decrease the financial impact of losses.

Usual participants in claim reviews are

- representatives of the insured business, such as the risk manager, safety manager, and human resources director,

- representatives of the insurer involved with the claims, such as an underwriter or captive manager,

- representatives of the insurance agent or broker,

- the claim adjuster, and

- legal counsel when appropriate.

BUSINESS USES

Claim reviews are a component in the ability to manage the financial impact of losses, which is discussed in Chapter 14. It is important that *loss reserves* be as accurate as possible because they represent the amount of money that is allocated for future payments on claims that already have been reported. The financial value of claims is important because it impacts a business's ability to purchase cost-effective insurance in the future, as well as the amount that a business may have to pay for claims that are covered by a risk-sharing program.

In addition, claim reviews can be used to develop programs to temper those aspects of business losses that are difficult to quantify, such as lost productivity when employees are injured and unable to work, loss of customers when orders cannot be filled, and loss of reputation when the public learns about damage the business has caused others. Claim reviews are particularly valuable for businesses that have large workforces and, consequently, numerous employee injuries and workers compensation claims.

The frequency of formal claim reviews depends upon the

- number of serious claims, and

- frequency of claims.

Claims should be reviewed at least once a year. But businesses with many claims—or a number of serious claims—may desire formal review sessions on a quarterly or biannual basis.

> ### Importance of Claim Reviews
>
> Regardless of where and how claim reviews are conducted, it is critically important that businesses pay attention to how claims are being adjusted and settled. The financial repercussions from poor loss experience can be extreme for a business that does not proactively manage its losses.
>
> Many online risk and claims management information systems provide real-time information on claims. Use of these may decrease the number of in-person claim reviews that are needed.

Reviews may be held in person—either at the insured's business or at the adjuster's office—or through conference calls. Claims involving all types of coverage should be considered. But claims that traditionally take a lengthy time to adjust and settle are the most obvious subjects for review. These are said to have *long tails*. Long-tail claims often take years to settle, and the longer the tail, the greater the possibility that the financial value of the claim will increase. Claims that typically have long tails arise from workers compensation and general liability exposures. Additional information on long-tail claims is contained in Chapter 13.

Formal reviews should be conducted periodically throughout the year, with the timing established by the number and the magnitude of losses. Therefore, businesses with a high frequency or severity of claims are the most obvious prospects for regularly scheduled claim reviews.

ADVANTAGES

There are several advantages to conducting regular claim reviews. They

- encourage open lines of communication with adjusters and legal counsel,

- facilitate the development of initiatives to temper claim *soft costs*, such as lost productivity and poor customer relations,

- help risk managers to focus loss control attention on areas of the operation that have a high claim frequency,

- help risk managers to focus loss control attention on areas of the operation in which serious claims have occurred, and

- lead to reductions in the financial value of claim reserves and claim payments.

DISADVANTAGES

There are several disadvantages to conducting periodic formal claim reviews. They

- require a commitment of time from a number of parties,

- may be resisted by insurance company representatives who believe they have sole authority in the way that claims are handled,

- may waste time and resources if the business is not fully committed to managing claims, and

- may require an investment of money today to save money in the future.

Risk Management Tip

Claim reviews are a part of the process of claim management. Businesses that want to avoid unpleasant surprises will take an active interest in claims on a day-to-day basis in addition to organizing formal claim reviews.

DESIGN FEATURES

Setting up the Process

Risk managers first must decide how often claims should be formally reviewed. For the purpose of this discussion, we will illustrate a business that has a large employee workforce with a moderate-to-high frequency of workers compensation claims. The business, ABC Restaurants, has averaged 181 workers compensation claims a year over the last five years. Figure 28.1 shows the company's workers compensation loss experience as of January 1, 2003.

During the five-year period, ABC purchased five retrospectively rated workers compensation programs

Figure 28.1

Workers Compensation Losses as of 1/1/03

Policy Term	# Closed Claims	# Open Claims	Paid Losses	Reserved Losses	Incurred Losses	ALAE	Premium
1/1/1997-98	173	7	$152,398	$52,169	$204,567	$7,632	$375,000
1/1/1998-99	185	4	$183,111	$149,575	$332,686	$8,111	$382,000
1/1/1999-00	168	3	$116,321	$98,423	$214,744	$2,621	$376,000
1/1/2000-01	153	14	$89,325	$143,652	$232,977	$1,995	$392,000
1/1/2001-02	146	54	$69,253	$198,158	$267,411	$4,312	$405,000
Total	825	82	$610,408	$641,977	$1,252,385	$24,671	$1,930,000
Total paid	$610,408						
Total reserves	$641,977						
Total incurred	$1,252,385						

from XYZ Insurance Company. Under a *retrospectively rated insurance program*, ABC's premium fluctuates with increases and decreases in the total cost of claims. As shown in Figure 28.1, $610,408 has been paid over the five-year span for workers compensation claims. An additional $641,977 has been earmarked as reserves for payments in the future. Reserves are established based on actuarial formulas that gauge how much individual claims will cost by the time they are completely settled.

Since ABC shares its workers compensation risk with the insurance company, ABC's risk manager requests quarterly claim reviews. Two are set up as conference calls, and the other two are held in person at ABC's headquarters.

At least one month prior to a review meeting, ABC's risk manager reviews her information on each of the eighty-two claims that remain open (have not yet been completely settled) during the five years. She looks for situations in which employees already have returned to work or are scheduled to return in the immediate future, as well as the medical prognosis for employees that remain off work. More than half of the fifty-four open claims from the 2001-2002 policy term are progressing well and probably will be closed in the immediate future. However, five serious claims in that policy period involve back injuries, and the employees remain off the job. In addition, three of the open claims from the 2000-2001 policy term involve long-term injuries, and all fourteen of the open claims from the prior three policy terms are very serious.

Based on this, the risk manager asks that twenty-two claims from the five-year span be discussed in depth and that shorter progress reports be supplied by the claim adjuster on the other sixty open claims. She asks the adjuster to list any claims that will be closed before the review meeting is held.

In preparing for the review, the adjuster reviews the claim files in depth and prepares written claim status reports on each of the open claims. Figure 28.2 is a sample status form, which describes the situation on the shoulder injury that a waiter sustained in the 2000-2001 policy term. (Insurance and adjusting companies will have their own style of status reports, and Figure 28.2 is shown for illustration purposes only. Figure 28.3 is a blank sample status report form, which may be used as a starting point for considering the type of information that is important.) The Figure 28.2 status report indicates that, of the $89,325 of claim payments in that policy period, $11,270 was spent for this one employee. The

$60,600 that is reserved on the case is included within the 2000-2001 reserved claims amount in Figure 28.1 of $143,652.

During the review, the participants discuss what measures can be taken to try to decrease the severity of the claim in an effort to reduce their financial impact. In the Figure 28.2 example, the management plan suggests that the treating physician is recommending a continuation of physical therapy and that ABC Restaurants should try to develop a modified job that will accommodate Mr. Smith's injury. Non-medical personnel cannot dictate medical options, and the injured employee's treating physician should approve modified job duties.

Risk Management Tip

Claim reviews are a good forum for discussing activities that could reduce the severity of claims. It is important to remember that state workers compensation laws and regulations dictate much of what employers and insurance companies can do to return employees to work after an injury. In addition, little can be done on products or general liability claims once they enter a stage of litigation. However, at the least, formal review of claims prepares business and risk managers for serious claim situations so there are no surprises.

Legal Aspects

Formal claim reviews provide a forum in which to discuss the status of claims and develop initiatives to decrease their severity. Some individuals believe that, once claims are filed with an insurance company, the insured business has given up the right to have input in how they are adjusted.

Contrary to this thought, some courts have held that insurers hold the absolute right to settle claims when only their money, and none of the insured business's money, is at stake. Therefore, the insurer has an obligation to work with the insured business to manage claims when a risk-sharing plan—such as a retrospectively rated or large deductible program—is involved. This is because both the insurance company's and the business's money are involved. An example is *Transport Indemnity Company v. Dahlen Transport, Inc.*, 161 N.W. 2d 546 (Minn. 1968), in which the Minnesota Supreme Court ruled that an insurer can be forced to produce evidence

Figure 28.2

Sample Workers' Compensation Claim Status Form		
Claimant: John Smith	**Age:** 31	**Date:** March 5, 2003
Policy term: 1/1/2000-2001		**Status:** Open
Date/Loss: May 21, 2000	**Average Weekly Wage:** $625	

	Indemnity	Medical
	Wage Loss Paid: $2,520	**Medical Paid:** $8,750
	Wage Loss Reserved: $35,000	**Medical Reserved:** $25,600
	Total Paid: $11,270	**Total Reserved:** $60,600
Total Incurred Claim Amount:		**$71,870**

Description of claim/injury:	Torn rotator cuff, right shoulder. Surgery performed but pain & restriction of movement continues.
Action since last report:	Claimant underwent surgery on Sept. 25 and was discharged. Surgery apparently successful, but claimant continues to complain of pain and lack of mobility.
Narrative/current prognosis:	Claimant is 31-year-old waiter who tore rotator cuff when twisting to pick up and stack cartons. Therapy was followed by surgery, which appeared successful. However, claimant still complains of pain, and mobility test shows 50% restriction of movement at current time. Claimant is participating in physical therapy. Independent medical exam (IME) will be scheduled after 6 weeks of therapy.
Management plan:	Continue PT & await IME results. HR department should talk to treating physician about modified duty job for claimant. Possible partial permanent injury if therapy is not successful. Claimant appears to want to return to work, but futher surgery may be needed.

that settlements were made in good faith and not as a tool to avoid responsibility for making payments under excess insurance policies that it provided. A number of other cases also discuss such responsibilities in risk-sharing arrangements. Reference to these can be found in the End Notes to Chapter 13.

Transport Indemnity and other cases support the theory that insurance companies may face conflicts of interest when adjusting claims under risk-sharing programs. This is because spending the insured's money to settle a claim quickly could ultimately result in the insurance company saving its money. The fact that several courts have ruled that the insured business has a right to participate in claim strategy supports the validity of formal claim reviews.

At all times, state and federal laws governing the rights of claimants must be respected.

Time Required to Implement

Claim reviews require both preparation and participation time by a number of individuals. The amount of time, quite naturally, relates to the number and severity of claims involved.

In addition to the time spent preparing for and conducting the claim review, follow-up time also is required. One tangible outcome of any review should be a succinct list of recommendations or action items with timeframes attached. These become blueprints for program improvements, subsequent day-to-day management activities, and future claim reviews.

Long–Term Ramifications

Instituting a process of active claim management should have a long-term positive effect on the financial

Figure 28.3

Blank Sample Workers' Compensation Claim Status Form		
Claimant:	Age:	Date:
Policy term:		Status:
Date/Loss:	Average Weekly Wage:	

	Indemnity	Medical
	Wage Loss Paid:	Medical Paid:
	Wage Loss Reserved:	Medical Reserved:
	Total Paid:	Total Reserved:
	Total Incurred Claim Amount:	

Description of claim/injury:

Action since last report:

Narrative/current prognosis:

Management plan:

impact of claims. In general, management commitment to this results in

- additional business-wide attention to preventing and managing claims,

- a reduction in the soft costs associated with claims, such as lost productivity, because claims tend to be resolved more quickly, and

- better cooperation among all parties involved in the claim, including claimants, risk managers, claim adjusters, and insurers.

WHERE CAN I FIND OUT MORE ABOUT IT?

Additional information may be obtained from most insurance companies, agents, and brokers.

GLOSSARY

Claim frequency. The relative frequency of claims filed against a business.

Claim reviews. Formal discussions about the status of a business's claims.

Claim severity. The relative severity of claims, usually illustrated by their financial value.

Claim status report. A form used to illustrate the status of a claim, such as the paid and reserve amounts, recent activity, and recommended action.

Long-tail claims. A commonly used term to describe the relative length of time before various types of claims are fully adjusted and settled. Long-tail claims may take years to adjust and settle.

Loss reserves. Loss or claim reserves represent the value of claims that have been estimated and set up for future payment.

Retrospectively rated insurance programs. A rating arrangement in which the final premium for insurance coverage is not determined until all claims are closed. The final premium is determined by the insured's actual financial loss experience during the policy period.

INDEX

S